P9-DFC-521

THE FONTANA ECONOMIC HISTORY OF EUROPE

General Editor: Carlo M. Cipolla

There is at present no satisfactory economic history
of Europe—covering Europe both as a whole and
with particular relation to the individual countries—
that is both concise enough for convenient use
and yet full enough to include the results of
individual and detailed scholarship. This series is
designed to fill that gap.

Unlike most current works in this field, the
Fontana Economic History of Europe does not end at the
outbreak of the First World War. More than half
a century has elapsed since 1914, a half-century that
has transformed the economic background of
Europe. In recognition of this the present work has
set its terminal date at 1970 and provides for sixty
contributions each written by a specialist.

The Fontana
Economic History of Europe
Volume 3

The Industrial Revolution

1700 – 1914

Editor Carlo M. Cipolla

Harvester Press/Barnes & Noble
In association with Fontana Books

This edition first published in 1976 by
THE HARVESTER PRESS LIMITED
Publisher: John Spiers
2 Stanford Terrace
Hassocks, Nr. Brighton
Sussex, England
and published in the U.S.A. 1976 by
HARPER & ROW PUBLISHERS, INC.
BARNES & NOBLE IMPORT DIVISION
10 East 53rd Street, New York 10022

The Industrial Revolution
This edition first published in 1976
by The Harvester Press Limited
and by Barnes & Noble
in association with Fontana
First published in paperback in 1973
by Fontana Books

The Harvester Press Limited
ISBN 0 85527 114 0
Barnes & Noble
ISBN 0-06-492178-6

Typesetting by Wm. Collins Sons & Co. Ltd.
London and Glasgow
Printed in Great Britain by Redwood Burn Limited
Trowbridge, Wiltshire
Bound by Cedric Chivers Limited, Portway, Bath

Contents

The Industrial Revolution   7
C. M. CIPOLLA

1. Population in Europe 1700–1914   22
ANDRE ARMENGAUD *translated by A. J. Pomerans*
Demographic Data – Population Growth – Natural
Growth – Migration – Bibliography

2. Patterns of Demand 1750–1914   77
WALTER MINCHINTON
Determinants of Demand: Geography and Climate –
Industrialisation and Technology – Population and
Urbanisation – Articulation of the Market – Fashion and
Social Custom – Role of Government – Components
of Demand: Food – Clothing – Housing – Other –
Bibliography

3. Technological Progress and the Industrial
Revolution 1700–1914   187
SAMUEL LILLEY
Technology before the Industrial Revolution –
Technological Change in the Early Industrial
Revolution – Some Thoughts about Causal Origins –
Science in the Early Industrial Revolution – Science and
Technology in the Later Industrial Revolution –
Bibliography

4. Banking and Industrialisation in Europe
1730–1914   255
BERTRAND GILLE *translated by Roger Greaves*
Credit Demand – Evolution of Banking Techniques –
Economic Behaviour Patterns – Bibliography

5. The State and the Industrial Revolution
1700–1914   301
BARRY SUPPLE
The State and its Policies – Mercantilism, Feudalism,
Individualism 1700–1815 – The State and the Diffusion
of Industrialism 1815–70 – The State and Economic
Immaturity 1870–1914 – Bibliography

6. The Service Revolution: The Growth of
    Services in Modern Economy 1700–1914   358
    R. M. HARTWELL
    Definition and Classification of Services – The Service
    Revolution – Individual Services – Structural Change
    and Growth – Conclusion – Bibliography

7. The Industrial Bourgeoisie and the Rise of
    the Working Class 1700–1914   397
    J-F. BERGIER *translated by Roger Greaves*
    Situation of the Bourgeoisie – The Advent of the Industrial
    Bourgeoisie – Towards the Cohesion of the Industrial
    Bourgeoisie – Towards the Mass of the Workers – The
    Condition of the Workers – Towards the Working-Class
    Consciousness – The Awakening of Class Consciousness
    on the Continent – Bibliography

8. Agriculture and the Industrial Revolution
    1700–1914   452
    PAUL BAIROCH *translated by Muriel Grindrod*
    The Agricultural Revolution – Reasons for Agriculture's
    Primary Role – The Influence of Agriculture in Industrial
    Development – Bibliography

9. The Emergence of Economics as a Science
    1750–1870   507
    DONALD WINCH
    Origins and Emergence – Classical Political Economy
    in Britain after Adam Smith – The Spread of Classical
    Political Economy – The Culmination: Karl Marx and
    John Stuart Mill – Bibliography

10. Industrial Archaeology   574
    M. J. T. LEWIS

    Notes on the authors   604

    Index of Persons   608

    Index of Places   615

    General Index   620

Introduction

C. M. Cipolla

Between 1780 and 1850, in less than three generations, a far-reaching revolution, without precedent in the history of Mankind, changed the face of England. From then on, the world was no longer the same. Historians have often used and abused the word Revolution to mean a radical change, but no revolution has been as dramatically revolutionary as the Industrial Revolution—except perhaps the Neolithic Revolution. Both of these changed the course of history, so to speak, each one bringing about a discontinuity in the historic process. The Neolithic Revolution transformed Mankind from a scattered collection of savage bands of hunters, whose life in Hobbes's famous phrase was 'solitary, poor, nasty, brutish and short', into a collection of more or less interdependent agricultural societies. The Industrial Revolution transformed Man from a farmer-shepherd into a manipulator of machines worked by inanimate energy.

Before the Industrial Revolution the animal and vegetable kingdoms had provided the largest part of the energy needed by Man to keep himself alive, propagate the species, and make a living. For thousands of years the Paleolithic hunters had lived off plants and animals as prey. From the Neolithic age onwards, Man learnt to domesticate animals and cultivate plants, to improve their quality and to use them in a progressively more rational and efficient way. Separating the Paleolithic hunters and the Neolithic farmers there is a chasm; on one side, the savage state: on the other, civilisation. For centuries, however, the world of Mankind remained a world of plants and animals. The Industrial Revolution opened up a completely different world of new and untapped sources of energy such as coal, oil, electricity and the atom, exploited by means of various mechanisms— a world in which Man found himself able to handle great masses of energy to an extent inconceivable in the preceding bucolic age. From a narrow technological and economic point of view, the Industrial Revolution can be defined as the process by which a society gained control of vast sources of inanimate energy; but such a definition does not do justice to this phenomenon, neither as regards the distant origins of the phenomenon itself, nor as regards its economic, cultural, social and political implications.

I have already said that the Industrial Revolution brought about a discontinuity in the course of history. Crescenzi in the thirteenth century, and agronomists in the fifteenth and sixteenth centuries could still usefully refer to the treatises written by the Romans. The ideas of Hippocrates and Galen continued to represent the basis of official medicine well into the eighteenth century—two centuries after the revolt of Paracelsus. It did not seem absurd to Machiavelli to refer to the Roman constitution when he planned an army for his times. At the end of the eighteenth century Catherine II of Russia had transported from Finland to St. Petersburg an enormous stone to place at the base of the monument dedicated to Peter the Great; the method of transporting this huge stone was much the same as that used thousands of years before by the Ancient Egyptians when building the pyramids. Palladio and his successors could still draw inspiration and instruction from the buildings of Classical Antiquity. As Cederna writes: 'From the Pharaohs to Baron Haussmann certain things have remained constant and immutable in the architecture of the past, even after a thousand changes of style: the materials—stone, lime, brick —and certain fundamental unchanging relations between supporting and supported elements: wall and roof, column and arch, pillar and vault, and so on. It is easy to give examples of monuments which have been formed from those already in existence. The travertine of the Colosseum proved useful in the building of St. Peter's in the Vatican, in the sixteenth century.' A basic continuity characterised the pre-industrial world, even throughout great upheavals like the rise and fall of the Roman Empire, of Islam, and of the Chinese dynasties. As has been written: 'if a Roman of the Empire could be transported some eighteen centuries forward in time, he would have found himself in a society

which he could, without too great a difficulty have lea
to comprehend. Horace would have felt himself reasor
at home as the guest of Horace Walpole, and Catullus
would soon have learned his way among the sedan-chairs,
the patched-up beauties and the flaring torches of London
streets at night.'[1] This continuity was broken between 1750
and 1850. In the middle of the nineteenth century, if a
general studied the organisation of the Roman army, if a
doctor paid attention to Hippocrates or Galen, or if an
agronomist read Columella, he did it purely for historical
interest and as an academic exercise. Even in faraway, unchanging China, it became evident to the most enlightened
of the scholar-officials of the Celestial Empire that the
ancient classical values which had given continuity to
Chinese history throughout invasions and changes of
dynasty, were no longer valid for survival in the contemporary world. In 1850 the past was not merely past—it
was dead.

On the other hand, if the Industrial Revolution created
in the course of three generations an irrevocable disruption
in the course of history, its roots nevertheless reached deep
into the preceding centuries. In order to discover the origins
of the Industrial Revolution one must go back to that profound change in ideas and social structures that accompanied the rise of the urban communes in Northern Italy,
in Northern France and in the Southern Low Countries,
between the eleventh and the thirteenth centuries. To
understand the essential significance of the rise of these
urban centres and their new culture, one must emphasise its
revolutionary character, the revolt against the predominant
agrarian-feudal order. It was the beginning of the end of a
society in which power and economic resources were based
exclusively on landed property and were monopolised by
social groups whose ideals were chiefly fighting, hunting, or
praying. In its place there began to grow a society based on
commerce, manufacturing and the professions, inspired by
the ideals of expediency, profit and, to some extent, reason.
The warlord and the monk were replaced by the merchant,

1. C. H. Waddington, *The Ethical Animal*, Chicago 1960, p. 5.

and the professional. The civilisation based on these two characters developed quickly and within a few centuries had conquered Western Europe. A cumulative process reinforced and refined its structures, both institutional and human. In the sixteenth and seventeenth centuries a severe crisis slowed down or even reversed this movement, in its two original areas: Italy and the Southern Low Countries. But it continued and reached its height in two other areas of Europe—the Northern Low Countries and England. At the end of the seventeenth century the salient features of these two areas were an extraordinary expansion in commerce and manufacturing; the presence of a large merchant class endowed with remarkable managerial ability, economic power and social and political influence; an impressive stock of manpower—both artisans and professionals; a relatively high degree of literacy, and a relative abundance of capital. These were the material facts. In the realm of ideas, the main characteristic was an aptitude for things mechanical, and a strong and growing inclination towards quantitative measurement and experiment. The Baconian philosophy and the mechanical conception of the universe marked the point reached by the movement of ideas which had begun centuries earlier in the urban communes of Italy and Flanders. There is an obvious continuity between Honnecourt's sketches, Leonardo da Vinci's machines and Newton's discoveries. At the end of the seventeenth century in England and Holland the movement reached its peak and spread through all classes of society. 'Men had become mechanics.' And a growing number of scholars, amateurs and craftsmen devoted themselves ever more industriously to mechanical invention and experiment.

If, at the end of the seventeenth century, a man with imagination, culture and common sense had been asked which of the two countries, Holland or England, had the greater chance in the next 150 years of bringing about an explosive revolution in the field of production, his reply would have favoured Holland. In all essentials Holland had the advantage over England. But she was imperceptibly ossifying into conservatism and she was losing leadership in a progressively greater number of fields. Moreover England possessed coal and Holland did not.

The use of coal for heating and iron ore smelting in England went back to the sixteenth century,[2] and the presence of abundant deposits of coal almost at surface level facilitated progress in the techniques of its use. Towards the end of the eighteenth century Watt's steam engine made possible the transformation of the chemical energy of coal into mechanical energy. After 1820, when the steam engine was used for rail transport, the use of coal began on a large scale in widely varied processes of production. The world production of coal and equivalent energy developed in a spectacular way:

	millions of tons of coal	equivalent in millions of megawatt hours
1860	132	1,057
1880	314	2,511
1900	701	5,606
1920	1,193	9,540
1940	1,363	10,904
1960	1,809	14,472

Watt's discovery was no accident. It was not accidental either that such a discovery had an overwhelming application in the field of production, and that it was followed by a whole series of similar inventions. As Whitehead wrote, man 'had invented the method of invention', and new discoveries would allow the exploitation of new forms of energy and the more efficient use of the forms of energy already known. Between 1860 and 1890 the industry of oil extraction was begun, and the internal combustion engine was brought to perfection. The end of the century saw the introduction of electricity. In the middle of the twentieth century man had begun to exploit atomic energy. Towards the middle of the twentieth century absolute world production of coal continued to increase but the percentage of energy produced from coal as against the total energy derived from the various inanimate sources was continually decreasing. The

2. J. U. Nef, *The Rise of the British Coal Industry*, London 1932, Vol. 1.

world production of energy from all inanimate sources developed as follows:

	milliards of megawatts
1860	1·1
1880	2·6
1900	6·1
1920	11·3
1940	15·9
1960	33·5

As I have already mentioned the availability of coal was a strategically important element in the process of development until the middle of the nineteenth century. The early industrial development of Belgium was undoubtedly connected with the presence of important coal fields in Belgian territory. However, if coal was a necessary condition for industrial growth it never was a sufficient condition. An Industrial Revolution is above all a socio-cultural fact. Coal by itself does not create and does not move machines. One needs men capable of mining the coal, of devising, building and operating the steam engines, of organising the factors of production and assuming the risks and responsibilities of enterprise. From the middle of the nineteenth century onward the diminution in the cost of transportation of coal and the economic exploitation of alternative types of energy made industrialisation possible in those areas which were not endowed with coal fields. This greatly helped the geographical diffusion of the Industrial Revolution. But that the Industrial Revolution was essentially and primarily a socio-cultural fact becomes evident when one notices that the first countries to industrialise were those who had the lowest percentage of illiterates and the greatest cultural similarities with England.

To date the beginning of the Industrial Revolution of a country is an arbitrary act, no less arbitrary than to date the beginning of the Middle Ages or the Renaissance. Geographical areas, economic sectors and social groups within the same country move with different tempos, according to different dynamics; new activities and new forms of life develop while a number of traditional activities and old institutions manage to survive. Indulging in the need for chronological classification one might however assert that by 1850 the Industrial Revolution had penetrated into Belgium, France, Germany, Switzerland and the United States. By 1900 it had extended to Sweden, Italy, Russia, Japan and Argentina. Presently it is penetrating into India, China and Africa.

Japan is one of the most interesting cases as it has been the first non-western country to import the Industrial Revolution. In Japan the Industrial Revolution began relatively early and developed at a very rapid rate. On the other hand Japan is an Asian country which in the second half of the nineteenth century had little in common with the socio-cultural scene of the English Island. To interpret and explain the Japanese case we must take into account two circumstances. Japan had a long tradition of importing foreign techniques and cultures. For centuries Japan had imitated China and when China declined and the West developed, Japan simply changed its model. Moreover, recent studies amply show that in the second half of the nineteenth century when Japan had started on the road of industrialisation the country was already exceptionally developed from the point of view of education. Illiteracy in Japan was no higher than in England and it was much less than in France. Once more cultural factors obviously played an important role in the history of the Industrial Revolution.

J. K. Galbraith once wrote that countries in the process of developing can be looked at as pearls that move along a necklace. From a historian's point of view the statement is both incorrect and unrealistic. It may easily generate the fallacious idea that the road to be followed in the process of industrialisation is the same for all countries independently from the peculiar conditions of time and space. Such an idea may easily become the source of dangerous mistakes not only at the level of historical interpretation but also at the level of economic policy. When the Industrial Revolution developed in Germany, Italy, the United States and Japan times were quite different from those of England in the 1780's. Germany, the United States, Italy and Japan had to face an industrial power already established, namely Great Britain. They had the advantage of having a model but the disadvantage of having to face a formidable competitor. Moreover between 1780 and 1870 technology had made enormous progress. The amount of fixed capital and the quality of human capital necessary for industrial development after 1870 were quite different from what had been necessary a century before. Banks and technical schools played a considerably greater role in the German industrialisation than in the English. If today in the industrialisation of the so-called Third World the State plays an increasingly important role, the reason is essentially the same, namely that times have continued to change and the effort required today for an agricultural country to industrialise is such that neither the individual entrepreneurs nor the banks can be adequate. The Industrial Revolution is always essentially the same but the method in which it is accomplished varies according to the different historical conditions.

I have already said that through the Industrial Revolution man comes to master new and formidable types of energy. These can be used for destruction or production. In both these fields the results of the Industrial Revolution have been amazing. There is no need here to analyse and emphasise the powers of destruction held by man as a result of the Industrial Revolution, although this is an argument of vital importance in the question of the survival of civilised life on our planet. Custom and tradition require that we concentrate on the other side of the medal.

Reasonably reliable indices for the progress of world industrial output are available dating from the second half of the nineteenth century when the process of industrialisation had crossed the frontiers of England and was becoming apparent for the first time in France, Germany, Switzerland and the United States:

	general index (1953 100)	world production of iron steel (millions of tons)	
1860	4	5	—
1900	16	40	29
1920	26	60	72
1940	51	102	142
1960	140	260	380

The spectacular growth in output was accompanied by a spectacular growth in population. The population of England and Wales rose from about 6 million in 1750 to about 9 million in 1800 and about 18 million in 1850. Between 1750 and 1850 the population of Europe (Russia excluded) rose from about 120 million to 210 million. In 1950 it reached 393 million.

Amazing as it was, the growth in population was still lower than the growth in national product. Because this was so in the past is no guarantee that it will continue to be so in the future; however the fact remains that in the course of the last two centuries national output of industrial countries has increased more than population, and that means an increase in income per head.

In the ten years before 1780 income per head in England ncreased by about 0.3 per cent per annum. Between 1850 and 1900 it increased by more than 2 per cent per annum.[3]

TABLE I

Country	period considered	annual increase per cent		
		population	national income	income per head
France	1845–1950	0·1	1·5	1·4
Germany	1865–1952	1·0	2·7	1·5
Italy	1865–1952	0·7	1·8	1·0
United Kingdom	1865–1950	0·8	2·2	1·3
Russia	1870–1954	1·3	3·1	1·5
Switzerland	1865–1952	0·7	3·6	2·8
United States	1875–1952	1·7	4·1	2·0
Canada	1875–1952	1·8	4·1	1·9
Japan	1885–1952	1·3	4·2	2·6

Sources: S. Kuznets, *Economic Growth*, Glencoe III, 1959, pp. 20–1.

3. Phyllis Deane, *The First Industrial Revolution*, Cambridge 1965, pp. 222 ff.

Table I provides similar data for other countries which became industrialised in the course of the nineteenth century.

The results of this growth in income per head can be set out in other indices which may be more immediately significant. In a pre-industrialised country the expectation of life at birth is less than 30 years. In a pre-industrialised country over half the average personal income is absorbed by the cost of living, and in frequent years of famine the whole of the average personal income is not enough to buy the food needed simply for subsistence. In an industrialised country hunger has disappeared, food expenditure absorbs no more than a quarter of the average personal expenditure, expectation of life at birth is well above 60 years. Consumption and investment have increased dramatically and no matter what index is drawn up, a rise in the figures takes place corresponding to the Industrial Revolution, which has no precedent in history; a leap forward into a completely new world.

The data which I have set out above concerning the growth in population and production are related to other data concerning the massive growth in international communications and their speed. By communications here I mean the movement of merchandise and people as well as the exchange of news and information; I therefore refer to the progress of shipping, railways, road transport and air transport, as well as to that of books, newspapers, the telephone, radio and television. The extraordinary growth in world production in the last two centuries is inconceivable unless one takes into account the development of communications and the greater specialisation and efficiency which derived from it. The implications of the phenomenon are not only economic, however. Societies which for hundreds and thousands of years had been practically unaware of each other, and then developed according to completely diverse and alien forms of culture, were suddenly placed in immediate contact—and, if the occasion arose, positions of conflict. Even 200 years ago, it took months, as well as the participation of ambassadors and dignitaries, for a message from the King of England to reach the Emperor of China. Nowadays the President of the United States can telephone direct to the President of the Soviet Union and discuss immediately the matter in hand without the need of itinerant intermediaries.

It is in matters like this that the historical discontinuity represented by the Industrial Revolution which I mentioned earlier is dramatically obvious. I must take up this point again. Before the Industrial Revolution 60 to 80% of the active population of any country was employed in some form of agricultural activity and lived in the country. An industrialised country has no more than 5 or 10% of its active population employed in agriculture, and the greater part of the people tend to live in large urban agglomerations. A transformation of this kind has implications which obviously go beyond demographic and economic areas and invade the whole socio-cultural sphere. But that is not all. The quantitative leap forward resulting from the Industrial Revolution which is illustrated by the demographic and economic indices that I gave earlier, is of such proportions as to force through in every area of human activity radical qualitative changes which combine with those which are connected with the abandonment of the land. Stendhal was profoundly right when, referring to the Industrial Revolution, he wrote that it was not only limited to the sphere of production but involved a total, drastic change 'in customs, ideas, beliefs.'

The socio-cultural change required and imposed by the Industrial Revolution is shown in all its global and radical vastness in the case of the so-called 'underdeveloped' countries, i.e., pre-industrial countries, which are facing problems of industrialisation. The fact that the Industrial Revolution began in England depends amongst other things on the fact that in this country in the sixteenth and seventeenth centuries social and political structures, mental attitudes and scales of value had developed which were favourable to industrialisation. The Industrial Revolution gained easy access on the continents of Europe and North America because the societies in these areas had a good many socio-cultural patterns in common with English society. When it is a question of bringing about a revolution outside Europe or North America, one realises that the introduction of new machinery and new productive technology is part, and a small part only, of the desired renewal, and that machinery and technology only have significance and can only operate in the context of a new socio-cultural atmosphere. What to a casual observer might appear merely an economic and technological problem, instead turns out to be a formidable and much more complex problem of political, social and cultural upheaval.

'Industrial Revolution' is a label. The validity of any definition cannot be judged in absolute terms: it depends how it is used to interpret the phenomena under examination or to demonstrate a given thesis. I am certain that we are denying ourselves a satisfactory understanding of the problems which afflict mankind today if we adopt a definition of 'Industrial Revolution' which limits the concept to those socio-economic-cultural developments which took place in Western Europe between 1750 and 1900. It seems more rational to me to look at it from a wider point of view, and to say that in those more industrially advanced countries such as the United States, Russia, Great Britain, Sweden and Japan, the Industrial Revolution has not ended: only the first stage is over. This fact is so obvious that those who cling to a narrow definition of 'Industrial Revolution' are then obliged to speak of a 'second Industrial Revolution'. If it were merely a question of words, the matter would not be particularly important. But it is not simply a question of definitions. If the Industrial Revolution has not ended but is continuing and is only now entering its second stage, this means that even the more advanced industrial societies are having to face problems of social restructuring and cultural and political renewal, which are no less formidable than those problems which beset the so-called underdeveloped countries. In the middle of the nineteenth century the social and political structures, ideologies and culture of England, the United States, France, Switzerland and Belgium were adapted to the completion of the first stage of the Industrial

Revolution. But technological progress and demographical development are now relentlessly imposing the second stage of the Industrial Revolution. Once we have set out on the road to industrialisation it is unthinkable to turn back and it is impossible to stop. Machines dictate the rate of our development. And paradoxically that process which solved the problems in the past is beginning to pose other problems which we are neither used to nor prepared for.

The industrial society of the future requires a new type of man. The agriculturalist might have been illiterate, but there is no place for illiteracy in the industrial society. In order to live and survive in such a society the individual needs several years' instruction and the development of a new mentality in which intuition is replaced by rationality, approximation by precision, emotion by calculation. On the other hand, an industrial society is characterised by continuous and rapid technological change. In such a society established systems quickly become obsolete and men are no exception to the rule. The agricultural worker could live his whole life on a few ideas learnt in adolescence. Industrial man is subjected to a process which is continually forcing him to become up-to-date and is forever leaving him behind. In the agricultural society the old man is the wise one: in the industrial society he is a has-been. The annoying division of labour, and the introduction of team-work involve more continuous, more precise and yet more impersonal and oppressing relations with one's fellowmen. 'Privacy' is a habit and a virtue in agricultural society, but it is a singularity in industrial society. The ethical status of most acts had a personal basis in the agricultural society, but in the industrial society most inter-personal relationships tend to be regulated by statistics on probability.

The pre-industrial family unit is traditionally an institution of large numbers and patriarchal in character, which, besides its basic function of procreating, raising and educating new generations, accepts responsibilities for what is now called 'social security'. The family in the industrial society is a numerically restricted unit, relatively less stable, with greatly reduced functions because society and the state are taking over many of its traditional duties. The changed numerical relationship reflects characteristically the reduced role of the family: in the agricultural world the family is a large nucleus in a numerically small society; in the industrial world the family is a numerically small nucleus in an ever-increasing society.

These are facile diagnoses and forecasts. But there are other and much more difficult problems. The new dimensions on which mankind works, whether as regards our numerical entity or our productive and destructive potentiality or our cognitive and organisative levels, impose a world-wide restructuring of human society, both internal and external—i.e., in relations between members of the same society or between different societies. This is another reason for the great anguish of our generation—because the problems are many, formidable and pressing and there is no area of human activity, no corner of our society which does not need new solutions. And we seem to lack the necessary time and imagination to solve these problems, encumbered as we are with institutions inherited from a world now dead, impeded by tradition, out-of-date scales of values, customs and points of view, unable to distinguish between fact and fantasy. I said before that the only event historically comparable to the Industrial Revolution is the Neolithic Revolution. But apart from every other consideration, the Neolithic Revolution developed in the course of thousands of years. It took more than 5,000 years to move from the Middle East to Scandinavia and about 2,500 years to pass through from Mexico to the source of the Ohio river. Man had time to adapt gradually. The Industrial Revolution has invaded the world, turned our very existence upside down and overthrown the structures of all existing human societies in the course of only eight generations. And today it is beginning to press with great urgency new problems of such enormity that the human mind can hardly grasp them —the uncontrolled increase in population; the hydrogen bomb; the pollution of the atmosphere, the destruction of the natural surroundings by industrial waste; the demand for further mass education; the presence of an ever-increasing number of old people kept alive but rejected by the rest of society; the breaking up of the traditional state; the scientific organisation of uncontrolled centres of power; the unlimited possibilities held out by geneticists and biologists of influencing nature and the behaviour of man. Under the weight of these problems the old structures crumble. The conservatives complain that they do not understand what is happening and they deceive themselves by trying to keep alive a past which is already dead. Those who understand what is happening do not know of and cannot conceive adequate solutions to these pressing and formidable problems. The young people protest when they realise the inadequacy of the old institutions and the older generation, but they too have no better diagnoses and no better cures, and they give vent to their frustration in surges of violent anarchy and curious hatred against their inheritance, or try to escape reality either by destroying their consciousness or by a desperate search for new religions. Everyone has been taken by surprise. It is the story of the 'Sorcerer's Apprentice' which would be funny if it were not tragic.

1. Population in Europe 1700–1914

André Armengaud

INTRODUCTION

The period from 1700 to 1914 was marked, in Europe, particularly towards the end, not only by vast economic changes but also by an unprecedented increase in population. This was by no means the first demographic expansion, since vast population increases had also taken place in the eleventh, twelfth and thirteenth centuries, and again in the sixteenth. However, in the period under consideration this increase took on dramatic dimensions—the population of Europe, which amounted to about 110 millions in about 1700, had climbed to over 450 millions by 1914. Increases on this scale were quite unprecedented. Moreover, the very pattern of population movements had begun to change, at different times in various European countries—and above all in the West. Previously, and also at the beginning of our period, the mortality rate had been permanently and consistently high, to reach calamitous proportions in times of famine, war, or epidemics. This meant that the population could only increase by virtue of a relatively high birth rate which, in favourable years, helped to make good the losses sustained in hard times. But now this age-old pattern began to give way to a new order in which man's will played an increasingly important part. The mortality rate was greatly reduced by advances in medical science, hygiene and in the economic field, and shortly afterwards the birth rate, too, decreased to new low levels thanks to the more widespread use, at different dates in different countries, of voluntary birth control methods. Since, in general, the drop in the mortality rate anticipated the fall in the birth rate by several decades, the population increased by leaps and bounds during the interval, and would have increased further still had it not been for the exodus of some millions of Europeans who, from about the middle of the nineteenth century, started to pour into the new colonies, and quite particularly into North America and Australasia.

Now, while the broad outlines of these events are well known, many of the details have remained obscure. In particular, we are uncertain of the causes, the nature, and the precise timing of the decline in the mortality and birth rates, questions into which many demographers have begun to look more closely especially since the Second World War. What then are the precise sources on which they can draw?

DEMOGRAPHIC DATA

During the period under consideration, governments in various countries tried increasingly to initiate statistical surveys of various kinds, for purposes of more efficient tax collection, army recruiting or general administrative reasons. It was in the eighteenth century, for example, that all the Scandinavian and some of the German countries first introduced a regular, and several other countries a partial, census. Hence it is often said, somewhat glibly no doubt, that the eighteenth century was the cradle of the statistical age.

In fact, demographic data began to be compiled much earlier, although primarily for ecclesiastical reasons. Chief among these compilations were the parish registers of births, marriages and deaths. Occasionally the registers also contained complete lists of parishioners and even of persons who had come into, or left, the parish during a particular year. In the eighteenth century, parish registers in general began to be kept more meticulously and far more universally, and the number which has been preserved is correspondingly greater. In France, King Francis I had ordered as early as 1539 (Edict of Villers-Cotterets) that all parish priests must keep a full record of births, marriages, and deaths, but the crown had, time and again, to enforce and modify this edict before a satisfactory system of records was at last established. In England, the oldest Anglican parish records go back to 1538, but the majority date from after 1600 and those of dissenting and other churches are still more recent. In Norway, where the oldest parish registers extant date from 1623, it was only towards the end of the seventeenth century and in the first half of the eighteenth that their use became widespread—most of the registers that have come down to us start between 1685 and 1755. The position is much the same in Sweden, where the keeping of parish registers was made compulsory in 1686.

On the far side of Europe, in Rumania, the custom of keeping parish registers was introduced by the Catholic Church in the sixteenth century. Other churches followed suit—Protestants at the beginning, Uniates at the end, of the seventeenth century, and the Orthodox Church a century later. The Uniate and the Orthodox registers were drawn up in Rumanian, the Catholic ones in Latin, the Protestant ones in Hungarian, and the Lutheran in German.

Many other examples could be cited: suffice it to say, however, that there is scarcely a country in Europe in which some sort of parish register was not introduced. According to a Swedish law of 1748, quite elaborate reports, drawn from the current records, were to be filled out each year (later every three years) by the pastor of each parish— giving births in each calendar month by sex and by legitimacy; marriages and annulments; and deaths by sex, by age, and by cause, with some additional information. It has been said that each pastor's office became 'a small statistical laboratory.'

A Tabular Commission was established in Sweden in 1749 to consolidate and analyse all the parish returns. Sweden was thus the first country to compile a series of reliable reports on its population.

France under the monarchy also tried to analyse her vital statistics by the scrutiny of parish registers. The first analysis of this kind was made by Colbert for Paris only, and covered the years 1670 to 1683 inclusive. His trial effort was repeated on a wider scale in the eighteenth century. From 1772, at the request of Controller-General Terray, a yearly account of the numbers of births, marriages and deaths was established for each *généralité* (administrative district) and some of the statistics were published by the French Academy of Sciences. Thus when the new science of population studies saw the light of day at the end of the eighteenth century, it could draw on a wealth of reliable data. Moreover, in most countries, the state began gradually to establish its own registers of births, marriages and deaths. The civil administration was thus separated from the clerical in yet another field, and this was one of the most important developments in demographic history. In France, the revolutionary government made the registration of vital events a public responsibility, assigned, by a law passed on 20th September, 1792, to the mayor of every commune. All records had to be made out in duplicate: one set going to the Records Office at the end of the year, and the other being kept in the Town Hall. This system, with a few minor improvements, is used throughout most of Europe to this day—in the countries annexed by Napoleon it was introduced as part and parcel of the Napoleonic Code. Elsewhere, the change came about later. In Great Britain, it was not until 1837 that the State took charge of civil records, and not until 1874 that the registration of births and deaths was made compulsory. Hungary introduced secular records as late as 1894. In any case, soon after they took over the job of keeping such records most European governments also began to publish statistical surveys.

Another important source on which demographers can draw is the census count. For a long time, many European countries had taken regular censuses of 'hearths' or households in the statistical sense of the word, chiefly for tax purposes; but in the period under review, general census counts began to be made as well. They may therefore be considered a characteristic feature of modern Western civilisation—previously the need for gathering such information had neither been felt nor, for that matter, could it have been adequately met: a government can only conduct a reliable census count once it has built up an efficient administrative machine. Often special government departments had to be set up to collect and analyse the results of these early surveys. In France, an official department responsible for statistics was first founded in 1800, disbanded in 1812, and re-established on a broader basis in 1833. In

England, in the same year, the Board of Trade set up a Statistics Office, and in 1837, the General Register Office. Prussia established an official bureau of statistics in 1810, Bavaria followed suit in 1813, and Austria in 1828. The German Empire set up a *Statistisches Reichsamt* in 1872, by which date, general census counts had ceased to be exceptional. German, Italian and Scandinavian countries were the first in modern Europe to publish such counts. The first census to be published was that taken in 1695 in the Habsburg Empire. It listed the number of persons, their sex, age and social status. Later, national censuses were taken in Prussia (1725), in Hesse-Darmstadt (1742), in Hesse-Cassel (1747), in Finland and Sweden (1749), and in Norway and Denmark (1769).

In many countries the regular census was preceded by regional surveys. In France, for instance, the Ancien Régime tried several times to establish the number of inhabitants in a particular Généralité. The first national censuses were taken during the French Revolution—in 1790, 1793 and again in 1796. The Revolution, in effect, ushered in the era of continuous population studies, but it was only in 1801 and 1806, under Napoleon, that the results of a general census were first published. Great Britain, too, took her first national census in 1801, followed by Prussia in 1810, the Netherlands in 1829, Spain in 1842, Italy in 1861, and Russia in 1867.

Soon afterwards, it became common practice to take censuses at regular intervals. Here, too, the Scandinavian countries led the way at the end of the eighteenth century, along with the United States. The chosen interval was ten years in Scandinavia, Great Britain, Italy and Spain, and five years in France and Germany. By about 1860 seventeen European countries were taking censuses at least every ten years; by 1910 the number had grown to twenty-three.

The oldest of these censuses cannot unfortunately be considered reliable in all respects. Moreover, they often fail to provide more than the most rudimentary data. In France, for example, the distinction between rural and urban populations was not introduced until 1846, and detailed information on the distribution of the population by ages and nationality did not become available until 1851, But these defects cannot obscure the fact that these early censuses represent an enormous step forward, and that they provide the demographer with essential information, with data that were sorely lacking in the past.

Finally, the demographer can also draw on a number of other documents, some going back to the eighteenth century but the greater number, and the most detailed among them dating from the nineteenth. These in the main comprise: tax rolls, electoral lists, conscription lists, and replies to administrative enquiries.

In short, the period under review is extremely well documented, and despite many gaps it is true to say that the analysis of all the available material has barely been begun.

POPULATION GROWTH

From what we have said, the reader will have gathered that it is extremely difficult to determine the precise population of Europe in the late seventeenth or early eighteenth centuries. We are forced to fall back on estimates, and it cannot be stressed enough that these can only be uncertain and approximate. With this reservation, we may say that the most probable inferences suggest that Europe, at that time, had a population of from 100 to 120 million. It might be mentioned in passing that this figure had barely changed since the middle of the seventeenth century.

How were these numbers distributed geographically? Without going into details, and supposing the figure to be closer to 120 than 100 million, the largest and most important states in order of size had the following populations: the German Empire, including Austria and her possessions, 20-22 million; France approximately 20 million; European Russia, 9 million; Great Britain, 9 million; Spain, 7-8 million. Again it must be emphasised that these figures are highly speculative.

Now, until 1740, the population increased very slowly, as it had in the previous century: there was no clear demo-

graphic break at this juncture. However, from about 1750
onwards, when Europe counted some 120-140 million inhabitants, the rate of growth began to accelerate rapidly so
that, by 1800, the population had increased to between 180
and 190 million. In other words, the growth rate must have
doubled within 50 years. The reasons for this remarkable
change will be examined below.

Because the data are so imprecise, we cannot establish to
what extent this sudden growth benefited some countries
rather than others—whether Western Europe, thanks to its
high degree of development and its more advanced economy
expanded more rapidly than other parts of the Continent
or whether the rest of Europe took the lead thanks to its
higher birth rate. In any event, the general European
growth rate increased once again in the nineteenth century,
and there was even a relative acceleration in the second half
of that century with respect to the first. It is generally
thought that the population of Europe increased from 187
million in about 1800, to 266 million in 1850, 401 million in
1900 and 468 million in 1913. The increase expressed as a
percentage, which may be roughly put at about 34% for the
second half of the eighteenth century, thus went up to 43%
for the period 1800 to 1850, and to 50% for the period 1850
to 1900. The annual growth rate rose from 7·07‰* in the
first half of the nineteenth century to 8·23‰ in the second,
reaching 12·84‰ in 1900-1913.

Clearly, therefore, not only did the population of Europe
increase in absolute terms but its growth rate kept increasing
as well. This fact is the more remarkable in that, in 1800,
Europe was probably the most highly populated part of the
whole world, with a density of about 18·7 inhabitants per
square kilometre, while the corresponding density of Asia
was barely 14 and that of Africa and America less than 5.
And yet the population of Europe kept expanding even
further, reaching 26·6 inhabitants per square kilometre in
1850 and 40·1 in 1900, by which time it was almost twice as
great as Asia's.

In effect, Europe's share of the world population in-

* ‰ signifies per thousand.

creased from about 21% in 1800 to 22·23% in 1850, and at least to 25% in 1900. It is true that Asia, thanks to its enormous size and the extremely dense population of the monsoon countries, still harboured about 57% of mankind in 1900, but this was a decrease with respect to 1800, when the corresponding figure had been about 64%.

It must be stressed that the population did not increase evenly in all parts of Europe. Unfortunately, so many frontier adjustments took place during the period under consideration that it is extremely difficult to make comparisons. Taking the population within the frontiers established at the dates shown, we obtain the following picture:

Estimated Populations of Various European Countries
from 1800 to 1910 (in millions)

	1800	1850	1900	1910
Denmark	0·9	1·6	2·6	2·9
Finland	1·0	1·6	2·7	3·1
Norway	0·9	1·5[1]	2·2	2·4
Sweden	2·3	3·5	5·1	5·5
Belgium	3·0	4·3[2]	6·7	7·4
Holland	2·2	3·1	5·1	5·9
Gt. Britain	10·9	20·9	36·9	40·8
Ireland	5·0	6·6	4·5	4·4
France	26·9	36·5	40·7	41·5
Spain	11·5	15·5[3]	18·6	19·9
Portugal	3·1	4·2[4]	5·4	6·0
Italy	18·1	23·9	33·9	36·2
Switzerland	1·8	2·4	3·3	3·8
Germany	24·5	31·7	50·6	58·5
Austria-Hungary	23·3	31·3	47·0	51·3
Bulgaria	—	—	3·7	4·3
Russia	—	—	59	112[6]

[1] In 1855; [2] In 1845; [3] In 1857; [4] In 1867; [5] In 1858; [6] In 1897.

While population increases were thus general, except for Ireland which was not, in fact, an independent country at the time, we can see that the growth rate varied greatly from one European country to the next. To take only a few examples, between 1800 and 1910, the population more than tripled in Denmark, Finland and Great Britain, more than doubled in Belgium, Holland, Germany and Austria-Hungary, doubled in Italy, and increased by less than 55% in France. The differences are even more strongly marked for the period from 1850 to 1910. In these 60 years Great Britain, after having doubled her population in the previous half century, doubled it once again, while the population of France increased by only 5 million, i.e. by less than 14%.

Similar differences can be observed in the average annual growth rate during 1850-1910. With the exception of Ireland, where there was a decrease in population, it ranged from 2·2 per thousand inhabitants in France and 4·2 in Spain—the only countries in which the increase was less than 5‰—to 10·2 in Finland, 10·3 in Holland, 10·4 in Denmark and 15·3 in Great Britain.

This uneven development led quite naturally to profound changes in the relative numerical importance of the leading European States. In 1800, Great Britain accounted for only 5·8% of the total population of Europe, in 1900 this proportion had risen to 9·2%. In France, on the other hand, the corresponding proportions decreased from 14·3% at the beginning of the nineteenth century to 10·1% in 1900, with the result that, in 1910, the population of the United Kingdom outstripped that of France for the first time. By contrast, the relative numerical strength of Germany and of Austria-Hungary remained more or less constant throughout the period 1800-1910; the birth-rate in both countries was close to the overall European average.

As a result of all these developments, population densities varied considerably on the eve of the First World War. The highest densities were found in North-Western Europe, and more precisely in some of the countries bordering on the North Sea: Belgium with 259 inhabitants per square kilometre, the Netherlands with 171, England and Wales with 239. Considerably lower population densities were recorded in Italy (121), Germany (120), Austria (95), Switzerland (91), France (74), and Spain (39). Lower densities were also the rule in Eastern Europe (Hungary: 64; Bulgaria: 45;

Rumania: 55; Russia: 26) and particularly in Scandinavia (Sweden: 12; Finland: 8; Norway: 7). Nevertheless, the general population of Europe had been increasing ever since 1700, and much new land had been brought under the plough, from the Low Countries to Russia, but above all in the most sparsely populated areas of Eastern Europe. In the West, agriculture was greatly stimulated by the introduction of new methods (such as the replacement of 'bare fallow', a device for thoroughly cleaning the land, with turnips and other root crops) and of new laws (enclosure acts, etc.), and finally, in the second half of the century, by the rise in agricultural prices which led directly to increased production. In Holland, the reclamation of land from the sea was tackled with new energy, and in the province of Groningen, in particular, a host of peat bogs began to be drained. In France and Ireland, vast tracts of previously uncultivated land were gradually transformed into arable fields. Thus French farmers applied for permission to clear more than 400,000 hectares in 1766-1780. In Schleswig-Holstein, fields reclaimed from fens and heaths added 24% to the existing arable area. At Hainault, in the province of Namur, the Duke of Ahremburg drained 600 hectares of fenland in 1785. Similar cases could be cited from many other regions, and this expansion of agriculture continued into the nineteenth century. In Germany, a great deal of land was reclaimed in the 1770s, particularly in Brandenburg and Hanover, and in Italy reclamation continued well into the twentieth century. It should be mentioned that all this newly reclaimed land was not enough to feed the growing population, and that a great many pastures had to be transformed into arable fields as well. While small peasants still had to supplement their meagre incomes by means of cottage industries, many rural areas, especially in Western Europe, became relatively over-populated. Thus though Great Britain made an early start with industrialisation, her countryside had never before been as highly populated as it was in the first half of the nineteenth century, and this concentration was accompanied by widespread hardship. Ireland, on the brink of the Great Famine,

and with special economic and social problems, was particularly hard hit. In France, the rural population reached
its peak during the reign of Louis Philippe, when some
regions in particular were bursting at the seams. In
Southern and Eastern Europe, the increase in rural
population continued for a long time, so that, despite the
rather low overall growth rate there were still more people
than the land could support at the end of the nineteenth
century, especially in countries with large landed estates.

What is the reason for these marked differences in population trends in various parts of Europe? Basically, it is because cities developed earlier, faster, and on a far larger
scale in Western than they did in Eastern Europe. In effect,
when industrialisation appeared first in the West, it was
associated with a massive increase in urban population.
Since, in most towns, the mortality rate was higher than the
birth rate, and since, even when this was not the case, the
extra births were still insufficient to supply the increasing
demand for labour, the towns kept drawing in an ever
larger number of rural inhabitants. Even so, urban growth,
although considerable, especially after 1750, failed to over-
take rural growth in the eighteenth century. We have, unfortunately, neither enough nor sufficiently accurate data to
allow of a general description of this process, but we do
know that the growth in urban population accelerated even
further during the nineteenth century. One fact alone will
suffice to make this clear: in 1800 there were twenty-three
towns of more than a hundred thousand inhabitants in
Europe, with a total of $5\frac{1}{2}$ million inhabitants; in 1900 there
were 135, with a total of 46 million. The growth of capital
cities was particularly striking. Within a single century, the
population of St. Petersburg increased by 300%, that of
London by 340%, that of Paris by 345%, that of Vienna by
490%, and that of Berlin by 872%.

How did this sudden influx into the towns affect the
leading countries of Europe? Great Britain, in about 1800,
had only one major city, namely London, which had something like a million inhabitants. It was the greatest city in
the world, and far outstripped the rest of Great Britain—

Edinburgh, Liverpool, Glasgow, Manchester, Birmingham
and Bristol numbered from 50,000 to 100,000 inhabitants
each. By 1850 the population of London had grown to
2,363,000 and there were nine other British cities with over
100,000 inhabitants, and eighteen with from 50,000 to
100,000 inhabitants. These twenty-eight cities accounted for
a total of 5·7 million people, roughly a fifth of the entire
population of Great Britain. By 1910, there were 46 British
cities with over 100,000 inhabitants, and the population of
London had leapt to 4·5 million, thanks largely to the
incorporation into the city of outlying towns and villages.

Across the Channel, Paris had a population of 547,000 in
1801, and only two other French cities numbered slightly
more than 100,000 inhabitants each, namely Lyons and
Marseilles. By 1851, Paris counted just over one million
people, Marseilles 195,000 and Lyons 177,000. In 1911,
these figures were respectively 2·8 million, 550,000 and
523,000. By that time, sixteen French cities, including Paris,
Marseilles and Lyons, had populations of more than
100,000 inhabitants.

Germany and Austria together had only three cities with
more than 100,000 inhabitants in 1800, namely Vienna
(247,000), Berlin (172,000) and Hamburg (130,000). Four
other cities—Dresden, Breslau, Königsberg and Cologne—
counted from 50,000 to 60,000 inhabitants each. Fifty years
later, there were five German cities with over 100,000 inhabitants: Vienna (444,000), Berlin (419,000), Hamburg
(132,000), Breslau (114,000) and Munich (110,000). At
that time, the future giants of the Ruhr basin were still
mere villages; Essen, for example, had only 9,000 inhabitants and Düsseldorf 27,000. Altogether some 1,850,000
people lived in fourteen German and Austrian cities of more
than 50,000 inhabitants each. From 1850 to the beginning
of the twentieth century, German industrialisation gave an
enormous impetus to urban development. By 1900 there
were 73 German and three Austrian cities with over 50,000
inhabitants, accounting for a total of 13,650,000 people.
This growth continued; by 1910, Berlin had a little over
two million inhabitants, Vienna had the same number,

followed by Hamburg with 1·1 million. In addition, Munich, Cologne, Leipzig and Dresden all counted more than 50,000. But the most prodigious development took place in the Ruhr. Between 1850 and 1910, Essen increased her population from 9,000 to 295,000; Düsseldorf grew from 27,000 to 359,000 and Dortmund and Duisberg, which had been small hamlets in the middle of the nineteenth century, became major cities of 214,000 and 331,000 inhabitants respectively. By 1910, the German Empire could boast 45 cities of more than 100,000 inhabitants each. Thus, though urbanisation came later to Germany than it did to Great Britain, its ultimate effects were no less dramatic.

At the end of the eighteenth century, Italy, historically an urban civilisation, could boast the greatest number of cities in Europe. Naples at the time counted more than 350,000 inhabitants; Milan, Rome, Venice, Palermo and Genoa between 100,000 and 200,000 each; Florence, Turin and Bologna between 50,000 and 100,000. These nine towns together made up about 7% of Italy's total population. By about 1860 the situation had not greatly changed, only Messina was added to the list of towns with over 100,000 inhabitants. From 1860 to 1910, four other Italian cities grew to this size, but the most striking expansion took place in Rome (539,000) and the industrial centres of Milan (599,000) and Turin (427,000). Naples, too, despite its relative lack of industries, was growing fast and numbered 723,000 inhabitants in 1910, by which date thirteen Italian cities exceeded the 100,000 mark.

Finally in Russia, Moscow and St. Petersburg had over 200,000 inhabitants each by 1800. Unfortunately we do not have precise data on the size of other Russian cities. By 1850, St. Petersburg had taken first place with 485,000 inhabitants, followed by Moscow with 365,000, and there were five other cities with 50,000 to 100,000 inhabitants each: Odessa, Saratov, Kiev, Kazan and Tula. From 1850 to 1900, major Russian cities in general doubled or quadrupled their size. By 1910, the population of St. Petersburg had reached 1·9 million, that of Moscow around 1·5, and there were twelve other cities with over 100,000 inhabitants.

Among these, Odessa had grown to 479,000 and Kiev to 477,000. This was the belated beginning of a process of urban growth that was to accelerate prodigiously after the Revolution of 1917.

The intense growth of cities in the nineteenth century necessarily went hand in hand with marked changes in the relative distribution of the urban and rural populations. Comparisons in this field can only be made with caution, as the definition of these two categories varies considerably from one country to the next. In Great Britain and Scandinavia, the term 'urban population' has a purely administrative and legal connotation: it refers to people living in a district with a particular kind of administrative structure. In France, 'urban population' was defined in 1846 to comprise all those living in a commune with more than 2,000 inhabitants concentrated in the chief town. Elsewhere the distinction is based upon the total number of inhabitants in a given parish, and the lower limit varies from 1,500 in Ireland and 2,000 in Germany and Austria, to 5,000 in Belgium, the Netherlands and Greece, and 6,000 in Italy. Despite these differences, certain facts stand out. To begin with, the rural population, at least of Western Europe, which was still increasing in the first half of the nineteenth century, began to decrease slightly in those countries where the total population was growing most quickly, and more steeply wherever the total population remained relatively stable, for instance in Ireland and France.

In England, for example, the rural population increased from 6·6 million in 1801 to 9·9 million in 1851, decreased to 9·2 million by 1891 and then remained stable for a long time. Similarly, in Germany and in Italy, the rural population remained fairly stable from 1870 to 1914. In France, however, the rural population, which comprised 26·7 million people in 1846, went down to 24·9 million in 1876, to 23 million in 1901 and to 22·1 million in 1911.

The point at which the urban population out-stripped the rural was reached at different dates in different countries— it occurred in 1851 in England and Wales; in 1891 in Germany; and as late as 1931 in France. When looking at these figures, we must remember that 'rural population' is not identical with 'agricultural population'—over much of Western Europe, agriculture ceased to be the most important activity during the second half of the nineteenth century. This change came first in England and Belgium; Germany followed in 1850-1870; France at the end of the Second Empire or the beginning of the Third Republic, and Scandinavia towards the end of the nineteenth century. By contrast, the majority of people living in the Balkans, and in Eastern and Central Europe (with the exception of Bohemia) continued to follow agricultural pursuits until well into the twentieth century. This was true also of Italy (54% of the population employed in agriculture around 1910), and of Spain and Portugal. All these differences reflect disparities in the development of agricultural techniques. As agriculture became increasingly mechanised in various countries at various times, the demand for manpower in this sector of the economy diminished—consumption failed to keep up with agricultural productivity.

In those countries where the fall in agricultural population was most pronounced, it went hand in hand with an expansion of the urban proletariat, with a shift to what Colin Clark has called the secondary (industrial) and tertiary (service) sectors of the economy. Three examples will be sufficient to illustrate this point: between 1851 and 1901, the number of people employed in French agriculture was reduced from 53% to 42%, with a corresponding increase from 25% to 31% in the secondary and from 22% to 27% in the tertiary sector. In Germany, these three sectors employed respectively 42%, 39% and 19% of the working population in 1882; by 1907 these figures had changed to 35%, 42% and 22%. In Sweden, the proportion of agricultural workers fell from 72·4% to 48·8% from 1870 to 1910, while the number of workers employed in the secondary sector rose from 14·6% to 32%, and from 13% to 19·2% in the tertiary sector. This was the beginning of a process that was to culminate in a complete change in European employment patterns.

Now, the increase in urban populations had other repercussions as well. To begin with it led to a geographical spread of the existing towns and cities by the growth of suburbs. Suburban housing offered the advantage of lower costs and freedom from town taxes, and was greatly facilitated by the development of better transport systems. In London, no more than 13% of the total population lived in the suburbs in 1861; by 1891 this figure had risen to 25%, and it continued to go up. Fifty-seven thousand people lived in the suburbs of Berlin in 1871; 500,000 by the end of the century. In France, the suburbs of Paris grew more rapidly than the capital itself. From 1801 to 1856 the population of Paris increased by 65%, that of the Départment de la Seine by 496%. In 1861, the suburban communes closest to the city were incorporated into Paris, but the remaining suburbs more than compensated for this loss in population. From 1861 to 1896, Paris itself increased its population by 50%, the rest of the Départment by 203%. Similar developments took place in most other European capitals.

The expansion of the cities introduced a host of special problems. Gross overcrowding in many districts not only produced insanitary living conditions but also lowered moral standards and administrative efficiency. As the cities grew, public transport systems capable of carrying more and more passengers had to be developed. In rapid succession came the omnibus, the tramway—first horse-drawn and later electric—followed by metropolitan railways. In some cases, special plans were drawn up to meet the new conditions, the most famous example being the reconstruction of Paris by Baron Haussman during the reign of Napoleon III. However, in most cases what plans were put forward were piecemeal and came too late.

The teeming cities had to be provisioned, and this raised fresh problems of transportation. Water, too, was needed in great quantities by the new cities, and a host of waterworks and reservoirs had to be constructed. Meanwhile, the overcrowding of cities contributed to the deterioration of public health: the spread of tuberculosis and the recurrent epidemics of cholera resulted directly from the rapid growth of the urban population.

The vast influx of new inhabitants altered the very nature of city life, and especially its social and moral quality. Social segregation became more marked as different districts were taken over by one class or another. The hold of religion grew weaker, particularly as the churches proved too slow to adapt to the changing conditions. Crime became increasingly frequent and the suicide rate mounted.

Finally, insofar as the urban population was made up of new immigrants, its structure as regards, age, sex, married status, birth and mortality differed from the national average in many ways. A detailed analysis of this phenomenon would take us too far afield.

NATURAL GROWTH

How can we explain the enormous growth of population in Europe which, as we have just seen, continued from the eighteenth century to the beginning of the twentieth? Did its causes lie in an altered birth or mortality rate, or in a combination of the two? There can be no simple answer to this question, if only because population increases were not uniform throughout Europe, and also because demographers disagree in their analyses, particularly of developments during the first half of the period under review, for which there is a marked lack of data.

It would seem that somewhere between 1750 and 1800 the mortality rate began that process of decline which, with a few breaks, has continued until today. As one would expect, the decline began in the 'crisis death-rate'; i.e. the death-rate caused by famines, epidemics and wars. It was followed by a decline in the ordinary death-rate. This decline was a turning point in the history of European demography.

If we look, first of all, at the period from 1750 to 1825, we discover that several factors contributed noticeably to this process. To begin with, agricultural productivity was greatly increased due to improved farming methods, and quite particularly to the introduction of artificial manures, of new methods of crop rotation, and improvements in livestock resulting from planned in-breeding and cross-fertilisation. Large fluctuations from one harvest to the next were reduced, and with the exception of Ireland (1845-50), famine disappeared from Western Europe. (In Great Britain, the last famine occurred in 1709-10.) However, minor shortages continued to occur, above all on the Continent, until the third quarter of the nineteenth century.

It seems likely that Europeans, better fed than ever before, became more resistant to disease. Hence, despite the frightful conditions of the urban proletariat in the first half of the nineteenth century the overall picture was one of gradual progress.

Moreover, notable advances were made in medicine. Up till then, doctors had understood so little about their subject that they probably killed more people than they cured. However, once again, although we do not fully understand the precise mechanics of the change, the situation began to improve in the eighteenth century.

This is not to say that epidemics had disappeared. Thus plague swept through Marseilles in 1720, through the Ukraine in 1737, through Messina in 1743, and through Moscow in 1789-91. Nevertheless, it was not so grievous as in the past. But typhus was common in times of war and typhoid fever at all times. In 1761, a violent influenza epidemic struck at the whole of Europe. Whooping cough, now considered a minor children's disease, often proved fatal—in Sweden alone it is thought to have caused the death of 40,000 children from 1749 to 1764. But the most formidable killer diseases in the eighteenth century were undoubtedly the infectious fevers, and quite particularly smallpox. It would take us too long to enumerate even the most important outbreaks; suffice it to say that in 1719 it killed 14,000 people in Paris alone and that, in 1770, it ravaged most of the major European cities. In 1830-37, cholera made its first appearance in Europe, claiming 100,000 victims in France and more than 50,000 in the United Kingdom. There were fresh outbreaks in 1847-49, 1851-54, and again in 1855, when the disease struck at the Eastern Mediterranean and decimated the armies fighting

The Cholera Epidemic in Europe (1829-1837)

August 1831
Helsinki

St. Petersburg
June 1831

Kazan

Nizhny-Novgorod
September 1830

Moscow

Orenburg
August 1829

Russo-Polish War

wow
May 1831

Astrakhan

Aral Sea

(in 1823)
July-August 1830

Odessa

Galatz

Bucharest
July 1831

Black Sea

Tiflis
August 1830

Constantinople
June-August 1831

Trebizond

Erzurum

TURKISH EMPIRE

Smyrna

Aleppo

Russian war against
Turkey and Persia

PERSIA
September 1829

Baghdad

from India
since 1817

Turco-Egyptian
conflict

SYRIA
March 1831

Alexandria
July 1831

Cairo

EGYPT

*July 1830
from Mecca*

Persian Gulf

the Crimean war. Malaria, tuberculosis, and various deficiency diseases were also rife at the time.

The only known way of combating epidemic diseases was to establish a 'cordon sanitaire', a task that was generally entrusted to the soldiery, who also placed any suspected travellers into quarantine. In the eighteenth century, these and other preventive methods became very much more effective because of better administrative techniques. In addition, medical science now took enormous strides forward, not least in midwifery.

Many known diseases were accurately described for the first time, and could thus be distinguished from other infections. Treatment became more empirical, and purgatives, water, diet and bloodletting began to replace those magical cures that had for so long held pride of place. Quinine began to be used against fevers, and the plague, for reasons that have not yet been fully explained, did not recur in Western Europe after 1720. Finally, doctors were able to prevent smallpox by inoculation and, from the end of the eighteenth century, by vaccination.

The first of these new methods was popularised in England in 1720 by Lady Montague, the wife of the British Ambassador in Constantinople. In this process, healthy individuals were made resistant to smallpox by injections of pus taken from a convalescent subject. Inoculation was slowly accepted, at least among the wealthier classes, and spread from England, first to France, where its use was vigorously opposed, and then to Spain and the rest of the Continent. However, inoculation was not always as successful as it was vaunted to be; it had the disadvantage of tending to keep the disease alive and even to increase its spread, so much so that some medical historians think it had a negligible effect on the death rate. Nevertheless it remained in use until the great discovery of vaccination with cow-pox This idea first occurred to Dr. Edward Jenner when he observed that people who had had cow-pox were immune to smallpox. On 14th May, 1796, for the first time, he vaccinated a child and afterwards verified that he had immunised it. However, the effects of these discoveries barely made themselves felt until the nineteenth century, when the use of vaccination became widespread and smallpox began to disappear from Europe.

At the same time, medicine took new strides in other spheres as well, and for the first time became truly scientific, notably in the development of modern methods of diagnosis, for instance by Laënnec, and in the development of herbal and chemical drugs.

Progress in agriculture and medicine, then, brought about a widespread if not universal lowering of the mortality rate, particularly among young people and children, on which subject we have a wealth of information.

Since this decline in the mortality rate was not uniform, we shall examine its effects on the principal countries of Europe one by one.

Although we cannot be certain, it appears that the English mortality rate increased steeply from 1700 to 1740. According to Brownlee, it rose from 28-29% in 1701-10 to 35-36% in 1731-40. This high mortality has been attributed to heavy gin-drinking, but it seems likely that other factors were involved as well. In any case, the mortality rate started to fall after 1740, dropping from 35-36% in 1740 to 26-27% in 1791-1800. This long period of declining mortality was a new and even revolutionary fact in the history of European demography, the more so as it occurred well after famine had been reduced or eliminated. Did this decline become even more pronounced during the first twenty years of the nineteenth century, as used to be generally believed? Probably not, but it does seem likely that the English mortality rate continued its slow decline until 1850 (except, perhaps during 1820-40), despite several epidemics.

In Norway, mortality remained static throughout the eighteenth century; in Sweden, by contrast and despite temporary set-backs, it had already begun to fall appreciably by 1750 and continued to do so throughout the eighteenth century.

Similarly, in France, the mortality rate began to fall from the middle of the eighteenth century. Local studies show clearly that, during the last decades of the Ancien Régime, there was a particularly strong decline in infant and juvenile mortality, and a concomitant rise in life expectancy.

Bad harvests continued to exert a stronger influence than they had in England, but even there the general trend was observed. Though the revolutionary wars brought a temporary increase in the mortality rate, they did not halt the process for long. It is true that the mortality rate levelled out in the nineteenth century (decreasing from 26-27% in 1800 to about 23% in 1860-69), but even that represents a progressive decline.

The mortality in Belgium and Switzerland seems to have decreased in a similar manner, but, in the absence of general studies it is difficult to fill in the details for Europe as a whole. We also know that most of Central, Southern and Eastern Europe, in the grip of autocratic rulers, experienced famines, epidemics and wars which caused temporary but sharp increases in the mortality rate. In Hungary, for example, the famines of 1788-89 and of 1816-17 claimed more than 50,000 victims each. In Bohemia, the death rate rose steadily from 30·4% in 1785-89 to 39·5% in 1805-09, doubtless because population increases were not accompanied by a corresponding rise in food production. But in spite of everything there was gradual progress even in these parts: in Poland, for instance, there were no more great epidemics after the middle of the eighteenth century, and since the birth rate was relatively high, the population kept increasing steadily.

The data, fortunately, become more numerous and more detailed for the second half of the nineteenth century, and show beyond any doubt that the mortality rate continued to fall, sometimes extremely rapidly. This development was apparently due to continued economic progress, which benefited increasingly large sections of the population. Improved methods of transport (steamships and railways) greatly helped the elimination of local shortages, at least in Western Europe. There was no longer any correlation, for example, between the price of wheat and the mortality rate. In addition, further progress was made in medicine, thanks

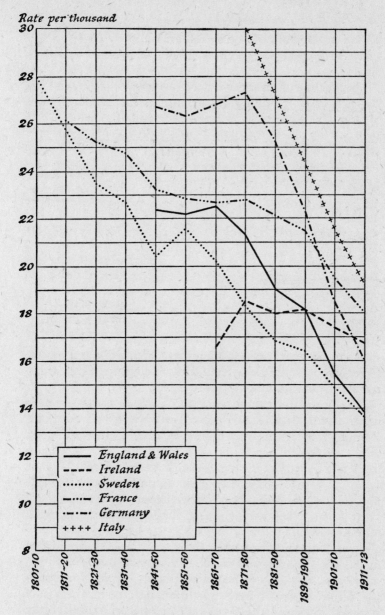

Rate per thousand

Death rate in several European countries in the nineteenth century

largely to the work of Louis Pasteur, whose new serums and vaccines helped to check a large number of epidemic diseases.

The decline in mortality may be clearly seen in the following table including all countries for which figures covering the dates under review are available:

MORTALITY RATE PER THOUSAND INHABITANTS

	1851–1860	*1901–1910*
Austria	31·4	23·2
Belgium	22·5	16·4
Denmark	20·6	14·2
England and Wales	22·2	15·4
Finland	28·7	18·0
France	24·0	19·4
Germany	26·4	18·7
Netherlands	25·6	15·1
Norway	17·1	14·2
Sweden	21·7	16·7

It can be seen that although the decrease is not uniform, it occurred in all these countries, including those which started off with a low mortality rate.

Finally on the eve of the First World War, the highest general mortality rates occurred in Eastern and Southern Europe. The figures were highest in Russia (approximately 29‰), followed by Rumania, Hungary, Serbia, Spain (22·8‰), Austria, Portugal, Italy (20·4‰) and France (18·6‰). The lowest rates were found in Germany (16·5‰) and, above all, in North-Western Europe, where England (14·1‰) and Denmark (13·2‰) had reduced mortality to an especially low level.

For a long time, mortality remained considerably higher in the cities than it was in the countryside. Little by little, however, the situation began to change, thanks largely to the introduction of new amenities and modern ideas of personal hygiene, etc. As a result, the urban mortality rate gradually became lower than the rural.

In conclusion, it must be stressed that the decline in

general mortality was largely due to the reduction in infant mortality. This occurred very early on in Scandinavia, followed by North-Western Europe, and much later and more slowly by Southern and Eastern Europe. In Sweden the infant mortality rate, i.e. the number of deaths per thousand births in the age group 0-1, dropped from 178·5 in 1801-10 to 146 in 1851-60, and 84·5 in 1901-10. France, for the same periods, had infant mortality rates of: 191, 173 and 132 per thousand respectively. In England and Wales, where figures are only available from the middle of the nineteenth century, the rate fell from 154 per thousand in 1851-60 to 127·5 in 1901-10. At the latter date the rate was still 186·5 in Germany, 159·5 in Italy, and more than 200 in Spain, Austria-Hungary, Rumania and Russia. Even so, the rate had begun to fall in the majority of these countries.

Taken as a whole, this long decline in the mortality rate was the most permanent and most pronounced in the recorded history of mankind.

It is still impossible to draw up a table covering the whole of eighteenth-century Europe, although current research into parish registers will no doubt enable us to do so one day. All we can say for the moment is that in France, for example, the life expectancy at birth could have been no more than about 29 years. This figure represents the average, and varied widely for different classes and in different parts of the country. Thus we know that, in nearby Geneva, the life expectancy at birth for members of the ruling class rose from 41·6 years in the first half of the century to 47·3 in the second half. Now it seems certain that the population of the city as a whole could not have enjoyed so high an expectation of life. In Sweden, the corresponding figures for the second half of the century were 33·7 years for men and 36·6 for women. Between 1791 and 1815, they went up to 35·3 and 38·4 respectively. In this matter, Sweden was far in advance of the rest of Europe and remained so for a considerable time.

In the nineteenth century, despite very great class and sex variations, and differences in economic development, there was an increase in life expectancy throughout Europe, as the following figures illustrate:

		Men yrs.	Women yrs.
England and Wales	1838-1854	39·9	41·8
	1901-1910	48·5	52·3
France	1817-1831	38·3	40·8
	1908-1913	48·4	52·4
Sweden	1816-1840	39·5	43·5
	1901-1910	54·5	56·9
Denmark	1835-1844	42·6	44·7
	1911-1915	56·2	59·2
Germany	1871-1881	35·5	38·4
	1910-1911	47·4	50·6
Spain	1900	33·8	35·7
	1910	40·9	42·5
Italy	1876-1887	35·1	35·4
	1901-1911	44·2	44·8
Russia	1896-1897	31·4	33·3

It must be stressed that the increase in life expectancy resulted less from a prolongation of adult life than from the reduction in the mortality rate for young people, and especially for infants.

This led to an increase in the number of people of all ages. In France, for example, out of every 10,000 individuals born, the number of survivors was as follows:

Age	Male			Female		
	1801-07	1860-62	1900-02	1805-07	1860-62	1900-02
1 yr.	7930	8180	8410	8240	8440	8680
20 yrs.	5853	6505	7310	6231	6704	7566
60 yrs.	2870	3870	4179	3224	4046	4730

This development was even more marked in Sweden:

Age	1757-1763*	Male 1816-1840	1841-1855	1891-1900	1757-1763	Female 1816-1840	1841-1855	1891-1900
1 yr.	7800	8203	8366	8891	—	8451	8605	9079
20 yrs.	5700	6718	6881	7736	—	7012	7185	7900
60 yrs.	2930	3278	3578	5095	—	4089	4445	5640
*Both sexes								

These tables show clearly that the drop in the mortality rate was an important factor in the growth of European populations during the eighteenth and nineteenth centuries. In turn it influenced the birth rate, by reducing the number of marriage partners who died before the end of the woman's fertile period. Let us therefore take a close look at the birth rate.

The birth rate must be studied in conjunction with the marriage rate, since the majority of births in Europe are engendered by married couples. Now the marriage rate, although the most stable of the three factors controlling the size of population, nevertheless does, at different times and in different places, fluctuate considerably.

On this subject we still lack adequate information, at least as far as the eighteenth century is concerned. In France, if we can extrapolate from the records of certain villages which have been studied in detail, it seems that the marriage rate rose appreciably during 1700-1800. In effect, deaths recorded among women over 50 show that very few spinsters were involved. Moreover, the age at which women married during the whole of the eighteenth century seems to have been relatively high, generally 25 or thereabouts, and this had an important bearing on fertility.

In Belgium, similarly, the marriage rate was high; it is estimated at 12-17 ‰ in Flanders at the beginning of the eighteenth century, and in the countryside the rate appears to have been higher still.

In Scandinavia, on the other hand, the marriage rate was

relatively low. In Norway, where overall figures are only available from 1770 onwards, the marriage rate was around 7-8‰. In Sweden, it even declined; from 1750 to 1810 the proportion of married men (in the male population over 15) dropped from 60% to 55·3% and that of married women from 50·3% to 48·4%. Out of every ten thousand adults (men over 18 and women over 15) 913 men and 737 women were married annually in 1756-65, and only 723 men and 557 women in 1796-1805. (The discrepancy was probably due to the fact that the women were more numerous than the men.)

Data from Southern Europe are too fragmentary to allow of any generalisation. In Catalonia, the rate seems to have been relatively high, at all events higher than for Spain as a whole, but its chronological development is unknown. In Italy, by contrast, we know that the marriage rate decreased steadily over the century by about 33% in Venice, but increased slightly on the mainland. We lack precise details for the rest of Europe.

Even so, it is possible to trace the evolution of the birth rate during the eighteenth century, at least in broad outlines. In general the picture was affected by the persistence of old behaviour patterns, and the emergence of isolated geographical and social pockets in which these patterns tended to disappear.

Most married couples did not traditionally practise voluntary birth control. The results can be clearly seen in the French village of Crulai in the Départment de l'Orne, which has been studied by Etienne Gautier and Louis Henry. Here the fertility rate for married couples was very high in the first half of the eighteenth century, at any rate above the present average for Western Europe. Married women of under 39 had an average of two children every five years, and women under 30 gave birth to three almost as often as to two children in the same period. It should be noted in passing that, despite the common belief, most women did not conceive every year. In fact, women do not normally conceive while they are breast-feeding, and breast-feeding used to be the general rule. Families of fifteen or

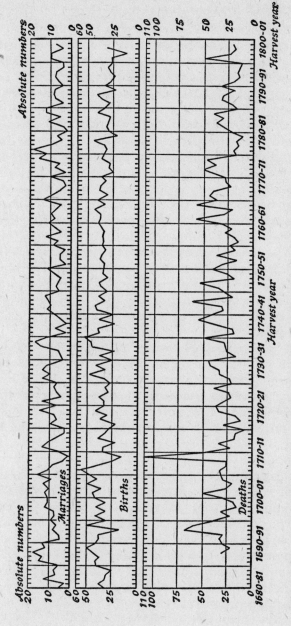

Marriages, births and deaths in a French Rural Parish in the eighteenth century.
(After E. Gautier and L. Henry; La population de Crulai, Normandy)

twenty children which have been cited as typical of the age were, in fact, few and far between. Nevertheless, the birth rate was high, and, in general, women who lived with their husbands until their menopause gave birth to eight, six or four children, depending on whether they had married at twenty, twenty-five or thirty. In addition, child-bearing used to continue throughout the fertile period in a woman's life, in contrast to the modern pattern in which all the children come during the first few years of marriage. In consequence, most married women under 40 were either carrying children or breast-feeding them. Finally, studies of the interval between marriage and the birth of the first child show that very few children were conceived before marriage, and since illegitimate births were also rare, we may conclude that pre-marital intercourse was extremely uncommon. Hence it is nonsense to talk of 'a natural fertility cycle'—social no less than psychological factors (late marriages, prolonged breast-feeding and the prohibition of extramarital sex relations) acted as so many brakes upon the physiological cycle.

It is true that Crulai is only one example, and that a rural one, and we can only extrapolate from its results with the utmost caution. The study of parish registers has shown that even within France the behaviour of married couples and the resulting birth rate was subject to many local variations, and when further research will enable us to analyse birth rates for the whole of Europe, even greater local differences will no doubt emerge.

In fact, many factors have a strong bearing on the birth rate: age of marriage, the average expectation of life of a married couple, temporary migrations, economic factors, the state of health and so on. Without going into details and without stopping to describe what we know of the conditions in the different countries, it is interesting to enquire how far voluntary birth control, which was to become the most important factor of all, was being practised in the period under investigation.

Although we do not have all the answers to this question, it would seem that some social groups, of small numerical importance, were already using birth control techniques by the beginning of the eighteenth century. This was certainly true of the bourgeoisie of Geneva, where the practice was introduced in the second half of the seventeenth century, and of the French nobility, whose legitimate birth rate dropped continuously or in stages from 1650 to 1750. The average number of children per noble family declined from 6·15 in 1650-99 to 2·79 in 1700-49, and to 2·0 at the end of the eighteenth century. In the meantime the average maternal age dropped from 31·2 to 25·1. The British aristocracy followed a different trend, but in Sweden, among the population as a whole, the average number of births per thousand married women between the ages of 15 and 50, dropped from 251 (1756-65) to 232 (1796-1800). This decrease is too great to be explained by late marriages, and we are therefore led to conclude that voluntary birth control must have been practised by at least some Swedish couples during the second half of the eighteenth century.

In France, on the other hand, it seems probable that voluntary birth control did not become widespread until the Revolution, when it took root so rapidly as to set France apart from all the other European nations.

There were, however, no concomitant changes in the French marriage pattern. Thus from 1811-20 there were 15·9 newly married people per thousand inhabitants, from 1851-60 the proportion remained the same, and from 1906-10 it decreased by a tiny fraction to 15·8. This shows a remarkable stability but was by no means exceptional. In England and Wales, the number of newly married people changed little as well: it dropped from 16·9 per thousand in 1851-60 to 15·3 in 1906-10. For Germany, the figures were 15·6 and 15·9; for Austria, 15·6 and 15·4; for the Netherlands, 15·8 and 14·9; and for Belgium, 14·7 and 15·8. A few countries had unusually high marriage rates; thus in Serbia, the proportion of newly married people was 23·6 ‰ in 1861-70 and it was still 19·9 ‰ in 1906-10. In Hungary, the rate was more than 18 ‰ at the beginning of the twentieth century. In Ireland, on the other hand, the rate was exceptionally low: 10·6 % in 1861-70, and 10·3 ‰ from

1906-10. This was largely due to the Great Famine of 1846-50 and to the massive emigration of young people that ensued.

In short, no definite or consistent trend emerges from the study of nuptiality, except possibly in Sweden and Norway, where there seems to have been a slight decline from 1811 to 1910. This is not to say that the marriage rate in general was free of minor fluctuations, caused chiefly by wars and economic crises. And often, too, a rise would be followed by a decline. In 1813, the marriage rate in France increased by 68% because married men were exempted from conscription, but the number decreased in the following year because many engaged couples, who would normally have married during that year, had already done so.

However, while the marriage rate remained more or less stable, the birth rate began to decline in most parts of Europe and quite especially in the West.

This happened first of all in France, where it dropped from 36-37‰ in 1770-89 to 35‰ in 1792, and to 33‰ under Napoleon. Despite temporary fluctuations the decline continued from 1820 to 1850. The rate tended to settle at around 26 births per thousand during the Second Empire, and then, with a few minor fluctuations, it continued to go down until the First World War. From 1860-1914, for example, the average rate decreased during every five-year period.

In Ireland, too, the birth rate fell early and dramatically after the Great Famine of 1846-50, and never regained its old level, because of mass emigration, which left an unequal proportion of women behind, and also because of the custom of contracting late marriages. After 1880, the Irish birth rate dropped even more dramatically, but the case of Ireland is quite exceptional.

In general, a sharp decline in the birth rate came much later. With the exception of France, all countries for which statistics are available had a relatively low birth rate in 1801-14. Throughout Scandinavia, the rate was below that of 1790-1800 but after 1815 it rose once again. In Sweden, the birth rate reached its nineteenth-century peak in 1821-

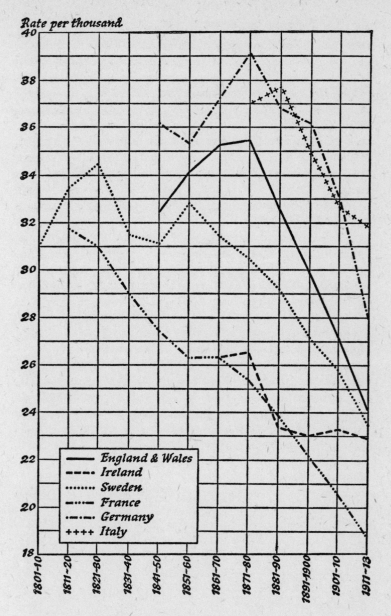

Rate per thousand

Birth-rate in several European countries in the nineteenth century

1830. A similar development occurred in Tuscany. Prussia, in 1816-26 and Austria in 1819-26 still had a very high birth rate, reaching or even exceeding 40‰. In Europe as a whole, the birth rate fell very slowly during the first three-quarters of the nineteenth century. In Sweden, it remained at about 30‰ up to about 1880 and then fell fairly rapidly. In England and Wales, where the rate had reached its peak of more than 35‰ from 1862-78, a marked decline began in 1879, and from 1896 on, the average birth rate was less than 30‰.

In Germany the decrease came later still. The birth rate reached 36‰ during 1896-1900 and fell to a minimum of 31·6‰ in 1906-10. In Southern Europe, where we have figures for only part of the period 1850-1914, the rate decreased as well, though not so sharply. In Spain, the birth rate averaged 36·2‰ in 1881-1890, and 34·4‰ in 1901-10. In Italy, it dropped from 36·9‰ in 1871-80, to 32·7‰ in 1901-10.

In Eastern Europe, natality appears to have remained high until at least the beginning of the twentieth century. Despite a lack of data for this part of the world, we can safely say that the birth rate was still over 40‰ in 1900. The gap between Eastern Europe and the West, which was probably traditional, was thus widened further.

Finally, the birth rates for the period immediately preceding the First World War, from 1908-13, were as follows:

European Russia	45·6‰	Netherlands	29·5‰
Rumania	43·1‰	Denmark	27·1‰
Bulgaria	41·0‰	Scotland	26·2‰
Serbia	38·2‰	Norway	26·0‰
Hungary	36·0‰	England	24·9‰
Portugal	34·6‰	Switzerland	24·7‰
Italy	32·4‰	Sweden	24·4‰
Spain	32·1‰	Belgium	23·4‰
Austria	31·9‰	Ireland	23·1‰
Germany	29·5‰	France	19·5‰

In short, the birth rate remained extremely high in Eastern and Southern Europe, was lower in Central Europe, lower still in North-Western Europe and particularly low in France.

A more detailed analysis also reveals marked differences between urban and rural areas: in general the cities had a lower birth rate for any given age group than the country. It also reveals differences reflecting social, class and religious distinctions, whose discussion would take us too far afield.

The general fall in the birth rate was due to a host of factors, all, however, closely related to economic and social changes: the decrease in infant mortality due to better sanitation; industrialisation; the trend towards individualism; the wish to rise in the social scale; the spread of education; the women's franchise; the decline of religious beliefs and their replacement by rationalist norms. We still cannot tell why it was in France that this development first took place.

In any case, the declining birth rate was accompanied, at least at its sharpest, by an increase in the average age of the population, or to put it another way, by an increase in the number of elderly, and a decrease in the proportion of young people. It has often been said that this increase resulted from declining mortality and increased life expectancy, but in fact this was not the case since a reduced mortality rate, as we have seen, benefits children as much as it does adults. It is evident that the primary factor was the falling birth rate. Moreover, the age of the population rose most sharply in France, where the birth rate fell quite dramatically at the same time. From the end of the eighteenth century, the French population comprised 8% of people over 60; the same percentage was reached by Sweden in about 1860 and in England and Germany only in about 1910. In detail, the composition of the French population changed as follows:

PROPORTION PER THOUSAND INHABITANTS (FRANCE)			
Age	*1778* (estimated)	*1851*	*1901*
0-19	440	361	347
20-59	489	537	529
60 and over	71	102	124

The change was greatest in the first period, that is during the first half of the nineteenth century. In Sweden, on the other hand, as we saw, mortality declined steadily from the middle of the eighteenth century, while the birth rate barely changed, so that the average age of the population only began to increase in about 1870-80.

PROPORTION PER THOUSAND INHABITANTS (SWEDEN)					
Age	*1750*	*1800*	*1850*	*1870*	*1910*
0-14	332	323	330	341	317
15-64	606	620	622	605	599
Over 65	62	57	48	54	84

As a result, France and Sweden found themselves, by 1911, the two countries with the highest proportion of old people in Europe:

DISTRIBUTION BY AGE AND SEX OF 1,000 INHABITANTS (1911)						
	0-19		*20-50*		*60 and over*	
	M	F	M	F	M	F
France	170	169	264	271	57	69
Sweden	209	201	227	244	53	66
Gt. Britain	201	200	247	276	38	47
European Russia	240	247	216	227	33	37
Austria	222	223	231	242	38	44
Hungary	227	227	228	236	40	42
Germany	220	217	237	245	35	44
Netherlands	222	218	231	240	42	47
Belgium	200	198	253	255	43	51
Spain	210	209	236	256	42	47
Italy	244	243	227	224	32	30

Moreover, France and Great Britain, followed by Sweden

and Belgium, had the lowest proportion of inhabitants under the age of twenty.

The changes in the birth and death rates which we have been discussing help to explain the mechanics of European population growth in the eighteenth and nineteenth centuries.

Before that time, as we saw, the population could only increase slowly because, while the marriage and fertility rates were both high, an equally high mortality kept them in check. In peacetime, with good harvests and the absence of serious epidemics, the population would increase in size substantially, but as soon as the harvest failed, as soon as there was an outbreak of disease, or of war, the mortality at once leapt to catastrophic proportions, more than off-setting the population increases of the previous years. And if by an extraordinary combination of favourable circumstances, the population growth continued for some time, the increased numbers would rapidly outstrip the limited economic resources, and mortality would once again gain the upper hand.

This 'classical demographic pattern' continued to hold sway in Europe until the late eighteenth century, when it slowly disappeared, though at different dates in the various countries. But the basic point to remember is that the decrease in mortality preceded the fall in natality. In the interval, the excess of births built up, and it is this fact which explains the rapid growth in the population of Europe. Subsequently the drop in the birth rate led to a gradual decrease in population figures.

In short, we can say that the period under review was characterised by a transition from a high birth and mortality rate to a reduction in both. So drastic was this transformation that the French demographer Adolf Landry has called it a 'demographic revolution'.

It occurred, on the whole, earlier in Western than in Southern and Eastern Europe, and the initial period of rapid change came to an end earlier in France than it did elsewhere. As we have seen, the drop in the mortality rate during the second half of the eighteenth century, led to a rapid rise in French population, the average excess of births over deaths reaching its peak during the ten-year period 1821-30 (5·9 ‰). This was followed by a drastic and steady decline to a mere 0·6 ‰ in 1891-1900, and a slight rise to 1·2 ‰ in 1901-10. France had, by this date, the lowest excess of births over deaths in Europe, even including Ireland. In England and Wales, for which we have no figures before 1841-50, the average rate of natural increase was consistently in excess of 10 ‰ and reached its peak of 14 ‰ in 1871-80; it was still 11·8 ‰ in 1901-10. In Norway and Sweden the trend was similar, but Germany and Denmark only reached their peak natural increase rates (14·2 and 14·4 ‰ respectively) in 1901-10. The same was true of Spain and Italy and very probably of most of Eastern Europe; in 1911-13, at any rate, the natural increase rate was still over 15 ‰ in Russia, Bulgaria, Serbia and Rumania.

This time lag introduced considerable contrasts in the population movements of many countries, some of them next door neighbours. From 1901 to 1910, for example, the population of Germany increased on the average by 866,000 people annually, whereas that of France increased by only 47,000. However, the important point to remember is that there was a substantial excess of births over deaths in most parts of Europe, so much so that it became one of the chief causes of mass emigration.

MIGRATION

What information we have on migratory movements before the end of the eighteenth century is fragmentary and often unreliable. We know far more about the nineteenth century but even here migratory trends can only be retraced in broad outline. Thus while many countries made some attempts to keep track of emigration and immigration, they were thwarted by the fact that frontiers were, more often than not, crossed illegally. Moreover the different countries did not adopt the same definition of 'migrant', so that their figures often differ. For example, there is a considerable discrepancy between the European figures for the number of emigrants who embarked for overseas and the colonial figures for the number of European immigrants who arrived! And yet the statistics for intercontinental migration are more reliable than those for intracontinental migration, because they were both more important and also simpler to record.

The difficulties are even more marked in the case of intra-national migration, i.e. population movements within a given country. Wherever it was mandatory to register changes of address, or where regular population records were kept, we can study migratory movements in detail, but these conditions were only fulfilled in a small number of countries: notably in Holland, Belgium and Denmark. In any case, in this paper we shall be examining the pheno-menon of international rather than intranational population movements.

In the eighteenth century, international migration was of two types: spontaneous or government sponsored. The kings of Spain and Portugal tried, by various measures, to direct and control the emigration of their subjects to America; similarly the kings of France attempted to in-crease the French population of their overseas colonies, notably the West Indies, Guiana, Louisiana and Canada. Often the government did not intervene directly but left the task to private companies, which were granted special con-cessions or privileges. Emigration plus natural growth led to a remarkable increase in the number of Europeans living overseas; the number of French Canadians, for example, increased from 20,000 under Louis XV to 56,000 in 1763 and 100,000 by the end of the century. This was partly the result of an extremely high birth rate. Similarly, the European population of the British colonies in America rose from 250,000 in 1715 to over 5 million by 1800. It has been estimated that during the eighteenth century, about 1½ million people migrated from the British Isles to the New World, of whom 500,000 were Ulster Presbyterians and some 50,000 were convicts. A flood of emigrants left Ger-many, too, and in 1766 an estimated 200,000 Germans were living in what was later to become the United States of

America. Moreover, a large number of Germans crossed to America as mercenaries during the War of Independence, and many decided to stay on. Thus 17,000 of them took up residence in 1784. A number of Swedish and Dutch emigrants also settled in North America from 1700 to 1800. By contrast, Spanish emigration to Latin America fell off sharply during the eighteenth century.

Besides emigration to the colonies there was also a considerable movement of peoples from one European country to another, and quite particularly to the East, which was far less densely populated than the rest, and where 'enlightened despots' frequently tried to attract new immigrants. Frederick the Great, who said that 'a country's wealth is the number of its men' brought in 300,000 immigrants as settlers into more than 900 Prussian villages. In the Habsburg Empire, the Hungarian plain, which had been depopulated by the Turks, was resettled with descendants of its former inhabitants together with people from neighbouring countries. In Russia, the Empress Catherine II tried to settle the southern steppes with Russians and Germans. Russians also emigrated to Siberia, which counted 575,000 settlers towards the end of the eighteenth century.

Nor were these movements the only ones to take place in Western Europe. Though France, as we saw, was the most highly populated country in Europe, the crown encouraged certain categories of immigrants: mercenaries for the army, and specialist workers for the new industries. Unfortunately precise details are lacking, but it has been estimated that by 1775 there were around 50,000 foreigners in France. At the same time, Frenchmen were emigrating to other Continental countries, notably to Catalonia. By 1780, there were probably 230,000 Frenchmen living abroad.

By far the largest number of emigrants from France and the British Isles left their homes as a direct result of religious and political persecution. French Protestants departed in very large numbers during the reign of Louis XIV, and this process continued throughout the whole of the eighteenth century. They travelled to Switzerland, Holland, England, Germany, the Scandinavian countries, and even to Russia and the Cape of Good Hope. Then, at the end of the century, the Revolution produced a new wave of French emigrants.

Meanwhile, many Germans settled in the Baltic states, in Poland and Russia, as administrators and traders, and as founders of important new settlements.

For the Swiss, emigration was traditional; some 300,000 of them served as mercenaries under neighbouring rulers; others left for Eastern Germany, Russia, Spain and America, especially in times of local famine, for example in 1710-11, and again in 1770-71.

In this field, too, the data are extremely sparse, so that we can only sketch briefly what future research will no doubt be able to fill in one day.

From about 1830, migration, not only to the New World, but also within the Old, began to climb to new peaks. Let us look at inter-European migration first.

In general, the movement was from underdeveloped countries to under-populated or highly industrialised ones. This seems to show that industrialisation, far from reducing, tends to increase the demand for labour, at least in the long run.

In France, immigration began to exceed emigration from 1800 onwards. The latter reached its peak in 1881-90, when on average 47,000 people left France, one-third of them for other European countries. Meanwhile, immigration continued to grow apace. Thus, 100,000 people entered France each year in 1906-10. The French migratory rate, i.e. excess of immigrants over emigrants was positive for almost the entire nineteenth century. From 1851-1911, the number of foreigners in France rose from 380,000 to over 1,150,000, most of them coming from neighbouring countries.

In Great Britain, the largest number of immigrants were Irish; they started to arrive well before the beginning of the nineteenth century, and came in particularly great numbers after the Famine of 1846-50. This influx slowed down at the end of the century, but by 1911 there were more than 550,000 Irish immigrants in Britain. At about the same time, religious persecution in the Russian Empire brought many

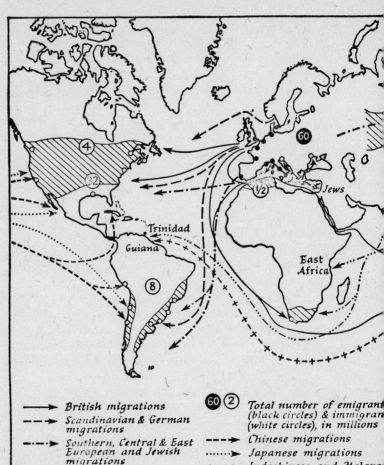

→		British migrations
- - →		Scandinavian & German migrations
-·-·→		Southern, Central & East European and Jewish migrations
●		European ports of embarkation
○		Ports of disembarkation
▨		European immigration zones

⓺⓪ ② Total number of emigrant (black circles) & immigran (white circles), in millions

- - → Chinese migrations

······→ Japanese migrations

+-+→ Indochinese and Malaya migrations

--→ Indian migrations

The inset shows the total number of European emigrants

The Great Migrations

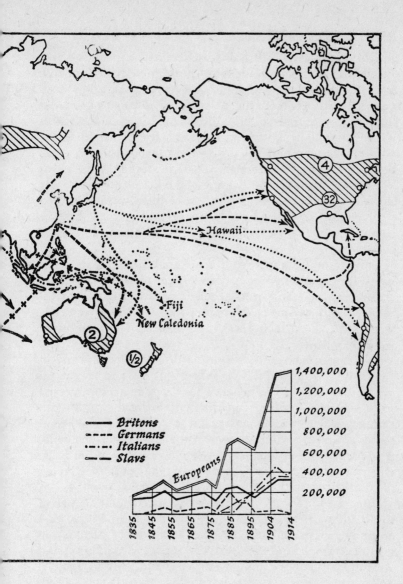

Hawaii

Fiji

New Caledonia

Britons
Germans
Italians
Slavs

Europeans

1,400,000
1,200,000
1,000,000
800,000
600,000
400,000
200,000

1835 1845 1855 1865 1875 1885 1895 1904 1914

Jewish immigrants to Britain, particularly from 1881-1914. In all, the number of aliens in the United Kingdom rose from 105,000 in 1871 to about 300,000 in 1914.

Finally, in Germany, there was a great deal of Continental immigration of a seasonal nature. This began in the 1880's when Ruthenians, Poles and Italians came to take the place of Germans who had left for overseas. From 1911 to 1914, the annual entry of foreign seasonal workers rose to an average of 710,000, of whom 200,000 to 300,000 were subjects of the Czar. A proportion of these workers settled permanently in Germany. In 1910, the German Empire contained 1,236,000 foreigners from other European countries.

Emigration from Europe to the rest of the world involved much larger numbers still. Until 1840, more than 30,000-40,000 people left Europe each year, making a total of some $1\frac{1}{2}$ million during the period 1801-40. These, it seems, were chiefly farm labourers or domestic staff thrown out of work by industrialisation.

In some countries the state subsidised emigrants, and in England, Edward Gibbon Wakefield evolved a special system of state-aid. In general, however, migration ceased to be officially organised in the first half of the nineteenth century, when most emigrants left their homes for personal motives, and made their own arrangements for the long, costly and arduous journey to relatively unknown parts. To emigrate was no small adventure and many of those who left died either on the way or shortly after arrival.

After the 1840's, there was another, spectacular change in the pattern of emigration. As a result of the political and economic crises of 1845-48, the abolition of serfdom in Central Europe, and the discovery of gold in California and Australia, European emigration leapt suddenly to 200,000 and even 300,000 per year. Even after this peak was passed, emigration ran at a much higher level than it had during the first half of the century. It was encouraged not only by rapid population increases in Europe but also by the development of steamships and railways, which made the journey much safer, speedier, and cheaper. At the same time, the development of industrial capitalism led to periodic slumps which forced unemployed workers to seek their fortunes abroad. Similarly, many farm-workers were made redundant by population increases, improvements in agricultural productivity and, from 1873 to 1896, the low price of farm produce. At the same time, the new countries were becoming better known, which helped to make migration look less of a hazard. Many settlers began to send for their relatives or friends, and steamship and railway companies did their utmost to encourage emigration, while colonial governments offered special incentives to newcomers from Europe.

It has been estimated that in the period 1841-80, 13 million Europeans emigrated from the Old World. Most of them came from Great Britain, Ireland and Germany—in 1845-50, Britain alone accounted for 80% of all these emigrants, and for 50% of them from 1850-75. The pace of emigration slackened slightly in 1857-75, due to the sudden boom in industry and the American Civil War. Then it regained its old impetus and, after 1880, climbed to new levels. In the next twenty years alone, 13 million Europeans left their continent.

Their number grew until 1890. From 1875-80 an annual average of 280,000 emigrants crossed the Atlantic. From 1880-1885, the number had increased to 685,000 and by 1885-90, it had reached 780,000. After 1890, it levelled out but the annual average was still more than 730,000. Emigration reached its peak in about 1910 with an annual exodus of 2 million Europeans. From 1871-1914, a total of 34 million Europeans left for the New World and 25 million of them became permanent settlers.

The massive increase in emigration went hand in hand with a change in national migration patterns. From 1880 to 1890, the number of British migrants decreased in favour of Germans and also of Scandinavians. From 1885, and still more so from 1890, East and South Europeans came to the fore, with particularly large contingents from Spain, Portugal, Italy, and the Austro-Hungarian and Russian Empires. By the beginning of the twentieth century, these countries were providing the major proportion of European emigrants.

Since the nature and rhythm of emigration differs from country to country, we shall now briefly consider the most important of these in turn.

In the United Kingdom, emigration increased fairly steadily during the first half of the nineteenth century, involving a total of 400,000 emigrants in 1841-5. In 1846-50, this total rose sharply to 1,030,000. After this date, it never fell to below 600,000 for any five-year period, and was often considerably higher. Thus in 1881-85, and again in 1886-90, the totals were more than 1,200,000 and from 1901-15 the five-year totals were 1,170,000; 1,670,000 and 1,789,000 respectively.

More than 50% of these emigrants went to the United States, but at the beginning of the twentieth century they began increasingly to be attracted by British and other possessions.

England, Scotland, Ireland and Wales contributed un-equal proportions of emigrants: it has been estimated that of the 2,370,000 British subjects who emigrated between 1815 and 1850, 1,830,000 were Irish. In 1845-50 alone, a particularly critical period for Ireland, there were 949,000 Irish emigrants and a further 892,000 left during the next five years. The peak year was 1851, when 250,000 Irish crossed the sea. Then Irish emigration began to fall off (except for another increase in 1885-90)—Ireland was rapidly running out of people.

The flow of German emigrants was interrupted by the Napoleonic wars but, after 1815, it increased considerably in the wake of poor harvests and political unrest. From 54,000 in 1841-45, the number of German emigrants rose to more than 182,000 in 1846-50, and to about 374,000 in 1851-55. Then, it declined again but rose once more after 1866 to reach a peak of over 857,000 in 1881-85. Then the growing needs of German industrial and economic expansion reduced emigration to extremely low figures: after 1896 a maximum of 150,000 Germans emigrated during any 5-year period.

From 1870 to 1910 a total of some 2,800,000 Germans left
for overseas.

Although much smaller, French emigration overseas
involved at least 800,000 people in 1870-1910. They went
chiefly to Algeria, North America and to Argentina. An
unusual feature of French emigration was that it was chiefly
made up of industrialists and managers, merchants, members of the liberal professions—not, as elsewhere, of farm
labourers and unskilled workers.

Spanish and Portuguese emigrants went predominantly
to their former colonies in the New World. Spanish emigration reached its peak of 318,000 in 1906-10. In Portugal the
flow of emigrants kept increasing until the outbreak of
World War I. During 1911-15, 271,000 Portuguese left their
homes; more than 90% went to America, principally to
Brazil, where some 1,160,000 Portuguese settled between
1857 and 1924.

Little is known about emigration from Italy before 1876.
It seems to have been fairly slight during the first half of the
nineteenth century but to have increased to some importance
after the unification of the kingdom in 1860, due to increased population pressure and general poverty. From
1876-1910, Italian emigration overseas continued to grow:
133,000 Italians set sail in 1876-80; 655,000 in 1886-90;
810,000 in 1896-1900; and 1,970,000 in 1906-10. After
that, emigration fell off slightly: 1,546,000 Italians set sail
in 1910-15, doubtless because of the outbreak of war. In
1876-85, most Italian emigrants went to other parts of
Europe, but after 1885 inter-continental emigration began
to predominate, with the United States, Argentine and
Brazil as the chief objectives. Different Italian provinces
had their own favourite destinations, and followed their own
pattern of emigration. The North initially provided the
largest number of emigrants, and it was only after the First
World War that it was overtaken by the South. From 1876
to 1915, a total of more than $7\frac{1}{2}$ million Italians left Europe
and a further $6\frac{1}{2}$ million left for other parts of Europe.
However, many of them came back to Italy eventually.

Turning now to Central Europe, we find that overseas

emigration from Austria-Hungary was relatively slight during the first half of the nineteenth century but rose to 59,000 in 1876-80, topped the million mark in 1901-05, and reached 1,327,000 in 1906-10. Altogether, more than 2,300,000 Austrians and 2,000,000 Hungarians embarked from European ports in 1875-1913. No more than 75% of these were, however, true Austro-Hungarians—the Habsburg Empire had a large Slav population. These emigrants went almost entirely to North America, chiefly to the United States (approximately 90%).

In Eastern Europe, Russia poured large numbers of her population into Asia, but strictly speaking this was a form of intra-national migration. However, overseas emigration was by no means negligible either. Net emigration accounted for 4,500,000 in 1828-1915. Practically non-existent before 1828, very slight up to 1859, Russian emigration increased rapidly in 1860-99 and became of considerable importance after 1890. All the races of European Russia were represented. From the end of the nineteenth century, Jews, fleeing from persecution, made up the great majority, followed by Poles, Russians and Finns in that order. Here, too, North America was the chief destination. From 1891-1900, 71·9% of emigrants from the Russian Empire went to the U.S.A., 4% to Canada, and 3·7% to Argentine and Brazil.

Finally, at the end of the nineteenth century and the beginning of the twentieth, the Balkans began to account for an important flow of emigrants, chiefly made up of Greeks, and Turks, who again went mostly to the United States.

Taken as a whole, European emigration probably represents the greatest transfer of populations in the history of mankind. Its consequences were enormous, in demographic no less than in economic, terms. Emigration not only slowed down the population expansion in Europe but also led to a considerable two-way movement of capital: money taken out by the emigrants themselves and money sent back to their dependents. Emigration also opened up new commercial markets to the exporting nations, because emigrants continued to buy the products they had become used to at home. Finally, emigration tended to bring about a general increase in wages by reducing the supply of labour, and a lowering of land prices by decreasing the demand. In some parts of Europe, however, these trends were cancelled by the continuing expansion of the remaining population. In fact, several authors have argued that, far from reducing the population pressure, emigration helped to raise the birth rate because parents came to feel that their children could always make their way abroad. Others contend that there is no immediate correlation between emigration and the birth rate. They point out, for instance, that although the birth rate at the beginning of the twentieth century was very low in both Ireland and France, the number of emigrants from Ireland was high whereas the number from France had always been low. If, therefore, emigration does constitute a factor in increasing natality, its effect must be masked by other factors.

One noticeable consequence of emigration was that it raised the average age of Europeans. Emigrants, in effect, were almost invariably young adults and, in the long run, their departure also helped to raise the European mortality rate and to decrease the birth rate.

Furthermore, emigration produced an unbalance between the sexes: male emigrants outnumbered female by far. The higher mortality rate for men, both in normal and in war times, had the same effect, but emigration greatly increased this tendency. In England and Wales, for example, there were 253,000 more women than men in 1801; by 1914, the surplus had risen to 1,197,000. Thus emigration tended to slow down the birth rate indirectly as well, i.e. by reducing the marriage rate.

In more general terms, the vast exodus from Europe in the nineteenth and early twentieth centuries had a profound effect on the geographical distribution of mankind. Thus while the great majority of Jews had always lived in the Old World, above all in Central and Eastern Europe, by 1914, the United States had a Jewish population second only to Russia's. Similarly, on the eve of the First World

War, almost 50% of Irish and Portuguese people were living overseas.

Above all, emigration extended European civilisation or at least a copy of it, across most of the North American continent, Australia, the temperate regions of Africa and even part of Asia, galvanising vast new areas and forcing them to play an active part in the world economy. Never before had one continent exercised so great an influence on the rest. In short, the emigration of millions of Europeans was a predominant factor in ensuring the supremacy of Europe.

CONCLUSION

The study of European population movements is of great interest not only to the demographer but also to the student of economic history—by increasing or decreasing the number of producers and consumers, demographic processes have had direct repercussions on industrial growth.

In the agricultural sector, too, population increases have helped to stimulate production, whether by increasing the area of cultivated land or by leading to the introduction of more rational methods of cultivation. True, during the period under review, the more highly industrialised countries tended to concentrate more on the export of finished goods and preferred to make up their agricultural deficit with imports from abroad, but these could not have been produced in sufficient quantities without the help of European emigrants, most of whom had left their old homes because of overpopulation. And wherever population growth was not accompanied by a corresponding growth in industrial production (e.g. in Russia), social problems became extremely acute; particularly in the late nineteenth century.

However, increasing population pressure was only one factor in the rise of industrial societies—a large pool of manpower cannot be tapped in the absence of technicians, capital and a spirit of enterprise. But wherever these are found, a rising population invariably stimulates industrial production. The examples of Great Britain during the entire nineteenth century and Belgium and Germany after 1890, illustrate this point abundantly. Conversely, the slow population increase of France during the last quarter of the nineteenth century was no doubt one reason why she was so slow in building up her industries.

Technical progress and the new needs it brought in its wake altered the relative importance of many established industries and even, as we saw, of the three economic sectors. This led inexorably to changes in the distribution of labour. Now such changes are always painful and hence resisted by the working class whose opposition can act as a brake on industrial progress. However, population growth helps to counteract this tendency since young people, who are abundant in all growing populations, tend to seek work in expanding rather than in stagnant or declining branches of the economy.

It must be emphasised, however, that the population of Europe often grew faster than the economic resources, so that, as we saw, part of the labour force was thrown out of work and forced to emigrate. This fact notwithstanding, the labour force in the United Kingdom increased from 5,800,000 at the end of the eighteenth century to above 18,350,000 in 1910; in France it increased from 13,000,000 to 20,700,000 during the same period; in Italy from 8,700,000 to 16,400,000, and in Belgium from 1,450,000 to 3,230,000. It was this great new labour force which helped to create new wealth and to raise the average standard of living to unprecedented levels.

Hence, while population growth was not the sole factor in developing the economy of eighteenth- and nineteenth-century Europe, it played a crucial role in this process, quite particularly so in Western Europe.

BIBLIOGRAPHY

STATISTICAL SURVEYS:

Sundbärg, *Aperçus statistiques internationaux*, Stockholm, 1906.
   Historisk Statistik för Sverige. I. Befolkning, 1720-1950, Stockholm, 1955.
Mitchell, B. R. and Deane, P., *Abstract of British Historical Statistics*, Cambridge, 1962.
Institut National de la Statistique et des Etudes Economiques: *Annuaire statistique. Résumé rétrospectif*. Paris, 1951, 1961 and 1966.
Köllmann, W., *Bevölkerung und Raum in neurer und neuester Zeit*, A. G. Ploetz, Würzburg, 1965.

GENERAL HISTORY

The Cambridge Economic History of Europe.
Habakkuk, H. G. and Postan, M., The Cambridge Economic History of Europe. VI, *The Industrial Revolution and After*, Cambridge, 1965.

Histoire generale des civilisations
Mousnier, R., Labrousse, E. and Bouloiseau, M., Vol. V *Le XVIIIᵉ siècle*, Paris, 1953.
Schnerb, R., Vol. VI, *Le XIXᵉ siècle*, Paris, 1955.
Chaunu, P., *L'Europe classique*, Paris, 1966.

Demographic Studies
Landry, A., *Traité de démographie*, Paris, 1949.

Chevalier, L., *Démographie générale*, Paris, 1951.
Hauser, P. M. and Duncan, O. D., *The study of population. An Inventory and Appraisal*. Chicago and London, 1959.
Fromont, P., *Démographie économique. Les rapports de l'économie et de la population dans le monde*. Paris, 1947.
Armengaud, A., *Démographie et Sociétés*. Paris, 1966.
Beaujeu-Garnier, J., *Trois milliards d'hommes—Traité de démo-géographie*. Paris, 1965.

POPULATION STUDIES

a General:

Landry, A., *La révolution démographique.* Paris 1934.

Population in History. Essays in Historical Demography. Edited by D. V. Glass and D. E. C. Eversley. London, 1965.

Reinhard, M., Armengaud, A. and Dupäquier, J., *Histoire générale de la population mondiale.* Paris, 1968.

International Population Conference. New York, 1961. Vol. I. London, 1963.

b Parish Registers:

Fleury, M. and Henry, L., *Nouveau manuel de dépouillement et d'exploitation de l'état civil ancien.* Paris, 1965.

Henry, L., *Manuel de Démographie historique.* Geneva and Paris, 1967.

Eversley, D. E. C., Laslett, P. and Wrigley, E., *An Introduction to English Historical Demography.* London, 1966.

Gauthier, H. and Henry, L., *La population de Crulai, paroisse normande. Etude historique—Cahiers de l'Institut National d'Etudes Démographiques, No. 33.* Paris, 1968.

Ganiage, G., *Trois villages d'Ile de France au XVIIIe siècle. ibid. No. 40.* 1963.

Valmary, P., *Familles paysannes au XVIII- siécle en Bas-Quercy. ibid. No. 45.* 1965.

See also

Henry, L., *Anciennes familles genevoises. Etude démographique—XVIe—XXe siècle. ibid. No. 26.* 1956.

Hollingsworth, T. H., *The Demography of the British Peerage* (Supplement to *Population Studies*, XVIII, 2). London, 1964.

Levy, C. and Henry, L., *Ducs et Pairs sous l'Ancien Régime.* Population, 1960, 5, pp. 807-30.

c Urban Population:

Meuriot, P., *Des agglomérations urbaines dans l'Europe contemporaine.* Paris, 1897.

Weber, A. F., *The growth of cities in the nineteenth century. A study in statistics*. New York, 1899.

d *Mortality:*

Chevalier, L. (ed.), *Le choléra, la prémiére épidémie du XIXe siècle*. Collective studies.
Bibliotheque de la Révolution de 1848, Vol. XX. Paris 1958.
Sauvy, A., *Les limites de la vie humaine*. Paris, 1961.
  Problèmes de mortalité—Méthodes, sources et bibliographie en démographie historique. International Conference held at the University of Liège from 18th to 20th April, 1963. *Les Congrès et Colloques de l'Université de Liège*, Vol. 33. University of Lèige, 1965.

e *Migration:*

Gonnard, R., *Essai sur l'histoire de l'émigration*. Paris, 1928.
Willcox and Ferrenczi, *International Migrations*. 1929-31.
Sorre, M., *Les migrations des peuples. Essai sur la mobilité géographique*. Paris, 1955.

JOURNALS AND PERIODICALS

Population Studies. A journal of Demography. London.
Population. Revue de l'Institut National d'Etudes Démographiques, Paris.
Annales de Démographique historique. Paris (since 1964).

2. Patterns of Demand 1750–1914

Walter Minchinton

Consumption is the sole end and purpose of all production
Adam Smith, *Wealth of Nations* (Cannan ed.) II, 159

Between the eighteenth century and the outbreak of the first world war radical changes took place in the economic, social and political life of Europe which affected the pattern of demand. A vital revolution led to sustained population growth, the concentration of a greater number in towns and substantial emigration. Agricultural productivity rose and food supplies were further augmented by the widespread adoption of new crops and by the strengthening of links with the wider world by the steamship and refrigeration. After 1750 comparatively few famines occurred. Based on a developing cumulative technology, the tide of industrialisation moved across Europe. Means of communication—the railway, the telegraph, the newspaper—and institutional developments—such as the spread of banking and the operation of stock exchanges—helped to reduce market imperfections, to facilitate the greater mobility of the factors of production and to make demand more effective. Mass production then became possible for a mass market. But the distribution of wealth remained uneven and some even held that while the rich got richer, the poor got poorer. Cumulatively these changes were much more radical than Europe had previously experienced. While the Europe of 1700 had many similarities with the Europe of 1300, the Europe of 1900 was markedly different.

In many ways the experience of industrialisation helped to knit Europe together and to give it some degree of corporate identity. Capital, skills and goods circulated comparatively freely. Some experiences, like price movements and demographic trends, were shared to a greater or lesser degree and so diversity narrowed. Yet marked differences remained—and in some respects the gulf tended to widen between the developed countries of Europe—

between Great Britain, France, Belgium and Germany—and the less developed—Spain, Italy and the Balkans and eastern Europe. And as the pace of industrialisation differed, so there were significant differences in social structure and in patterns of private consumption. As business varied and the nature of state involvement took different forms, so the pattern of public demand also differed. Variations between countries, between classes and over time need therefore to be borne in mind throughout the ensuing discussion.

THE DETERMINANTS OF DEMAND

In aggregate terms the stock of goods and services available for current consumption depends on the current level of consumption, imports and the net balance between saving and dissaving less exports. For a modern community such a calculation is not easy to carry out. It is therefore *a fortiori* more difficult for past times. In the first section of this chapter we shall examine the level of wealth available which is itself a function of climate, of geography, of the level of technology and the degree of industrialisation, and of the kind of economy practised. We shall also discuss how wealth was distributed, which depends on social structure, population pressures and other matters, and the pattern of spending, which can be influenced by fashion and social custom, by the distribution between private and public expenditure and by other factors. Then, secondly, the components of demand will be looked at: the demand for food, clothing and other consumer goods, for lighting, heating and shelter, for labour and for services, both by individuals and corporate bodies.

GEOGRAPHY AND CLIMATE

First, geography and climate affected demand. The needs of those who dwelt in northern and central Europe and had to cope with long dark winters differed in some degree from the inhabitants of the Mediterranean just as the requirements of those who lived in the mountains were not entirely coincident with those who inhabited the plains. And those who lived on the coast and went down to the sea in ships required articles of which their compatriots who lived far from great waters had no need. And the reciprocal of these differing situations was that for purely geographical and climatic reasons the stock of goods available for consumption varied to a substantial degree from one part of Europe to another. There was a Europe of beer and a Europe of wine, a Europe of brick, of timber and of stone. Nor are we dealing purely with physical limitations alone. Europe continued to have a considerable diversity and man's response to similar circumstances differed. While many might keep cows, the animals which they reared were of varying breeds and the cheese which they made, like the beer which they brewed or the bread which they baked, was not of a standard kind. A similar variety was visible in clothing and in manufactures. The geography of vernacular architecture reflects to a considerable degree the availability of building materials; stone, brick, cob or timber were employed because they were the materials to be had locally. To a large extent factor endowment imposed a control upon what could be done but the individual or collective skills of particular communities gave their products a distinctive local, regional and, where the term was appropriate, a national appearance.

Conditions of work also modified patterns of consumption. The agricultural worker required a different diet from the clerk, the muscular and the mental, the active and sedentary. They took different amounts and sorts of nourishment. They also needed different clothing, tools and equipment and involved different types of capital expenditure. Their patterns of work also differed and so did their leisure hours and needs. These and other considerations need to be taken into account in any discussion of patterns of consumption. But there was nonetheless an underlying unity which linked Europeans together. Despite the differences in geography and climate and in much else besides, the needs of Europeans differed in degree rather than in kind.

INDUSTRIALISATION AND TECHNOLOGY

The major development which transformed the patterns of demand in this period was the spread of industrialisation based on improved technology. By a growing specialisation of function between countries and between regions, which was no longer dependent on local factor endowment but on skills and capital investment, output was increased and production costs fell. The new economic order which was based on the extended use of machinery and the employment of a developing range of techniques replaced the customary, tentative and fitful by the contractual, cumulative and rational. Beginning in Britain, the whole organisation of production was transformed. In the first phase new processes in textiles and in iron and steel increased output and reduced costs and markets were extended by the improvement of roads, the construction of canals and the development of shipping. Then came the railway, which enabled larger volumes of goods to be transported cheaply, and the spread of more developed financial institutions which enabled more capital to be mobilised so that the replacement of high-cost labour intensive processes by low-cost capital intensive methods could continue. And, towards the end of the nineteenth century, when the initial impact of the massive developments in textiles, in iron and steel and in transport was beginning to wane, there came a further batch of product inventions which brought a range of consumer durables, like sewing machines and bicycles, to a wider market and introduced the motor car and refrigeration to a more limited range of consumers.

To a greater or lesser extent productivity in agriculture also increased through new crops, improved rotations, chemical fertilisers and better stockbreeding. Average crop yields were increased and added significantly to grain supplies, while the demand for meat was satisfied not only by increasing the number of cattle, which increased in average weight, but also by killing them at an earlier age. So farming was able to escape to a limited degree from the trap of diminishing returns. And total output was also increased by taking more land into cultivation. Improvements in transport helped to eliminate local food shortages, and to augment European production it became possible to import foodstuffs and agricultural raw materials from the wider world. While from the 1870s a number of European countries protected their farmers from the full brunt of the competition of American wheat and later of Antipodean and Latin American meat and dairy produce, these net additions to supplies, particularly important as far as Great Britain was concerned, brought with them a trend towards whiter and more digestible bread and reversed the centuries' long trend towards lower meat consumption.

As trade augmented European food supplies, so it opened up new and expanding sources of raw materials—of cotton, wool, timber, iron ore and other metals—and sources of new materials such as rubber and petroleum. Trade also provided a market for European manufactures and enabled economic growth to proceed at a faster pace than it could have done if it had been dependent solely on the internal European market. Thus overseas trade helped to raise European output per head and hence European incomes and consumption. But the overall benefits from trade varied over time.

The gain from trade depended on the terms of trade. In the early nineteenth century some of the benefits of industrialisation in Britain were enjoyed by her customers overseas rather than by her own inhabitants as the falling price of industrial products moved terms of trade against her. But this decline was arrested by 1855 and the great expansion of agricultural production overseas brought a marked reduction in import prices from the 1880s to the end of the nineteenth century as the terms of trade moved in favour of the European metropolis and against the periphery. In the early twentieth century, with a massive expansion of capital investment overseas, the terms of trade once more moved against European manufactured goods and the gains from trade were accordingly reduced.

Overall, however, it cannot be denied that the spread of industry had many consequences affecting both demand and supply. Most importantly, it served, by increasing output per head, to raise per capita incomes and so enabled more people to demand a wider range of goods and services. The development of industry also brought with it new demands for labour, for skills and for services, for an extended range of raw materials and for an enormously greater amount of capital equipment. It also made necessary the improvement of the economic and social infrastructure —transport, commercial services, power supplies and the like. On the supply side, it facilitated both an expansion of production at lower cost and a wider range of products and services. These served not only to increase the quantity of goods available but to improve their quality and with it the whole quality of life. Industry also helped to transform work patterns and hence in the longer run it affected the way in which people spent their incomes. It made possible a clear delimitation between work and leisure. Further, it created demands for an educated working force and growing literacy widened the market for reading matter, for books as well as for newspapers and periodicals. Yet there were costs as well as benefits, at least for some. Industrial and technical changes could sometimes adversely affect living standards as they did in the case of the handloom weavers.

At this point it should of course be said that demand and supply are not independent variables but are inter-related. The demand for some products is inelastic, as it was by and large for working clothes in this period: some products such as bread have a backward-sloping demand curve—as incomes rise people tend to reduce their consumption of bread and to eat other foods, notably meat, instead: while the demand for other products is price-sensitive. Mass production was impossible without mass demand which meant that prices had to be low enough for working class demand to be effective. While the price of tea and coffee was high they remained luxury drinks but when their prices fell, they became beverages of wider consumption. Although the pressure of demand may lead to a rightwards movement of the supply curve, an extension of supply may also result in an increase in effective demand. Then differential price movements may have a substitution effect. When the price of margarine fell below that of butter the sales of the former increased and of the latter fell. And the market for some products, such as sugar and tea, is complementary.

Further, it is a truism worth stating that there can be no effective demand for a product until it is available. In the nineteenth century the development of gas and electricity and of consumer durables such as bicycles, sewing machines and motor cars provide illustrations. Similarly supply may be a response via developments in technology to a changed demand situation. As cities grew in the nineteenth century proper arrangements for the disposal of effluent and sewage were necessary and this new need provided a stimulus for the development of cheap non-porous pipes (which did not become available in England before 1846), traps, gullies and hydraulic devices. Some inventions were developed before there was a need for them but in other cases a challenge was necessary to evoke a response. Needless to say, not all challenges were met.

Finally, the pattern of immediate consumption was to some degree affected by capital formation. Some writers have suggested that in the first phase of industrialisation European living standards were depressed in order that capital formation should take place but this is a view which not all historians support.[1] In the early days of industrialisation in Britain it is now argued that the role of fixed capital has been exaggerated but in other European countries railway building, by and large, preceded industrialisation and required large inputs of capital. Factory-housed power-driven machinery required more capital equipment: agriculture became somewhat more capital intensive: and

1. See Ronald Max Hartwell, 'The Standard of Living Controversy: a summary' in Ronald Max Hartwell, ed. *The Industrial Revolution* (Oxford: Blackwell, 1970) pp. 173–8.

transport, not only on the railways but on the roads with the first motor vehicles and on the sea with the growth of steam shipping, was much more so. Building for houses and government buildings as well as for factories, railway stations, warehouses or port facilities made a substantial claim on resources. In the late seventeenth century in England, capital formation accounted for perhaps 5 per cent of the national income; by the 1840s this proportion had climbed to 10 per cent. More detailed figures are available for Britain for the later nineteenth century. The following table shows gross domestic capital formation as a percentage of the gross national product:

TABLE 1: Gross Domestic Capital Formation as percentage of Gross National Product in Britain, 1861–1914

1861–4	*1865–9*	*1870–4*	*1875–9*	*1880–4*	*1885–9*
7·1	7·1	7·4	8·7	6·9	5·3

1890–4	*1895–9*	*1900–4*	*1905–9*	*1910–14*	
6·1	7·6	9·2	6·6	5·5	

Source: Phyllis Deane and William A. Cole, *British Economic Growth, 1688–1959: Trends and Structure* (Cambridge U.P., 1962) pp. 332–3.

For certain countries, as the following table shows, estimates have been made of the distribution of national product (at current prices) between private consumption, government consumption and capital formation:

TABLE 2: Percentage Distribution of National Product (at current prices)

	Private consumption	*Government consumption*	*Capital formation*
UNITED KINGDOM			
1860–69	83·0	5·1	11·9
1870–79	82·3	4·6	13·1
1880–89	81·8	5·4	12·8
1890–99	81·9	6·3	11·8
1900–09	78·8	7·7	13·5
1905–14	78·4	7·1	14·5

	Private consumption	*Government consumption*	*Capital formation*
GERMANY			
1851–60	82·6	3·8	13·6
1861–70	80·5	4·2	15·2
1871–80	73·8	5·5	20·7
1881–90	72·5	6·3	21·3
1891–1900	69·9	6·8	23·3
1901–13	67·8	7·4	24·8
ITALY			
1861–70	87·9	4·7	7·5
1871–80	86·7	3·8	9·5
1881–90	84·7	4·6	10·6
1891–1900	84·1	5·0	10·9
1901–10	78·4	4·2	17·3
1906–15	77·9	6·9	15·3
SWEDEN			
1861–70	86·3	4·5	9·2
1871–80	84·4	4·3	11·3
1881–90	86·3	5·5	8·1
1891–1900	83·6	5·2	11·2
1901–10	83·5	5·4	11·1

Source: Simon Kuznets, 'Quantitative aspects of the economic growth of nations, VII. The share and structure of consumption', *Economic Development and Cultural Change*, X (1962) 72–3.

POPULATION AND URBANISATION

A second major factor in this period was the unprecedented growth of population. From the middle of the eighteenth century Europe went through a vital revolution which took its population from an estimated 100–120 million in 1700 and 120–140 million in 1750 to 180–190 million in 1800, about 260–270 million in 1850 and over 450 million in 1914. The Victorians had pointed out the consequence of this increase for production: 'with every mouth God gave a pair of hands', but the significance for consumption was not less. The mouths had to be fed if the hands were to work. Moreover, rapid population growth, in part at least a consequence of lower infantile mortality, meant also for a period that the proportion of the population of working age (between 15 and 59) grew.[2] European population as a whole therefore became more productive. And the demand of this growing population was mainly responsible for the technological innovations of the eighteenth and early nineteenth centuries.[3]

But at some periods it is clear that the growth of European population outstripped available resources. Although diminishing in frequency and seriousness, there were a number of occasions in various parts of Europe between 1750 and 1914 when death stalked the land in the wake of food shortages. In 1769 five per cent of the French population are said to have died from starvation and in the following year 168,000 died in Bohemia and 20,000 in Poland and Russia. 1771 and 1772 were famine years in Austria and Hungary. The bad harvest of 1786 which brought with it the threat of rural famine helped to exacerbate popular discontent in France. Food was rationed in France in 1793 and harvest failures in England in the mid-1790s caused alarm. Floods led to food shortages in Poland in 1812. Ten years later the failure of the potato crop, which had substantially augmented food supplies in many parts of Europe, foreshadowed the catastrophic famine in Ireland, which had become tragically dependent on the potato, in 1845–7 when disease and malnutrition caused 2–3 million deaths and reduced the population by one-half. There were serious food shortages in the Rhineland, too, in 1847 which, as in Ireland, led to emigration. Not till the 1860s was the threat of famine exorcised in western European countries as far apart as France and Sweden. It was the spread of the potato, the development of transport both on land and sea and the increasing availability of food from other parts of the world which largely helped to banish subsistence crises

2. For the United Kingdom the proportion of the population aged 15–64 years was 56 per cent in 1821, 60 per cent in 1851 and 62 per cent in 1901 (Brian R. Mitchell and Phyllis Deane, *Abstract of British historical statistics* (Cambridge U.P., 1962) pp. 12–13).

3. See Chapter 3, p. 187

from the face of the European continent in the half century before the first world war. But outbreaks still occurred. There were famines in Russia after the bad harvests of 1891, 1906 and 1911. In 1912 more than 30 million of the Russian rural population endured starvation.[4]

Not only did European population grow but there was unprecedented migration and urbanisation and this affected patterns of demand. Of some importance was migration within Europe, into France, into Great Britain, into Russia, both seasonal and permanent. But of greater importance was emigration from Europe.[5] The motives for this were complex but both the 'push' of adverse conditions at home and the 'pull' of better prospects overseas were major factors. Until the 1850s the major flows were from northern and western Europe, with the emigration of the Irish after the potato famine of the mid-1840s the most spectacular movement, while later in the century the majority of the migrants came from southern Europe. For obvious reasons no precise figures exist but it has been calculated that in the first half of the nineteenth century 4 million people left Europe, mainly for the western hemisphere, while in the second half the 24 million who emigrated spread themselves more widely over the earth's surface. This emigration was of importance in many directions but as far as the pattern of consumption in Europe at this time was concerned it had two consequences of importance. First and directly, it served to relieve the pressure of population on resources. Partly as a consequence of this massive emigration, although European population continued to grow, Europe escaped from the low-income poverty trap into which other parts of the world have fallen at different times and so was able in many cases to enjoy a rising standard of living. And by making labour less plentiful in some cases, it led to a rise in the wage levels while by reducing the pressure on land it helped to reduce the price of land. Secondly and indirectly the emigration

4. Philip Hanson, *The Consumer in the Soviet Economy* (Macmillan, 1968) p. 21.
5. For details see Chapter 1, p. 22.

from Europe facilitated the exploitation of the primary resources of the rest of the world and so made possible the production of food on which Europe was able to call to supplement its own supplies and the raw materials—cotton, wool, timber, oil, tin and other commodities—which were essential for the expansion of European industry. Emigration also affected capital movements. While some emigrants took money out, others, particularly from southern Europe, sent remittances home which increased family incomes and so extended their claim on resources.

The major development, however, was in the changed balance of population between town and country. Although in the first phase of industrialisation the towns were great consumers of people, the urban population grew more rapidly than the population as a whole. Whereas in 1800 there were 23 European cities with over 100,000 inhabitants with a total population of 5·5 million (out of 192 million or less than 3 per cent), in 1900 there were 135 such cities with a total population of 46 million (out of 423 million or over 10 per cent). Most of the new or expanding towns were either multi-functional metropolises, industrial towns or commercial centres: but the nineteenth century saw also the growth of spa and resort towns to meet the leisure needs of a small but growing proportion of the population. Inevitably this process of urbanisation was uneven. By the early twentieth century 77 per cent of the population of the United Kingdom, 56·1 per cent of Germany, 41 per cent of France, 40·5 per cent of the Netherlands but only 22 per cent of Switzerland and 21·5 per cent of the population of Sweden were urbanised.

The growth of towns had widespread implications for the pattern of demand. It stimulated specialisation and so helped to rise per capita incomes, it affected the structure of expenditure, it resulted in a vastly increased market for food and other agricultural products and shifted some activities, such as food processing and tailoring, which had previously been carried out on a customary basis within the family or the village, into the market and by extending the use of money aided exchange. It also led to the extension of central and local government provision of services: piped water, sewage and refuse disposal, public health facilities, urban transport and housing as well as the provision of markets and cultural activities such as libraries, museums and art galleries. And finally the anonymity of the city helped to break down some of the restraints on expenditure. By allowing greater opportunity for competitive emulation and by increasing sensitivity to new types of goods, the growth of cities may have led to higher levels of consumption. The late nineteenth century saw a further phase of town growth, the expansion of the suburbs made possible by transport developments, which made increasing demands on supplies and services.

THE ARTICULATION OF THE MARKET

Adam Smith once suggested that a prerequisite of economic advance was the widening of the market. Such a development can take place in a number of ways: by population growth within an area, by the geographical extension of the market area, by the removal of obstacles to the free movement of goods or by various technical developments which improve both the transport of goods and also the circulation of information about market opportunities. Some aspects, such as population growth, industrialisation and urbanisation have already been discussed, but the others merit consideration.

As much as anything, transport improvements transformed the European market situation: they made local markets into national markets and national markets into international. Particularly in western Europe, improvements in land and water transport helped to eliminate local shortages. More widely, transport development had a number of consequences. It physically extended the size of markets, it increased considerably the volume of commodities which could be transported, it lowered the cost of transport and so permitted a further extension of the market by a reduction in price and it facilitated a different disposition of financial resources since by shortening the period from manufacture to sale it reduced the amount of capital tied up in stocks. A graphic illustration of the effects of transport improvement is provided by the growth of traffic carried by the Danube Steamship Company. Founded in 1831, it possessed 41 steamships and numerous smaller vessels by 1847. In 1835 this company carried 38,529 centner of freight: in 1847 3·2 million centner, mostly of agricultural products.[6] Cases could be multiplied but this single example must suffice to make the point. Similarly the enormous development of oceanic steam shipping in the later nineteenth century enabled European demand for food and raw materials to be met with increasing ease from the four corners of the earth.

Other developments also facilitated the articulation of demand. There was a considerable reduction in the variation of weights and measures. Backed by legislation, the Napoleonic reforms which gave the movement towards decimalisation considerable impetus, were particularly important. Similar improvements took place as far as currency was concerned. In the eighteenth century a bewildering variety of coins (both foreign and domestic), of notes and of bills were in circulation while there was from time to time a shortage of coin. Improvements in minting and the growth of the banking system were amongst the means by which this problem was solved and the imperfections of the market reduced.

Political developments also helped. The unification of Germany and of Italy eased currency problems and reduced the number of variations of weights and measures prevailing, continuing the movement towards standardisation set on foot by Napoleon. The creation of bodies such as the International Bureau of Weights and Measures, the International Postal Union and the international commissions for the control of navigation on the Rhine and the Danube helped to reduce the frictions in trade. The late

6. Jerome Blum, *Noble Landowners and Agriculture in Austria, 1815–1848: a study in the origins of the peasant emancipation of 1848* (Baltimore: Johns Hopkins Press, 1948) p. 91.

nineteenth century saw a considerable increase in the number of such bodies in existence:

TABLE 3: Numbers of International Organisations, 1850s–1910

Before 1857	1870	1880	1890	1900	1910
7	17	20	31	61	108

Source: Frederick L. Nussbaum, *A History of the Economic Institutions of Modern Europe: an introduction to* Der moderne Kapitalismus *of Werner Sombart* (New York: Crofts, 1937: New York: Kelley, 1969) p. 280.

In the machinery of marketing there were substantial changes. For the most part the fairs which had provided periodic wholesaling facilities declined and their place was taken by a variety of provisions: some manufacturers sold their products through their own sales organisations, sometimes using travelling salesmen; with the development of the postal system orders were sought by means of catalogues and samples. Commodity exchanges were established to deal in certain primary products. Thus in London exchanges for wholesale trading in coal and other commodities were established while corn exchanges were more widely set up in provincial cities as well. A few fairs, such as the Leipzig fair, found a continuing role as a mart for particular products such as furs. And for the new industrial products international exhibitions, beginning with the Great Exhibition of 1851 in the Crystal Palace in Hyde Park, London, came to be held. There was also a considerable expansion of wholesaling which came to be more highly organised.

Retail trade also underwent a transformation. Daily and weekly markets continued to be held and were particularly important for agricultural produce and perishable food-stuffs. Still in the mid-nineteenth century most of the food purchased in England was obtained in this way. But there were also the street traders who plied their trades, mostly from fixed stalls. And there was that rather shadowy figure, the itinerant trader, who peddled his wares from village to village, bringing news of the wider world as well as commodities for sale. Alongside these older forms, retail shops had become firmly established in the more developed parts of Europe by the mid-eighteenth century, catering particularly for the middle classes and the well-to-do. Regarded as a skilled occupation, shopkeeping also underwent change. Some built up their businesses by engaging in wholesaling as well. Others prospered on the basis of 'small profits and quick returns' by developing display and advertising and by refusing to give credit. In them, too, the haggling of the market came to be replaced by fixed prices. By such means, 'by increased skill', wrote an English shopkeeper in 1851, 'the same amount of capital is made to do a greater quantity of work than before. In fact the substitution of quick for slow sales is precisely like an improvement in machinery which cheapens the cost of production'.[7] Already far advanced in England by this time, the growth of retail trading took place elsewhere in Europe as countries industrialised and urbanised. In Prussia, for example, there were three times as many retailers per thousand of the population in 1900 as there had been in 1850.

But in addition there were four major developments in retailing which were a product of the growth of towns, the increasing purchasing power of an urban working class and the growing standardisation of products. These were the establishment of co-operative societies, of department stores and of chain stores of two types, multiple and bazaar. In the industrial north of England, after a number of abortive attempts, co-operative stores were set up from the 1840s to provide the better-off sections of the working class with cheap sound articles and unadulterated food. Their success was due not so much to their deals as to their effective operation of a vertically integrated system of wholesaling and retailing through branches enabling them to take advantage of the economies of scale and the benefit from price reductions from bulk orders. Towards the end of the nineteenth century, as a recognition of these economic

7. W. N. Hancock, *Competition Between Large and Small Shops* (1851) cited by Dorothy Davis, *A History of Shopping* (Routledge & Kegan Paul, 1966) p. 259.

possibilities in a situation where both purchasing power was growing and the range of pre-packed and standardised products under brand names and supported by advertising was increasing, chain stores were established in England, particularly to trade in mass-produced footwear, chemist's goods, ready-made clothing, books and stationery and imported foodstuffs. Thomas Lipton was one of the salesmen who seized the new opportunities for marketing a range of fairly standardised foodstuffs in England. Beginning with a single shop in Glasgow in 1872, he had set up 245 branches throughout the country before the end of the century. This development helped to reduce price—and so extend demand—in two ways. First, the multiple retailers like Lipton who set their gross profit margins at 10–15 per cent —between one-half and one-third of the mark-up adopted by independent wholesalers—not only directly reduced their own prices but indirectly forced other retailers to do the same.[8] And secondly, by acquiring sources of supply, such chains were able to market products more cheaply. Lipton, for example, acquired tea estates in Ceylon and so was able to offer his own blends at 1s 2d to 1s 9d per lb against the going rate of 3s to 4s. In France, too, a number of regional chains of grocery stores had been established by the end of the nineteenth century and in Belgium the grocery business of Delhaize Frères, founded in 1871, had 565 branches throughout the country by 1904.

In the case of the third retailing innovation, the department store, it was France which took the lead. The Bon Marché and the Louvre were set up in the 1860s and these examples were followed quickly elsewhere. In Germany similar stores were established at Tietz in 1879, at Karlstadt in 1881 and at Althoff in 1885. In England a number of stores catering largely for the upper classes were established in London in the last quarter of the nineteenth century or so including William Whiteley's which boasted that the store could sell 'Everything from a pin to an elephant'. Like

8. See Peter Mathias, *Retailing Revolution: a history of multiple retailing in the food trades based upon the Allied Suppliers group of companies* (Longmans, 1967) p. x.

the supermarkets of today, the department stores were able to offer a wide range of goods, clearly priced, and their sales were inflated by 'impulse buying' which was denied the specialist shop. Finally there were the bazaar-type chain stores pioneered by Woolworth's in America and copied by Marks & Spencer's Penny Bazaars in England, which with a minimum of service made available a wide range of cheap and standardised necessities for easy inspection by the public. Together these four developments effectively increased competition in retailing, extended the range of goods which could be easily supplied and generally increased the efficiency of marketing. They thus helped to make consumer demand more effective.

Since many changes in retailing took place not as a result of the actions of a relatively limited number of entrepreneurs using capital-intensive innovations but as the outcome of the separate decisions and actions of numerous individual retailers, change was of necessity slow and patchy. Nevertheless the broad lines of development are clear. Direct exchange between producer and retailer declined as the wholesaler increasingly intervened. The street trader lost ground and came to cater for the poor. Markets changed their form and fairs, by and large, were reduced to places of entertainment rather than of trade. The retail shop grew in importance and new forms, the department store and the chain store, emerged. And all these changes were largely the consequence of the emergence of a substantial urbanised working class demand in the context of a communications situation which made it possible to carry out such changes on a large scale.

Newspapers were a further way in which the machinery for articulating demand was improved in the period between the middle of the eighteenth century and the outbreak of the first world war. In the course of the eighteenth century a wide range of local newspapers and journals had been founded. Newspapers of national standing followed. *The Times* (which took its present name in 1788) was started in 1785 and *Le Moniteur Universel* in 1789. These newspapers were important both for the information they carried about general market conditions and political events which might affect the course of trade and as a vehicle for advertisements for particular products or consignments of goods. With the growth of literacy there emerged a wider range of magazines and journals which catered for specialist interests, accountants, engineers, farmers and many others. Nor was it just a man's world; there were a large number of women's magazines which brought, *inter alia*, news of the latest fashions. Before the end of the nineteenth century newspapers had ceased to be a middle class preserve. But a landmark was the foundation of the *Daily Mail* in 1896 which was the first English newspaper to recognise the existence of a large working class readership. So the spread of newspapers helped to reduce the imperfections of the market.

Newspapers were able to operate more effectively because of developments in communications: the telegraph, the oceanic cable, the telephone and, on the eve of the first world war, wireless helped to bring both news and commercial information more quickly and effectively. Ships no longer had to 'call for orders' but could be given instructions as their voyages progressed, notably as they neared European ports with their cargoes of foodstuffs or raw materials.

Finally there was the monetary factor in the articulation of demand. While many workers were paid in kind, their purchasing power was restricted. An important development therefore was the replacement of such methods of remuneration by money wages. In agriculture there was considerable change. In Italy in the nineteenth century day workers on the land came to be paid in money while after the emancipation of the serfs in Russia, they were paid money wages. More important still was the growth of industry which greatly increased the number of workers paid money wages. And demand became more effective as the machinery of wage payment was improved. Truck—the payment of wages in kind—was abolished and so the worker gained greater freedom of choice in expressing his purchasing power. The period of wage payment, too, was shortened as the volume of circulating media grew. Monthly pays became weekly pays while Friday rather than Saturday became pay day and these changes too gave the worker more choice in the use of his money. As has already been indicated, a major factor in the retailing revolution of the nineteenth century was the emergence of a considerable working class demand for food, clothes and other products. Among financial developments, particularly important for capital investment though also of importance on current account was the development of financial institutions which enabled the cash surpluses of a wider range of the population to be mobilised by the proliferation of institutions such as stock exchanges and banks and the widening range of devices which combined risk and return in varying proportions. Legal developments—joint stock and limited liability legislation—which provided greater security for the investor were also of significance.

FASHION AND SOCIAL CUSTOM

But patterns of consumption are not entirely an individual matter. As John Hobson noted: 'Current Prestige, Tradition, Authority, Fashion, Respectability supplement or often displace the play of individual taste, good or bad, in moulding a class and family [and, one should perhaps add, a regional or national] standard of consumption'.[9] The number of deviant members of a community is commonly small and so the life-style of most members of a society is usually largely socially determined. Patterns of food consumption are generally slow to change but the initial vogue for tea and coffee, for example, was largely a matter of fashion. The purchase of luxury items and furniture is often very little a functional matter and to a greater extent one of taste. The style of housing is affected by similar considerations. But clothes are the aspect of consumption where fashion, a sort of socially recognised caprice, 'la passion papillone', as Fourier described it, has held the greatest sway. Here the influences were international. For

9. John A. Hobson, *Work and Wealth: a human valuation* (Macmillan, 1914) p. 139.

most of the period between 1750 and 1914 Paris was the centre of upper class fashion and the high-born and well-to-do in other countries did their best to emulate the French in style, colour and fabric. In the main the pace was set by the aristocracy and conventional consumption was often formed by imitation of the class above. But the display of the aristocracy in some parts of Europe at least came to be challenged if not emulated by the rising wealth of the bourgeoisie. Though sometimes pejoratively described as 'the nouveaux riches', their purchasing power formed the basis of their competitive emulation. Nor was the fashionable traffic all in one direction. Some fashions in clothes were taken over from the lower classes. A further trend was also visible. The sports clothes of one generation tended to become the formal clothes of the next.

Convention or fashion also influenced the way in which people spent their time. The old aristocratic landowning society had a high leisure preference. To fill their waking moments a highly ritualised round of visits, entertainments and functions was accepted and pursued. Sport was subject to the restraints of convention and had its hierarchy of prestige. Para-military pursuits such as hunting, shooting and fishing were the preserve of the landowner. For the working classes the pattern of such leisure as was available was largely socially determined. There was a sequence of folk festivals which persisted with some vigour in the face of industrialisation while new practices developed. Paternal employers came to organise works outings while religious organisations, friendly societies and the like arranged special functions for their members. With living space at a premium, the pub, the beer house and the café were places of public resort and centres of social activity. And expenditure on drink, not seldom a response in industrial areas to an instinct to escape from a narrow cramping environment, was affected by social attitudes. Throughout society the conventional use of living space tended to be rigidly determined. While in the upper reaches of society houses tended to provide rooms for each activity, the use of living space lower down the social scale was highly ritualised.

And in death as in life there were conventions to be obeyed. The funeral provided an occasion to establish individual identities often denied in life. In many directions conspicuous consumption was one obvious way in which status and standing could be asserted.

Though convention was conservative, it was not immutable. The changing pattern of industrial activity, the changing requirements of labour had their effect on patterns of behaviour. The spread of fashion, the volatile element in social customary behaviour, was facilitated within Europe by the existence of countries having relatively similar ideals of culture and by the absence of political and social barriers to the general adoption of new modes. It was assisted by the development of newspapers and journals, by the improved articulation of the market, by developments in transport and by travel. And there was a major development, the democratisation of fashion. While the pace of fashionable change was perhaps no more rapid than it had been in earlier times,[10] the pursuit of fashion, competitive emulation, tended to reach further down the social pyramid. This spread of fashion was aided not only by personal contact between mistress and maid and by the demonstration effect but also by the enhanced circulation of fashion magazines and by the invention of the paper pattern.

Most important for consumption was the attitude of mind. The Puritan was typically associated with a wish to limit material desires. He was reputed to dress soberly and to live unostentatiously. Members of religious orders commonly took a vow of poverty. Such attitudes seemed appropriate when output was growing slowly but when with industrialisation the speed of growth not only increased but appeared sustained, the old precepts of poverty ceased to appeal. The quickening pace of technological change began to provide glimpses of abundance which could make dreams of affluence possible. To reinforce the material desires, philosophers and economists came to expound a

10. Caroline A. Foley, 'Fashion', *Economic Journal*, III (1893) 458–74.

hedonistic calculus rather than asceticism. One element in the expansion of demand was the growing attitude of acquisitiveness of European society. But not all influences operated in the same direction. With advancement possible, the perceptive worker saw that thrift provided a route to wealth and the 'self-made man' became an object of esteem. The gospel of wealth was preached by Samuel Smiles and given institutional form in friendly societies, mutual clubs and savings banks.

THE ROLE OF GOVERNMENT

From the late eighteenth century and particularly from 1850 the efficiency of government intervention improved and its range extended, a consequence of the changes in European society such as industrialisation, urbanisation, population growth and other factors such as burgeoning nationalism and military expenditure which required an expanded bureaucracy, of rising real incomes which made the finance of a wider range of governmental functions possible and of a change in attitude to governmental intervention. While in the mid-nineteenth century, 'that government is best which governs least' was a sentiment which commanded support in England at least, before the century had drawn to a close the retreat from laissez-faire had begun. Dicey commented on 'the growth of collectivism' and Bismarck's interventionist policies were being emulated elsewhere.

Government action affected consumption in a number of ways. As far as clothing was concerned, sumptuary laws wasted away in the later eighteenth century and attempts to control by legislation what people wore were abandoned. Some controls over food supplies dating from the middle ages, like the assizes of bread and ale in England, were also brought to an end. But governments soon found that laissez-faire was not completely possible. Since market forces sometimes operated like Gresham's law, the bad driving out the good, the force of law was required. As far as food was concerned, they had to intervene, for example, to prevent the adulteration of foodstuffs.

Then governments were able either to reduce or remove both internal and external barriers to trade. When Voltaire had travelled in France in the mid-eighteenth century, he had complained that he had crossed a customs barrier every time he changed horses, but these impediments were removed during the Revolution. In Germany, too, local tolls abounded. In the early nineteenth century there were no less than twenty-two tolls on the Weser between Munden and Bremen. These, and many others, the Zollverein removed but in other parts of Europe, such as Italy, internal barriers to trade remained late in the nineteenth century.

Tariffs on imports particularly affected the consumption of foodstuffs. When, from the 1840s, English tariffs on imported foodstuffs were either reduced or abolished, consumption, particularly of sugar and tea, grew.[11] More generally, the spread of free trade reduced barriers to the importation of commodities and by reducing their price helped to widen the market for them. Tariffs tended to distort the pattern of expenditure, the degree of distortion depending upon the elasticity of demand. But the free trade interlude in the middle of the nineteenth century was only brief. The 1860 Anglo-French treaty led, as a result of the operation of the most favoured nation principle, to reductions in trade barriers between France and practically all other European countries. Throughout Europe trade was either freed or subjected to low duties. Agricultural products were more affected than industrial. Grain duties were abolished by the Zollverein in 1853, by Britain in 1860, by France and the Netherlands in 1862, by Italy in 1870, by Belgium in 1871. But the retreat from free trade came from the late 1870s: in Italy in 1878, in Germany in 1879, in France in 1881, in Bulgaria in 1883, in Switzerland in 1884, in Rumania in 1886, in Belgium and Sweden in 1887, in Austria-Hungary, Spain, Portugal and Russia in the same

11. Though coffee provided an opposite example. While the duty was reduced sharply, consumption fell. See Mathias, *Retailing Revolution*, pp. 11, 30.

decades and only Great Britain and Denmark held to free trade.

But, whatever the effects of protection on farmers in France and Germany—and Michael Tracy has argued it was only the larger farmers who benefited—protection was certainly against the interests of consumers in general. Studies published by the British Board of Trade before the first world war suggest that urban workers in France and

---

TABLE 4: Wages and Hours of Work of Workers in Certain Trades in Different Countries, as a percentage of the Corresponding Figures for England

	France	*Germany*	*Belgium*
Weekly money wages	75	83	63
Hours worked per week	117	111	121
Hourly wage rates	64	75	52

Source: Board of Trade (U.K.), *Cost of Living in Foreign Towns* (Cd 4032, 1908; Cd 4512, 1909; Cd 5065, 1910) quoted in Michael Tracy, *Agriculture in Western Europe: crisis and adaptation since 1880* (Cape, 1964) p. 39.

Germany had to pay considerably higher prices for their food than similarly placed workers in England, although the continental workers worked longer hours for less money. With more moderate protection in Belgium, the workers there were less affected. As the following table suggests, agricultural protection in France and Germany substantially aggravated the gap in the standards of living of their working population as compared with England. The pattern of expenditure of French and German workers was affected by protection which largely deprived them of the opportunity to buy cheap imported food. Paying more for food, they consequently had less to spare of a given income for expenditure in other directions.[12] While protection affected the urban consumer adversely, at the same time it served to shield the farmers from the worst effects of the late nineteenth-century fall in agricultural prices and so helped

12. See Michael Tracy, *Agriculture in Western Europe: crisis and adaptation since 1880* (Cape, 1964) pp. 35–40.

to check the fall in farm incomes. It also slowed down movement off the land and, particularly in France, reduced the pace both of modernisation on the farm and of industrialisation.

TABLE 5: Cost of an Average Working-man's Food Budget in Different Countries in 1905[a] (in pence)

| | At English consumption levels, but foreign prices | | | | At foreign consumption levels and foreign prices | | |
	England and Wales	France	Germany	Belgium	France	Germany	Belgium
Bread	27½	31¾	39¾[b]	26⅛	41¾	35¼[b]	41
Flour	12¾	19¾	18	13¾	..	3½	1
Potatoes	7¼	7¼	6¼	6¾	6¾	9¾	13
Sugar	10¾	15¼	12¾	16	5	4¾	3
Bacon	12	..	14¾	11¾	..	7½	6
Cheese	5¼	..	4¼	6⅜	..	3	4¼
Butter	26½	25	27¾	26	15¾	17¼	29¼
Milk	17½	12½	13¼	11¼	10	17	9
Beef	30½	33¼	37	29¼	22⅛	18¼	17⅞
Mutton	9½	12½	13¼	10½	8⅜	–	1¾
Pork	4	4⅝	5	4¼	7	15¾	8½
Total of above	163½	(161⅞)[c]	192	162	(116¾)[c]	132	134⅝

[a] Data for Belgium refer to 1908.
[b] Consists of an 'equivalent' amount of wheat flour.
[c] Incomplete total.
.. Not available.
– Nil or negligible.

Source: Board of Trade (U.K.), *Cost of Living in Foreign Towns* (Cd 4032, 1908; Cd 4512, 1909; Cd 5065, 1910) quoted in Tracy, *Agriculture in Western Europe*, p. 39.

Taxation also affected the pattern of consumption. Although revenue from customs still bulked large in governmental income, there was other taxation both direct and indirect. While direct taxation, such as the land tax, reduced total purchasing power, by and large without distorting individual expenditure,[13] indirect taxation

13. Since elasticities are not equal for all goods, direct taxes may affect consumption patterns

affected the pattern of consumption. In the middle of the eighteenth century in England the net was cast wide. In 1769 a foreigner commented that 'the people are taxed in the morning for the soap that washes their hands; at 9 for the coffee, the tea and the sugar they use at breakfast; at noon for the starch that powders their hair; at dinner for the salt that savours their meat; in the evening for the porter that cheers their spirits; all day long for the light that enters their windows, and at night for the candles that light them to bed'.[14] And other items such as carriages, playing cards and wallpaper might have been added to the list. The effect of the window tax is still visible in England while the consumption of soap, tea and sugar increased sharply when the taxes on them were removed. Not only in England but in other countries as well, taxation was used in order to raise revenue and also on occasion to reduce the consumption of alcoholic liquors. Together with rising prices of production, increased taxes brought about a sharp reduction in gin-drinking in England from 1750. In most countries, however, the effect of taxation on consumption has been little studied. In general the effect of indirect taxation was regressive. As it fell relatively more heavily on the poor than on the rich it tended to restrict the purchasing power of the mass of the people and to maintain a markedly unequal distribution of incomes. In many parts of Europe, combined with the exactions of landlords and the Church, government taxes kept the peasant at or near subsistence level and so prevented the development of markets for consumption goods. And when changes took place the burden of taxation on the mass of the population often remained heavy. Even in England until 1913 the working man contributed more to the revenue of the state than he benefited by its social expenditure.

But total demand was not just a summation of the needs of individual consumers; it also had a corporate component. Most important in these years was the public demand of

14. *Annual Register*, March 1769, cited by Thomas S. Ashton, 'Changes in Standards of Comfort in Eighteenth-century England', *Proceedings of the British Academy*, XLI (1955) 178.

the state, most visible in two respects; first in relation to war and second on account of the demands of growing industrial societies for social services. Early modern Europe had seen the institutionalisation of war. From being a casual and spasmodic business, war had grown in scale and increased in complexity. So its demand on resources on both capital and current account increased. Standing armies were established, the number of men under arms increased and their demands for equipment grew. Barracks and dockyards were built, warships grew in size, uniforms, weapons and supplies were required on an unprecedented scale. In the second half of the eighteenth century these trends continued. While still limited, the wars for empire involved an increasing claim on resources. But there was also development in warfare. With the publication of his *New principles of gunnery* in the 1740s, Benjamin Robins put the practice of gunnery on a much more scientific basis, transformed the art of fortification and rendered Vauban's system obsolete.

In a number of ways the intensification of warfare was reflected in the Napoleonic Wars, a conflict for European domination. The first war fought by civilian armies, it saw a great increase in the number of men under arms. On his advance to Moscow in 1812, Napoleon had an army of 612,000. The accuracy and frequency of firepower increased as did the mobility of artillery. And more weight of arms could be mustered for battles which were once more fought *à l'outrance* because once again soldiers took lodgings where they could and were able, because of the spread of the potato, to live off the land. While it apparently played no part in the Seven Years War, twenty years later the War of the Bavarian Succession was nicknamed the 'potato war' because many of the soldiers lived on the new food which they claimed from the fields on their progress.[15] At sea, too,

15. Hans Delbrueck, *Geschichte der Kriegskunst in Rahmen der politischen Geschichte* (9 vols. Berlin, 1900–36) IV, 479, cited by John U. Nef, *War and Human Progress: an essay on the rise of industrial civilisation* (Routledge, 1950) p. 323.

there were developments. New types of warships appeared in greater numbers.

The influence of the Napoleonic Wars on consumption was far-reaching. The armies and navies provided employment for some and raised the incomes of others. The need to clothe, provision and arm many thousands of soldiers created an enormous demand for certain commodities. In the absence of British competition, striking growth was evident in the cotton industries of Ghent, Paris, Mulhouse and Saxony and in the metal-working industries of Belgium, Germany and Switzerland. Great engineering works, such as John Cockerill's works at Liège and the Escher-Wyss plant at Zurich, came into being. French experts were sent into the less developed regions of French occupied Europe to carry out geographical surveys, prospect for minerals and supervise the operation of mines and factories.[16] But war also brought devastation and inflation. And to finance hostilities, governments had to divert income from the private to the public purse. It was these wars which led to the first major direct tax levied on the individual, the income tax, to be introduced into Britain.

From 1815 until the middle of the nineteenth century, Europe enjoyed a period of peace and military expenditure was limited. At sea Britannia ruled the waves and used her ships to limit the African slave trade. Then the flurry of limited wars in the third quarter of the century had momentous consequences. Before the Crimean War the main casualties in war were not those who were killed in battle but those who died of illness or subsequently of their wounds. The activities of Florence Nightingale confirmed the importance of proper medical care in reducing casualties and provided a great stimulus to nursing and medical care not only for the military but for civilians also. Economic growth in Russia was at least in part a function of military exigencies. The Crimean War was a spur to the emancipation of the serfs and the construction of a railway system

16. William O. Henderson, *The Industrialisation of Europe, 1780-1914* Thames & Hudson, 1969) p. 27.

while the Turkish War of 1876 led to attempts to expand Russian heavy industry.

From 1870 to almost the end of the century there was a lull in hostilities in Europe and then there came a series of regional wars which were accompanied by more widespread preparation for war. The size of standing armies was increased and an armament race began which was particularly evident in the naval sphere. In response to the growth of the German navy came the demand for Dreadnoughts in England. 'We want eight and we won't wait'. Expenditure on arms therefore grew. The following table gives figures for Great Britain, France and Germany.

TABLE 6: Expenditure on Arms, 1875–1914 ($ million)

	Great Britain	France	Germany
1875	133 ·2	137 ·4 (1873)	106 ·5 (1881–2)
1907–8	291 ·8	243 ·7 (1908)	290 ·5
1913–14	385 ·0	277 ·2	352 ·7

Source: Nussbaum, *Economic institutions*, p. 278.

And expenditure per head of population also increased: in Great Britain from $4.00 per head in the 1870s to $8.50 on the eve of the first world war: in France from $3.80 to $7.10 and in Germany from $2.36 to $5.87 in roughly the same period.

The second expansion of public demand—in the social field—was a product of industrialisation and urbanisation. Social pressures grew to control the progress of industrialism. Factory acts were passed to control hours and conditions but were only effective when an inspectorate was appointed to see that they were enforced. Public health provisions were needed in the growing towns and again required both material resources and officials to make them effective. The necessity for consumer protection from false products or adulteration also resulted in an extension of governmental intervention. Other problems of an industrial society, unemployment, sickness and old age, proved beyond the capabilities of competing private agencies and again led to a growth of state intervention. And more positively advancing industrial nations required a higher standard of literacy so that education passed from private hands into those of the state. Some developments occurred first in England, others in France and yet others in Bismarck's Germany, but all increased the number of persons employed by the state and the public claim on resources.

On the whole governments played a relatively small part in capital formation but there was one important exception. While English experience differed, in other European countries public investment was important in the construction of the railways.[17] And the importance of the government as investor varied considerably. In Russia, for example, between 1890 and 1917 the government was the largest customer for an important part of heavy industry.

Local government also extended its activities. In England Joseph Chamberlain campaigned as mayor not for minimum expenditure but for 'high rates and a healthy city' and municipalities came to take an increasing interest not only in poor relief and highways but also in hospitals, schools and public health. The production of gas and electricity and the provision of transport—municipal socialism—also became the responsibility of town governments. Interest in the arts was also evident, in art galleries, theatres, libraries, concert halls and opera houses. As Table 7 shows, government consumption as a proportion of total consumption increased in a number of (but not all) European countries for which information is available in the half century or so before the first world war.

Military expenditure was clearly the reason why the figures for Germany and the United Kingdom were higher than those for other countries. The growth of the public sector was also evident in terms of employment. By 1911, for every 10,000 inhabitants, Belgium had 200 public officials, France 176, Germany 126 and England 73.[18]

17. See Chapter 5, p. 301.
18. Ronald Max Hartwell, *The Industrial Revolution and Economic Growth* (Methuen, 1971) p. 217.

TABLE 7: Government Consumption as percentage of Total Consumption, 1851–1920

United Kingdom	*1860–79*	*1880–99*	*1900–14*
	4·8	5·8	7·4
Germany	*1851–70*	*1871–90*	*1891–1913*
	4·0	5·9	7·1
Italy	*1861–80*	*1881–1900*	*1901–10*
	4·2	4·8	4·2
Norway	*1865–74*	*1875–94*	*1895–1914*
	3·8	4·8	6·6
Sweden	*1861–80*	*1881–1900*	*1901–20*
	4·4	5·4	5·8

Source: Simon Kuznets, *Modern economic growth: rate, structure and spread* (New Haven: Yale U.P., 1966) pp. 236-7.

INCOME

From the side of the consumer, three aspects need to be considered: first, the level of income, then the social distribution of private income, and thirdly the division of income between the public and the private sectors.

During the early modern period, from 1500 to 1750, the growth of wealth in Europe was slow and hesitant. Professor Kuznets sets the possible (and perhaps the maximum) long-term rate of growth of output per head in the developed countries of western Europe during these two and a half centuries at about 0·2 per cent per year, giving a total rise in per capita product over the period of about 65 per cent.[19] As population growth during the same years occurred at a rate of 0·17 per cent per annum there was some slight overall increase in per capita income between 1500 and 1750 in western Europe but, as will be indicated below, the benefits of this growth were very unevenly distributed. In the rest of Europe increase in average per capita income did not reach

19. Simon Kuznets, 'Capital Formation in Modern Economic Growth and some Implications for the Past', *Third International Conference of Economic History* (Paris 1968) pp. 30-1.

the level of western Europe and in some places the standard of living may actually have declined during the early modern period.

The period from 1750 to 1914 provides a distinct contrast with the previous two hundred and fifty years. Although poverty was by no means abolished, although there were considerable differences both social and geographical, although there were costs in industrialisation in terms of dirt, noise and loss of individual liberty and falling living standards for some, it is undeniable that the average standard of living rose. One very crude index is provided by increased longevity. While life in pre-industrial Europe was nasty, brutish, short, in this period life expectancy increased throughout Europe. To take but two examples of countries which enjoyed rather different experiences in the nineteenth century: in England life expectancy for males increased from 39·9 years in 1838–54 to 48·5 years in 1901–10 and in Italy for males from 35·1 years in 1876–87 to 44·2 years in 1901–11.[20] Much of the decline in general mortality was due to the reduction in infantile mortality but not all. Further, while it is true that happiness cannot be measured by the length of days and life can be dragged on as well as cut short, is it not probable that these figures imply an increase in the sum of human well-being? Such arguments are admittedly inferential but more direct calculations also show that with industrialisation, with developments in technology and the growth of market opportunities, output per head rose and so did average incomes in proportion.

The course of events in the United Kingdom can be followed in more detail. During the first three-quarters of the eighteenth century there is evidence of a rise in real incomes per head. Writing in 1776 Adam Smith believed that 'the real quantity of the necessaries and conveniences of life which it [labour] can procure to the labourer, has, during the course of the present century, increased perhaps in a still greater proportion than its money price.'[21] Then,

20. For more details see Chapter 3.
21. *An Inquiry into the Nature and Causes of the Wealth of Nations*, ed. Edwin Cannan (Methuen University Paperbacks, 1961) I, 87.

with the onset of industrialisation, and despite the far-ranging qualitative changes in the economy, there appears to have been a check to the rise in real incomes between 1790 and 1815. Similar checks appear to have been experienced by other countries as they industrialised. The rise in incomes was halted in Germany between 1820 and 1850 while real incomes in Russia rose more slowly between 1860 and 1880. The severity of the check varied from country to country. [22]

A marked acceleration in the growth of real incomes after the removal of wartime restrictions was followed in the 1840s by a period of stagnation or decline. Then from about the mid-century the pace of growth quickened again to reach a high level in the last thirty or forty years of the century and our period comes to an end with a renewed check to the increase in real incomes in the early twentieth century. On the basis of these figures it appears that real incomes approximately quadrupled in the United Kingdom in the course of the nineteenth century. But such estimates do not take account of all the changes involved. First, they do not take account of changes in kind and quality. Gas lighting was not available in the early nineteenth century. Similarly the quality of food changed and with the reduction of adulteration may have improved. And, secondly, there are non-pecuniary aspects of the standard of living which need to be taken into account. In the course of the nineteenth century, for example, average hours of work were reduced and people were able to enjoy more leisure.

If comparisons within a country over time are fraught with difficulty, how much more fragile are comparisons between countries over time. Yet some attempt must be made. In the early eighteenth century, the three richest countries in Europe were the Netherlands, France and England. The course of events in England has already been described. Since this increase in real wages was largely a

22. For a theory explaining the differences which arose, see Alexander Gerschenkron, 'The Early Phases of Industrialisation in Russia: after-thoughts and counterthoughts' in Walt W. Rostow, ed. *The Economics of Take-off into Sustained Growth* (Macmillan, 1963) p. 152.

function of economic growth, other countries tended to lag behind Britain. In those areas of Belgium, France and Germany where industry developed and towns grew, living standards began to rise in the first half of the nineteenth century but in the less-developed parts of Europe there was little change. Still in 1860 living standards in Russia were much below those which obtained in western Europe. While with the advance of industry, particularly between 1880 and 1913, real income per head increased in Russia, it did no more than keep pace with the European average of 1·0 per cent per annum between 1860 and 1913 and so the gap between the richer countries of Europe and the poorer tended to widen in the later nineteenth century. By the eve of the first world war it has been estimated that real income per head in Russia was equal to that of Italy but only half that of Germany and one-third of that of the United Kingdom. There were thus in 1913 wide variations in living standards between different parts of Europe. The following table presents a comparison for four countries for the end of our period:

TABLE 8: Gross National Product per capita (rubles)

	Great Britain	France	Germany	Russia
1897	273	233	184	63
1913	460·6	—	300·4	101·4

Source: Rondo Cameron, *Banking in the Early stages of Industrialisation: a study in comparative economic history* (Oxford U.P., 1967) p. 184.

It provides some indication of the relative position of four countries in 1897 and of the development between 1897 and 1913 of three of them.

And what was true between countries was also evident within countries. By and large the course of economic change enriched the towns and industrial areas more than the countryside. Within England these changes brought about a shift in the balance of wealth. At the end of the seventeenth century, southern England, the regions south of a line drawn from the Severn to the Wash, included the richest part of England but in the next two centuries industrialisation enriched the north of England and south Wales and average incomes per head rose above those of the less developed rural areas of southern England. Similar shifts were visible in other European countries. Industry enriched the Ruhr, the Saar and the areas around Lille and Liège.

Also to be noted are other changes which the shift from agriculture to industry involved. In early modern times agricultural workers had intermittent employment largely conditioned by the seasons but some at least had bye-employments and enjoyed income in kind, both food and housing. While industrial wages were in many cases higher than agricultural wages, industrial work was also inter-mittent as the result of fluctuations in the level of demand, bye-employments were usually impossible and income in kind was less frequent. In the crowded industrial towns, the urban worker had no garden in which to grow his vegetables or common on which to keep his pig or poultry, no wood from which to gather kindling or game to trap or poach. When these factors are taken into account, inter-regional comparisons become much more difficult to assess.

As there was marked inequality in the distribution of income geographically, so there was socially as well. It is possible that there had been some narrowing of social distance in material terms in the previous centuries. But between 1688 and 1812 there would appear to have been a marked increase in the inequality of incomes in Britain. The upper classes in general seem to have expanded their incomes by more than the national average while the small farmers, unskilled labourers and the poor who grew as a proportion of the total population seem to have increased their standard of living by less than the average. To some extent the rich appear to have increased their standard of living by reducing the size of their households as the poor appear to have lost ground by increasing the size of their families.[23] But 'eminent merchants' not only increased their families but also raised their living standards

23. See Volume 4, Chapter 3.

more than any group of comparable size in the community and the professional and commercial classes improved their relative real incomes while the armed forces appear to have fared relatively badly.

Nor did all sections of the community suffer equally from the check to consumption where it occurred. Merchants and industrialists gained relatively while the aristocracy of labour, the skilled factory workers, appear to have been able to maintain their living standards better than their unskilled counterparts in the factories or their fellows employed in shops or in the fields.[24] In a sense the controversy about the British standard of living between 1790 and 1850 is explicable in these terms. The 'pessimists'—the Hammonds, Hobsbawm and Thompson—have been discussing the fate of that section of the working class who bore the brunt of the check while the 'optimists'—Clapham, Ashton and Hartwell—have focused their attention on those workers who benefited relatively from the first phase of industrialisation. But both parties are agreed that British living standards rose from the 1850s and more particularly from the 1870s and then received a further check between 1900 and 1913. And what was true of Britain was true of other countries too. Once the initial phase of industrialisation was over, real incomes began to rise.

While land was still a reservoir of wealth, the great change in the period of industrialisation was that landowners found themselves joined and sometimes outflanked by the new wealth of the bankers, the industrialists and the merchants. Though not always given full social recognition, the Rothschilds, Krupps, Schneiders, Levers, Rhodes &c became forces to be reckoned with. In France, for example, in 1902 there were 15,000 fortunes over 1 million francs. In many countries the noble landowners displayed resilience by exploiting their lands for profit, for mining, industrial development or urban housing, or by marrying into the

24. For the Rhineland, see Thomas C. Banfield, *Industry of the Rhine, series I. Agriculture: embracing a view of the social condition of the rural population of that district; series II. Manufactures: embracing a view of the social condition of the manufacturing population of that district* (London, 1846, 1848).

families of new wealth. At the other end of the scale, the conditions of the poor remained wretched whether they were in Ireland, in southern Italy, in Russia or in the Balkans. The rich had certainly become richer and wealth continued to be very unevenly distributed. Figures available for England and Wales on the eve of the first world war show that under 1 per cent of those over 25 owned two-

TABLE 9: Distribution of Wealth among people of 25 and over, England and Wales, 1911–13

Amount of capital	No. of persons	% of all persons	Amount of capital £ millions	% of all capital	Average holding
Above £25,000	32,000	0·2	2,685	41·3	84,000
£10,000–25,000	57,000	0·3	930	14·3	16,300
£5,000–10,000	81,500	0·4	635	9·8	7,800
£1,000–5,000	426,000	2·3	1,030	15·8	2,400
£100–1,000	1,766,000	9·4	670	10·3	380
Below £100	16,382,500	87·4	550	8·5	34
Total	18,745,000	100·0	6,500	100·0	350

Source: Mark Abrams, *The Condition of the British people, 1911–45* (Gollancz, 1946) p. 110.

thirds of the national wealth while over 87 per cent shared 8·5 per cent of the total and this clearly consisted of little more than their clothes and furniture. In less detail, figures are available which show the shares of national income enjoyed by the richest, and in some cases the less rich, in Denmark, Prussia, Saxony and the United Kingdom in the later nineteenth century.

While inherited wealth served to reinforce the current incomes of the rich, poverty was a function of lack of inheritance, of low incomes and also in some cases of unwise expenditure. According to one view, the distribution of incomes in Edwardian England was just about as unequal as it had ever been anywhere.[25]

25. Peter Laslett in *The Listener*, 28 December 1961, cited by Marghanita Laski, 'Domestic Life' in Simon Nowell-Smith, ed. *Edwardian England, 1901–1914* (Oxford U.P., 1964) p. 142.

TABLE 10: Shares in National Income of Ordinal Groups, selected countries

DENMARK	*1870*			*1903*	
top 5 per cent	36·5			28	
top 10 per cent	50			38	

PRUSSIA	*1854*	*1875*	*1896*		*1913*
top 5 per cent	21	26	27		30
top 20 per cent		48	45		50
[top 40 per cent		66			67]
lowest 60 per cent		34			33

SAXONY	*1880*	*1896*	*1912*
top 5 per cent	34	36	33
top 20 per cent	56	57	55
lowest 60 per cent	27	26·5	27

UNITED KINGDOM	*1880*	*1913*
top 5 per cent	48	43
top 20 per cent	58	59

Source: Kuznets, *Modern economic growth*, pp. 208-9.

THE COMPONENTS OF DEMAND

Man's basic material requirement is for food, and after that clothing and shelter. Customarily only after these needs are met does man seek other outlets for his expenditure and satisfy his needs for entertainment, luxuries and other conspicuous expenditure or is able to postpone consumption and invest. Notably, as Ernest Engel suggested, the proportion of income spent on food falls as income rises.[26] But since, as we have already seen, a substantial proportion of the population had very little in the way of money income, it is not easy to discuss patterns of expenditure. Nevertheless

26. But, as Eric Jones has pointed out, 'in societies where elementary physiological needs are far from satisfied, it is certainly not self-evident that expenditures will be devoted to achieving the satisfaction of those needs' and he provides a twentieth-century example from Columbia which suggests that 'it may literally be necessary to advertise food to a starving man' ('The Fashion Manipulator: consumer tastes and British industries, 1660-1800' in L. P. Cain and P. A. Uselding, ed. *Business Enterprise and Economic Change* (forthcoming)).

some attempt must be made. Private consumption will be discussed and then corporate and institutional expenditure.

First, then, how did a private person spend his income? Until the later eighteenth century few family budgets have survived and so for previous periods it is only possible to give an impressionistic picture for different social groups. In the 1790s in England, however, the curiosity of two investigators led to the publication of a series of working class budgets.[27] Biased by his interest in the poor law, David Davies set out in *The Case of Labourers in Husbandry* information relating to 127 poor families. Though probably not typical of agricultural workers as a whole, these budgets (summarised in the following table) show that food accounted for about 70 per cent of expenditure, clothes for about 10 per cent, rent and fuel for another 8 per cent, leaving 10 per cent or so for medical care and other needs.

TABLE 11: Budgets of Families of Agricultural Workers in Great Britain, 1787-1793

	Annual Family Income (£)				
	10–20	20–25	25–30	30–45	All
	1. Percentage of Expenditures				
Category of Expenditure					
Food	70·1	69·5	75·3	81·8	72·2
Rent	5·3	5·1	4·9	4·3	5·0
Fuel	2·6	3·0	4·2	3·1	3·2
Clothes	9·1	11·3	7·7	4·9	9·3
Medical care	5·2	4·5	2·3	1·6	3·9
Sundries	7·8	6·7	5·7	4·2	6·5
	2. Absolute Data				
No. of families	34	58	25	10	127
Average No. of persons in family	5·2	6·0	5·8	7·5	5·9
Average income (£)	18	22	27	36	23
Average expenditure (£)	23	27	29	38	27

Source: David Davies, *The Case of Labourers in Husbandry Stated and Considered* (London, 1795) quoted in George C. Stigler, 'The early history of empirical studies of consumer behaviour', *Journal of Political Economy*, LXII (1954) 97.

27. Earlier Arthur Young had analysed the actual outgoings of four families in his *The Farmer's Letters to the People of England, containing the sentiments of a practical husbandman on various subjects of the utmost importance* (3rd ed. 2 vols. London, 1771) especially letter V.

In the middle of the nineteenth century, Ernest Engel analysed the expenditure of 153 Belgian families. This showed a pattern of expenditure for these working class families very like that of their English counterparts half a century or so earlier. Noting that the better-off families spent a smaller proportion of their income on food and a somewhat larger share on clothing, Engel put forward a law of consumption which has become associated with his name. 'The poorer the family', he stated, 'the greater the proportion of its total expenditure that must be devoted to the provision of food'. Other investigations followed which it is not possible to follow in detail here[28] but for the early

TABLE 12: Percentage Composition of Belgian Workmen's Family Budgets, 1853

Category of Expenditure	*I* (On relief)	*II* (Poor but Independent)	*III* (Comfortable)
Food	70·9	67·4	62·4
Clothing (including cleaning)	11·7	13·2	14·0
Housing	8·7	8·3	9·0
Heat and light	5·6	5·5	5·4
Tools and work supplies	0·6	1·2	2·3
Education, religion, etc.	0·4	1·1	1·2
Taxes	0·2	0·5	0·9
Health, recreation, insurance, etc.	1·7	2·8	4·3
Personal services	0·2	0·2	0·4
Total	100·0	100·0	100·0
Average income (francs)	565	797	1,198
Average expenditure (francs)	649	845	1,214
Minimum expenditure (francs)	370	440	541
Maximum expenditure (francs)	1,256	1,769	2,823

Source: 'Die Productions- und Consumtionsverhältnisse des Königreichs Sachsen' in Ernest Engel, *Die Lebenkosten belgischer Arbeiter-Familien* (Dresden, 1895) p. 27 quoted in Stigler, 'Studies of consumer behaviour', p. 98. Stigler notes 'the table contains some errors; I have added the last four lines of the table'.

28. See, for example, Frederic Le Play, *Les ouvriers européens: études sur les travaux, le vie domestique et la condition morale des populations ouvrières de*

twentieth century it is possible to make a comparison between four countries, Great Britain, Germany, France and Belgium, of the proportion spent on food by different income groups:

TABLE 13: Percentage Expenditure on Food, 1905

Weekly Income in Shillings	Great Britain	Germany	France	Belgium
Under 20		68·7	62·7	66·1
20 to 25	67·3*	64·5	60·8	64·8
25 to 30	66·2	62·3	58·6	63·6
30 to 35	65·0	59·2	57·9	62·1
35 to 40	61·0	57·7	56·1	61·2
40 and over	55·9	56·3	52·8	57·0

* This figure is for weekly incomes of under 25 shillings.

Source: Board of Trade (U.K.), *Working class rents, housing and retail prices* (Cd 3864, 1908); *Cost of living in foreign towns* (Cd 4032, 1908; Cd 4512, 1909; Cd 5065, 1910) quoted in Edwin R. A. Seligman and Alvin Johnson, ed. *Encyclopaedia of the Social Sciences* (New York: Macmillan, 1930) IV, 297.

Here, too, expenditure on food declined proportionately with an increase in income.

The consequence of such a heavy percentage concentration of expenditure on food was two-fold. It meant that demand for other goods was limited: and, since food was a prime necessity, it meant that normally expenditure on other goods was extremely responsive to changes in the price of foodstuffs. In particular, as *The Economist* pointed out in 1864:

l'Europe: précédées d'un exposé de la méthode d'observation (Paris, 1855; 2nd ed. 6 vols. 1877) which presents budgets for workers in central Europe, England, France, Germany, Russia, Scandinavia, Spain and Switzerland; and Henry Mayhew, *London Labour and the London Poor: a cyclopaedia of the condition and earnings of those that will work, those that cannot work and those that will not work* (4 vols., London, 1861–2). Later investigations were carried out by individuals (for example, Charles Booth, B. Seebohm Rowntree in England, Gottlieb Schnappe-Arndt in Germany, Marcus Rubin in Denmark and Carl Landolt in Switzerland) and by governments. See Edwin R. A. Seligman and Alvin Johnson, ed. *Encyclopaedia of the Social Sciences* (New York: Macmillan, 1930) VI, pp. 73–8.

A bad harvest, and a consequent great rise in the price of food, has its effect—its immediate bad effect—upon every industry in the kingdom . . . The price of food is so large an item in the outlay of most families that, when it is augmented by some 40 or 50 per cent, of necessity there is decreased consumption of all things, and the manufactures which are dependent on the consumption and prosperity of the great mass of the working classes are one and all at once depressed.[29]

As in personal terms it appears to be broadly true that food consumption as a proportion of total consumption falls as income rises, so it can also be said that overall as a country grows in wealth so it spends a smaller proportion of its income on food.[30]

Because the expenditure of the poor was so limited it is not necessary to set it out in any detail. But the patterns of expenditure of other sections of the population deserve to be considered a little more fully. One difference between the poor and the better-off working class which became more apparent in the course of the nineteenth century was the increased provision which was made for savings. An analysis made in Germany which compared the family budgets of 853 families of working men and officials with the average expenditure of the country as a whole, showed that the poorer group saved 4·6 per cent of their income compared with a national average of 17 per cent.[31]

Empirical evidence appears to suggest that the richer sections of European society were able to spend a greater percentage of their incomes on personal services, on luxuries, on education, on entertainment, on travel and on

29. *The Economist*, 1864, p. 1133, repeating, in effect, an oft-expressed view. See, for example, Sidney Pollard and Colin Holmes, *Documents of European Economic History, vol. I. The Process of Industrialisation, 1750–1870* (Arnold, 1968) p. 151.

30. For an analysis of changes in the distribution of private consumption for the United Kingdom (1880–1919), Germany (1851–1913), Italy (1861–1920), Norway (1865–1910) and Sweden (1864–1913), see Simon Kuznets, 'Quantitative Aspects of the Economic Growth of Nations, VII. The share and structure of consumption', *Economic Development and Cultural Change*, X (1962), pp. 80–92.

other forms of conspicuous consumption. While such differences between the rich and the poor can be stated in general terms, perhaps the most vivid way to indicate differences in expenditure is to present individual budgets. Set out in table 14, therefore, are the ways in which six English families disposed of their incomes. Taken from articles in the *Cornhill Magazine* in 1901, they represent, as the editor of that journal stated at the time, an attempt to put down in £ s d the proportions of the yearly earnings which are devoted to rent, food, clothing, education, amusements, &c in average families throughout the kingdom, ranging from the household of a working man in receipt of 'good weekly wages' to that of a wealthy man 'whose income reaches the magic figure of £10,000 a year'.[32]

FOOD

As the budgets have shown, food was a major item in the expenditure of the majority of the population of Europe in these years. Still a great gulf existed between the gluttony of the rich and the exiguous food supplies of the poor but famine was virtually banished from the face of the continent. As a broad generalisation it may be said that Europeans were better fed in the early twentieth century than they were in the early eighteenth century. Nevertheless throughout these years the very poor were badly fed. In the poorest parts of Europe, in Ireland, Spain, Italy and Sicily, Bulgaria and Russia, their basic food consisted of maize porridge or rye bread and vegetables (potatoes, cabbage, turnips, beans and onions), water, tea or coffee, some alcoholic liquor depending on the locality and meat was taken but rarely. There was only limited dependence, except in times of stringency, on imported foods and the dietaries therefore largely consisted of what could be grown locally. In the Mediterranean region, for example, wheat rather than rye tended to be grown and fruit was much more plentiful than in northern Europe. Wine was drunk

31. See Table 1, *Encyclopaedia of the Social Sciences*, IV, 296.
32. Edgar Royston Pike, *Human Documents of the Age of the Forsytes* (Allen & Unwin, 1969) pp. 157–75.

TABLE 14: Budgets for Selected Income Levels, 1901

	£78 p.a.		£150 p.a.		£800 p.a.		£1800 p.a. (in town)		£1800 p.a. (in country)		£10,000 p.a.	
	£ s. d.	%	£ s. d.	%	£ s. d.	%	£ s. d.	%	£ s. d.	%	£ s. d.	%
Housing (rent, rates and taxes)	18.4.0	23·3	31.3.5	20·8	130.0.0	16·3	360.0.0	20·0	180.0.0	10·0	3450.0.0[11]	34·5
Heating and lighting, etc.	9.8.6	12·1	9.17.0	6·6	21.0.0	2·6	60.0.0[5]	3·3	80.0.0[5]	4·4	200.0.0	2·0
Servants' wages and house expenses												
Food	32.3.3[1]	41·2	47.9.0	31·6	88.0.0[2]	11·0	250.0.0[6]	14·0	250.0.0[6]	14·0	600.0.0[12]	6·0
Clothes	5.4.0	6·7	25.0.0	16·7	208.0.0[3]	26·0	550.0.0[7]	30·5	450.0.0[7]	25·0	1200.0.0[13]	12·0
Insurances and benefit club	2.12.0	3·3	4.8.3	2·8			200.0.0	11·1	180.0.0	10·0	570.0.0[14]	5·7
Alcohol and tobacco	7.3.0	9·2	2.5.0	1·5	30.0.0	3·8	60.0.0	3·4	50.0.0	2·8	200.0.0	2·0
Travel and holidays			12.0.0	8·0	50.0.0	6·2					750.0.0[15]	7·5
Newspapers, books, stamps and stationery, etc.	5.2.0	3·4	5.2.0	3·4	18.0.0	2·2	30.0.0	1·7	30.0.0	1·7	280.0.0[16]	2·8

TABLE 14 (continued)

	£ s. d.	%	£ s. d.	%	£ s. d.	%	£ s. d.	%	£ s. d.	%
Entertaining, presents and charity	1.10.0		35.0.0		40.0.0⁸	4·4	40.0.0⁸	2·2	750.0.0¹⁷	7·5
Doctor, etc.		1·0	30.0.0		100.0.0⁹	3·8	100.0.0⁹	5·5	100.0.0	1·0
Husband's and wife's allowances			140.0.0⁴						900.0.0⁴	9·0
Balance	3.5.0	4·2	6.1.4	4·0	50.0.0	17·5	150.0.0 6·2	440.0.0¹⁰ 8·3	440.0.0¹⁰ 24·4	1000.0.0 10·0

1. Meat and fish, £14 1s 8d; bread and flour, £5 10s 6d; grocery, £4 6s 8d; cheese, butter, bacon and eggs, £4 19s 8d; greengrocery, £3 5s 0d.
2. Wages, £38; repairs, £50.
3. Including washing and window cleaning.
4. Including clothes.
5. Coal.
6. Repairs, insurance, cleaning, painting &c, £100; wages, £130; linen, £20.
7. Including washing and lighting.
8. Charity.
9. Including journeys.
10. Minus £130 for pony carriage and groom and £150 for garden expenses.
11. Country property, £2,200; London house including rates, taxes, decoration and repairs, £800; taxes, £450.
12. Wages, £400; linen &c, £200.
13. Including beer and washing.
14. Education and children's clothes, £500; liveries, £70.
15. Stables, £600; small journeys and visits, £150.
16. Including hampers, cabs and small bills.
17. Entertainment and amusements, £350; charity, £400.

Source: Cornhill Magazine, 1901, quoted in Edgar Royston Pike, Human Documents of the Age of the Forsytes (Allen & Unwin, 1969), pp. 157–75.

in southern Europe with beer in the north and cider in Brittany and parts of England. Local supplies of spirit varied with potatoes in northern Europe providing the commonest source.

While many were poorly fed, the spread of economic activity resulted in many more people than in previous centuries indulging themselves to excess. If Adam Smith held that the desire for food is limited in every man by the narrow capacity of the human stomach and varies in quality rather than in quantity,[33] such a view underestimates the range of consumption between 1750 and the first world war. The gluttony of not merely the rich but of the well-to-do as well, which in the English case can be well-documented from the pages of Mrs Beeton's *Book of Household Management*—the nation which knows how to dine, she opined, has learnt the leading lesson of progress—provided a marked contrast to the limited dietaries of the poor. In Berlin the rich enjoyed Rhenish wines and Dutch cheeses, ate well at dinner, *à la francaise*, and then consumed jelly cakes and cream buns late in the evening while the poorer Berliners ate, usually at midday, porridge or ryebread and potatoes and perhaps some lard or pork washed down with thin beer. Similarly the *haute cuisine* of the well-to-do in France bore little relation to the bread and cider of a Norman farm hand or the fish stew and sour wine of the Marseilles dockworker.[34]

But dietaries were not unchanging. There were significant developments between 1750 and 1914. First, there was an increased consumption of starchy or sweet foods including potatoes, biscuits and cakes. Then there was a move with growing purchasing power towards whiter bread and lower bread consumption and an increased demand for meat and fish. And, towards the end of the period, for poorer people a greater variety of other foodstuffs, largely imported, became available. Nevertheless differences between countries continued to be of importance as even a limited comparison of the quantities of food consumed by working class families

33. Smith, *Wealth of Nations*, I, 183.
34. Franklin L. Ford, *Europe, 1780–1830* (Longmans, 1970) p. 378.

in the United Kingdom, France and Germany in a normal week in 1905 shows:

TABLE 15: Family Weekly Consumption of Specified Foods, 1905

		U.K.	France	Germany
Tea	lbs	0·6	—	—
Coffee	lbs	—	0·6	¾
Sugar	lbs	5⅓	1¾	2
Bacon	lbs	1½	—	¾
Eggs	no.	12	10	10
Cheese	lbs	¾	—	½
Butter	lbs	2	1¼	1¼
Potatoes	lbs	17	16	26
Flour	lbs	10	—	2
Bread	lbs	22	29	25
Milk	quarts	5	4	6½
Beef	lbs		3	2·2
Mutton	lbs	6½	1	—
Pork	lbs		¾	1·6
Veal	lbs		1¼	—

(U.K. Beef/Mutton/Pork/Veal braced = 6½; France braced = 6; Germany braced = 3·8)

Source: Board of Trade (U.K.), *Working Class Rents, Housing and Retail Prices* (Cd 3864, 1908) p. xxviii; *Cost of Living in Foreign Towns* (Cd 4032, 1908) p. xxvii, (Cd 4512, 1909) p. xxiv, quoted in Ernest H. Phelps Brown and Margaret H. Browne, *A Century of Pay: the course of pay and production in France, Germany, Sweden, the United Kingdom, and the United States of America, 1860–1960* (Macmillan, 1968) p. 50.

And there were significant variations in diet within countries as well as between countries, between Scotland and southern England, between Provence and Brittany, between Schleswig-Holstein and Bavaria, which could profitably be explored if space allowed.

Comparatively little information is available about the food value of nineteenth and early twentieth century dietaries. An analysis of the dietary surveys of Dr Edward Smith in 1862–3[35] suggests that indoor workers had a daily calorie intake of 2,190 and rural workers of 2,760. Bowley's figures for 1860 were somewhat higher at 3,240 a day rising

35. Theodore C. Barker, D. J. Oddy and John Yudkin, *The Dietary Surveys of Dr Edward Smith, 1862–63: a new assessment* (Staples P., 1970) p. 43.

to 3,470 in 1880 and an average of 3,900 in 1914[36] but this latter figure falls short of Heckscher's estimate for the total population of Sweden in 1912–13 of 4,402 calories.[37] If normal calorie requirements are taken as 3,000 to 3,300 calories a day, while the later dietaries were adequate, the English diets of the early 1860s were insufficient for healthy living.

Inevitably more information is available about institutional dietaries than about individual. Schools, poor law institutions, hospitals and the armed forces all provide evidence. In 1773 at the military orphanage in Copenhagen, three meals were served a day: in the morning bread and tea with milk, at midday soup with meat and bread and in the evening bread and butter or dripping, and ale.[38] Of English prisons in the early nineteenth century it was said of all the hardships the prisoners had to suffer none was worse than the inadequacy and dreadful quality of the food. At a generous estimate, the dietary of the Millbank penitentiary in 1822, which consisted of $1\frac{1}{2}$ lb of bread, 1 pint of gruel and 1 pint of soup a day for males, gave them 2,000 calories daily and was deficient in vitamins. No wonder scurvy caused trouble in prisons.[39] But schools and workhouses were little better. When the half-starved Brontë girls pleaded for more to eat, they were lectured on the sin of caring for carnal things and of pampering greedy appetites. Like Oliver Twist, who had the temerity to ask for more, and his unfortunate companions in the workhouse, schoolchildren and prisoners were persistently underfed. But, despite complaints, it was not until the later nineteenth century that English institutional dietaries were much improved.

36. Arthur L. Bowley, *Wages and Income in the United Kingdom since 1860* (Cambridge U.P., 1937) p. 36.

37. Eli F. Heckscher, *An Economic History of Sweden* (Cambridge, Mass: Harvard U.P., 1954) p. 69.

38. Poul Thestrup, *The Standard of Living in Copenhagen, 1730–1800: some methods of measurement* (Copenhagen: Institute of Economic History, 1971) p. 37.

39. Jack C. Drummond and Anne Wilbraham, *The Englishman's Food: five centuries of English diet* (2nd ed. Cape, 1958) pp. 366–7.

In theory, at any rate, the English sailor fared better. In 1811 the daily naval ration provided for $1\frac{3}{4}$ oz cheese, $4\frac{1}{4}$ oz meat, $2\frac{1}{4}$ oz pork, $\frac{7}{8}$ oz butter, $\frac{1}{4}$ oz suet, $\frac{7}{8}$ oz sugar, 3 oz flour, 1 lb bread and 1 qt beer.[40] His counterpart in the French navy in 1759 got biscuits instead of bread and wine instead of beer together with some vegetables, giving him 2,353–2,766 calories a day for an equally monotonous diet which may have proved to be much less attractive in fact than in prospect.[41] The biscuits could be mouldy, the bread weevily and the dried meat hard and difficult to eat. Nor did food for the armed forces improve much over time. At the beginning of the Crimean War the English troops, who were reputedly worse fed than the French, had a daily ration of, on paper, $1\frac{1}{2}$ lb bread or 1 lb biscuit and 1 lb of fresh or salt meat a day. Apart from any question of vitamins, this diet was clearly inadequate since it supplied scarcely 2,500 calories a day where 3,500–4,500 were needed. And scurvy, as Florence Nightingale reported, occasioned more loss of life amongst the British troops in this war than any other cause.[42]

For the years immediately before the first world war it is possible to obtain a picture of the annual expenditure on food in the United Kingdom for an average of the years 1909–13. In terms of financial outlay, more than twice as much was spent on meat as on bread; dairy products also accounted for more than bread as more milk and butter were eaten while margarine had begun to make headway as a cheap substitute for butter.

Now to look at individual foodstuffs in more detail. And first, bread which bulked large in the dietaries of most of the European population. From the eighteenth century, two trends are visible. There was the gradual spread of wheaten bread instead of bread from coarser grains. In northern Europe this trend appears to have taken place earliest in

40. Drummond and Wilbraham, *The Englishman's Food*, p. 465.

41. Jean-Philippe Filippini, 'Le regime alimentaire des soldats et des miliciens pris en charge par la marine française au XVIIIe siècle', *Annales*, XX (1965) 1157–62.

42. Drummond and Wilbraham, *The Englishman's Food*, pp. 395–6.

TABLE 16: Average Annual Expenditure on Food in the United Kingdom, 1909–1913

	£ million	%
Bread and cereals	468·21	14·3
Meat, poultry and eggs	1,029·01	31·5
Fish	109·77	3·4
Dairy products	533·81	16·3
Margarine and other fats	85·83	2·6
Vegetables	263·58	8·1
Fruit and nuts	180·37	5·5
Sugar, cocoa and confectionery	282·53	8·6
Tea and coffee	124·85	3·8
Other foods	197·42	5·9
Total	3,272·15	100·00

Source: Alan R. Prest and Arthur A. Adams, *Consumers' Expenditure in the United Kingdom, 1900–1919* (Cambridge U.P., 1954) table 46, p. 74.

England. One estimate suggests that about two-fifths of English bread was wheaten in 1696 and three-fifths in 1764.[43] By 1859 barley and oat breads had virtually disappeared, rye bread was little made and wheaten bread was almost everywhere consumed.[44] The campaign in England in the early nineteenth century for the repeal of the corn laws was one to maintain and cheapen the wheaten loaf. This change was made possible by the great improvements in agricultural productivity, particularly between 1750 and 1850 in England and then from the 1870s by imports of American grain. What is a well-documented trend in Britain was also visible in continental Europe.[45] 'In the nineteenth century',

43. William J. Ashley, *The Bread of our Forefathers: an inquiry in economic history* (Oxford: Clarendon P., 1928) pp. 5–8.

44. Hartwell, *The Industrial Revolution and Economic Growth*, p. 330, citing John R. McCulloch, *A Dictionary, Practical, Theoretical and Historical of Commerce and Commercial Navigation*, ed. Hugh G. Reid (London, 1869) p. 197.

45. According to Henri Sée (*La vie économique de la France sous la monarchie censitaire, 1815–1848* (Paris, 1927) p. 21), it was not until the Restoration that wheat acreage began to surpass that of rye in France while as late as 1883 in Germany (according to Theodor A. G. L. von der Goltz, *Leitfaden der landwirtscharftlichen Betriebslehre* (Berlin, 1897) p. 49) rye occupied three times as much of the acreage under cereals as wheat and one and a half times as much as oats, the other most widely diffused

Professor Landes has written, 'one can almost follow the rise in per capita income and the diffusion of higher living standards among the poorer sections of the population, into rural areas, and into central and eastern Europe by the wheat frontier.'[46] The second trend was a decline in bread consumption. Though some evidence now appears to suggest that, when incomes were reduced in England in the 1840s, families did not switch from meat to bread but reduced consumption all round,[47] a rise in living standards seems to bring about a decline in bread consumption. Reaching a peak annual average consumption of 270 lb per head in 1870, the demand for wheat and wheat flour had fallen to 211 lb in the early twentieth century (1900–13). Thus the demand curve for bread was backward-sloping from 1870. And what was true of Britain began to be true of other developed European countries as well.

TABLE 17: Annual Consumption of Cereals (as flour) per head, 1914

	Belgium	France	Germany	Italy	Switzerland	United Kingdom
kgs	135·0	185·0	127·7	149·0	102·8	95·0

Source: Paul Lamartine Yates, *Food, land and manpower in western Europe* (Macmillan, 1960) p. 27.

Perhaps the single most important change in the dietary of Europe in the period of industrialisation was the introduction of the potato. 'It is difficult for the modern mind to realise', wrote Sir John Clapham, 'that until almost the end of the eighteenth century the food problem in Europe

crop. In Belgium rye was said in 1878 to be 'the foundation of the food of the Flemish population'. See Ashley, *Bread of our Forefathers*, pp. 20–1.

46. David Landes, *The Unbound Prometheus: technological change and industrial development in western Europe from 1750 to the present* (Cambridge U.P., 1969) p. 47.

47. John C. McKenzie, 'The composition and nutritional value of diets in Manchester and Dukinfield in 1841', *Transactions of the Lancashire and Cheshire Antiquarian Society*, LXXII (1965) 132. In the 1860s, however, in the cotton depression in England, consumption of bread fell by about 35 per cent and of meat by about 70 per cent or more. See Barker, Oddy and Yudkin, *Dietary Surveys of Dr Edward Smith*, p. 41.

had to be faced without potatoes, or that French menus contained no *pommes frites*'.[48] Known since the late sixteenth century, the potato made slow progress in Europe apart from Ireland until the end of the eighteenth century. Then, with wheat prices rising sharply as a result of harvest failures in the 1790s, the efforts to popularise the potato, already espoused by Turgot and adopted in the north of England, made ground elsewhere. In France, except in the lowlands of the south where the climate was unfavourable to its growth, it made progress in all districts and in Germany by 1815 it was widely grown. The contribution of the potato to war has already been noted. In England it is estimated that per capita daily consumption increased from 0·4 lb in 1795 to 0·6 lb in 1838[49] but whether this was a net addition to the dietary or the substitution of an inferior vegetable for wheaten bread is a matter of dispute.[50] 'Increasing consumption was due', Hartwell has argued, 'to the simple facts that people liked potatoes and that they were good food'. In Ireland, Germany and elsewhere they were more, they were also a source of alcohol, of starch and of meal. Professor Connell has vividly described the poteens of Ireland:[51] in Prussia in 1831 there were 23,000 distilleries of which between a half and two-thirds used potatoes. In the course of the nineteenth century the potato was more widely adopted throughout most of Europe as a staple item of the dietary. Less liable to failure than cereals, it was, according to Roscher, *the* cause of the increased growth of European population. But when failure came, as the Irish potato famine showed in 1846–7, its effect could be catastrophic. In the later nineteenth century the potato made rapid advances. Between 1850 and 1882 the area of potatoes

48. John H. Clapham, *The Economic Development of France and Germany, 1815–1914* (4th ed. Cambridge U.P., 1963) p. 22.

49. Redcliffe N. Salaman, *The History and Social Influence of the Potato* (Cambridge U.P., 1949) p. 613. Hartwell notes that English potato consumption in the late 1950s was almost exactly the same as it was in 1838 (*The Industrial Revolution and Economic Growth*, p. 332).

50. See Hartwell, *The Industrial Revolution and Economic Growth*, p. 332.

51. See Kenneth G. Connell, *Irish Peasant Society: four historical essays* (Oxford: Clarendon P., 1968).

under cultivation in France increased by 66 per cent. And yields grew too. France had a low yield as did Germany but Great Britain was to France as $1\frac{5}{8}$ to 1 and Holland and Belgium were about twice the French yield. While the potato began to lose ground in Britain from the 1880s[52]— despite the fish and chip shops—as a result of a rise in working class living standards, it remained a major part of the dietary of European countries in the later nineteenth century. Comparative figures for 1910–14 are as follows:

TABLE 18: Annual Consumption of Potatoes per head, 1910–1914

	Belgium	France	Germany	Italy	Switzerland	United Kingdom
kgs	206·5	176·0	199·0	27·8	127·0	97·0

Source: Yates, *Food, Land and Manpower*, p. 27.

Though there has been little discussion of the subject, other vegetables—cabbages, onions, tomatoes, turnips, beans and peas—appear to have been widely eaten in Europe. Salad greens—lettuces, radishes and cucumbers—were less commonly consumed. Some of the rural population at least were able to grow their own vegetables but they often became scarce in the industrial cities, despite the establishment of market gardens in their neighbourhood. Greater knowledge of nutrition led to an increased consumption of vegetables, particularly amongst the better-off, in the later nineteenth century.

Fruit consumption varied considerably in Europe. In the Mediterranean countries olives, grapes, oranges and melons were plentiful and melons were eaten also in eastern Europe in Hungary and Russia. In northern Europe, while the rural poor were able to enjoy some fruit, consumption was limited. Particularly was this so in England. Until the 1870s the urban working class ate little fruit and many of the middle and upper classes considered it a luxury while some thought fruit-eating unhealthy, particularly for children. The growth in demand in the later nineteenth century appears to have been the result of a change in taste.

52. About 12 per cent fall from the 1800s to the late 1890s.

And demand was stimulated by increased supply. Expanding imports encouraged home production as farmers retreated from cereal production in the face of foreign competition and canned fruit provided a further source for the more wealthy. An important new item from about 1900 was the banana which rapidly won a large sale, particularly amongst the urban poor. Further, the fall in sugar duties stimulated the manufacture of jam in England. As a result, England moved in the course of the late nineteenth century from a low to a high consumer of fruit.

TABLE 19: Annual Consumption of Fruit per head, 1910–1914

	France	Germany	Italy	United Kingdom
kgs	13 ·4*	23 ·6	23 ·7	33 ·0

* Believed to be a considerable underestimate.

Source: Yates, *Food, Land and Manpower*, p. 27.

Abel has argued that the annual consumption of meat in Germany declined from the fifteenth century from an average of 100 kilograms or more per person (a sort of biological maximum) to not more than 14 kilograms per person in the mid-nineteenth century.[53] And what was true of Germany, it has been stated, was sooner or later true of the rest of Europe. But quite obviously there were differences between countries and classes and over time. In England in the later eighteenth century there were two conflicting developments. As a result of the work of Bakewell and others, sheep came to be bred for meat as well as wool and more mutton became available. But for the rural poor the position was worsened since a consequence of the enclosures from the mid-century was the savage invocation of the game laws which robbed the poor of the chance of trapping game or rabbits or of fishing. In the towns, too, the urban poor appear to have had little meat but the effect of livestock improvement, not only of sheep but also of cattle and pigs,

53. See Edwin E. Rich and Charles H. Wilson, ed. *The Cambridge Economic History of Europe, vol. IV. The Economy of Expanding Europe in the Sixteenth and Seventeenth Centuries* (Cambridge U.P., 1967) p. 414.

began to be visible. Earlier than in some parts of Europe
the declining trend of meat consumption appears to have
been reversed and Dr Hartwell holds that 'in the first fifty
years of the nineteenth century, the English working class
came to expect meat as a part of the normal diet'.[54] Though
there were wide regional divergences, by 1863 average
weekly meat consumption in England amounted to about
one pound. In the later nineteenth century more meat was
eaten as the result of the expansion of imports. To the cattle
brought from Ireland was added canned meat from the
USA and frozen meat from Australia, New Zealand and
later the Argentine. Annual per capita meat consumption,
stimulated by falling meat prices, rose from 108 lb in
1880–4 to over 130 lb (63 lb beef, 32 lb mutton, 35 lb pork)
in 1900–4. By the first decade of the twentieth century,
almost entirely because imports were available to augment
home production, meat consumption (excluding bacon
which accounted for another 13 lb a year) in England, as
the following table shows, was higher than in European
countries:

TABLE 20: Annual Consumption of Meat per head, 1903–1911

	Austria-Hungary	Belgium	France	Germany
kgs	46·0	29·5	33·6	48·2
	Italy	Russia	Switzerland	U.K.
kgs	17·5	22·0	54·2	60·2

Source: *Encyclopaedia of the Social Sciences*, IV, 297 (Austria-Hungary and
Russia); Yates, *Food, land and manpower*, p. 27 (others).

By and large much less important than meat was fish. Of
the amount of freshwater fishing it is impossible to estimate.
Fish abounded in many streams, rivers and lakes in Europe
and continued to do so throughout this period where the
rivers and lakes were not polluted by the spread of industry.

54. Hartwell, *The Industrial Revolution and Economic Growth*, p. 333,
though the 'pessimist' would add, 'for the man and on Sundays only'.

But public consumption was often limited by private fishing rights and so freshwater fish were frequently confined to the tables of the landowners. Supplies of sea fish, which were normally salted or smoked, were obtained from the seas around the coasts of Europe or brought, chiefly to the Mediterranean, from the Newfoundland banks. The availablity of supplies fluctuated considerably but fish was an essential part of the dietary of many parts of Europe. In some countries, fish was less important. In England in particular, before 1815, except during gluts, fish was expensive and appeared regularly only on the tables of the well-to-do.[55] After that date with better marketing, transport, increased supplies and therefore falling prices, English consumption of fish appears to have grown. The use of ice which led to a fall in the market for salt or pickled fish also enabled the North Sea grounds to be more fully worked while fish could also be brought to England from the further European waters. By the mid-century Mayhew reported that 'the rooms of the very neediest of our needy metropolitan population always smell of fish; most frequently of herrings'.[56] And more generally in continental Europe, these developments which enabled fish to be marketed widely in a fresh state, converted it from a luxury article in many places to one within reach of the bulk of the population.[57] In England in the 1880s a significant new development took place. Using the new supplies of cheap cod and vegetable oils, fried-fish shops were established and fish and chips, augmenting its protein content, became a part of the working class dietary in England. Besides the fried-fish shops, canning, particularly of sardines and salmon, helped to increase fish consumption not only in England but in other parts of Europe as well.

55. Hartwell, *The Industrial Revolution and Economic Growth*, p. 335.

56. Henry Mayhew, *London Labour and the London Poor; a cyclopædia of the condition and earnings of those that will work, those that cannot work and those that will not work* (4 vols. London, 1861–62) I, 62.

57. Charles Singer, Eric J. Holmyard, Alfred Rupert Hall and Trevor J. Williams, ed. *A History of Technology, vol. IV. The Industrial Revolution, c. 1750–c. 1850* (Oxford: Clarendon P., 1958) p. 51.

TABLE 21: Annual Consumption of Fish per head, 1910–1914

	Germany	Italy	Switzerland	United Kingdom
kgs	7·7	2·8	2·1	19·4

Source: Yates, *Food, Land and Manpower*, p. 27.

As far as drink is concerned, water, polluted though it might be, was the main drink of the poorest. But otherwise alcoholic beverages were widely consumed. In England in the early eighteenth century, the production of gin and other cheap raw spirits expanded rapidly to meet the demand, particularly of London and the industrial areas. While it is impossible to estimate how much illicit gin was distilled, the consumption of gin on which duty was paid rose from 0·5 million gallons in 1700 to more than 5 million gallons in 1735. The corrupting effects of this high consumption, satirised by Hogarth in his 'Gin Alley', led to increases in taxation in 1736 and 1751 but it was the sharp rise in the price of grain that led to a rise in price of cheap spirits and the public then of necessity returned to beer. Although increases in production barely kept pace with the growth of population, consumption of beer was high in the later eighteenth century. In 1800 it amounted to 33·9 gallons a head a year. Per capita consumption then declined in the following half century to 19·6 gallons per head but as beer shifted from being a national drink to a masculine drink, consumption remained high for those for whom the quickest way out of the squalor of the new industrial towns was by drink. The increased availability of beer which was a consequence of the Beerhouse Act of 1830 led immediately to a brief boom in consumption but in the long run it had the more serious consequence of greatly increasing adulteration. In the third quarter of the nineteenth century the activities of the public analyst reduced adulteration and the short-run reaction to rising incomes led to a substantial increase in beer consumption which reached a per capita peak of 34·4 gallons a year in 1876. From that level consumption fell to 30 gallons in 1900 and the fall continued until the outbreak of the first world war (1910–14, 27 gallons).[58] In the mid-century drink had accounted for £15–20 a year (out of a total income of £80). In the later nineteenth century self-interest allied with the propaganda of the temperance societies to bring about a realisation that poverty was not just a question of low incomes but also of the wrong allocation of incomes and heavy drinking fell to the bottom of the social scale. With the changes in consumption patterns came also a change in taste. Beginning in London and spreading west and north, a taste for lighter beers gained ground and consumption of the heavier beers declined.

Elsewhere in Europe alcohol consumption was high in the nineteenth century. In Germany drunkenness was said to be common because spirits were cheap and it was prevalent in Belgium too. In France per capita wine consumption expanded in the mid-nineteenth century from less than 50 litres a year in 1840 to nearly 90 litres a year in the mid-1870s. According to one report a startling amount of 440 litres of alcohol per head per year was consumed by the inhabitants of Rennes in Brittany—9 litres of beer and 9 of spirits, 22 litres of wine and 399 litres of cider.[59] No wonder there were temperance campaigns and agitation for government control which, though very limited in effect, did something to check and then turn downward the trend of per capita consumption. Not till the first world war, however, was effective legislation enacted. The relative per capita annual consumption of pure alcohol (litres) in

58. Wine and spirits consumption was small by comparison and fluctuated with the level of duty:

gallons	1800–04	1850–54	1900–04	1910–14
wine	0·43	0·23	0·34	0·25
spirits	0·80	1·08	1·04	0·67

Source: George B. Wilson, *Alcohol and the Nation: a contribution to the study of the liquor problem in the United Kingdom from 1800 to 1935* (Nicholson & Watson, 1940) p. 331.

59. Robert Mandrou, 'Les consommations des villes françaises (viandes et boissons) au milieu de XIXe siècle', *Annales*, XVI (1961) 743. Traditionally, Professor Cipolla tells me, per capita consumption of wine in Italy was more than one litre per day but most of the wine consumed by the mass of the population had a low alcoholic content.

certain European countries in 1904–05 was estimated to be:

TABLE 22: Annual Consumption of Pure Alcohol per head, 1904–1905 (litres)

Great Britain & Ireland	Germany	Austria-Hungary	France	Russia	Italy
10·5	9·5	9·0	22·4	2·6	14·1

Source: Emil Struve, *Handwörterbuch der Staats-wissenschaften*, IV (3rd ed. Jena, 1909) p. 761, quoted in *Encyclopedia of the Social Sciences*, IV, 297.

Thus, in the beer-drinking countries consumption was very much on the same level but alcohol-intake was much higher in the wine-drinking countries and particularly in France. On the basis of these figures, Russian consumption was low.

Coffee drinking began in the seventeenth century and coffee houses appeared in many European cities in the following hundred years. Apart from England where the taste for coffee declined in favour of tea, coffee became the most common non-alcoholic drink in Europe but annual consumption varied considerably. In the early twentieth century the Dutch consumed 14–15 lb per head, the Belgians, the Swedes and the Norwegians nearly as much. Germany, which took about one-fifth of the world's coffee crop, used 6–7 lb per head and France about 5 lb per head but in Austria-Hungary consumption amounted to about 2 lb per head while in Italy under 1 lb per head was used.

While the price of tea was high it remained a luxury drink but consumption grew in England as the price fell when duties were removed. Arthur Young noted in 1767 'the custom, coming in, of men making tea an article of their food, almost as much as women'. When the duty was further reduced by Pitt in 1784 the consumption of tea doubled and then trebled to reach 1·4 lb per head per year in 1800–9. A substantial further increase occurred in the later nineteenth century. By 1871, when it was nearly 4 lb per head, this trend was criticised. The poor people found that they could enjoy a quite deceptive feeling of warmth after drinking hot tea, whereas, in fact, a glass of cold beer would have given them far more real food. But the trend continued and in the early twentieth century annual tea consumption in England reached 6·2 lb per head. Consumption elsewhere in Europe was low. In 1906 the figure in Holland was 1·45 lb per head, in Russia 0·94 lb, in Germany 0·11 lb and in France 0·06 lb.

For an Englishman used to advertising campaigns exhorting him to 'drinka pinta milk a day', the low milk consumption of previous generations comes as something of a surprise. In the eighteenth century in the pastoral parts of England the poor could obtain milk if they were able to keep a cow on the common but the supply of milk to the towns was almost indescribably bad, either contaminated or watered or both. With enclosure and urbanisation milk supplies for both town dweller and country dweller became more difficult. Some relief came with the construction of the railways though cows were still being milked on London doorsteps in the 1830s and it was not until the 1870s, by which time the railway companies had learned to keep milk cool, that larger supplies became available. Even in the 1880s the total supply to London was only 110,000 gallons, enough for a daily per capita consumption of about one-fifth of a pint, and 21·5 per cent of this milk still came from London cowsheds. From the 1880s more milk was drunk in England, mainly by children and invalids, facilitated by increased production and improved transport. But the needs of some sections of the population for milk, which was used chiefly for puddings and in tea, was met by condensed milk, developed in America in the 1850s and in Switzerland in the 1860s. Milk powders also became available in the 1900s. Despite such developments a report in 1902 showed that Britain was the smallest milk drinker of all European countries. Whereas in Saxony 46 gallons per head per year were consumed and in Sweden and Denmark the figure was 40 gallons, in France it was 16 gallons and in the United Kingdom only 15 gallons per head per year were drunk.[60]

60. John Burnett, *Plenty and Want: a social history of diet in England from 1815 to the present day* (Nelson, 1966) p. 158.

Other dairy produce also had its place in European dietaries. Butter consumption was determined partly by price and partly by availability. In the later eighteenth and early nineteenth century it was not infrequently rancid and was often too costly for daily use. But other fats, such as lard, were also used. Invented about 1869, margarine, after a fight against prejudice, won a market for itself in the quarter of a century before the first world war, particularly when the use of ground nuts and palm oil in the 1890s enabled its price to be reduced. Where peasants were able, they often kept chickens and there was a substantial foreign trade in eggs. Cheese, too, was widely manufactured and sheep and goats' milk was used where cows' milk was not available. Improved transport gave some cheese which had previously had only a local sale a wider market. Rising standards of living brought increased consumption of these dairy products but there were still wide variations between European countries as these figures for annual per capita consumption for 1910–14 show:

TABLE 23: Annual Consumption of Fats, Eggs and Cheese per head, 1910–1914 (kgs)

	Belgium	France	Germany	Italy	Switzerland	United Kingdom
Fats	15·5	18·0	18·4	9·8	—	11·6
Eggs	6·8	8·0	6·5	6·4	7·3	7·3
Cheese	—	4·5	3·5	4·5	11·1	3·9

Source: Yates, *Food, Land and Manpower*, p. 27.

From the early eighteenth century sugar ceased to be the luxury of the wealthy few and was increasingly used as a sweetener in coffee and tea, in jams and preserves, and in chocolate, puddings, cakes and confectionery. Sugar consumption in Britain rose from 6–8 lb per head a year in the 1750s to about 25 lb in the 1850s and, with the abolition of the sugar duties, more sharply to 78 lb in the 1900s. In France and Germany there was a similar marked rise in the later nineteenth century. In both countries sugar consumption per head trebled between 1840 and 1900. On the eve of the first world war annual per capita consumption of sugar (and syrup and honey) in Belgium amounted to 14·3 kilos, in France to 14·7 kilos and in Germany to 19·5 kilos.[61] The general rise in demand led to an expansion of sugar beet production, sometimes with government assistance and protection, in many parts of Europe.

After drink, the 'harmful and useless habit' of tobacco smoking provided solace. In England snuff-taking gained ground in the eighteenth century and so tobacco consumption fell from just under 2 lb a head in 1700 to under 1 lb in 1786. During the Napoleonic Wars the cigar was introduced and became somewhat more socially acceptable than the pipe but per capita consumption remained stable at about 1 lb per head throughout the first half of the nineteenth century. With the introduction of the cigarette in the 1850s, however, and with rising mass purchasing power, tobacco consumption grew in England in the later nineteenth century, rising from 1·3 lb a head in 1885 to 2 lb in 1900 and 2·3 lb in 1913.[62] In France a similar trend was visible in the later nineteenth century and tobacco consumption rose from 0·5 kilos per head in 1852 to 0·8 kilos in 1872, 0·9 kilos in 1892 and 1·0 kilos in 1904.[63] The demand for tobacco led to an extension of its cultivation, particularly in eastern Europe. According to some writers, the introduction of tobacco growing also helped to raise the standard of living of the peasants and brought great prosperity to Dalmatia, to cite but one example, in the 1890s.[64] In a number of European countries tobacco manufacture became a state monopoly and in many it was taxed.

61. Colin Clark, *The Conditions of Economic Progress* (2nd ed. Macmillan, 1951) pp. 370–73.

62. Alfred Rive, 'The Consumption of Tobacco since 1600', *Economic History*, I (1926) 73. Between 1888 and 1914 cigarette consumption rose from 100,000 lb to 50 million lb a year (Alan R. Prest and Arthur A. Adams, *Consumers' Expenditure in the United Kingdom, 1909–1919* (Cambridge U.P., 1954) p. 8.

63. Clark, *Conditions of Economic Progress*, pp. 372–3.

64. Doreen Warriner, ed. *Contrasts in Emerging Societies: readings in the social and economic history of south-eastern Europe in the nineteenth century* (Athlone P., 1965) p. 366.

Although there were some improvements in diet, the situation in Europe on the eve of the first world war was far from satisfactory. For some at any rate there had been little or no change. And all change was not beneficial. There was considerable ignorance in dietetic matters. Children suffered from the decline in breast-feeding and the use of artificial milk foods instead; roller-grinding produced whiter but less nutritive flour. In English towns the dietary of the poor was low in bone-forming elements and resulted in a decline in the general state of teeth in the course of the nineteenth century and in poor physique. While the reports of Rowntree which drew attention to the inadequacy of the food consumed by the poor went largely unregarded, the condition of recruits for the Boer War drew attention to the situation. Over the country as a whole nearly 40 per cent of the potential recruits were not called up, chiefly on grounds of bad teeth, heart affections, poor sight or hearing and deformities. 'A startling number', the official report stated, 'were found physically unfit to carry a rifle'.[65] 'The opening of the twentieth century', it has been said, 'saw malnutrition more rife in England than it had been since the great dearths of medieval and Tudor times'.[66] So even in the developed parts of Europe while the rich fed well, the poor fed badly.

CLOTHING

After food, clothes, which accounted for about 10–15 per cent of the budget, were an essential need for almost everyone. While gipsies in Rumania in the early nineteenth century apparently went about naked and children more widely wore little, most other people wore clothes of a sort. But throughout these years the very poor were miserably clad in rags and often went barefoot. When Garibaldi and his thousand landed in Sicily in 1860 they were surprised to find young boys dressed in skins like savages. The clothing of the day workers in Italy at this time too was

65. Drummond and Wilbraham, *The Englishman's Food*, p. 404.
66. Drummond and Wilbraham, *The Englishman's Food*, p. 403.

frequently little above the category of rags. By contrast the well-to-do were often splendidly dressed. Expenditure on clothing for the mass of the people was a function of income. On the eve of the first world war per capita consumption of textiles was higher in industrialised countries than in those less developed:

TABLE 24: Annual Consumption of Textiles per head in the 1900s

	Austria-Hungary	France	Germany	Italy	Russia	United Kingdom
Marks	32	66	59	31	20	66

Source: *Encyclopaedia of the Social Sciences*, IV, 297.

While social and regional differences were of considerable importance, several general influences also affected the fashionable scene. First, the industrial revolution brought cheaper fabrics. 'Now', wrote David Macpherson in 1806, 'cotton yarn is cheaper than linen yarn; and cotton goods are very much used in place of cambrics, lawns and other expensive fabrics of flax; and they have almost totally superceded the silks. Women of all ranks, from the highest to the lowest, are clothed in British manufactures of cotton, from the muslin cap on the crown of the head to the cotton stockings under the sole of the foot'.[67] And cotton, which had the advantage of being more easily washable than wool, made further advances in the nineteenth century. Then, perhaps a reaction to the dirt produced by the dark satanic mills of the nineteenth century, people lost their love of colour and for men's dress particularly dark colours came to predominate. A growing number of magazines appeared in western Europe from the 1770s which brought news of the changing fashions, largely emanating from Paris, which were copied with all due speed in the other capitals of Europe. The elaborate clothes and wigs of the ancien régime were followed by the clinging muslins and near nudity of the revolutionary years. The classical lines of the Empire style gave way to the exuberance of the mid-

67. Ashton, 'Changes in the Standards of Comfort', p. 183.

century with the crinoline having a brief period of dominance. Then clothes became less extravagant and the new outdoor activities for women—tennis, cycling and motoring —gave them a more practical aspect. From the mid-century two broad trends are discernible. With improving communications, the general outlines of fashion became less personal and more international. But at the same time the foundation of haute couture houses which followed the establishment of the house of Worth in 1858 fostered the individual taste of the wealthy. Clothes continued to provide an opportunity for conspicuous display. By contrast, men's dress became more austere and, according to the time of day, was strictly regulated by convention. 'A man away from home', it was stated in 1894, 'should never be separated from his hat, whether on a visit, out to dinner or at a ball'.

The clothing needs of the poor peasant and town worker continued to be extremely modest. As late as 1913–14 the average working class family in England spent just over one shilling per head per week on clothes. Meantime, throughout Europe many who lived on the land continued to weave their own cloth and to tan their own leather. For the mass of the rural population the influences which determined what clothes they wore included the availability of raw materials—woollen or cotton cloth and linen for clothes, leather, felt or wood or bark for footwear—local climatic conditions and occupational needs—whether their work was outdoor or indoor, at sea or on land—and local customs or tradition. The Russian peasant, for example, customarily wore blue linen or hemp trousers and red shirts on holidays while his womenfolk wore dresses of printed linen. For working dress kaftans were worn over shirts and trousers. Their sandals were made from birch bark while leather boots were kept for special occasions. From the 1870s felt boots were increasingly worn. In cold weather, the men wore jackets of untanned sheepskin and fur hats.

Since industrial employment was more demanding in time than agriculture, many industrial workers were forced to go to the market for clothes though a good many continued to be made in the home. Knitwear—stockings, scarves, pullovers and such like—were frequently home knitted and shirts and underclothing could be made by the womenfolk and dresses could be made with the aid of paper patterns. But outer clothing and footwear came to be purchased. Cotton cloth, which fell in price in England by one-third between 1830 and 1850, made ground at the expense of woollen. In response to this sizeable and growing demand, from the 1870s the sewing machine led to the development of ready-made clothing, which, like ready-made footwear, began to encroach on the bespoke market. For the more thrifty poor in England there grew up also a market in second-hand clothes which enabled them to dress reasonably respectably at lower cost. So fashionable clothes came within the reach of at least the better off working class.

Then there was an institutional demand for clothing, for armies and navies, for the church, for schools, for hospitals and for other uniformed occupations such as the railways, the customs service, the police and the like. As far as the armed forces were concerned, minor modifications were made in the uniforms which had become universal by the middle of the eighteenth century. Demand for hardwearing coarse cloth for such purposes expanded sharply in time of war and particularly during the Napoleonic Wars when an unprecedented number of men were under arms in Europe. There was then need for footwear, headgear and other articles as well. In the course of the nineteenth century a utilitarian trend in uniform became more evident but the most marked change came as a result of the guerilla activity during the Boer War which forced the thin red line of the British army to abandon its bright—and extremely visible— uniforms for khaki which had first been used in India in the middle of the century. Standardisation of naval uniforms came much later than military. During the Napoleonic Wars, sailors wore what they pleased. A uniform for the British navy was prescribed as a regulation in 1857 and its general lines were subsequently adopted by other navies. The churches continued their demand for broadcloth, for black and brown and white and red. In some schools, workhouses and similar closed communities the inmates were dressed in institutional garb and with the growth of hospitals there came a demand for nurses' clothing designed to meet the needs of hygiene and decency. 'I devised this little train', the Lady Superintendent of the Middlesex Hospital announced in the 1870s, 'so that, when you lean over the bed to attend to your patient, your ankles will be covered and the students will not be able to see them'.[68] It was only the exceptional employer such as Matthew Boulton at the Soho Mint in the 1790s who put his workers into uniform but it was the Metropolitan Police, who had been given a distinctive dress by Peel in 1829, which provided the example for the railways. While there had been no standard clothing for the stage coaches, the railways provided uniforms for their station staff almost from the start but enginemen and firemen, at least in England, were not so equipped but were required to appear on duty dressed in a standard fashion.

HOUSING

Housing, the third major material need of mankind, was in some form required by everyone.[69] Here there was an enormous range from the palaces, châteaux and country seats of rulers and nobility to the hovels of the poorest. Particularly in the country, many people in every part of Europe lived in primitive conditions throughout this period. Often without windows and with floors of beaten earth, their dwellings were usually made of the materials available locally. In Russia the huts were of timber, in Ireland of sod, in Portugal of stone, in England depending on the area of brick, of stone, of wood or of dried mud. Some were of such insubstantial construction that they

68. Phyllis Cunnington and Catherine Lucas, *Occupational Costume in England from the Eleventh Century to 1914* (Black, 1967) pp. 321–2.

69. Or almost everyone. In 1851, 18,249 houseless people were recorded by the census in London. Of these, 9,972 were living in barns and 8,277 in the open air. (See Gareth Stedman Jones, *Outcast London: a study in the relationship between the classes in Victorian society* (Oxford: Clarendon P., 1971)).

could be destroyed by gale or flood while others were more durable. But almost without exception such dwellings had small openings for windows, not always glazed, and many had no chimneys. They were dark, smelly, smoky, uncomfortable and overcrowded yet often insufficiently warm. The housing of the rural poor underwent little change or improvement between 1750 and 1914. But for the richer peasant farmers there was change. The growing population meant an expanding demand for food and so led to growing farm incomes which were reflected in housing improvements. In some places houses were extended while in others new-style farmhouses appeared. In England the longhouse, where living quarters and accommodation for the animals were under one roof, was replaced in many cases by a more lavish two-storey farmhouse and separate stabling was built.

During the eighteenth century the example of Versailles stimulated other great landowners to build enormous country houses set in landscaped gardens but then the enthusiasm for such immense houses faded and the romantic movement brought with it a change in landscape setting from 'formal' to 'natural'. Instead of the large palace, numbers of modest country houses were built, some of them in the developing parts of Europe such as England by the nouveaux riches merchants or industrialists. And this trend continued in the nineteenth century.

But a major feature of this age of industrialisation was the growth of the towns. It was here that the pressure on housing was most acute. In the first phase of industrialisation, which varied in time throughout Europe, European cities shared a common experience. The movement of people into towns led to desperate overcrowding and to problems of water supply, refuse disposal and public health for which neither the thinking of the day nor the administrative machinery available were appropriate. Every available inch of accommodation was pressed into service and houses were quickly built—sometimes too quickly built—to provide what the Hammonds called the barracks of the working classes. In England back-to-back housing was put up by speculative builders with little regard for amenity and houses were crowded together in the lee of smoke-belching, noisy and sometimes smelly factories. Conditions were worst in the older industrial towns such as Manchester where even the cellars were pressed into use as accommodation and less desperate in the newer industrial towns such as Bolton and Middlesbrough. And what was true of England was often true elsewhere. When industrialisation first began to gather pace almost everywhere housing provision fell short of need.

Since some industry was established in new areas, industrialists in such cases had not only to erect their works but also had to provide housing for their workers. A considerable number of new industrial towns or villages were built which set new standards of working class accommodation. Towns like New Lanark in Scotland, Saltaire in England or Le Grand Hornu near Liège in Belgium included not only housing but also shops and places of entertainment. In Germany later in the nineteenth century, Krupp, the Baden Aniline & Soda Works, the Hoechst Colour Works and the United Machine Works of Augsburg and Nüremberg were among the firms who erected dwellings for their workers. When the English railway companies built their new engineering works at Wolverton, Swindon and Crewe social hierarchies were carefully preserved. This is how *Chambers's Edinburgh Journal* described the new railway housing at Crewe:

> First, the villa-style lodges the superior officers; next a kind of ornamented Gothic constitutes the houses of the next in authority; the engineers domiciled in detached mansions, with accommodation for four families, with gardens and separate entrances; and last, the labourer delights in neat cottages of four apartments, the entrances within ancient porches. The first, second and third, have all gardens and yards; the fourth has also gardens.[70]

70. Cited by William H. Chaloner, *Social and Economic Development of Crewe, 1780–1923* (Manchester U.P., 1950) p. 48.

In other occupations also houses were provided with the job. Many farm workers in England had tied cottages as did tollhouse keepers, some railway employees, some teachers, ministers of religion and some members of the armed forces (and their wives). The advantages of reasonable accommodation and some hedge against changes in rent were to some extent offset by the lack of security this sometimes involved. Loss of the job meant loss of the house or flat as well.

For the growing urban middle class, the industrialists, merchants, professional men and bureaucrats, there was a great expansion of provision. In England the eighteenth-century terrace houses came to be superseded by the town version of the country villa, detached or semi-detached and of such a size that it could only be run with the aid of a small army of domestic servants. Many of the houses of the English provincial industrialists were enlarged from comparatively modest town houses by successive stages to palatial dimensions. For the less affluent middle class, housing was provided by the speculative builder. Alongside overcrowding for the mass of the population went lavish provision for the better-off. And the higher-paid artisans in the later nineteenth century were able to move into better accommodation.

In the course of the nineteenth century a number of forces combined to bring about an increase in house rents and a growing proportion of income appears to have been spent on housing. In England rents in 1801 accounted for about 5 per cent of total consumer expenditure; by 1851 this percentage had risen to 8 and by 1901 to nine. And it is clear that, as Schwabe argued, 'the proportion spent on rent increased with decreasing income'. A Victorian manual suggests that in England 10 per cent of an income of £250 a year should be spent on accommodation but those with smaller incomes had to pay a greater proportion of their income in rent. Those with £100–125 a year paid about £25 in rent (one-quarter to one-fifth) while those with an income of about £40 a year paid about £6 10s in rent or about one-sixth of their income. Comparative figures for German towns between 1868 and 1880 are as follows:

TABLE 25: Proportion of Income spent on Rent in selected German towns, 1868–1880

	Berlin		Hamburg		Breslau	Leipzig	Dresden
Income	1876	1868	1874	1882	1880	1875	1880
Under £30	—	22·3	24·2	26·5	28·7	29·9	26·8
£30–60	24·7	18·8	20·9	23·5	21·0	21·2	18·4
£60–90	21·8	19·9	21·1	18·9	20·8	19·7	16·3

Source: William J. Ashley, *The Progress of the German Working Classes in the Last Quarter of a Century* (Longmans, 1904) p. 35.

Rents were usually lower in country districts than in towns, and in small towns than in great cities.

When real wages rose urban workers sought better accommodation. As table 26 shows, there was a general though not universal tendency in Germany for the proportion of workers occupying dwellings or apartments with two heatable rooms rather than one to rise in the later nineteenth century.

Although a functional division between the rooms was still not possible, it is clear that the larger apartments were less crowded than the smaller ones. In the dwellings with two heatable rooms there was an average of two persons per room in major German cities in 1905, whereas in the dwellings with one heatable room the average was over three persons.[71] The decrease in overcrowding showed itself everywhere in Germany[72] and was also apparent elsewhere, as in England where the number of people per house fell sharply, especially between 1890 and the first world war.

In recognition of the failure of market forces to provide adequate accommodation for the urban poor, philanthropic

71. See Ashok V. Desai, *Real Wages in Germany, 1871–1913* (Oxford U.P., 1968) p. 26.

72. It was most marked in Frankfurt according to W. J. Ashley. See his *The Progress of the German Working Classes in the Last Quarter of a Century* (Longmans, 1904) p. 139.

TABLE 26: Proportion of the Population of Selected German Towns Living in Dwellings with One or Two Heatable Rooms, 1875–1910

	1875		1880		1885		1890		1895		1900		1905		1910	
	Number of heatable rooms															
	1	2	1	2	1	2	1	2	1	2	1	2	1	2	1	2
Old Leipzig	21·4	25·9	21·7	27·3	19·1	26·4	15·9	25·9	15·1	25·7	—	—	—	—	—	—
Dresden	—	—	48·3	21·9	48·1	22·8	42·9	25·9	41·8	27·1	37·4	28·4	—	—	—	—
Berlin	45·3	26·6	43·9	27·7	44·1	28·6	44·2	28·9	43·7	29·5	43·0	30·7	41·0	33·8	—	—
Breslau	—	—	—	—	37·1	14·8	48·4	26·3	44·3	30·1	40·9	32·5	37·1	34·2	—	—
Hamburg	—	—	—	—	29·5	31·3	24·1	31·6	20·6	31·5	19·2	31·2	16·6	30·9	25·5	34·8
Leipzig	—	—	—	—	19·1	26·3	30·4	33·8	28·2	36·2	21·9	37·2	19·0	38·5	12·7	40·5
Lubeck	—	—	—	—	—	—	45·0	24·8	39·3	28·4	37·6	31·4	34·6	34·0	27·0	31·8
Magdeburg	—	—	—	—	—	—	49·7	24·5	49·1	23·3	45·4	23·5	42·3	23·8	40·7	24·2

Source: 1875 and 1880: H. Lindemann, 'Wohnungsstatistik', *Schriften des Vereins für Sozialpolitik* (Munich and Leipzig) 94, I (1901), 291, table IX; 1895: 7 (1898) 61, table 5; 1900: 11 (1903) 76, table 4; 1885: *Statisches Jahrbuch deutscher Städte* (Breslau) I (1890) 74, table 4; 1905: 16 (1909) 445, table 5A 1890: 3 (1893) 41, table 6; 1910: 21 (1916) 866, table 13; quoted in Ashok V. Desai, *Real wages in Germany, 1871–1913* (Oxford: University Press, 1968), p. 123.

associations such as the Peabody Trust were set up in England to provide model dwellings and these blocks of working class apartments can still be seen in London and other large English cities. National legislation and urban by-laws were also enacted to ensure that housing met the barest minimum of standards and in some areas programmes of slum clearance were started. But, as Stanley Chapman has argued, there were:

> endless difficulties involved in the improvement of working-class housing in the second half of the nineteenth century. Reformers, philanthropists, and local-authority officials struggled to set and maintain adequate standards of sanitation and ventilation, and to provide accommodation at rents which working-class families could regularly afford, but unemployment, widespread casual employment, low earnings and desultory habits frustrated repeated attempts to reach better standards. The problem was exacerbated by relentless demographic pressure, by hordes of immigrant Irish inured to primitive conditions, by the mass destruction of cheap property for building central railway termini and, more generally, by lack of education and failure to appreciate elementary cleanliness.[73]

To attempt to meet the demand for houses which grew as real wages rose some manufacturers in England, like Cadbury and Lever Brothers, made renewed attempts to house their workers and following enabling legislation some municipal authorities began to build houses too. But little progress was made and between 1890 and 1914 only 5 per cent of the new working class houses in England were provided by local authorities.

As urban transport systems developed in the later nineteenth century, cities began to escape from the confines of their earlier boundaries and the growth of suburbs proceeded apace. In London suburban expansion was facilitated by the construction of the underground from the

73. *The History of Working-class Housing: a symposium* (Newton Abbot: David & Charles, 1971) p. 11.

1860s. In Germany there was a steady acceleration of town growth from 1870 but the momentum increased as the result of the adoption of the electric tram in the 1900s. In 1890 there were 35 electric trams as compared with 4,044 horsedrawn trams and 141 steam trams in Germany but by 1910 practically all German suburban passengers were carried by electric trams which not only increased the ease of movement but did so at reduced cost.[74]

In England garden suburbs were laid out for the middle class in London in the early nineteenth century and in the provinces later. In the early twentieth century such ideas of town planning were expanded and the concept of the garden city—*rus in urbe*—found favour, with Letchworth as the first example, but this movement made little progress before the first world war. Of more significance was the continued failure of the private sector to keep pace with housing demand. The building industry in England tended to be active when the demand for capital overseas was slack, thus there was a strong cyclical element to house-construction. In the 1880s and early 1890s there was a considerable increase in house-building in industrial areas for renting but this trend was checked by the export finance boom which reached a peak between 1909 and 1913. On the eve of the first world war there was still a grave housing problem in Great Britain. Many slums remained and, according to the definition of the 1911 census, one-tenth of the population lived in overcrowded conditions.

Although there was still severe overcrowding in some places, although slum conditions existed in many industrial cities, although the standard of some rural housing, particularly in southern and eastern Europe, was deplorable, rising living standards had begun by the early twentieth century to be reflected in better housing. And with improvements in the standard of accommodation went other developments. The provision of pure piped water made some progress and sewage and refuse disposal became properly organised but perhaps the greater part of the population of Europe lacked individual water supply and sanitation by

74. See Desai, *Real Wages*, pp. 93–4.

1914. The condition of country dwellers was possibly better as far as water supply and sanitation was concerned than that of the poor in the towns. Public health facilities were improved. The towns were no longer, as they had been in the first phase of industrialisation, great killers of people. There were improvements too in heating and lighting. But for the poorest in the countryside there was little change. In Italy, for example, farm workers slept with the animals in their stables or barns for warmth in winter. While other rural workers still tended to rely on the peat, dung or timber available locally, the spread of railways made coal supplies cheaper and more easily available and, with the development of the iron industry, iron stoves and kitchen ranges could be obtained cheaply and more readily from the 1860s. Better heating was accompanied by better lighting. Candles continued to be widely used but improved oil lamps came onto the market from the 1840s and mineral oils replaced vegetable oil or animal oil for illumination, giving both a better light and causing less smell. Discovered in the late eighteenth century, gas made progress first for street lighting. In London, Westminster was lit by gas as early as 1814 and by 1816 the city had 26 miles of gas-mains. Gas lighting in Paris began with the Palais Royal in 1819 and by the mid-century the majority of large French towns were lit by this method. Due to problems in developing a satisfactory burner, gas made progress more slowly for domestic illumination. Gas cookers were coming into use in the 1870s and heaters from the 1880s. In some places electricity was used as a source of light. Electric arc-lights were employed in a number of public places and commercial establishments in London and Paris in the 1870s while the development of the incandescent lamp in the 1880s made electricity more suitable for domestic use. They were in use in London, Madrid and Barcelona early in the decade and by 1900 electric lighting by incandescent lamp was an accepted feature of urban life.

If cleanliness was next to godliness, here too there was progress. The water closet began to make headway after 1870 and before the end of the nineteenth century fixed

TABLE 27: Use of Gas and Electricity in Breslau Dwellings, 1910 (per '000 dwellings)

	Dwellings with				
	0–1 living room	*2 living rooms*	*3 living rooms*	*4 living rooms*	*All dwellings*
Gas in living rooms only	8	8	8	10	10
Gas in living rooms and kitchen		10	57	164	189
Electric light		2	3	4	18

Source: Desai, *Real Wages*, p. 27.

cast-iron baths were installed in some houses but bathrooms were not provided in the dwellings of the great majority. House cleaning was made easier with the development of carpet sweepers and vacuum cleaners late in the century. Nevertheless, while domestic service did not lack recruits change was slow. Few lifts were installed, there was little full-scale central heating and convenience was rarely a relevant consideration in the design of kitchens. The idea of the house as a machine for living in had not yet been born.

OTHER EXPENDITURE

Once food, clothes, shelter, heating and lighting had been accounted for, there was for many little if any surplus left to spend in other directions. The majority of the population were able to acquire something in the way of crockery and cutlery, a few pots and pans for cooking and the meagrest sticks of furniture—a bed, a table and perhaps a chair or two. Some bedding was necessary, a few rags for domestic purposes and some cleaning materials (soap, soda, grate-black &c) would also be numbered amongst the purchases of all but the very poor. The use of soap began to spread. Going up the income scale an increasing amount would be spent on furniture. Aping the middle class and aristocracy, the artisans tended to crowd their rooms with furniture, any available flat surfaces with ornaments, their walls with cheap prints. Glass was generally employed for the windows, there would be much fabric used in wall hangings and curtains, however inappropriate all this was for rooms illuminated by smoky lamps and warmed by smoky fires. Regional differences were important in the style of furnishings and there were variations in the patterns of expenditure. The English worker, it was said, tended to acquire movable property rather than spend money on a good diet. He had an over-furnished home and an under-nourished body whereas the French placed greater emphasis on . food. Some mechanisation of the manufacture of furniture tended to cheapen and standardise what was available and there was a growth of organised markets in second-hand furniture in some parts of Europe. Wallpaper was more widely adopted and linoleum came to be employed as a floor covering. The middle class home and upper class dwelling were lavishly filled with expensive and elaborate furniture, some of which was imported as foreign styles gained a vogue in furnishings as with clothes. With the spread of literacy and the emergence of a wider reading public, more books were bought both for education and for entertainment. Cheap reprints of the classics as well as contributions to scholarship widened the market for books and the novel emerged as the most popular form of litera-ture, sometimes issued in weekly parts or on an enormous scale as a three-decker volume. The detective story became fashionable before the first world war. Musical instruments were also acquired. Traditionally the shepherd had had his pipe while other musical instruments were to be found in peasant homes. But in the nineteenth century the piano—first the grand and then the upright—was acquired by the more well-to-do sections of society for music-making. With no place in the home for such activities, working men in England took up brass instruments—sometimes with religious fervour—and formed bands, and small orchestras were to be found in village churches though these were driven out as the organ was more generally adopted to accompany congregational worship.

With industrialisation and the need for timekeeping the clock found itself a place in a growing number of homes even though for many of the working class the factory hooter or the knocker-up served instead. For the kitchen a number of mechanical items became available such as mincers and coffee grinders but perhaps the most important consumer durable to appear was the sewing machine which, from the middle of the century, was increasingly employed for making uniforms and other clothing commercially but also gave an impetus to the manufacture of women's and children's clothing in the home. It was also used for other domestic purposes, such as the making of sheets, curtains and tablecloths. And transport was transformed by the bicycle and the motor car. Rapid improvements were made in the bicycle which quickly moved from the penny-farthing to a boneshaker which could transport the worker to his factory, the clerk to his office or provide recreation for the ladies. At first the plaything of the rich, the motor car was also adopted in some countries before the first world war by professional people. But circumscribed by law, the number of motor cars grew comparatively slowly. By 1913 there were 106,000 registered in Great Britain, 91,000 in France, 50,000 in Germany, 20,000 in Italy and 7,000 in Russia.[75]

For the majority of the people in Europe, their daily needs exhausted and oft-times exceeded their resources. But for a small but growing number a surplus existed. Higher up the social scale, more would be spent on education, provision would be made for medical treatment and some entertaining would be done.

LABOUR AND SERVICES

A consequence both of industrialisation and urbanisation and the rising standards of consumption which accompanied them were significant shifts in the demand for labour. In aggregate terms the most important change was an altera-

75. Walt W. Rostow, *The Stages of Economic Growth: a non-communist manifesto* (Cambridge U.P., 1960) p. 170.

tion of the allocation of labour between the three sectors of demand: agriculture, industry and services. With a different chronology and to a varying extent the proportion of those who were engaged in agriculture fell and those who were engaged in industry rose. As the following table shows, the proportion of those engaged in the tertiary sector altered little but the overall figures conceal considerable changes. While the numbers of those employed in domestic service fell, the numbers of those engaged in government service, in the professions, in entertainment and other such services grew.

TABLE 28: Distribution of National Product between three major sectors, selected countries

	Agriculture	*Industry*	*Services*
FRANCE			
1825–35	50	25	25
1872–82	42	30	28
1908–10	35	37	28
GERMANY			
1860–69	32	24	44
1905–14	18	39	43
ITALY			
1861–65	55	20	25
1896–1900	47	22	31
NORWAY			
1865	34	21	45
1910	24	26	50
SWEDEN			
1861–65	39	17	44
1901–05	35	38	27
UNITED KINGDOM			
1801	32	23	45
1841	22	34	44
1901	6	40	54

Source: Kuznets, *Modern economic growth*, pp. 88–93.

For women, the most important source of employment continued to be in the home. Many wives and daughters worked hard to look after the needs of their—oft-times extended—family. And for the upper and middle classes, the running of a home also continued to be a very labour-intensive operation. In England at the end of the seventeenth century, the ability to command personal services was an important index of wealth. According to Gregory King, peers had an average household of 40 while eminent merchants had an average of eight. In London in about 1700, servants formed 17 per cent of the population. While with the decline of hospitality, eighteenth-century establishments were smaller than medieval, by modern standards they were still impressively large. In the nineteenth century the number of domestics continued to vary with the wealth and position of the head of the household. In the early part of the century in England, on an income of £250 a year, a maidservant could be kept. On an income of £1,000 a year, the household would be larger. A family consisting of a gentleman, his wife and three children would have an establishment of three female servants, a footman and a coachman, who was responsible for their carriage and a pair of horses.[76] All upper and middle class people kept servants, but servants were often kept in at least the upper working classes as well, not so much to maintain the pattern of a formal and complicated way of living as for needed assistance in the often painfully hard task of maintaining even a poor home in early twentieth-century England.[77] In 1801 there were 600,000 domestic servants in Britain while in 1851, out of a total population of 21 million, 905,000 women and 134,000 men were employed in domestic service, forming after agriculture the largest occupational group. In the third quarter of the nineteenth century the demand for domestic service grew, the number of domestic servants in Great Britain rising to 1·8 million in 1881. And

---

76. Dorothy C. [Mrs C. S.] Peel, 'Homes and Habits' in George M. Young, ed. *Early Victorian England, 1830–1865* (2 vols. Oxford U.P., 1934) I, 105.

77. Laski, 'Domestic Life', p. 145.

only then did continued expansion begin to fall off as better-paid occupations became available to women. 'The young working-girl of to-day', wrote Mrs Peel in 1902, 'prefers to become a Board School mistress, a post-office clerk, a typewriter, a shop girl, or a worker in a factory—anything rather than enter domestic service'.[78] Even so in 1911, 38·6 per cent of all occupied women in Britain were employed in domestic service. In other countries in western Europe, domestic service was important but the same factors curbing its growth had begun to operate before 1914.

Inevitably female domestic servants sometimes found themselves fulfilling sexual roles. But there was also more deliberate provision to meet man's sexual demands. Courtesans earned themselves a place in the highest ranks of society while prostitutes were in wider demand. In his *Journal*, Boswell describes how he obtained satisfaction through casual encounters on the streets of London. In the nineteenth century theatres earned themselves an ill-reputation as places of assignation but females could be picked up on the streets of many a European city. In many towns brothels existed. It is obviously not easy to discover how many prostitutes there were. But in 1810 there were reputed to be 175 brothels and 3,000 prostitutes in Berlin which then had a population of over 150,000. In 1844 Faucher estimated that there were 750 known prostitutes in Manchester, 250 in Paisley, 300 in Hull, 2,000 in Liverpool and 15,000 in London. In some countries, in an effort to limit the spread of venereal disease, registered prostitutes were given free and regular medical examinations. Complaints about double standards led also to pressure to control prostitution. In 1843 regulations to control their activities were passed in Paris, in 1846 brothels were closed in Prussia (but allowed to reopen in 1851) and abolitionist legislation was enacted in Norway in 1890 and in Denmark in 1901. But the legislation appears to have had only a limited effect. The pattern of provision changed but prostitution continued to exist. In 1900 it was estimated

78. Dorothy C. [Mrs C. S.] Peel, *How to Keep Houses* (Constable, 1902) p. 133.

that there were 60,000 prostitutes in Paris and London, 50,000 in Berlin and 25,000 in Vienna.

This is not the place to describe in detail the changing pattern of employment in services because that is the subject of another chapter in this volume.[79] But certain points related to consumption need to be made. First, the nineteenth century saw an expansion of professional services, including lawyers, architects, surveyors, land agents, engineers, secretaries, accountants, bankers, insurance agents, auctioneers and so on. Then there was a growing demand for medical services, for doctors, nurses, chemists, dentists (and veterinary surgeons). Inevitably all these changes affected the scale of another service, education. Here two developments are worthy of note. First, the spread of industry greatly expanded the need for a literate working class. And, when literacy was not enough, technical education had to follow. Then there was a transformation of higher education to meet the wider demands for professional skills. The growth of retail and wholesale trading discussed above also led to an expanded demand for employment in these sectors of the economy, as did the growth of central and local government, the judiciary, the police and the armed forces.

There was also a demand for leisure services. The poor entertained little and in industrial centres had little leisure but in the country the round of traditional festivities continued to punctuate with revelry and some feasting the tedium and short commons of the daily round. In the towns as in the village, the hostelry, inn or café provided a social centre with light and warmth and refreshment. Travelling fairs also brought a touch of the exotic and bizarre as well as providing a link with the outside world. The ceremonies of state, gild and municipality as well as the year-round ritual of saints' days and festivals provided occasions for popular entertainment which became transmuted in industrial countries. Such were the daily changing of the guard, military parades for special occasions, secular displays like the London Lord Mayor's show and religious

79. See Chapter 6, p. 358.

parades for Mardi Gras or Corpus Christi. And then there was the popular culture of folk song, legends, superstitions and oral tradition which provided more informally and casually for the leisure hours, such as they were. But much still remains to be written about the history of popular entertainment.

For the better-off, alongside the private entertainment at dinner parties, receptions, balls and weekend parties in the country of near-feudal splendour, there was a considerable expansion of organised entertainment. The theatre, the opera and ballet flourished and for more popular tastes there were the music hall and the pantomime. The provision of music also grew and became institutionalised on a secular basis. As skilled musicians were available cheaply and choral singing became a popular pastime, composers such as Mendelssohn, Berlioz, Mahler and Elgar were able to write works for large orchestras and choirs of enormous size.

One leisure pursuit which was all-pervading, both geographically and socially, was gambling. Enormous sums were placed on bets by members of the aristocracy. The English, it was said, would bet on anything from a horse race to the antics of a couple of flies on a window-pane. Lotteries, both private and public, were organised in many European countries. In England public gambling on games of chance or cards was made illegal by successive acts in 1745, 1845 and 1892 but illicit gambling in clubs catering for all classes continued to take place. Elsewhere in Europe, the casino became a feature of public life, notably at Homburg (Hesse) and at Monte Carlo where gaming was introduced in 1856.

Outdoor entertainments or pastimes were predominantly the preserve of the upper classes. Blood sports —hunting, shooting and fishing—which called for almost military virtues in a civilian setting predominated. But 'although the manly amusement of foxhunting' was regarded as 'the best corrective to those habits of luxury and those concomitants of wealth which would otherwise render the English aristocracy effeminate and degenerate', this sport could be shared by the farmers over whose land the hunt pursued its quarry. But fraternisation existed only out-of-doors. Prize-fighting could also cross class barriers and provided an opportunity for gambling. In the course of the eighteenth century too horse racing, the sport of kings, also grew in popularity. In England courses were established at Ascot, Doncaster, Epsom, Newmarket, Nottingham and Manchester before 1800. And the sport grew in the following century. Not only did it provide a wildly fluctuating income for the gambling fraternity but it gave rise to considerable expenditure on both current and capital account. Accommodation, entertainment and transport had to be provided, race courses built, stables erected and bloodstock bred. While its operation and finance remained a predominantly upper-class pursuit, the man in the street could also enjoy it. Late in the nineteenth century greyhound racing in England gained for itself a more plebeian support. In the course of the century working class sports became less barbarous. Bull-baiting, bear-baiting, cock-fighting, rat-killing and badger-drawing diminished in importance in England but the bullfight continued to have a ritual significance in Spain. In England, too, cricket extracted itself from its gambling context and gained a wider following while with the shortening of working hours professional football was more widely supported from the 1870s. For the better-off, lawn-tennis gained favour both as a social and a sporting occasion late in the century.

Lastly the rise of the holiday trade deserves mention. The grand tour had provided the finishing of a rich man's education but new pleasures developed in the eighteenth century, the spa and the holiday resort. At first the preserve of the well-to-do, taking the waters at spas became somewhat more widely diffused before 1914. Of much greater importance was the growth of the holiday resort and particularly the seaside resort. Again until the middle of the nineteenth century, this form of pastime was the prerogative of the rich. But as industry more sharply differentiated work from leisure and as transport facilities grew, the patronage of holiday resorts began to extend down the social scale. Though still a predominantly upper and middle class activity on the eve of the first world war, attempts had already been made to cater for the working class who visited such resorts more on day trips than to stay. Resorts such as Ostend, Boulogne, Blackpool and Southend catered for a wider public and the growth of demand led to increased provision.

The period covered by this volume therefore saw a radical alteration in the demand for labour. It saw an expanded market for a wider range of skills and an altered and extended demand for services.

CAPITAL AND CAPITAL GOODS

Little is known about the needs of individuals for capital. For the majority of the population of Europe, their need was for cash advances from time to time in order to meet the day-to-day costs of living. Since earnings often varied considerably from week to week or from time to time because of seasonal employment, it was the shopkeeper who, by allowing credit, enabled the poor to obtain the necessities of life—food, fuel and clothing. Those who sometimes had slightly larger incomes borrowed money, usually at very high rates of interest, from a moneylender while others obtained money from a pawnbroker. Sometimes such loans for which goods were pledged were to meet emergencies; on other occasions they were part of a regular pattern of life. In England the pawning of the best clothes often took place. They would be pledged on Monday to provide spending money for the week and redeemed on Saturday when the week's wages were paid, worn on Sunday and then pledged again on Monday. Indebtedness was therefore a constant thread in the fabric of the lives of the poor in the nineteenth century. For the better-paid workers, friendly societies and savings banks were established to provide security for their savings. And since with rising expectations, houseownership became an aspiration amongst artisans, building societies emerged to meet the needs for capital for house purchase. Money could be raised in other ways also. With jewellery or plate as collateral, the pawnbroker made loans; banks would permit overdrafts on suitable security; while for the landowner, the mortgage or some such similar device continued to be employed.[80]

But much more important was the finance of industrialisation. Between 1750 and 1914 the demand of industry, agriculture and commerce in Europe for capital rose almost continually and changed sharply. Though he deals only with the experience of England and France, Professor Gille has set out in Chapter 4 the ways in which shifts in the need for short-term, medium-term and long-term capital were met by appropriate institutional change and innovation. At the same time in real terms the process of industrialisation involved a shift in demand from tools to fixed equipment. To discuss this change here in detail would mean embarking on a far-ranging study of industrial growth in Europe but certain points can be made. The debate about the relative importance of fixed and working capital in the first phase of industrialisation is one which is still in process, but it is clear that until 1914 there remained throughout Europe to a greater or lesser extent a wide range of domestic or handicraft industries whose capital demands in terms of tools and equipment were small. And these were usually met, as they had traditionally been met, by the carpenter, the blacksmith and by other skilled artisans. But the new feature of the industrial scene was the growth of machine-driven, factory-housed manufacture. In pre-industrial Europe, shipyards had provided one of the fairly limited number of examples of capital-intensive manufacture, but from the later eighteenth century textiles, iron and steel, brewing, and later other food processes, chemicals and other metal manufactures came to employ more fixed equipment. In this process there were three elements of capital expenditure: the power supply, the

80. In 1845 Sándor Petófi (1823–49), the Hungarian poet, wrote:
> *Tax I do not pay; that's fine!*
> *Few the lands that I call mine,*
> *But debts enough to reach the sky:*
> *A Magyar nobleman am I !*

quoted in Warriner, *Contrasts in Emerging Societies*, p. 60.

equipment and the buildings in which not only the power units and the machinery but also the administration, which made their employment possible, was housed.

All the new textile processes adopted in the eighteenth century demanded power on an unprecedented scale. Some increased use was made of animal power but water provided the major source of power. In England until at least as late as the 1830s water power was developed and its use extended, not only for textiles but for metal working, timber, paper and flour milling, and for other purposes as well. In the following decades water power was still employed on a considerable scale. In 1844, for example, the French iron industry was using hydraulic engines of 21,710 hp compared with steam engines of 5,982 hp, while as late as 1850 more than one-third of the power for the woollen textile industry (12,600 hp steam; 6,800 water) and about one-eighth of the power for the cotton textile industry (71,000 steam; 11,000 water) in England came from water.[81] To meet such needs mills and wheels were built and ponds, dams and leats constructed. Not only streams and rivers were harnessed, but the tides too. A recent survey has shown that half of the tidemills known to have existed in the south-west of England were erected after 1790. Such demands led to improvements in the efficiency of waterwheels. Poncelet's undershot wheel with curved vanes was a considerable technical step forward, and the water turbine which developed from the work of Fourneyron not only increased the efficiency of water power, but in due course made the generation of hydro-electricity possible.

More important, however, than water power was steam. For some purposes, such as mine drainage, the Newcomen engine was readily adopted, but the greater economy of the Watt engine enabled it to meet the demand for power where cost considerations were of greater importance. By 1800 more than 1,200 steam engines were in operation in Britain. In the early nineteenth century an increasing number of low-pressure engines were used as steam gained

81. Landes, *Unbound Prometheus*, pp. 104, 182.

superiority in the textile industry, but, for a range of purposes, the high-pressure engine resulting from the work of Woolf and others also came to be employed. To meet the demand for greater efficiency and more compact units, improved engines were developed. Some indication of the growth in demand for steam power as more powerful engines came both to replace water power and to be employed for a wider range of uses is provided by the following table:

TABLE 29: Capacity of all Steam Engines ('ooo horse-power)

	1840	*1850*	*1860*	*1870*	*1880*	*1888*	*1896*
Great Britain	620	1,290	2,450	4,040	7,600	9,200	13,700
Germany	40	260	850	2,480	5,120	6,200	8,080
France	90	270	1,120	1,850	3,070	4,520	5,920
Austria	20	100	330	800	1,560	2,150	2,520
Belgium	40	70	160	350	610	810	1,180
Russia	20	70	200	920	1,740	2,240	3,100
Italy	10	40	50	330	500	830	1,520
Spain	10	20	100	210	470	740	1,180
Sweden	—	—	20	100	220	300	510
Netherlands	—	10	30	130	250	340	600
EUROPE	860	2,240	5,540	11,570	22,000	28,630	40,300

Source: Mulhall, *Dictionary of Statistics*, p. 545; Wl. Woytinsky, *Die Welt in Zahlen* (7 vols.; Berlin 1926), IV, p. 59. Woytinsky correctly stresses the approximate character of these estimates. (Landes, *Unbound Prometheus*, p. 221.)

Thus, steam engine capacity available in Europe almost quintupled between 1840 and 1896. With the progress of industrialisation the demand for power proved cumulative. As water power was supplemented and then supplanted by steam power, so other energy sources were called upon. While steam became the dominant source of power not only for extractive and manufacturing industry but for rail and sea transport as well, gas engines, internal combustion engines (both gas and oil), and electrical motors were also pressed into service.

Then there was the second aspect, the mechanisation of processes and their operation on a larger scale. The textile industry was amongst the first industries to undergo the move from simple to more complex and expensive machines. The early textile equipment was simple, used in limited numbers, and was comparatively cheap. A 40-spindle jenny cost about £6 in 1792; scribbling and carding machines £1 for each inch of roller width, while a slubbing billy with 30 spindles cost £10 10s.[82] In the early nineteenth century the situation had radically changed: the mule had become a long machine of up to a thousand spindles, workable only by steam or water power and costing more than a thousand pounds. In iron making, blast furnaces, puddling furnaces, rolling mills and coke ovens also grew in size, as did plant for brewing, soap, sugar and chemicals. The coming of the railways brought an expanding demand for locomotives. In the later nineteenth century, while the trend in textiles was towards more spindles and looms, in other industries economies of scale operated more obviously and larger plants were built for iron- and steelmaking, chemicals, sugar, soap and other industries. And more powerful locomotives were used on the railways, while steam came to replace sail at sea.

The demand for machinery had two important consequences: it led to the creation and expansion of engineering firms and it brought about the establishment of a machine tools industry. The history of engineering is a comparatively neglected aspect of industrial industry. Apart from a few notable exceptions, such as Boulton & Watt, little attention has been paid to the firms which made the machines. Yet their ability to meet the demands for the new prime movers and the new equipment was crucial to the process of industrialisation. In the early stages in the textile industry some of the firms built their own machines, but they soon became too expensive and complicated for this to be done. Most of the engineering firms were general manufacturers who made comparatively small numbers of varying types of equipment. In 1834, for example, William Fairbairn 'equipped waterwheels equivalent to 700 horses' power

82. William B. Crump, ed. *The Leeds Woollen Industry, 1780–1820* (Leeds: Thoresby Society, 1931), pp. 212–13, 293.

and steam engines to 400 horses' power from his engineer factory alone'.[83] But where demands were greater, as for textile machinery, a degree of specialisation occurred, and some firms came to concentrate on this particular branch of engineering. Otherwise, by a process of adaptation within old firms or by the formation of new, the changing demands for engineering products, which occurred as the nineteenth century advanced, were met.

As the cradle of the industrial revolution, Britain became an important source of machinery for developing industries in Europe. Steam engines and textile mill equipment loomed large amongst the machinery exported from Britain. But local attempts were made to meet local needs. While steam engines were made in Belgium, Germany and Sweden in the eighteenth century, the main development of the engineering industry in Europe came after 1800. By the middle of the century most of the leading firms such as Calla, Gouin or Schneider in France, Cockerill in Belgium, and Borsig, Egells and Hakort in Germany were able to undertake anything ordered, from locomotives and marine engines to distilling apparatus and lathes. Some even tried their hand at textile equipment, although it was soon recognised that this was a product best left to specialists.[84]

Since the new machines could not be made efficiently and in quantity with existing tools and the prevailing level of skill, a second consequence of the demand for capital equipment was the emergence of a machine tools industry. In particular, it was 'the tireless driving power of the steam engine that called the engineer's heavy machine tools into being and led to the establishment of the first heavy machine shops'. While the origins of this development can be found in the eighteenth century, as late as the 1810s William Fairbairn found that in Manchester 'there were then no self-acting tools. The whole of the machinery was executed by hand. There were neither planing, slotting nor shaping machines; and, with the exception of very imperfect lathes and a few drills, the preparatory operations

83. Andrew Ure, *Philosophy of Manufactures* (1835), p. 39.
84. Landes, *Unbound Prometheus*, p. 103.

of construction were effected entirely by the hands of workmen.' Through the work of Jesse Ramsden, Joseph Bramah, Henry Maudslay, Richard Roberts, Joseph Whitworth, James Nasmyth and others in Britain, the situation was transformed and a whole range of machine tools— lathes, presses, planing, punching, milling and gear-cutting machines—were developed. As a further and important step, the efforts of Whitworth led to the standardisation of screw-threads. The second half of the nineteenth century saw the spread of the 'American system' of fully interchangeable parts, particularly important for small arms manufacture but of significance also for the production of typewriters, sewing machines and other articles. It saw also the range of machine tools widened and developed under the pressure of demand for machines which could deal with a greater range of materials at a faster speed and with more flexibility and precision. In the last two decades of our period the automobile industry began to exert an important influence on the development of machine tools as it has continued to do since 1914.

The need to keep the new steam engines and machinery fully employed had yet other less direct consequences for capital investment. In the first decades of the nineteenth century, for example, gas lighting was installed in textile mills, replacing oil-lamps or candles, giving a stimulus to the expansion of the gas industry. And the raw material and fuel demands of industry provided an incentive to transport improvements.

Finally there were the buildings. Steam engines had to be housed, machinery protected, and office and administrative staff provided with accommodation. This was often the most expensive—and durable—aspect of industrialisation. In many parts of the British Isles empty engine houses now stand gaunt sentinel, while the mines are abandoned and the machinery has gone: mill buildings, like those at Belper or New Lanark, also provide an impressive reminder of a past phase of industrialism. Not only manufacture but distribution also required capital investment. Warehouses had to be built at the ports, and main distribution centres and exchanges for dealing in coal, corn and metals had to be erected. Banks put up solid edifices in towns and cities throughout Europe and brokers, wholesalers, insurance agents and a wide range of other ancillary services demanded accommodation. As factories towered over the new industrial towns, so extensive commercial buildings formed a new and dominant feature of many cities. Such demand for buildings was less specific than the industrial demand for machinery, but it was not without its influence on building techniques. It encouraged, for example, the use of cast iron instead of wood for the frames for buildings. It also played its part in extending the market for bricks, timber, glass, stone, iron and other building materials.

Like industry, but to a much lesser degree, agriculture gradually became more capital-intensive. To meet the growing demand for food and industrial raw materials more land was brought into cultivation. Money had therefore to be spent in clearing the ground and enclosing it by fences and hedges as well as on legal charges. Rough calculations of the cost of enclosure in England before 1845 indicate the course of events there:

TABLE 30: Cost of Enclosure in England, 1727–1845

	Acres enclosed ('000)	Estimated cost (£000)
1727–60	75	34
1761–92	478	459
1792–1815	1,013	2,245
1816–45	200	450

Source: Phyllis Deane, 'Capital formation in Britain before the railway age', *Economic Development and Cultural Change*, IX (1961), p. 358.

To enable some land to be worked, it had to be drained. In England and the Netherlands considerable investment took place in the construction of banks and dams, drainage channels and pumping windmills or engines. Elsewhere, as in Italy and France, irrigation was necessary. In Hungary, works to control the River Theiss increased the cultivable area. While advance was slow, some additional investment also took place in farm machinery. Drilling machines, threshing machines (patented in 1786), reapers (from 1826) and other forms of equipment were used, and the steam engine made its appearance. As farming in the more developed areas of Europe invested more, so its demand for labour declined and the numbers employed in agriculture fell. There was also the construction of barns, cattle sheds and other farm buildings. Thus the demands of agriculture for capital also grew between 1750 and 1914.

In addition, the services increasingly and more widely enjoyed by the European peoples could not be taken advantage of without capital investment. House-building has already been discussed since the provision of shelter was an essential prerequisite for its enjoyment. Similarly, certain services could not be made available without capital investment. Among the most important of these were transport, the functions of central and local government, distribution, cultural and recreational facilities, and religion.

First, transport. In order that people should be able to travel both within their own countries and abroad in Europe, roads had to be improved, bridges built and more regular coach services provided. To meet this expanding traffic, more roadside provision was necessary so hotels, inns and hostelries proliferated. The travels of one English nobleman alone, the earl of Bristol, appear to have led to the establishment of a large number of hotels in various towns in Europe. Then, while the railways were originally constructed for the carriage of goods to facilitate consumption, they soon became consumption goods in themselves. It early became apparent that passenger traffic provided an additional and profitable source of revenue. While in Spain the Minister of Public Works and in Russia the requirements of the Tsar might predominate, in other countries economic considerations were taken into account. The railways accordingly invested in passenger rolling stock, with marked class distinctions between first, second and third. Later, more sophisticated provision was made for dining and sleeping and Pullman cars and corridor coaches with steam heating and electric light were introduced. Larger locomotives were designed to haul heavier trains at higher speeds. Hotels were built by the railways and waiting rooms were provided for the comfort of passengers. Among the more impressive buildings of the new industrial age were the main line termini, whether in London, Paris, Berlin or Milan. Similarly, steamship lines were established to provide pleasure cruises to foreign parts or short day trips along the coasts and rivers and lakes of Europe. And not only were vessels required but piers and landing stages had to be built. While the grand tour had followed the whim and interest of particular participants, the needs of the new travelling public were catered for by travel agencies, among the first of which was Thomas Cook's, founded in 1845. And for the improvement of urban and suburban services the bus and tramway companies had to build garages and sheds, provide terminals and purchase vehicles so that their routes could operate. And before the private motorist could range far afield garages and petrol stations were necessary. The expansion of the postal services and the introduction of the telegraph and the telephone also required investment in post offices and transmitting equipment.

Then, there were the public utilities, water, sewage and refuse disposal, gas and electricity. As cities grew, needs for water could not be met by the traditional means of wells or the direct use of streams or rivers since such supplies were often both inadequate and polluted. As early as the 1790s James Watt wrote to Robert Mylne, engineer of the New River Water Company, 'People now have such a rage for washing their b-ms' that more water and therefore more pumping engines were needed.[85] Reservoirs had therefore to be built to supply the large urban centres. In Scotland, Edinburgh was supplied by a reservoir by 1823. In France, the Zola dam was built on the Infernet between 1843 and

85. Harold Perkin, *The Origins of Modern English Society, 1780–1880* (Routledge & Kegan Paul, 1969) p. 96.

1854 to supply water to Aix-en-Provence and the Gileppe dam in Belgium was built between 1870 and 1875. In England there were sixteen water companies by 1825 but the major developments came later. The Dale Dyke dam was built in 1858 to create the Bradfield reservoir to supply Sheffield with water and in the 1880s Lake Vyrnwy was formed to provide water for Liverpool. An alternative method, drawing on existing lake supplies by means of long pipe lines, was adopted by Manchester.

Other aspects of the social infrastructure also required capital investment. As the process of urbanisation gained momentum, the problems of sewage and refuse disposal became much more acute. Practices which had been tolerable in villages or small towns became insupportable in large cities. So sewers had to be constructed, pumping engines installed and corporate provision made for the disposal of sewage and the collection of refuse. Similarly, while oil or candles were used for illumination, only lamps or candle-holders were required, but neither gas nor electricity could be used for street lighting, domestic illumination and heating or for industrial purposes without the establishment of gas plants and electricity generating stations and distribution networks of pipes or wires. By 1859 there were nearly 1,000 gas works in England in urban centres but this number was reduced as the advantage of distributing gas from large central works became apparent. In this way gas set a pattern which, from the 1880s, electricity was to follow. Coal provided the initial fuel both for the production of gas and the generation of electricity but from the later nineteenth century water supplies were harnessed to supply hydro-electricity. France and Italy led the way. In Italy the first scheme was inaugurated in 1883 to supply Genoa while in France the Avignonet plant was started in 1899.

Welfare and medical services, too, required capital investment. Many hospitals were built and maintained by charitable or religious organisations. In eighteenth-century England fifty-seven hospitals, mostly founded after 1750, were added to the five royal hospitals previously in existence while in the nineteenth century not only were nearly 800 more built but specialised provision was made for maternity, tuberculosis, mental disorder and so on. By the early twentieth century, Professor Perkin has argued with perhaps a degree of exaggeration, the 'hospital had changed from a last, dangerous refuge for the sick poor to a highly sophisticated fortress in the war against disease'.[86] For the able-bodied poor, workhouses were built.

There was also considerable investment in education. Schools, colleges and universities were built to extend the range of provision and to enable a growing proportion of the population to be educated. And when private provision failed, the state had to step in. In the later nineteenth century in England, the School Board schools towered over the surrounding houses and provided a rival focus on the skyline to the towers and spires of the churches.

The administration of law and order required buildings. In the capitals and provincial centres of Europe new law courts were built. Such were the Royal Courts of Justice in the Strand, London and those in Brussels (1866–83). And for the custody of the convicted, prisons were built, many on Bentham's Panopticon principle which was also used for workhouses and factories in order to provide easy and effective supervision. The most famous of English prisons, Dartmoor, was begun in 1806.

The government of state or municipality demanded an appropriate setting as the democratic principle spread. In London the Houses of Parliament were re-built between 1836 and 1860; in Vienna new Parliament and city offices were built on the Ringstrasse. For the conduct of government, offices had to be provided and much of Whitehall dates from the nineteenth century when these buildings were erected to provide accommodation for the widening scope of government. And rulers had to be provided with dignified residences. What was apparent on the national scene was duplicated locally. Prominent in the major provincial English cities such as Leeds, Birmingham and Liverpool are their nineteenth-century townhalls and

86. Perkin, *Origins of Modern English Society*, p. 121.

rathäuser or mairies can similarly be seen on the continent. Often, too, the mayor or burgomaster was provided with a residence. So the changing governmental arrangements which were necessary for administrative, welfare and other services gave rise to a considerable amount of building.

In many European towns the old fortifications were demolished in the nineteenth century but defence required some capital investment. Fortifications were erected, barracks and arsenals built, as in Paris or at Woolwich, and naval dockyards, such as Toulon and Karlskrona, were extended. The shift from sail to steam, moreover, required the establishment of coaling stations as ports of call. Finally, there were the examples of national display, the Brandenburg Gate in Berlin, the Arc de Triomphe in Paris and the Albert Memorial in London. And on a smaller scale, statues were erected to honour distinguished men.

For culture, recreation, entertainment and leisure, an enormous investment was necessary. Libraries such as the British Museum (begun in 1823) and the National Library, Munich (1831), museums such as the Altes Museum, Berlin (1822–30), art galleries like the Rijksmuseum, Amsterdam (opened in 1885) were built and their range extended. Before the first world war folk museums were set up in Scandinavia. Then, as drama, ballet, opera and music flourished, theatres, opera houses and concert halls were established in many European capitals, for example, the Dresden Opera (1837) and the Paris Opéra (1861–74), and in smaller towns and cities as well, such as the Bordeaux theatre (1772–80) and the Parma Teatro Regio (1821–9), as the patronage of the arts moved from the courts and was taken up by the middle class. The music hall and pantomime were also provided with appropriate stages like the Carré Theatre, Amsterdam which opened in 1887. And then there was provision for sport. Sports arenas were constructed and stadiums built to provide both for individual and team exercise and to cater for the growth of spectator sports such as association football, support for which grew in the later nineteenth century. Parks were created. Such were the Englischer Garten (Munich), the

Bois de Boulogne (Paris) and Kew Gardens (London). In many European cities the passing into disuse of town fortifications gave an opportunity for laying out extensive promenades and public gardens as at Cologne, Magdeburg, Vienna and Frankfurt. Some pleasure gardens—the Tivoli in Copenhagen dating from 1843 and the Tiergarten in Berlin—were also set up. And to cater for the resident as well as the traveller, restaurants, inns and taverns were built. Public halls for more general purposes such as the Free Trade Hall, Manchester or St George's Hall, Liverpool were provided. There was thus an enormously extended range of facilities provided for public enjoyment between the eighteenth and the early twentieth century. And to cater for the needs of rich Englishmen, the nineteenth century saw the emergence of the club, the Reform, the Athenaeum, the Traveller's and others.

To meet the needs both for the increased population with its altered distribution and for the fragmentation of denominations, large numbers of places of worship were established. In England, to take one example, between 1801 and 1873, 4,210 new Anglican churches were built, an increase of about one-third, and about 20,000 non-Anglican chapels or nearly a ten-fold increase.[87] To take account of the altered distribution of the population, new dioceses were created and new cathedrals built, notably at Truro and at Liverpool where rival Anglican and Roman cathedrals were begun. All this, which was replicated in continental Europe, required considerable capital investment.

While most building continued in a traditional fashion, the nineteenth century saw the employment of new methods and materials. Particularly notable was the use of cast iron to enable the large areas of railway stations or exhibition halls, such as the Crystal Palace, to be roofed. Then there was the growing employment towards the end of the nineteenth century of concrete for buildings. And thirdly, the quantity production of mouldings and castings greatly reduced the cost of ornamentation and enabled architects

87. Perkin, *Origins of Modern English Society*, p. 122.

and decorators to indulge in elaborate decoration. These new methods and materials gave architects a new freedom. A new generation of architects emerged, of whom perhaps the most distinguished was Walter Gropius.

CONCLUSION

While there is some debate about the course of the standard of living in Europe in the early modern period between 1500 and 1750, there is little about the trend between the late eighteenth century and the early twentieth century. Though the share of the mass of the population in total output may not have changed much if at all during the course of this century and a half, there was a substantial increase in output per head. According to one source, the index of real wages in France increased from 55·5 in 1820 to 100 in 1900 and in Great Britain from 37 in 1790 to 100 in 1913.[88] Because average real wages approximately doubled, there was a significant rise in the general standard of living. The majority of the population of Europe was better-off on the eve of the first world war than they had been before the French Revolution. But wide social and geographical differences still remained within Europe. Everywhere the wealthy lived extremely well; a greatly enlarged middle class had an enhanced standard of living. 'Surely there never was any time in the life of the world when it was so good, in the way of obvious material comfort, to be alive and fairly well-to-do', wrote C. E. Montague, 'as it was before the [first world] war'.[89] The condition, too, of some industrial workers had improved but, as the social surveys revealed, there were still a large number of industrial poor who led overcrowded, under-paid, unhealthy, underfed lives. For the peasantry in the less developed parts of Europe life had changed remarkably

88. Frederick L. Nussbaum, *A History of the Economic Institutions of Modern Europe: an introduction to* Der moderne Kapitalismus *of Werner Sombart* (New York: Crofts, 1937; New York: Kelley, 1969) p. 327.

89. Charles E. Montague, *Disenchantment* (Chatto & Windus Phoenix Library, 1928) p. 218, quoted in Arthur J. Taylor, 'The Economy' in Nowell-Smith, *Edwardian England*, p. 105.

little in the two hundred years or so covered by this chapter. Still in 1907–8 in Russia the peasant dietary consisted of 'cabbage, rye bread, potatoes, fat, and a little milk. Beef is given occasionally. Boots are of bark and all dress is of home manufacture'.[90] Regional and class differences—and for that matter, particularly for rural communities, year to year variations—were of considerable importance.

Nevertheless there was change. Amongst the more significant achievements of the nineteenth century was that it reduced and then removed the age-long threat of famine from most of the people of Europe.[91] Further, a considerable improvement in the dietary was visible, at least in western Europe where white bread had driven out black, the consumption of meat had greatly increased, reversing a centuries' long trend, and a wider range of other foodstuffs was available. In many instances people were better dressed. Cotton clothing had replaced linen in western Europe and leather boots had supplanted sabot or bare feet. For the peasant, housing conditions had, however, shown little change and many industrial workers were poorly housed in dirty, noisome, noisy dwellings. Agriculture had become in the more developed parts of Europe a residual industry and the benefits of industrialisation had to a considerable extent passed it by. So while certain groups of organised workers were able to influence their hours and working conditions, the life of the agricultural labourer remained as arduous as ever. Though the industrial worker benefited to some extent from legislative and collective action, it may well be that before 1914, the effect of mechanisation was to increase the intensity of work. Better nourished and better clothed they might be, but hard work was still their lot. 'Never', wrote d'Avenel in 1896, 'never has this French people of ours been so happy as it is to-day, and never has it believed itself more to be pitied. Its grievances have grown with its comfort; and in proportion as its condition became better it deemed it worse.

90. James Mavor, *An Economic History of Russia* (2nd ed. Dent, 1925) II, 351–2, quoted in Hanson, *The Consumer in the Soviet Economy*, p. 22.
91. Clapham, *France and Germany*, p. 402.

The mark of this century, favoured among all the centuries, is to be dissatisfied with itself'.[92] And as prices rose more sharply than wages from about 1896, standards of life were threatened. In the ten years before the war, English specialists noted that German rags were not quite as good as they used to be. 'This', as Sir John Clapham noted, 'is a sure test; for prosperous nations and classes throw away their clothes early. The best rags on the market are American and Canadian; the worst Italian and Greek'.[93]

Engels had forecast that the progress of industrial capitalism would bring the immiserisation of the poor and there were others who argued that while the rich had got richer, the poor had got poorer. Engels' prophecy was certainly falsified and it is doubtful whether the poorest could have got any poorer. But whether the gap had in fact widened it is very difficult to estimate. To some extent any conclusion depends not only on material welfare but also on value judgments. As the foregoing pages have suggested, much work still remains to be done before well-substantiated conclusions can be obtained about changes in the pattern of demand between the middle of the eighteenth century and the first decade of the twentieth. A chapter such as this can do no more than sketch rather impressionistically the outlines of the subject, indicate something of its scope and set out, where appropriate, the rather tentative generalisations which are possible at the present time.

92. Clapham, *France and Germany*, p. 406.
93. Clapham, *France and Germany*, p. 407.

BIBLIOGRAPHY

Demand has been a neglected subject both because source material, although voluminous, is not easy to handle, particularly with respect to individual consumers, and because economists and historians have tended to be more interested in production, in supply than in demand. The consumer has been little discussed except by:

Elizabeth W. Gilboy, 'Demand in the Industrial Revolution', *Facts and Factors in Economic History: Articles by Former Students of Edwin Francis Gay* (Harvard U.P., 1932) pp. 621–39; reprinted in Ronald Max Hartwell, ed. *The Causes of the Industrial Revolution* (Methuen, 1967) 121–38.

Simon Kuznets, 'Quantitative Aspects of the Economic Growth of Nations, VII. The Share and Structure of Consumption', *Economic Development and Cultural Change*, X (1962) 1–92.

Ada E. Levett, *The Consumer in History* (Benn, 1929).

General works of relevance include the following:

Colin Clark, *The Conditions of Economic Progress* (Macmillan, 2nd ed., 1951; 3rd ed. 1957).

Alexander Gerschenkron, *Economic Backwardness in Historical Perspective* (Cambridge, Mass: Belknap P., 1962).

Cambridge Economic History of Europe, Vol. VI. The Industrial Revolutions and After: incomes, population and technological change (Cambridge U.P., 1965).

John A. Hobson, *Work and Wealth: a human valuation* (Macmillan, 1914).

Simon Kuznets, *Modern Economic Growth: rate, structure and spread* (New Haven: Yale U.P., 1966).

David Landes, *The Unbound Prometheus: technological change and industrial development in western Europe from 1750 to the present* (Cambridge U.P., 1969).

Frederick L. Nussbaum, *A History of the Economic Institutions of Modern Europe: an introduction to* Der Moderne Kapitalismus *of Werner Sombart* (New York: Crofts, 1937; New York: Kelley, 1969).

For some relevant statistics in summary form, see:

Thomas S. Ashton, 'Some Statistics of the Industrial Revolution in Britain', *Transactions of the Manchester Statistical Society*, 1947–8, reprinted in Eleanora M. Carus-Wilson, *Essays in Economic History*, III (Arnold, 1962) pp. 237–51.

Brian R. Mitchell and Phyllis Deane, *Abstract of British Historical Statistics* (Cambridge U.P., 1962).

Axel Gustav Sundbarg, *Aperçus statistiques internationaux* (Stockholm, 1908).

There is an embarrassing volume and variety of source material of varying degrees of reliability since the 'standard of living' question has frequently given rise to polemical writings. First, some collections of documents which contain relevant material:

Robert Forster and Elborg Forster, ed. *European Society in the Eighteenth Century* (Macmillan, 1969).

Sidney Pollard and Colin Holmes, *Documents of European Economic History*, Vol. I. *The Process of Industrialisation, 1750–1870*; Vol. II. *Industrial Power and National Rivalry, 1870–1914* (Arnold, 1968, 1972).

Peter Putnam, *Seven Britons in Imperial Russia, 1698–1812* (Princeton U.P., 1952).

Doreen Warriner, *Contrasts in Emerging Societies: readings in the social and economic history of south-eastern Europe in the nineteenth century* (Athlone P., 1965).

Then a few selected contemporary works:

Thomas C. Banfield, *Industry of the Rhine*, series I. *Agriculture: embracing a view of the social condition of the rural population of that district; series II. Manufactures: embracing a view of the social condition of the manufacturing population of that district* (London, 1846, 1848).

Isabella Beeton, *The Book of Household Management* (London, 1861: Cape, 1968).

Charles Booth, *Life and Labour of the People of London* (17 vols., Macmillan, 1902–4).

William Coxe, *Travels into Poland, Russia, Sweden and*

Denmark, Interspersed with Historical Relations and Political Inquiries (3 vols., London, 1784).

David Davies, *The Case of Labourers in Husbandry Stated and Considered* (London, 1795).

Sir Frederick Morton Eden, *The State of the Poor or an History of the Labouring Classes in England from the Conquest to the Present Period* (3 vols., London, 1797).

Friedrich Engels, *The Condition of the Working-class in England in 1844*, ed. William O. Henderson and William H. Chaloner (Oxford: Blackwell, 1958).

Frédéric Le Play, *Les ouvriers européens: études sur les travaux, la vie domestique et la condition morale des populations ouvrières de l'Europe; précédées d'un exposé de la méthode d'observation* (Paris, 1855; 2nd ed. 6 vols., 1877).

Henry Mayhew, *London Labour and the London Poor: a cyclopaedia of the condition and earnings of those that will work, those that cannot work and those that will not work* (4 vols., London, 1861–2).

Benjamin Seebohm Rowntree, *Poverty: a study of town life* (Macmillan, 1901).

Hippolyte A. Taine, *Notes on England*, ed. William F. Rae (London, 1872); ed. Edward Hyams (Thames & Hudson, 1957).

Arthur Young, *Travels in France During the Years 1787, 1788 and 1789*, ed. Constantia Maxwell (Cambridge U.P., 1929).

Government reports also contain a vast amount of material.

For Great Britain, there are a number of works which deal with aspects of this subject, see, in particular:

John Burnett, *A History of the Cost of Living* (Penguin Books, 1969).

———, *Plenty and Want: a social history of diet in England from 1815 to the present day* (Nelson, 1966).

George D. H. Cole and Raymond Postgate, *The Common People 1746–1938* (Methuen, 1938).

Phyllis Deane, *The First Industrial Revolution* (Cambridge U.P., 1965).

Phyllis Deane and William A. Cole, *British Economic Growth, 1688–1959: trends and structure* (2nd ed., Cambridge U.P., 1967).

Sydney Pollard and David W. Crossley, *The Wealth of Britain, 1085–1966* (Batsford, 1968).

Alan Prest and Arthur A. Adams, *Consumers' Expenditure in the United Kingdom, 1900–1919* (Cambridge U.P., 1954).

For other European countries, material in English is not plentiful but see:

William J. Ashley, *The Progress of the German Working Classes in the Last Quarter of a Century* (Longmans, 1904).

Jerome Blum, *Noble Landowners and Agriculture in Austria 1815–1848: a study in the origins of the peasant emancipation of 1848* (Baltimore: Johns Hopkins, 1944).

John H. Clapham, *The Economic Development of France and Germany 1815–1914* (4th ed., Cambridge U.P., 1936).

Shepherd B. Clough, *The Economic History of Modern Italy* (New York: Columbia U.P., 1964).

Kenneth G. Connell, *Irish Peasant Society: four historical essays* (Oxford: Clarendon P., 1968).

Michael Drake, *Population and Society in Norway, 1735–1865* (Cambridge U.P., 1969).

Philip Hanson, *The Consumer in the Soviet Economy* (Macmillan, 1968).

Eli F. Heckscher, *An Economic History of Sweden* (Cambridge Mass: Harvard U.P., 1954).

Hajo Holborn, *A History of Modern Germany, vol. II. 1648–1840; vol. III. 1840–1945* (Eyre & Spottiswoode, 1964, 1969).

Brynjolf J. Hovde, *The Scandinavian Countries, 1720–1865: the rise of the middle classes* (Ithaca, N.Y.: Cornell U.P., 1948).

Gerald T. Robinson, *Rural Russia under the Old Regime: a history of the landlord-peasant world and a prologue to the peasant revolution of 1917* (New York: Macmillan, 1949).

Jaime Vicens Vives, *An Economic History of Spain* (Princeton U.P., 1969).

For a discussion of food and food supplies, see:

Wilhelm Abel, *Agrarkrisen and Agrarkonjunktur in Mittel-europa vom 13 bis zum 19 Jahrhundert* (Berlin: Paul Parey, 1935).

William J. Ashley, *The Bread of our Forefathers: an inquiry in economic history* (Oxford: Clarendon P., 1928).

Theodore C. Barker, John C. McKenzie and John Yudkin, ed. *Our Changing Fare: two hundred years of British food habits* (McGibbon & Kee, 1966).

Bernard H. Slicher van Bath, *The Agrarian History of Western Europe, AD 500–1850* (Arnold, 1963).

Jack C. Drummond and Anne Wilbraham, *The English-man's Food: five centuries of English diet* (Cape, 1939; 2nd ed. revised by Dorothy D. F. Hollingsworth, 1957).

Mancur Olson, jnr., *The Economics of Wartime Shortage: a history of British food supplies in the Napoleonic Wars and in World Wars I and II* (Durham, N.C.: Duke U.P., 1963).

Redcliffe N. Salaman, *The History and Social Influence of the Potato* (Cambridge U.P., 1949).

Paul Lamartine Yates, *Food, Land and Manpower in Western Europe* (Macmillan, 1960).

For retailing and distribution, see:

David Alexander, *Retailing in England During the Industrial Revolution* (Athlone P., 1970).

Dorothy Davis, *A History of Shopping* (Routledge & Kegan Paul, 1966).

James B. Jeffreys, *Retail Trading in Great Britain, 1850–1950* (Cambridge U.P., 1954).

Peter Mathias, *Retailing Revolution: a history of multiple trading in the food trades based upon the Allied Suppliers group of companies* (Longmans, 1967).

Henry Pasdermadjian, *The Department Store, its origin, evolution and economics* (Newman Books, 1954).

For clothes and consumption goods, see:

François Boucher, *A History of Costume in the West* (Thames & Hudson, 1967).

Caroline A. Foley, 'Fashion', *Economic Journal*, III (1893) 458–74.

James Laver, *Taste and Fashion from the French Revolution to the Present Day* (new ed. Harrap, 1945).

Alfred Rive, 'The Consumption of Tobacco since 1600', *Economic History*, I (1926) 57–75.

Edith Saunders, *The Age of Worth, Couturier to the Empress Eugénie* (Longmans, Green, 1954).

Werner Sombart, *Luxury and Capitalism* (Ann Arbor: University of Michigan P., 1967).

Thorstein B. Veblen, *The Theory of the Leisure Class: an economic study in the evolution of institutions* (New York: Macmillan, 1899).

For building and the growth of towns, see:

Sidney D. Chapman, ed., *The History of Working Class Housing: a symposium* (Newton Abbot: David & Charles, 1971).

Harold J. Dyos, ed., *The Study of Urban History: the proceedings of an international round-table conference of the Urban History Group at Gilbert Murray Hall, University of Leicester, on 23–26 September 1966* (Arnold, 1968).

John Parry Lewis, *Building Cycles and Britain's Growth* (Macmillan, 1965).

Lewis Mumford, *The Culture of Cities* (Secker & Warburg, 1940).

John N. Tarn, *Working Class Housing in 19th-century Britain* (Lund Humphries, 1971).

Adna Ferrin Weber, *The Growth of Cities in the Nineteenth Century: a study in statistics* (New York: Columbia College, 1899).

For wages and the standard of living, see:

Thomas S. Ashton, 'Changes in the Standards of Comfort in Eighteenth-century England', *Proceedings of the British Academy*, XLI (1955) 171–87.

——, 'The Standard of Life of the Workers of England 1790–1830', *Journal of Economic History*, IX (1949) supplement, pp. 19–38.

Gosta A. Bagge, Erik Lundberg and Ingvor Svennilson, *Wages in Sweden 1860–1930* (2 vols., P. S. King, 1933–5).

Arthur L. Bowley, *Wages and Income in the United Kingdom since 1860* (Cambridge U.P., 1937).

Ernest H. Phelps Brown and Sheila V. Hopkins, 'Seven Centuries of Building Wages', *Economica*, new series, XXII (1955) 195–206 reprinted in Eleanora M. Carus-Wilson, ed., *Essays in Economic History*, II (Arnold, 1962) pp. 168–78.

———, 'Seven Centuries of the Prices of Consumables, Compared with Builders' Wage-rates', *Economica*, new series, XXIII (1956) 296–314 reprinted in Carus-Wilson, ed. *Essays in Economic History*, II, 179–96.

Ernest H. Phelps Brown and Margaret H. Browne, *A Century of Pay: the course of pay and production in France, Germany, Sweden, the United Kingdom and the United States of America, 1860–1960* (Macmillan, 1968).

Ashok V. Desai, *Real Wages in Germany, 1871–1913* (Oxford U.P., 1968).

Elizabeth Gilboy, 'The Cost of Living and Real Wages in Eighteenth Century England', *Review of Economic Statistics*, XVIII (1936), 134–43.

Ronald Max Hartwell, *The Industrial Revolution and Economic Growth* (Methuen, 1971).

Eric J. Hobsbawm, *Labouring Men: studies in the history of labour* (Weidenfeld & Nicolson, 1964).

Jürgen Kuczynski, *A Short History of Labour Conditions in Germany 1800 to the Present Day* (Muller, 1945).

Karl Gunnar Myrdal, *The Cost of Living in Sweden 1830–1930* (P. S. King, 1933).

George G. Stigler, 'The Early History of Empirical Studies of Consumer Behaviour', *Journal of Political Economy*, LXII (1954) 95–113

Poul Thestrup, *The Standard of Living in Copenhagen, 1730–1800: some methods of measurement* (Copenhagen: Institute of Economic History, 1971).

For other topics, see:

Cyril B. Falls, *A Hundred Years of War* (Duckworth, 1953).

Roy Lewis and Angus E. U. Maude, *The English Middle Classes* (Phoenix House, 1949).

Dorothy Marshall, *The English Domestic Servant in History* (Historical Association, 1949).

John U. Nef, *War and Human Progress: an essay on the rise of industrial civilisation* (Routledge & Kegan Paul, 1950).

Sir Alexander M. Carr Saunders and Paul A. Wilson, *The Professions* (Oxford: Clarendon Press, 1933).

Charles Singer, Eric J. Holmyard, Alfred Rupert Hall and Trevor I. Williams, *A History of Technology, vol. IV. The Industrial Revolution, c. 1750–c.1850; vol. V. The Late Nineteenth Century, c. 1850–c. 1900* (Oxford: Clarendon Press, 1958).

3. Technological Progress and the Industrial Revolution 1700–1914

Samuel Lilley

TECHNOLOGY BEFORE THE INDUSTRIAL REVOLUTION

To the economic and social historian the Industrial Revolution of the eighteenth and nineteenth centuries is characterised by a host of novelties — the more or less rapid transition from domestic or workshop to factory production, and from *manu*facture in the literal sense to *machino*facture; a spectacular development in the capitalistic form of industrial organisation, and the growth — for the first time on a significant scale — of a proletariat that owned nothing but its ability to work; the development of national and international markets in run-of-the-mill products rather than luxuries; the attainment within a few decades of a stage at which an industrial economy could continue to expand indefinitely by the plough-back of its own profits as capital; and a great deal more.

In technological history the first impression is also of novelty — a spate of revolutionary inventions entirely transforming the technological scene. But more sober consideration tends to change the emphasis from novelty to continuity. The technological aspect of the Industrial Revolution (or at least its earlier phases) is better regarded as an acceleration — an *enormous* acceleration, it is true — in a process that had been going on since early in the Middle Ages.

There have been two great Technological Revolutions in the story of mankind[1]. The first began with the advent of agriculture about 8000 B.C. It gave us all the basic agricultural techniques, including irrigation. It created the textile, pottery and metallurgical industries, and the technology of fermentation — for both bread and beer. To transport it contributed the sailing ship and the wheeled

1. Apart from the tool-making and fire-using revolution that started the human story.

cart, together with the harnessing of animals to draw cart
and plough. It developed specialisation enough to cope with
the complexities of mining and metallurgical industry; and
an organisation of labour that could build the pyramids. It
brought mankind from savagery to civilisation.

But around 2500 B.C. technological advance ground almost to a stop; and during the next three thousand years
rather little progress took place. Iron metallurgy, which
came around 1400 B.C., was of crucial importance. The
Greeks made some modest applications of animal power to
drive machinery. Late in the pre-Christian era the water
wheel was invented — but used only for corn milling, and
even for that only to a very small extent. A few other devices
— like gears, screws and cams — date from the classical
period. But when compared with the revolution that preceded them, these three millenia constitute a technological
stagnation.

It was early in the Middle Ages that men began to find
a way out of this impasse[2] From the sixth century on the
water-driven corn mill spread rapidly in western Europe.
And from the eleventh century water power was applied
to an ever-widening range of industrial processes — fulling
cloth; driving forge hammers and metallurgical bellows,
sawmills and grindstones; crushing ore, woad, tan bark and
other materials, and grinding pigments; water-lifting and
irrigation; pulping paper and driving lathes. By the mid-
fourteenth century water power could in principle be
applied to drive almost any machine, if the load of work
warranted it. The windmill appeared in the late twelfth
century and was in turn used for industrial power (though
less widely than water).

The ancient harness, developed first for oxen, was ill-
suited for the horse — wasting at least two-thirds of its
power. Yet it remained unchanged until the development
of the modern harness between the ninth and twelfth centuries. With the addition of iron shoes and the tandem

2. Many of the following inventions were anticipated in, and may
well have come from, China. But for our purpose it is the European use
of a technique that matters, and only European dates are given below.

harness about the same time, the horse at last became available as an efficient source of power in agriculture and transport, and as yet another industrial prime mover.

The inefficient steering oar, which had lasted unchanged in principle since prehistoric times, was replaced from the thirteenth century on by the modern sternpost rudder. The greater control that resulted permitted the rapid development of rigging, culminating in the full-rigged ship of the fifteenth century. Other medieval contributions to transport included the ship's compass (twelfth century) and the canal lock (fourteenth).

The spinning-wheel arrived in the thirteenth century — the first advance on the free-hanging spindle which had appeared some nine millennia earlier, and a typical example of how the Middle Ages took things that were little more than tools in the ancient world and turned them into true machines. The flimsy ancient loom, with its minimum of mechanical aids, was transformed into a machine that was set in a sturdy frame and equipped with rollers, a suspended reed, a shedding mechanism worked by treadles and other devices.

Metallurgy (as mentioned above) came to use much water power — another example being water-driven wire drawing from the mid-fourteenth century. Plant increased greatly in size. And — purely as a result of scale changes — cast iron was produced in the thirteenth century[3], though not widely used till the fifteenth.

Higher levels of mechanical sophistication are implied in the development of the mechanical clock (fourteenth century) and of printing (key transitions in mid-fifteenth century). And in the course of all this, medieval man came to understand the use of such basic devices as crank, connecting rod, treadle, and cord (or belt) drive — to which the fifteenth and sixteenth centuries added a wide variety of contrivances for linking one mechanical motion to another.

This great flow of inventions reached a maximum in the thirteenth century and after about 1350 there was some slowing down. But heavy power-driven machinery in min-

3. Previously only wrought iron could be made.

ing and metallurgy grew rapidly in scale during the fifteenth to seventeenth centuries. And the textile technology, which was to prove so important in the Industrial Revolution, benefited from several key inventions: the flyer added to the spindle[4] in the fifteenth century, the knitting machine or stocking frame (1589), the ribbon loom (early seventeenth century) and gig-mills for raising the nap (mid-sixteenth).

Despite occasional hesitations this second Technological Revolution has been going on continuously from the early Middle Ages up to our time — and beyond. And the technological changes of the Industrial Revolution are to be thought of as a phase — a crucially important phase, but still only a phase — of this long-term movement.

The early stages of the Industrial Revolution — roughly up to 1800 — were based very largely on using medieval techniques and on extending these to their limits. For example, though the increasing application of power is one of the typical trends of the time, it is quite misleading to think of this mainly in terms of steam. The cotton mills that led the change from cottage to factory were powered by water wheels — most of them a good deal smaller than those of 36 foot diameter that Agricola had described in 1556. The first mills were a generation old before steam seriously entered the picture[5]. The long slow expansion of the iron industry was similarly based on ever increasing amounts of water power — though the advent of the Watt engine for providing blast (1776) and driving forge-hammers (1783) perhaps came in the nick of time. And one has only to wander about England with the eyes of an industrial archaeologist to notice that until well after 1800 *new* projects in al-

4. To enable spinning and winding the thread onto the bobbin to be done simultaneously instead of alternately.

5. The first application of steam to cotton-spinning in 1786 (not 1785, as usually stated) was a mill owner's desperate response to arbitrary interference with his water supply by the Fifth (or 'wicked') Lord Byron. See J. P. Marshall, 'Early Applications of Steam Power: the Cotton Mills of the Upper Leen', *Transactions of the Thoroton Society of Nottingham* 60 (1956), 34–43. A good many years were to pass before many thought it worthwhile to change to steam.

most every industry commonly adopted water[6] rather than steam to drive the machinery. The first phase of the Industrial Revolution relied heavily on medieval sources of power.

The transport system that had to cope with moving ever increasing quantities of raw materials and finished goods was again based entirely on perfected versions of medieval techniques, used on a grander scale. Exports and imports were carried in ships that were in principle the same as those that had developed in the two centuries after the introduction of the sternpost rudder. Changes in scale and improvements in design there had certainly been in plenty during the sixteenth and seventeenth centuries. The steering-wheel was introduced in 1705, but (surprisingly enough) no startling progress took place during the eighteenth century[7]. Internally the goods were carried in vehicles made efficient by medieval developments in the harness (though on a much better road system) or on canals that could climb hills to reach almost any destination thanks to the fourteenth-century invention of the lock. Only when these existing techniques had been pushed to their limit did the nineteenth century turn to the development of railways and steamships.

Cast iron was the last important addition to the catalogue of materials available for engineering before the coming of cheap steel in the 1850s[8]. The eighteenth and early nineteenth centuries, despite the enormous increase in demand, were content to develop methods that would make existing materials — particularly iron — available on a greater scale. And a similar tale could be told in other spheres. By contrast, it would *not* be possible to regard medieval technology as mainly a continuation of trends begun in classical times. The real break in technological continuity came at the beginning of the Middle Ages, not in the eighteenth century.

6. Or less frequently wind or animal power.
7. *A History of Technology* (ed. by Charles Singer and others) *3* (London, 1957), 495, and *4* (1958), 574.
8. Huntsman's crucible steel of the 1740s was costly, and was used mainly for cutlery.

TECHNOLOGICAL CHANGE IN THE EARLY INDUSTRIAL REVOLUTION

Bearing in mind, then, the idea that much of the eighteenth century technology is less a new departure than a completion of medieval developments, let us now survey some of those lines in which the biggest changes did occur. And we must obviously begin with cotton — the industry which first demonstrated the possibility of growth at completely unprecedented rates. Production of the British cotton industry expanded ten times between 1760 and 1785, and more than ten times again between then and 1827[9].

Curiously enough the two most original of the inventions that contributed to this progress were made long before the expansion started, and were (naturally) aimed at the then much more important woollen industry. These were Kay's flying shuttle of 1733, which roughly doubled the weaver's output, and Lewis Paul's use of rollers to draw out the rovings as part of a power-driven spinning machine (patent 1738; in action 1741 powered by two asses, and water-driven in 1743). Neither of these had much immediate effect, but when the flying shuttle came into general use in Lancashire in the 1750s and 60s — at a time when the market was expanding vigorously — it led to a shortage of yarn[10]. One natural consequence was a series of inventions designed to improve the productivity of the ordinary cottage spinning-wheel. But these were a mere prelude to the machines of Hargreaves, Arkwright and Crompton which were to revolutionise the industry.

Hargreaves's 'spinning jenny' (perfected 1768) merely imitated the actions of a spinner using the cottage wheel in its primitive form without flyer[11]), and linked these together in such a way as to allow one operator to work

9. As measured by its consumption of raw cotton (retained imports).

10. Previously it had taken 3 to 5 spinners to keep one weaver going. Now the disparity was much increased.

11. The flyer was not well suited to cotton spinning and was more used for wool and linen.

several spindles (eventually 100 or so). It was not adaptable to power drive. Arkwright's 'water frame' or 'throstle' (1769), on the other hand, was specifically intended for use with water or animal power. It used rollers (in the manner of Paul, perhaps re-invented independently) to draw out the rovings, but otherwise it was essentially the late medieval spinning wheel (*with* flyer this time) with power drive added. At first it even employed the traditional device of placing pins on the flyer to allow a spinner to guide the thread evenly on to the bobbin[12] — thus demonstrating how closely Arkwright was imitating his model.

Arkwright's rollers apart, both these machines were constructed entirely from the elements that made up the old spinning wheel. There had to be more interlinking than formerly of the motions of the various parts, but all the requisite linking devices had been developed well before the end of the sixteenth century and would be familiar to anybody interested in machinery. Much the same might be said of Crompton's 'mule' (completed 1779), which combined elements of both earlier machines, though it was already growing a little more complicated. Like the jenny it was merely a device for multiplying the number of spindles that could be operated by a skilled spinner, who must intervene several times in its complicated cycle; and it was not at first suitable for power drive.

From 1790 attempts were made to adapt the mule for power. And by 1800 it had become a power-driven factory machine, though still requiring the services of a skilled operator to control it. Between 1825 and 1830 Richard Roberts developed the fully self-acting mule — an automatic power-driven machine that no longer required skilled attention. During these later phases the mule had been growing very much more complicated, and it is significant that the final version was not created by a carpenter and weaver (Hargreaves) or a barber and hair dealer (Arkwright) or a weaver and farmer (Crompton) — all of whom were self-trained in the mechanical arts — but by a man whose trade was machine-maker and who had worked

12. This was replaced by an automatic mechanism a few years later.

under that king of mechanics, Henry Maudslay, and was himself the inventor of an improved lathe and a planer.

As the productivity of the spinning industry increased by factors of a few hundred to one, it was the weaving end that now formed the bottleneck. The obvious answer was a power loom. But, just as the hand loom is a much more complicated machine than the spinning wheel, so it was far more difficult to create an effective power loom than to invent a jenny or water frame. Cartwright's machine of 1787 need not be thought of as more than a brave pioneering effort, and it took the work of more than a generation of industrious and gifted men to produce a power loom productive enough and reliable enough to displace the hand loom weaver from what had become almost a privileged position. The model that eventually 'broke through' was, significantly enough, again produced (about 1822) by that same machine-building specialist, Roberts, who created the self-acting mule[13]. Even then the power loom was for many years only suitable for the coarser weaves.

Needless to say, the transfer of the cotton industry from cottage to factory depended on the effective mechanisation of many auxiliary processes — carding, drawing and roving at the start and various finishing processes at the end. But a detailed study of these would throw little further light on the conditions in which the cotton expansion took place.

In summary, we may say that, apart from the one really novel idea of drawing out by rollers, the cotton-spinning inventions up to about 1800 were essentially a matter of connecting together in new combinations the parts of the spinning wheel which had been familiar for centuries. These were 'easy' inventions to make in the sense that they re-required no special qualifications or training. They could be made by any intelligent man who had sufficient enthusiasm and sufficient commercial vision. Merely 'wanting to' strongly enough was in itself almost all that was required. (At a later stage — that of the power loom and self-acting

13. Basing himself largely on the work of William Horrocks a decade earlier.

mule — the technical difficulties became much more severe. But by then the industry, cross-fertilised with some branches of engineering, had already created a new type of expert in machine building.)

This is not a story of sophisticated inventions breaking through some critical technological barrier, and so *creating* the conditions for expansion. Developments that were technically so simple can only be *responses* to social and economic conditions that offered widening opportunities for self-advancement through innovation. The statistics of the expansion support this view. As Figure 1 shows, the eighteenth-century story of cotton falls into three distinct periods, in each of which production increased at a remarkably constant rate. From the first decade of the century to the 1740s the rate of growth was about 1.4 per cent per annum[14]. Then it changed suddenly to 2.8 per cent per annum, maintaining that rate till the seventies. And in the third period, from then till the early nineteenth century, the annual rate leaped up to 8.5 per cent. The key inventions of Hargreaves, Arkwright and Crompton follow two or three decades *after* the first of these accelerations in the industry's growth rate, and can reasonably be inferred to be consequences of the new incentives and opportunities which more rapid expansion created[15].

The inventions did not initiate cotton's explosive expansion. But — as the third sector of the graph clearly shows — once they had been made, the rate of expansion could rise to levels that would previously have been quite impossible. The hundred-fold growth in production between 1760 and 1827 could not have been achieved by a hundred-fold increase in the labour force, but only by the rises in productivity which the spinning machinery and eventually the power looms provided. The improved quality, as well as the lower prices, of the yarn produced by the new machines enabled cotton to take the place of linen and silk for many

14. Compound interest.
15. The delayed introduction of Kay's and Paul's earlier inventions also seems to indicate that market demand, not supply of inventions, dominated the situation.

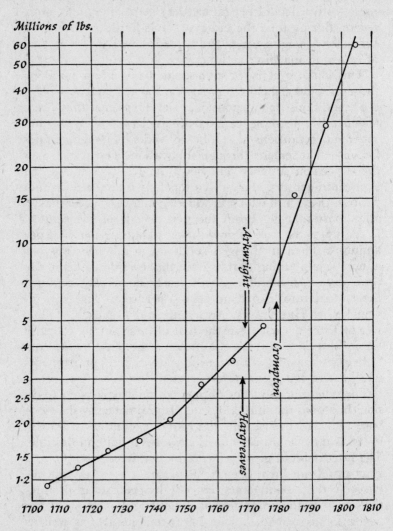

Fig. 1. The growth of cotton production in Britain during the eighteenth century. Each plotted point shows the average quantity of retained imports of raw cotton (in millions of lb., logarithmic scale) for a decade, 1700–09, 1710–19, etc. The straight lines show the general trends (as determined by statistical methods).

purposes, and British cotton to oust its competitors from practically every market — and so the hundred-fold increase could be sold.

No other industry underwent the explosive development of cotton. But in two cases —iron and steam power — a long, slow or hesitant evolution, throughout the century and beyond, produced changes which in the long run were perhaps more significant. During the last two-thirds of the seventeenth century and the first third of the eighteenth the British iron industry had been in slow decline. If the trend had continued, there would have been small chance of the Industrial Revolution ever getting beyond the pre-liminary cotton outburst. The trouble was not lack of de-mand — English consumption of iron was high (compared with other countries) and rising sturdily, but was being supplied by increasing imports, chiefly from Sweden. The industry was, in fact, being slowly starved by a growing shortage of wood[16] —for the available supplies, never very ample in Britain, grew increasingly inadequate to cope with population expansion and industrial growth.

In principle the way out of the difficulty had been under-stood since the early seventeenth century — the substitution of coal for wood. But the technical difficulties were immense. The idea of using coke[17] — obtained from coal essentially as charcoal is got from wood — was perhaps fairly obvious. But problems of choosing appropriate ores and coals, estab-lishing correct proportions between materials and so on could only be solved by laborious trial and error. Abraham Darby produced coke-smelted cast iron in 1709 at Coal-brookdale in Shropshire, but the scanty evidence suggests that it was another decade or so before a reliable process had been evolved — at first much unusable metal was pro-duced and even the best output was of poorish quality.

16. From which was obtained the charcoal for smelting. This explana-tion still seems to be basically true, even if its detail has had to be modified since Nef drew attention to it in 1932. (J. U. Nef, *The Rise of the British Coal Industry.*)

17. Coke had been used in malting since before 1650. In one way or another coal had replaced wood in many British industries during the sixteenth and seventeenth centuries.

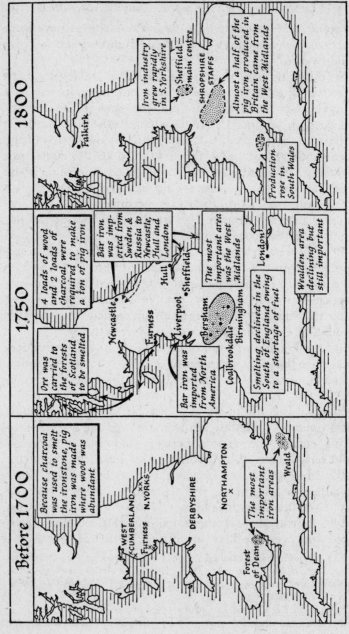

Fig. 2. *The changing locations of the iron and steel industry.*

Before 1700

Because charcoal was used to smelt the ironstone, pig iron was made where wood was abundant

WEST CUMBERLAND
Furness ×
N.YORKS ×
DERBYSHIRE ×
NORTHAMPTON ×

Forest of Dean ×××
The most important iron areas
Weald

1750

4 loads of wood and 2 loads of charcoal were required to make a ton of pig iron

Ore was carried to the forests of Scotland to be smelted

Bar iron was imported from North America

Newcastle
Furness
Liverpool
Bersham
Coalbrookdale
Birmingham

Bar iron was imported from Sweden & Russia to Newcastle, Hull and London

Hull
Sheffield

The most important area was the West Midlands

London

Smelting declined in the South of England owing to a shortage of fuel

Wealden area declining but still important

1800

Falkirk

Iron industry grew rapidly in S.Yorkshire

Sheffield main centre
SHROPSHIRE
STAFFS

Almost a half of the pig iron produced in Britain came from the West Midlands

Production rose in South Wales

J. L. Gayler et. al. A Sketch-map Economic History of Britain (Harrap 3rd ed. 1965).

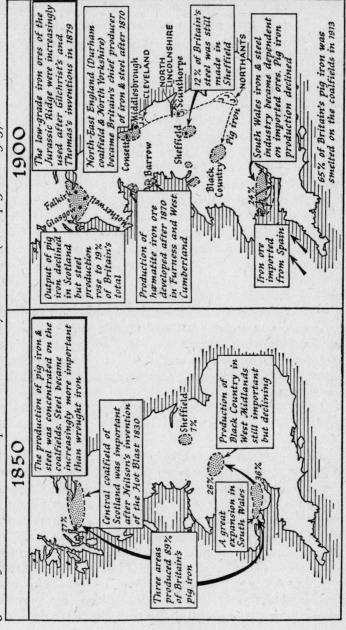

However Darby was a foundryman[18], and for this side of the trade — as contrasted with the then more important conversion of pig to wrought iron — coke-smelting had important advantages. It gave a more liquid metal, which permitted much finer, and eventually much larger, castings to be made. And so the Darby firm flourished, at first in the making of small articles like bellied three-legged cauldrons, fire grates, smoothing irons, pestles and mortars and the like — all of higher quality than the charcoal furnaces could produce — and later in producing much bigger castings to cater for the larger and more elaborate machinery that expanding industry was demanding. Cylinders for Newcomen steam engines were at first made, expensively, of brass. But the Darby firm demonstrated in 1722 that it could successfully cast even such large pieces. This became an important part of the firm's trade — reaching in 1763 a 7 ton cylinder of 74 inch diameter, 10½ feet long. In fact, around the mid-century cast iron was rapidly replacing wood in many engineering uses: Smeaton specified it in 1754 for the main shaft of a windmill; soon it came into use for gear wheels, water-wheel shafts, and the like; and Abraham Darby III demonstrated its structural possibilities in the iron bridge over the Severn (1779), the main ribs of which are 70 feet long.

These later developments were much facilitated by the practice of re-melting the iron in a second furnace, instead of casting it direct — which considerably improved the quality — and by advances in the means of providing blast. About 1760 Smeaton replaced the traditional bellows with cast-iron cyclinders; and in 1776 Wilkinson installed one of the first Watt engines to blow a furnace. Yet despite all this, the industry was very slow to change. Even in 1760 there were only 17 blast furnaces in Britain that used coke for smelting; and the number had only reached 31 in 1775.

The fact is that the production of *castings* — in which the new process was eminently successful — was then much less important than the conversion of cast (pig) iron into wrought iron, whose malleability and tensile strength made

18. A maker of castings.

Thousands of tons

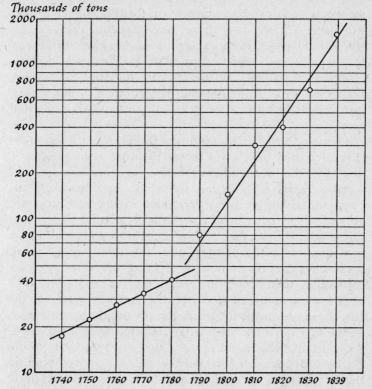

Fig. 3. *The expansion of pig iron production (thousands of tons, logarithmic scale) in England, 1740–1839.*
A History of Technology *ed. Singer, vol. 4 O.U.P.*

it the prince of useful metals till the coming of cheap steel. Coke-smelted iron was at first of a quality that made it unsuitable for conversion to wrought iron. But around 1750 Abraham Darby II started producing a metal that was much better adapted for conversion. Yet the forge-masters[19] seem to have been unnecessarily reluctant to use the new material. The break came when Henry Cort perfected in 1784 his puddling process for converting pig to wrought iron in the reverberatory furnace. Besides substituting coal

19. Makers and workers of wrought iron.

for wood in this second stage of production, Cort's process was more efficient than its predecessors. And this, coupled with some agreement to accept a rather lower quality in return for a much reduced price, led to the rapid adoption of coke-smelted pig as the starting material for conversion to wrought iron. By 1790 there were 81 coke-fuelled furnaces in Britain, against 25 using charcoal. Coke had won.

Though Darby's invention was far more fundamental in character than Cort's, yet it was the latter that eventually liberated the iron industry from the restriction of fuel supply. Figure 3 illustrates the point forcibly. From the 1740s to the 80s pig iron production in England increased at the fairly steady rate of 2 per cent per annum (compound interest). But from then to the 1830s, and presumably as a consequence of Cort's invention, the rate rose to about 6 per cent[20]. If one thinks in terms of the industry's own expansion, then iron's industrial revolution started with Cort's work in the eighties. If one thinks in terms of the size of establishment involved, the revolution began earlier — the Carron works in Scotland started with a capital of £12,000 in 1760, raised to £150,000 in 1774; by 1776 the Darby firm had several furnaces with a turnover of more than £80,000 each. But it is surely more important to think in terms of the contribution of iron to the efficiency of industry in general. And this came in two (overlapping) stages. First there was the development of the casting side to the point where it could provide major parts of machinery and structures. Then, after Cort's work, came the possibility of using wrought iron on a greatly increased scale. This led to reductions in the cost and improvements in the quality of producer durables, and so helped to stimulate further industrial expansion and further invention. And of course developments like the railway system would have been unthinkable without easily available wrought iron.

It may be that future generations will have to revise the accepted view that cotton was the leading sector in the

20. It will be noticed that the detailed figures plotted on the graph show only a very mild effect of war-time boom and post-war slump.

Industrial Revolution. It is at least possible that the fundamental changes were the less spectacular ones that took place in iron and other producer-goods industries, and that the cotton outburst was more in the nature of a symptom exhibited by one particular sensitive organ. One can imagine an Industrial Revolution and a transition to sustained growth without an explosion in cotton; without an expansion in iron it would be inconceivable.

It has already been stressed that the machinery of the early Industrial Revolution was driven by prime movers that had been inherited from the power revolution of the Middle Ages. The development of the steam engine came, as it were, hesitantly and reluctantly as and when it proved no longer possible to cope with expanding needs by the traditional means. The first break was in coal mining. The great seventeenth century expansion in the use of coal, which was so vividly documented by Nef[21], led to a progressive deepening of the pits and so to an enormous increase in the power needed to pump them dry. In 1702 one Warwickshire colliery was using five hundred horses to keep the water at bay. Similar problems were being experienced in tin and lead mining. The limit was being reached.

This was the urgent demand that led to Newcomen's development (1712 or perhaps earlier) of the first commercially successful steam engine (or 'atmospheric' engine). Eminently successful though it was at coal mines, where cheap waste fuel was available[22], the Newcomen engine was too inefficient, too costly in fuel, to be of much service elsewhere[23].

By the 1750s the demand for power was again seriously straining available resources, Newcomen engine included. Scattered as it was over a wide industrial range (the only big concentration outside the mines being in iron working,

21. *Op. cit.* A fourteen-fold expansion occurred between the 1550s and the 1680s.

22. There were 57 engines near Newcastle in 1769.

23. Though it did have some temporary success, because of the high value of the product, at Cornish tin mines and even Derbyshire lead mines.

where water wheels reached 40 feet in diameter by the mid-century), the increased demand would be hard to demonstrate directly. But it is clearly reflected in the strong interest which arose about that time in the improvement of prime movers. Smeaton in the fifties applied scale model techniques to improve the design of both water wheels and windmills. This was the beginning of a long series of highly sophisticated advances in design and construction that brought the water wheel to virtual perfection by about 1830. The windmill, too, was perfected by the addition of the fantail mechanism in 1745, the increasing use of cast iron working parts, the development of devices for automatically adjusting the sails to wind strength (1772-1807), and consistent careful attention to questions of scale and proportion. Around 1770 Smeaton undertook a systematic study which enabled him to bring the Newcomen engine to about the limit of its development. This last was by far the most powerful prime mover then available — reaching up to about 75 horse power in the seventies. But it was a pumping engine only, not adaptable to drive machinery. It is surely a sign of desperation that the Newcomen engine was frequently used to pump water to supply a water wheel to drive machinery — the Darby firm, for example, installed one in 1742 to keep ten wheels going.

These were the conditions in which James Watt was urged on to turn the Newcomen engine into an efficient and versatile source of power. He naturally started by improving the existing pumping engine (and in any case mine drainage still provided the largest single demand). He recognised the basic weakness of the Newcomen engine in 1763, conceived the remedy — his separate condenser — in 1765; and finally, after overcoming immense practical difficulties, delivered the first engines to customers in 1776.

When the pumping engine was safely launched, Watt was persuaded rather reluctantly to turn his attention to a rotative version for driving machinery. The patent was taken out in 1781, and further improvements followed[24].

24. Double-acting engine and expansive working, 1782; centrifugal governor, 1788; steam engine indicator, 1796.

Over the next three decades the steam engine was applied in almost every industry, though it was a long time before its victory over water power was complete.

There is no space to trace the later history of the steam engine, but some important lessons can be learnt by glancing at its applications in the field of transport. The railway story is indeed a strange one. One side of it begins with the crude railways that were in use at German mineheads by 1500, and were introduced at English coal mines shortly after 1600. These were essentially a matter of providing the ordinary horse and cart with a better running surface than a road could give. Before the end of the eighteenth century such railways had become common at British mines and ironworks. Sometimes they catered mainly for internal transport — the Darby iron works had 20 miles of them. Sometimes they connected the works to port or canal, when the nature of the terrain made a feeder canal impossible — the Pen-y-Darran iron works in Glamorganshire had a line 9¾ miles long serving this purpose. By 1820 that county had nearly 250 miles of such railways, and the Newcastle district had almost 400 miles.

In an age that was outgrowing the existing transport system it was natural to think of the application of steam power to traction. Richard Trevithick, working on the problem from about 1797, produced moderately successful road carriages, and then thought of applying his engine to the works railways of the previous paragraph. In 1804 he demonstrated a locomotive on the Pen-y-Darran line, which pulled 10 tons of ore and 70 passengers at 5 miles per hour. The need for something more powerful than horses was being increasingly felt, and so many men worked on this problem — the most successful, of course, being George Stephenson.

Meanwhile a sociologically more novel idea was developing: that of the public railway. This, however, meant a line on which anybody could use his own carriages on paying a toll — a hybrid of works railway and toll road. One was opened in 1805, chiefly for carrying stone and lime from Merstham (Surrey) via Croydon to Wandsworth on the outskirts of London. Nearly 200 miles of such railways began working between 1800 and 1820.

It was with similar intentions that the Stockton-Darlington railway was projected. The Parliamentary Act of 1821 laid down that it should be worked 'with men and horses or otherwise'. On Stephenson's recommendation the amended Act of 1823 also permitted the use of locomotives. But although the company did possess a locomotive when the line was opened in September 1825, and had four by the following spring, yet for some years the bulk of the traffic was conveyed in the vehicles of mine owners and private carriers, horse-drawn[25]. The passenger traffic was carried entirely in converted stage-coaches, operated on the railway by stage-coach companies and using horse traction exclusively. On a single-track railway, provided with sidings at roughly quarter mile intervals and no signalling system, it can be imagined that this mass of unco-ordinated traffic led quickly to confusion. Conventions were worked out as to who should go back if vehicles or trains met between sidings, but eventually the company had to take over the entire working — though not till after the Liverpool-Manchester line had benefited from these experiences.

These details have been given in order to illustrate the sleep-walking manner in which the early railways were developed, with the projectors failing completely to understand what they were doing. Likewise, they were worlds away from appreciating the economic consequences of their acts. They made large profits — but not from the traffic they had taken into account in their estimates. Originally they expected to draw their greatest gains from the haulage of coal from the pits of the Bishop Auckland region for sale at points along the line. They had no hopes of profits from carrying coals to the sea for shipment to London and elsewhere. Yet within a few years they were shipping about half a million tons annually — getting on for a quarter of the London market. When the line was extended four miles along the coast in 1830 to create a new coal-carrying seaport, there was one farmhouse on the spot. Ten years later,

25. With stationary engines and cables for steep inclines.

6,000 people lived there — the town of Middlesbrough.
Before the coming of the line, coach traffic between Stockton
and Darlington carried fourteen or fifteen passengers a
week. And it was on that basis that the meagre passenger-
carrying arrangements were made. Nobody foresaw how
the carriage of coals and merchandise would create its own
passenger traffic — soon amounting to five or six hundred
a week[26]. Of course this was still a small part of the total:
$2\frac{1}{2}$ per cent of receipts in 1828, 7 per cent in 1835. But (to
look ahead for a moment) receipts for passenger traffic on
the Liverpool-Manchester line had by 1835 reached six
times' expectations and formed 53 per cent of total receipts.[27]
And before the end of the thirties passenger traffic had
become the main source of railway income.

The canals, the eighteenth century's first attempt to cope
with transport problems created by growing towns and expanding industry, were by this time turning out to be very
inadequate. The restricted amount of water available put
a limit to the number of canals that could be constructed,
so that the owners enjoyed a monopoly imposed by natural
law rather than by economic manipulation. This monopoly
they ruthlessly exploited, thus providing one of the main
motives for the growth of the railways as described hitherto,
and especially for the establishment of the line that took
the crucial step into modernity. Manchester cotton merchants complained that it took longer to bring their raw
material by canal from Liverpool than to carry it across the
Atlantic. Hence there arose about the year 1821 the idea
of a railway between these two towns. But delays, stemming
mainly from the opposition of landowners and of canal,
coaching and turnpike interests, enabled the projectors to
learn from the Stockton-Darlington experience. And so the
Liverpool-Manchester line, when it was opened in 1830,
was the first public railway in the modern sense of the word

26. The passenger figures are from John Francis, *A History of the
English Railway* (1851, reprint Newton Abbot. c. 1967), 55, and must
not be taken too literally. But the general impression is correct.

27. H. G. Lewin, *Early British Railways* (London and New York, c.
1925), 38.

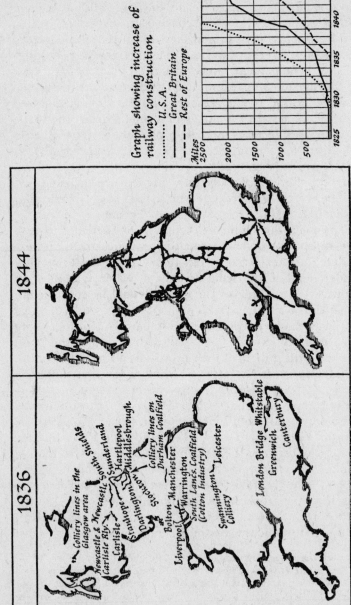

Fig. 4. The growth of the railway network in Britain.

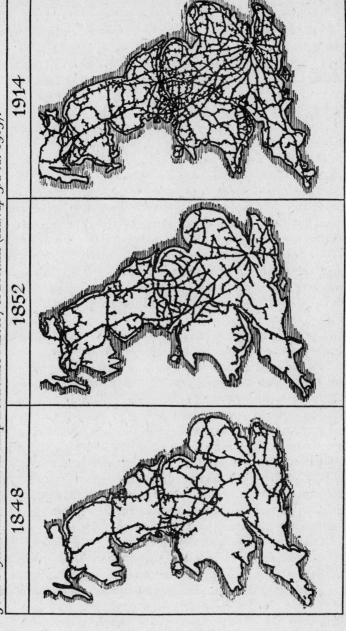

J. L. Gayler et al. A Sketch-map Economic History of Britain (*Harrap 3rd ed. 1965*).

1848   1852   1914

— operated entirely by the company and carrying passengers and freight for a charge in its own trains, hauled by steam locomotives.

The Liverpool-Manchester line demonstrated all the basic principles of railway technology and organisation. It showed, too, that railways paid — by 1833 share values had more than doubled. The rest of the country followed, somewhat cautiously at first (less than 500 miles in operation in 1838), and then with enthusiasm that expanded into the railway booms and yielded 6,000 miles by 1850.

So the railway story down to the eighteen-thirties is far from being a tale of vision and well-planned effort. Various people at various times and places made piecemeal attacks on the several sorts of problems arising from the saturation of the canals and inadequacy of the roads. Nobody envisaged the railway in anything like the form that eventually emerged. But so desperate was the need for improved inland transport that sheer quantity of ill-directed effort led, and within a moderate time, to the railway system which, more than any other single factor, was to ensure that the Industrial Revolution would not be a mere flash in the pan.

The railways flourished almost as soon as the technical and organisational problems had been solved. It was far otherwise with steamships. Though it was by no means obvious how to apply steam power to propel a ship, yet the paddle steamer was convincingly demonstrated in the first decade of the nineteenth century, and by 1815 steam navigation was well established on the rivers of the U.S.A. In Britain there was less need and less opportunity for the inland use of steamships. But on short sea crossings, where regularity was more important than economy, some progress was made with steam packets from 1818 on.

Yet in the great nineteenth century expansion of long distance shipping it was sail, not steam, that made the running. Released from its eighteenth century stagnation, the sailing ship developed more elegant and efficient design, culminating in the 'clippers' of the 1850s. For long journeys steamships could not compete. Too much cargo space had to be sacrificed for carrying coal; and this difficulty was exaggerated by the poor efficiency of the engines. However by the middle of the century engine efficiency was improving rapidly — and could have advanced much faster if the promise of economic reward had been sufficient. The more efficient screw was ready to take over from the paddle as soon as it should be worth anybody's while to tackle the rather simple task of producing engines working at somewhat higher speeds. In 1865 Alfred Holt, engineer turned shipowner, demonstrated that the technical problems had been solved, when his ship carried 3,000 tons of cargo nonstop on the 8,500 mile voyage to Mauritius.

Yet sail continued to dominate the long sea routes, and it was not till 1880 that steam ships accounted for half the carrying power of the chief maritime countries[28]. The point is that economic factors far outweighed technical ones. Steam could not conquer until economic developments gave speed and regularity[29] a value that outweighed the cost of the fuel (for wind is free!) and the loss of cargo space to accommodate engine and fuel. Above all, steam could not win until the volume of international trade justified the establishment of a world-wide system of coaling stations — a process that did not begin till the fifties. It was really the opening in 1869 of the Suez Canal (which itself favoured steam at the expense of sail) that sufficiently stimulated the provision of bunkering facilities. From then on, steam's victory was assured.

What emerges from all these case histories, different though they may be in many respects, is that in every instance it was the general movement of the economy, and not the technical innovations as such, that dictated the pace of change. The inventions came — or at any rate were seriously developed — when economic conditions were ripe.

28. C. Ernest Fayle, *A Short History of the World's Shipping Industry* (London, 1933), 247. Steamships then constituted 25·1 per cent of the tonnage, but (because of their greater speed) could carry an estimated 50·2 per cent of the traffic.

29. Steam's superiority in this regard had been demonstrated as early as 1838, when the *Great Western* crossed the Atlantic *westward* in 15 days, against a normal 40 days or more for fast sailing packets.

Most of the developments studied above also share (in varying degree) another characteristic, typical of the time — they emerged largely from attempts to find a supplement to or substitute for some commodity which, by the laws of nature, could not keep pace with the demands of an expanding economy[30]. The shortage of water or the difficulties of terrain set a limit to the further extension of the canal system. And so — in the curiously blind manner already described — desperate merchants or pit owners were driven to create the railway. The amount of wood available to industry is limited by nature, and so a great deal of technological effort in the seventeenth and eighteenth centuries was concerned with how to use coal in its place. The two key inventions in the iron industry — Darby's near the start of the century, and Cort's towards the end of it — were part of that effort.

Since it was questions of quality that restricted the use of coke-smelted iron until after the middle of the century, one might feel that in this case technical rather than economic factors played the decisive role. But though the improvement of quality involved the solution of difficult technical problems, yet these were of a type that involved no major discovery — merely gradual improvements in operating conditions, arrived at by patient trial and error. The speed of advance would be proportional to effort. While only the Darbys were trying, progress was necessarily slow. But when the expanding market brought in others — like Wilkinson — in the 1750s and after, the accumulation of multiple experience led fairly rapidly to a product of the desired quality.

The case of the steam engine is perhaps less simple. The Newcomen engine came into being because the coal-for-wood trend pushed mine drainage beyond the capacity of the existing prime movers. And it is no insult to Newcomen to say that the scientific and mechanical knowledge avail-

30. In this respect cotton was an exception. Though the market was favourable, there was never any serious threat of a famine in cotton goods.

able at the turn of the century was such that once the need grew strong enough, once enough people started trying to use steam for pumping, *somebody* was bound to succeed. Since the separate condenser was conceptually much the most difficult invention of the century, it will perhaps be urged that this advance at least could not be just a matter of response to economic demands. And that might well be true, though it should also be remembered that many others were trying to improve steam engines, and that the genius is simply the man who arrives first at some point that others are striving towards. The rush of customers shows that the improved pumping engine did not appear ahead of its market. And the drive to develop the rotative engine came less from Watt the inventor than from Boulton the entrepreneur, with his remakable market sense.

It appears, then, that the inventions of the early Industrial Revolution were *primarily* — for we have yet to consider their ultimate consequences — were *primarily* responses to economic demands. Inventors did not act, nor did the social environment encourage them to act, unless the need was already clear — indeed, pressing. This is not surprising. The idea of invention as good in itself, as something that can be reasonably undertaken even when the need is doubtful — this idea is one that could only arise in a world that has passed through an industrial revolution and discovered (as in the case of television) that new techniques, in sufficiently affluent societies, create their own demands. In the eighteenth century or the early nineteenth, one did not normally invent simply because an invention was possible. And what happened when some enthusiasts tried to do just this is shown by the story of steamships. Once the steam engine was established, the idea of applying it at sea was obvious. It attracted quite a large crowd of inventors and projectors — including some of the best pioneer inventors around 1800 and some of the best professional engineers from the 1830s on. Technically these enthusiasts succeeded fairly well, and with a little more support they could have done much better. But the steamship still had to await the slow ripening of economic conditions.

SOME THOUGHTS ABOUT CAUSAL ORIGINS

In the eighteenth century, then, technological innovation was more effect than cause. On a longer time-scale, however, extended back to embrace the medieval period, it may be that technology played a much more important causal role. Dwarfed though they were by subsequent developments, the technological changes of the Middle Ages were greater in scale — by a very large factor — and more radical in kind than any since the start of civilisation. It would not be surprising if they should be found to have played a major part in promoting the sequence of economic, social and political changes that led, in the very long run, to the Industrial Revolution. It could, in fact, be argued (though this is not the place to do so) that trends like the development of large-scale machinery, the increasing complexity of the means of production, and transport improvements that facilitated trade were among the more important factors promoting the break up of the medieval economy and the emergence of the capitalistic type of production.

These long-term speculations apart, it is certainly true that the sixteenth and early seventeenth centuries witnessed a remarkable growth of capitalist enterprise within what was still, when taken as a whole, a modified form of the feudal economy of the Middle Ages. As a result of peculiar historical-geographical circumstances that cannot be discussed here, the lead in this new type of production was taken by the people of what had hitherto been a rather underdeveloped island on the fringe of the European economy. Pre-capitalistic elements might still be quantitatively dominant in seventeenth-century England, but already the capitalist sector — in both agriculture and industry — was beginning to govern the pace and direction of new development. It was here, too, that the political transformations which necessarily accompany such large-scale economic changes first came to fruition, culminating in the revolutions of 1640 and 1688-89.

Despite all the complications that appear when these

revolutions are examined in concrete detail and despite the compromises that emerged from them, it remains true that before the end of the seventeenth century political power in England (to which we can now begin to add Scotland) had been redistributed in a way that favoured the merchant, banker and capitalist farmer — and to a lesser extent the industrial entrepreneur — at the expense of the nobility, big landlords[31] and small craftsmen. Constitution and custom might in theory be supposed to protect the landed interest. In practice, through the borrowings of needy governments and the corruption of a House of Commons whose members were 'more interested in the spoils of office than in political principles'[32], it was money, and anybody who held it, that ruled the country. At first the mercantile interests predominated, but industry was left room to manoeuvre — and eventually to take the major share of political power.

Freed (by and large) from the legal and customary restrictions of the past, capitalistic commerce and capitalistic industry went on to expand at an unprecedented rate. The real output of industry and commerce multiplied nearly four times during the eighteenth century[33]. It was this expansion, and the increasingly bourgeois environment in which it occurred, that constituted the essence of the Industrial Revolution. The technological changes of the eighteenth century were merely some of those things that were bound to arise when ambitious men in these conditions sought a way to the top. The following attempt to trace these connections in more detail owes a great deal to several detailed studies of recent years[34].

31. And in any case the English aristocracy had by now become distinctly bourgeois in outlook — at least in comparison to its continental equivalent.

32. Christopher Hill, *Reformation to Industrial Revolution* (London, 1968), 177.

33. Phyllis Deane and W. A. Cole, *British Economic Growth, 1688–1959* (Cambridge, 1964), 78.

34. To mention but a few, D. S. Landes, 'Technological Change and Development in Western Europe, 1750–1914', being pages 274–601 of *The Cambridge Economic History of Europe 6* (Cambridge, 1965), particu-

Market demand, it was suggested above, was what chiefly brought forth the technological innovations of the eighteenth and early nineteenth centuries. And without question demand was rising vigorously. As a result of the sixteenth and seventeenth century developments mentioned above, England entered the eighteenth century with the highest level of material welfare in the world—having recently overtaken Holland in that respect. The population began to grow[35]—presumably at least in part as a result of higher living standards. The ability of English agriculture (still easily the dominating sector of the economy and now largely capitalist in structure) to expand at a comparable rate avoided Malthusian complications. Living standards continued to rise (or at the worst times did not fall). After buying food and other basic needs, the ordinary family had an increasing (if still small) amount of purchasing power left over for buying manufactured goods. The virtual disappearance of the peasantry meant that almost all economic life passed through the market — contrast the peasant economies still common in Europe. So growing population, rising standards of living and almost universal commercialisation combined to produce a steady expansion of the home market. With income more evenly distributed than on the continent, the demand was largely for articles of everyday use, which could form the basis of mass production industries. As a result of freedom from internal customs barriers (which still afflicted most continental countries) and steady improvements in transport (turnpike roads, 'navigations', and later

---

larly pages 275–314; Phyllis Deane, *The First Industrial Revolution* (Cambridge, 1967); M. W. Flinn, *The Origins of the Industrial Revolution* (London, 1966); R. M. Hartwell (ed.), *The Causes of the Industrial Revolution in England* (London, 1967). What follows can only be the briefest summary of some of the ideas that have emerged from these and other studies, set in a framework for which the present author must take responsibility.

35. Probably not significantly till the 1740s, though the statistical evidence is so uncertain that significant growth even from 1700 on seems plausible to some authorities.

canals) there was a potential *country-wide* mass market for any entrepreneur with the skill to capture it.

The export trade, though smaller in volume than the home, was capable of greater and more rapid expansion — by the 'simple' device of capturing markets from other exporting countries or destroying domestic competition (chiefly in the colonies). And it was here that the British economy derived its most obvious benefits from the political changes of the seventeenth century[36]. The Navigation Acts of 1651 and 1660 laid the foundation of the policy which ensured that Britain would rule the commercial waves — reserving, as they did, a monopoly of trade with British colonies. 'No state was more responsive to the desires of its mercantile classes; no country more alert to the commercial implications of war'[37] — as a result of which most of the best colonial territories were won for Britain. And when the export trade, having advanced fairly steadily since before 1700, put on a spurt in the middle decades of the century[38], it was chiefly to the colonies that the new goods flowed.

The colonies had to depend on Britain for all those manufactures which in a balanced economy would be produced at home — 'nails, axes, firearms, buckets, coaches, clocks, saddles, handkerchiefs, buttons, cordage, and a thousand other things'[39]. And so it was largely the colonial trade that enabled the home country to become an exporter of manufactures in general, instead of depending almost

36. Not that Government action to help home trade was lacking. Parliament's willingness to overrule landed opposition to road and inland navigation improvements served the interests, above all, of merchants and manufacturers. Tariff protection sometimes even favoured manufacturers at the expense of oversea traders.

37. Landes, *op. cit.*, 285–6. And war itself provided another very useful market — as almost certainly the greatest consumer of iron, for instance.

38. A rise of perhaps 75 per cent in domestic exports between 1740 and 1760. But there are many snags in interpreting the statistics (and even more for the statistics of the home market, which were therefore entirely avoided above).

39. R. Davis, 'English foreign trade, 1700–1774', *Economic History Review*, 2nd series, *15*, 290.

exclusively on woollen goods. These exports, it will be noticed, are mainly articles for everyday use, not luxuries — articles, therefore, with mass production possibilities. And it is mass production, with a small profit per unit, rather than the supply of expensive luxuries, that offers the biggest reward for technological innovation. It was, of course, the export market — with a ten-fold increase between 1750 and 1770 — that gave the cotton industry its impetus at a crucial time. Even after that expansion the cotton trade was still tiny compared to wool — by a factor of something like 20. But an entrepreneur seeking a band wagon to jump on would certainly find the cotton prospect more attractive.

This is not the place to discuss the thorny question of the relative importance of the home and export markets. Suffice it to say that they seem often to have complemented each other, the one expanding when the other slackened. The home demand provided reliability — some security for one's investment. The risks and big prizes of the export field provided outstanding opportunities. Between the one and the other there is no difficulty in explaining the demand that led to industrial expansion and technological innovation.

But why should the response to this challenge have come so overwhelmingly in the form of technological innovation? It is not enough to say that the demand could not have been satisfied by any other means. For of course it could have gone unsatisfied. History is littered with instances where much needed technical advances were *not* made, though they were well within the reach of skills available at the time. What factors make one society eager to innovate and leave another content with what it has inherited?

Much of the answer would seem to lie in the class structure of the society. A particularly relevant point concerns the extent to which those who derive unearned wealth from industry[40], and who thus command resources that *could* be

40. Or agriculture, where relevant.

used for its further development, themselves take direct responsibility for the actual processes of production[41]. To take an extreme case, the Bronze Age civilisations of Egypt and Mesopotamia, once they had passed beyond their formative period, settled down to a class structure in which the wealthy ruling class of kings, nobles and priests hardly concerned themselves at all with how things were produced. They focused attention on the process of compelling the peasants and craftsmen to hand over to their masters virtually the whole of their surplus product above what was needed for bare subsistence. This concentration on the art of exploitation, rather than production, left them unaware of obvious deficiencies in production methods and devoid of the knowledge to effect improvements. The peasants and craftsmen must have had the knowledge; but they lacked all incentive, since increased production would benefit only their masters. And so the extreme polarisation of classes in these states led to the technological stagnation — virtually complete for over a thousand years — mentioned near the beginning of this essay[42].

The capitalist industrial organisation provides the extreme opposite of these conditions. Here the entrepreneur who derives his wealth from cotton mill or blast furnace also undertakes complete responsibility for decisions about how production is carried out. In theory, if not always in practice, his employees are mere robots who do what they are told. And so the capitalist entrepreneur is aware — to a degree that no previous exploiter is aware — of how much he stands to gain from this or that technical change. He probably also has enough technological knowledge to judge the practicability of an invention, perhaps even to invent

41. This thesis, if found unsatisfactory, must not be blamed on any of the authorities cited in note 34. The author derived the idea from the works of V. Gordon Childe — particularly *Man Makes Himself* (London, 1937) and *What Happened in History* (Harmondsworth, 1942), but must himself take responsibility for its application to the matter in hand.

42. For a somewhat fuller discussion of this theme and some examples of easy inventions that were not made for millennia, see S. Lilley, *Men, Machines and History* (London, 1965), 18–24, 50–1, 53.

for himself. And the cold steel of competition reinforces this awareness and eliminates those who do not possess it. Hence derives the extreme sensitivity of response to technological opportunity that eighteenth century entrepreneurs repeatedly exhibited.

And so, with the strong capitalist sector that had grown up within the economy in the sixteenth and seventeenth centuries, and with the new freedom won from the revolutions of 1640 and 1688-89, England (with Scotland not far behind) was able to answer the challenge of expanding markets with an unprecedented outburst of technological innovation. English inventive effort was already turning sharply upwards in the 1690s[43]; and soon after that the first important results were achieved — Newcomen's engine, Darby's coke smelting. It is surely significant that the wave of innovation first got going in those sections of industry that were already fully capitalistic, and came much later in fields like cotton, which only arrived at a high degree of capitalism under the influence of the new machines.

The sensitivity of the entrepreneur to the potentialities of profit through technological change probably reached its highest development in the Britain of the eighteenth and early nineteenth centuries[44]. And it offered the inventor far fairer prospects than at any previous time or in any other country. If he was not himself an entrepreneur (like Darby) he seldom had difficulty in getting enough financial backing[45].

Barriers between social classes had been losing their rigidity even before the seventeenth century revolutions, and more rapidly since. So now the country gentleman —

43. W. H. Chaloner and A. E. Musson, *Industry and Technology* (London, 1963), 33; Charles Wilson, *England's Apprenticeship, 1603-1763* (London, 1965), 187-8.

44. Later is was to be modified by the advent of the non-participating shareholder and the financier, who do not take such direct responsibility for what actually goes on in the works.

45. One notes Watt's nine years of inadequate finance before he teamed up with Boulton. But the development costs in this case were of quite exceptional magnitude.

even the noble lord — sought to jump on the entrepreneurial band wagon by developing mines or iron works on
his estate or digging canals. And since he did not himself
know the ins and outs of the business, some ambitious young
man got his chance as manager. More important, in the
more flexible society industrial success became an attractive
avenue to social advancement. Barber's apprentice Arkwright and colliery worker Stephenson could rise to the
top. Members of the middle classes — physician's son Lewis
Paul; Edmund Cartwright, clergyman and son of a clergyman — could find it worthwhile to seek their fortunes in
industry and invention. In earlier tradition, of course, they
would have followed their fathers in some middle-class
profession, free from the taint of trade. A very special role
in the chemical industries was played by Scottish medical
graduates who opted for industry rather than practice[46].
Despite relics of old-fashioned snobbery in sections of what
had once been the aloof aristocracy, industry acquired a
degree of social esteem quite unparalleled in any previous
era; and as a result it could, at last, attract an adequate
proportion of the country's best brain-power.

This social mobility was paralleled by the ease with which
talent could move from one industry to another, following
the prospect of profit. Watt started as an instrument maker.
His partner, Boulton, began as a 'toy-maker' (manufacturer
of trinkets) and went on to make a name for himself, not
just in the steam engine business, but in several other lines
like Sheffield plate, silver plate, minting and mint machinery
and so on. Thus one man's enterprise led to minor revolutions in several distinct manufactures. John Roebuck (pages
228-229 below) moved from medicine to chemical industry,
and then to iron, and tried his hand unsuccessfully with
the steam engine.

To almost every sentence in the last three paragraphs
could be added another contrasting the British position
with that of her rivals — inventors on the continent failing
only for lack of financial backing; an aristocracy standing
aloof from and despising the world of commerce and in-

46. See page 227 below.

dustry; avenues of advancement for ambitious members of the middle classes still confined to the traditional learned professions; industry regarded as socially degrading and therefore left in the hands of the second best; and so on. And finally one would contrast the extent to which continental industry was bound by government regulation and guild control with the comparative freedom of its British counterpart. The contrast must not be overdrawn, for there was not then and never has been, in Britain or anywhere else, an era of unadulterated *laissez faire*. But in practice (though often not in legal theory) British industry was usually allowed to develop in the direction that the profit motive and competition would take it, whereas on the continent guild restrictions and mercantilist controls were maintained and even sometimes strengthened through the eighteenth century. The state-supported industries — intended as forcing houses of industrialisation — were in practice stunted by bureaucratic inefficiency. The story on page 229 below — the Director of a French state industry showing that a revolutionary technique would work, small-scale English and Scottish firms developing it in practice — is a fair symbol of the contrast.

Several other factors can only be mentioned: the supply of capital (there seems to have been no great increase in the rate of capital investment during the eighteenth century, and no shortage of funds for investment, but occasional difficulty in channelling resources where most needed); the role of dissent in creating the ideology of industrial progress (how much was the dissenter's outlook a product, and how much a cause, of industrial success?); and the creation of a proletariat to work the factories (the role of agricultural improvement in releasing labour, and of enclosure in compelling migration to the towns).

In summary it can reasonably be said that, if one takes for granted the state which the world had reached towards the end of the seventeenth century — and particularly the ascendency of capitalist practice and bourgeois attitudes of mind in Britain, and the contrasting situation elsewhere —

then a very plausible explanation can be given of why there should have been an Industrial Revolution in the eighteenth century, why it should have happened in Britain, and why it should have produced the enormous acceleration in technological progress. It may be more difficult to understand the exact timing of the Revolution. But in any case before that problem can be solved, it would be necessary to agree as to just what the dates of the crucial transformation are. When we say Industrial Revolution, do we primarily refer to the cotton explosion in the closing decades of the century? Or was this outburst merely a spectacular flare-up that occurred when more fundamental changes in market conditions and entrepreneurial attitudes, within an economy that was growing in stature all round, impinged on an industry in which the technological problems were peculiarly easy? If the latter, then is the period of crucial transition really the years from 1740 to 1770 when various indices of industrial and commercial activity (as well as population growth) appear to turn sharply upwards? Or could the critical phase even be right back at the beginning of the century, when capitalist industry and bourgeois attitudes had already gone far enough to produce the first major technological changes? The analysis that has been offered in the last few pages — with its emphasis on bourgeois conditions and attitudes encouraging technological answers to questions posed by the market — would seem to favour this last possibility. Let us leave the thought in the air, and return to an earlier point to correct a one-sided formulation.

Having repeatedly emphasised that the inventions of the earlier stages of the Industrial Revolution were effects, not causes — merely results that one would expect when eager men sought to take advantage of the expansionist opportunities that had opened out — having said this, it is necessary to redress the balance by pointing out that the technological changes had economic effects that went far beyond the wildest dreams of the inventors and innovators. The cotton-spinning pioneers, hoping (one assumes) to gain

modest wealth[47] by cheapening one process in the manufacture of cloth, could have had no notion that they were
going to make cotton the largest single industry in Britain
within a generation, that this minor textile would by 1815
account for 40 per cent by value[48] of domestic exports, that
it would demonstrate the possibility of creating a world
market in the cheapest of cheap consumer goods, that it
would provide a 'dramatic object lesson in the profitability
of mechanisation'[49], inspiring hundreds of inventors to attempt the like in other fields, and thus providing one of the
main psychological stimuli of technological advance for a
couple of generations.

But this theme of 'unforeseen consequences' — of innovations producing economic and social effects far different
from anything the innovators intended — is best illustrated
from the later story of the railways, whose 'sleep-walking'
origin has already been discussed. Far from being appen-
dices to or substitutes for other modes of transport — as
they were originally conceived — the railways rapidly became the backbone of inland transport. The resulting improvements in speed and reliability, and the cost reductions,
were of a different order of magnitude from those envisaged
by the pioneers. And yet perhaps even these are to be regarded as a minor part of the railways' economic effects.

They made competition more effective, squeezing out
inefficient units that had hitherto been protected by isolation, raising the general technological and managerial level.
They made demands for coal, iron and steel that stimulated
the rapid growth of these industries. For a decade and a
half from 1856[50] railway supplies made up nearly a third
of all U.K. iron and steel exports. British world supremacy
in engineering, both civil and mechanical, in the period

47. Arkwright can hardly have anticipated that the official value of
all cotton exports in 1769, when he introduced his invention, would be
exceeded twofold by his personal fortune at death 23 years later.
48. Even though cotton prices had fallen sharply as a result of the
innovations.
49. Phyllis Deane, *op. cit.* (as in note 34), 89.
50. Earlier statistics not available.

1840-80 was largely based on skills learnt from railway building and organisational forms worked out for this purpose.

The huge capital demands of railway construction raised investment rates to quite new levels. Even down to about 1830 British investment, as a percentage of national income, remained at a level which today would be regarded as typical of underdeveloped countries—and most of this still went into land, buildings, public property and farming. It was from about 1835 to about 1870 that the investment rate rose to the level characteristic of a modern industrial state — and the railways took a far greater share of this capital than any other industry, with their suppliers of coal and of iron and steel absorbing a good deal of the rest. It was the railways, too, that in effect established the pattern of investing one's savings in enterprises with which one has no other connection — the capital of the Industrial Revolution hitherto had been obtained from friends or business associates or other sources whose interest was not *purely* financial.

In sum, when the effects which have been inadequately sketched in the last few paragraphs are taken together, the development of the railways begins to look like the central event in the maturing of the Industrial Revolution. The eighteenth century, particularly its last few decades, saw technological changes on essentially modern lines — power-driven machinery, factory production, and so on — in several industries. But it was only in the Railway Age, and largely as a result of the impact of railways, that modern industry became dominant in the economy as a whole. Not till then, one might feel (even if proof seems impossible), was it certain that the process of industrialisation would continue.

So an earlier conclusion has to be modified. Though they *originated* as mere consequences of the economic drives of their times, the spinning machines and the railways had effects that went far beyond the trends that produced them — and the same, *mutatis mutandis*, would apply to other inventions[51]. They amplified the expansionist drive so powerfully and turned it in such unforeseen directions as to make it virtually a new phenomenon. The feeling that the inventions were the *cause* of the Industrial Revolution, though not a historical truth, is almost justified by this outcome.

SCIENCE IN THE EARLY INDUSTRIAL REVOLUTION

During the nineteenth century the balance between technological innovation and economic incentives changed radically. New technologies arose which were not in any important degree extensions of previous ones (as the spinning machinery had been) or substitutes for resources in short supply (coke-smelting, railways). They arose very nearly as if invention were regarded (by the inventor and by society) as a good in itself. In varying degree they created their own markets, instead of merely catering more efficiently for existing ones. And yet some of these innovations had social and economic effects that transcended even those so far described. The synthetic chemical industry and parts of the electrical industry are two outstanding examples. These, it will be noticed, are cases of technological innovation derived from the application of science. And a fuller survey[52] would confirm that wherever, in the course of the nineteenth century, technology takes on more fully the mantle of *initiator* of economic change, it is a technology based on science. As a prelude to examining the major role of science in some nineteenth century technology, it will be useful to glance at the lesser, but not negligible, part which it played in the eighteenth century.

The *machinery* which revolutionised the textile industries owed nothing to science. But the production of cloth depends on other processes besides the mechanical ones of

51. For a fuller treatment of the effects of these and other technological changes, see Phyllis Deane's contribution on *The Industrial Revolution in Great Britain* in volume 4, particularly pages 174–188 and 209–223.

52. For regrettably it will only be possible to use selected examples to illustrate the topics covered in the rest of this article.

spinning, weaving and the like. There must also be chemical treatments, of which the most important is bleaching. The main part of the bleaching process was exposure to the sun for many days, and 'There was not enough cheap meadow-land . . . in all the British Isles to whiten the cloth of Lancashire once the water frame and mule replaced the spinning wheel'[53]. The revolution in machinery demanded a revolution in bleaching.

Now the processes of invention in industrial chemistry are conceptually different from those involved in mechanical matters. An untrained worker can visualise combinations of levers, wheels, pulleys and belts and can then construct the machine he has imagined, test it and modify it as necessary. The 'wheels' of chemical processes — the molecules, atoms and electrons, as we should think of them nowadays — are well hidden. The untrained worker is reduced to the slow process of trial and error. To advance industrial chemistry fast enough to keep pace with mechanical developments required the special insights of men who were educated in chemistry as a science. In the eighteenth century that usually meant medical men — for medicine was the only profession that included a chemical education. And in Britain it almost always meant Scottish medical men — for, while the English Universities were moribund, a Scottish medical student got a first-class chemical training from Professors like William Cullen and Joseph Black.

One important stage in the traditional bleaching process was *souring* — soaking for about 48 hours in a weak acid, usually buttermilk. And a shortage of this raw material developed long before the advent of the spinning inventions. Thus the first revolution in eighteenth-century bleaching was the introduction of sulphuric acid for the souring process. And so we must turn aside to look at the development of sulphuric acid manufacture[54]. For this material is widely

53. Landes, *op. cit.*, 338.
54. As with mechanical devices, so also most of the chemical substances which the early Industrial Revolution was to use were inherited from the Middle Ages — including sulphuric acid and the alkalies. The problem now was to develop methods of large-scale production.

used in industry; and already quite early in the eighteenth century the demand for it had been outrunning the potentialities of the existing production method — which was to burn sulphur, along with saltpetre, under a glass bell-jar and condense the product in water[55].

The first improvement, by Joshua Ward in 1736, was the substitution of large glass globes, of about 40 gallon capacity, for the bell-jars of the apothecary's shop. The price per pound of acid fell from about 30s. to about 2s. Ward was a druggist and quack doctor, and it is not known whether his partner, John White, had any scientific knowledge of chemistry. But there is no doubt about science lying at the basis of the crucial improvement that was carried out by Dr. John Roebuck at Birmingham — a town whose very varied trades, many of them using the acid for metal-pickling or cleaning, provided a rapidly expanding market.

Roebuck was a product of both the Edinburgh and the Leyden medical schools. With Samuel Garbett, a progressive business man, he established what was in effect a chemical laboratory to service the Birmingham metal and 'toy' trades. They improved methods of refining gold and silver, and of recovering them from scrap, and acted as general consulting chemists to manufacturers. Thus Roebuck's business was a scientific one, and his improvement in sulphuric acid manufacture depended on a piece of knowledge that only a trained chemist would possess — namely that lead is one of the very few materials that is not attacked by the acid. Here was the key to industrial production, since it broke through the limitation of scale which the fragility of glass had imposed on Ward's process. Roebuck's Birmingham plant started in 1746; another followed at Prestonpans in Scotland in 1749. The price now fell to 3½d. a pound. It had thus dropped by a factor of a hundred in just over a decade — even the cotton spinners could not rival that.

There is some evidence that Roebuck and perhaps others knew that dilute sulphuric acid could be used at the souring

55. Another established method need not concern us, since it was not capable of expansion to industrial scale.

stage of bleaching. But its introduction in practice in the 1750s arises from the researches and lectures which Francis Home[56] undertook on behalf of the Board of Trustees for Fisheries, Manufactures and Improvements in Scotland. Home was paid £100 for his work — a goodly sum for those times, and evidence that the master bleachers not only knew the value of science, but were even prepared to *pay* for it — provided the money did not come from their individual pockets. The souring stage now used a cheap and plentiful raw material, and into the bargain had become more efficient. The time taken was reduced from a couple of days to a few hours. The industry took a leap forward.

Mere substitution of a new raw material for an old one was not, however, enough. The main bleaching process — exposure to sun and air — took several months. And the clearing of that bottleneck depended, not merely on the application of existing scientific knowledge by men competent in science, but on using the latest chemical discoveries of some of the best brains of Europe.

In 1774 Karl Scheele of Sweden, one of the three or four most eminent names in the field of pneumatic chemistry, discovered the gas which we now call chlorine. Dissolved in water it was found to bleach vegetable dyes[57]. C. L. Berthollet, director of the French state dyeing industry and perhaps the second greatest French chemist of the century, experimented with its use for bleaching cloth in 1785-6; but the process had no future in pre-Revolution France. Two men were mainly responsible for transmitting Berthollet's idea to the practical Scottish bleachers: Patrick Copland, Professor of Natural Philosophy at Marischal College, Aberdeen; and James Watt, who was a chemist of eminence as well as 'the celebrated improver of the steam engine', one of three who share the honour of discovering that water (hitherto thought to be an element) is a compound of oxygen and hydrogen. By 1787-8 the process was being

56. Later (1768) to become Edinburgh's first Professor of Materia Medica. His *Experiments on Bleaching* was published in 1756.

57. The actual bleaching is done by nascent oxygen released by the action of chlorine on water.

used by two firms in Scotland and one near Nottingham, and a little later it spread to Lancashire.

Chlorine, however, is a difficult and dangerous substance to handle. Over the next few years many attempts were made to tame it. And at last, in 1798-9, Charles Tennant and Charles Macintosh invented bleaching powder (from the action of chlorine on slaked lime), which was the final solution to the problem. The bleaching bottleneck was broken and it is surely clear that the nineteenth-century expansion of the textile industry depended as much on chlorine bleaching as on the machinery for spinning and weaving.

For some fifty years starting from the 1820s the kingpin of the chemical industries was alkali manufacture — the production of sodium carbonate ('washing soda') from common salt with the aid of sulphuric acid, coal and chalk. Its product was used in glass-making, soap boiling, various auxiliary textile processes, and many other trades. Its by-products were involved in making bleaching powder and in paper-making. In addition, a developed chemical industry involves a highly complex interlocking of various processes, each of which produces end products for use outside the industry and intermediates that form the raw materials for other processes. And in the period under discussion the alkali process lay at the centre of these complicated interactions.

The modest amounts of alkali needed for medieval and early modern industry were derived from plant ashes (land plants yield potash, seaweed gives soda). Inevitably even the moderate industrial expansion of the early eighteenth century created a shortage. This led, for example, to the development of the Scottish kelp industry[58], whose product for a time kept the alkaline wolf at bay, and indeed was still of major importance till the 1830s. But industry's growing greed for alkalies could not be satisfied from any organic source. And so, almost from the very moment in 1736 when

58. Described in A. and N. L. Clow, *The Chemical Revolution: a contribution to social technology* (London, 1952), Chapter III.

chemical science had shown it to be a theoretical possibility, there began the search for a practical method of producing soda from sea-salt.

No proper history can be attempted here of how this struggle led to eventual success. But a mere list of those involved will show that here again science, at the highest level then available, was the key to technological innovation. They include Scheele, Roebuck and Watt, who have already been mentioned; Joseph Black, the undisputed father of modern chemistry; Guyton de Morveau, one of Lavoisier's chief associates in the antiphlogistic revolution that put chemical theory on essentially modern lines; James Keir, typical example of Scottish medical man turned to chemical industry, member of the Lunar Society (in itself almost a guarantee of scientific excellence), one of the first chemists to accept the antiphlogistic theory in Britain (where it was long resisted), a very competent chemical investigator (as witnessed by his published papers); the ninth Earl of Dundonald, industrial adventurer who appreciated the value of scientific advice, rather than scientist in his own right, better known as a pioneer of the coal tar industry[59]; Duhamel du Monceau, who first clearly distinguished potash from soda, discovered (1736) that the latter contained the same base as common salt, and almost immediately sought to exploit his discovery commercially (too early for success, of course); Malherbe, de la Metherie, Brian Higgins, Alexander and George Fordyce, who are known to historians of chemistry to be scientifically competent, though the general reader will probably not have met their names; and several others.

In so far as details are available, they indicate that these researchers and projectors made full use of all that science could offer. Keir, for example, began by finding a weak point in the well-established doctrine (as it then appeared

---

59. Wood tar, essential to maritime power, was yet another example of an organic product that could not keep up with economic expansion. Dundonald's work was also concerned with the various by-products obtainable in the distillation of coal tar — foreshadowing the central chemical industry of the later nineteenth century.

to be) of 'elective affinities'[60], and his transformation of a chemical observation into a working process depended on a subtle point that could only have been noticed by one who was highly knowledgeable and skilled as both 'pure' and industrial chemist — a point, in fact, that was missed by German chemists considering the possibility of reviving the process during the First World War[61].

Keir's process seems to have been an economic success in the last two decades of the century (though only because sodium or potassium sulphate was then cheaply available as a waste product from other industries). Dundonald's process was also a success, and during the last few years of the eighteenth century and the first twenty or so of the nineteenth, synthetic alkali works were operating profitably on Tyneside and in the Glasgow area. All this was *before* the introduction into Britain of the Leblanc process which marked the final victory over the supply of alkalies from organic sources.

Leblanc, trained as a pharmacist and then as a surgeon, was presumably no great chemist — but good enough to benefit from the work of other French experimenters mentioned above. His process, which differs from several earlier ones only in quantitative details, was patented in 1791. Both Leblanc and his project suffered in the confusions of the revolutionary years, though before 1815 France had become independent of natural alkali supplies. But what really counts was James Muspratt's establishment of a large-scale works using the Leblanc process near Liverpool

60. The desired reaction,
$$Na_2SO_4 + Ca(OH)_2 \rightarrow 2NaOH + CaSO_4$$
(sodium sulphate + quicklime → caustic soda + calcium sulphate), normally goes the other way. Keir discovered that if one trickles a very dilute solution of sodium sulphate very slowly over lime, then the reaction goes in the desired direction.

61. J. L. Moilliet, 'Keir's caustic soda process — an attempted reconstruction', *Chemistry and Industry*, 1966, 405-8. This is a pioneer effort in a type of investigation that must be undertaken more often if the the role of chemical technology in the Industrial Revolution is to be understood — the use of modern knowledge to reconstruct the old process and find the conditions in which it will work effectively, together with some attempt to calculate its economics on this basis.

in 1823[62]. In 1825 Tennant (page 230 above) established the process in Scotland. The core of the chemical industry, as it was to be for half a century, had been formed.

Science played a similar, if not always so central a part in all the chemical industries of the eighteenth century, and in other industries that rely heavily on chemical transformations, such as pottery, glass and paper-making[63]. The infant science of geology also gave some help to mineral prospectors. But the only other development in which a key part can be claimed for science was that of the steam engine. Starting from a problem concerned with pumping, the science of vacuums and atmospheric pressure had been developed by Galileo, Torricelli, Guericke and Boyle. It was consciously applied by Huygens in an attempt to make a gunpowder engine, and by his assistant and successor, Papin, who produced a demonstration model of a cylinder-and-piston steam engine. Papin's work — and indeed all the scientific work of the times — was readily available in printed form and otherwise, and we can reasonably presume that Newcomen[64] benefited from it, even though we have no direct evidence as to how skilled he was in science.

Smeaton used the methods of a scientifically-minded engineer in his work on improving the steam engine and other prime movers (pages 202-203 above). But engineering informed by scientific method was not enough. And it was no accident that the man who discovered the fundamental defect in the Newcomen engine, and invented and perfected the crucial improvement of the separate condenser, was instrument maker (semi-official) to Glasgow University, where Joseph Black was developing his theory of latent heat (1761-4). This theory as such could only make a small contribution towards unravelling the steam-engine problem.

62. Muspratt had some experience as a chemical manufacturer, but a negligible background of chemical science. However, by this time chemical treatises and reference works had reached a high enough level to enable such a one to obtain the required knowledge.

63. The technological developments in all these are discussed in Clow and Clow, *op. cit.*, which is also informative about economic and social effects.

64. And his immediate predecessor on a rather different line, Savery.

But surely Watt's work — which included much experimental investigation of the properties of steam — was made possible only by living and working in an environment where Black and his colleagues (with whom Watt was on terms of friendly co-operation) were constantly discussing the properties of heat and performing experiments thereon. Watt's success depended on the fact that his experiments were quantitative; and the science of measuring heat (as contrasted with temperature) was a recent Glasgow creation. It seems likely, too, that Black's theoretical generalisations were necessary to enable Watt to understand his experimental results. But when all this has been said, it has to be added that the scientific effort of the years 1763-5 in which Watt conceived his invention is far outweighed by the engineering effort of a further decade needed to make a practical machine.

Apart from these special cases, the more rapid technological changes of the last few decades of the century kept constantly throwing up problems — often problems of detail. And sometimes the solution could be obtained by using a piece of scientific knowledge or applying a touch of scientific thinking. Progressive manufacturers were well aware of this and took good care to have scientific advice on tap. They did not employ scientists, but they arranged that life should be made pleasant for any gentleman with scientific leanings who would agree to settle near by and act as consultant when required[65]. Matthew Boulton was mainly responsible for easing two scientifically-minded physicians in succession, William Small and William Withering, into a prosperous Birmingham practice. He took the lead in raising a subscription to provide Joseph Priestley

65. For contacts between industrialists and scientists in the Manchester area, see A. E. Musson and E. Robinson, 'Science and Industry in the late Eighteenth Century', *Economic History Review*, 2nd series, *13*, (1960), 222–244. Details of similar relationships in the Midlands can be extracted from R. E. Schofield, *The Lunar Society of Birmingham* (Oxford, 1963) and are summarised on pages 474–80 of S. Lilley, 'La Scienza agli Inizi della Rivoluzione Industriale', *Studi Storici*, anno 2 (1961), 465–495. The last chapter of Clow and Clow, *op. cit.*, also discusses relations between scientists and industrialists.

with a supplementary income that would enable him to settle as minister of religion in Birmingham. And in one of its aspects — though this, of course, is not the whole story — the famous Lunar Society of Birmingham was simply a grouping of industrialists needing scientific advice and medicos, clergymen and others who could give it — with James Keir functioning in both capacities.

From this discussion it will be clear that in the eighteenth and early nineteenth centuries science did not *initiate* industrial trends. It merely solved some problems which the general movement of industry had created. When the old methods of bleaching or of making sulphuric acid or soda proved hopelessly inadequate to satisfy the needs of expanding industry, then and only then was research undertaken to find alternatives. If, as suggested earlier, most technological innovation of this period has something of the character of a reluctant response to an overwhelming demand, then the same is doubly true of innovation based on science. If persistence, ingenuity and craftsmanship could speed up the process or find the substitute as required, that was good enough. If they could not, then as a last resort science was called in.

It follows that where science *was* used, it played an absolutely essential role. A working bleacher, suffering from shortage of buttermilk, *might* have hit on the idea of using sulphuric acid as a substitute; he could never have conceived that chlorine could take the place of bleach-fields (!) — to say nothing of discovering chlorine itself. Nor could a practical kelp burner have conceived that the product of his craft could be produced from such unlikely ingredients as salt, coal and chalk. To make these discoveries, the special kind of knowledge and the special kind of procedure that constitutes science were absolutely essential. And without these discoveries, the progress of the Industrial Revolution would, at the very least, have been severely retarded.

Science, in the sense in which the term is used here — an effective science that could be used to control and alter nature as well as to understand — was a mere 150 years old at the period under review. The chemical knowledge was mostly discovered only a few decades before it was used. Are we, then, to regard it as a singularly fortunate co-incidence that intellectual developments, largely divorced from contemporary social and economic changes, should have created this science just in time to prevent the In-dustrial Revolution from choking under a mountain of cloth that it could weave but could not bleach? There is no space to discuss the question fully. The author can only state his dissent from this view, highly fashionable though it be among historians of science. In his opinion the Scientific Revolution of the seventeenth century is what emerged from the impact of rising capitalism and of the bourgeois revolution on existing quasi-scientific thought[66]. And the chemical knowledge (for example) that was so vital to eighteenth century industry emerged when it did because the enquiring minds of the scientifically inclined were also sensitive to the various social and economic needs of their times. There was a two-way interaction between chemical science and chemical industry.

SCIENCE AND TECHNOLOGY IN THE LATER INDUSTRIAL REVOLUTION

It would obviously not be possible, in the space available, to give a well-rounded account of nineteenth-century technological change[67], still less to discuss the drives that promoted it and the effects it produced. A few examples of major trends may help the reader to connect the movements described in other essays in these volumes with at least some parts of technology. Further consideration of the developing role of science in technological change will pro-

66. This is not the same as the crude statement that modern science arose because various groups of capitalists *wanted* it for the purpose of solving this or that problem.

67. A particularly grave omission is the question of how the rest of Europe in due course followed Britain into the industrial era. See the excellent treatment in Landes, *op. cit.* (note 34 above), particularly pages 353–458.

vide a convenient framework to which these samples may
be pegged.

As the nineteenth century rolled on the part played by
science was to become a much more revolutionary one[68].
Yet many industries continued to make progress in very
much the old way — using science only as a desperate
device when nothing else would serve. So far as concerns
machinery, which by the end of the century had entered
almost every productive sphere, it remained true that 'the
typical inventor was usually a workman or amateur
who contrived to find the most convenient arrangement of
wheels, rollers, cogs and levers designed to imitate the movement of the craftsman at higher speed and using steam
power'[69].

And the creation of the steel industry — that is to say,
the industry making steel that was cheap enough for general
use instead of merely for cutting edges, which must be regarded as by far the most important innovation in the second
half of the century — the creation of this steel industry
owed less to science than did the revolution in bleaching
sixty years earlier. Bessemer certainly made use of a modi-
cum of scientific knowledge, but his invention of the 'converter' for producing steel from pig iron (1856) came mainly
from his persistence and his acute observation of accidental
happenings, coupled with his ignorance — as an outsider
to the industry — of what could not be done. Siemens, who
developed the alternative open hearth process in the following decade, came from a family of scientifically trained
engineers[70] and certainly made systematic use of his own

68. This is not, of course, to deny that science in turn was profoundly
influenced by social and economic trends. But in some cases the connection now became so remote and indirect that it is often good enough
to think of science almost as an outside influence impinging on the
economy.

69. J. D. Bernal, *Science and Industry in the Nineteenth Century* (London,
1953), 28–9.

70. Who played a leading part in giving to German industry, now
beginning to rise from its long sleep, that scientific bias that distinguished
it from British and American industry in the latter part of the century.

scientific education; yet the main novelty in his process — the regenerative use of waste heat — surely owes more to the science of economics than to the whole of natural science.

To make good steel both these processes required ores of low phosphorus content. And it was in learning how to use the much commoner phosphoric ores that science at last made a notable contribution to the industry. Sidney Gilchrist Thomas, a junior police court clerk, was studying chemistry at night school when he learnt from a lecturer that there was a fortune waiting for anybody who could solve this problem. He set out to find the solution by scientific analysis — reading the technical literature, visiting iron works when time allowed, experimenting in a cellar laboratory. Having decided on the answer — a lining of magnesian limestone to absorb the phosphorus — he was able to have it tested on a small scale in 1877 by a cousin who was chemist at an iron works. Full scale production began in 1879. Since it freed the industry from dependence on the rather rare phosphorus-free ores, the Thomas process was the real start of the age of steel. By 1890, 64 per cent of the steel of continental Europe was being produced by this method, as against only 14 per cent in Britain — dread symptom of the unprogressive attitude that was by this time arising in more than one British industry.

World output (from all processes) rose from a bit over half a millions tons in 1870 to almost 28 million tons in 1900. Steel substantially replaced wrought iron for rails during the seventies and in shipbuilding by 1890. The first all-steel bridge was built across the Firth of Forth in 1883-90. From 1888 on steel began to take over from wrought iron in skyscrapers, while the following year saw the completion of the Eiffel Tower.

Not one of the scientific ideas used by Bessemer, Siemens or Thomas dates from later than 1790 — a very good indication that economic demand, rather than scientific and technological possibility was still the dominant factor. By contrast, the development of the aluminium industry was carried out on highly scientific lines from the very beginning. The invention of the electrolytic production process[71] independently by Hall in the U.S.A. and Héroult in France came at the earliest possible moment technologically (1886), since it depended on the availability of cheap electric power. And it had to create its own market. World production was 7,300 tons in 1900 and 20,000 tons in 1907 — with a very long way to go (via two world wars) to reach the millions of tons per annum of recent years.

If the pattern of development in steel was not very different from the typical eighteenth-century pattern, the growth of the electrical industries exhibited some striking novelties. Instead of an overwhelming economic demand — often for a substitute for some commodity whose supply was limited by nature — leading to an almost reluctant technological innovation (aided, if no other way would serve, by science), we find the electrical developments beginning in scientific researches which had only the remotest (if any) connection with economic demand. Indeed the reason why much of eighteenth-century electrical research was carried out was simply that this was a *clean* branch of science which, in the age of the Enlightenment, could be pursued by gentlemen without greatly dirtying their hands or clothes. These researches revealed technological possibilities that could not even be thought of before the scientific work had been done. And in many cases enthusiastic inventors were experimenting with new machines and gadgets long before any real economic demand had emerged. Attempts at electric telegraphs, for example, started in 1753.

After Volta's 'pile' of 1800[72] had provided the means of producing steady currents, the progress of discovery became much more rapid; and by 1831 workers like Davy, Oersted

71. Earlier processes can be ignored, since they produced the metal at such a price that it was used by the rich and the royal for conspicuous display.

72. As a result of which electricity got mixed up with the distinctly dirtier science of chemistry, and research tended to move from the *salon* to the laboratory (if one existed) or cellar or shed.

and Faraday had discovered all the phenomena involved in the telegraph and in electric light and power, as well as such industries as electroplating.

The railways — both directly (for their own signalling needs) and indirectly (since there is always a desire for communication rather faster than available transport) — created the first economic demand that electricity was to supply: the telegraph. The requisite scientific phenomena had been known for nearly twenty years, and so the actual inventor might be anything from an eminent professor of physics (Wheatstone in England) to an artist who had attended a few lectures on electricity and knew how to get help from the more knowledgeable (Morse in the U.S.A.). For a couple of decades after the first practical installations (1837) empiricism, ingenuity and drive were enough for the expansion of the telegraph. But the step up to the trans-Atlantic scale introduced new problems whose solution required all the mathematical-physical erudition of William Thomson (later Lord Kelvin). Success came in 1866, after ten years of trying — including a classical case of the 'practical' man ignoring Thomson's advice and plunging, as a result, into disaster.

The invention of the telephone (1876) was again the result of much scientific research — but less in electricity than in acoustics, for which Bell was peculiarly well equipped by family tradition and personal profession[73]. There was, of course, virtually no demand for the telephone until it had been invented. It was one of the earliest cases of that important phenomenon of the present age — invention as the mother of necessity.

One need hardly add that nobody — unless he were a believer in magic — could even have thought of asking for a telegraph or telephone that dispensed with wires, until after Maxwell had proved theoretically that what we now call radio waves exist (1864) and Hertz had demonstrated them experimentally (1886 onwards). Then the possibilities

73. Naturally a great deal more electrical knowledge was involved in further developments, particularly those of Edison.

became immediately obvious, and several inventors had at least demonstrated the feasibility of radio communication before Marconi's success from 1896 on.

Faraday's conversion of mechanical motion into electric current in 1831 completed the scientific discoveries on which the electric light and power industry was based. Yet it was to be another fifty years before that industry really got going. There were many engineering problems to be overcome before laboratory demonstrations could be converted into economical machinery. But it has been suggested that these could have been dealt with in a decade or two if they had been subjected to the intense attack that industrial society could by this time deploy when its incentives were clear. Bernal has urged the thesis that the delay arose mainly from an economic structure which had no effective mechanism for encouraging innovation unless this could promise almost immediate profitability. 'The promoters of electrical devices could not sell them because there was no cheap source of current. At the same time there was little urge to develop generators because there was no demand for the current'[74]. As a result, the industry developed by a series of steps in which one use for current promoted some improvement on the generating side, which made power cheap enough for some other application to be tried, and so on.

The first industrial use was for electroplating. In the thirties and forties this stimulated developments in generators to replace costly batteries. These made electricity an economic proposition for lighthouses in the late fifties and sixties. Hence derived a new incentive to improve the generating side that led to the replacement of permanent magnets by electromagnets — and by 1870 the modern dynamo had arrived in principle. Now arc-lighting was cheap enough to be worth installing in such places as railway stations, docks, theatres, iron works and markets. There remained the problem of 'subdividing the light', which was solved about 1880 by the incandescent filament lamp invented (independently) by Swan in England and Edison in the

74. Bernal, *op. cit.*, 120.

U.S.A.[75]. Edison also put almost the finishing touches to the generator, and worked out most of the distribution system.

The incandescent lamp, by turning electricity into a consumer good, provided the type of demand to which nineteenth-century capitalism most eagerly responded. And so the electric supply industry boomed in the eighties. With consumption now assured, improvements in generation, transmission and distribution went on apace, and soon electricity could be used for many other purposes (which before long consumed more power than did lighting): electric trains and trams (from the eighties on), the production of aluminium (page 239 above) and other electrochemical processes which depended on enormous supplies of energy, the electric furnace in metallurgy and, in the early years of the twentieth century — for the industry was very slow to see the potentialities in this field — the provision of power, in small units, in industrial workshops, and eventually in the home. The economic effects — such as allowing industry to move away from the coalfields and giving the small industrial unit a renewed chance to compete with the large one — hardly need stressing.

In terms of sheer time and effort, empirical engineering still bulked far larger than science in the process of innovation, even at the end of the nineteenth century. Yet in retrospect it is quite obvious that even some decades earlier industrial civilisation had started to move into a new phase in which the future would lie with those individuals, those companies and those nations who could make the best use of science. And even as early as the 1840s and 50s a few far-sighted men had been saying so. Let us therefore turn to one other field in which the economic effects of using or failing to use science showed up with most exemplary clarity — the synthetic dyestuffs industry.

In the 1850s organic chemistry (the chemistry of carbon compounds) was in the process of rapid transition from a sort of intelligently directed cookery to a science with a

75. And could, one feels, have been solved a generation earlier if cheap enough current had made it economically attractive.

well established theoretical basis. And in 1856 William Henry Perkin, searching in youthful enthusiasm for a way of making quinine synthetically, discovered instead a brilliant and fade-resisting dye, later called 'mauve', that could be made by a reasonably simple process from raw materials abundantly present in coal tar. After receiving only moderate encouragement from dye makers and users, he undertook the manufacture himself and — despite the entire novelty of the processes involved, and his own total ignorance of industrial chemistry — was marketing the dye in December 1857. This was the beginning of the synthetic dye industry, which in due course was to become the synthetic everything-else industry. It was the first important instance of a whole new industry arising directly and immediately from a scientific discovery.

There had been no effective demand, before this time, for synthetically produced dyestuffs; and — despite occasional vague prophecies by eminent chemists anxious to advertise the importance of their vocation — nobody had even tried to find them. The new industry created a market for its wares on a completely unforeseen scale, simply because it provided the goods at a price, and particularly of a quality, that nobody had even faintly envisaged before Perkin made his discovery.

In a rush to profit from the new opportunities many other dyes were created during the following years. The next major step was the first synthesis of a dye that had previously been obtained from natural sources — alizarin, the dye in madder. In a race for a patent, three German chemists beat Perkin by one day (in 1869), but Perkin still got into production first. Some alizarin figures[76] will serve to illustrate the new industry's economic impact. Before 1869 British madder imports varied in annual value in the range £750,000 to £1,000,000. By 1878, imports had fallen to

---

76. These and later statistics are quoted from contemporary estimates given in papers collected in *The British Coal-tar Industry: its Origin, Development and Decline*, ed. W. M. Gardner (London, 1915). Some corrections might result from modern statistical methods, but not enough to upset the general picture.

1,700 tons at a price that synthetic competition had brought down from about £45 to £10 a ton — in fact they were already negligible. By 1880 world production of synthetic alizarin paste (10 per cent pure) was 14,000 tons at £122 — totalling £1.7 million. This was the equivalent of about 126,000 tons of madder[77], which (at the pre-1869 price) would have cost nearly £5.7 million — a saving of £4 million from one dye alone.

Synthetic indigo, marketed in Germany in 1897, after more than thirty years of research by German chemists, may be regarded as the culminating achievement of the dyestuffs industry. Within ten years it had almost completely superseded the natural product. In parts of India the effect was catastrophic.

As might be gathered from the last two paragraphs, this industry that began in Britain had become almost a German monopoly within two or three decades. In 1870 Britain produced 40 tons of alizarin; Germany less than a ton. The following year Britain still led, but only by 220 tons to 150. And by 1873, British production was a mere 435 tons, against 1,000 tons from Germany. By 1883 Britain imported two-thirds of her alizarin. World production of synthetic dyestuffs in general rose from zero in 1856 to £400,000 in 1862, mostly British, some French. By 1878 it was £3,150,000, to which Britain contributed £450,000 and Germany £2,000,000. Statistics collected from typical British dyeing firms during the eighties and nineties showed that few of them used as much as 10 per cent of home-made dyes. By 1900 Germany held 90 per cent of the world market.

This commercial victory was based on a 'technological take-over'. Between 1886 and 1900 the six largest German firms took out 948 British patents; the six largest British firms took out 86. The German industry worked to higher manufacturing standards. Dyers had no doubts but that German dyes offered superior quality and better value for money. So far as this industry was concerned, Britain took

77. Actually pre-1869 world madder production was in the range 50,000–90,000 tons — so the market had not just been captured; it had been expanded.

on the appearance of an underdeveloped country, with a 'colonial' economy, exporting raw materials (in the form of primary and intermediate coal tar products) to Germany, and buying back from that country the highly finished and valuable manufactured dyes. It has become fashionable in recent years to study the earlier steps in the Industrial Revolution with a view to facilitating the 'take-off' of under-developed countries into 'sustained growth'. The study of these later stages might provide equally valuable lessons as to how advanced countries can avoid the 'dive-back' into a state of underdevelopment.

The more superficial reasons why Germany was able to steal the synthetic industry from Britain are not hard to come by. Their factories were thoroughly modern, with pro-duction highly rationalised. They were prepared to make huge capital investments: in 1900 the six largest German firms had a capital of about £2½ million; while total British capital in the industry was probably less than £½ million. The German industrialists took enormous pains to ensure that they had a sufficiency of scientific talent in their em-ploy. In 1900 the same six largest German firms employed about 18,000 workpeople, 1,360 commercial staff, 350 engineers and technologists *and* 500 chemists. The number of chemists in the whole British dyestuffs industry was at that time estimated at some 30 to 40. Furthermore the German chemists were on average the products of a more advanced education than their English counterparts. And the German industry employed several men who would have figured in the world ranking list for chemists, while except for Perkin himself (who retired early) the British industry attracted no man of scientific eminence.

At a slightly deeper level, the enquiry as to why the leaders of industry should have behaved so differently in Germany and England would lead us to consider the achievement of German national unity in 1871, and the very conscious efforts of the German government (and be-fore 1871 several state governments, notably the Prussian) to help, even to *drive*, their nascent industries into making up for three centuries of disunited economic backwardness.

One would discuss, for example, the way in which patent laws were first allowed to be ineffective, making it easy for the young industry to pirate the discoveries of the British and French, later tightened up to prevent theft in the reverse direction[78]. One would note the part played by the banks, with state backing, in providing the German chemical firms with capital on a scale that could not be matched in Britain, where the private investor still reigned supreme[79]. The resulting large-scale structure gave the German industry great advantages in financing and using research, in being able to offer customers a complete range of dyes (where English firms could only provide a few) and so on.

In Britain three generations of 'practical men' had been making very good profits, and the role played by science in even a small proportion of these was far from obvious. The methods that had made Britain the workshop of the world could surely be expected to keep her so. Why take a risky gamble (as it would seem) on the brainstorms of laboratory egg-heads? The Germans, on the other hand, had no hope of overcoming the disadvantages of a late start, except by maximum use of science and by concentrating, when possible, on industries based on science. Industrial leadership was put in the hands of scientists, not financiers; and even the banks had their scientific advisers.

But still we have hardly dug beneath the surface. No matter how willing entrepreneurs might be to employ chemists and develop industry based on chemical science, no matter how willing the government to promote or the banks to finance these efforts, nothing at all could have been achieved unless the educational system could supply a sufficient number of chemists, trained to a high enough level. The German capture of the dyestuffs industry was possible only because that country had been leading the

78. See J. I. Beer, *The Emergence of the German Dye Industry* (Urbana, Ill., 1959), 54–6, 105–8.

79. On such matters, which can only be alluded to here, see Knut Borchardt's *The Industrial Revolution in Germany* in volume 4, and Bertrand Gille, *The Bank and the Industrial Revolution*, in volume 3, *passim*.

world in the science of organic chemistry for twenty-odd years before Perkin's original discovery. Clearly German science in the thirties, forties and fifties was not developed for the purpose of serving industry — for the very good reason that there was almost no industry in existence which it could serve.

The roots of this chemical pre-eminence were not economic. Its origins are to be found in German national pride trying to re-assert itself after the ignominies of Napoleonic defeat. The 'normal' roads to greatness — industrial power, empire building and the like — must remain closed until the problem of national unity had in some way been solved. And so — as the only possibility that remained open — there developed a powerful movement to demonstrate German greatness through high intellectual endeavour. The emphasis was on *endeavour*, on painstaking scholarship and research in any field where an infinite capacity for taking pains is more important than any of the other senses of the word 'genius'. And that description applies most fitly to organic chemistry.

Justus Liebig studied chemistry in the remarkable schools which had been produced by the French Revolution, and returned home in 1824 very conscious of his country's inferiority and very determined to rectify it. And it was the school of organic chemistry which he founded that ultimately made possible the German dyestuffs victory.

Liebig and his pupils had tremendous faith in the practical benefits that were to result from their chemical researches. But if the researches could be done in Germany, the practical application must be carried out elsewhere. Having made notable advances in agricultural chemistry, Liebig looked hopefully to England for action. His speeches, reports and lobbying led eventually to the foundation of the Royal College of Chemistry in 1845. Its first professor was one of his best pupils, August Wilhelm Hofmann, who promptly switched the work of the College from agricultural chemistry to the chemistry of coal tar. And it was under Hofmann's tuition, and under the stimulus of a remark by Hofmann concerning quinine that Perkin made his discovery of mauve. So in a sense, even the very beginning of the synthetic dye industry was more German than English[80].

Meanwhile at home Liebig was constantly agitating for improved facilities for scientific education. And the Prussian government, well on its way to the Prussian Empire, thinking already of industrialisation and doubtless impressed by the successes of Hofmann and his pupils in England, was persuaded to establish magnificent chemical laboratories at the Universities of Berlin and Bonn[81], and to call Hofmann home to plan them and then to take the Chair at Berlin in 1865. From the sixties onwards the Polytechnics, also with government support, were educating engineers and chemists to almost as high a level as the universities, though along more vocational lines. From these institutions — constantly improved, with even more government help, after 1871 — came the flow of manpower that enabled the German dye-stuffs industry to forge ahead so rapidly. In the eighties, Munich University alone had about 50 research students working under Von Baeyer (one of the pioneers of synthetic indigo). By contrast, from Hofmann's departure till 1874 there was no chair of organic chemistry in Britain. No wonder the initial lead in the industry was so rapidly lost!

From the eighties onwards, the synthetic dyestuffs industry widened out into the synthetic chemical industry in general — making pharmaceuticals like aspirin, novocaine, veronal (first of the barbiturate drugs) and salvarsan (followed in the 1930s by the sulpha drugs and the general flowering of chemotherapy), synthetic perfumes and flavourings, saccharine and a host of other products. In nearly every case Germany took the initial lead, and it needed a long hard struggle in the inter-war years before Britain

80. The work of the College depended on a steady stream of help from Germany (Beer, *op. cit.*, 23). And Hofmann himself contributed far more to the industry than any of his English pupils, even Perkin. Furthermore, in the early days English firms depended on employing German chemists, some of whom subsequently became leaders of the industry in the Fatherland.

81. Themselves founded (1809, 1818) as part of the intellectual movement of national re-assertion described above.

and the U.S.A., having at last recognised their folly[82], could catch up. Even so, the Germans shot ahead between the wars in the field of synthetic rubber (with the young U.S.S.R. as their only serious rival). Meanwhile their chemical strength enabled I. G. Farbenindustrie to organise a network of international cartels which was perhaps Hitler's most effective secret weapon during the Second World War[83]. These few lines may perhaps give a faint indication of the consequences that followed from allowing organic chemistry to become virtually a German monopoly.

Not every case in which Britain lost the technological initiative is explicable in terms of the use of science and in terms of education. The American lead in mass-production engineering methods, for example — which eventually produced the great expansion in consumer durables — takes its origin largely in that country's response to its scarcity of skilled labour. To catch up — at first even to avoid falling further behind — the U.S.A. *had* to find methods of substituting routine operators for craftsmen, and of building the skill into the machine. Britain — and on the whole the rest of Europe — having a better supply of skill available, dallied with the old methods till well after the American lead had been established.

Nevertheless the story of the synthetic dye industry taught a lesson that has often been repeated since: to maintain technological progress in the conditions that were already maturing towards the close of the nineteenth century, not only must industry make ample use of science (which implies that scientifically and technically qualified men should have a large share in directing it), but also the educational system that is to provide the scientists and scientifically trained engineers must be set up a whole generation in advance[84].

82. Recognised it fully? Or only in part?

83. See, for example, J. Borkin and C. A. Welsh, *Germany's Master Plan* (London, n.d.) and G. Reimann, *Patents for Hitler* (London, 1945) — both written in heat, but perhaps nonetheless truthful for that.

84. Unless, of course, the necessary talent is to be obtained by brain-drain. But the British synthetic dyestuffs industry was created by means of a brain-drain from Germany. Is its fate to be taken as an awful warning?

BIBLIOGRAPHY

The following list must not be regarded as a systematic bibliography, but rather as the sort of reading and reference list that the author would personally recommend to his own, non-specialist and non-vocational, adult students with a view to amplifying some aspects of the preceding article. The addition of an asterisk (*) to the date of publication indicates that the work listed contains a useful bibliography that would facilitate further exploration. A double asterisk means that the bibliography will probably be more than usually helpful as regards the theme(s) of the present essay.

The only full-scale attempt to set the technological changes of the Industrial Revolution solidly inside the economic and general history of the period—seeking to discuss on the one hand what historical factors called them forth and on the other what effects they produced—is the work of Professor D. S. Landes. This first appeared as an extended essay, 'Technological Change in Industrial Development in Western Europe, 1750–1914', which constituted pages 274–601 of *The Cambridge Economic History of Europe*, ed. H. J. Habakkuk and M. Postan, vol. 6 (Cambridge, 1965**). With some revisions, an introduction en uiring why Western Europe should have become the scene of this world-shaking change and two additional chapters bringing the story down to the present day, it has now been published as *The Unbound Prometheus: Technological Change and Industrial Development in Western Europe from 1750 to the Present* (Cambridge, 1969). It is regretted that the latter version arrived too late to be used in the present essay.

For the history of technology as such—largely ignoring its relations to historical change in general—the most comprehensive work available in English is *A History of Technology*, ed. Charles Singer, E. J. Holmyard, A. R. Hall and Trevor I. Williams, 5 volumes (London, 1954–58). Volumes 4 and 5, together with some parts of volume 3, are relevant to our period. The contributions—divided by branch of technology and chronologically—are very uneven in quality. The standard of the plentiful illustrations is high. Most of the articles carry bibliographies, which again vary widely in quality. Much of the material that went into the making of these five enormous volumes has been condensed into 750 pages in T. K. Derry and T. I. Williams, *A Short History of Technology from the Earliest Times to A.D. 1900* (Oxford, 1960**). Being again divided into chapters each dealing with a single branch of technology (with chronological division only into the periods before and after 1750!), this cannot be read as continuous history. Its quality, however, is more even than that of its gigantic parent, and it would frequently be the best work to consult first in seeking the answer to some question.

W. H. Chaloner and A. E. Musson, *Industry and Technology* (London, 1963*) is concerned, despite its general title, only with Britain. It consists of 238 excellently chosen pictures, with more than usually informative captions, and a quite short accompanying text (25 pages cover the eighteenth and nineteenth centuries). *Technology and Western Civilisation*, vol. 1 (covering the period from the beginning to 1900, but mostly post-1600), ed. M. Kranzberg and C. W. Pursell, Jr. (London, 1967**) again collects essays referring to particular technologies in five main chronological periods, together with more general 'framework' articles like 'Prerequisites for industrialisation', 'The social impact of industrialisation', etc. The level is again uneven, but the book is a mine of useful information and interesting ideas. S. Lilley, *Men, Machines and History: the Story of Tools and Machines in Relation to Social Progress* (2nd edition, London, 1965) is concerned with the part played by technology in the broad sweep of history, but it could also serve as a brief introduction to those parts of mechanical technology which space considerations have squeezed out of the present article.

To get the 'feel' of a historical period one ought to study it at least in part through the eyes of contemporaries. For the general reader, who probably has little access to contemporary sources, a useful substitute is F. Klemm, *A*

History of Western Technology (London, 1959*). Despite its title, this is a collection of extracts from such sources as Watt's patent specification, a letter from Abraham Darby's daughter-in-law concerning smelting with coke, Edward Baines's early (1835) book on the development of the cotton industry, and so on. Similarly the atmosphere of the early railway endeavour can probably be better appreciated from recent reprints of works written while the railways were still growing than from present-day histories—for example, John Francis, *A History of the English Railway, its Social Relations and Revelations, 1820–1845* (1851, reprinted Newton Abbot, c. 1967), and W. W. Tomlinson, *The North Eastern Railway: its Rise and Development* (1915, reprinted Newton Abbot, 1967). The latter will help greatly towards understanding the 'sleep-walking' development of the Stockton-Darlington line. And for recapturing the enthusiasm of the Industrial Revolution there is still nothing to beat the works of Samuel Smiles (whose too heroic attitude can be forgiven him)—particularly, *Lives of the Engineers*, 3 volumes (London, 1862) and *Lives of Boulton and Watt* (London, 1866). For a careful scholarly account of steam engine history one can turn to H. W. Dickinson, *A Short History of the Steam Engine* (Cambridge, 1939).

It is curious that in many branches of technology there is still no good general study that can be recommended. This applies to electricity, even though there is much of value in M. MacLaren, *The Rise of the Electrical Industry during the Nineteenth Century* (Princeton, 1943*), and most surprising of all to the cotton industry, where one has to make do with excellent books on particular topics, such as R. S. Fitton and A. P. Wadsworth, *The Strutts and the Arkwrights, 1758–1830* (Manchester, 1958*).

The iron and steel industry has been much better served ever since T. S. Ashton's classic, *Iron and Steel in the Industrial Revolution* (Manchester and London, 1924; 2nd edition, Manchester, 1951, 3rd edition, Manchester, 1963*). Among more recent works one can mention W. K. V. Gale, *The British Iron and Steel Industry: A Technical History* (Newton Abbot, 1967), written by one who understands the technology of the industry from inside and takes the trouble to explain it to those outside; and Alan Birch, *The Economic History of the British Iron and Steel Industry, 1784–1879* (London, 1967)—a curiously rambling and ill-arranged work which nevertheless contains lots of useful material.

For understanding the role of chemical technology and therefore of chemical science in the earlier phases of the Industrial Revolution one turns to the superb book by A. and N. L. Clow, *The Chemical Revolution: a Contribution to Social Technology* (London, 1952**), which contains a mass of well documented information. Later developments can be followed in the more pedestrian work of D. W. F. Hardie and J. D. Pratt, *A History of the Modern British Chemical Industry* (Oxford, 1966), which supplements its general historical treatment with 63 pages of brief accounts of individual firms. F. S. Taylor, *A History of Industrial Chemistry* (London, 1957*) covers a vast canvas rather shallowly, but would be useful to those approaching the subject for the first time.

The story of the German take-over in synthetic dyes is carefully told in J. J. Beer, *The Emergence of the German Dye Industry* (Urbana, Ill., 1959*). But the reader is likely to gain more insight from *The British Coal-Tar Industry: its Origin, Development and Decline*, ed. W. M. Gardner (London, 1915). This is a collection of papers, originally written by eminent men in the industry or closely connected with it over the period 1868–1915, reprinted when the outbreak of war had revealed British weakness, in the hopes of starting a revival. If it is unobtainable, the reader will find much of its material palatably served up in J. G. Crowther's essay on Perkin in *British Scientists of the Nineteenth Century*, vol. 2 (Pelican edition, Harmondsworth, 1941*—the other editions do not include this essay), which in any case gives a racy and generally accurate account of the dyestuffs industry.

The Science Museum, London, publishes (through Her Majesty's Stationery Office) a series of (mostly excellent) pamphlets on various industries and technologies, which cannot be detailed here.

The developing discipline of industrial archaeology

provides the amateur with the opportunity for direct contact with some of the evidence of technological history. No bibliography can be attempted here, but the reader may care to sample the series 'The Industrial Archaeology of the British Isles' being published by David and Charles of Newton Abbot, or to dig in the journal *Industrial Archaeology*.

Two other journals should be mentioned. *The Transactions of the Newcomen Society* deals almost entirely with the history of British technology. Regrettably the approach is often too antiquarian, doing little to relate the technological material to history in general. *Technology and Society*, as its title indicates, *is* concerned with broader questions. It contains many useful papers, but one has to note that other contributions are remarkable more for their enthusiasm than for their historical judgement.

4. Banking and Industrialisation in Europe 1730–1914

Bertrand Gille

Banking *and* industrialisation: the link seems unbreakable. The whole rise of the banks in the nineteenth century runs parallel to the rise of industry; it is impossible to consider the one without the other. Yet this obvious truth, as it seems today, was for many years far from obvious to a previous age.

It may help us to keep things in their proper perspective if we deal with this topic under three main headings. For the sake of clarity, we will take them one by one.

The first has essentially to do with quantities. In all three sectors of credit — the short term, the middle and long term, and the formation of fixed capital — the demand for capital rose continually. We can determine the demand for short-term credit from the amount of discount handled by the central banks. But the demand for medium- and long-term credit — the latter a relatively recent development — is much harder to evaluate; and the investment in fixed assets in this period is virtually unknowable, even approximately, in quantitative terms. We may say, however, that the demand for capital necessarily tallied in every respect with the growth of the economy in general. We hardly need to insist on this point. However, we *should* perhaps insist on the fact that the structure of that demand was subject to evolution. At the start of our period, the demand was low and relatively dispersed. At the close, it was considerable and (up to a point) concentrated in large production units. This concentration in the demand was met by a gradual concentration in the supply, with the emergence of the large financial institutions.

The second aspect of the question is no less important, but has perhaps not received all the attention it deserves, despite the relative abundance of the sources. I am referring to the technical media of credit and financing. The things that concern us here are, of course, the volume and the structure of the demand for capital, but also the various forms of financial operations and their legal framework. A history of the techniques of banking or of capitalism in general would probably be an easy undertaking, seeing that very many handbooks on this subject were published in both the eighteenth and nineteenth centuries. The methods used for the circulation of capital and, what is more relevant to our topic, those used for its investment are on the whole well known. It remains to be shown how those methods evolved. Some interesting spadework has been done in this field, but much ground remains to be covered. The introduction of securities representing capital was necessarily bound up with the development and organisation of stock markets, and to a large extent conditioned the expansion of the deposit banks, then the appearance of investment banks, followed by that of the investment companies. Money, whose history has still to be written, was not the least important of these media: we know what a boon paper money and artificial exchange rates were for certain countries whose capital resources long remained low, both in volume and in accumulation.

Lastly, the question of economic attitudes has to all extents and purposes never been studied. Attitudes towards the banks — the almost indispensable bridge between demand and supply — differed at the outset and evolved considerably. Relations between bankers and industrialists necessarily belong to a sphere quite different from that of financial techniques or economic circumstance. Every relationship supposes at least two points of view on any given question. Certain hankerings after dominance and the fears that they inspired, the desire to go it alone — attitudes such as these had a direct bearing upon industry's relations with the bankers, and it would be wrong to neglect them. We should also note that the very type of the industrialist changed greatly in the course of the century. The family businessman, the great speculator, the chairman or director of joint-stock companies, the banker, or the financier cannot react in the same way to identical problems, and the variety of combinations possible is very large.

Hence the questions to be considered are very wide-ranging. We cannot hope to cover everything here: some points will regrettably have to be left in the dark, and several important questions will have to be left aside until further research or the discovery of new sources has given us more to go on. A further difficulty is that in this field there are no 'typical' structures or lines of development. The European economies all have their peculiarities to start with, and the staggered inception of industrialisation and industrial backing introduces further diversity from one country to another. This makes it difficult to view our essentially analytic subject in the round. Identical problems give rise to different solutions: this diversity is the inescapable consequence of structural differences on both the economic and the psychological planes.

After this definition of our subject, and before examining its various aspects one by one, we need to give a brief account of the situation in the second half of the eighteenth century. We shall limit our remarks to two countries: England (whose industrial revolution was already well under way) and France (where industrialisation was just beginning).

The English banking system does not appear to have been fully equipped to cope with the needs of modernised (and therefore generally larger) industrial units. The merchant bankers were much more interested in large-scale international trade and its concomitant financial transactions; as well as the state's requirements. The interest that they could take in industrial investment and credit facilities for industry was limited by the size of their available capital, and it was rather low in relation to the sudden high demand. When they backed industry, they did so first and foremost to support their own business activities. The English provincial banks, in their turn, were very small affairs with limited funds put up by small groups of partners. They received deposits and made payments; discounting

I

bills was the only activity open to them in the absence of any long-term commitments.

At the end of the eighteenth century the use of shares was more widespread in England than in any other country. This meant that English industry could draw on the vast wealth of the gentry and nobility, many of whom were willing to invest: the industrialist had relatively large amounts of capital to work with, and the capitalist held securities that were more or less negotiable. In many instances, however, it is difficult to distinguish between direct participations and long-term loans: a case in point is the arrangement that Lloyds Bank (founded in 1765) made with the Darby family at Coalbrookdale, and with Crowley, Wilkinson or Walker. David Landes has shown that the large London houses were relatively slow in entering the promotion field.

Long-term loans to industry were probably fairly common. Boulton, for one, got credits from Elliott & Praed, the Truro bankers, and from Lowe, Vere & Co. in London. Short-term credit, which was so hard to come by elsewhere, was certainly much easier in England owing to the spread of the provincial banks. English industry did not really get off the ground until the very end of the eighteenth century; its good fortune was to get permanent capital from a wealthy and favourably-disposed public as well as fairly generous facilities from the bankers.

On the continent, technical improvements and, correspondingly, the first large industrial ventures were very largely supported by the governments. Mines, mills and forges in France, Germany and Russia were able to start transforming themselves in the eighteenth century thanks to public money. This state interventionism was a direct extension of mercantilist practices. In France, indeed, a public organisation, the Caisse du Demi pour cent, had been founded to finance industrial development and transformation.

Research on the French and Belgian coal industry in the eighteenth century has shown that the demand for capital was very broad, but that almost all the supply came from

the private sector — merchants' class or even nobles.
Industrial investment during this period took the form of
illiquid shareholdings. Living off their deposits, the banks
could not afford this kind of risk, and having no securities
to offer their customers, could not act as brokers. They
shunned long-term commitments and only discounted bills
indirectly in order to provide themselves with instruments
of payment and exchange.

In France at this time, certain public figures played a
highly important role. Their functions were complex.
Nominally charged with the administration of public funds,
but true bankers in all but name, they involved government
money, entrusted capital and their personal fortunes in vast
industrial speculations. One of them, Baudard de Saint-
James, Treasurer-General of the Navy, invested capital in
the Le Creusot works — in which the king himself (i.e. the
state) had interests — in the Saint-Denis sheet lead enterprise, the Decize mines and glassworks, the mines at
Baigorry and Mons, a sailcloth mill, the famous Compagnie
des Eaux de Paris, and the Caisse d'Escompte.

True, we do come across bankers in France, Belgium and
Germany with interests in industrial ventures, particularly
those exploiting new techniques. Here we need to underline
two important points, which hold for much of the nineteenth century as well. It is not always possible to distinguish
between the investment of the bank and the personal investment of the banker. In either case, what was perhaps a
search for a flow of new banking business resulted in the
tying up of capital, which could be an excessive burden.
With investments amounting to 15.2 per cent of his assets,
Baudard de Saint-James went bankrupt in 1787 because
he was unable to mobilise his investments. The second point
is equally important: in the eighteenth century, banking
was still a very undifferentiated branch of business, and
many bankers were also industrialists. Two cases in point
are the textile manufacturers Périer at Grenoble and
Eichhorn at Breslau. Others belonged to the class of
merchant bankers so common in England: these men
invested to increase the turnovers of their businesses. The

Portalès family were bankers at Neuchâtel in Switzerland, but they also dominated the European calico trade. They financed the Le Pescheux spinning-mill at Saint-Véran near Lyons, and also provided capital for Bourgoin-Jallieu.

The main difference between the continental countries and England lay in the credit facilities available to industry. They were much lower on the continent, perhaps because the larger banks, which in many cases had links with the Geneva banks, got a large proportion of their profits from government financing. The long term was practically unknown and discount hard to come by.

At the start of the nineteenth century the situation was much as it had been at the end of the eighteenth: the private banks were still in control of the flow of money, on the continent at least; in England the joint-stock banks were beginning to spread (though not without causing some disturbances), ultimately to the great benefit of industry, especially as regards the short term. But the situation soon began to evolve rapidly. Increased industrialisation created an increased demand for capital: the setting up of protective customs barriers around 1820–1822 gave continental industrialists the power to stand up to English competition and brought in sufficient profits to make investment a paying proposition. Thanks to the rise of the joint-stock companies, investments became stable enough to suit the needs of the industrialists, and sufficiently mobile to suit those of the investors. Joint-stock companies spread in France and Belgium after 1830, in Germany after 1840, and in almost all the other countries after 1850.

As we have seen, the primary sources in our field are sadly lacking in detail. No serious inventory of bank archives has ever been made; the archives themselves are often badly conserved or simply not conserved at all. The printed sources are abundant enough, but they are often hard to interpret. The banks' balance sheets merely give a few lines of figures; the commentaries on the figures are almost always elliptic and can only give us a very rough idea of what the banks' policies may have been.

Until recently, the secondary sources were almost as

lacking. Over the past few years, however, historians have begun to take more interest in this fundamental sector of the economy, and several important studies have been published. But it cannot be overstressed that our greatest need is for monographs, of which we still have far too few.

This essay, then, can only be a temporary stopgap, as will be readily appreciated from the sketchy bibliography at its close. Therefore, over and above general and quantitative considerations, the interest of which is not denied, I would like to discuss the two essential problems that I have already defined: the evolution of banking techniques and the persistence of psychological behaviour patterns.

The technical problems were much easier to appreciate than to solve. As regards the short term, the problem was not really technical at all; the reason why it was hard to come by was perhaps due more to competition from other banking opportunities, in some countries at least, than to any difficulty of a practical kind, for it was technically simple. In England, where the joint-stock deposit banks spread very rapidly, discounting of bills was practised on a large scale. On the continent, by contrast, the private banks that controlled the flow of money for many years were not particularly interested in deposits, but got their profits from exchange and by acting as brokers. Hence, on the continent, discount long remained an adjunct of exchange — and a very limited adjunct into the bargain. This goes a long way towards explaining both the fairly high cost of discounting bills and the low amount of credit available.

As regards investment, however, bank support (issues of capital or long-term loans) was dependent on the introduction of appropriate techniques. What had to be found was a way of ensuring the stability of the investment from the industrialist's point of view while enabling the investor, if need be, to mobilise his investment. Shares, the instrument much used in England as early as the eighteenth century, took longer to catch on in continental Europe. Here again, certain considerations have to be taken into account. For a share to be easily negotiable, it had to be in the form of bearer securities; but this meant that the issuing enterprise could lose track of its shareholders. Also, just as important, the enterprise had to find a sufficiently receptive and active market for the issue and negotiation of its securities. To get itself known, and to keep its shares at a certain level — an essential condition for future issues — were both immediate and long-term preoccupations for the firm.

The problem was exactly the same as regards long-term credit, with the additional requirement of a guarantee, which the shareholder had no reason to expect since he was a part-owner of the enterprise. It was impossible to get loans from a single source for more than a certain sum. For many years, the guarantee took the form of a mortgage, and in many countries mortgages were cumbersome instruments until the indispensable techniques for dealing with them had been devised — fairly early on in Germany, but not until the second half of the nineteenth century in France and Belgium. Well before then, in fact before 1830, the Basle banks split their industrial loans into notes of equal value which they placed with their customers; the loans themselves were guaranteed by mortgages. This was an industrial adaptation of the government loan notes that had formerly made the fortunes of the Geneva banks. After 1830 it was the borrower himself who split his loan by offering securities of equal value covering the whole of the loan: these were called bonds, and the first of their kind were issued for the French railways from 1837 onwards. The methods used for placing these new instruments were much the same as those used for shares.

Having defined the situation as regards the demand, we now need to take a brief look at the structures of the supply. Savings were much more dispersed. Would-be investors had no means of knowing what investments might interest them, nor, even if they had known, any way of subscribing directly. To be sure, the increase in the numbers of bank outlets had considerably narrowed the gap between supply and demand, just as the extension of the post and telegraph services had quite considerably modified the techniques used by the banks. But, this apart, we have to consider quite different factors, the most important of which, perhaps, were psychological. In the first place, the investor had to choose between variable-yield securities and fixed-yield securities — between shares and bonds. By far the most security-minded of the European peoples, the French preferred fixed-yield securities, hence (later) the crashing success in France of foreign loan bonds, the other aspect of which we shall discuss below. The Germans and English were much keener on shares. (The French prefer financial secrecy and bearer securities, perhaps with an eye on evading taxation. In England, registered shares are much more common: not only are dividends and coupons payable via cheque through the banks or even at the shareholder's home, but also the companies know who their shareholders are and can keep them informed without resorting to the often excessive publicity used elsewhere.) In some European countries, those whose development did not become sure until the very end of our period, the accumulation of capital was extremely difficult. This situation made international transfers of capital imperative; up to the eve of the First World War, there was total freedom of action in this domain, but the technical problems were much greater.

The point where supply and demand meet is the market. Considering all the difficulties involved, the organisation of a market for capital could only be complex. Several stages need to be distinguished. 1. As was natural, the negotiation of existing stocks took place on the bourse, thanks to a whole series of middle-men, among which we must surely include the banks. 2. A much more important stage was that concerned with issues. In reality, no direct issues of industrial stocks were ever possible, except in the case of a few railway companies whose stations served as outlets. In most cases it was necessary to resort to the banks as go-betweens.

Hence the banks stood at the centre of the market, gathering in savings on one side and putting them back into circulation on the other. But the banker himself was in business to make money; and the nature of his own business had changed appreciably. At all events, the very principles of banking procedure made the adoption of two complementary rules imperative: the conditions under which funds were borrowed must correspond to those under which they were lent. This was the only way the banking institution could maintain its liquidity, i.e. be able to liquidate its business within a given period of time. In this respect it was aided by its own capital — itself a guarantee rather than ready cash.

It follows, then, that the banks had to have resources equal to the industrial policy that they wished to pursue. Now, the resources of the private banking system, which was the system of all continental Europe, were necessarily limited. With a very few distinguished exceptions, the private banks had low capital and relatively low deposits. Thus their policy was concerned neither with investment, which they would have been hard put to practise, nor even with credit, but almost entirely with business on commission. The only deposit banks in existence were the English banks, and they alone discounted bills. These private banks, then, were not particularly interested in deposits, which were a heavy burden owing to the interest that had to be paid on them; and what deposits they had were only accepted if the depositer's wealth or bond guaranteed that the deposits would be relatively stable.

With regard to industry, therefore, the only long-term aid that could be made available consisted of loans, which were limited in both quantity and duration. True, some bankers successfully carried on this kind of business with mortgage guarantees; but they only did so insofar as their deposits were stable.

The launching of new ventures was much more difficult, as was the placing of large debenture loans. Some banks could count on their reputations to find a public for the securities that they were asked to place; but they were few, and were generally very choosy about the securities that they accepted. They were not greatly hampered by any lack of outlets, for their network of tried and trusted correspondents reached a fairly wide public. But only a very few enterprises could benefit from this arrangement, and the banks were keener on using their outlets for the distribution of government bonds and the like: this enabled them to furnish the capital needed by the railway enterprises, whose shares and obligations, with interest guaranteed by the government, had much the same status as the government's own issues.

Inasmuch as industrialisation — by which I mean the creation of large industrial enterprises — required increasing amounts of capital from an ill-informed or uninformed public, it was imperative that other banking structures and techniques be devised. An answer had to be found for the long-term, not merely by bringing in savings from every possible quarter, but also by bridging the gap before public investment. Finally, in many instances, bank credit, known and trusted, had to stand in, at least for a time, for the unknown credit of industrial enterprises.

Were the Saint-Simonians the first to form an idea of the extensive role that the banks could play in an industrial economy? As early as the first decades of the nineteenth century, the shortage of capital for industrial development was patent everywhere but in England. 'In a society where some possess the tools of industry without being able or willing to put them to work, and where others, who are industrious, lack the tools to work with, the aim of credit must be to get the tools from the former, who own them, to the latter, who know how to put them to work.'

Though true, the text is vague. Banks did not create capital, but they stimulated the circulation of capital, headed it in the right direction, and harmonised the uses to which it was put. Some thought the banks should be centralised, each particular bank playing a specialised role within the whole. Inheritances and state capital would provide this 'Banque centrale de Crédit industriel' with additional funds.

But the germ of several new technical notions is already present in these writings. The Saint-Simonians believed that bills payable on demand were of no practical use; for long-term credits, the bank would issue bills payable at the same dates as the credits: this was the bank's own credit standing in for that of the industrial enterprise. For the capitalisation of industrial companies, the bank should act solely as a go-between. To help approved industrial ventures, it should issue long-term loans pending public buying up of these shares. Even at this early date, it was believed that the bank would eventually absorb public credit, extend its activities beyond national boundaries and bolster those countries where capital was in insufficient supply. To ensure that the money available was suitably distributed among the applicants, three committees would be set up to advise the board: a committee of scholars, a committee of technicians, and a third committee dealing with 'finance and political economy'. In part, this was basically the system that was in fact adopted during much of the nineteenth century.

In fact, the first practical experiment slightly preceded the expression of the Saint-Simonians' ideas. We find the first mention of the Société commanditaire de l'industrie by the Paris banker J. Laffitte in June 1825. Its declared aim was to 'contribute to and participate in the success of any enterprise, invention or improvement relating to agriculture, industry or commerce', with certain restrictions that we will discuss below.

The plan provided for a capital of 100 million francs, but no details were given as to how aid was to be applied for. But we know that applications were to be examined by a specialised sub-committee of the board of directors. Most of the Paris bankers and politicians subscribed for shares, and the enthusiasm of foreign bankers such as Baring, Irving, or Ricardo in England, Hentsch in Switzerland, and various bankers in Germany gave Laffitte's project a thoroughly international look.

The company was to take the form of a *société anonyme*; this meant that it had to get government approval, which was refused. In addition, the crisis that set in in November 1825 was hardly favourable for the setting up of a venture of this scope and importance. In the present state of our knowledge it is not possible to list all the similarities it may have had with the ideas of the Saint-Simonians.

The case of the Société générale de Belgique is frequently

cited. It was founded in 1822, during the period of Dutch domination, under the aegis of the King of Holland, at a time when the Belgian economy was in almost complete stagnation. Its title, Société générale des Pays-bas pour favoriser l'industrie nationale, is a fair summary of its aims: 'to contribute to the progress, development and prosperity of agriculture, industry and commerce, yet without being able to trade in anything except gold or silver'. By the terms of its charter, it was effectually limited to the issue of bills payable on demand and the ordinary operations of a discount bank. People still believed that aid to industry should bear less on capitalisation — which was the industrialists' business — than on a more extensive use of discount. However impressive the bank's capital may have appeared on paper, it was tied up right from the start in government stocks and a large forestry estate. Hence, at first, this institution was a far cry from the ideas of the Saint-Simonians and the aspirations of Laffitte. Up to 1830, the Société générale de Belgique managed its estates, dealt in deposits and public credit and, so far as industry was concerned, contented itself with working a slate mine in one of its forests and opening a lead mine that was soon abandoned.

The revolution and crisis of 1830 threw it willy-nilly into industry. The liquidation of several private banks brought masses of industrial shares into its hands. Also, to justify its existence, it had to bring some life back into the Belgian economy, in the first instance by granting aid to industry. When the recovery came in 1835, the Société générale de Belgique had been obliged to take up quite a considerable quantity of industrial securities in this way, and to create others besides. What had merely been an expedient thereupon became a deliberate policy. 'The Board of the Société générale has applied itself to creating and spreading the spirit of association as a means to prosperity and development for this country's industry. The Board, focusing its attention on our beautiful provinces, has been struck by the immensity of the wealth with which several parts of our soil have been endowed by Nature; but, at the same time, it has appreciated that it is frequently the case for the proprietors of the wealthiest of mines and the most useful and efficient of manufactories to lack sufficient means for the development of production. At a time when coal has become the main element of industrial wealth, when iron is of such paramount utility and such widespread employment, could our mines and forges continue to languish, without results for those whose fortunes are invested in them, and without increasing the wealth of our land? When each day the applied sciences discover new techniques which fundamentally transform the system of manufacture and which, whilst reducing the cost of production, increase and improve the product, when new industries are brought to us from abroad, were we to see them refused for lack of capital? Were we to see our raw materials exported only to be brought back to us with their cost increased by the manufacturing profit? The Board has deemed that it should not be so and that, in these circumstances, it was fulfilling its mandate by lending its support and by furnishing, with prudence, capital for industry.'

The Société générale de Belgique immediately ran up against the major difficulty: the impossibility of mobilising short-term deposits. New methods had to be devised. In 1834 it studied a plan for a 'Caisse des capitaux accumulés avec ou sans intérêt'. In 1835 it founded two finance companies, the Société de Commerce de Bruxelles and the Société nationale pour les entreprises industrielles et commerciales. These were equivalent to our modern investment companies. The company's capital was subscribed by the public, and the company held a portfolio carefully designed to avoid losses. In addition to their own stocks, these companies issued long-term loans that enabled them to finance commercial or industrial enterprises, founded as or converted into joint-stock companies, by taking up part of their shares, which were then gradually sold off to the public. Hence, at one and the same time, they worked as investment companies and, thanks to the capital brought in by the sale of fixed-yield bonds, as temporary finance companies for unproved enterprises.

Industrialisation went ahead so fast that in 1837 the

percentage of permanent investments in the Société générale's balance sheets stood at 70 per cent. The finance companies were also at the end of their resources. Thereupon an attempt was made to reach the small saver. The Société générale founded the Société des Capitalistes réunis, a real open-end investment company (unit trust), whose resources came from small amounts of long-term capital investments. Here again, the portfolio was designed to take the minimum of risks. It was hoped by this scheme to reach the small 'capitalist' whose savings were insufficient for him to invest directly.

Founded in 1835, the Banque de Belgique followed the same course of action. In October the same year, the chairman was authorised to take shareholdings in industry. Encountering the same obstacle, the Banque de Belgique founded a Société des Actions réunies, which had the same aim as the subsidiaries of the Société générale.

The aim of these finance companies was, then, to favour investment. Société de Commerce and Société nationale aimed above all at providing starting capital and temporary backing for companies. Mutualité and Actions réunies were a kind of industrially-minded savings bank. They were active in France and Germany as well as Belgium.

In 1837 Laffitte founded the Caisse générale du Commerce et de l'Industrie, which made use of some of his earlier ideas. This bank seems to have been essentially a deposit bank dealing in all the current short-term operations. Like the private banks, it naturally attempted to secure stable forward deposits by issuing what were still called bills — 'a secure and profitable shelter for temporarily unemployed capital'. But it was intended that this capital was to be used first and foremost for making more or less long-term advances.

There was more to come, however. 'I will hide nothing from you,' Laffitte writes in his circular. 'My first step is to establish an ordinary bank, but I have in mind to convert it, with the co-operation of picked associates, into a real commercial and industrial bank.' It rather looks as if, returning to his ideas of 1825, and more or less imitating the Société générale de Belgique, Laffitte wished to create a second Société commanditaire de l'industrie designed to promote 'industrial association'. This society was to have been headed by Laffitte and Arago: the financial abilities of the former and the scientific knowledge of the latter would have enabled them to judge the merits of the concerns asking for aid. In September 1838 the statutes were ready. Government hostility and the crisis of December 1838 once again brought the proceedings to a halt.

Deposit banks modelled on the Caisse Laffitte appeared in Paris and throughout France. Those of their founders who were aware of the workings of finance statutorily excluded the right to invest in industry, often with the exception of companies working state concessions (mines and railways).

Yet mention must be made of an interesting experiment that managed to survive for quite some time. The Société lyonnaise d'Emploi de fonds et de crédit, usually known as the Omnium lyonnais, was founded in 1838. In addition to the sale and purchase of securities and tendering for loans, it invested in industry and held an investment portfolio, thereby aiding the Lyons merchants with regard to their investments, most of which went into coal mines and bridge-building and gaslight companies.

The Belgian and French examples won little following in the other continental countries. In Prussia, an active *homme d'affaires*, whom we shall meet again later, tried as early as 1845 to form a joint-stock bank in Cologne, one of the aims being to assist the development of industry in Westphalia, the Rhineland and Prussia. This attempt was no doubt premature. The Berlin Seehandlungs Gesellschaft, founded in 1772, had for all intents and purposes become a department of the Bank of Prussia. After 1830 this company also began financing industry on quite a big scale: mechanical engineering, weaving, spinning and flour-milling.

The crisis of 1848 revealed, especially in France, that these techniques could not cope with the increase in industrialisation and the appreciable increase in the size of the firms. Its immediate result was to focus attention on the reconstruction of the short-term credit system. The very titles of the French Comptoirs d'Escompte, founded in 1848, and the Disconto Gesellschaft, founded in 1851, show what was expected of them. When the recovery set in in 1852, an attempt was made to take up the ideas that had gone before in the light of what proved to have been a salutary setback.

The founding of the Péreire brothers' Crédit mobilier marked an important step forward. 'The policy behind the Crédit mobilier has been inspired by the insufficiency of credit resources available for the organisation of industry in this country, by the state of isolation to which our financial forces have come, and by the absence of a sufficiently powerful co-ordinating centre.' This was a clear indictment of the existing bank system.

Leaving aside the ordinary banking business that the crédit mobilier was to perform as a deposit and discount bank, we shall examine the way in which it was to function as an industrial finance company. One of its first aims was certainly the centralisation of the different credit operations required by large enterprises: capitalisation, issues of bonds, long-term credits. Hence its activities covered at one and the same time the placing of securities with its clients, temporary investment pending resale of these securities, and probably permanent investment as well, insofar as the bank intended to keep a say in the management of the companies it patronised. This intervention had to go hand in hand with a change in the industrial structure: enterprises had to join forces to form units large enough to cope with foreign competition on the day free trade was introduced.

Long-term capital was necessary for this plan to be feasible. To begin with, there was the capital stock of 60 million francs. For the rest, the crédit mobilier counted on the issue of debentures (*obligations à échéance*). The maturity dates would be made to tally with those of the bank's commitments — real dates in the case of advances and credits, supposed dates in the case of temporary investment. It should thus be possible to get sleeping cash and idle capital back into circulation. The form of the obligations enabled those who invested their ready cash in these loans to benefit from their mobility. A further advantage, not the least in the eyes of the sponsors, was that this system made it possible to substitute bank credit for the unknown or suspect credit of the ventures that came to it for aid. The statutes had wisely laid down restrictions on issues, exactly like those imposed on the central banks.

That was not all, however. The Péreires' plan embraced the whole of Europe. Their wish was to create similar establishments abroad to help in the development of industrially backward countries. What they wanted more than anything was to maintain close links with all the banks founded in this way. 'While ensuring that these establishments remain free to act according to the special requirements of each nation's industry, we must carefully avoid the dangers of isolation. We must strive to develop their capacity for expansion and association; links must be forged between them, for that is how we shall put capital to its most efficient use and give it, once a certain stage has been reached, the broadest and most influential range of action.' The obligations issued by the various crédits mobiliers, the interest on which would be payable at a standard rate, might then become an all-embracing security for the whole of Europe. According to its sponsors, this system would result in the available capital dispersed and perhaps trapped in diverse European lands being grouped together in great financial centres, in the direct application of this capital in the most efficient and satisfactory way, in a general lowering and standardising of rates of interest, in the introduction of a European credit paper, in the gradual disappearance of most of the obstacles that made credit transactions so difficult, slow and costly within Europe, and eventually in a single credit and currency system for the whole of Europe. The hope was for a kind of common market for capital with a view to the generalised development of industry.

The first imitation in Europe of the Crédit mobilier de Paris was the Darmstädter Bank für Handel und Industrie, founded in 1854. The idea was Mevissen's: he conferred with a Cologne banker, Oppenheim, who called in the crédit mobilier. The latter went into the deal in force and took out a very large share in it. The aims of this bank were the same: 'to provide German industry with temporary capital to meet special needs; to make it easier for these industries to increase their capital by advancing it to them for a specified period; but also to participate in these industries on a lasting basis, founding them if need be, and helping them in an advisory capacity ... To help the expansion of important and responsible enterprises by participating in them in its own right and with its own funds: it will also strive, as far as possible, to orientate the spirit of enterprise and German capital towards the real needs of the moment — the development of German industry.'

In 1856, after some hesitation, other imitations followed in astonishingly rapid succession. Every region in Europe, and in some countries every town, wanted to have a 'crédit mobilier' of its own. These establishments fall into three broad groups. There were those founded under the aegis of the Crédit mobilier de Paris and based on the concept of internationalism. There were those, generally purely national, founded under the auspices of the Rothschilds, who entered this field, which they did not approve of, to counterbalance the influence of the Péreires. And lastly, there were those that were independent of these two financial groups. Whatever the affiliations of these new 'crédits mobiliers' as they were known whatever their exact title, many private banks participated in their establishment, as they had already done for that of the Crédit mobilier de Paris. The Péreires failed in their bid against the Rothschilds in Vienna and Turin. Their bids were turned down in Amsterdam, Antwerp, Naples, Rome, and in Russia: the reason given in the first two countries was that there were enough banks already, and in the last three countries that the state's economic development was insufficient to warrant the foundation of a crédit mobilier. In Berlin, both the Péreires and the Rothschilds were sent packing. In Madrid, however, there was a welcome for everyone, and three crédits mobiliers were founded.

Germany was particularly affected by this craze for crédits mobiliers: fifteen institutions of this kind were founded in 1855–1856. The Disconto Gesellschaft itself, founded as a deposit and discount bank, restyled itself as a crédit mobilier in 1856. Switzerland, despite its plethora of powerful private banks, witnessed the arrival of three crédits mobiliers, the most important of which, or at least the longest-lived, was the Schweizerische Creditanstalt. Even Sweden got its crédit mobilier, the Stockholms Enskilda Bank.

The crédits mobiliers were at one and the same time deposit and discount banks and investment banks. But the early enthusiasm soon gave way to caution in the face of banking inflation. The crisis of 1857 proved that things had gone rather too far. The sobering-up process that followed was marked, in France, by the creation of three large institutions that dealt exclusively in deposits, Crédit industriel et commercial (1859), Crédit lyonnais (1863), and the Société générale de France (1864). The financing of industrial ventures was forbidden by the statutes, or remained extremely limited.

The years 1863 and 1864 were marked by the recovery of the crédits mobiliers, again under the impulsion of the Crédit mobilier de Paris, which returned to its policy of expansion. United Italy took part in this movement: the Italian Crédit mobilier, remodelled by its French homonym, began a brilliant, if stormy, second career. Its complement, the Credito italiano, became Italy's main deposit bank.

Even at that early date, however, it seems that the Péreires' implementation of the Saint-Simonian notions was doomed. A move was afoot towards a new kind of institution, the *banques d'affaires* or investment banks. There was potential danger in the issue of obligations, with which, moreover, many industrialists refused to deal. *Banques d'affaires* act with capital of their own, take up shareholdings and issue securities through associated deposit banks, the latter providing the retail outlets lacked by the former. For indeed the deposit banks spread rapidly throughout Europe, opening thousands of branches. This policy seems to have been inaugurated by the French Société générale in the very year it was founded, 1864. In 1870 it already had thirty-three agencies scattered throughout France. On the eve of the First World War, the Crédit lyonnais had 374 permanent branches and agencies as against the 594 of the Société générale de France. All these outlets — France in particular was almost saturated with them — aimed at gathering in private savings. The *banques d'affaires*, for their part, had no agencies (at the very most a few subsidiaries abroad) and used their funds to take out shareholdings in industry, the aim of which was to bring in not so much income or capital gains as a permanent flow of business.

In France, the first — and for many years the only — bank of this kind was the Banque de Paris et des Pays-bas, founded in 1872 from the merger of two banks. Its fairly close links with the Société générale de France provided it with the funds that it lacked. The second great *banque d'affaires* in France was the Banque de l'Union parisienne, founded in 1904 by a group of private (and mostly Protestant) banks in Paris to make sure of a strong position on the stock market.

A relative latecomer on the French financial market, the Banque des Pays-bas was very active abroad: government loans, railways and industrial enterprises. It founded two foreign subsidiaries (Brussels and Geneva) and elsewhere took out participations in various foreign banks — in Spain (1878: Credito general espanol), Italy (1896: Banca commerciale italiana), Russia (1899: Banque russo-chinoise), Egypt (1908) and South America (1910: Banque italienne et française pour l'Amérique du Sud).

In the other countries, the crédits mobiliers, variously remodelled or completely transformed, served as *banques d'affaires*. The network was completed after various calamities had resulted in a simplification of the banking map. We may mention: in Germany, the Deutsche Bank (1870), the Dresdner Bank (1872), the latter a transformation of a private bank, and the National Bank für Deutschland (1881); in Italy, after the crash of 1893, a new network was built up with support from certain German banks, a network based essentially on the new Credito italiano and the Banca commerciale italiana.

In fact, this move from the crédit mobilier type of bank to the *banque d'affaires* was partly due to the European public's growing familiarity with industrial stocks and to the spread of the banks. From then on, there was much less need for the stopgap type of bank founded by the Péreires and their imitators.

We began this discussion by stating that the evolution of the banking system seemed roughly to follow the evolution of industrial enterprises on the one hand and that of the stock market on the other. That statement, as we have seen, is amply borne out by the facts. The banks had to adapt continually to changing conditions. If we look for periods in that evolution, we find: (i) between 1815 and 1848, a period of uncertainty, with a growing tension between industrial evolution and varying degrees of banking immobility; (ii) the period 1850–1870 saw the craze for crédits mobiliers, which were perhaps more effective in other countries than they were in France; and (iii) after 1870, the *banques d'affaires* took over from the crédits mobiliers. Surprisingly enough, England alone was unaffected by this long chain of developments. England had contrived to create types of banks that suited its rapid rise to economic refinement. Thanks to the English public's rapid adoption of deposits and to their country's well-rooted banking tradition, England managed to avoid the unwieldiness of the continental system, which was, so to speak, encumbered by its metal money. The English banks were the hub of world trade, of course.

I have referred to the importance of psychological factors, or economic behaviour patterns. They are important despite the fact that they vary greatly in kind and intensity from one country to another. We often find, on the one hand, industrialists refusing to have anything to do with the banks, and on the other, banks hesitating to take the plunge into industrial ventures. The situation was not so much one of active strife as of fundamental opposition, for reasons that were generally completely different from one person to another.

We need to remember the position of the entrepreneurs. In the nineteenth century very many family firms still existed. Clannish and proud, many of them refused to let strangers into their business. The joint-stock companies themselves often continued in the family tradition, or passed into the hands of small closed groups. In the large enterprises founded by economic adventurers, the possessive instinct was perhaps even stronger. On either side, the major concern was with keeping one's independence, with going it alone. The fear of distraint and eviction was very great. The immediate corollary of this attitude was the one that maintained that the bankers knew nothing of the industrialists' problems and were incapable of framing their policy accordingly. Industry required special knowledge, mainly technical knowledge, that the bankers neither had nor were capable of appreciating or acquiring.

It should be possible to collect a great many examples of this state of mind, which was so firmly anchored, even in England. We come across them especially after 1850, when the banks became more active; but they reflect a situation that existed long before then. 'There's no getting on with men like these,' wrote Ferdinand de Lesseps when launching his Compagnie universelle du Canal de Suez. '. . . The bankers are trying to get me to toe the line. I won't. I'll go it alone.' De Lesseps's biographer adds the comment that the founder of Suez had only the sketchiest understanding of finance. Krupp, for his part, developed his businesses so fast between 1855 and 1866 that he ran out of capital. The banks could not help him individually, and it seemed to him that the proposed consortium would put a rope round his neck. He demanded twenty million and no interference. He eventually had to seek a solution to his financial problems elsewhere.

Other sentiments besides these were involved. The nobility of work in industry was often contrasted with the parasitism of the moneybags, the utility of work with the futility of the banks. The banks, as the catchphrase went, did not create capital. Bank policy was blamed for the crisis of 1838–1839. During much of the nineteenth century, it was commonly held that the industrial regions did not need banks and never would. Here is what the chairman of a bank in Lille had to say as late as 1869: 'There is no scope for a deposit bank in Lille. Lille is not a capitalist town, it is first and foremost a great industrial and commercial centre where savings are consolidated as soon as they are produced, where floating capital is the exception rather than the rule, and where the true role of a bank is to lend money rather than receive it. Nor are we in a suitable environment for an issuing bank. Important deals are never planned in the provinces; no provincial bank has enough scope for it to become an efficient and influential issuing bank.'

This was only a short step from thinking that industry and imagination were as synonymous as banking and sterility. Though he belongs to a later period, we may cite the example of the great French automobile manufacturer, André Citroën. What would there be left of him, his biographer writes, if he accepted backing from the bankers? Was he to become a mere branch of the Union parisienne, the Banque Rothschild, or the Banque Lazard? 'He will have nothing to do with the bankers . . . he will have nothing to do with accountants, figure-jugglers, decimal-point fusspots.' Citroën himself typically declared, 'I'll have no truck with the bankers, banking is the death of the spirit.'

In many countries on the continent, credit was held to be the same as debt, and the dread of debt was universal. François de Wendel was wracked by this fear from 1807 to 1822, despite the fact that his calls for credit were numerous, amounting as they did to close on three million, a considerable sum for his day. But his notebooks reflect the nagging care this caused him. We should add that, contrary to general practice in England, the interest rate on money was very high in continental Europe.

Are we to infer that this situation was universal? In all truth, we lack precise information for the other countries. The entrepreneur class in Belgium was smaller than in France. Belgium's sole very great industrialist between 1830 and 1848 was Cockerill, an Englishman. He did not turn to the banks until he began to run into trouble: first the Banque de Belgique then, when the crisis of 1839 put the Banque de Belgique in a bad way, the Société générale de Belgique. All the anniversary albums published by the great industrial firms, including Cockerill's, cast a coy veil over relations between industrialists and bankers, as if there was something improper in mentioning them. This is true of the most recent of them as well.

It is safe to say that in the first part of the nineteenth century industrialists only called in the banks when they were absolutely forced to. Often, indeed, the call came when the situation had become desperate or utterly hopeless. Aid was requested in particular to develop the manufacturing process; but over-rapid development in this branch merely led the industrialists into still deeper waters. This policy resulted in trouble for the banks and encouraged mistrust on the part of the bankers, about whom we shall have something to say later.

This negative attitude seems to have persisted, not to say worsened, when the credit institutions gradually took over from the private banks. One could always get on with a banker one knew well, a personal friend or fellow-councillor; everything was different when one had to deal with an anonymous body of strangers who bombarded you with questions and laid down conditions. As we have seen, changes in the structures of industry had already been proposed by the Péreires' Crédit mobilier; concentration resulted in individual enterprises being engulfed by larger groups: the industrialists' mistrust of the banks was consequently all the greater. On the other hand, the large industrial enterprises could argue with the banks on an equal footing: we shall see how important the consequences of this were in Germany. For their part, the railway companies had fairly rapidly succeeded in ensuring their financial independence and had technical resources that enabled them to deal directly with the public; to be sure, the guarantee of interest put their securities on a par with government stocks in most of the continental countries.

This attitude in industry had important consequences. Enterprises, particularly in France, often wildly resorted to self-financing. This practice necessitated relatively high selling prices and their inevitable corollary, severe ·tariff protections. Throughout the nineteenth century, the industrialists of most countries were fervent protectionists, providing they had no interests in foreign markets. There can be no doubt that Italian industry, buttressed as it was by forced currency, did not grow appreciably until a measure of protectionism was introduced after the 1880s.

Self-financing also presupposed slow growth, inefficiently small enterprises, prolonged use of plant and, quite frequently, a fair share of mistrust for technical innovations. This resulted in the survival, in some sectors at least, of small to middling family enterprises — an uncompromising fragmentation of industrial production. It is very probable that the same symptoms were present in the industrial structures of England.

For the older type of firm, self-financing was the only way it could conserve its family status. For the joint-stock companies it was the only means of restricting the number of shareholders and keeping one's independence. All that was required from time to time, when investment was needed both urgently and on a sizeable scale, was a call on medium- or long-term credit, thus mobilising in advance self-financing that would otherwise have come too late and been too small. We would need to tabulate balance sheets to appreciate this movement in the accumulation of capital, which partly demolished the banks' raison d'être. It is a pity that such balance sheets have rarely come down to us, for a study of them would be much more instructive and interesting than any study of profits, those ephemeral reflections of a changing situation. Here, nonetheless, are a few figures drawn mainly from French enterprises.

The Wendels' capital stock moved from 1,230,401 francs on 30th June, 1825, to 30,000,000 in 1870, all from self-financing, since no outside calls were made apart from a few bank loans as stopgaps. From 1830 to 1846, Decazeville increased its stock by around 7,000,000 — as much again as it had started out with — by withholding dividends. In 1880, Forges de Terrenoire had financed themselves to the tune of 17,000,000 since their début, whereas the capital had remained virtually the same. In 1848, Saint-Gobain had a reserve of 9,000,000, as much again as its capital.

It might reasonably be thought that this policy changed somewhat in the late nineteenth and early twentieth centuries. But it seems not. One example will suffice. The founding of new industrial enterprises, especially in the traditional sectors, made no call on the banks. The founding of Aciéries de Longwy in 1880 was due exclusively to industrialists, twelve of them in all, who shared the initial capital investment. From 1880 to 1914 the capital stock of this important enterprise merely doubled, from 15 to 30 million. Gross profits accounted for close on 145.5 million, distributed profits for around 50.5 million, and self-financing (including depreciation) for 87.7 million, excluding sundry write-offs doubtless included in the trading accounts, amounting to over 77.5 million. This example typifies the policy pursued by French industry; similar facts would be found in many other enterprises.

France was perhaps an extreme case, but the same situation may well have existed in England. Let us be quite clear about the two things we are considering. Self-financing was only possible in the case of enterprises that had been established and flourishing for a long period of time. They had had a whole century, so to speak, to digest technical progress and growth. This in itself led them to create a mentality that is often found in the older industrial countries with firmly-established traditions of management. There are indeed two cases to consider, each slightly different from the other.

The first concerns the younger industrial countries with little or no tradition of management. To make up for lost time, considerable capital and reliable management were needed. This was generally where the banks came in, inasmuch as they could find the necessary capital and insofar as they could supply guidance in the absence of proven management. This was striking in Belgium in the aftermath of independence, and in certain industries formed from domanial or feudal units in central Europe — in Austria and certain regions of Germany, for example. Differences of this kind are clearly reflected in the different results obtained by the various European crédits mobiliers.

This is also true of the industries that mushroomed at the end of the nineteenth century as a result of technical progress. Here again, we are obliged to make a few distinctions. Certain industries undoubtedly had no particular appeal for the banks, to begin with at least. Here the field was wide open for the economic adventurers: the automobile industry is a striking example. Other mushroom industries, by contrast, whose tremendous potential was instinctively grasped almost from the start, got considerable backing and guidance from the banks: the obvious example is electricity. Over and above this distinction between different sectors of industry, we can perhaps make another distinction, this time by countries. France, apart from its automobile industry, which did not really become an 'industry' until the First World War, produced none of the rocketing self-made tycoons that the United States turned out by the score; in Germany, by contrast, such men were relatively common, even in the electrical industry. We shall discuss their relations with the banks a few lines farther on.

To close this brief (and tentative) discussion of the industrialists' attitude towards the banks, we need to consider a further aspect, which is not the least complicated. Beyond a certain stage in its development, industry could not help feeling the need for the services of the banks. In the first half of the nineteenth century, however distant they may have been, relations between industrialists and bankers were not too difficult: business was conducted on a personal basis; as we have seen, industrialists and bankers often had social contacts over and above their business connections. The very smallness of the banking institutions, almost all of which were private banks, meant that their fears were as yet modest ones, just as requests for aid were limited by the scope of the industrial enterprises. As soon as the first mighty financial institutions came along, however, as soon as the demand for capital grew in size and spread, the types of relationship changed. This gave rise to the notion that industrialists might found their own banking institutions. But it took time, many false starts, and a good deal of experimentation before the notion was successfully put into practice.

One of the earliest experiments in France came during the July Monarchy. Founded in 1837, the Caisse Laffitte, as we have seen, was a purely financial organisation directed by bankers. However, there was good reason for industrialists with linked interests — one can barely call them 'groups' — to form similar institutions to meet their own ends. This came about in 1846, with the founding of the Caisse Baudon, which was largely modelled on the Caisse Laffitte. This institution resulted from the collaboration of a group of bankers (the same ones who had founded the Paris-Orleans railway) and industrialists with whom they had common interests: Alais, Decazeville and Fourchambault, and Mines de la Loire, who had recently pulled off a spectacular merger. The Caisse Baudon did not last very long; it went under in the great crisis of 1848.

The experiment was important, however. When the banks became joint-stock companies, the industrialists could take out interests in them, join their boards and help to shape their policies. In a way, the industrialists did to the banks what they feared the banks would do to them.

The way the Crédit mobilier de Paris was founded and the composition of its board of directors are equally revealing. So long as the reins were held by bankers and financiers, the industrialists refused to touch the shares of any new banking venture. There can be no denying that the declared policy of the Crédit mobilier had enough in it to frighten French industrialists. It was also a cause for concern in political circles, despite all the benefits the latter had reaped from it. This may explain the subsequent reaction, which we have already discussed. This reaction was reflected in the creation of new finance institutions with a different outlook.

At the same time, however, there was a re-emergence of

the link between industrialists and finance institutions that had already been apparent on the eve of the revolution of 1848. Industrialists may be found on the boards of these new finance organisations, sometimes in force. In 1859 the following were members of the board of the Crédit industriel et commercial: Arlès-Dufour, the Lyons silk-merchant, Hochet, the head of Fourchambault, who had already belonged to the board of the Caisse Baudon, West and Delahante, who had been directors of the great Compagnie des Mines de la Loire, Parent, a public works contractor, Dehaynin, a contractor to the gas and coal industry, and Montané, a shipbuilder. The professional bankers were almost the minority.

The board of the Crédit lyonnais, founded in 1863, is just as revealing. Henri Germain was at Mines de Montramebert, Hauts-fourneaux de Marseille, Forges de Commentry, and Ateliers de la Buire; Jullien was the head of Forges de Terrenoire; Colongeat and Ferouillat were directors of the Firminy steel plant; Ferouillat was chairman of Forges de l'Horme; Basset was at Forges de Commentry and Forges de Saint-Etienne, Bouthier at Hauts-fourneaux de Chasse, Brölemann at Aciéries de la Marine, Desseilligny at Le Creusot and Decazeville. On the Société générale de France, founded in 1864, the financiers were present in greater numbers, but the industrialists were not absent, far from it. Parent belonged both to the Crédit industriel et commercial and the Société générale. Schneider, the chief of Le Creusot, was for many years chairman of the Société générale.

To be sure, the provision of finance for industry was forbidden, or extremely restricted, in all these institutions. In point of fact, French industrialists, whose need for short-term capital was permanent owing to the fact that they were forever investing their working capital, helped to found deposit banks in order to get round this difficulty. Their aim was to provide themselves with a facility that English industrialists had enjoyed since the end of the eighteenth century.

Elsewhere in Europe, the founding of crédits mobiliers

seems to have been due solely to financiers. But we may wonder whether industrialists in these countries were as yet powerful enough to get a hearing on the boards of these institutions. Probably not, particularly since the industrial role of these institutions, as we shall see, was of considerable depth and spread.

The period from 1870 to 1914 was marked by a certain reversal in the situation. Whereas in France the links between industrialists and financial institutions undoubtedly slackened, in Germany, by contrast, the industrialists set out to conquer the credit establishments. Elsewhere, we again find industrialists founding establishments of their own.

We may take an example from Belgium. Ernest Solvay started out in 1863 with a modest partnership limited by shares, with a capital of 136,000 francs put up by members of his family and a few close friends. The business always conserved this narrow, family status, since the transfer of shares was attended with numerous formalities. In 1906 it acquired the Banque générale belge, which became the bank of the firm. In France, just before or just after the First World War, large firms similarly acquired or founded banks: the Wendels, the Pont-à-Mousson group, and Le Creusot, for example. These banks were particularly useful in aiding the foreign expansion of these industrial groups.

In Germany, the evolution was slightly different. The great industrialists only slowly came round to colonising the boards of existing financial institutions. Borsig joined the board of the Berliner Handelsgesellschaft as early as 1869; then came the turn of Emil Rathenau in 1890, and Walther Rathenau in 1908. We may say that this put the Allgemeine Elektrizität Gesellschaft on an equal footing with its bank. Around the turn of the century, Siemens similarly came to dominate the Deutsche Bank, and Georg Siemens eventually became its chief. More important still, in order to act abroad, these electrical firms also resorted to founding banks of their own, generally outside Germany to avoid friction on their home front. True, in 1895, in order to found the Bank für elektrische Unternehmungen in

Zurich (Switzerland), the A.E.G. was helped by several financial institutions, in particular by the Banque de Paris et des Pays-bas, the Schweizerische Creditanstalt and the Banca commerciale italiana. Similar examples may be found in other industries. Some big industrialists established relations with several banks so as not to come under the sway of any one in particular: Thyssen with the Disconto Gesellschaft, the Dresdner Bank and the Deutsche Bank; Stinnes with the Dresdner Bank, then the Darmstädter Bank, of which he had virtual control.

Not surprisingly, therefore, German industry was much more wont to call on the banks than French industry was, more frequently undertaking increases of capital while continuing to practise a large measure of self-financing. The example of the A.E.G. mentioned above will suffice. Its balance sheets for 1883, 1890–1891 and 1899–1900 give the following figures (in millions of marks):

	shares	loans	depreciation and reserves
1883	5		
1890–1891	20	5	5.63
1899–1900	60	14	27

Other industries also attempted to break away from the banks. Although the German coal industry had other motives in forming its producer syndicates, the syndicates were a great help in getting it away from the banks, by lessening the need for the banks' intermediary. In their turn, moreover, they gradually began to take over the banks. In 1905 the main banks' sway over the mining companies had never been less. In 1910, to take three large enterprises, we find them figuring on the boards of the following banks:

Harpener Bergbau A.G.   Berliner Handelsgesellschaft
                           Dresdner Bank
                           Deutsche Bank
                           Darmstädter Bank

Phönix	Deutsche Bank
	Disconto Gesellschaft
	Dresdner Bank
	Darmstädter Bank
Gelsenkirchener	Deutsche Bank
	Disconto Gesellschaft
	Dresdner Bank
	Darmstädter Bank

Inversely, to take just one of the main banks, the Berliner Handelsgesellschaft, we find the following industrial enterprises represented on its board:

Consolidation
Hibernia
Bochumer Verein
Harpener Bergbau
Internationale Kohlenbergwerks
Braunkohle und Brikett Industrie
Riebeck'sche Montanwerke
Schlesische Kohlen und Kokswerke

We may say, then, that there was a great deal of inter-penetration between the banks and the world of the industrialists. We shall return to this point.

Elsewhere, the evolution was less clear-cut. Both in Austria and in Italy, banks and industrialists went their own fairly distinct ways up to the First World War. The situation was doubtless much the same in countries like Sweden, which also possessed long-established and thriving industrial firms.

To turn now to the other side of the question, we may say that the bankers were by no means unaware of the fact that most industrialists mistrusted them. They could all the more readily appreciate this fact as they felt the same way about industry. Even those private banks that were the products of industry — it is fair to say that they were far fewer than those produced by trade — proceeded with a great deal of caution and circumspection.

There were many reasons for this. The first will be readily appreciated, since it has to do with a question that we have already discussed. Prior to 1850, the private banks did not have a great deal of capital to work with: their capital was often very limited and their deposits only covered a very narrow field owing to the fact that the banks were frightened that a slump would burden them with excessive costs. Even if these deposits were relatively stable, they could not readily be put to use on a long-term basis, since the banks insisted on maintaining a broad margin of liquidity.

That was not all. Loans, advances or industrial investment did not belong to the normal business of the private banks. As we have seen, both in England and on the continent, the two fundamental banking procedures were commission and exchange transactions. Between 1830 and 1847 the earnings of Rothschild's in Naples show that interest on money brought in slightly more than banking profits, which merely proves that Naples was no longer important either as a trade centre or as a banking centre. Besides, the interests came essentially from annuities held by the bank and advances made to the government; its business had absolutely nothing to do with industry. This limitation of the bank's activity was such that discounting bills was in fact never practised in its own right but as a branch of exchange. Lastly, we may say that almost all the banking houses put fairly large amounts into international trade, but neither needed nor desired to launch out into what were rather disapprovingly called 'industrial speculations'.

Bankers sometimes worried over whether a given 'ordinary' transaction did not in fact mask some kind of industrial investment. The Paris bankers André & Cottier turned down a request for credit from Forges de Basse-Indre in 1825 because they suspected the request of being a roundabout way of getting finance for purchases of plant. In the same year, another Paris banker, Sartoris, refused the custom of the Compagnie des Mines de fer de Saint-Etienne — like Silhol of Nîmes in 1833 with regard to the Compagnie des Forges d'Alais — for fear of being forced into making more or less permanent advances.

There was a twofold reason behind this attitude. The bankers were frightened of a rapid rise in the demand for capital; if they followed the movement, there would come a time when they would simply be unable to refuse credit. In 1836 the Paris banker Seillière, who had regularly advanced cash to the Wendels, came back from a visit to Hayange 'scared out of his wits by the investment going on' — investment here being synonymous with risk. The same thing happened later between Stinnes and his banks: he led them on until it was technically difficult for them to refuse his requests for credits and funds.

There can be no doubt that the bankers knew little about the problems of industry, particularly from the technical point of view. The introduction of industrial departments in the banks is an important question about which we know far too little. Laffitte's first project in 1825 had provided for the setting up of an industrial committee. When he returned to his plan in 1837, he envisaged partnership with a scholar, Arago, who was perhaps not best suited for the role. Nonetheless, the need had been felt for a team of experts capable of informing the bank boards about the problems peculiar to industry. Some of the big private banks employed outside advisers, either for specific deals or on a full-time basis. Rothschild's banks in Paris and Vienna — its other three houses probably took no interest in industry — had extremely capable advisers: the great Paulin Talabot in Paris and Riepl in Vienna. In addition, the Paris house retained Michel Poisat, a distinguished chemist. Other firms may have done a similar sort of thing. The Seillières had also recruited a technician, Eugène Schneider, who directed and controlled their industrial establishments: it was in this capacity that he headed Le Creusot, bought by the Seillières in 1836 and gradually taken over by the Schneider family.

Did the financial institutions have technical departments?

The question has never been studied and the sources have little to say on the matter. It would appear that the Péreires' Crédit mobilier was fairly well equipped on this score. It had an economic fact-finding department, perhaps the first of its kind; but it does not seem to have employed engineers except occasionally. Bontoux, the future founder of the Union générale, was one of those it commissioned in this way. As early as 1866, the board of the Société générale de France had decided to set up an industrial committee to vet applications for aid, but we know very little about the way it worked. In special cases, the Société générale also had recourse to consultant engineers before deciding to recruit one on a permanent basis — Callon, a professor at the Ecole des Mines retained by Mines de la Grand Combe and the Régie des Forges d'Aubin. A few years later, an industrial department was formed with an engineer on the staff. After 1870, Rothschild's also retained a group of engineers led by an *ingénieur des mines*, Aron. We do not know what the situation was with regard to the other European banks. Research in this field should be encouraged, for the appearance of these permanent institutions was an important element in the evolution of the banks' attitude to industry. An institutional history of the banks (or the enterprises, or any number of fields for that matter) explaining such changes of attitude could be most valuable.

'This system of personal contacts,' writes J. Bouvier in his history of the Crédit lyonnais, 'put the bank in touch with the main industrial concerns in its region. Whether it was able to get complete information on their real situation is, however, another question . . . Even its own committee members were extremely reticent about their own affairs . . . As industrialists, they were each other's competitors.' Hence, in this respect, the entry of industrialists on to the boards of the banks probably did not bring the results that might have been expected.

Turning now to discuss the ways in which the banks participated in industry, we need to draw a few distinctions. To begin with, there was what we may call the traditional

kind of participation — direct investment on the part of
the banks or bankers. In France, if not elsewhere, this
participation fell into two periods, up to and beyond the
two great crises of 1825–1830 and 1839–1840, and affected
the two commanding heights of industry, steel and coal. In
the first period, it would seem that the banks' attention was
focused on the steel industry. Investment was more rational
in some cases than in others. Milleret's, in Paris, for instance,
owned interests in the following firms:

Aciéries de la Bérardière
Usines d'Allivet et de Bonpertuis
Hauts-fourneaux de Saint-Laurent
Forges d'Articole
Hauts-fourneaux de Rioupéroux
Hauts-fourneaux de Saint-Hugon
Forge de Pinsot
Fonderie de Vizille
Société des fonderies de Decazeville
Compagnie des Mines de fer de Saint-Etienne

With the exception of the last two, all these firms were
small, old-fashioned concerns, mostly in the Dauphiné, and
quite incapable of becoming large factories on the English
pattern. Milleret's applied antiquated notions of concen-
trations that had no solid foundation; needless to say, they
went out of business in 1830.

Alongside these experiments based on old-fashioned
notions there sprang up large enterprises of the modern type,
completely new foundations generally based on coal.
Though the banks that took part in the founding of Alais
were as yet few in number, they were in a clear majority
at the founding of Decazeville. But both ventures merely
ticked over for many years, lacking the necessary backing
with raw materials and transportation.

In the second period, coal was the main preoccupation.
The banks were very active here, but, it seems, more on a
speculative basis than with a view to permanent investment.
Only two large enterprises were bolstered by bankers; they

were Le Creusot, bought by Seillière's in 1835, and Mines
de la Grand Combe, founded in 1836 with the backing of
Rothschild's. Neither bank went into these deals without
some misgivings. In Belgium the Rothschilds took an
interest in large industrial enterprises such as Charbonnages
belges or Forges de Sclessin, but they were rather dragged
into it by the Société générale de Belgique. At the same time,
in Austria, they were aiding the recovery of the Witkowitz
iron works. But we may wonder whether, for many bankers,
this sudden interest in industry was not merely part and
parcel of their interest in the railways.

In fact, most investment between 1835 and 1848 went
into the railways, and thence to all branches of industry.
The railways were the banks' main targets — much more
on the continent than in England, curiously enough. But it
is clear that, in this field, the banks were really pursuing a
financial policy: the guarantee of interest put shares on a
par with annuities, and the companies' purely financial
business (deposits, transfers and interest payments) was
largely commission business. The banks acted in the same
way over the insurance companies they created at this
period, above all in France and Germany. The banks'
presence on the railway boards (as on the insurance
boards) was mainly to make sure that this lucrative
business continued to come their way. Having missed their
chance at home, the English banks took an active part in
the building of the railways on the continent.

As regards credit, the banks were as mistrustful as ever.
What we need here, for at least some of the banks, is a split-
up of the credits, in order to calculate both their size and
where they went to. The Paris banker Vassal opened credits
for a foundrymaster in Doubs, a spinning-mill owner in
Saint-Quentin, a sugar refiner and a colliery owner: in all
3.7 million, when his capital amounted to 2.5 million. He,
too, went out of business in 1830.

Such was the position in France. But was it not universal?
Similar instances are found in Germany: Oppenheim in
Cologne, Eichthal in Munich, Kaskel in Dresden, Mendels-
sohn and Bleichröder in Berlin had exactly the same

attitude as their counterparts in Paris or in France as a whole. They helped industry in their regions with credits and helped to place railway shares. Elsewhere, industrialisation was only beginning, and industry asked nothing of the banks; needless to say, the banks made no attempt to start the ball rolling. We lack knowledge of the Italian and Austrian private banks, but they probably neither could nor would play a role in industry. The examples that are cited were no doubt exceptions. The English quickly realised that the size of a bank's deposits could enable it to render service even when the terms of its commitments were fairly remote. There were also crises and rushes on deposits and, inevitably, thundering crashes. Both in England and on the continent, people were quick to realise that these disasters often stemmed from generous aid to industry.

Was this position changed by the appearance of the first big financial institutions? Probably not. The crédit mobilier had seen the light of day with an impressive prospectus, but its desire to change the face of industry cannot have pleased everyone. The loss of the archives of this institution will ever be a great misfortune for the economic history of France. As we have seen, the balance sheets are disappointingly vague. Here, for instance, is that for December 1862. Total assets amounted to around 213.4 million francs. Long-term investments are listed under two headings:

annuities:	50,000,000
shares and bonds:	97,870,000
	making a total of 147,900,000
Fixed deposits are as follows:	
bills held:	11,900,000
carried forward:	17,500,000
advances to companies:	17,441,000

Hence the total aid to industry amounted to:

investments:	97,870,000
advances:	17,441,000
making a total of:	115,311,000

i.e. around 54 per cent of the total of the balance sheet. At first sight, this figure might seem high. We need to know exactly what it stood for; and that is where the trouble starts. Analysis of the board reports reveals that 'investments' (investments and long-term loans) were exclusively concerned with service companies: public transport (railways and town transport), gas and water companies, but no industry proper. We know from other sources that the crédit mobilier attempted on several occasions to take interests in industry — steel, coal, glass — but without success. Founded to play a major role in industry, the crédit mobilier missed its vocation. No doubt we have to make allowance for the industrialists' refusal to be dominated by the bankers, which, as we have seen, was very common in France. The crédit mobilier's desire to assume a large share in the direction of industrial ventures could but confirm the industrialists' misgivings. As we have seen, the financial institutions that were founded later on denied themselves the right to finance industry. Though their advances to industry were not altogether negligible, they did not add up to much.

If the crédit mobilier had little success with industry in France, it did considerably better in the other continental countries. The Spanish crédit mobilier largely copied its initiator in Paris and concerned itself almost exclusively with public transport, gas and insurance, taking out a few shares in mines in northern Spain. In the Germanic countries, by contrast, the institutions founded in 1855–1856 and 1863–1864 made an effective contribution to the industrial development of their respective regions. Prior to 1848 already, Schaafhausen's in Cologne had become interested in the industrial development of the Ruhr — its steel rather than its coal. Transformed into a joint-stock company on the advice of Mevissen, the A. Schaafhausen'sche Bankverein backed numerous enterprises in the region (Hörder Bergwerks und Hüttenverein in 1851, Kölner Bergwerksverein in 1852; it assisted the début of Klöckner and helped to found the Cologne machine works). Prior to 1870, the Disconto Gesellschaft had a hand in the Dortmunder

Union, a Bochum mining company, and the large Phönix firm: it subsequently moved into Silesia and intervened in heavy industry and textiles. In 1857 Germany had five big banks: Disconto, Berliner, Schaafhausen, Credit Anstalt in Leipzig, and Darmstädter Bank. Their total aid to industry amounted to 20 to 25 million thalers, i.e. 25 to 28 per cent of their capital. This eloquently proves that the German banking system was more prepared to favour industrial development than any other system.

The Credit Anstalt in Vienna followed similar lines. It helped to launch a steel venture in Prague (a merger of several coal and steel firms), founded the great locomotive and mechanical engineering works at Wiener Neustadt, had a hand in lignite mines and glassworks and provided the initial capital for the great Montanwerke company in 1868.

In those countries where the traditional type of enterprise did not exist and where industrial management lacked both tradition and economic strength, the banks were able to intervene insofar as industrialisation became a concerted policy. The banks did not beget industry, they aided its birth. The Italian banks had much the same set-up as the crédits mobiliers, but their efforts to get Italian industry off the ground were for many years unsuccessful.

We have already touched on the characteristics of the period that followed. In France the situation remained much the same as before: industry clung to its independence and only asked for aid when it had to. For their part, the banks remained as mistrustful as ever, and stuck to finance. The official history of the Crédit lyonnais highlights the few occasions when this institution seems to have wished to play a role in industry, and its lack of success. The founding of the first *banques d'affaires* at the very start of the Third Republic made no difference. France had an oversupply of capital for which industry's demand was very low; this naturally resulted in a migration of capital, partly in the form of capital for new industries (to Russia in particular), but above all in the form of loans to impecunious and generally insolvent foreign governments. After 1880 came the creation, in France itself, of industries exploiting new techniques. Here there were no established firms, no traditions of hostility towards the banks. It was the banks that took the initiative, dealt with the public and kept the biggest say in industry. Such was the case for the electrical industry and for non-ferrous metals. All the same, there were exceptions: we have already pointed to the automobile industry; and the official history of the great French firm Péchiney tells us that the founder of the modern aluminium industry, Héroult, was turned down by at least some of the banks that he approached for aid.

In Germany things were quite different: industry had colonised the banks and the links between the two were many and varied; but industry had got the upper hand and banking had been relegated to a secondary role. For instance, it was not a bank that joined the Banque de Paris et des Pays-bas to found the Société norvégienne de l'azote in 1906, but an industrial firm, Badische Anilin. Long-term loans and shares in the balance sheets of the Disconto Gesellschaft moved from 6.2 million marks in 1894 to 104 million in 1907; in those of the Deutsche Bank, from 3.24 million in 1871 to 80 million in 1906.

This situation was less marked elsewhere. Between 1870 and 1890, the Stockholms Enskilda Bank gave appreciable aid to Swedish mining, iron and paper, tying up part of its capital in the process. From 1901–1902 onwards, it launched out into the equipment of the Norwegian waterfalls and the production of electricity, and took part in Russian telephone projects. All kind of difficulties arose, however, and the bank was obliged to retrench. It practically dropped out of the Norwegian deals and subsequently cut back its permanent investments severely.

At the end of our period, for political as much as economic reasons, the Swiss banks recovered the important role that their precursors had played in the eighteenth century. The Zurich Schweizerische Creditanstalt did much to aid the large mechanical engineering firms in its city. It formed connections with other banks to promote electrical firms. Along with the German banks and A.E.G. it founded the

Elektrobank in 1896, and with the Geneva Union financière, the Schweizerische Bankverein, the Banque de Paris et des Pays-bas, and the Schneider firm, it founded in Geneva the Société franco-suisse pour l'industrie électrique, which was subsequently active in France and Italy also.

In truth, on the eve of the First World War, the overlapping of interests was considerable. The structures had become completely different; there was no longer any clear distinction between industry and banking; a world of finance had been born, an industrialist's world as much as a banker's world, embracing very many aspects of economic activity. Some differences continued to exist, however; there were countries where, as in France, industry held on to a large part of its autonomy and the banks were sent packing abroad. In others, the industrialists gained the upper hand, as in Germany, and the banks became the servants of industry. Lastly, there were countries whose industrial development was initiated by the influx of foreign capital and whose industry consequently fell into the hands of this new world of finance. There were countries where the public's familiarity with industrial speculation rendered the role of the banks less important. And finally, there were countries like Belgium, where circumstances left the field virtually wide open for bank intervention.

To give a more precise account of the situation would be presumptuous. We can only hope that many monographs dealing with both sides of the question will come along to provide us with the primary information that we still so sorely lack.

BIBLIOGRAPHY

A complete bibliography of this subject would be out of place here as it is very extensive and of very uneven quality. General economic histories and those relating to specific countries have not been cited as, for the most part, these contain nothing of particular value on the problems of banking.

Industrial history sometimes contains interesting matter, and the works of Beaumont and Benaerts on German industry are worthy of notice.

There is little on the history of banking in one particular epoch or country. For the eighteenth century the notable work of Luthy, *La banque protestante en France*, Paris, 1959 and 1961, and Madame Ozanam's careful reconstruction, *Baudard de Saint-James*, Geneva, 1969, are recommended. For the nineteenth century there is far more material. For France see Gille, B., *La banque et le crédit en France 1815–1848*, Paris, 1959; and for Belgium, Chlepner, B. S., *La banque en Belgique*, Brussels, 1926. For Germany there are many works of reference, often concentrating on one particular centre of banking; one might mention Poschinger, H. von, *Bankwesen und Bankpolitik in Preussen*, Berlin, 1878–1885, and Diouritch, *L'expansion des banques allemandes à l'étranger*, Paris, 1909. A study of Austrian banks is at present being prepared. For England see L. S. Pressnell *Country Banking...*, Oxford; W. F. Crick and J. E. Wadsworth *A Hundred Years of Joint Stock Banking*, London, 1936, and R. S. Sayers *Lloyds Bank in the History of English Banking*, Oxford, 1969.

There are extremely interesting and thorough studies of international capital transfers, and attention is drawn particularly to Jenks, *The Migration of British Capital to 1870*, New York, 1927; Crihan, *Le capital étranger en Russie*, Paris, 1934; Cameron, *France and the Economic Development of Europe* (1800–1914), Princeton, 1961; and the recent thesis of Poidevin, R., *Les relations économiques et financières entre la France et l'Allemagne 1898–1914*, Paris, 1969.

On the same subject as this study see Levy-Leboyer, M., *Les banques européennes et l'industrialisation internationale, dans la première moitié du XIX siècle*, Paris, 1964; and Cameron, R., Crisp, O., Patrick, H. T. and Tilly, R., *Banking in the Early Stages of Industrialisation*, Oxford, 1967.

Monographs are still the most valuable source. It would be useful to have a critical and scholarly survey of the commemorative volumes with which companies celebrate their anniversaries, some of which are real works of history.

FRANCE

La Société générale (1864–1964), Paris, 1964.

Bouvier, J., *Le Crédit Lyonnais de 1863 à 1882*, Paris, 1961, 2 vols.

Bouvier, J., *Le krach de l'Union générale (1878–1882)*, Paris, 1960.

Gille, B., *Histoire de la Maison Rothschild*, Geneva, 1965–67.

ENGLAND

Fulford, *Glyn's*, London, 1953.

GERMANY

Disconto Gesellschaft (1851–1901), Berlin, 1901.
Berliner Handels Gesellschaft (1856–1956), Berlin, 1956.
A study is in progress on Bleichröder.

AUSTRIA

Ein Jahrhundert: Creditanstalt und Bankverein, Vienna, 1956.

BELGIUM

Le centenaire de la Société générale de Belgique 1822–1922, Brussels, 1922.

SPAIN

Sanchee-Albornoz, N., *La Sociedad general del credito mobiliario espagnol 1856–1902* in *Moneda y Credito*, June 1966.

ITALY

There is almost nothing except Pantaleoni's article on the fall of the Italian Crédit mobilier. A study is being prepared on the Banca commerciale italiana.

SWEDEN

Gasslander, O., *History of the Stockholms Enskilda Bank to 1914*, Stockholm, 1962.

SWITZERLAND

Johr, W. A., *Schweizerische Kreditanstalt (1856–1956)*, Zurich, 1956.

5. The State and the Industrial Revolution 1700-1914*

Barry Supple

I saw clearly that free competition between two nations which are highly civilised can only be mutually beneficial in case both of them are in a nearly equal position of industrial development, and that any nation which owing to misfortune is behind others in industry, commerce and navigation . . . must first of all strengthen her own individual powers, in order to fit herself to enter into free competition with more advanced nations.[1]

INTRODUCTION

In the long perspective of history the Industrial Revolution is an *international* phenomenon — extending, in its processes and consequences, over the whole world. In spite of this worldwide significance, however, it is customary for economists and historians to examine its origins and impact in terms of individual nations. And this is a logical feature of the study of industrialisation, for the flow of goods and men and ideas, the patterns of culture and ambitions, the elements of social structure, are all best understood, in the first instance at least, in terms of the distinctive frameworks created by national boundaries. Frontiers are more than lines on a map: they frequently define quite distinctive systems of thought and action. The state is, of course, preeminently such a system; and it is therefore through the history of nations that we must begin any empirical study of the role of the state in the international phenomenon which we call the Industrial Revolution.

Modern industrial society originated in Britain when laissez-faire was an important part of the emerging economic ideology. This is not to say that the British classical econ-

* I am greatly indebted to Professor Donald Winch for his extremely useful comments on the penultimate draft of this chapter.

1. Preface to first edition of Friedrich List's *The National System of Political Economy* (1841), quoted in 1904 edition, p. xi.

omists ignored the case in favour of direct participation by the state in the workings of the economy. But the balance of their argument about the efficient allocation of resources and the best way of encouraging economic progress came down heavily on the side of non-interference. Even more important than this was the associated fact that the initial phase of modern economic growth in Britain was a market-based phenomenon — owing little directly to the activity of the state.[2] On the other hand, however, although other nations imported Britain's Industrial Revolution with vigour and enthusiasm, they did not on the whole adopt the official policy — or, rather, the lack of policy — which was associated with the pioneer episode of industrialisation. Indeed, in the context of modern world history, a laissez-faire economic policy seems less like an orthodoxy than a brief aberration from a norm of detailed government intervention in economic affairs. Certainly by the second half of the twentieth century, whatever the controversy about particular policies, it is generally acknowledged that the state must take a leading role in the attainment of the objective which haunts the nations of the world: sustained industrial development. Moreover, as far as economic theory is concerned, even as applied to a market economy, extensive government action to induce industrial growth is justified by at least two sorts of circumstance.

First, there is what might be called the 'prerequisite' or 'institutional' argument. This holds that state action is necessary where economic growth is being held back by institutional 'obstacles', the reform or elimination of which can only be undertaken by official action. The transition from a traditional to an industrialising society, for example, may be held to depend on the abolition of feudal land tenures (which impede the effective use of natural resources and labour power) or of the taxation power of local authorities and magnates (which prevent the creation of truly national markets). Equally, it may be thought necessary to adjust a distorted taxation system, provide for a stable currency system, or reform the legal system in order to

2. But see below, pp. 314-316.

ensure security of contract. And as long as economic growth depends on such institutional change, there is a potential role for the state, because the state is the only authority capable of reforming entrenched institutions. Put another way, whatever the prospective efficiency of market forces, public action may be needed to improve the 'non-economic' environment within which private agencies can allocate resources most effectively.

Second, the important distinction between social and private costs and benefits can justify state action to stimulate economic growth simply because the unmodified price system may not ensure an optimum allocation of economic resources. Thus, where private action or inaction (in response to market prices and opportunities) imposes costs or benefits on other people which are not taken into account by the original decision-maker, there is a divergence of private and social costs or benefits. As a result, purely private action may not maximise social product. It may well be, for example, that a particular type of project — such as the provision of technical information and training, the creation of an educational system, investment in an irrigation scheme, or an electricity network or a new road system — would return only a moderate profit to a private investor, but has 'external economies' of such dimensions, in relation to its cost-reducing effect upon other sorts of enterprise, as to warrant government sponsorship or help. More broadly, in an underdeveloped economy the risks of private investment in a particular industry may prevent its expansion, even though such an expansion would be justified in the long run or in terms of other, complementary, activities. Here, too, it would be appropriate for the state to initiate or subsidise the activity (by tariffs, favourable loans or subsidies, guaranteed markets, direct participation, etc.). And, at the most general level, since aggregate and rapid growth may itself have a considerable social benefit, but be in no particular private interest actually to encourage, the state may 'justifiably' intervene to accelerate overall expansion.

Neither the idea of the institutional prerequisites of

economic growth nor the concept of social costs and benefits is particularly modern. For example, classical economists were well aware of the importance of government action either to reform feudal and traditional institutions in order to encourage private economic activity or to ensure the efficient operation of private enterprise in a modern economy. The evil of backward countries with abundant land but indolent populations, wrote David Ricardo, 'proceeds from bad government, from the insecurity of property, and from a want of education in all ranks of the people. To be made happier they require only to be better governed and instructed.'[3] In addition, the concept of 'externalities', with its associated social-private cost-benefit distinction, was known to Adam Smith — who argued that an important 'duty of the sovereign or commonwealth is that of erecting and maintaining those public institutions and those public works, which, though they may be in the highest degree advantageous to a great society, are, however, of such a nature that the profit could never repay the expense to any individual or small number of individuals, and which it therefore cannot be expected that any individual or small number of individuals should erect or maintain.'[4] The elaboration of the idea of externalities came with the development of neo-classical economics in the late nineteenth and early twentieth centuries. It is, however, only recently, with the modern preoccupation with worldwide economic growth and economic backwardness, that they have become important and explicit elements in economic analysis and planning.

Although these rationalisations of state intervention in

3. *The Principles of Political Economy and Taxation*, Chapter V ('On Wages'). John Stuart Mill was even more explicit: the first requirements of an improvement in the condition of Asiatic countries, and 'the less civilised and industrious parts of Europe, such as Russia, Turkey, Spain and Ireland', he held, were 'a better government: more complete security of property; moderate taxes, and freedom from arbitrary exactions under the name of taxes; a more permanent and more advantageous tenure of land, securing to the cultivator as far as possible the undivided benefits of the industry, skill and economy he may exert.' *Principles of Political Economy* (edited by W. J. Ashley, 1909), pp. 189–90.

4. *Wealth of Nations*, Book V, Chapter I, Part III.

the economy provide a useful starting-point for the historian of industrialisation in the eighteenth and nineteenth centuries, it is not really possible to use them to appraise the efficiency of government policy in the period — if only because the quantitative data on which firm judgments might be based are scanty and imperfect. Consequently, the principal objective of this chapter is to examine why and how the state actually intervened in the initiation of industrial growth in a few leading examples of industrialisation before 1914, and to see if the varying role of the state in that industrialisation can be placed in any systematic framework.[5]

THE STATE AND ITS POLICIES

European history in the period under consideration — and more particularly in the period between the French Revolution and the First World War — was dominated by the emergence of the modern state. This meant, on the one hand, that the pattern of international relationships and rivalry, and the fabric of men's lives, were increasingly affected by the growing coherence of national institutions and attitudes. On the other hand, the nation state was 'modernised' by the advent of industrialisation, with its enormous impact on social structures and ambitions and its revolutionary implications for worldwide networks of power. Some relationship between the state and industrialisation is, in fact, necessarily involved in the idea of modernity. Britain's relatively brief but spectacular period of unchallenged economic supremacy, French history after the Revolution, the creation of a powerful, imperial Germany and its industrial rivalry with late Victorian

5. The chapter will be exclusively concerned with pre-1914 history and, therefore, with capitalist examples of the Industrial Revolution. It will also be confined to the initiation of industrial growth — distinguishing this from the role of the state in extensive growth in pre-industrial economies, in the maintenance of economic growth in reasonably mature economies, and in the pursuit of objectives other than growth (e.g. in the field of welfare, income distribution, the protection of minority or relatively weak groups, etc.).

Britain, the unification of Italy — all exemplify the role of the national concept in modern history. The state — in the sense of the sovereign institutions of society — was an obvious expression of that concept in the international arena. At the same time, however, it was a potential instrument of nationhood and of industrial power, since its sovereignty (where it could be successfully asserted) implied an ability both to transform national institutions and to dispose of economic resources by legislative or administrative means.

The extent of state political and economic activity obviously varied from country to country. Yet, even where it was at its most extreme, it cannot be treated as an entirely independent element in socio-economic processes — i.e. as an institution which, with or without consent, imposes its will on all other institutions. Although its power *was* virtually absolute, the state must also be seen as *part* of society, reflecting particular social forces and representing (however confusedly or narrowly) specific group or class interests. Such an institution can conceivably act arbitrarily in the political sense. But it cannot act entirely independently of causes located in the society with which it is associated. Hence, although in some respects 'the state' shapes 'society', it is more useful to envisage 'the state' as the institutional arrangements which a group or interest (or shifting alliances of groups or interests) within society uses in order to exercise its dominance in the political arena. This is not to say that the state always, or ever, reflects the exact distribution of effective power within a society. (For example, in Britain the political authority and influence of the industrial middle classes lagged behind their effective economic power for much of the nineteenth century.) But it *is* to say that a government draws its aims as well as its legitimacy from existing elements in a particular society.

The purpose in emphasising this obvious point is to help systematise our understanding of the historical role of economic policy. For, insofar as it is directed towards economic expansion, such expansion must be the objective not merely of 'the government' but also of a group or groups *in society.* This aspect of the role of the state in industrialisation makes it difficult to accept Professor Hoselitz's interesting distinction between 'autonomous' and 'induced' patterns of economic growth — a distinction which depends upon whether crucial economic decisions are made by private individuals (in pursuit of 'self-oriented' goals) or by governments (in pursuit of 'public' objectives).[6] The argument that the state's policies reflect as well as shape social and economic forces obviously blurs this distinction, or at least reduces its usefulness. For the dichotomy between autonomous and induced patterns could well mask the fact that what is called 'induced' is often, in terms of its origins and key personnel, merely 'autonomous' in a different institutional setting. In other words, the state becomes an institutional device (perhaps the most important institutional device) by which groups seek to secure ends which, in other circumstances, they might conceivably secure by private means.[7] Correspondingly, therefore, the important question becomes: in what circumstances will groups or classes in the society use the state to encourage industrial development? And the important point to remember is that the state enters the arena of industrial development not as an arbitrary and unpredictable force, but as the agent of 'old' or 'new' forces or classes within society, acting either in their own self-interest or in pursuit of an ostensibly national purpose, within which their own role can be rationalised. The state, like the entrepreneur or the labour movement, is a social phenomenon.

Historically, the most important way in which the state stimulated industrial growth in a capitalist setting was through its ability to restructure the institutions of society — i.e. through its ability to *create* a capitalist setting in the first instance. As we shall see, the eradication of the power of

6. Bert F. Hoselitz, 'Patterns of Economic Growth', *Canadian Journal of Economics and Political Science*, 21 (November 1955), pp. 423–6.

7. This, of course, applies to direct economic policies — rather than to fundamental institutional reforms which can only be carried out by government action.

feudal institutions (land tenures, guilds, etc.) in revolutionary France, the abolition of internal tariffs in France and Germany, the maintenance of an orderly system of law in Britain, the political unification of Germany and Italy — all depended on state action, and all moulded the framework of enterprise in ways which increased entrepreneurial security and helped the free flow of resources and men. Less extensively, but still significantly, the conventional role of the state in providing services with fairly large external economies could be harnessed to the needs of industrialisation. This was the case, for example, with state aid to formal technical education (which occurred much earlier on the Continent than in Britain) and with official information services such as some German states used to diffuse technological ideas. Thirdly, and illustrating an even longer and more widespread tradition, the state could manipulate taxes, subsidies or markets in order to stimulate the development of private enterprise. It could, for example, protect favoured industries by custom duties, provide specific firms or industries with subsidies or monopolistic privileges, guarantee sales or the payment of interest on private investment in order to attract capital to particular ventures, or itself lend money on favourable conditions. Finally, although it rarely did so outside the field of railways, the state could directly assume the tasks of investment and enterprise.

The 'tool box' of the state in relation to the encouragement of industrial growth was, in fact, potentially very extensive. Moreover, virtually all of its contents — institutional reform, the provision of public services, financial support or protection to private business, public enterprise — had been created and used by European governments before modern industrialisation began in the nineteenth century. It was not, therefore, the discovery of new means of stimulating growth, but the perception of new *opportunities* and *reasons* for doing so which led the state to associate itself with industrialisation in the modern era.

Generally speaking, the timing, extent and form in which industrial growth, and the desire for it, came to individual European countries depended on three sorts of factors: their character and ambitions as nations, their level of backwardness, and their receptivity to example and market forces (including the inflow of foreign entrepreneurs and skilled labour). By the same token, these three factors were also relevant to the use of state institutions to promote industrialisation. In addition, the ease and extent to which the authority of the state was used for industrial ends were further influenced by the historical experience of the different societies, and by the political institutions and assumptions which they inherited.

First, state action was obviously necessary when the initial, fundamental task was to *create a new nation* (as in Italy and Germany), to standardise such basic arrangements as currency, taxes, weights and measures (as in revolutionary France); or to modernise the institutions of an existing traditional society (as in Prussia in the early years of the nineteenth century). And although such activity was not necessarily seen as a means of industrialisation, the consequent effect (in terms of political security, national cohesion, institutional uniformity and predictability) on markets and other economic institutions was, in fact, likely to be favourable to growth.

Second, state action was obviously *desirable* when the dominant elements in a relatively backward (or new) nation wished to build up and assert its power as quickly as possible. In some circumstances this might be seen as a need to promote *general* industrial growth, as when the Tsarist state promoted economic development by subsidy and direct investment from the 1880s; in other circumstances, as a need to expand and strengthen a strategic sector or sectors (e.g. the railroad network or an armaments industry). Such a process could obviously be initiated in an 'established' society. In addition, however, industrialisation was the object of what Rostow has called 'reactive nationalism': the assertion of independence by a pre-industrial society threatened by the expansion of more advanced ones.[8] (Tsarist Russia is perhaps the best example.)

Moreover, even without nationalist overtones, given the

8. W. W. Rostow, *The Stages of Economic Growth* (1960), p. 26.

ambitions for industrial growth of a dominant economic group, state action might be seen as either necessary or desirable depending on the degree of backwardness. Thus, basic institutional arrangements might have to be reformed in order to create, in a now unfashionable phrase, the 'prerequisites' of growth. Finally, and quite apart from a possible need for social reform, backwardness of economic arrangements and attitudes might severely limit the availability or flow of investment funds or enterprise or ideas. And the state could therefore intervene to make up for some of the deficiencies of market forces — by direct investment in industry or transport, by guaranteeing sales (and therefore profits), or by the extension of valuable commercial privileges.

The variety of possible motives for state intervention makes it impossible to systematise its chronology or taxonomy in any simple way.[9] If backwardness alone were the main cause of official action, and if underdeveloped countries had industrialised in rough order of increasing backwardness, then we should expect to see examples of more and more active and widespread state intervention as time went by. In fact, however, backwardness was not the sole determinant of the chronology of development, and even more important, the variations introduced by the elements of nationalism and imitativeness and political tradition preclude any such simple, sequential analysis.[10] It is true, as we shall see, that Britain and Russia, the first and last major European countries to begin industrialisation in the period before 1914, were, in fact, at polar extremes of the spectrum of state-induced industrialisation in pre-1914 Europe. But generally considered, the role of the state in industrial growth under capitalism was per-

9. It will be appreciated that only more or less explicit attempts to stimulate or provide the framework for expansion have been mentioned in the text. Any comprehensive account of the role of the state would have to acknowledge the economic consequences of policies which were ostensibly concerned with non-economic ends — and, in particular, the indirect consequences of changes in budgetary policies, social and military expenditures, state educational systems, etc.

10. See pp, 351-353.

vasive (it was of considerable indirect importance even in Britain) and its precise forms and extent in different countries were functions of a variety of pressures and individual circumstances.

MERCANTILISM, FEUDALISM, INDIVIDUALISM: 1700–1815

Attempts to promote industrial development by public policy antedate the Industrial Revolution. For example, in continental Europe in the eighteenth century — although on the whole not in Britain — what we have come to call mercantilism continued a long-established tradition of state aid and stimulus to particular manufacturing sectors.[11] Although based upon general objectives — the creation of strategic industries, the increase of national strength and power, the redressing of trade imbalances — these policies were by and large directed towards the expansion of individual sectors of the economy rather than towards overall economic growth. And they reflected, in quite clear-cut ways, the shortages of capital, entrepreneurship and technical skills which in traditional, pre-industrial societies severely hampered the emergence of 'modern' large-scale industry. In France, the precedents of the Colbertian policy of the late seventeenth century were continued through the *manufactures royales* (state-run enterprises) and *manufactures privilégiées*, with monopoly rights, fiscal privileges, subsidies, and the like, awarded in armaments, metallurgy and luxury industries. In Prussia, the government, notably that of Frederick the Great (1740–86), stimulated the establishment of 'factories' in textiles, glass, chemicals, metals, etc. — and itself promoted coal mines and iron works in Silesia. Similarly, other German states, and Austria under Maria Theresa (1740–80), pursued a policy of selective 'industrialisation'; while in Russia Catherine the Great (1762–96) revived the policies of Peter the Great through a wide range of factories, mines and iron works using serf labour, and

11. It also continued the tradition of 'nation-building' — i.e. attempts to unify nations through the harmonisation of economic institutions.

either wholly owned by the state or jointly sponsored with private businessmen.

Such economic activities as these fitted very well into a regime of 'enlightened absolutism'; they were promoted by centralised, authoritarian (at least in ambition) governments, and served by professional civil servants.[12] Autocratic royalty and central bureaucracy were basically concerned with the power of the state. And by the second half of the eighteenth century they were stimulated by a new example and potential threat: the beginning of Britain's successful Industrial Revolution made abundantly clear the power and potential of the new technology in the critical metal industries, in armaments and in textiles. Hence, in addition to channelling domestic resources and demand towards new industrial enterprises, eighteenth-century governments turned to British technical skills to provide the basis of innovation; continental visitors flocked to Britain to observe and learn; and continental governments employed British technicians and entrepreneurs to stimulate their own manufactures: John Holker in French textiles, and as an Inspector-General of Factories; William Wilkinson in iron and cannon manufacturing in France and lead smelting in Silesia; John Baildon in coke furnaces at the state ironworks in Silesia; Charles Gascoyne in royal iron foundry and engineering works in Russia.

Yet superficially dramatic as some of these policies were, their success — measured in terms of general economic or industrial growth — was very limited. While, admittedly, it is possible to trace some continuity between eighteenth-century establishments and later industrial developments, and continental civil servants established a tradition of technical education and official concern for industrial progress which was later to be of considerable importance, nevertheless, the extent of state activity and its effect on

12. In France their authority was checked by other forces, notably the 'judicial aristocracy'. In Prussia the central civil servants became an 'increasingly bold and independent corps of bureaucrats'. See Hans Rosenberg, *Bureaucracy, Aristocracy and Autocracy: The Prussian Experience 1660–1815* (1966), pp. 109–36.

industrial production in general were restricted. Industrial growth, even of a moderate sort, did not become 'self-sustaining' and the state-sponsored sectors tended to remain enclaves within pre-industrial societies. This relative failure of mercantilist industrial policies can be attributed in part to the inefficiency and lack of skill with which the new enterprises were often established or run — but perhaps even more to the fact that there was a profound lack of balance between their progressive character (technologically and organisationally) and the social and economic settings within which they were. promoted. The general shortage of entrepreneurial skills, the reluctance to invest risk capital in new ventures, markets fragmented by high transportation costs and local trade barriers, low levels of effective demand, poor labour supplies, lack of mobility of resources or of complementary technologies — all meant that government efforts could have only a very limited 'inducement' effect on the economy as a whole. Put another way, the backwardness of agrarian, semi-feudal and basically pre-industrial economies could not be overcome by partial experiments in industrial development: private institutions and market forces were simply not ready to respond to this degree of stimulation. Like other social agencies, the state could not ignore the environment within which it operated.

The lessons implied in the history of mercantilist policies in traditional settings are, in fact, brought home by contemporaneous events in Britain. For in terms of the relationship between government and manufacturing Britain was perhaps the least mercantilist of the major powers — and yet was the first to industrialise. Obviously, this is not the place to enter into a discussion of why the Industrial Revolution occurred first in Britain, or why it occurred in the late eighteenth century.[13] But it is reasonably clear that among the advantages she enjoyed were precisely those institutional and economic advantages which continental

13. See Phyllis Deane's contribution, *The Industrial Revolution in Great Britain 1700–1914* in Volume 4, chapter 3; M. W. Flinn, *Origins of the Industrial Revolution* (1966).

societies lacked: a well-developed level of entrepreneurial and technical skills, readily available capital for industrial investment, a compact market with low transport costs, social and political arrangements which encouraged mobility of men and resources. In other words, the existing economic and technical 'balance' was such, and the flexibility of attitude and resources such, that a much lower stimulus was needed to trigger off a 'self-sustained' (i.e. market-based and autonomously reinforcing) process of industrial expansion. And although there remains considerable controversy as to the proximate cause or causes of British industrial growth, they are surely to be found in market, rather than in government, pressures — in overseas trade or demographic change or agricultural development or technological innovation.

Compared with the continental experience, therefore, the British Industrial Revolution was a triumph of individualism — not merely in the sense that its innovators and entrepreneurs were characterised by a striving, profit-oriented individualism, but also because its mechanisms of supply and demand and resource allocation were geared to the decisions of individual economic agents. To this extent, starting from a position of international dominance and economic sophistication, there was little justification for state action, on grounds of either nationalism or backwardness, to induce industrial growth. Whether or not governments need intervene with economic processes, argued Jeremy Bentham, depended on 'the different circumstances of the several political communities', and 'In England, abundance of useful things are done by individuals, which in other countries are done either by government or not at all.'[14]

Yet before we conclude that the first Industrial Revolution owed everything to the market and nothing to government, it is worth remembering that the very characteristics of the market environment which distinguished Britain's position from that of other European countries were in

14. 'Manual of Political Economy', in *The Works of Jeremy Bentham* (1838–43), III, 35n.

large part a function of state action. Thus, the whole
evolution of government since the civil strife of the seventeenth century had resulted in an unmatched degree of
political stability and social harmony, while the early
political and administrative unification of the country
helped create a relatively compact and unified market. In
addition, compared with its neighbours, Britain enjoyed
the benefits of a standard currency, tax and tariff system,
and a sound structure of commercial law. Finally, and in
some respects most significantly, the governing classes in
what was still a heavily landed society were broadly sympathetic to, and, indeed, representative of, the commercial
and financial interests which helped transform Britain's
economic institutions and opportunities from the late
seventeenth century onwards.[15] Perhaps the most striking
indication of this is the powerful role which the state played
in the creation and defence of the Empire, in the extension
of an international trading network of which Britain was
the centre, and in the regulation of commercial and imperial
relations so as to benefit the domestic economy and British
businessmen. This was, in fact, 'mercantilism' of a different
sort: navigation laws which attempted to monopolise imperial trade for British and colonial business interests;
which obliged colonial exports to come first to Britain and
colonial imports to pass through Britain; and which stipu-
lated the use of British or colonial ships. It also meant wars
which were ultimately successfully fought to expand and
defend Britain's colonial possessions and trade. If by the
1760s Britain was indeed the centre of the world's biggest
free trade area, if her trade and shipping enjoyed a world-
wide dominance, if her merchants and manufacturers had
privileged access to large markets in Asia and America, if
she was a major entrepôt for Europe, and if, as seems likely,

15. However, a further important distinguishing feature of British
society was the extent to which the landed and business classes enjoyed
relatively harmonious relationships. British society was certainly less
compartmentalised, attitudes and social respect were less rigid, and men
and resources flowed more easily in *both* directions. As a result, it is less
surprising to find the state, even when its institutions were manned by
men of the land, also acting in the interest of men of trade.

these developments were critical components of her 'readiness' for industrialisation — then the state did play an important, albeit indirect, role in the pioneer Industrial Revolution.

The fact remains, however, that the role *was* indirect; that as with its influence on law, on social and political institutions, on the freedom with which men could apply their efforts and use their resources, the state in Britain had, over generations, helped create the framework within which individual action could initiate an Industrial Revolution. Relatively deficient in such a framework, as we have seen, continental countries found it difficult to industrialise even with the *direct* help of the state. Indeed, in an important respect the 'direct-action' policies of the eighteenth century were premature until a more appropriate environment for directly productive activity had evolved. The changes necessary for growth — the erosion of the institutions and relationships of traditional society — commenced before modern industrialisation, and continued throughout the nineteenth century and beyond. Nevertheless, in this process of social change the French Revolution and its immediate aftermath played a critical role.

Of course, the French Revolution, the Napoleonic conquests and the reverberations of revolutionary upheaval did not completely replace a feudal with an individualistic structure in continental Europe, or even in France, between 1789 and 1815. For one thing, various aspects of the older traditional society — much of the effective powers of the guilds, some of the fragmentation of political authority — were already eroded by 1789; for another, the institutional arrangements of continental society after 1815 remained both more authoritarian and more influenced by traditional survivals than the progressive society of contemporaneous Britain. Nevertheless, the fact remains that in France the Revolution dealt a decisive blow to feudalism (in land tenures, in tax rights and feudal dues, in personal status): henceforth, a peasant society, not always progressive, but certainly individualistic and independent, dominated the land. The National Assembly also took the profound step of abolishing the guilds (1791) and declaring that everyone was 'free to do such business as and to exercise such profession, art or trade as he may choose'. Moreover, this provision for free trade in men had been anticipated by a decree for internal free trade in goods (1790): after replacing the traditional provinces with departments, the National Assembly abolished the internal tariffs and tolls which had formerly so restricted the domestic market. And in its early years the Revolutionary government made further contributions to the environment of enterprise by introducing the metric system as a standard basis for weights and measures, decimalising the currency, providing a protective patent system for inventions, and establishing a Mining College and a Polytechnic for the training of government engineers. Napoleon in power followed this by the centralisation of control over local departments, by the systematic provision of a better road network, by the formulation of state legal codes, by protection to the rights of private property and to its owners, by the stabilisation of financial affairs, and by the formation of the prize-giving *Société d'encouragement pour l'industrie nationale de la France* under government patronage in 1802.

Although the immediate effect of the Revolution and the Revolutionary Wars on the development of continental industry was probably harmful,[16] their institutional ramifications — and, therefore, their long-run indirect effects — were considerable. In France, where they were carried furthest, they helped create the institutional preconditions of a new, nationwide, unified market — a market not merely for commodities, which could now move more freely and at lower cost between the regions, but also for land, men and ideas. To a large extent, no doubt, the restructuring of the business environment which was associated with the Revolution and its aftermath can be seen in terms of the reforms of a hitherto frustrated middle and professional class for whom the overthrow of the *ancien régime* meant new

16. See, for example, François Crouzet, 'Wars, Blockade and Economic Change in Europe, 1792–1815', *Journal of Economic History*, XXIV, 4 (December 1964).

influence and new opportunities to create 'their' sort of society. Yet this was by no means the only set of forces at work: on the one hand the abolition of feudalism and the fragmentation of estates was directed towards the creation of a peasant, rather than a capitalist, agriculture. On the other, the assertion of French power — first in defence of the Revolution and then in an aggressive attempt to impose French hegemony on Europe — reflected a new and keener nationalism, sharpened by ideological fervour, which found domestic expression in the modernisation of institutions, the search for social and political coherence, and the drive for meritocratic mobility and administrative efficiency.

By the same token, the influence of Revolutionary and Napoleonic reforms was transmitted into other lands not merely by the forces of liberalism or capitalism — but by conquest, by nationalism, and ultimately by reaction against French dominance. At the height of its power France ruled or controlled the areas which now comprise Belgium, the Netherlands, Switzerland and Italy, and much of Germany. And its soldiers and administrators diffused not merely a new set of political ideas and expectations, but also institutional change: the abolition of feudal forms and, to a large extent, realities, systematic legal codes, and rationalised administrative structures (there was, for example, a drastic reduction in the number of small states which made the German political scene so chaotic). Moreover, while much of this was the direct effect of the spread of the revolutionary influence, and was even welcomed within the relevant countries, perhaps the most spectacular consequence was indirect — a reaction in the form of a counter-nationalism to the humiliating conquests by the French armies. This happened in Prussia, where the defeats at Jena and Auerstadt (1806) led to a sense of political humiliation and to an essentially correct deduction that the problems of Prussian strength and independence could best be tackled by agrarian and social reform: local government and the taxation system were overhauled, hereditary serfdom was abolished and regulatory restrictions and burdens on industry were reduced.[17] As a result, although the practice took some time to accomplish, the foundations of a more flexible and therefore more efficient society were laid down, and the way was prepared for the freer movement of men between occupation and of capital between uses. These reforms were necessarily undertaken by the state — operating through an increasingly powerful bureaucracy — and logically based upon an intensified nationalism. They helped lay the basis of modern Prussia and for its later role in the economic shaping of a new Germany.

In this, as in other respects, therefore, the French Revolution was a major watershed in modern European history. Even if, as seems likely, the immediate economic consequences of revolution and conquest were harmful, they played a vital role in the acceleration of institutional change. Indirectly they gave firmer shape to the business system which was to create the Industrial Revolution.

THE STATE AND THE DIFFUSION OF INDUSTRIALISM, 1815–70

The main countries of western Europe emerged from the Napoleonic Wars with a framework of socio-economic institutions which were far better suited to the needs of economic growth than those of the mid-eighteenth century. And the process of modernisation, although initially retarded by the political reaction which set in with the final defeat of the French had, quite inescapably, to be continued in the new conditions of the nineteenth century. Yet the removal of potential obstacles to industrialisation was not, alone, sufficient to promote it — although it *was* sufficient to encourage the beginnings of the emergence of a newly important class of entrepreneurs in industry, finance and commerce. What actually stimulated industrial growth in western Europe in the early nineteenth century was a combination of Britain's continuing example, economic pressure and national ambition.

17. Less extensive, but comparable types of reforms were instituted in Austria.

For most of this period, the British economy, which had initiated the Industrial Revolution without the direct intervention of the state, prolonged and heightened its supremacy on the basis of market forces. Indeed, the main trend of British legislation after the Wars (which, if anything, increased the industrial gap between the British and continental economies) was precisely in the direction of a continued dismantling of the structural, fiscal and economic barriers to the mobility of men and resources. Flexible use of land had, of course, already been achieved (it was confirmed by the General Enclosure Act of 1801 which aimed at a simplification of agricultural reorganisation). And in the postwar years a formidable series of reforms took place. Tariffs were reduced from the 1820s and the campaign for free trade led to the repeal of the Corn Laws (1846) and later to the virtual abolition of significant duties on almost all imports. The Navigation Laws were liberalised in the 1820s and abolished within a generation. In the mid-1820s the remaining laws ostensibly regulating the manufacture and quality of various goods were repealed. A new Poor Law in 1834 was in part designed to 'free' labour from the enervating pull of local wage-subsidies and relief payments, by substituting the disincentive of harsh workhouse conditions. The capital market was made much more efficient by easier facilities for forming joint-stock companies, which culminated in limited liability legislation in 1856. And the confidence of British manufacturers was reflected not merely in the advent of free trade, but in the abolition of the Combination Acts (1824), which had hindered trade-union development, in the further liberalisation of trade-union laws, and in the repeal of the legislation (which was in any case by then somewhat ineffective) forbidding the emigration of skilled artisans (1825) and the unlicensed export of machinery (1843).

It can, of course, be argued that, with respect to the international economy, British manufacturers could well afford to be liberal. Their superior technology and productivity, and the rapid growth rate of their investment and output, ensured that they would suffer no direct loss. Yet even so, it is of considerable significance that the government — increasingly influenced, although by no means yet dominated, by industrial interests — should have exercised its power not in any direct stimulus of economic expansion but in the dismantling of old institutional restraints and the creation of new arrangements which extended even farther the freedom of British entrepreneurs and the mobility of British factors of production. Admittedly, these are also grounds for claiming that in the sphere of social and welfare legislation, as also in such areas as the nominal regulation of railway affairs, the balance was tipping towards state intervention rather than laissez-faire. But even here, much of the legislation can be rationalised as the attainment of 'a refined laissez-faire regime' which '*demands* positive state action' to control monopoly or to make externalities explicit.[18] And as far as the allocation and flow of productive resources were concerned, there was no doubt that Britain was closer to the ideal of liberal capitalism in 1851 than it had been in 1815 — and that the task of shaping the institutional prerequisites of the move had been willingly adopted by a state which proved admirably accommodating to new economic forces and social trends.

Sustained by an environment which was outstandingly favourable to their private enterprise, British businessmen forged ahead in the industrial race. In fact, it seems likely that growth rates, capital accumulation and accompanying social change were at their most rapid in the 1830s, 1840s and 1850s. Yet the dramatic qualities of Britain's industrialisation were not — indeed, could not be — ignored on the Continent, while the new pressures of demand and supply (of men and capital and techniques as well as goods) which flowed from Britain's Industrial Revolution were also powerful stimulants of change. Emulation and competitive forces therefore served to diffuse industrialisation in western Europe in the first half of the nineteenth century. By the 1850s it had begun decisively to transform the economies

18. R. L. Crouch, 'Laissez-faire in nineteenth-century Britain: Myth or Reality?' *The Manchester School of Economic and Social Studies*, XXXV, 3 (September 1967), p. 215.

of France, Belgium and parts of Holland, while its influence was already felt in various of the German states.

This transformation was based in large part on domestic resources and skills. And even when resources or skills were lacking, continental entrepreneurs were active and ambitious enough to secure them from Britain. As a result, British capital, sometimes accompanied by entrepreneurs, flowed into continental industries and, from the 1840s, railways. In the early years of the century thousands of British workers (ranging from the navvies who constructed early railway lines to locomotive drivers, textile machine operators and iron makers) gravitated to new centres of industry across the Channel; and even when a basic labour supply had been developed in particular industries on the Continent, British foremen and supervisory personnel were still much in demand: 'We find in France,' it was said in 1840, 'that the principal foremen at Rouen and in the cotton factories are from Lancashire; you find it in Belgium, in Holland and in the neighbourhood of Liège,' while in the Viennese cotton mills 'the directors and foremen [are] chiefly Englishmen or Scotsmen, from the . . . manufactories of Glasgow and Manchester.'[19]

Yet the considerable potential of private enterprise and market forces on the Continent in the years after 1815 did not mean that the role of the state was as neutral as in Britain. First, the example of British technology, which was an invitation and opportunity to businessmen, was a threat and a challenge to those who assessed the national interest in terms of the distribution of economic and military power. Modern growth rates also accelerate the rate at which the international balance of power is disturbed; and, as a result, the quest for economic expansion was harnessed to the ends of national power.

Writing in 1841, Friedrich List, the German political economist, argued that:

At a time when technical and mechanical science exercise

19. John Macgregor, Secretary to the Board of Trade, quoted in J. H. Clapham, *Economic History of Modern Britain* (1930), I, p. 491.

such immense influence on the methods of warfare, when
all warlike operations depend so much on the condition
of the national revenue, when successful defence greatly
depends on the questions, whether the mass of the nation
is rich or poor, intelligent or stupid, energetic or sunk in
apathy; whether its sympathies are given exclusively to
the fatherland or partly to foreign countries; whether it
can muster many or but few defenders of the country —
at such a time, more than ever before, must the value of
manufactures be estimated from a political point of
view.[20]

Industrialisation thus became an adjunct of political policy.
Second, there were still some areas even in north-western
Europe where institutional reform was needed — and two
at least (the German and Italian states) where the basic
political prerequisites of unified nationhood still had to be
achieved. Underlying both these ambitions — for national
power and for national coherence and independence — was
a newly importance force in European ideology: nationalism. The concept of the unity, character and uniqueness of
individual nations had roots which went far back in European history. But with the opening of the post-Revolutionary
age, with the sense of opportunity and threat derived from
the twin forces of modernisation and economic growth, the
drive for national strength became a pervasive force in
continental Europe. To some, the idea of the nation was
largely a metaphysical concept; but many also recognised
its economic implications. As List argued:

between the individual and entire humanity . . . stands
THE NATION, with its special language and literature,
with its peculiar origin and history, with its special
manners and customs, laws and institutions, with the
claims of all these for existence, independence — reflection and continuance for the future . . . Meanwhile,
however, an infinite difference exists in the condition and
circumstances of the various nations . . . but in all of
them . . . exists the impulse of self-preservation, the

20. List, *National System of Political Economy* (1904 edition), pp. 168-9.

striving for improvement which is implanted by nature. It is the task of politics to civilise the barbarous nationalities . . . to secure to them existence and continuance. It is the task of national economy to accomplish *the economical development of the nation,* and to prepare it for admission into the universal society of the future.[21]

Consequently, while a desire to defend and extend the nation state provided a reason for governments' concern with the Industrial Revolution, the relative backwardness of those seeking to imitate Britain, combined with the importance of achieving a fairly rapid growth rate, provided a strong incentive for its positive encouragement. Finally, and again in contrast to Britain, the early nineteenth-century governments of continental Europe shared a tradition of direct participation in industrial and technological development. Their institutions and their official outlook both meant that it was logical for them to play an active role at a time of genuinely modern industrialisation.

In relation to the last point, for example, in both Belgium and the German states (more rarely in France) the state itself invested money in industrial enterprises. In Belgium — which was dominated by the Dutch until 1830 — the government channelled funds towards shipbuilding and manufactures in the 1820s, although this was in part a placatory move by the Dutch towards the Belgian provinces, and the flow declined to an insignificant trickle after Belgium secured her independence in 1830. (Belgian nationhood, however, brought a much more active state policy in the field of railways.) In Prussia, the state ironworks and coalmines in Silesia retained their importance,[22] while new government funds were ploughed into transport (which will be dealt with below) and manufacturing

21. *The National System of Political Economy* (1904 edition), pp. 141-2.
22. David S. Landes, *The Unbound Prometheus: Technological Change and Industrial Development in Western Europe from 1750 to the Present* (1969), p. 179. In 1850 some 20 per cent of Prussia's coal output came from state-owned mines: Wolfram Fischer, 'Government Activity and Industrialisation in Germany (1815-70)', in W. W. Rostow (ed.), *The Economics of Take-off into Sustained Growth* (1963), p. 83.

industry — including Prussia's first mill to weave worsted with power looms, in 1842. Yet even here there was a reaction: by the 1840s the use of official subsidies to industry was under attack as a threat to 'pure' private enterprise and as a losing proposition. By the mid-1850s the Overseas Trading Corporation (*Seehandlung*) which had handled most of these funds had disposed of the bulk of its investments. As far as direct investment in manufacturing industry was concerned, state action in the leading economies of western Europe — France, the Low Countries, Prussia — was becoming less necessary, and therefore less desired by industrial entrepreneurs who were increasingly capable of raising needed capital privately.

There was, however, another type of state action which was eminently acceptable to private enterprise and which was of *increasing* relevance to the needs of industrialising societies. This was the pattern of aid to technical education and to the diffusion of technological and business ideas which had been established in the eighteenth century. The authorities in France and the German states, for example, sent officials to Britain and the United States to bring back technical information, and shaped their trading, taxation and patent policies to encourage and subsidise inventors, immigrant businessmen and imported machinery and ideas. Individual German states established offices to provide local technical assistance. And in Prussia, it has been said, a 'benevolent bureaucracy' undertook a programme of industrial promotion, on the basis of which 'the middle-class citizen was educated for entrepreneurship.'[23]

In such high level institutions as the French *Ecole Polytechnique*, the Prussian *Hauptbergwerks-Institut*, and the Technical Universities in various German states, or more modestly in numerous mechanical training schools, as well as in the subsidising of their students, the state provided means of industrial advancement which had very high social benefits, albeit low private profit potential. The long-run benefits of such varied encouragement to

23. Fischer, 'Government Activity and Industrialisation in Germany', in Rostow (ed.), *The Economics of Take-off*, p. 90.

a rationalised technological and industrial system were enormous.

This participation in the technological and educational externalities of manufacturing industries obviously suggests that the reluctance of the French or Prussian governments to invest money directly in manufacturing was a pragmatic rather than an ideological response to economic circumstances. And this is confirmed by the attitude of continental governments towards the railway.

European governments had, of course, long been concerned with the social overhead capital embodied in national transport systems. Now, from the 1830s onwards, the relationship between the state and the creation of nineteenth-century railway networks provides a striking example of government 'intervention' in a capitalist system. In this respect it is significant that Britain — less overtly nationalistic, more explicitly individualist — was once again an exception. There, private market forces determined the shape and extent of the railway network and provided the necessary resources for its construction. But in Britain the railways *followed* the Industrial Revolution: they came to a powerful and wealthy society which did not need the help of the government to mobilise financial resources. On the Continent, by contrast, the timing of the technological 'availability' of the railway, and its potential importance for rapid economic growth, meant a new role for the state. Thus, on the one hand, it was clear that the pattern, as well as the extent and speed of construction, of railway systems would help determine the pattern and coherence of national development itself. Railways could unite a nation as could no other technological development, and their potential role in military hostilities was soon apparent. National consciousness and national strategy therefore combined to give the state a crucial basis for action — especially where large land masses emphasised the superiority of rail over water transport. On the other hand, the economic incentive to railway construction encountered financial difficulties precisely because of its timing: although they were potential stimulants of general economic growth, railways were themselves large and expensive investments, the return to which might take years to appear. Private costs were unprecedently high; private benefits conceivably remote, certainly risky. In these circumstances there was a straightforward economic motive for government participation to reduce private costs or guarantee private benefits. As a consequence of these twin incentives — the political-strategic and the economic — the state played an important part in the development of railways in the newly industrialising nations.

In the 1830s in Belgium, newly freed from Dutch control, the desire to assert national sovereignty, independence and competence led to a decision to construct the railway network as a national enterprise, and on a systematic pattern. (Private lines were permitted — but were negligible in extent until the 1850s and 1860s.) From the start, however, its economic implications were not ignored: rates were kept low and a deficit built up as the state used the new system to encourage national development and capture much of the transit trade between the North Sea ports and central Europe. Even so, by the 1850s the state system (about 900 kilometres in 1850) was returning a steady profit and had achieved its main political and economic purposes: Belgium was strong and independent and had greatly enlarged its industrial system and particularly its output of coal, iron and textiles.[24]

In France (whose size made the question of inland transport even more important) the state's conventional concern with improving communications was continued in the early nineteenth century. Louis Philippe's government — heavily representative of financial interests — mobilised capital for road and canal construction. Efforts to encourage the railway were even more important. After initial private ventures to serve the mining and manufacturing area around St. Etienne, the state was enlisted in a far more extensive

24. In fact, the 1850s and 1860s saw no new public initiatives in Belgian railway construction — although private lines grew from some 150 kilometres in 1850 to 2,100 kilometres in 1870. After 1870, however, the state began to buy up competing private lines.

scheme. Partly aroused by the modernising drives of the followers (many of them active capitalists) of Saint-Simon, the French government acknowledged the arguments in favour of a national rail network. In 1833 the Department of Highways and Bridges was charged with designing such a network: having studied British and American lines, a systematic plan was drawn up, with main lines radiating from Paris and serving military as well as presumed civil demand. After prolonged public discussion (meanwhile almost 900 kilometres of line had been constructed — much with state aid or loans or guarantees to the promoters) the Railway Law of 1842 provided the general lines of a solution to the critical question of finance.[25] The provision of capital was to be a joint effort of public authorities and private interest, with the authorities being principally responsible for the 'infrastructure' (i.e. land, track, bridges, tunnels), although they were sometimes obliged to pay for much of 'superstructure' (stations, rails, equipment) or provide more direct financial aid to companies, before handing over the lines to private concessionnaires. In return for its aid, the state secured representation in management, supervised charges and safety, and retained the right to nationalise the lines when the concessions expired. In the mid-1840s, subsidised by government policy and attracting British contractors, navvies, engine drivers and capital,[26] French railway construction boomed. By 1847 there were some 1,800 kilometres of track.

Brought to a halt by the crisis of 1847 and the revolution of the next year, the railway boom was revived in the 1850s under Napoleon III's Second Empire — by which time

25. The specific provisions of the 1842 Law (e.g. with regard to the proportions into which financial responsibility was to be divided between the state and private investors) were not, in fact, retained. However, the general principle implicit in them (i.e. the assumption that the state should be an active and enterprising partner in the financing and running of the railway system) was the basis of future action.

26. Some 5,000 British workmen were said to have worked in France for Thomas Brassey, the great contractor; and by 1847 it has been estimated, half of French railway share capital was owned in Britain: W. O. Henderson, *The Industrial Revolution on the Continent* (1961), pp. 113–14.

extended aid to railways had become part of a broad-based stimulus by the state to industry, banking and urban development. It had started with grants by Louis Napoleon's republican government (1848–52) and quickened appreciably when he became Emperor, when the government decided to accelerate the construction of lines and to merge them for strategic and economic efficiency. Following precedents set in 1851 and 1852, interest payments on railway capital was guaranteed, much longer concessions were granted, and amalgamations were encouraged. As a result of this and private initiative, the French network grew from under 4,000 kilometres in 1851 to almost 7,000 in 1857 (by 1870 it reached 17,000 kilometres), and in the mid-1850s almost thirty companies, accounting for about half France's mileage, were fused into six companies. By 1860 the original plan of 1842 had been completed — and the French railway system had been successfully established by a distinctive partnership of public and private resources and efforts.

The new mode of transport was also of vital importance to the other large land mass of western Europe: Germany. In Germany's case, however, the early years of the railway were also years of political fragmentation. And the lack of national unity was reflected in the fact that the various states made no attempt to plan a national system when the first railways were constructed in the 1830s and 1840s. On the other hand, public and private needs were clearly recognised: by 1850 there were almost 6,000 kilometres of line in the various German states (compared to only 3,000 in France). In contrast to Belgium's state-owned system and France's public-private co-operation, however, German railways were 'mixed' systems, with private and public companies running separate lines. In Prussia, there was, in fact, no state enterprise until the early 1840s, when the financial difficulties of the early lines led to government investment in, and guarantees to, private companies. The first Prussian state railway was initiated in 1847. Thenceforth the government rapidly extended its control over large parts of an expanding network. The drive for Prussian dominance in Germany, the military implications of

German nationhood, and the concept of economic unification and growth all played a part. Altogether, by 1875 there were some 28,000 kilometres of railways in Germany (by now a federal entity); the federal states controlled almost half (12,000 kilometres), private owners about as much (12,600 kilometres), and the balance was privately owned but managed by the various federal railway administrations. In Prussia, which had the best developed strategic sense and the maximum economic opportunity, over 9,000 of the total of 16,000 kilometres were privately owned and run. In the southern German states nearly all the lines were nationalised.

The cost, external economies and strategic implications of railways gave them a special importance in nineteenth-century economic development, and readily explains the involvement of public authorities in their construction and management.[27] Yet, distinctive as they were, they really only provide a particular example of a general situation: the state's necessary concern with nation-building and market unification. That concern was manifest in the history of three countries: France, Italy and Germany.[28]

As we have already seen, the French state was accepted as an agent of socio-economic change in the somewhat ineffective schemes of the *ancien régime* and, much more significantly, in the period of upheaval from 1789 onwards. Most of the state's work then had been structural and institutional. After the downfall of Napoleon, however, there was less pressure for fundamental reform. On the other hand, the turbulent history of France, and the suc-

27. By the last two or three decades of the century the economic problems of railway transport in advanced economies had produced an even more extensive role for the government — in terms of ownership, management and regulation — throughout Europe. Public ownership increased, and the state came to play a more explicit role, even in Britain. All this, however, was a reflection of the problems of relative maturity rather than the needs of growth.

28. For the course of industrialisation in these countries, see the relevant chapters of Volume 4: 1, 2, 5: Claude Fohlen, *The Industrial Revolution in France 1700–1914* Knut Borchardt, *The Industrial Revolution in Germany 1700–1914* Luciano Cafagna, *The Industrial Revolution in Italy 1700–1914*.

cession of different regimes until the establishment of the Third Republic (1870), ultimately implied considerable pressure on government to encourage economic development.

In the immediate aftermath of Napoleon's defeat, with the restoration of the Bourbons (1815–30), governments and policies were dominated by the conservative landed aristocracy — a fact which, together with financial stringency, meant that .the state played a relatively small part in the general encouragement of industry. At the same time, however, a very high industrial tariff was imposed in 1816 and in subsequent years the government helped promote new canals — which were related in part to the coal and iron trades and, therefore, to the interests of landowners. This regime, largely as a result of liberal dissatisfaction with its reactionary structure and policies, was succeeded by the 'July Monarchy' (1830–48) under Louis Philippe, which was much more directly representative of elements in the new business classes — particularly of financial capitalists. As a result, as we have seen, the government financed and encouraged significant programmes of road, canal and railway improvements. It also favoured the growth of the embryonic banking system. In general, however, the Monarchy's increasing conservatism encountered rising unrest and radicalism, and in 1848, the year of Revolutions, Louis Philippe was overthrown. France became a Republic, briefly in a radical mould, and subsequently more moderately under Prince Louis Napoleon Bonaparte, who was President until 1852. In that year Bonaparte, as Napoleon III, created the Second Empire. Meanwhile beneath the froth of political change, steady if not spectacular industrial growth was releasing new forces and tensions in French society: not merely a left-wing labour movement but also a 'radical' bourgeoisie, which was represented by men of thought as well as men of action. And among the most curious of the resulting trends was the appearance of a class of financial and industrial capitalists very much influenced by the ideas of a utopian socialist, Saint-Simon, who was persuaded of the need for systematic industrial development and had a vision of a golden industrial age. In this respect, indeed, Saint-Simonism has been seen as one of the possible 'ideologies of delayed industrialisation' — as the intellectual and emotional stimulus needed 'to break through the barriers of stagnation in a backward country, to ignite the imagination of men, and to place their energies in the service of economic development.'[29] Capitalists and publicists, influenced by this sort of a vision of a rational, technocratic, industrial order, occupied positions of power and influence in France in the middle years of the century. Thus Michel Chevalier, the economist, the Péreire brothers of the Crédit Mobilier, and Ferdinand de Lesseps, the promoter of the Suez Canal, were Saint-Simonians. And as a group they were largely instrumental in the development of the French railway network and investment banking. At the same time, with Napoleon III's rise to imperial power, the government made a much more sustained effort at economic development. The extension and rationalisation of the railway network in the 1850s and 1860s was perhaps the most important aspect of this 'programme'. Napoleon III himself was influenced by Saint-Simonian ideas, although his 'sweeping vision of planning and state action' was reflected in a far more nationalistic form at the level of actual railway planning.[30] Another striking move by the government, and one that had psychological as well as ramified economic effects, was the virtual rebuilding of Paris (under the direction of Baron Georges Haussmann), as part of the extension of public works. In addition, the government removed the state's previous inhibitions on the formation and growth of joint-stock banks. This, together with the enactment of specific legislation (in 1863 and 1867) to facilitate the foundation of such companies without state control, encouraged their development as channels for large-scale investment in industry and railroads — a de-

29. Alexander Gerschenkron, *Economic Backwardness in Historical Perspective* (1962), pp. 22, 24.
30. Charles F. Kindleberger, *Economic Growth in France and England 1851–1950* (1964), pp. 186–7.

velopment which was of crucial importance in France's mid-century growth. Finally, too, the Napoleonic state began to reduce the tariffs which for years had cocooned rather than stimulated French industry and mining. Ingrained conservative attitudes were changed as the economy was exposed (albeit briefly) to competition through the reduction of tariffs and the Cobden-Chevalier Treaty (1860), although the state cushioned the blow to some industries by providing temporary financial help where the lower tariffs had their main effect.[31]

Although the state continued to support economic development after 1870, it should perhaps be emphasised that its direct role in France's industrialisation was far from dominant. And certainly the account given so far is in danger of underestimating the importance of private initiatives and capital, of the profit motive, of industrial entrepreneurs, and of the great financial capitalists. Yet government action was an obvious factor in French economic growth in the early nineteenth century. In addition to the heritage of structural reform, the railway network was heavily dependent on state action, technical advice and assistance were liberally supplied, and by the 1850s specific initiatives — with regard to public works, the positive encouragement of private enterprise, and the reform of trade policy — were all having an effect. Matching this variegation of effort, no single motive or explanation can be adduced for the pattern of state aid to French industrial development. In part it was the survival into a new industrial age of a traditional concern with national development; in part the result of the efforts of newly-influential capitalist classes to extend the system within which their ambitions could be achieved and rationalised; and in part the effort of new regimes (particularly the Second Empire) to forge national support on the basis of national economic effort. As might be expected too, the various policies sometimes reflected a haphazard and unnecessary subsidy to private capitalists, sometimes the

31. For this period see Volume 4, chapter 1, Fohlen, *Industrial Revolution in France*, pp. 20–22 and *passim*.

strategic and military aims of nationalism, sometimes very long-run socio-economic goals, and sometimes the need for collective action, in costly projects, to generate the 'externalities' so important to more diversified economic development.

If we turn from France in the early nineteenth century — an 'established' nation with reasonably well defined economic objectives — to Italy in the same period, some clear and obvious contrasts emerge. Admittedly, in the case of Italy, as with all new nations, the state played an indispensable role in the process of unification. On the other hand, although economic ambitions were indissolubly linked to nationalist sentiment, and the individual state governments were moderately active in the encouragement of railways and industry, Italy remained at a level of substantial economic backwardness throughout the period leading up to its unification in 1861 — and, indeed, experienced rapid industrial growth only at the very end of the century. In other words, the process of Italian nation-building was not immediately associated with a process of economic growth, and state action was largely confined to the creation of the national framework of an economy and the eradication of many of the political and institutional obstacles to subsequent expansion.

Nevertheless, it is important to emphasise that nationalism was itself interpreted in economic terms. As with other west European countries, the Italian states had been profoundly affected by the French Revolution and its consequences. The French conquests, in fact, served to develop a strong liberal-nationalist feeling (both positively by encouragement and, ultimately, negatively by reaction against French policies). And after Napoleon's fall, by which time most of Italy's agriculture had become 'free' of feudal constraints,[32] a powerful nationalist movement agitated for political unification and the abolition of restrictions on enterprise in order to secure both the market-basis for economic expansion and the essentials of national identity

32. Much, particularly in the north, had been attained even before Revolution. It was the centre and the south which were especially affected by institutional reform in the revolutionary era.

and strength. In the main, however, the process of unification — which took another two generations — was accomplished by political and military means, and without, as yet, any transformation of the Italian economy.[33]

In the case of Germany the basis of ultimate unification was laid (even before the individual states had begun to play a crucial role in the creation of their various railway networks) by the establishment of the *Zollverein*, or Customs Union (1834). Here, as in so much of subsequent German history, the lead was taken by Prussia — where the government had already unified and energised the domestic market in 1818 by abolishing a complex mixture of duties levied at provincial and town boundaries and replacing them with a single (albeit very low) tariff at the state frontier. In fact, the abolition of tariff barriers within Germany was widely acknowledged to be a prerequisite of extensive development — although inter-state rivalries held up the attainment of this end for many years. Ultimately, after smaller customs unions had been founded, the *Zollverein* came into operation on 1st January, 1834, with its duties based upon the Prussian tariff and Prussia undertaking its negotiations with foreign countries. The free trade area created by these moves covered about four-fifths of Germany and contained about 33 million people.[34] By facilitating interregional mobility, competition and specialisation, and by strengthening Prussia's hand in international commercial negotiations, the *Zollverein* — a classic example of market-creation by the state — greatly encouraged private industrialisation.

In the long run the Prussian-dominated *Zollverein*, which grew in size as it was extended to more states, was a powerful agent of political as well as economic change: the unification of political institutions in Germany was based upon the unification of market institutions.[35] Thus the

33. For the role of the state in the period of Italy's rapid industrial growth at the end of the century, see pp. 340-350.

34. Britain's population at the time was 17 million, and Ireland's just under 8 million.

35. It is significant that in 1848 when, as a result of the Revolution

rivalry between Prussia and Austria was frequently expressed in terms of a rivalry over extending the central European customs union, and although special economic relationships between Austria and the *Zollverein* were established, Prussia ultimately asserted its economic leadership by securing the renewal of the *Zollverein* Treaties on the basis of a free trade policy — reflecting the relative unimportance of industry in Prussia and the dominance of the Junker landed class. This was in 1865, and was a symbolic prelude to Prussia's speedy military defeat of Austria and her German allies in 1866.[36] Various German states were thereupon annexed to Prussia, which now controlled a North German Federation; the *Zollverein* was extended, with new rules which gave Prussia more power over the south German states; and a Customs Council and a Customs Parliament replaced the *Zollverein* Congress as administrative agencies — although Prussia was not in the event able to transmute them directly into political institutions for a more unified Germany.

The 1860s saw the birth of modern Germany under Prussian hegemony, and while France was being defeated by Prussia in the war of 1870–1, the German Empire was formally established in January 1871. The creation of the new state was underpinned by the forces of economic growth. Prussia, the most powerful of German states, naturally took the lead externally as well as internally; the economic prospects of unification anticipated the political reality; and the *Zollverein* and the railway — two structural prerequisites of the extension of the market — shaped the framework of the new state. Moreover, the ideology of nationalism took close account of its economic implications: not merely in en-

---

of that year, a short-lived National Parliament met in Frankfurt, its Economic Committee drafted articles for a proposed constitution which would have given Germany a single tariff, cost-based river tolls and a single authority for controlling tariffs, custom administration and common taxes and excises.

36. A defeat which was facilitated by Von Moltke's strategic use of extensive railway and telegraph lines — another indication of the nationalistic implications of industrial technology.

visaging that national power had to be based upon national wealth, but in asserting that economic achievement (e.g. tariff policy and industrial growth) could be both cause and effect of nationhood.

As with the French case, one should guard against an exaggeration of the role of the state in Germany's industrialisation. Certainly, the actual processes and proximate causes of industrial growth were firmly embedded in market forces — not merely in the sense that (with the main exception of the railways) the principal units of production were privately managed and financed, but also in that some of the most important agents of change for the industrial sector — the joint-stock banks — were successful innovations of private enterprise to overcome the problems of capital mobilisation.[37] Nevertheless, even more than in nineteenth-century France, the state institutions of Germany did exercise a considerable influence on the course of economic development. In terms of direct actions this was achieved through help to industry in its early stages, the sponsoring of technical education and information, and participation in the construction and, even more, the management of railways. Less directly, but in the last resort more significantly, the state was responsible for creating the very fabric of nationhood — a fabric within which market forces could be unleashed to produce industrialisation. More than this, the attainment of nationhood, although associated with war, was also the consequence of economic policies. An arrangement like the *Zollverein*, followed a generation or so later by the political drawing together of the various German states into one *Reich*, provided the basis, as no private activity could have done, of accelerated economic growth.

By the 1850s and 1860s the twin forces of nationalism and industrialism had changed the political appearance and economic prospects of Europe. The Industrial Revolution, initiated in Britain with little direct help from the state, had spread almost everywhere as an idea, and in a few

37. Gerschenkron, *Economic Backwardness*, pp. 11–16.

countries as a reality — but compared with Britain, it had done so with more, and sometimes far more, explicit en- couragement from the state. To some extent collective action can be seen as the consequence of relative economic backwardness. Yet substantial direct government activity had taken place only in one area where capital and tech- nological needs were considerable: the railways. In other directions, with nation-building as a principal incentive, state institutions tended to be preoccupied not so much with mobilising resources for investment or directly en- couraging industrial development, as with creating what in retrospect, and sometimes in prospect, were the pre- conditions for ultimate industrial growth.

It would, in fact, be wrong to contrast a laissez-faire Britain and other European countries committed on doc- trinaire grounds to the use of state resources for growth purposes. First, because the extent of government inter- vention can be best explained not in terms of basic systems of political economy but as the outcome of economic needs and national ambitions. Second, because what might be called 'negative intervention' — the use of the state to make *institutional* adjustments designed to encourage market ac- tivity — was a common feature of British and continental economic history. We have already seen that in the early nineteenth century successive British governments, without abandoning their theoretical commitments to laissez-faire, greatly improved the framework and liberalised the pattern of commercial policy within which goods, capital, enter- prise and labour could flow freely. And it is a strong feature of continental economic development in the middle years, and particularly the third quarter, of the nineteenth century that they exemplified a comparable liberalisation of trading relationships and of the legal institutions of a nascent industrial capitalism.

The tendency to free trade was perhaps the most striking aspect, if the most transitory, of this 'negative intervention- ism' — if only because it came at a time of economic nationalism, a phenomenon more frequently associated with protective tariffs (as it was to be later). Indeed, since most adjustments of commercial policy were effected by international agreement and since all were related to world trade, it might be better called 'economic internationalism'[38] — an internationalism in which Britain's influence and example were almost as strong as in the field of technology. Free trade was an attempt to achieve at the level of the international economy something of what was achieved *within* a country by the lowering of internal trade barriers. There were, in fact, two principal types of such commercial policies: first, the abolition or reduction of levies on trade on international waterways;[39] second, commercial treaties resulting in a lowering of tariffs between the main industrial nations of Europe.[40] Nor was it merely a phenomenon of industrial countries: Cavour, as Prime Minister of the Kingdom of Sardinia in the 1850s, reduced tariffs in trade treaties with Belgium, France and England.

Free trade exposed developing industries to competition and enhanced specialisation and the diffusion of ideas and technology. Nevertheless, it was only a temporary phase in continental economic policy. Far more long-lasting in its effects, was the series of adjustments to the framework of enterprise. The adaption of legal institutions to the needs of the freer and more secure allocation of capital and enterprise, already had a long history by the middle of the nineteenth century. Nevertheless, it was so far accelerated in the third quarter of the century as to mark a new era in the relationship between industrialism and its legal base. This applied to the spread of limited liability by simple registration, which had an immense effect on the ease of company formation; to the repeal of the prohibition on usury; to the legalisation of such important commercial instruments as cheques; to the extension of patent laws to

38. Landes, *The Unbound Prometheus*, pp. 199–200.

39. E.g. on the Danube (1857), Rhine (1861), Scheldt (1863), Lower Elbe (1861), Upper Elbe (1863 and 1870), and through the Danish Sound (1857).

40. E.g. between Britain and France (1860), France and Belgium (1861), France and Prussia (1862), France and the *Zollverein* (1866), Prussia and Belgium (1863–5), Prussia and Britain (1865), Prussia and Italy (1865).

cover and protect trademarks; and to the modification of commercial and company law.[41] The industrial system had apparently come to stay, and its progenitors naturally ensured that the socio-legal institutions of society did not impede its progress.

THE STATE AND ECONOMIC IMMATURITY, 1870–1914

Economic liberalism was only a brief episode in the history of industrial capitalism. In the last quarter of the nineteenth century the tide turned in the leading industrial economies. Thenceforth a larger and much more 'positive' economic and social role was found for the state. To differing degrees in such countries as Germany, Britain, France and Belgium, economic nationalism took a far more restrictive turn as tariff barriers were raised and the intensified rivalry of the international economy led to the nationalistic control of markets and the extension of exclusive empires. Meanwhile, the state moved to tackle the economic and social problems of growth, to salvage railways systems, to bolster weak sections of the economy, and to ameliorate the increasingly apparent social tensions and problems of urban and industrial maturity, which demanded more welfare legislation and social reform. Obviously, all these developments — and notably the rise of protection and the increasing knowledge of the structural imperfections of liberal capitalism — greatly extended the scope of the state's economic role, as governments wrestled with the problem of instability, poverty and urbanism. Laissez-faire, which in any case only ever existed in a very specific form, was dead; killed not by the prerequisites but by the consequences of industrialisation.

Given our primary concern with the role of government in the *initiation* of Industrial Revolutions, this is not the place to explore the social and economic policies of the most advanced countries in the period 1870–1914. Yet it was not only the problems of relative maturity which

41. For a summary statement, see Landes, *The Unbound Prometheus,* pp. 197–8.

intensified the state's participation in economic affairs in the last decades of the nineteenth century. The problems of backwardness also led to a heightened emphasis of the state's economic role, as European latecomers to the process of industrialisation recognised the need to call on the power of government.[42] Two contrasting examples deserve mention in this respect: Italy and Russia.

In the case of Italy, unification in 1861 had not been immediately followed by any significant industrial advance, although between the 1860s and the 1890s some of the structural and technological foundations of later progress were being laid as basic industries (textiles, metallurgical, shipbuilding) grew more sophisticated, and the railway system was extended from some 1,600 kilometres (1861) to 16,000 kilometres (1896). Between 1895 and 1908, however, there was a sharp spurt (manufacturing output grew at almost 7 per cent annually), and this was followed by a more moderate growth (2.4 per cent) until 1914. Although Italy's growth rate was slower than that of Sweden, Russia or Japan, and although manufacturing industry still only accounted for just under 25 per cent of total national product in 1911–15, Italy's industrialisation had obviously begun. What role did the government play?

The Italian government was an active participant in industrial expansion. First, it mobilised a very high proportion of the capital needed for the railway system: between 1861 and 1914 the state spent 12,600 million lire, an amount equal to the national income in 1900, on railway construction,[43] owning 6,000 out of just under 10,000 kilometres in 1884 and (after an unsuccessful interlude in which the main networks were operated by private companies under government supervision) some 15,000 out of 17,000 in 1905. Second, the government extended direct aid to various industries. In the years after unification subsidies were given to shipping and tax advantages to

42. The same could be said of Japan which, however, is excluded from this survey.

43. Shephard B. Clough, *The Economic History of Modern Italy* (1964), p. 67.

shipbuilding (which, like the railways, was heavily capital intensive and involved the use of expensive materials and technology), while from 1885 onwards, direct subsidies were extended to shipbuilding and progressively increased.[44] In iron and steel, where Italy suffered from severe competitive disadvantages in the chronic shortage of iron ore and coal,[45] the government gave some direct assistance (e.g. in 1884 to the steel works at Terni) and used its ownership of the iron ore mines at Elba to provide cheap raw material to encourage metal production; and generally gave favourable orders to metallurgical and engineering enterprises. Third, and following an increasing fashion, the state in Italy pursued an active policy of agricultural and industrial protection, with the main help in industry going to cotton textiles and ferrous metal-making from 1878, and to machinery from 1887.[46]

Obviously, therefore, it is possible to associate a marked acceleration of industrial development in Italy with reasonably vigorous government efforts to provide scarce capital for high-cost industries, and to protect and subsidise specific industrial interests. On the other hand, however, there is room for some doubt about the precise effect of the state's actions.[47] It has been argued, for example, that the timing of its efforts did not always match the actual pace of industrialisation, since much of its actions (e.g. a good deal of railway construction, the protective tariff, industrial subsidies) antedated the period of real growth by a decade and more; and that much of its policy was misplaced, since it was 'onesided' and concentrated 'on the least deserving branches of industrial activity'.[48] The examples given are

44. When the generous arrangements of 1896 proved to involve fairly heavy official expenditure, an overall limit was imposed (1901) and the rates were reduced (1911 and 1913).

45. In 1914 Italy's coal production was 700,000 tons — as against almost 300 million in England and 220 million in Germany.

46. Grainstuffs were also protected from 1887. By 1895 Italy's wheat tariff was the highest of the principal European countries.

47. See Gerschenkron, *Economic Backwardness*, Chapter 4 ('Notes on the Rate of Industrial Growth in Italy, 1881–1913').

48. Gerschenkron, *Economic Backwardness*, p. 80.

cotton, which was an old industry with only limited potential for Italy, and iron and steel, which were heavy users of high-cost coal and the consequent high prices of which impaired the development of those sectors which were potentially heavy users of ferrous metals. Relatively neglected by the tariff policies were such promising industries as engineering and chemicals. From this viewpoint it is difficult to avoid the conclusion that Italy's tariff policy, although designed to benefit some industrial sectors, was largely fashioned by existing vested interests — concerned far more with protecting their established position than with stimulating new and progressive industrial growth on a broad front.

Yet even if Italy did lack a really effective government development programme, and thereby failed to overcome its intense backwardness with a spectacular and broadbased industrial 'push', one must not underestimate the pace and degree of industrialisation which *did* take place. And in that industrialisation, the state was called upon to play a familiar role: to shield private enterprise from external competition, to draw together scarce capital to build and run the railways which private companies could not, and to provide selective financial and market help. In their origin these policies may sometimes have been selfish or misguided; but in their results they were expansionist.

To a greater extent than with the Italian example, the history of Russia's economic development apparently provides an almost classic instance of the state's successful initiation of industrial growth in an essentially capitalist system.[49] The actual period of growth came, quite spectacularly, from the mid-1880s onwards: by the 1890s the average annual rate of *industrial* expansion was about 8 per cent (higher than that of any other leading European economy at comparable periods of development), and relative stagnation between 1900 and 1905 was followed by

49. For Russian industrialisation, see Volume 4, chapter 8, Gregory Grossman, *The Industrialisation of Russia.*

renewed growth at a rate of about 6 per cent up to 1913.[50] By the outbreak of the First World War Russia was still seriously backward in terms of structure and its per capita output, which was probably only a third of that of Great Britain and about half of Germany's. Nevertheless, it had achieved a vast amount in terms of the growth of its industrial sector, the provision of a relatively modern transport network, and the beginnings of a fundamental economic transformation.

The Russian government's direct stimulation of industrial growth was, in fact, largely confined to a burst of activity in the last fifteen years of the century. And its main details can be relatively easily summarised. First, as with other continental countries, albeit with more intensity because of the greater land mass and strategic problems of the country, the state assumed prime responsibility for the railway systems. In earlier years (after the Crimean War) the government had subsidised and regulated the pioneer main lines. Now, during the great railway boom of the 1880s and 1890s, the state went even further in constructing and acquiring lines — the most spectacular being the Trans-Siberian railway (over 5,000 miles long), commenced in 1891, although taking a decade to complete. Significantly, the state-sponsored railway boom coincided with Russia's industrial spurt and can be seen as 'the main lever of a rapid industrialisation policy'.[51] Second, direct help was extended to manufacturing industry, and especially to technologically 'modern' sectors (e.g. heavy industry in iron and steel and machinery): particular enterprises were subsidised and given tax advantages; the state helped with the provision

50. Gerschenkron, *Economic Backwardness*, pp. 129–33. (In relation to these aspects of Russian economic history and the role of the Tsarist government, one is particularly reliant on Professor Gerschenkron's work.) It should, however, be noted that these growth rates refer only to manufacturing industry — which was still a relatively small proportion of total output. Between the mid-1880s and the outbreak of the First World War total output of goods and services probably grew at just under 3 per cent annually: see Raymond W. Goldsmith, 'The Economic Growth of Tsarist Russia, 1860–1913', *Economic Development and Cultural Change*, IX, 3 (April 1961), p. 443.

51. Gerschenkron, *Economic Backwardness*, p. 19.

of investment funds; favourable, high-priced contracts were awarded by public enterprises (e.g. the railways, the army and navy). Third, and perhaps the best evidence of the *systematic* nature of the state's efforts, commercial and financial policies were generally attuned to the needs of growth. Thus, after a period of free trade, designed to encourage the country's agricultural specialisation, the interests of the landed aristocracy were spurned and a system of protection adopted from 1877. In 1891 highly discriminating duties were imposed to encourage manufacturing in all its processes (i.e. raw material and semi-finished as well as final products). The state also encouraged a vast influx of foreign capital both indirectly by ensuring an appropriate level of agricultural exports to service interest payments and directly by using its credit to issue substantial amounts of public loans. Moreover, government budgets were shaped with an eye to the need to gather in resources and allocate them to strategic uses, while the state's extensive ownership, management or regulation of enterprises (agricultural land, railways, distilleries, timber, sugar, banks, etc.) were similarly deployed in a sustained attempt to secure industrial growth.

From the present viewpoint, the actual details of government policy in Russia are less important than the explanation of why the state should have assumed this role — and why it should have assumed it *then*. In this regard, it is important to remember that the Russian state had always been a leading agent of social and economic change: not merely in the sense that it had given direct aid to various sorts of industrial enterprises, but also because the Tsarist government had traditionally combined an almost unique authoritarian and coercive role with a proprietary as well as a governing status in Russia.[52] The concept of the state as the owner as well as the ruler of society, together with the fact that its perennial ambition had been to secure a 'big-power' role for a backward society, naturally led to the imposition of heavy official burdens on the mass of the population and to the assumption by government of vast,

52. The state was, for example, the biggest landowner.

although not always well fulfilled, responsibilities. This pattern intermittently characterised Russia from the sixteenth to the twentieth centuries.

Various points follow from this, which are relevant to Russian economic history in the late nineteenth century. Thus, the coercive authority, and wealth, of the state meant that it normally had no need to consult other elements and groups in society. More than other European governments, the Tsarist government could hope to act autonomously with respect to the social groups which it ruled. On the other hand, however, particularly given the backwardness of the Russian economy, the state could decidedly *not* act autonomously with respect to the international society of which Russia was a part. It had to pay particular attention to strategic and military matters, and to the economic implications of pre-industrial Russia's vulnerable position. The national humiliation of military or political defeat would be felt the more keenly by a government powerful at home but weak abroad; and its very power would stimulate it to action in the event of such defeat. In the second half of the nineteenth century there were, in fact, two important examples of such humiliation. The first was Russia's defeat, on her own soil, in the Crimean War (1853–6), which was marked by a loss of control of the mouth of the Danube and by the neutralisation of the Black Sea. In the aftermath of the war, keenly aware of the logistic factors which impaired its defence capabilities and of the general backwardness of the society it ruled, the Tsarist government set about encouraging railway construction (principally on strategic grounds), and undertook a series of social reforms — notably the emancipation of the serfs in 1861, the provision of some measure of local self-government with the Zemstvo Law of 1864, and the reform of municipal government in 1870. Nevertheless, such changes were not in themselves sufficient to transform the military or economic position of Russia. And in 1878 she had once more to submit to international ignominy: the Congress of Berlin, in paring away much of the national gain secured in the war against Turkey (1877–8), demonstrated the weakness of a pre-industrial nation when confronting the might of industrial economies such as Britain and Germany.

Events such as these, together with a heightened awareness of Russia's backwardness and of the opportunities and dangers implied in west European economic development, made the late nineteenth century a time of intellectual and political ferment in Russia, and a period of anxiety and hope for national strength and the national future. At one level, the rise of liberal and radical opposition posed a threat to Tsarist autocracy. This threat was often based on a desire for national strength and renewal, although radical movements had an understandable preoccupation with the problems of the peasant and land rather than with the potentialities of industrial growth, and were therefore predominantly agrarian in orientation, and sometimes heavily traditional in outlook. At another level, the Tsarist government's efforts at reform in the 1860s were part of a relatively new mood — a mood that culminated in the 1880s and 1890s with an unprecedently vigorous programme of railway building and industrialisation, even while (from 1881 onwards, after the assassination of the relatively 'liberal' Tsar, Alexander II) the autocratic system of government was re-emphasised, radicalism savagely repressed, and the reform movement arrested.

There was obviously little immediate and direct connection between national defeat in the 1850s and the intensive beginnings of Russian industrialisation some thirty or forty years later. Indeed, there was only one critical reform (albeit a supremely important one) which emerged from the events of mid-century: the emancipation of the serfs. The emancipation was an essential long-run prerequisite of economic growth — and, to this extent, the state played a traditional role in re-shaping the social framework in a way ultimately favourable to expansion. Nevertheless, the emancipation and subsequent laws neither stimulated a new phase of expansion nor took place in a way directly favourable to such an expansion. In particular, both agricultural productivity and labour mobility were impeded by the setting of high quit rents for the land transferred to the peasantry: by the devolution of authority to the village communes rather than to individual peasants; by the provision for the regular reallotment of the land by the communes to peasant families (a reallotment in large part based upon the size of the family); and by the fact that in order to leave the land peasants had to pay for their release and secure the consent of the head of the household.

On the other hand, the fact that agrarian reform was not in the first instance favourable to higher productivity or the effective application of competitive forces to the market for land, goods and men, was not an inhibition to all types of growth. In particular, in measure as the 'non-market' force of state-induced expansion relied upon a *restraining* of the growth of peasant wealth, and substituted governmental purchasing power and investment for potential peasant demand and consumption, so agrarian progress and mobility were the less needed — at least in the short-run. In this, as in other respects, 'Government action took the place of what in other countries was achieved through the pull of a growing free market, or through . . . credit creation or . . . previously accumulated [capital]'.[53]

Thus, indirectly and unwittingly, agrarian reform in the 1860s was a prelude to industrial growth in the 1880s and 1890s. And in that growth, as we have seen, the role of the state — seeking, through a combination of autocracy and nationalism, to strengthen Russia — was paramount. In this regard it is significant that Sergei Witte, a successful businessman who was Minister of Finance in the most vigorous phase of Tsarist expansion and who led the drive to industrial growth, was deeply influenced by the industrial nationalism of Friedrich List's *National System of Political Economy* (1841) and by Bismarck's contribution to German economic strength.[54] Autocracy and nationalism were still the most powerful forces in Russia's economic history. 'The

53. Gerschenkron, *Economic Backwardness*, p. 126: 'A central principle of governmental policy was to impound a larger share of the peasant's output rather than to take active steps to raise that output.'

54. Theodore H. Von Laue, *Sergei Witte and the Industrialisation of Russia* (1963), pp. 2, 262.

experience of all peoples clearly shows,' wrote Witte to the Tsar in 1900, 'that only the economically independent countries are fully able to assert their political power.' And in later years, after he himself had fallen from power with his work uncompleted, he wrote in his *Memoirs* that 'It was imperative to develop our industries not only in the interest of the people but also of the state. A modern body politic cannot be great without a well-developed national industry.'[55]

The ambition and role of the state in late nineteenth-century Russia was in part a familiar echo of previous episodes in Russian history — when the weight of Tsarist power had been brought to bear on economic and social activity in an attempt to 'westernise' and modernise at least selective aspects of that activity.[56] And as happened earlier, the economic repression which was the inevitable concomitant of this form of autocratic 'growth policy' ultimately led to a reaction which impeded the process of expansion itself. By the end of the nineteenth century, heralded by an economic crisis in 1900, economic stagnation arrived — a stagnation accompanied by extreme unrest on the part of the class, the peasantry, which had been obliged to pay most heavily for incipient industrialisation, and by the social and intellectual dissatisfactions of an industrialising society. Both sets of forces culminated in the Revolution of 1905 and the peasant rebellions which were associated with it.

In fact, and to a large extent without precedent, the

55. Quoted in Von Laue, *Sergei Witte and the Industrialisation of Russia*, pp. 2, 262. In 1900 Witte argued that in the absence of rapid industrialisation Russia, and its Asiatic hinterland, would be vulnerable to economic invasion by more efficient nations who 'would drive their roots into the depth of our economy. This may gradually clear the way also for triumphant political penetration by foreign powers . . . Our economic backwardness may lead us to political and cultural backwardness as well.' (Von Laue, *Sergei Witte and the Industrialisation of Russia*, p. 3.)

56. For an appraisal of the long-run historical significance of government policy in the generation or so before 1914, see Alexander Gerschenkron, 'The Early Phases of Industrialisation in Russia', in W. W. Rostow (ed.), *The Economics of Take-off into Sustained Growth* (1963); *Economic Backwardness*, pp. 119–42.

Tsarist state followed its vigorous encouragement of growth in the period 1885–1900 with a period of withdrawal and relative quiescence in the period after 1905. This was partly the result of the financial stringency which followed war (against Japan, 1904–5) and revolution; and partly, perhaps, a response to the problems attached to earlier more 'forward' policies. At the same time, however, the inheritance from the earlier phase of growth — an adequate base of social overhead capital, an embryonic capitalist system and monetary institutions, a vigorous class of entrepreneurs — made the role of the state less vital to continued industrialisation. Even so, there were structural changes yet to be undertaken. With Stolypin's agrarian reforms of 1906 and 1910, the position of peasants and land-ownership was radically altered. In effect, peasants were afforded much greater liberty to sell land, to move away from their villages and to consolidate their holdings (although the outbreak of war in 1914 prevented the full implementation of reforms). And the permissiveness reflected in structural reform was matched by a permissiveness towards newer modes of capitalism: the rise of investment banks and the continuing activities of the new class of industrial entrepreneurs. All this was accompanied by renewed expansion, although the industrial growth rate of 1906–14 was less than it had been in the 1890s. And it is tempting to interpret this episode in Russia's economic history as part of a 'normal' progression of industrial development: from extreme backwardness necessitating large-scale state intervention, to a more advanced position where the capitalist economy could discard the crutches of government aid and initiative, and develop and elaborate its own institutions for the gathering and application of capital, and for industrial innovation and expansion. Yet whatever the explanations of events after 1905, it is significant that in the 1880s and 1890s government action was explicitly related to the problem of initiating industrialisation in a backward economy, and that the problem was defined and tackled in terms of the fear of national weakness, the drive to national power, and the exercise of coercive authority. Russia's industrialisation exemplified nationalism as well as capitalism, tradition as well as novelty.

CONCLUSION

The varied experience of pre-1914 Europe offers little scope for firm generalisation about *'the'* role of the state in initiating and sustaining industrial growth. There was, in fact, a *variety* of roles — ranging from the permissive shaping of 'prerequisite' institutional arrangements to the positive and autocratic mobilisation of capital and entrepreneurship in strategic sectors of the economy. One can certainly say that the basic framework of state action was capitalist economic development; and to that extent the role of governments was either to stimulate and encourage private enterprise (by tariffs, subsidies, the provision of information, etc.) or to replace it in key areas in order to encourage it more generally. But, beyond this, confronted with the varieties of historical experience, one must seek for the generalisations which will make sense of the widely contrasting intensities with which the weapons of government policy were deployed on behalf of the Industrial Revolution in different countries. Was the variation systematic? What factors tended to shape it?

As had already been implied, perhaps the single most useful explanatory concept for these purposes derives from the idea of economic backwardness. It is the idea that the greater the degree of underdevelopment the more likely it was that the intervention of the state would be needed in order to overcome the resulting obstacles to industrial growth. If, for example, and following Professor Gerschenkron's lead, we see Britain, Germany and Russia as three paradigms in which the accumulation of capital necessary for growth was attained in the first by diffused private action, in the second by the partial substitution of investment banks for the 'missing' private capitalist, and in the third by the temporary substitution of the state for the banks, then we have the possibility of systematic generalisation; 'once we view the industrial development of Europe in this fashion, it appears indeed as a unity, but not as the simplicist, homogeneous unity, as it appeared to stage theorists . . . but as a complex, graduated unity where the degree of backwardness of the under-developed areas is the dominant factor determining the nature of the substitutions that have taken place.'[57]

Yet the idea of backwardness is, by itself, an insufficient explanation of the historical data which we observe (after all, many countries which remained backward also 'needed' government action — but never got it). At the very least it would be necessary to explain not merely why industrial-isation presupposed a role for the state, but also why and how the state played that role when it did. It is this aspect of the problem — an aspect which is perhaps implicit in Professor Gerschenkron's concept of the ideological aspects of 'tension' between the degree of backwardness and the potential gains of growth — which presupposes other deter-minants of government action than the degree of under-development.

In this regard we have to take account of strategic as well as economic ambitions; and of nationalism and the com-pulsion towards nation-building as well as industrialisation and the compulsion towards economic power. Moreover, just as political backwardness may in some circumstances have been as important as economic backwardness, so the political situation in its broadest sense — the access of potential entrepreneurial groups to power, the nature and traditional objectives of the state — could be an indepen-dent determinant of the intensity, extent and direction of the state's economic policy. It is, of course, clear that some of these determinants are themselves functionally related to the level of economic backwardness. Others, however, had only a tenuous connection, while even those that were closely related to the level of development were not always related to it in consistent ways. As a result, therefore, no single plane of explanation is entirely satisfactory: the role of the state in industrialisation under capitalism was a

57. Alexander Gerschenkron, *Europe in the Russian Mirror: Four Lectures in Economic History* (1970), p. 103.

function of levels of economic underdevelopment, of degrees of national autonomy and rivalry, of the intensity of national feeling, of the particular forms of political inheritance, and of the political penetration of the new capitalist class. Yet connecting all these apparently different elements was a single, large theme. For in the last resort, as we broaden our angle of vision, so the state's varied role in industrialisation must be seen not as the product of unique, national histories, but as part of a European-wide phenomenon — as a prolonged international upheaval in which nationalism, capitalism and industrialism all played their part in ushering in the modern world.

BIBLIOGRAPHY

This brief list is confined to books and articles available in English

GENERAL AND COMPARATIVE

Hugh G. J. Aitken (ed.), *The State and Economic Growth* (1959). A useful although somewhat discursive collection, with chapters on aspects of growth in Russia, Germany, Switzerland and eastern Europe—as well as on non-European countries and on comparative aspects of the problem.

Rondo E. Cameron, *France and the Economic Development of Europe, 1800–1914* (1961). An important study of influence and connections, with data on other European countries but relatively little on state policy.

Alexander Gerschenkron, *Economic Backwardness in Historical Perspective* (1962). As well as containing case studies of Italy, Russia and Bulgaria, this indispensable collection also reprints various comparative and systematic analyses of economic growth before 1914.

W. O. Henderson, *Britain and Industrial Europe, 1750–1870* (1954). Studies of the influence of British techniques, capital and skills.

David S. Landes, *The Unbound Prometheus: Technological Change and Industrial Development in Western Europe from 1750 to the Present* (1969). A substantial and detailed synthesis of factual and analytical history.

David S. Landes, 'Japan and Europe: Contrasts in Industrialisation', in William W. Lockwood (ed.), *The State and Economic Enterprise in Japan* (1965). A lively comparison, dealing primarily with Germany and Japan.

Friedrich List, *The National System of Political Economy* (1841; translated into English 1856, 1904, 1922).

W. W. Rostow, *The Stages of Economic Growth* (1960). A generalised attempt to see growth as an orderly sequence of stages.

Gustav Schmoller, *The Mercantile System and its Historical Significance illustrated chiefly from Prussian History* (1884, 1931). A classic study of 'mercantilism'—interpreted as the government promotion of economic growth and nation-building.

Barry E. Supple (ed.), *The Experience of Economic Growth: Case Studies in Economic History* (1963). Reprints various general articles as well as case studies.

FRANCE

Rondo E. Cameron, *France and the Economic Development of Europe, 1800–1914* (1961).

Rondo E. Cameron, 'Economic Growth and Stagnation in France, 1815–1914', *Journal of Modern History*, XXX, 1 (March 1958).

J. H. Clapham, *Economic Development of France and Germany, 1815–1914* (1963 edition). First published in 1921 and still one of the most useful introductions.

S. B. Clough, *France: A History of National Economics, 1789–1939* (1939). Principally concerned with the nature of government policy.

C. W. Cole, *Colbert and a Century of French Mercantilism* (1939).

A. L. Dunham, *The Industrial Revolution in France, 1815–1848* (1955). A detailed survey.

W. O. Henderson, *The Industrial Revolution on the Continent* (1961). A factual treatment of the details of industrialisation in Germany, France and Russia.

GERMANY

Ingomor Bog, 'Mercantilism in Germany', in D. C. Coleman (ed.), *Revisions in Mercantilism* (1969).

Ralph H. Bowen, 'The Roles of Government and Private Enterprise in German Industrial Growth, 1870–1914', *Journal of Economic History*, Supplement X, 1950.

J. H. Clapham, *Economic Development of France and Germany, 1815–1914* (1936 edition).

Wolfram Fisher, 'Government Activity and Industrialisation in Germany (1815–70)', in W. W. Rostow (ed.), *The Economics of Take-off into Sustained Growth* (1963).

T. S. Hamerow, *Restoration, Revolution, Reaction: Economics and Politics in Germany, 1815–71* (1958).

W. O. Henderson, *The State and the Industrial Revolution in Prussia, 1740–1870* (1958).

W. O. Henderson, *The Zollverein* (1959 edition).

W. O. Henderson, *The Industrial Revolution on the Continent* (1961).

W. G. Hoffman, 'The Take-off in Germany', in W. W. Rostow (ed.), *The Economics of Take-off into Sustained Growth* (1963).

David S. Landes, 'Japan and Europe: Contrasts in Industrialisation', in William W. Lockwood (ed.), *The State and Economic Enterprise in Japan* (1965).

Gustav Schmoller, *The Mercantile System and its Historical Significance illustrated chiefly from Prussian History* (1884, 1931).

Richard Tilly, 'Germany 1815–1870', in Rondo Cameron (ed.), *Banking in the Early Stages of Industrialisation* (1967).

Thorstein Veblen, *Imperial Germany and the Industrial Revolution* (1915; 1939 edition). An idiosyncratic but stimulating interpretation, with little on the actual course of industrial growth.

GREAT BRITAIN

T. S. Ashton, *The Industrial Revolution* (1948). A slim classic of knowledge and insight.

J. H. Clapham, *An Economic History of Modern Britain*, Vol. I, 'The Early Railway Age, 1820–1850' (1939 reprint). Still an important source.

Phyllis Deane, *The First Industrial Revolution* (1965). An analytical approach with chapters on various aspects, including the role of government.

M. W. Flinn, *The Origins of the Industrial Revolution* (1966). A brief but broad survey on various aspects of economic growth in the eighteenth century.

W. O. Henderson, *Britain and Industrial Europe, 1750–1870* (1954).

ITALY

S. B. Clough, *Economic History of Modern Italy* (1964).

Alexander Gerschenkron, 'Notes on the Rate of Industrial Growth in Italy, 1881–1913', in *Economic Backwardness in*

Historical Perspective (1962). Deals with the role of the state.

K. R. Greenfield, *Economics and Liberalism in the Risorgimento: A Study of Nationalism in Lombardy, 1814–1848* (rev. ed. 1965).

RUSSIA

Alexander Baykov, 'The Economic Development of Russia', *Economic History Review*, 2nd series, VII, 2 (December 1954). A general survey of causal factors.

Alexander Gerschenkron, 'The Early Phases of Industrialisation in Russia: After-thoughts and Counterthoughts', in W. W. Rostow (ed.), *The Economics of Take-off into Sustained Growth* (1963). A comparative appraisal of different 'models' of Tsarist development, and the role of the state.

Alexander Gerschenkron, 'Russia: Patterns and Problems of Economic Development, 1861–1958', in *Economic Backwardness in Historical Perspective* (1962).

Alexander Gerschenkron, 'Economic Development in Russian Intellectual History', in *Economic Backwardness in Historical Perspective* (1962).

Alexander Gerschenkron, 'Agrarian Policies and Industrialisation: Russia, 1861–1917', in M. M. Postan and H. J. Habakkuk (eds.), *Cambridge Economic History of Europe*, VI, Part 1 (1965).

Raymond A. Goldsmith, 'The Economic Growth of Tsarist Russia', *Economic Development and Cultural Change*, IX, 3 (April 1961). A quantitative analysis.

W. O. Henderson, *The Industrial Revolution on the Continent* (1961).

P. I. Lyaschenko, *A History of the National Economy of Russia to the 1917 Revolution* (1949). A Soviet interpretation.

Roger Portal, 'The Industrialisation of Russia', in M. M. Postan and H. J. Habakkuk (eds.), *Cambridge Economic History of Europe*, VI, Part 1 (1965).

Theodore H. von Laue, *Sergei Witte and the Industrialisation of Russia* (1963). An extended study of the Tsarist Finance Minister and his policies.

6. The Service Revolution: The Growth of Services in Modern Economy

R. M. Hartwell

DEFINITION AND CLASSIFICATION OF SERVICES

'Studying economic progress in relation to the economic structure of different countries', Colin Clark wrote in 1940, 'we find a very firmly established generalisation that a high level of real income per head is always associated with a high proportion of the working population engaged in tertiary industries.' 'From Sir William Petty's day to the present time', he also noted, 'the transfer of working population from primary production to secondary and tertiary has been continuing, and perhaps will continue for as many centuries more'. 'What much careful generalisation of available facts shows to be the most important concomitant of economic progress . . . [is] the movement of working population from agriculture to manufacture, and from manufacture to commerce and services.'[1] Here are the themes of this chapter: first, the importance of structural change in the process of economic growth, involving the transfer of resources from lower to higher productivity sectors; second, the time sequence of structural change, in which the decline of agriculture is followed in succession, by the expansion of industry and services; third, the importance of services in growing economies, and the high correlation between services and income. The focus, then, is on growth, structural change and services, and the relation between the three. By growth is meant, using the economists' definition, a substantial and sustained (long-term) rate of growth of real income (real output) per head of population. By structural change is meant the transfer of resources between the three sectors of the economy—the primary (agriculture), the secondary (industry) and the

1. C. Clark, *The Conditions of Economic Progress* (London, 1940), pp. 6–7, 176, 341.

tertiary (services)—so as to alter their percentage shares of employment and output.

While growth and structural change are relatively easy to define, however, it is more difficult with services. But since this chapter is primarily concerned with the historical growth of services, it is necessary to define the tertiary sector, and/or the services which comprise it, in a way at least potentially useful to the historian. The economists, who evolved the concepts 'a service industry' and 'a tertiary sector', have no general agreement about the definition of 'a service', or about the classification and aggregation of services.[2] The origin of the idea of a service lay in the distinction between goods (tangible objects) and services (non-tangible objects) made by Adam Smith. But, as another great economist, Alfred Marshall, pointed out, 'Man cannot create material things' and in both goods and services he produces utilities. Thus all productive activities by men can be seen as producing services.[3] Indeed still in French, there is no distinction between 'goods' and 'services'; the term '*bien*', as M. Lengellé has pointed out, 'denotes anything which is useful, profitable or attractive'.[4]

Definitions of 'a service' have tried to isolate what is uniquely characteristic about services by establishing criteria with analytical usefulness. Three main groups of characteristics have been identified: the first, which centres on intangibility, includes lack of durability, unstockability, producer-consumer intimacy, as well as intangibility; the second is concerned with the unit of production, and argues that services are produced in small, labour-intensive rather than capital-intensive units of production, with a high ratio of value added to the value of total inputs; the third concentrates on the labour force of the service sector which includes a strategically important, but relatively small, professional group (of high value human capital), and, in comparison with other sectors, a high proportion of female,

2. See V. R. Fuchs, *The Service Economy* (New York, 1968), pp. 14–17.
3. A Marshall, *Principles of Economics* (8th ed., London, 1929), p. 63.
4. *Manpower Problems in the Service Sector. Supplement to the Report* (O.E.C.D., Paris, 1966), p. 20.

self-employed and part-time workers. But these characteristics have certain disadvantages for identifying services:
individually, or in combination, they apply in varying
degree to activities in other sectors; they do not uniquely
describe all services; and, most important for the historian,
their usefulness for describing services has changed over
time.

Intangibility is the most generally accepted criterion of a
service, but it is obvious that many services either are
associated continuously with the handling of tangible goods
(for example, retail trade), or transform, or partly transform, tangible goods (for example, all repair and maintenance services). Thus it is difficult, historically, to
separate out the service component of the work of the
engineers and mechanics who planned, designed, built and
repaired the capital equipment of the industrial revolution
(machines, factories, canals, railways, ships, etc.). It is the
same with durability; the work of the new or expanding
professions, for example in education, lived on beyond the
point of purchase or consumption. And on the closeness of
the producer and consumer, it is easy to point to a range of
services directed either at producers or at middlemen, and
not at consumers; indeed, it was the expansion of such
intermediate services as banking, discounting, accounting
and wholesaling, which was such a notable feature of the
industrial revolution. It is obvious, therefore, that the range
of distinctions which centre on intangibility are neither
unique to the services nor measurable, so that other criteria
of demarcation must be sought. On the small size and
labour-intensive bias of production units in the services,
there is now, and was during the industrial revolution, one
great exception—transport—in which units were often both
large in size and capital intensive in nature, making
extensive use of physical capital equipment.[5] Generally,
however, services were produced during the industrial

5. It is fair to say that some economists exclude transport from the
service sector, probably for this reason (for example, Fuchs, *op. cit.*); but
transport is so obviously a 'service' that exclusion merely compounds the
definitional difficulty.

revolution, and up to the twentieth century, in small enterprises, of which the self-employed doctor, lawyer, barber, restaurant-owner and clergyman were obvious examples. Similarly the high value-added-component, the result generally of a low input in services of raw materials, underlines the importance in the development of services of human capital, and especially of skilled human capital. On the nature of the labour force in the services—with a high proportion of female, part-time and self-employed workers—it is less certain that these characteristics were so important historically. The proportion of females in the labour force of the services is now fifty per cent or more, but the expansion of female employment in the initial stages of industrialisation—domestic service excluded—was in industry rather than in services; the female invasion of certain important service categories, like teaching, came only later. On the other hand, self-employment certainly increased with economic growth, as labour mobility increased, and as the opportunities for such employment expanded (for example, in personal services of various types, and in the artisan services required in homes and workshops).[6]

What, then, is the solution to the problem of definition? While recognising the usefulness of the above criteria for the analysis of any particular service, and for comparing (contrasting) the service sector with other sectors, these criteria do not give either an unambiguous historical or analytical framework for discussion. Because of this, it is probably easiest, and most useful historically, to think of the tertiary sector as a residual, what is left of total employment after subtracting employment in agriculture and industry.[7] There is certainly more agreement about what constitutes

6. A. D. Smith points out another characteristic of services (p. 6), but one with little historical relevance; 'methods of measuring real output changes in the service sector differ significantly from those used in the remainder of the economy'. *The Measurement and Interpretation of Service Output Changes* (National Economic Development Office, London, 1972), p. 6.

7. Thus Lady Hall ('Foreword' to A. D. Smith, *op. cit.*) equates the service sector with 'those sectors not classified as either manufacturing, agriculture or extractive industry' (p. iii).

those productive activities which are defined as agricultural or industrial, and, historically, the employment and output of these sectors have been more easily identified and traced. It is also obvious historically, as will be shown below, that the expansion of activities that were neither agricultural nor industrial was a new and important feature of the structural change that came with industrialisation. Whether services can be defined accurately or not, the expansion of 'the service sector' (in this residual sense) and, in the long run, the occurrence of 'a service revolution', have been part of the history of modern economic growth. It is important to remember that industry had long co-existed with agriculture, and that the expansion of industry, even in the new form of factory production, was not entirely a novel phenomenon for mankind. What was novel during the industrial revolution was the expansion of a group of activities which we now call services, activities which had been of minimal importance in pre-industrial economy. It was the expansion of the non-agricultural and the non-industrial sector—the service sector—which created the most significant break with the past with the onset of industrialisation in the advanced economies.

What, specifically, were these activities? Historians could use, as a list of services, selected subsectors of the *International Standard Industrial Classification* as follows: Group 1—wholesale and retail trade; Group 2—banks, other financial institutions, insurance, real estate, other business services (e.g. legal, accounting, technical); Group 3—community services (education, medical, research, religious, welfare, professional and labour organisations, library, museum, etc.); Group 4—recreation services (motion picture, theatre, etc.); Group 5—personal services (domestic, restaurant, hotel, laundry, barbering, beauty shop, photographic, etc.). Such a list, however, includes services not historically important, and, moreover, does not give a functional picture of the present role or past history of services. The great pre-industrial services were law, medicine and religion; the services which expanded most obviously with economic growth were transport, distribution, finance and government. It is significant, for example, that the historians who argue for prerequisites of the industrial revolution include in those prerequisites not only an agricultural revolution, but a number of service revolutions—a commercial revolution, a financial revolution, a transport revolution, and, finally, a revolution in government.[8] All these 'revolutions' caused fundamental changes in the quality of economic life—its sophistication, its linkages, its mobility, its adaptability, and its speed of response—by the expansion of services; they were thus an essential part of the industrial revolution and modern economic growth.

It is doubtful, nevertheless, whether any classification of services would suit the needs of the historian, and the following classification is suggested, therefore, only as a reasonably appropriate framework for an historical account of the growth of services in modern economic history:

I.

SOCIAL OVERHEAD SERVICES
  (i) Transport and Communications (including Post and Telegraphs)
 (ii) Public Utilities
        (*a*) Education
        (*b*) Police, Defence, Justice
        (*c*) Welfare Services (including Public Health)

II.

BUSINESS SERVICES
  (i) Retail and Wholesale Trade (including Land Agents, Auctioneers, etc.)
 (ii) Finance (Banking, Insurance, Brokerage, etc.)
(iii) Professional Services (Accountancy, Surveying, Architecture, Engineering, other Technical Services, etc.)

8. See M. Flinn (*The Origins of the Industrial Revolution*, London, 1969) for a general discussion of prerequisites. On particular revolutions see W. T. Jackman (transport), P. G. M. Dickson (finance), R. Davis (commerce), and E. Lipson (government). For a criticism of the prerequisite thesis see A. Gerschenkron (*Economic Backwardness in Historical Perspective*, Harvard, 1962) and R. M. Hartwell (*The Industrial Revolution and Economic Growth*, London, 1971).

III.

PERSONAL SERVICES

  (i) Domestic
 (ii) Artisan Personal Services (Barbers, Cleaners, Plumbers, Gardeners, Cafes, Hotels, etc.)
(iii) Professional Personal Services (Medicine, Law, Architecture, etc.)

IV.

COMMUNITY AND COOPERATIVE SERVICES

  (i) Religion
 (ii) Professional Associations, Trade Unions, Friendly Societies, Cooperatives, etc.

V.

RECREATION AND CULTURE

  (i) Entertainment and Sport
 (ii) Cultural Services (Theatre, Museums, etc.)

Thus classified, the size and importance of the service sector becomes obvious, as does its changing role in history. Thus classified, also, a number of important historical questions suggest themselves: How much and why did the service sector expand with industrialisation? What was the effect of this expansion on economic growth? How did the growth of services affect the quality of life in industrial society? How did the productivity of services compare with those of agriculture and industry? What were the national differences in the growth of services and how are they to be explained? Why have historians relatively neglected the history of structural change, and of the service sector? What are the lessons of history from the growth of services?

THE SERVICE REVOLUTION

In the history of services the industrial revolution marks the beginning both of rapid expansion and increasing specialisation. Services existed before the industrial revolution but were catered for either by a very small group of specialised producers, or, more generally, as a part-time activity by most adult members of society. The specialised producers included a small urban business sector, a tiny bureaucracy, a narrow range of professions and a largish domestic servant class. The business sector centred in the activities of merchants and traders, with a very small group of financiers and bankers, and lacked more specialised professional services (as, for example, that later given by accountants). This was a sector, nevertheless, which had been growing steadily since the late middle ages with the growth of towns and of trade, and its importance had been underlined by all historians of 'the rise of capitalism'. Indeed, most historians have seen the beginnings of modern economic growth in the activities of this sector, especially its role in extending the market and in accumulating capital. The bureaucracy grew with the establishment of national states and its size varied with the degree of centralisation; much local administration was performed as a part-time service (for example, by the magistrates of England). The professions of the period before industrialisation were confined mainly to 'divinity, law, and physic',[9] and of these, only divinity reached the mass of the population. Education, which in the nineteenth century became increasingly biased towards professional training, was in the eighteenth and earlier centuries mainly liberal in content, and only in law and medicine was appropriately specialised education deemed desirable or necessary. Other professional services were provided mostly by amateurs (for example, in architecture) or by members of the family (for example, in education). The largest service group was undoubtedly in domestic service, varying in work units from the few who served the urban artisan or merchant to the hoards of retainers who thronged the great houses and palaces of the rich and

9. Addison, in the early eighteenth century, wrote of the 'three professions of divinity, law, and physic'. Quoted by A. M. Carr-Saunders and P. A. Wilson, *The Professions* (Oxford, 1933), p. 294.

aristocratic. In contrast with the economy of the twentieth century where services are omnipresent, the peasants and artisans of distant pre-industrial economy, the majority of the population, rarely encountered specialised services except those of the priest or clergyman, the occasional travelling peddler or performer, and, perhaps the soldier or administrator. By the seventeenth and eighteenth centuries this situation was changing slowly as more services appeared, but there was no substantial increase proportionately in the service sector until the industrial revolution.

Industrialisation could not have occurred, or would have occurred more slowly, had there not been an expansion of social overhead services like transport and education, and of intermediate services like retail and wholesale trade, which were necessary as productive activities became more specialised, more localised and more roundabout. At the same time there was a less necessary but important growth of recreational and cultural services, which increased with increasing wealth and which helped to change the way of life. The growth of such services can be seen, on the supply side, as part of the growth of specialisation and the division of labour, of the more varied and more sophisticated use of labour, and on the demand side, as the result of the changing and expanding tastes which came with increasing wealth. As sustained growth commenced and as, in consequence, wealth increased, the demand for services of all kinds increased faster than the demand for goods. As specialisation increased, more and more business and professional services, which were formerly satisfied within the existing framework of industrial enterprises (for example, engineering ̀and architecture) were developed as independent professions operating as separate business units. A similar specialisation and separation took place as work moved from the home and workshop to the factory and office: as more work was institutionalised, and as more men and women were drawn into full-time employment, services like education, and even medicine, which were formerly satisfied within the home, were increasingly provided by trained professionals. As more population was drawn into the cities, new services were created (for example, in crime prevention, public health and factory inspection), and old services (for example, in entertainment) which had been satisfied previously in the homes, taverns, town squares and village greens, were also professionalised. As the complexity of social organisations increased, managerial functions which had once centred in one man, were now divided, and a new range of business professions emerged (for example, in accountancy). As government expanded, for reasons intimately connected with industrialisation and urbanisation, there was a proliferation and specialisation of the bureaucracy. Generally, as living standards rose, there was increasing demand for professional and other services which had previously been used only sparingly. These trends became obvious statistically, as soon as statistical records began to be kept systematically early in the nineteenth century.[10]

Services grew, as has been indicated, in response to market forces. The productivity of services before the industrial revolution was low, the cost of services was high, and the demand was small. Thus, for example, professional services, like those of doctors, were very expensive to the consumer and were used, generally, only by the rich. The smallness of the service sector, and its cost, was certainly a barrier to growth; in the case of transport, for example, only a drastic reduction in the cost of transport enabled the mobility of factors that was vital for growth. The expansion of the service sector at a decreasing cost was certainly an important factor in the general trend towards the reduction of costs which occurred during the industrial revolution. The essential link between services and industry ensured the expansion of both, and complementarity explains the rapid growth of even those services (like retail trade) whose productivity only increased slowly. By the end of the

10. See, for example, the statistics gathered together in the late nineteenth century by G. Fr. Kolb (*The Condition of Nations, Social and Political*, trs. Mrs Brewer, London, 1880), M. G. Mulhall (*The Dictionary of Statistics*, London, 1892) and A. D. Webb (*The New Dictionary of Statistics*, London, 1911).

nineteenth century a pattern of services had emerged which was to change significantly in the twentieth century (for example, with the further expansion of government and public utilities, and the decline of domestic service) but which in outline can be described with the classification suggested above (p. 363). Over much of Europe a service revolution was well under way by 1900 and service economies were already taking shape.

The result, then, of economic growth and industrialisation in the advanced economies was, ultimately, *the service revolution*: those economies with the highest per capita real incomes are today experiencing service revolutions comparable with the industrial revolutions of the eighteenth and nineteenth centuries. This new stage of development is the culmination of a long process of growth and structural change from which are emerging economies with fifty per cent or more of their employed population engaged in the production of non-tangible goods. Only the United States of America has attained this proportion; in other advanced economies the process of change has not gone so far, but in the richer economies of Europe today services already occupy between thirty and forty per cent of total employment (more in Great Britain), and the proportion is growing steadily. Moreover in most countries of the world the rate of growth of services since 1945 has been faster than that of total employment.[11]

Viewed in longer perspective, since the beginnings of industrialisation, the growth of services had closely followed, and sometimes preceded, the growth of industry. Unfortunately disaggregated figures for employment are unreliable or non-existent for most economies except for the very modern period, although statistics accurate enough for some international comparisons do exist for the period since 1870. And if a comparison is made of the figures for the years 1860–70, 1900–10 and 1930–40, the last before the great European economic growth after 1945, a pattern of development can be seen. In 1870 there were three clear

11. See *Manpower Problems in the Service Sector. Supplement to the Report*, *op.cit.*, particularly the paper by M. Lengellé.

divisions among the countries of Europe according to the percentage employment of services in total employment: in the first group, c. 35%, Great Britain and Belgium;[12] in the second, c. 25%, Germany, Holland and Norway; and in the third, from 12 to 20%, France, Italy, Spain, Denmark, Austria-Hungary and Portugal. By the first decade of the twentieth century, the pattern was already changing but the dispersion was just as great: in the first group, Britain now stood alone with 45%; in the second group, 30 to 35%, Germany, Belgium, Norway and Holland; in the third group, from 16 to 25%, France, Denmark, Austria-Hungary, Italy, Spain and Portugal. By the 1930s, the pattern was still changing; Britain now led with a percentage in the forties; an expanded second group, 35 to 39%, included Germany, France, Denmark, Holland, Norway and Belgium; and the third group, with c. 23% employment in services, consisted of Austria-Hungary, Italy, Spain and Portugal. In the period after 1945 most West European countries moved into the 30 to 40% bracket, with a few over 40%, and Britain approaching a service employment of 50% of total employment. Overseas, the United States of America, with only 25% service employment in 1870–80, had already reached the 50% proportion.[13] Even the most casual correlation of these figures with those of economic growth shows that the most advanced economies have had the highest service employment, and that countries which grew quickly also enlarged employment in the service sector, both absolutely and as a proportion of total employment.

This service revolution can be understood only in the context of the structural change that accompanies economic growth. Economic growth, defined usually in terms of a sustained rate of growth of real output per capita, is also a process of structural transformation, so that the definition

12. Although a small economy, and 'the second industrial nation' chronologically there is reason to be sceptical about the Belgian percentage.

13. S. Kuznets, 'Industrial Distribution of National Product and Labor Force', *Economic Development and Cultural Change* (July 1957).

of growth only in terms of an aggregate trend in output disguises, or ignores, the basic change in structure. Historically the relationship between growth and changing structure seems obvious, even though the historians have not much concerned themselves with it. Indeed, over the two centuries since the beginning of the first industrial revolution two distinct structural transformations in the economies of the developed countries can be distinguished: the transformation during the first phase of growth of a predominantly agricultural economy into one in which industry was much more important, but in which the services were also growing —the industrial revolution; and a subsequent transformation involving the further decline of agriculture, a slowing down in the rate of growth of industry, or even stability, and the substantial growth of services—the service revolution.

This long-term structural history, common to all countries experiencing growth, can be seen clearly in the case of Britain, as the following table shows:

Sectoral Change in the British Economy, 1801–1901[14]
A. Percentage of National Income contributed by Sector.
B. Percentage of Total Occupied Population employed by Sector.
C. Millions of Persons Employed by Sector.

Sector	*1801*			*1851*			*1901*		
	A	B	C	A	B	C	A	B	C
1. Agriculture	33	36	1·7	20	21	2·1	6	9	1·5
2. Industry	29	30	1·4	42	43	4·1	48	46	7·9
3. Services	38	34	1·4	38	36	3·3	39	45	7·2
4. Total Occupied Population (m)	4·8			9·7			16·7		
5. Total Population (m)	10·7			20·9			37·1		

14. Source: P. Deane and W. A. Cole, *British Economic Growth, 1688–1959. Trends and Structure* (Cambridge, 1967). The 1801 figures are much more doubtful than those of 1851 and 1901.

The over-all pattern of change which emerges has, as its most obvious feature, the decline of agriculture, in its contributions both to income and employment. Agricultural employment, about 50% of total employment in the mid-eighteenth century, was declining continuously from the beginning of the industrial revolution. From 1700 to about 1850 industry and services both increased their proportions, as that of agriculture declined; from 1850 to 1900, the service proportion increased, industry remained relatively stable, and the agricultural proportion continued to decline; after 1900, when the agricultural proportion was below ten per cent, the service proportion continued to increase, now at the expense of industry. A similar picture of change emerges when the contributions of the various sectors to national income are compared. And the relating of the employment percentage to the income percentage gives a measure of the changing productivity of the sectors. In the case of agriculture, the employment proportion is always higher than the income proportion; in the case of industry, the proportions are much the same; in the case of services, the proportion of income is higher than that of employment, but decreasing (a trend accelerating in the twentieth century). These ratios of employment to income reflect inter-sectoral differences in productivity, with industry and services consistently more productive than agriculture, and help to explain inter-sectoral transfers of resources. A similar picture of structural change, for example, can also be observed for Germany, as the work of W. G. Hoffmann shows.[15]

The dynamics in this history of structural change lay, on the one hand, in sectoral differences in productivity, and on the other, in the changing demands for goods and services as incomes rose: resources moved from sector to sector to benefit either from higher productivity and/or from greater demand. The marginal rate of return from

15. W. G. Hoffman, *Das Wachstum der Deutschen Wirtschaft seit der Mitte des 19. Jahrhunderts* (Berlin, 1965). See, for example, Tabelle 7, 'Die Struktur der Gesamtbeschäftigung nach Wirtschaftsbereichen' (p. 35) which shows how the proportion of agricultural employment fell from 54·6% of total employment in 1849–58 to 35·1% in 1910–13, while the proportion in industry increased from 24·3 to 35·1%.

investment in expanding sectors and industries was high and increasing, and played an important role in economic growth, while the returns in stagnant or declining sectors and industries were low, or even negative, and slowed down growth. Thus the industrial revolution in England can be viewed, partly at least, as structural change, as the transfer of resources, with the result of the more rapid growth of high productivity industry, compared with lower productivity agriculture, while the climacteric, or the slowing-down in the rate of English growth at the end of the nineteenth century can be attributed to overcommitment to slowly growing or stagnant industries, and to a failure to transfer resources to newer and more productive industries.

But structural change must be related also to changes in demand: as incomes increased during growth the proportion of income spent on food declined and the proportion spent on services increased. The income elasticity of demand for food was low, while that for services was much higher than that for goods. And when the demand for services is considered along with the productivity of services, there is an obvious explanation for the rapidly increasing proportion of service to total employment in the advanced economies of the twentieth century: demand for services has increased but the rate of growth of productivity of services has tended to be less than that of industry, with the consequent absorption into services of an increasing proportion of labour. There may have been no diminishing returns to agriculture in the century of Malthus and Ricardo, but certainly in the twentieth century it has required an increasing diversion of resources to produce the services demanded at a rate of growth of productivity consistently below that for the production of goods. This slow advance in the productivity of the service sector, in the long run, may act as a brake on growth. However, this is happening in the richer economies in which the consequences for living standards are not serious and in which, moreover, the technologically unemployed in the higher productivity growth goods sector may well be absorbed in the continually growing service sector, whose rate of growth of productivity is lower.[16]

INDIVIDUAL SERVICES

It is obviously impossible, in one short essay, to deal satisfactorily with all, or even one, of the services listed above. In any case, although there is a considerable literature on individual services, it is concentrated in certain services like transport and in certain areas like England, and there is nowhere a general historical survey, or general analysis, of the growth of services in modern economy. Of particular services,[17] transport and communications (I.i) retail and wholesale trade (II.i) and domestic service (III.i) were quantitatively the most important in terms of employment. In terms of strategic importance for growth, certainly financial services (II.ii), professional services (II.iii and III.iii) and some public utilities (I.ii) were equally necessary for growth, if less impressive as employers of labour. In terms of politics, and of the social problems of the transition from a rural-agricultural to an urban-industrial service economy, the expansion on the one hand, of public utilities in the forms of adequate internal security services and increasing welfare services (II.ii, b and c), and on the other, of working-class defensive associations, like the trade unions and cooperatives (IV.ii), were essential ingredients in the establishment of the varying degrees of consenting democracy which characterised the advanced economies in the nineteenth century. In terms of way of life, the expansion of personal services (III.i, ii and iii), of religion (IV.i) and of recreation and cultural services (V.i and ii) were also conditioning and reconciling influences in the creation of an industrial society. It was the beneficial combination of

16. See V. R. Fuchs, *Productivity Trends in the Goods and Service Sectors, 1929–61. A Preliminary Survey* (National Bureau of Economic Research, Occasional Paper 89, 1964).

17. The identification (in brackets) of the services discussed below is that of the classification suggested above (p. 363).

economic growth, which provided an ever-increasing stream of goods and services, of political democracy, which ensured the emergence of powerful forces, political and industrial, to protect and enlarge the interests of the working classes, and of a new and acceptable urban culture, which ensured, in the words of J. M. Keynes, 'the magnificent episode of the nineteenth century'. In this evolution, services had the balancing role, and it was the improvement in human capital, largely but not entirely because of the expansion of education, which was perhaps the single most important ingredient in the economic, political and social developments that come with industrialisation.

On the existing literature on services, transport (I.i) and finance (II.ii) have been the most extensively treated;[18] for the rest, only trade unions (IV.ii), education (I.ii, a), welfare services (I.ii, c) and religion (IV.i) have received detailed attention, but without consideration, generally, of the relationship between their particular histories and that of society or economy.[19] The most serious gap in the econo-

18. See, for example: on transport, L. Girard ('Transport' in *The Cambridge Economic History of Europe*, vol. VI, *The Industrial Revolutions and After*, part I, ed. H. J. Habakkuk and M. Postan, Cambridge, 1965); and on finance, B. Gille ('Banking and Industrialisation in Europe, 1730–1914', in this volume), M. Lévy-Leboyer (*Les banques européennes et l'industrialisation internationale, dans la première moitié du XIX siècle*, Paris, 1964) and R. Cameron *et al.* (*Banking in the Early Stages of Industrialisation*, Oxford, 1967).

19. On trade unions, see the bibliography of the article on 'Labor Unions' in the *International Encyclopaedia of the Social Sciences* (vol. 8, pp. 522–3, 532–3, 540); on education, see M. C. Kaser, 'Education and Economic Progress: Experience in Industrialised Market Economies' (in *The Economics of Education*, ed. E. A. G. Robinson and J. E. Vaizey, London, 1966) and *Education and Economic Development*, ed. C. A. Anderson and M. J. Bowman (London, 1966); on welfare services and the growth of government see E. Barker (*The Development of Public Services in Western Europe, 1660–1930*, Oxford, 1944), W. H. Beveridge (*Full Employment in a Free Society*, London, 1944), W. A. Friedlander (*Individualism and Social Welfare: An Analysis of the System of Social Security and Social Welfare in France*, New York, 1962), J. H. Richardson (*Economic and Financial Aspects of Social Security: An International Survey*, London, 1960), F. N. and P. R. Anderson (*Political Institutions and Social Change in Continental Europe in the Nineteenth Century*, Berkeley, 1967), J. Cramer (*The World's Police*,

mic history of services is undoubtedly in the area of retail
and wholesale trade, although equally surprising is the
dearth of literature on the learned professions generally, on
artisan services and on domestic services.[20] Considering the
massive social importance of domestic service, the lack of
research into this subject is perhaps the most surprising
feature of service literature. On culture, entertainment and
sport there is practically no analytical literature of worth.
As R. H. Tawney reminded us, long ago, 'We know at
present next to nothing of the relations between the artistic
achievements of an epoch and the character of its economic
life, and the only candid course is to confess that if, as
seems probable, such elusive links exist, the secret of their
interaction is as yet beyond our grasp'.[21]

Accepting the lacunae in our present knowledge, nevertheless, something can be said about each of the services
classified above.

I.i, Transport and Communications. Historians have argued
that 'a transport revolution' preceded and accompanied all
industrial revolutions; economists, similarly, have shown
that modern economic growth is correlated positively with
transport facilities, and that investment in transport is of
strategic and quantitative importance in inducing and
sustaining growth.[22] Improved transport is part of the
essential infrastructure of an advanced economy, and

London, 1964). The literature on religion is vast; a useful introduction,
again, is in the *International Encyclopaedia of the Social Sciences* (vol. 13).

20. On retail and wholesale trade see J. B. Jeffreys and D. Knee
(*Retailing in Europe. Present Structure and Future Trends*, London, 1962,
especially Appendix, part II on sources), and, for a particular country
see the two recent books of D. Alexander (*Retailing in England during the
Industrial Revolution*, London, 1970) and G. L. Rees (*Britain's Commodity
Markets*, London, 1972). On the professions see C. Morazé (*The Triumph
of the Middle Classes*, English translation, London, 1966), A. Carr-
Saunders and P. A. Wilson (*The Professions*, London, 1933), J. Mills (*The
Engineer in Society*, New York, 1946), R. Pound (*The Lawyer from Antiquity
to Modern Times*, St Paul, Minn., 1953), T. Parsons (*Structure and Process
in Modern Societies*, Glencoe, Ill., 1960).

21. R. H. Tawney, *Social History and Literature* (Leicester, 1958), p. 28.

22. See, for example, C. P. Kindleberger, *Economic Development* (New
York, 1958), p. 96.

absorbs today from five to ten per cent of national income. The development of transport, and especially of railways, has been reckoned, by many historians to have been the leading sector in the growth not only of national economies in the nineteenth century, but also of the international economy.[23] And if the prime role of the railways has now been revised, that of transport generally (and the social saving from improved transport) has not.[24] Improved transport not only directly lowered the structure of costs throughout economies, it also made markets accessible (allowing the growth of larger scale enterprises) and labour mobile. On occasions changing transport costs led to radical change; for example, when cheaply transported and cheaply produced American wheat reached European markets in the eighteen-eighties leading either to the decline of wheat farming or to its protection.[25]

Social effects were equally impressive: before the industrial revolution, residence and work-place tended to be identical for most people; after the development of the railway, for example, towns grew in size, suburbs separated people's homes not only from places of work but also from other social classes; the railway thus led to the social fragmentation of cities with their spectrum of housing from working-class slums to middle-class ghettos, separated by commercial and industrial areas. Some statistics of the growth of transport facilities are impressive enough to underline their importance: European mileage of railways increased from 1,679 in 1840 to 31,885 in 1860 to 135,000 by 1890, and millions of passengers carried over the same period increased from c. 340 to c. 1,750; by 1890, there were in Europe 13,000 miles of canals and over 63,000 miles of navigable rivers; world tonnage of steam shipping increased from c. 30,000 in 1830 to c. $7\frac{1}{2}$ millions by 1890, while the

23. L. H. Jenks, 'Railroads as an Economic Force in American Development', *Journal of Economic History* (1944).

24. The revision of the railway thesis of nineteenth century growth owes most to R. W. Fogel (*Railroads and American Economic Growth: Essays in Econometric History*, Baltimore, 1964).

25. C. P. Kindleberger, 'Group Behaviour and International Trade', *Journal of Political Economy* (1951).

tonnage of sea-borne merchandise increased from *c.* 10 to *c.* 150 million tons over the same period.

Equally important as transport services to shift goods and people, was the development of other types of communication, especially those like posts and telegraphs, which reduced the costs of information to producers and consumers.[26] Here, again, there was a decisive break with the past, with the more systematic collection of information and the more effective diffusion of it. The examples of the businessman sending forth cargoes of merchandise to distant and foreign countries, with the flimsiest of information about the market he was serving, and the politician preparing his annual budget, on the basis of economic doctrine rather than of carefully collected statistical information, indicate the revolution of information which was to make these two activities more rational. It was this 'inherent essentiality' of transport and communications which made them from the beginnings of expansion a matter of public interest, and, quickly, of public control. Transport and communication facilities became the first important public enterprises in many industrialising economies, and in others, the first industries to be controlled by extensive government regulation. Transport and communications industries, also, were spearheads of technological advance, large absorbers of capital (thus playing an important role in the development of capital markets), and large creators of income (sometimes, as in the case of Britain, large earners of foreign exchange) with extensive linkages and externalities.

I.ii, Public Utilities. A notable feature of twentieth century economies has been the growth of government and its agencies, providing some tangible goods but predominantly a variety of services. Much of this growth of government can be summed up in the phrase 'the welfare state', which came into being initially to redress income inequalities

26. See, for example, the outstandingly original and early contributions to the history of communications in this sense by H. A. Innes (*The Bias of Communication*, Toronto, 1951; *Empire and Communications*, Toronto, 1950).

and to remedy poverty, but expanded later for macro-economic management of economies in the interests of greater efficiency and faster growth. Welfare plus growth have been the twin aims of government and bureaucracy. Indeed so ingrained has become the uncritical acceptance of the essential role of government in the working of economies that it is often assumed that only strong government leadership will promote growth in the underdeveloped countries of the world.[27] And it is certainly true that it was during the industrial revolution that there was an expansion of the traditional responsibilities of government—in areas of public finance, police and defence, foreign and colonial affairs, for example—as well as in new areas, especially those connected with industrialisation, population growth and urbanisation. Retrospectively it can now be seen that the expansion of government services occurred also as a result of three other developments: first, to remedy the social costs of industrialisation which sometimes outweigh the private and social gains (for example, in areas of public health and factory work); second, to take over from other institutions jobs which they had been doing, sometimes for centuries (for example, the responsibility of Church authorities for vital statistics); third, to improve national economic efficiency (for example, by taking over industries and services, like education,[28] the Post Office and the railways, and by regulating important economic activities like banking, for example by controlling the issue of currency). Because of the increasingly complex nature of the problems raised in these areas of interference, there was

27. See, for example, W. A. Lewis, *The Theory of Economic Growth* (London, 1955).

28. Education deserves a chapter to itself, and the rapid increase in educational services in the nineteenth century, mainly but not exclusively the result of government intervention, was intimately connected with the process of economic growth. Those countries which had substantial growth rates also had high levels of formal education; those economies which adopted modern technology most quickly already had high school attendances by 1830. On education generally see C. M. Cipolla, *Literacy and Development in the West* (Pelican Books, London, 1969); also M. C. Kaser, *op. cit.*, and R. M. Hartwell, *The Industrial Revolution and Economic Growth* (London, 1971), Ch. 11.

an expanding bureaucracy of control, which not only collected information (often statistical in nature) but which also inspected and in varying degrees controlled a variety of social and economic activities. Social criticism was channelled into a regular bureaucratic process: identification of a problem and publicity about it; official inquiry and report; remedial legislation; government enforcement and inspection. Thus by 1910 it was estimated that 'for every 10,000 inhabitants Belgium had 200 public officials, France 176, Germany 126, the United States 113, and England 73'.[29] This variation in the size of the bureaucracies between countries, and the varying dates of the beginnings of industrialisation and the rates of growth subsequently attained, has led to a lively debate about the role that governments played in inducing growth in the developed economies. The literature on the economic growths of Germany, Russia and Japan, for example, is much concerned with this problem, but the 'paradox' of England remains to puzzle the advocates of intervention. The first industrial revolution was almost entirely a free market phenomenon.

II.i, Retail and Wholesale Trade. As with transport and financial services, economists have shown that the share of wholesale and retail distribution in total economic activity rises with economic growth. Retail and wholesale trade have become one of the largest sectors of any advanced economy; in 1955, for example, there were 14·5 million people in these trades in eighteen countries of Western Europe, representing about eleven per cent of the total European labour force. Moreover, those countries with the highest per capita real incomes (like France, Germany, Great Britain and the Netherlands) had a relatively high proportion of labour in trade, compared with countries of lower average income (like Greece, Italy and Spain).[30] The

29. F. N. and P. R. Anderson, *op. cit.*, p. 167. It is noticeable that England achieved the first growth with the smallest bureaucracy, but, critics might argue, at greater social cost

30. J. B. Jeffreys and D. Knee, *op. cit.*, pp. 7–9. The employment figure in the late 1920s was less than nine per cent.

economic functions of distribution are, for producers, to widen the market, for consumers, to provide 'place and time utility', and for both, to provide information. As manufacturing became more localised, commodity production was geographically separated from the consumer market; as more raw materials were produced commercially, there was also geographical separation between raw material producer and manufacturer; as production became more roundabout, there was a proliferation of the production of intermediate and semi-processed goods between raw material producer and the final producer of a finished product. Thus raw material producer, manufacturer and consumer, who in past ages often lived and worked together, were increasingly separated during the industrial revolution, and there was the development of necessary market linkages to complete the circular flow of production, trade and consumption.[31] The evolution of commodity markets, the decline of auctions and the rise of forward trading, the decline of fairs and local markets with a compensating rise of the retail shop and wholesale warehouse, were all important developments of the nineteenth century. Nevertheless, although the facilities for trade, both internal and external, expanded continuously with industrialisation, the productivity of trade services lagged behind that of industry. The substantial rise in distribution's share of total employment reflected its lesser advance in productivity compared with that of commodity production.[32]

II ii, Financial Services. 'It is a fact', writes R. W. Goldsmith, 'that financial intermediaries in the modern sense of the term—business enterprises most of whose assets are financial rather than tangible and most of whose activities are concerned with financial instruments such as money, claims and stocks—hardly existed before the industrial

31. See, for example, the excellent chapter on 'The Rationale of Markets' in *Britain's Commodity Markets* by G. L. Rees, *op. cit.*

32. See J. B. Jeffreys, S. Hausberger and G. Lindblad, *Productivity in the Distributive Trade in Europe* (O.E.E.C., Paris, 1954) and V. R. Fuchs, *Productivity Trends in the Goods and Service Sectors, 1929–61. A Preliminary Survey* (N.B.E.R., New York, Occasional Paper 89, 1964).

revolution of the eighteenth century. Almost the only exceptions are a few banks of issue in Europe.'[33] The industrial revolution was accompanied by a rapid expansion of financial intermediaries, whose role in growth was positive and beneficial.[34] Growth generated an increased demand for money, short-term credit and long-term capital, and hence, for institutions which could provide them, institutions to link surplus- and deficit-spending units, and to facilitate borrowing and lending by substituting the financial intermediary's liabilities for those of the borrowing or lending unit.[35] There was, to meet financial needs, the expansion of banks, money and exchange markets, discount houses, stock exchanges and capital markets, brokerage, etc. Such institutions laid the firm foundations of a well-integrated system of public and private finance. Important, also, was the development of a well disciplined insurance sector which allowed the efficient off-setting of business risks. Most remarkable of all financial centres was the City of London, with its complex network of complementary institutions so well described by W. Bagehot.[36] A measure of the significance of financial services is the ratio of the assets of all financial intermediaries to national wealth, a ratio which increased in Europe and America from perhaps a tenth in 1800 to a quarter or more by the outbreak of World War II in 1939.

II.iii and III.iii, Professional Services. A. M. Carr-Saunders and P. A. Wilson have written that, 'for several centuries some half-dozen professions provided all those skilled intellectual services upon which the day-to-day functioning of society depended'. With the industrial revolution, however, 'the flood-gates opened. New vocations arose and filled the ears of the public with demands for places

33. R. W. Goldsmith, *Financial Institutions* (New York, 1968), p. 3.

34. See J. G. Gurley and E. S. Shaw, 'Financial Aspects of Economic Development', *American Economic Review* (1955).

35. See Goldsmith, *op. cit.*, on 'Functions' of financial institutions, pp. 22–33.

36. W. Bagehot, *Lombard Street* (London, 1873), esp. Ch. 2.

alongside the ancient professions'.[37] In addition to expanding old professions, the industrial revolution added a wide range of new professions (for example, architecture, engineering, industrial management, accountancy, dentistry, veterinary science, surveying, journalism, brokerage, etc.). This development was important in two ways. First, it multiplied the absolute and relative size of the most skilled proportion of human capital in economies, and hence boosted economic growth. For this reason Colin Clark correlates growth, not so much with the expansion of the tertiary sector, as with the expansion of one of its sub-sectors, the professions.[38] Second, it produced a new and independent 'class' with occupations different from those which figured in ideological and social analysis, a class which has increasingly dominated twentieth century society. Hence Talcott Parsons' judgment that, 'The development and increasing strategic importance of the professions probably constitutes the most important change that has occurred in the occupational system of modern societies'.[39] Increasingly business and government have become dependent on professional services (for example, on accountants and scientists); increasingly, also, individuals have become dependent (for example, on school teachers and doctors). As the demands made on the professions became more exacting and as professional specialisation increased, then the professions began to organise themselves into professional guilds, and to guarantee standards by insisting on well-defined and exacting professional training which was, in the long run, also guaranteed by govern-

37. Carr-Saunders and Wilson, *op. cit.*, p. 295. Compare with the remark of F. M. L. Thompson (*Chartered Surveyors: The Growth of a Profession*, London, 1968), p. 64: 'Professionalism was in the air in the later eighteenth century. There was a stirring among the old professions of the law and medicine to modernize their archaic organisations ... Simultaneously there was a stirring of awareness among the practitioners of newer skills or services, that they constituted distinct new professions'.

38. Clark, *op. cit.*, pp. 186, 208.

39. 'Professions', *International Encyclopaedia of the Social Sciences*, vol. 12, p. 536.

ments.[40] Increasingly, also, the universities took over the education and formal training of most professions from the professional associations, thus reasserting an ancient tradition,[41] and independently assuring standards of competence.

III. Personal Services. Personal services during the industrial revolution increased on three broad fronts: as wealth increased, and especially as 'the middle classes' expanded, there was an increasing demand for household servants; for the same reason, and also because of the increasing division of labour, more artisan services were demanded (for example, the services of plumbers, cleaners, gardeners, barbers, cafe proprietors, etc.); and finally, increasing wealth also enabled the greater use of the learned professions (for example, of law and medicine). Domestic servants increased as a percentage of the total labour force throughout the nineteenth century whereas, proportionately and absolutely, they have declined in the twentieth. In Britain, for example, numbers of domestic servants increased from 0·6 millions in 1801 to 1·3 millions in 1851, to 2·2 millions in 1901, making domestic service throughout this period one of the largest occupational groups; by 1910 their numbers were declining.[42] The growth of personal services, generally, was important in the increasing division of labour that went with industrialisation; in particular, it released the time and talents of the professional and middle classes for more productive activity outside the home. There was, undoubtedly, a degree of conspicuous consumption in the employment of servants, and hence an opportunity cost; and it was the decline of domestic service in the twentieth

40. See, for example, for England, W. J. Reader, *Professional Men. The Rise of the Professional Classes in Nineteenth-Century England* (London 1966), Chapters 7, 8, 9 and 10 on the education of the professions.

41. Note that England was an exception before the industrial revolution with the training of law and medicine largely outside the universities.

42. Comparable figures for other countries are: France, 1901, 956,200 domestic servants in an active working population of 19·7 millions; the Netherlands, 1899, 197,500 in 5·1 millions; Hungary, 1900, 360,000 in 8·8 millions; U.S.A., 1900, 1,560,800 in 29·1 millions. See A. D. Webb, *The New Dictionary of Statistics, op. cit.*, article on 'Occupations'.

century which led directly to the expansion of the durable, consumer-goods industry.

IV. Community and Cooperative Services. There is some doubt as to whether the supply of religious services failed to keep up with the growth of population in the nineteenth century, or whether the demand for such services declined. The result, in any case, has been a secular decline in religious observance, differing between sects and between countries, but consistently downwards. Although firm figures are available only for the period after 1900, the data is extensive and conclusive.[43] The doubt still remains, however, whether the supply of religious services has been maintained, or has declined; proportionately, their importance has certainly declined.

With professional associations, trade unions, friendly societies, cooperatives and other cooperative associations, the story, generally, is different from that of religion; these services expanded with industrialisation. Perhaps the most dramatic story is that of the trade unions. And there is no doubt that trade unions came into being as the direct result of industrialisation, because industrialisation changed the relationship between master and worker, collected large bodies of workers together in the same working and living areas, created new social problems for the working classes, and made workers more self-reliant and more ambitious, politically and industrially. At first trade unions were seen as criminal organisations—laws were passed against them in England and France—but gradually their status became legalised, and their membership and power increased. Although pioneered by Britain, the European trade unions developed separately and had few organisational features in common. Their main importance in modern societies has not been industrial, although they have acted effectively in the economic interests of the workers, but political: trade unions formed the essential 'countervailing power' which

43. See M. Argyle, *Religious Behaviour* (London, 1958) for English figures, and F. Boulard, *An Introduction to Religious Sociology: Pioneer Work in France* (London, 1954) for France. In France, Boulard shows, there has been a decline since 1850, especially in industrial-urban areas.

made social democracy in Europe acceptable to the mass
of the population, and workable. By 1906, there were in
Europe nearly eight million workers organised into trade
unions, distributed as follows: Germany, 2·2 millions;
United Kingdom, 2·1 m.; France, 0·9 m.; Italy, 0·64 m.;
Austria, 0·45 m.; Russia, 0·25 m.; Sweden, 0·2 m.; Spain,
0·17 m.; Belgium, 0·16 m.; Hungary, 0·15 m.; the Netherlands, 0·13 m.; Denmark, 0·1 m.; Switzerland, 0·09 m.;
Norway, 0·025 m.; and Finland, 0·02 m.[44]

V. Recreation and Culture. The line between recreation and
culture is not an easy one to draw, but both are consumption
goods whose demand expands with increasing income and
leisure. Generally, both are fields neglected by the economic
historian, yet the organisation and supply of both changed
significantly with industrialisation, and the resources
devoted to them increased markedly. In general this meant
three things: first, a change from a rural to an urban setting,
with a decline of traditional rural sports and pastimes;
second, a change from the amateur and part-time provision
of services to the professional; and third, the development
of new institutions, privately endowed or profit-making, to
cater for both entertainment and cultural activities. Thus
popular entertainment, which in the eighteenth century
had been found mainly in the taverns and on the streets,
was in the nineteenth century institutionalised into music
halls. The supply of music was enhanced by the emergence
of the modern orchestra (in the sense of a standardised
combination of instruments), for which Beethoven's first
symphony of 1800 marked the real beginnings; the supply
of art to the public increased with the increase in public
exhibitions and galleries and the formation of the great
public galleries (for example, the English National Gallery,
founded in 1824). But even at this level of generality little
can be said about the economic history of sport, entertainment and culture. Their histories remain still to be written,
and it is possible only to guess about their quantitative and
qualitative importance. They must be, certainly, amongst
the most important consumption goods of modern societies,

44. Webb, *op. cit.*, p. 602.

and it is significant that their cost, which the individual consumer has been increasingly unwilling to pay, has been increasingly subsidised in the twentieth century by government.

STRUCTURAL CHANGE AND GROWTH

'We may first enunciate the simple but important principle', Colin Clark has written, 'that economic progress in any country, in the sense of a rise of the average real national income per head of the working population, may take place (a) as a result of improvement in real output per head in all or any of these three fields [agriculture, industry, services], or (b) as a result of transference of labour from the less productive to the more productive fields.'[45] During the process of growth, indeed, there are structural changes in an economy which take three forms: a change in the geographical distribution of labour (usually manifested in growing urbanisation and the localisation of industry); a change in the structure of output (with more industrial goods and services being produced, and in different proportions); and a change in occupational distribution (with labour being transferred from agriculture into industry and services, and also between particular activities within these three broad sectors of activity). The importance of structural change for economic growth, however, was not generally recognised before the work in the 1930s of A. G. B. Fisher and Colin Clark. A. G. B. Fisher first popularised the conceptual breakdown of the economy into three sectors—primary, secondary and tertiary—and noted that economies could be classified structurally in terms of wealth, according to the proportion of population employed in agriculture.[46] Colin Clark, after noting 'the flow of labour to tertiary production', classified according to the proportion employed in services. Following Fisher the most firmly established empirical generalisation about economic growth has

45. Clark, *op. cit.*, p. 344.
46. A. G. B. Fisher, 'Production, Primary, Secondary and Tertiary', *Economic Record* (March, 1939).

related to the decline of agriculture, to the secular decline
of both rural population and agricultural labour force, and
to the agricultural sector's declining share of the national
product. Following Clark the operational role of structural
change in economic growth has been firmly established,
showing that the switching of resources between sectors is
an indicator of, and a cause of, increasing productivity.

When Clark was writing in the late 1930s, the economics
of the tertiary sector—the services—had not been written,
and the history of services, though quite extensive, consisted of isolated studies of particular services without
attempts at synthesis. For economists, the picture changed
quite rapidly after 1945; for historians, as has been shown
above, the study of services remains today still largely
atomistic. The economists, however, have developed two
important types of literature of structural change, one
empirical and one theoretical. The empirical literature,
directly in line with the early work of Clark, has culminated
in the massive contributions of S. Kuznets whose 'Quantitative Aspects of the Economic Growth of Nations',
subjected the economic growth of the advanced economies
to detailed comparative statistical analysis.[47] The theoretical
literature had its origins more directly in neo-classical
theory, and has been concerned with structural change as a
dynamic of growth; in particular, this literature has been
interested in two-sector (or dualistic) models of economies
with a traditional (subsistence-agriculture) sector and an
advanced (capitalist-industrial) sector, and with change
resulting from increasing demand because of rising incomes.

Kuznets, in studying the changing composition of output
and employment during the growth of the advanced
economies, came to the following conclusions:[48] *as regards
output*, there has been a secular tendency for the share of

47. Ten articles in *Economic Development and Cultural Change* (1956–67);
see, in particular, Part II (July 1957), 'Industrial Distribution of
National Product and Labour Force'.

48. See B. F. Johnson, 'Agriculture and Structural Transformation in
Developing Countries: A Survey of Research', *Journal of Economic
Literature* (June 1970).

agriculture in total output to fall, for the share of manufacturers to rise, and for the share of services to have had no
systematic relationship with the growth of output (except
transport and communications, whose shares have risen); *as
regards employment*, there has been an unambiguous secular
tendency for the share of total agricultural employment to
fall, the share of manufacturing employment to rise, and
the share of service employment to rise substantially,
generally more than manufacturing employment; *as
regards productivity*, the productivity of agriculture has
generally been below the national average, while those of
manufacturing and services have been above. When the
productivities of manufacturing and services are compared,
however, the data is more difficult to interpret. Kuznets
has suggested that the productivity of services, generally,
has been higher than that of manufacturing, but, it is also
widely accepted that the rate of growth of productivity in
services in the twentieth century has lagged behind that of
manufacturing. Moreover some economists have argued
forcefully that the output of services generally has been
underestimated. Thus A. D. Smith, as regards Britain, has
written, 'After allowance is made for undervaluation of
service sector net output resulting from national accounting
conventions, imperfections in the pricing mechanism and
statistical estimation procedures, the difference in absolute
labour productivity between the goods and service sectors
is probably negligible'.[49] If this were so, of course, the
importance of services in modern economies is further
enhanced.

On the theoretical level, economists like H. B. Chenery
or A. Lewis,[50] in explaining the relationship between
structure and growth, have suggested various dynamic
elements in an economy with sectors of varying productivity
(or backwardness). Lewis' model of growth, for example,

49. *The Measurement and Interpretation of Service Output Changes, op. cit.*,
p. 131n.

50. H. B. Chenery, 'Patterns of Industrial Growth', *American Economic
Review* (1960); W. A. Lewis, 'Economic Development with Unlimited
Supplies of Labour', *Manchester School* (May 1954).

pictures a dualistic economy with a subsistence sector, in which the marginal productivity of labour is 'negligible, zero, or even negative', and a modern sector which absorbs labour from the subsistence sector; the emphasis is on the productive assymetry between the sectors and the consequent process of growth in which the supply of labour to the modern sector is virtually 'unlimited' because, at the prevailing wage rate, it exceeds demand. Using such a model C. P. Kindleberger has been able to explain European post-war growth as a process of transferring labour from a sector of subsistence agriculture in southern Europe, to a higher productivity industrial sector in the economies of northern Europe.[51] In such transfers the roles of changes in the composition of demand, and in supply conditions, have been emphasized: in particular, the decline in the rate of growth of demand for foodstuffs as incomes increased and the complementary increase in the rate of growth of demand for industrial goods and services; and the effect on the supply of goods from the increasing size of markets, resulting in economies from the increasing size of business and from their increasing localisation.

Here, then, in the work of the economists, are lessons enough for the historian about the role of structural change in growth. The historians, however, have generally neglected structural change as an historical phenomenon, and, in particular, have usually ignored its role in economic growth. In one respect only have the historians been interested in structural change: most historians of industrialisation have noted 'the decline of agriculture', but as a measure of change, rather than as part of explaining the process of growth. Thus, for example, P. Deane in *The First Industrial Revolution* recognises that the industrialisation of England resulted in a differing 'industrial and social structure', details some structural changes (with statistics) but concludes that 'probably the most significant difference in the labour force of 1850 as compared with the mid-eighteenth century was that it was a more specialised

51. C. P. Kindleberger, *Europe's Postwar Growth: the Role of Labor Supply* (Harvard, 1967).

labour force'.[52] C. Fohlen on 'The Industrial Revolution in France', similarly, notes 'the transfer from the primary into the secondary sector', but uses it almost exclusively as a measure of the slowness of France's industrialisation, rather than using it to analyse how growth occurred.[53]

The explanation for this neglect is two fold. In the first place, studies of agricultural change in the eighteenth and nineteenth centuries, up to the invasion of cheap American wheat, have concentrated on changes in agriculture itself, and especially on 'the agricultural revolution', on the increasing productivity of agriculture as a result of organisational and technological change.[54] And in the second place, studies of agriculture have been preoccupied with the social effects of agricultural change, and especially with such phenomena as 'the decline of the yeomen', the fate of the peasantry, and the social misfortunes of the agricultural labourer.[55] Thus there has been little consideration of the significance of the differences in productivity between agriculture and other sectors, and little discussion about the reasons which led men in increasing numbers to invest and work in industry and services rather than in agriculture.[56]

52. P. Deane, *The First Industrial Revolution* (Cambridge, 1965), pp. 254, 257.

53. R. Cameron (ed.), *Essays in French Economic History* (American Economic Association, 1970), p. 204.

54. Thus, B. H. Slicher van Bath, in the most comprehensive account of European agriculture up to, and during, the era of the industrial revolutions, notes that 'during the course of history the relative importance of non-agrarian production and non-agrarian population has steadily risen', but analyses agricultural change largely as a response to increasing external demand because or increasing population and industrialisation. He does not discuss structural change in relation to growth, and in analysing 'factors influencing the development of agriculture' concentrates on the formation of a market for agricultural goods through forces 'external' to agriculture: *The Agrarian History of Western Europe, A.D. 500–1850*, (English translation, London, 1963), pp. 18, 16.

55. See, for example, M. Fordham, 'The European Peasantry' in E. Eyre (Ed.), *European Civilisation. Its Origins and Development*, vol. 5 (Oxford, 1937), p. 112 *et seq*.

56. See, for example, the economists on 'The Role of Agriculture in Economic Development' (B. F. Johnson and J. W. Mellor, *American Economic Review*, 1961).

More fundamental, however, in the attitude of the historians to the industrial revolution and economic growth, has been preoccupation with Clark's first cause of economic progress, 'improvement' within sectors rather than 'transfer of resources' between sectors of differing productivity. The historians, generally, have explained the sustained gains in output that came with industrialisation by changes within industry itself: the changes in economic policy which allowed the more effective use of enterprise; the accumulation of capital which allowed the building and equipping of factories; the great technological inventions which allowed the remarkable increases in per capita productivity. The main characteristic of the analyses of economic growth by the historians has been their almost unqualified belief in the prime importance of the industrial sector with its increasing physical capital formation embodying improved technology. Generally there has been a comparative neglect of other factors within industry which raised productivity, like improved organisation and the improvement in the quality of human capital, and almost complete neglect of structural change as a source of increasing productivity. There has been recognition, noted above, that there was a transfer of resources from agriculture to industry, but even this idea of a transfer has been recently challenged. Traditionally the migration of labour from agriculture to industry during the industrial revolution was seen as a 'push' phenomenon, the result of changes in agricultural technology and organisation which reduced the demand for labour. But some historians have questioned this thesis, arguing, for example, that enclosures increased rather than decreased the demand for labour, and, generally, that agricultural improvements tended to be labour intensive. Similarly with capital, where historians now argue that it is not at all certain that agriculture was a provider of capital to industry; rather, that an agricultural revolution needed capital for exactly the same reasons as did an industrial revolution.[57]

57. For England, for example, see J. D. Chambers, 'Enclosure and Labour Supply in the Industrial Revolution', *Economic History Review*.

It is because of these preoccupations with certain aspects of industrialisation and growth that the historians, generally, have not given the services the attention that their combined impact as the service sector deserves. This, in turn, has led to other neglects, in particular to the neglect of the importance of improving human capital in growth, and in social and political change. It was the improved quality of labour in industry and agriculture which was perhaps the most important ingredient in modern growth, and that improvement, apart from better nutrition (the result of improved food supplies), depended mainly on the expanding service sector, particularly in the fields of medicine and education. But, also, it was the expanding tertiary sector which did much to reconcile a growing population to urban living and which facilitated the growth of political democracy.

CONCLUSION

This chapter has outlined the shift in employment and output in the growth economies of the last two centuries to services, and some of the reasons for, and effects of, that shift. It is important to stress that this shift has been more marked in employment than in output, and that the increasing importance of the service sector considered as an aggregate masks important structural change also within that sector. Thus, in the very modern period for Britain (since 1945), whereas employment in both distribution and financial services has been growing twice as fast as employment in industry, employment in transport and domestic service has been falling absolutely.[58] Similar changes occurred in the past, and there have been always 'old' and 'new' services, with differing rates of growth. Two other

---

(1952–3); and E. L. Jones, 'Industrial Capital and Landed Investment: the Arkwrights in Herefordshire, 1809–43', *Land, Labour and Population in the Industrial Revolution*, ed. E. L. Jones and G. E. Mingay (London, 1967).

58. C. W. McMahon and G. D. N. Worswick, 'The Growth of Services in the Economy', *District Bank Review* (December 1960), p. 11.

characteristics of services are also important in any consideration of their role in historic growth: the tendency, admittedly disputed, of the rate of growth of productivity in services in the twentieth century to be less than that of goods, with the possible long-term consequence of a slower over-all rate of economic growth; the tendency for service employment to be more stable than non-service employment, and to decline less than other employment during recession or depression.[59] It is probable, therefore, that the increasing share of service employment has meant, in the long-run, a slowing down in the rate of growth of output, but, also, a greater over-all stability of the economy.

On the demand side, the reasons for the continually increasing demand for a greater quantity and a greater variety of services in the developed economies has been the result of the varying income elasticities of demand for goods and services, and the relationship between the consequent spending patterns and the level of real incomes. Briefly, as real incomes rose (including leisure), the demand for goods rose less than the demand for services, and so the share of services in total output rose. This phenomenon, in the case of food, can be explained by theory; for goods, generally, it is more a matter of observation of behaviour patterns. Another important source of increasing demand for services was urbanisation; as the proportion of population living in cities increased, so did the demand for a range of particular services, for example, transport, street cleaning, public entertainment and police. It was similar with larger-scale and more complex business organisations in which the demand for specialised services was an inevitable concomitant of growth.

The importance of the services makes it possible to classify economies according to the proportion of their populations in the tertiary sector: (i) agricultural countries with a small industrial sector and in which the rate of growth of services is slow; (ii) industrialising economies, in which agricultural employment has declined and in which industry and services are both growing at comparable rates

59. *Ibid.*, p. 22.

of growth; (iii) industrial economies, in which agricultural employment has reached a minimum and industrial employment a maximum; and (iv) service economies, in which the service sector is growing at the expense of industry. This pattern can also be used historically; in the case of Western Europe, for example, stage (i) finished between 1800 and 1850, while stage (ii) occurred between 1840 and 1910, stage (iii) between 1920 and 1970, and stage (iv) is just beginning. The lesson of history is, undoubtedly, that what has already happened in the United States will happen elsewhere, and that the trend in employment towards the services in all developed and developing economies will result finally in a world-wide *service revolution*.

BIBLIOGRAPHY

There is no general history of services, but all work on this subject can best begin with two important contributions by economists:

C. Clark, *The Conditions of Economic Progress* (London, 1940).

S. Kuznets, 'Quantitative Aspects of the Economic Growth of Nations, II. Industrial Distribution of National Product and Labor Force', *Economic Development and Cultural Change* (July, 1957).

Specifically on the services the following should be consulted:

V. R. Fuchs, *The Service Economy* (N.B.E.R., New York, 1968).

M. Lengellé, *The Growing Importance of the Service Sector in Member Countries* (O.E.C.D., Paris, 1966).

R. Gallman and T. J. Weiss, 'The Service Industries in the 19th Century', *Studies in Income and Wealth*, vol. 34.

On structural change, see:

J. Akerman, *Theory of Industrialism* (Lund, 1960).

B. F. Johnson, 'Agriculture and Structural Transformation in Developing Countries: A Survey of Research', *Journal of Economic Literature* (June, 1970).

And Clark and Kuznets.

On particular services, see, for example:

L. Girard, 'Transport', *Cambridge Economic History of Europe*, vol. vi (Cambridge, 1965).

M. Lévy-Leboyer, *Les banques européennes et l'industrialisation internationale, dans la première moitié du XIX siècle* (Paris, 1964).

C. A. Anderson and M. J. Bowman, *Education and Economic Development* (London, 1966).

E. Barker, *The Development of Public Services in Western Europe, 1660–1930* (Oxford, 1944).

J. H. Richardson, *Economic and Financial Aspects of Social Security: An International Survey* (London, 1960).

J. B. Jeffreys and D. Knee, *Retailing in Europe. Present Structure and Future Trends* (London, 1962).

On particular economies, see, for example:

P. Deane and W. A. Cole, *British Economic Growth, 1688–1959. Trends and Structure* (Cambridge, 1967).

W. G. Hoffmann, *Das Wachstum der Deutschen Wirtschaft seit der Mitte des 19. Jahrhunderts* (Berlin, 1965).

J. Marczewski, *Introduction à l'histoire quantitative* (Paris, 1965).

L'industria italiana alla metà del secolo XX (Confederazione Generale dell' Industria Italiana, Rome, 1953).

The Industrial Bourgeoisie and the Rise of the Working Class 1700–1914

J-F. Bergier

INTRODUCTION

1769: two apparently insignificant events occur within a few months of one another. Nobody alive at the time could have any inkling of their importance; but they were to have a share in completely changing the face of the world. On January 5, an undistinguished Scots 'technician' obtained a patent for an improvement of the Newcomen steam engine commonly used for pumping water out of mines. In the space of a few decades, Watt's perfected machine modified profoundly the technical and social structures of industrial production; for the introduction of a new power source superseding that of man, wind, or running water soon wrought a clear distinction between the industrialist, who owned this comparatively expensive machine and the looms it drove, and the worker, who was paid to run it. A few months later, on August 15, Napoleon was born, the son of a family of such modest nobility that it seemed almost bourgeois: during his reign, the bourgeoisie, not merely in France but throughout western Europe, took up the reins of government and business.

The purpose of the following pages will be to give an outline of the reasons underlying this twofold phenomenon: the rise to power of the bourgeoisie via the economic, social, and political revolution that it brought about with an increasing awareness of its role and its strength; and the parallel formation of the working mass, which, created by the industrial activity of the bourgeoisie, gradually acquired the forms and values of a social class by attaining self-consciousness in its turn. Though partners in the growth of the economy, the bourgeois class and the worker class soon clashed over the radical opposition in their material interests and their social, political, or cultural aspirations. But, caught up as they both were in the irreversible trend of growth that defines the economy of the past two centuries, they were forced to come to terms with one another and to seek, on however illusory, however brittle a basis, some understanding.

The scope of the subject makes it a difficult and formidable one for the historian to tackle. Its importance for an understanding of the modern era and present-day society is fundamental. And its spread and diversity in both time and space are considerable: we shall limit the present discussion to those situations that seem to be the most significant in an all-round view. The literature on the subject is vast but variable, and there are few syntheses of sufficient completeness or objectivity. This last obstacle is not the least that we have to contend with: the problems that we shall be discussing have, not surprisingly, given rise to polemic; they had taken an impassioned turn by the end of the eighteenth century (with Thomas Paine, Babeuf, and the rest), and the passion rose before, during, and after the lifetime of Marx — and it is still far from dying out.

Bourgeoisie, proletariat, social classes: are we to attempt to define our terms at the outset? I am less convinced of the usefulness of such definitions as of their danger and, ultimately, of their uselessness within the historical perspective that concerns us here. These notions cannot be tied down to short, precise formulas. Those who have tried to define them in this way, whether historians or sociologists, have produced mere glosses that are either too vague or too restrictive. They have been unable to bring in simultaneously all the criteria worthy of mention; by stressing one more than another they have laid their definition open to immediate refutation. Some have limited themselves to legal considerations in which class is a function of, say, the possession of certain political rights; others, in greater number since Marx, have stressed the individual's role in production; others still have insisted on the importance of income. More recently, sociologists have underlined as the hallmarks of class the phenomenon of consciousness and collective action (i.e. the sense of the social function) of the classes and the restrictions instinctively placed by the classes

themselves on their permeability (in other words the phenomenon of social betterment). Each of these criteria no
doubt remains valid. But none of them can apply entirely
to the development of any of the classes. The bourgeois
who visited the Universal Exhibition in Paris in 1900 and
took pride in the achievements of his age was perhaps the
direct descendant of a bourgeois of 1789, but he was quite
unlike him in the way he lived, worked, and thought; and
as for the worker who joined the Section Française de
l'Internationale Ouvrière (S.F.I.O.) in 1905, what had he
in common with the illiterate wretch slaving away in a
smoky workshop for a paltry wage some sixty or eighty
years earlier, except that he too was still a proletarian?

Consequently it is the actual history of the bourgeoisie
and working class, more than even the best of glossaries, that
will provide us with the only definitions that are valid.

SITUATION OF THE BOURGEOISIE

At the dawn of the industrial age, the bourgeois was no
newcomer to the social scene. Indeed, he had existed for
centuries, ever since the urban renaissance that almost all
Europe experienced between the eleventh and fourteenth
centuries. Origially, the bourgeois was the burgher or
town dweller active as a merchant, official, artisan, lawyer
or man of letters and enjoying certain rights conferred by
the charter of his borough. But this original, legal notion of
the bourgeoisie gradually became more complex.

On the one hand, the bourgeois enjoyed real social and
material privileges with regard to the rest of society,
particularly vis-à-vis the mass of peasants. They were
therefore increasingly reluctant to share those privileges
with newcomers, and laid down conditions of entry. The
strictness of these conditions varied from one town to
another, or one period to another. In Paris, a stay of a
year and a day was all that was required for a man to
acquire bourgeois status, as well in the eighteenth century
as in the Middle Ages. But other towns imposed a longer
period of residence: five years in Bordeaux, ten years in

Lyons, Marseilles, and Périgueux. In Bordeaux, bourgeois also had to be householders, which created a kind of property discrimination between bourgeois and non-bourgeois. Elsewhere it was more common for access to the bourgeoisie and its privileges to be subject to the payment of a tax, which was sometimes low, sometimes very high: being free to fix the amoint of this tax as they chose, the bourgeoisie could allow or refuse entry to their group just as they saw fit, thereby giving it the characteristics of a self-conscious and selective class. Thus, in Geneva, an independent city-state whose bourgeois were in some sort their own seigneur, a register was begun as early as the fifteenth century for recording the names of newly-admitted bourgeois; their descendants gradually came to form a real bourgeois aristocracy of *citoyens*. In the eighteenth century, this aristocracy had become so inaccessible that it provoked a reaction from those who had failed to gain admission; and these social and political disturbances in 1770–80 foreshadow the revolution that was soon to convulse the neighbouring kingdom.

On the other hand, the bourgeois did not confine themselves to the cramped precincts of their towns. In a society which remained fundamentally rural, at least up to the threshold of the nineteenth century (and often much later, in Germany, or Russia, for example), and in which the social prestige pertaining to the nobility was linked with land-ownership, the townsfolk felt rather left out of things. They had an ardent desire to acquire land and have it worked by tenants. This brought two advantages: the prestige and authority conferred by the ownership of land; and ground rent, which generally yielded lower profits than business or industry, but which had the merit of being more stable. Hence, by the fifteenth or sixteenth centuries, the original meaning of the word bourgeois began to be lost, and by the eighteenth century it was no more than a remembrance of things past. On the eve of the Revolution, the French bourgeoisie, which was certainly not the wealthiest, held more than thirty per cent of the cultivated land. In Switzerland or certain regions of

Western Germany, almost all the land was in bourgeois hands. By contrast, in those countries where great domains were formed at a very early date and the towns' hold on the country was correspondingly weaker (northern Germany, central and eastern Europe, the Iberian Peninsula), the vast majority of land was held by the nobility or the church. England, where the bourgeoisie and the gentry were much more closely interdependent — to say the least — than elsewhere, stood halfway between the two extremes. But there too the acquisition of land was a constant aim of the early industrial bourgeoisie, whose members remained extremely attached to their largely rural origins.

At all events in this slow, uneven but unmistakable transformation the bourgeoisie very gradually lost the unity originally secured by its status in law. True, even in the eighteenth century the condition of 'bourgeois' still conferred certain privileges. But the privileges were increasingly losing their value because all kinds of divisions were occurring within the bourgeoisie. These divisions were due to the separation of the bourgeoisie into professions and to the emergence of discrepancies in the wealth of its members.

Without going into detail, and ignoring the innumerable regional differences, we can readily distinguish between four broad groups of bourgeois. The first comprises the rentiers, comparatively few in number (in France, around ten per cent of the total 'bourgeois' effective) and generally not very powerful within the bourgeoisie. Their role in the rise of industry was minor; and what share they had in it came generally late in the day: they had no profession, in most cases lacked drive and initiative, and for a long while remained distrustful of industrial investment, preferring the proven profits of ground rent, commercial income, or government loans. The second group comprises the members of the learned professions, the magistracy, or the administration: neither their duties nor their incomes led them to take much interest in industry. There were exceptions, however: there is evidence to show that the French notaries played a role as purveyors of capital (in small amounts) to small, recently-founded enterprises; but this role remained marginal and rarely led them to become industrialists themselves.

The two remaining groups are more interesting from our point of view. The first consists of the *bourgeoisie d'affaires*, the men who held all the reins at the close of the ancien régime. Their incomes were often higher than those of the nobility, whose equals they believed they were in many respects. This group produced the best State officials, and in places where the nobility was lightweight, the city republics for instance, it *was* the State — indeed, this was an ancient tradition in the great commercial cities of London, Paris, Lyons, Amsterdam, Geneva, or Frankfurt. These bourgeois were big merchants or bankers (the two pursuits were henceforth rarely combined as they had been during the Renaissance): a few families in the largest cities, closely linked by marriage and often linked from one city or country to another. The family connections of the Protestant bankers of Geneva, Paris, or Amsterdam, the shipowners of Marseilles, Bordeaux or Nantes, and so on were as wide as their business connections, and the solidarity that they created was astonishingly efficient. This tiny minority, then, held a large majority of the financial power and actual wealth of the European nations and their colonies. Hence this bourgeoisie also controlled the main manufactories — the nearest thing to what we would call industry. For, on the very threshold of the industrial revolution, the manufacturing bourgeoisie had still to acquire a personality of its own. The masters of the enterprises were the wholesale dealers. Either they already brought together wage-earning workers in their mines or factories (which was the case mainly in iron-working, with the Schneiders at Le Creusot, the Dietrichs in Alsace, and so on), or, more often than not, they resorted to the old *Verlag-System*, providing home workers with all or part of the tools and the raw materials and buying back the finished product at a price fixed by the dealer that virtually amounted to a wage.

The fourth and last group within the bourgeoisie, by far the most numerous, was that of the artisans and shop-keepers, the innumerable minor trades that were practised more or less independently. The separation between this group and the previous one is, of course, imprecise. When does an artisan become a manufacturer, or a shopkeeper a dealer? Yet on the whole the differences are glaringly obvious. Income, to start with, was much lower in this last group; and the way of life in each case was strikingly different. The man of affairs draws his profits from his investments, from the risks that he takes; his job is to direct, to calculate, and to take decisions. The artisan or shopkeeper live mainly off their own manual labour: the only difference between them and their employees is that they give the orders, while continuing to perform part of the work themselves.

These differences within the bourgeoisie, though obvious, are essential. For they ruled out all coherence between the groups, all sense of speaking the same social language, recognisably distinct and foreign to other social languages: in other words, the bourgeoisie had not yet become a class. Even if in some places it enjoyed certain juridical privi-leges which marked it off and conserved it — we have given the example of the Geneva bourgeoisie — it had no unity.

This accounts for all that was in store for the bourgeoisie: the difficulties that it was to encounter before it achieved complete political dominance; and the emergence of a new economic group, the industrial bourgeoisie, whose presence swiftly revolutionised the traditional structures that we have just been summarising.

THE ADVENT OF THE
INDUSTRIAL BOURGEOISIE

Charles Morazé's recent book has already become the standard account of the 'conquering bourgeois' (*bourgeois conquérants*). This expression is an admirable description of the bourgeois onslaught on all the levers of political and economic power, an onslaught that began as early as the eighteenth century and spread, with varying degrees of delay, from one country to another.

This is not the place to discuss the bourgeois seizure of political power. Besides, the circumstances, motives, and results differed appreciably from one country to another. The main thing is that everywhere, with or without violence and institutional discontinuity (very marked in France, barely apparent in England), the bourgeoisie took control. In some places it did so directly; in others it merely had to act upon the traditional framework of government. True, it did not meet with unqualified success everywhere. In those countries where industrialisation was early and rapid (Great Britain, France, Belgium and the Netherlands, Switzerland, Scandinavia), the success was clear and uncontestable. Elsewhere, it was slower and less effective, because the bourgeoisie still had to contend with either the dispersion of government (Germany, Italy) or the inertia of the economic and social structures, which gave predominance to the large domains (Austria, Hungary, Poland, Russia, Spain). Despite this diversity of attainment, however, there can be no denying that here was a universal trend of considerable force.

It is remarkable that, in a general way, the political bourgeoisie, which furnished all or part of the members of the governments, the parliaments, or the main administrations, did not merge for a very long while with the industrial bourgeoisie, whose climb was largely parallel and whose interests would seem at first sight to have coincided with those of the government and its officials. There were exceptions — Robert Peel, for instance. But the industrial entrepreneurs seem to have preferred to mind their own affairs rather than the affairs of state.

The question arises why. In the early phase of industrialisation, most of the entrepreneurs came from environments — we shall discuss them later — which were largely unprepared for political activity. They did not have the kind of prominence needed to win votes; and indeed, in those countries where the franchise was based on property, many of them would not have been eligible to stand in the first place. By the second or third generation, the more successful industrialists had largely attained the local prestige and acreage they needed to enter politics, yet they rarely did so. Biographies of industrialists are still far too few for us to form a satisfactory notion of the reasons for this abstention. It is probable, however, that it was due more to a lack of ambition in this field and to a lack of experience in or even taste for this kind of activity than to any lack of interest in government as such, on which, after all, the prosperity of the enterprises depended in two respects: in a general way, with regard to legislation (on labour, external trade, and so on) and taxation; and in a more particular way, in respect of government orders placed with the factories. The entrepreneurs did not stand aloof altogether, however. They had agents and spokesmen in the parliaments and occasionally even in the governments; though devoted to the cause of industry, these men were rarely industrialists themselves.

It is clear, then, that the industrial bourgeoisie merged neither with the upper bourgeoisie of the parliaments and administrations nor with the traditional upper bourgeoisie of trade and finance. The latter kept to themselves. They usually distrusted the parvenu industrialists, whose recent wealth seemed to flout theirs and to challenge the status quo that they were determined to defend. For several generations there was virtually no collusion or association between merchants and bankers on the one hand and industrialists on the other. The capital held by the former did not find its way into industry for a long while (in England and France, not until the middle of the nineteenth century; in the other countries, guided by the experience of the pioneers, the hesitation did not have to be so prolonged). In this respect, the absence, up to around 1850, of adequate banking structures and industrial credit institutions says much about this compartmentation of the bourgeoisie.

What, then, were the origins of this industrial bourgeoisie?

Where did the entrepreneurs come from? We may start by asking what is meant by an entrepreneur.

The word can mean two things, only one of which concerns us here. In its most usual sense, dating from the industrial revolution, the term 'entrepreneur' applies to anyone who directs, for his own account, an industrial undertaking (or even an enterprise producing nonindustrial goods or services), and who employs labour. But recent writers, notably the economists Joseph Schumpeter and François Perroux, or the historian Fritz Redlich, have limited the meaning of the word to the creator or rejuvenator of an enterprise — the man whose personal drive, inventiveness (in matters of management as much as — and often more than — production technique), and taste for competitive risk-taking results in 'progress': progress for his enterprise, if he is considered individually, in which case 'progress' is measured in terms of his profits; or, taking him as part of a collective effort, in the context of an industrial sector or a nation, progress in the material welfare of society as a whole.

In this precise sense in which we shall be using the word, the entrepreneur is a man with an original mental, not to say moral, make-up. For indeed the emergence of the entrepreneur class and the achievement by them — and by their workers — of the industrial revolution resulted from the historically exceptional combination of these personal qualities and the demographic, economic, social, and technical circumstances that are held to have been the prerequisites of the take-off. The entrepreneur sees everything in terms of profitability: ever since the earliest days of industrialisation he has possessed in the highest degree that spirit of capitalism that Max Weber, rightly or wrongly, associated with protestantism. The most remarkable instance in this respect — too remarkable to be characteristic, no doubt — is that of the industrial aristocracy of Mulhouse: a few families, Calvinists since the sixteenth century, 'a tightly-knit milieu linked by an intricate system of intermarriage . . . subscribing to the same religion, the same outlook, the same way of life — simplicity to the point of austerity, high standards of professional conduct, puritanism, and smug acquiescence in the tangible testimonials of divine favour' (Guy Palmade).

The spirit of capitalism had, of course, existed among the merchants and financiers before the industrial entrepreneurs came along. What the latter added, with help of circumstances that became particularly favourable to them, was their sense of adaptation and their genius for innovation that enabled them to appreciate the practical implications of the latest technical discoveries: their first aim was to get rich, but their second aim was to contribute to the progress of society by turning out a product that was cheaper, or better, or both.

Hence the entrepreneur was very different from the big capitalist that preceded him. If his thrift recalls the frugality of his predecessor, his kind as a whole imported an imaginativeness that the man of affairs before him (and for a long while alongside him) only displayed individually and in a much smaller way. All was grist to the entrepreneur's mill, everything counted, everything was possible; his only limitations were those of his market — and even these did not hamper him, since his innovations enabled him constantly to broaden the market, the global limits of which were still imprecise (and remained so at least until the first half of the twentieth century).

All this meant that the industrial entrepreneur broke free from the social limitations that capitalists before him had imposed upon themselves. This partly explains the social clashes that industrialisation was not long in producing. But was the entrepreneur's freedom with regard to social conventions a deliberate disregard for 'breeding' or merely a lack of it? This brings us back to the question of where the entrepreneurial class or group came from in the first place. We must also touch in the broad outline that we have just been tracing: the entrepreneurs of the industrial revolution, wherever it occurred, were obviously not all like the type that we have been portraying. The fact that they were not is clear from the splits that occurred within the industrialists' own social group — another question to which we must now turn.

Before the appearance of the industrial entrepreneurs, from 1760–80 in England then gradually elsewhere in Europe, 'industrialists' were, of course, already to be found. But some of them, wholesale dealers often called manufacturing merchants, merely organised commercially the output of a host of wage-earning artisans, without ever attempting to modify or rationalise the methods and techniques involved; their manufactories were more like communities of workers than industrial enterprises. The other 'industrialists', small independent artisans, mostly lacked sufficient means and (especially) sufficient imagination and breadth of mind to make significant innovations — from which they would constantly have been precluded in any case by the strict rules of the guilds.

Hence neither the manufacturing merchant group, through lack of interest, nor the artisan group, through lack of wherewithal, was able to mutate outright into an industrialist group. Not surprisingly, therefore, the other social and professional categories (nobility, peasantry, learned professions, and so forth) stood aloof from this great economic and social movement. So what we find is not a change of activity on the part of a group, but the quasi-spontaneous generation of a new group whose members came from every section of society. It was not birth, trade, or fortune that made the first industrialists, but initiative, ambition, and luck — if they succeeded, for the emergence of this new group was an affair for the fittest or luckiest; those who could not keep up helped to form the nucleus of the future proletariat.

The first industrialist groups gathered in the peak sectors of the industrial revolution: cotton and iron. It was there that needs were greatest and the demand seemingly insatiable; it was there also, in industries as new as spinning or as inorganised as ironworking, that the structures were most flexible and the prospects brightest. Hence these were the two fields in which enterprises proliferated — very rapidly in England, especially after 1785, rather more slowly but around the same time in France, and not much later in Switzerland (from 1801 onwards). Progress went ahead by leaps and bounds rather than constantly, with the braking effects and recessions provoked by the conjuncture as a whole (political and military events as much as the purely economic cycles).

In this mad rush, particularly in the cotton industry, almost anyone could set himself up as an industrialist. All that was needed to install a spinning frame was a small amount of capital (which could be got from a money-lender) and the services of a workman sufficiently acquainted with the technique to act as foreman. In almost every case, the biographies of these early industrial entrepreneurs show them to have started out from modest circumstances: shopkeepers, rural artisans, inn-keepers, farmers. Arkwright, the most famous (or at least the most typical) of them, who died in 1792 with a knighthood and worth a million, was a barber; whether or not he really invented the water-frame, he exploited it with the genius that others applied to the various new techniques. The Peels, who also built up a considerable fortune before one of them turned his hand to politics, had been well-to-do farmers; Sir Robert's grandfather had begun by dabbling in hand-spinning and cotton printing in the time left over from the land: from this he launched out into power-spinning and calico printing. William Radcliffe, also of farming stock, started out as an apprentice mill hand before founding a mill of his own, which became one of the most prosperous of all in the early nineteenth century.

Things were much the same in France: many of the great spinning or weaving dynasties began as humble artisan (rather than farming) families: the Peugeots, who built their fortune in textiles well before the motor-car, had been successively farmers, innkeepers, and millers before establishing a calico works near Montbéliard in 1759. But there were also a few former merchants among these entrepreneurs: 'dealers as long as the work was done by hand, they became industrialists as soon as mechanisation made it possible to set up spinning frames or power looms at little cost' (Claude Fohlen). In Switzerland, the first spinning mills, very modest affairs, were also opened by well-to-do farmers or artisans (they were usually both at once), before being taken over as early as 1800 by merchants such as Hottinger or Escher who were in a better position financially and commercially to acquire the already complicated and more costly English machines, or patents to build them on the spot.

The same can be said of the ironmasters. Many of them were of country extraction, such as the Darbys, Boulton, or Richard Crawshay, the 'iron king', whose father was a small farmer; John Wilkinson's father was a countryman before signing on as a labourer in an ironworks. But others belonged to an artisan milieu that naturally guided them towards the iron and steel industry: such were the New-castle blacksmith William Hawks, the nailsmith Aaron Walker, and many others. An extremely typical example is Peter Stubs: as a filemaker he had acquired a good know-ledge of his craft; but as an innkeeper at the same time he had managed to save part of his profits which he used as his initial capital.

Outside England, the iron industry was perhaps gen-erally more 'bourgeois' in its origins: beginning rather later, it necessitated a larger initial investment. In France, it was the main *maîtres de forges* traditionally established in the richest ore regions who became great industrialists. Here it was not so much the kind of activity that changed as the methods and scale of production. We find the same thing occurring in Saxony and the Rhineland later on (1820–40). It would seem, however, that the later industrial-isation began, the greater was the contribution of the upper strata of the bourgeoisie, with occasional financial aid or even direct participation from the landed aristocracy.

In spite of the undeniable diversity of the social and professional origins of the industrial pioneers in individual countries, the dominant trend was for them to come from the land. The towns — the large pre-industrial cities devoted to trade and the traditional crafts — made little contribution to industrialisation, which was the country-man's revenge, so to speak, on the society that neglected him. Further, the industrialist willingly returned to the land (in England more than elsewhere, perhaps): as soon as the fortune that he had built up allowed him to do so, he hastened to buy land (if possible the land formerly worked by himself or his ancestors) and to have it worked, in his turn, by tenants.

These industrialists were not technicians, still less scholars, but improvisers. They brought their inventiveness to bear, not on production techniques, but on their application, that is to say the internal organisation of the enterprise and the commercialisation of the products. An enquiry into the British cotton industry in 1803 showed that, despite the simple nature of the machinery, most of the entrepreneurs were incapable of taking their own technical decisions: 'The reason of it is, that the master was never acquainted with the art of weaving, he just puts in a man who understands the trade, invests his capital, and when he gets the price of the market, he goes forward' (quoted by Paul Mantoux). Hence a kind of division of labour was called for, not only in the appropriation of labour but in the management itself. It diminished, however, after a generation or two, when the heirs to an enterprise had managed to acquire specialist training. As we know, this division of technical and commercial responsibilities within the management reappeared at the end of the nineteenth century and from then on spread to all large and medium-sized enterprises.

In any case, the entrepreneurs had quite enough worries as things stood, without having to bother about actual production. They had to gather together a labour force, which was rarely as simple as the romantic tradition of a permanent host of unemployed would have us believe. (Right from the start of industrialisation the labour market underwent frequent variations that were not always to the workers' disadvantage.) The entrepreneurs had also to organise the commercial side of their enterprises — buying and selling. They had continually to cope with increasing competition, and, in order to do so, keep up with the needs and tastes of their customers and with the technical innovations that they had to be among the first to exploit if they were not to be crushed. Lastly, allowance made for the exigencies that we have been discussing, they had to make the best possible arrangements for financing their enterprises.

A great deal of ink has flowed on the question of capital for industry. Marx believed that the start of the process of industrialisation depended on the prior accumulation of capital, an idea to which most Marxist historians and economists have, of course, remained faithful. Yet this view is nowadays contested both by a number of economists and by historians. The former who, for the last fifteen years or so, have been making a careful scrutiny of the prerequisites for industrialisation, have come to the unanimous conclusion — though with some disagreement over priorities — that other factors were more decisive than the availability of capital: a prosperous agricultural system capable of feeding the people who quit the land for the factories; an infrastructure of trade and communications guaranteeing the supply of raw materials and the disposal of the products; an adequate level of technological development; and so forth. The historians, for their part, have established: (i) that the 'original accumulation' of capital that Marx traced back to the sixteenth century in fact went through many vicissitudes between then and the industrial period: the eighteenth or early nineteenth centuries were not 'wealthier' than the sixteenth; and (ii) that the initial investment of the industrial revolution, at least in those countries where it occurred first, remained very low.

The basic technical innovations — almost exclusively the work of amateurs or artisans of slender means — were characteristically very simple and therefore comparatively inexpensive. A frame or loom for working cotton, wool, or flax, even a steam engine or a blast furnace, did not involve enormous expenditure. The business became expensive when many looms, frames, or engines were used at once. Almost all the entrepreneurs started out with a small plant that they built themselves or bought, and with a correspondingly small labour force. They set themselves up on funds of their own or money loaned to them by a small circle of relatives, friends, or connections. They could not have done otherwise, moreover, since the large amounts of capital held by the bankers, merchants, or big landowners were only very rarely available to them. To expand or renew their plant, they had to rely on reinvestment of their profits.

Self-financing was the rule at the start of industrialisation. (The later-developing countries differed in this respect. Northern Italy, Russia, and so on, with their great agricultural domains, got less negligible aid from the landed capitalists and from the investments of foreign capital.) And in the second generation, self-financing enabled the large enterprises to expand and increase at the expense of the smaller and less profitable ones. The fact is that, even then, the men of affairs were still chary about industrial investment; and the banking system remained inadequate for industrial needs up to and beyond 1850.

Yet after 1800 in England, 1820 in France and Switzerland, self-financing in the strict sense ceased to be the rule entirely. The entrepreneurs had swiftly realised that it was in their interests to invest in other enterprises besides their own. It could be advantageous to take out interests in rival enterprises, already equipped but less successful, in order to gain more or less direct control of them: examples of this were frequent in the textile industry. Investment in other, complementary industries could enable the entrepreneur to improve his supply of raw materials (e.g. an ironmaster assigning assets to a mining concern) or his outlets (many owners of spinning mills gave financial aid to the weavers).

This soon led to concentration, vertical as much as horizontal. (The phenomenon was probably more accentuated in France or Switzerland than in England, and in ironworking more than any other branch). But this concentration was also simultaneously a cause and effect of the severe selection process which, as we have seen, eliminated large numbers of particularly ill-prepared industrialists and practically put them at the mercy of their more successful competitors. Concentration in industry had the further effect, which helped to shape the new bourgeoisie, of creating company enterprises with varying numbers of partners. Even if one or other of the partners emerged as a leader and acted the part of the 'entrepreneur' more than the others, all the active partners (as distinct from sleeping partners) took their place in the developing industrial bourgeoisie.

TOWARDS THE COHESION OF THE INDUSTRIAL BOURGEOISIE

The axiom that form follows function is as true in social history as it is in other fields. The industrial bourgeoisie was not the agent, but the product of the industrial revolution. It arose as the result of an identity of interests among a number of individuals whose social origins differed widely (despite certain dominants that emerge), and a common orientation in their activity.

But even though this industrial bourgeoisie shared the characteristic features of the entrepreneur, it had no self-awareness and no awareness of its collective role in society. It had no unity, no solidarity: it had no existence as a class. Too many differences stood between the individuals of whom it was composed: differences as regards social origins and hence education, and differences, fairly rapidly accentuated, as regards wealth. At the time of the group's emergence, cohesion was also obviated by the geographic spread of the different ventures within each nation. This obstacle was generally soon overcome, however, as the industrialists conglomerated in zones that were particularly favourable with regard to the availability of raw materials, communications, labour, and so on. The industrial towns that resulted — Manchester, Birmingham, Lille, Saint-Etienne, Zurich, Turin, the Ruhr cities, and so forth —

were not merely the overcrowded and insanitary seats of the working masses; they were also the rallying points of the industrial bourgeoisie. This development had a share in setting the industrial bourgeoisie apart from the other groups of bourgeois, who generally stayed on in the towns where they conducted their affairs, notably in the capitals of trade and traditional industry: London, Paris, Lyons, Milan, Berlin, etc. A final obstacle to the cohesion of the group was the keen competition among its members; and this obstacle was never completely overcome.

Gradually, however, this cohesion was achieved, at least partially. Two main factors which transcended national frontiers were largely responsible for this: (i) the development of an ethos, a culture peculiar to the industrial bourgeoisie; and (ii) the historical necessity, existing before it was felt or understood, for solidarity within the group — a kind of defence mechanism against the animosity of the rest of society, whose structures the industrial bourgeoisie, however small it was in actual numbers, had already wrecked.

Turning to a discussion of these two factors, we find that, at the outset, the industrial bourgeoisie necessarily had no culture of its own; that is to say, it produced no artifacts, and transmitted no ideas, bearing the mark of its personality (of which it had none) or its inventive genius, its dynamism. Indeed, its contribution to the cultural effort and progress of society as a whole was but a very humble one. In this respect also it differed considerably from the traditional bourgeoisie. Many, if not most, of the early industrial entrepreneurs had never got beyond the rudimentary schooling consistent with their station. Very few of them bothered to better their knowledge of things outside their profession; and sensibility was even rarer among them than knowledge. True, the refinement and taste of Wedgwood, for instance, are often justly praised: indeed such qualities were the famous potter's stock-in-trade. Boulton, the great entrepreneur, was a skilful mechanic, an art-lover, and the friend of many men of letters and science. The Mulhouse spinning-mill owners were highly educated and cultured. But those of the industrialists who belonged to the cultural élite of their day were still the exceptions (which made for further divisions within the group). The vast majority were self-made men whose stocks of knowledge, even technical knowledge, were very rudimentary. Owen, a notable exception in this respect, had harsh things to say around 1820 about the 'cotton barons': they were generally 'plodding men of business, with little knowledge and limited ideas, except in their own immediate circle of occupation' (quoted by Paul Mantoux).

Nonetheless, progress in this field was more or less rapid, depending on the country considered. It was particularly rapid in Switzerland, whose industrialised regions had long enjoyed a higher degree of literacy than most other countries. Gradually, the industrial countries (France was rather slow in this respect) opened higher institutions and trade schools in an attempt to make good the technological advance gained by England. As a rule, these innovations were not put forward by the industrialist group and do not appear to have had its support at the outset. But they were ultimately of service to it. Trained engineers capable of assuming increasingly complex professional responsibilities came to dominate the group; and thanks to their broader culture the group as a whole gained in refinement and maturity. And this attempt to form a body of qualified industrial managers contributed, of course, to the reinforcement of economic growth.

Having acquired a higher degree of education and culture, the industrial bourgeoisie of the time of Louis-Philippe or Robert Peel was proportionately more powerful and effective as a social force. But its potential remained limited by the fact that it had still not formed itself into a coherent group; before it did so, it had to encounter obstacles which only a united onslaught could overcome.

The first obstacles were political ones. As we have seen, the entrepreneurs were reluctant to get involved in politics. But it was important to them that government policy should suit their interests. When necessary, they managed to agree among themselves and put forward proposals, indeed demands. As early as 1784, for instance, Boulton was not merely speaking for himself but clearly for the whole group when he protested at the government bill for a duty on raw materials: 'Let taxes be laid upon luxuries, upon vices, and if you like upon property; tax riches when got, and the expenditure of them, but not the means of getting them' (quoted by Samuel Smiles in his *Lives of Boulton and Watt*). The puritanical, 'class-conscious' overtones in these words tell a story in themselves . . . Shortly afterwards, the English industrialists, led by Boulton and Wedgwood, formed a 'General Chamber of Manufacturers' which had a deep-reaching influence on the trade treaties with Ireland (1785), which they stopped, and France (1786). These early examples are revealing; many others could be cited for just about every country.

But these political obstacles revealed a latent conflict between the newcomers and the traditional bourgeoisie. This covert yet unremitting 'class struggle' within the bourgeoisie was fought over proposed legislation, economic doctrines (with the industrialists successfully disseminating the principle of laissez-faire), and social status. It would be interesting to trace the vicissitudes and evolution of this quarrel in greater detail than has been done hitherto.

At all events, there can be no doubt that sooner or later, in every country, the industrial bourgeoisie won the day. Nor can there be any doubt that its members kept to themselves, as is underlined by their tendency to religious dissent: many entrepreneurs in England were adherents of nonconformist sects and a number of the French entrepreneurs were protestants. From this religious or social dissent they derived vigour and, ultimately, cohesion. Everywhere they formed original, powerful, and greatly respected pressure groups. As early as 1821 there was talk in Alsace of a 'fabricantocratie'. And by the middle of the century the industrialist was universally hailed as the modern Prometheus, the begetter of a new society. Economists, philosophers, and social reformers (Saint-Simon, Enfantin, and Constantin Pecqueur) all gave him their blessing. 'The time has come,' wrote Isoard in 1834, 'for our industrialists to occupy the positions held since 1789 by successively, the priests, the soldiers, the lawyers, and the men of letters.' And did not Marx himself also stress the historically decisive role played by the entrepreneurs? But, for him, that role had already been fulfilled by 1848 . . .

For indeed behind the employers were the workers. From being an unorganised mass, the proletariat became conscious of its destiny, meaning its size and its strength. Faced with this challenge, the industrial bourgeoisie in its turn finally became conscious of itself and the privileges that the proletariat was beginning to contest. Just as the word capitalism would be coined some time later to answer its predecessor socialism, the industrial bourgeoisie became a 'class' in the full meaning of the word to resist the growing pressure of the working class.

TOWARDS THE MASS OF THE WORKERS

If the history of the entrepreneurs is not easy to grasp, that of the working masses is still less so. National differences, inequalities from one sector of industry to another, and the passion aroused very early on, for obvious reasons, by this question all put enormous difficulties in the historian's way and are particularly troublesome with regard to the kind of rapid survey that I should like to present here. We shall just have to skip the finer points and refer the reader to more complete accounts listed in the bibliography. (It is worth pointing out, however, that despite the enormous literature, much of which merely reproduces what has gone before, there are still considerable gaps in our knowledge, particularly as regards the continent.)

One thing is obvious: the working class, by which we mean a social entity with some awareness of its situation and aspirations, and more or less organised in relation to those aspirations, did not spring up overnight. It slowly emerged from the formless mass of the workers, and in so doing depended less on numbers than on the cultural level of its members, or rather its élite. Its formation came comparatively late. In the 'privileged' prototypal form that it took in England, it did not begin until the first quarter of the nineteenth century and did not culminate much before the 1830s. In the other countries, it came later still, depending on the level of industrialisation that they had reached; but here it developed rather faster, having been able to benefit, up to a point, from the previous examples. Nonetheless, analysis reveals that those examples cannot have been perceived and followed by any but the worker-élites (who accounted for all of the participants in the Working-Men's International); and that the masses in most of the countries had to cover in their own way and according to their own ideas, the same ground all over again later on. But comparative studies in this field are virtually non-existent (as they were until very recently in the field of industrialisation itself). Historians of the working class still confine themselves far too often to the history of labour movements, which is only the political aspect of the problem, and do not lay sufficient stress on the social and psychological realities involved.

It follows from our first remark that analysis of these questions must consider two phases: the formation of the working masses; and their maturing into a more or less clear-cut social class.

A proletariat already existed before the industrial revolution. The body of dependent artisans or journeymen in the towns already constituted a working population, in many cases a large one. The number of wage-earners in Paris in 1791 has been estimated at some 75,000, i.e. around 280,000 to 300,000 people if we include their wives and children — half the town. The actual proportion was doubtless higher as the towns were larger. But the journeymen were not the only components of the popular strata; we must add the domestic servants (very numerous), the casual workers of all kinds engaged in minor trades (gardeners, water- and wood-porters, messengers), the builders' labourers (often employed on a seasonal basis),

and lastly the destitute, of whom there were very many:
close on 70,000 people received poor relief in Paris in 1792
— one inhabitant in nine. The rural proletariat was also
very large: 40 per cent of the French agricultural population
at the end of the eighteenth century, with a higher proportion in England, and a higher proportion still, of course,
in the lowlands of northern, central, and eastern Europe.

The living conditions of this huge population had always
been bad. They sank lower still in the second half of the
eighteenth century (or in the nineteenth century in central
and eastern Europe) owing to the fact that this period had
by far the highest demographic growth rates — a phenomenon observed by Malthus with accuracy and anxiety.
This world was at the mercy of food crises, rising prices,
falling wages, unemployment, and the exchequer. It lived
and worked in the towns, in insanitary conditions, overcrowded and overworked, a state of affairs that industry
could generalise and prolong, but hardly worsen. Begging
and crime often became the only resource for many of
these poor wretches.

But this mass remained apathetic with regard to a
situation to which it had been subjected for centuries and
which it saw no way of changing. Apart from a few popular
revolts that remained strictly local — such as the *canuts*
(silk workers) in Lyons — or a few purely platonic protestations in the *cahiers de doléances* in France on the eve of
the Revolution, no group reaction and, especially, no sign
of solidarity can be detected. Solidarity in the ancien
régime societies was not horizontal but vertical. There was
solidarity between the worker and his employer and the
men with whom he worked, but not with those doing the
same job as himself in the workshop next door. The serf
might hate his lord, or the tenant his landlord, he nonetheless remained attached to him by bonds of custom that
were even stronger than human rights. Hence it was almost
unnecessary for the pre-industrial governments and
bourgeoisie to resort to repressive legislation with regard
to this mass.

The only exceptions were the guilds [*compagnonnages*] or

secret societies of journeymen artisans. Here indeed was a form of horizontal solidarity. But it was limited in its scope by the low membership of the guilds and their constant rivalry. In France, they lingered on through the process of industrialisation, from which they remained aloof however, clinging to a quasi-medieval outlook in the day of the great social upheavals. Their role in the formation of the working class can be regarded as non-existent, if indeed it was not negative.

In the space of a few decades, the industrial revolution swept away all these long-established structures, the persistence of which, it now seems, was due to mere inertia. They would have collapsed under the slightest shock — and the shock was far from slight; it swept the societies towards situations that were as new as they were unexpected.

The formation of the working mass around industry was due to two fundamental factors, one geographic, the other technical. On the one hand, a few sectors of industry (cotton, steel) grew very rapidly and in regions suitable for them. Their need for labour attracted available workers into these regions. On the other hand, the same industries generalised what had hitherto been confined to a few odd manufactories: they assembled the workers in a selfsame enterprise under the same roof, forming factories. The use of the steam engine as a motive force for several frames or looms at once, the need for rationalised production in bulk to amortise the working costs, lastly the employer's anxiety to keep a sharp eye on the work done by his men — these were the main motives for this revolution in the organisation of labour.

Yet the move to factory production was less universal than it is commonly held to have been. In some industrial sectors and (especially) in some regions, home work, often part-time (i.e. as an extra to farming) continued to exist and has survived down to the present day. In Switzerland, for instance, many specialised textile firms have persistently given preference to dispersed labour; certain simple skills to do with the clockwork industry are similarly performed by home workers. These exceptions confirm the rule: where industry remained dispersed, or became so, there was no formation of a working mass and no class-mindedness, and for that reason, later on, the socialisation of the workers remained very low. But, paradoxically enough, the same working milieux, more highly educated but individualistic, became more acutely aware of the working-class condition in general (for their own condition was comparatively privileged) and provided leaders for the working-class movement, anarchism in particular for which the Swiss Jura, with its clock industry, was a training ground.

Where it occurred — i.e. in all the great industrial zones — the concentration of the working masses was not automatic. Intervention from the entrepreneurs was necessary in order to overcome the series of obstacles that it encountered. The pre-industrial populations were particularly immobile. Not only because the available means of transport were inefficient — the railways were somewhat to modify the features of this problem — but mainly because moving was to these people so abhorrent that only great pressure could force them into it. It has been possible to observe that the idle population of London, where unemployment was rife, fiercely resisted being transplanted to the new centres in north and west England. The old Poor Laws, with their guarantee of parish assistance for the destitute, were an additional obstacle in England: the poor were unwilling to risk losing their livelihood by taking a job, when the job was so far away and so hypothetical; inversely, the distant communities were reluctant to take in people who might one day become a burden. Lastly, a solution had to be found to the problem of equipment: houses had to be built, food supplies laid on, and the circulation of low-value coins improved so that wages could be paid. This was a permanent and heavy worry for the early industrialists, particularly in England. Yet in England the concentration of the workers was more rapid and more accentuated than anywhere else because of the greater pressure of circumstances and needs.

To remove these obstacles, the entrepreneurs went to

enormous lengths. Not only did they build houses for their workers (as cheaply as possible, of course); they also strove to maintain a wages policy likely to attract labour. In the first stage of the industrial revolution, wages in England were comparatively high and above all stable (in real terms), much more so than in France, where the obstacles to recruitment were of much less consequence (except during the Napoleonic Wars). The situation was reversed around 1840, when English wages dropped to the minimum level that generally prevailed on the continent, even in Switzerland.

With the concentration of labour achieved, the formation of the working mass was complete. But where did the mass come from?

It used to be thought that the explanation was quite simple: the inexhaustible reservoir of industrial labour was the country, where the greater part of the population lived; where living conditions, on the continent, were almost universally deplorable; and whence, in England, so many land workers were driven into the towns and their factories by the enclosure movement.

There is no question of rejecting this explanation outright; but there are grounds for qualifying it considerably. It is a fact that the country furnished a large part of the new industrial labour force, but not in the proportions that used to be supposed. In France, farms were extremely fragmentary, with the result that agricultural workers were tied to the soil. The Revolution, which improved their lot by freeing them from seigneurial exactions and by putting the lands of the Church and the estates of the nobility on the market, played its part in this process. The wars up to 1815 drained off the rural population and correspondingly diminished the effectives potentially available to industry. When the army was disbanded, however, former soldiers flocked into the factories both in France and Switzerland and elsewhere.

In England, the rural exodus to industry captured the imaginations of poets and novelists long before it inspired historians such as the Webbs, Paul Mantoux, and many others. It was held that the enclosure of the commons was a cause of the industrial revolution in that it limited the number of farmers and labourers, who were alleged to have abandoned whole villages at a time (cf. Goldsmith's *Deserted Village*). It is true that many countrymen took the road to the mills. However, recent estimates by H. J. Habakkuk and J. D. Chambers have established: (i) that the exodus of the lesser peasantry was appreciable especially between 1660 and 1740, well before the industrial revolution, and did not coincide with the peak of the enclosures, which came around 1800; and (ii) that the beginnings of industrialisation correspond, quite on the contrary, with a *reinforcement* of agriculture, which had to produce more to satisfy an increased demand owing to the tremendous rise in population and the spread of the towns. As a result, the farmers' lot, at every level, actually improved. So much so that the number of agricultural labourers, as a percentage of the active population, was maintained and, in absolute figures, increased.

Yet by the late eighteenth century there was a reversal in the trend, the proportions of which reversal increased as time went on. Before the industrial revolution, the rural population constituted around 75 per cent of the English population (85-90 per cent in France). In 1801, at the first national census, it had dropped to 35 per cent (75 per cent in France), and 16 per cent in 1851 (around 55 per cent in France). The huge proportions of this regression are a fair reflection of the vastness of industrialisation in England. But we are still dealing in relative terms, and the *absolute* number of English peasants did not diminish: the real exodus came in the second half of the nineteenth century, as it did everywhere else (when foreign corn took over from home production).

These proportions in fact revealed another reality, in which we may see the explanation both of the origins of the English industrial proletariat and of England's overwhelming rise to supremacy: I am referring to the demographic growth that preceded and accompanied the industrial revolution. Whereas France moved painfully, from 1700 to 1800, from 20 to 25 million inhabitants (in round figures), England and Wales moved from $5\frac{1}{2}$ million shortly before 1700 to 9 million in 1801 and 18 million in 1851. The falling death rate, though still high, was matched by a rise in the birth rate from decade to decade after 1740. Thus the population of England, in striking contrast to that of the other nations, was rejuvenated. And it was the immense surplus of young people that constantly came in to swell the ranks of the working mass.

It is evident that the first wave of young people came from the country, like the popular urban masses already in existence: there was not enough work on the family farm for all the children. But this first movement was not of great size. As we have seen, the enterprises mostly began in a small way, hence with limited labour requirements. When the movement increased, in the period 1780–1800 and of course beyond, it was the industrial populations themselves, already in their second generation, that furnished a large part of the contingents required. But to this spontaneous generation, so to speak, of the working population, we must add the strong contingent of traditional artisans who, outstripped by techniques that they were not able or willing to adopt in time and ruined by the competition from industry, had no alternative to signing on at the mills.

What is true of England is true also of countries where the concentration of this population occurred more slowly, or came later. It is true of France, Switzerland, and Belgium, where the industrial boom followed closely, but less precipitously, on that of England; and it was to be true of Germany, Italy, and Russia, where the reserves of manpower were built up in the interim. Yet in each of these countries local conditions resulted in some variation from the English pattern.

The example of Switzerland is perhaps not particularly significant in this respect. Besides, an almost total lack of social statistics for the greater part of the 19th century makes it difficult to analyse the formation of a working mass which, in fact, never became very large, even in proportionate terms. In the 19th century, and even in the 20th, Swiss workers can hardly be called a mass at all. Around 1850, when industrialisation was at its peak, factory workers accounted for barely more than an estimated 2% of the total population, as against at least 5% in England (in 1841), around 3% in France, and 2% in Prussia (whose industrial take-off was much more recent). This is not to minimise the importance of the industrial revolution in the Swiss cantons, but to draw attention both to its gaps and to its real nature: virtually no mineral deposits, hence no heavy industry; and labour that was largely dispersed but often quite specialised. This meant that the agricultural and industrial populations were very incompletely differentiated. There was no sudden swing from one to the other; at the very most, there was a slow progression at the individual level. Numbers of peasants — many of them artisans already in their spare time — were led to give part of their time to industry in their village or in a neighbouring town; but most of them clung to their peasant mode of life and did not therefore constitute a working mass. If there was such a thing, it was composed solely of artisans thrown out of work by competition from industry, as happened everywhere. The real drain on the rural population, from 1860 onwards, came from the tertiary sector, whose labour force outstripped the active population of the rural areas around 1910.

Comparable situations existed in Bohemia and Moravia, and in Italy (in the closing decades of the century, in the textile industry of Piedmont, Lombardy, Tuscany, and the former kingdom of Naples). In all these countries, rapid demographic growth (incomparably less rapid than in England, however), coupled with the particularly high birth rate of the less privileged levels of society, accentuated the developments we have been discussing.

In Germany, the diversity of local conditions imposed further complications on the formation of the working masses which, moreover, were concentrated in the few development areas of large-scale industry: Saxony, Westphalia and the Rhineland, to a lesser extent Silesia, and the Berlin region. Between 1820 and 1850, large enterprises were still few and far between and the concentration of factory labour was low. Börsig, with around 1,000 employees in 1846, still seemed a giant; at the same date, Krupp employed less than 150. However, the liberation of the peasantry that took place in most of the German states between 1807 and 1850 had unexpected results; as in France, it tied the farming masses to the land, but it also impoverished the large majority of them, who were incapable of drawing sufficient income from the land that they had come to own. In the long run, many peasants were forced to sell, or to give up employing all the members of their large families. The extremely bad harvest of 1846–7 provoked the start of a rural exodus that continued through the decades that followed. From 1860 the disequilibrium between the booming industrial west and the still wholly rural regions in the east resulted in a vast movement of migration from east to west.

It is not without interest or significance for the economic, social, and even political history of Europe to point to the simultaneity, between 1850 and 1880, of the great currents of rural exodus. Whatever their level of industrial development, all these countries, even those whose industrialisation was only beginning, witnessed the draining of their countrysides in favour of the urban agglomerations with their factories and offices; developments in England or Germany had their equivalents even in Italy, where they initiated the famous *questione meridionale*.

If, then, the German peasant mass took an appreciably greater, though delayed part in the development of its country's labour force, the artisans were much less involved. Up to around 1806–10 in Prussia, later elsewhere, the German artisan class clung to powerful and vigorous corporative structures. The freedom of the artisan — his right to self-employment — was only gradually given legal recognition over the first half of the 19th century. The new legislation resulted in a rise in the numbers of artisans, when in the other countries that number was falling. In 1816, 31 townsmen in 1,000 were in business as self-employed artisans; in 1861, the figure stood at 59 in 1,000 — a progression out of all proportion to the demographic growth of the towns. In the absence of any progression in demand, individual incomes fell. In the heavily industrialised regions, artisan poverty became acute (as the young Marx saw for himself in the Rhineland) and led them to revolt (1844). But it was only after 1850, and particularly after 1860, that the usual swing from the crafts to industry (or, in many cases, to emigration overseas) took place.

Thus, sooner or later, in accordance with an ineluctable pattern of development, the vigorous and active forces of the nations, their working masses, converged on industry. They invariably encountered wretched living conditions. Just as invariably they gradually became aware of their situation, and reacted with what intellectual, legal, and political means they had or could create.

THE CONDITION OF THE WORKERS

The living and working conditions of the working masses in the early stages of industrialisation have often been described. Remarkably objective and accurate official enquiries as well as works of literature record the misery of these people in equally severe terms. (The most valid novels in the eyes of the literary critic are not necessarily the most reliable from the point of view of the historian, who can credit an Eugène Sue more readily than a Balzac . . .) Conditions were bad enough for most of the pre-industrial artisans; and they worsened in proportion as the factory proletariat increased, both in absolute numbers and as a proportion of the active population. In the earliest phase of all, that of the actual take-off, the industrialists' labour requirements may have made it possible (in England at least) to live slightly above the minimum subsistence level. But this phase did not last very long. By the second generation, the period of the first 'industrial' crises (1817–18, 1825), the standard of living went down steadily. Over the same period, profits rose, the industrialists gradually moved

away from the austerity of the puritanical early entrepreneurs and began to live up to their means, and the
relative divergence and the psychological gap between the
two industrial 'classes' increased proportionately.

This is no place to recapitulate the descriptions of
working life in the nineteenth century: the reader will find
them easily enough either in contemporary authors (Dr
Villermé, the author of a famous *Tableau de l'état des ouvriers
employés dans les manufactures de soie, coton et laine*, 1840; or
Marx and many others), or in more recent historians. Some
(the Hammonds, Paul Mantoux or, more recently, Eric
Hobsbawm, and others) have certainly been too pessimistic;
as a reaction, others (T. S. Ashton, T. Clapham, etc.) may
have gone too far in the other direction. But whatever the
nuance, everyone agrees that the workers' standard of
living was extremely low, with all that meant in the way of
misery, morbidity, illiteracy, and so on; and that the
industrialists perpetrated many grave wrongs, though we
must be wary of over-facile generalisations.

We shall limit our remarks to a few aspects of the problem
that had a particular but negative bearing on the formation
of the group and, in a later stage, the working class. The
workers' living conditions gave rise to the mass, but
hindered rather than helped its evolution towards an
organised and conscious class; they delayed and bedevilled
the inception of the workers' struggle against the industrial
bourgeoisie or the bourgeoisie as a whole, which meanwhile
gained control of government and used its power to defend
its positions.

With this prospect in mind, we shall discuss three
closely-related questions that are at once specific and universal within the phenomenon of industrialisation, i.e. they
were born of this phenomenon and its inherent exigencies,
and they appeared, with nuances that we cannot take into
account here, wherever the phenomenon occurred. I am
referring to the relation between men and machines; the
hours of work; and woman and child labour.

Work at the machines, for the men who were subjected to

it, constituted, to use the expression coined by Marx, an 'alienation'. It was not so much the machines themselves that estranged them, i.e. made their work unpleasant and uninteresting, as the obligation to accept the conditions imposed, to submit to an overall work plan, doing the same things over and over again without grasping their significance for the technical and social manufacturing process as a whole. This deprived them of the freedom that has always pertained to farming and the trades: to organise their work as they saw fit.

The working and living conditions of the early factory workers were generally deplorable. These circumstances were primarily responsible for the high level of morbidity (and a low expectation of life at twenty) and for the development of a number of vices in the working population — drinking in particular. The work itself was essentially monotonous, for the product was created by the machine, not by the worker who ran it. In addition, the men's work was generally laborious, for the lighter tasks were kept for the women and children. Hence the workers were tied down to a form of work and existence for which they were unprepared biologically, morally, or socially, and which turned them into brutes. This state of passive resignation from which it was hard, if not impossible, for them to escape prevented them from forming any sense of solidarity or community of interest within their work groups, still less within the group as a whole. It thus accounts in the first instance for the very slow maturing of the working-class consciousness.

The hours of work, the reduction of which — together with increases in wages — was to be one of the most constant demands of the future working class representative bodies, were another obstacle. The work was constant and unvaried throughout the year. The artisan, or still more the farmer, experienced seasonal variations in the intensity of his work. The industrial worker did not, unless he was unemployed. As for the length of the working day (discussed at length by Marx, for it is the basis of his theory of surplus value), which was limited only by the time biologically necessary for rest but not governed by any legislation or convention until much later, it was not a new thing in itself: artisans or farmers also worked long hours. What was new was the strict monotony of the work under permanent supervision. The working day left the worker no respite to think, to take stock of his situation, to organise his comrades, or ultimately to resist.

Woman and child labour all the year round in conditions almost identical to those inflicted on adult men remains the great moral scandal of the industrial revolution. It was the target of the first protestations, and it was the object of the first restrictive legislation; but the first timid reforms came only after 1830 (in Great Britain and France, much later elsewhere). Up to then (and even beyond, for it was some time before the legislation was widely respected), most workers' wives worked, which was a pretext for the employers to lower wages, considering the family was no longer kept on a single wage . . . It was not rare for entrepreneurs to set up subsidiary workshops for the women unable to work alongside their husbands. As for the children, who were tied to a working day of ten to twelve hours from the age of three (sometimes), or five or six (often), they could not receive any schooling likely to befit them for responsibility. If infantile mortality was not very high, infantile morbidity was rife, and it naturally had repercussions throughout the (brief) lives of those concerned.

This employment — and debasement — of children also had the effect of considerably retarding the formation of the working class consciousness. Conditioned by the work and discipline of the factories from their early childhood, individual adults, untaught and sickly more often than not, were incapable of appreciating their misery, much less of doing anything to remedy it.

Almost paradoxically, then, the larger the working mass became, the harder it was for it to progress towards self-consciousness and reaction, i.e. class warfare. It did so notwithstanding, but largely as the result of outside incitement, and not without many setbacks.

TOWARDS THE WORKING-CLASS CONSCIOUSNESS

To the sociologist, the pattern of this process may seem simple and universal, i.e. virtually the same everywhere. But for the historian, the phenomenon is much more complicated, not to say inextricable, owing to the great multiplicity of the circumstances in which it developed, which differed from one country or region to another. The social structures, economic foundations, ideas, attitudes, and political backgrounds were necessarily diverse; and it is most difficult today to find a universally valid explanation for them. Much essential data and the particular situation of several nations have not as yet attracted sufficient attention from the specialists; hence any attempt at synthesis remains very difficult and probably illusory. In this short essay we shall stress first of all the British model. Not merely because it is indubitably the one about which we know most, but above all because, as the first in time, it was also the most complete and therefore the most significant. The liberal institutions and policies of Great Britain also allowed each side in the struggle to manoeuvre or attack without hindrance, and this enables us to appreciate the ratios and relationships more clearly than elsewhere.

The problem with which we have to deal falls historically into three fairly distinct phases. In the first phase, which might be called the prehistory of class-consciousness, came the preparation of the forces that were to provoke the coming to awareness, in spite of the obstacles already referred to. These forces were generally exerted on the mass of workers from the outside: i.e. by individuals, groups, or institutions that either did not belong to the workers' world (personalities, policies, groups belonging to another social condition or profession, churches, benevolent societies, and so on), or belonged to it originally but differed from it by virtue of a privileged situation in the trade, by education, or by propensity for leadership.

In the countries where industrialisation occurred relatively late (Germany, Italy, Russia, etc.), the example given by the more advanced countries and, from 1864, the internationalisation of the working-class movement may have made a direct contribution to the swifter formation of an organised working class. In Russia, in particular, the class ideology defined and disseminated by a few intellectuals who had read Marx and other socialist writers preceded the class itself. It remains to be known, however, how far they really shaped that class, given the fact that the masses were largely illiterate and unamenable to abstract reasoning. The heroes of the working class were not so much its most original thinkers and teachers as those who contrived to translate the ideology into more readily-understood terms.

This is the second phase, during which the workers gained awareness of their condition — i.e. the exploitation (or alienation) to which they henceforth believed they were subjected — and of the struggle that they had to wage to transform it: this was the birth of the class (if we allow that it exists only in the consciousness that it acquires of itself and the struggles that it wages for power).

The third phase is the period of the struggle, the history of the institutions with which the class endowed itself (Chartism, syndicates, federations, confederations, International Working-Men's Associations, etc.), in a word the history of the labour movement. This history is deeply rooted in the structures of the economy and of the industrial society of Europe, and reflects these structures in dramatic and passionate terms. But the course and climax of this battle and the preparations for it belong to the field of political history: the clash is no longer concerned merely (or even mainly) with economic or social betterment, but with power. The centre of the stage is no longer dominated by the mass of the people, the factories, or the teeming industrial suburbs, except in the flames of revolutionary outbursts; it moves into the conference rooms at trade union and party headquarters, the committees and mass meetings. Economic history, social history, political history, and the history of ideas meet and merge. But we cannot hope to treat this question chronologically in the few pages available to us here, and the story has been told many times already. We shall confine ourselves to a very summary analysis that will be concerned mainly with the first two phases.

The working-class consciousness stemmed less from a collective realisation of the condition of labour, which as we have seen was virtually impossible, than from ideological movements that first appeared in the bourgeoisie, because the bourgeoisie alone was mentally capable of such reflection. But it remains most difficult to measure the impact of these various movements, which differed greatly and often contradicted one another; and it is most difficult to establish an order of importance or even occurrence.

The first realisation of the social problem created by industrialisation may have occurred, in England, in church circles. The churches involved were the nonconformist churches, which were numerous and active in this country and drew a large part of their membership from the industrial employer class and the petty bourgeoisie. The Church of England, aristocratic and conservative, remained impervious to social preoccupations. The same thing happened on the continent, where the Catholic Church, like protestantism where it was the official majority religion, long ignored this problem. Christian socialism, whether catholic or protestant, did not appear until very late in the day, not much before the middle of the nineteenth century (apart from insignificant exceptions), and for a long while remained distinct from the ecclesiastical hierarchy and authority.

From the very start of the industrial revolution, however, in the minority nonconformist churches (Presbyterians, Congregationalists, Quakers, Baptists, and so on), close to the people and evangelistic in outlook, ministers and a few deeply committed laymen expressed their concern at the social changes that were occurring and the new inequalities that they were leading to. They were the first to remind the bourgeoisie of its responsibilities and, more rarely, in the late eighteenth century, to propose concrete reforms for the improvement of the workers' lot. Their exhortations naturally went unheard. Even if they had gained a hearing nothing could have come of their proposed reforms, which were chimerical or inapplicable and did not attack the source of the malaise. But these early protests at least prove that the malaise already existed.

None of these churches thought of informing the mass; puritanical, they were all based on the principle of individual salvation, not on collective faith. Their action was charitable; they were, as E. P. Thompson has shown, churches *for* the poor. Only Wesleyan Methodism, perhaps, attempted to be the church *of* the poor. But after 1795, this church hardened and returned to conservative notions.

The poor were certainly numerous both in England and on the continent — around 1800, more than 100,000 people in London, out of slightly fewer than a million, were without visible means of sustenance — and the wealthier members of society saw the social problem as a mere problem of aid or (the more clearsighted of them, Malthus in particular) a problem of morals. The poor needed help (the Churches and Parliament took care of that) and encouragement — always individually — to put up with their misery, or to work for betterment, or to spend less on drink, or to have fewer children . . . A stricter police force was also needed, according to some. But no one as yet thought of linking poverty, which had always existed, with the social structures that were beginning to take shape. The bourgeoisie had still to realise that it had to deal with a new kind of poverty engendered by its attitude to industrial labour. But it got cold feet. There was a general fear of subversion similar to that which Jacobinism had brought to revolutionary France. And this scare caused the bourgeoisie to stick more firmly than ever to its conservative principles. 'Every man felt the necessity for putting his house in order,' wrote Frances Lady Shelley in her diary.

What about the employers? Could they really understand the problem? A few entrepreneurs (Wedgwood, or the Mulhouse spinning magnates, and others) tried to treat their workers more humanely. They paid decent wages, built better houses and schools, encouraged certain collective leisure pursuits, etc. This was paternalism. But at the outset (and throughout the nineteenth century) paternalism was the nearest the bourgeoisie got to an enlightened social attitude. The motives of its practitioners were not wholly pure, in any case, and evolved as time went on, even if the end result remained the same. In the early days, during the industrial 'revolution', paternalism drew its inspiration from the humanitarian and progressive outlook of a minority of clear-sighted entrepreneurs; at the same time it did not exclude the profit motive: there was a belief that a considerate employer would be rewarded with better work and the goodwill of his workers. In its second phase, however, paternalism was of a defensive nature. The cleavage must no doubt be related to the psychological effects of the revolutions of 1848. It aimed to divert the workers from the political temptations held out to them henceforth by the various forms of labour movement, trade-unionism or socialism. The attitude of the German industrial bourgeoisie after 1870 is extremely characteristic in this respect: its gestures to the workers (insurance cover, mutual aid, social clubs) were inspired by a fear of socialism. Addressing his employees in 1877, Krupp voiced a feeling prevalent in his class: 'Enjoy what is given you to enjoy. Relax, when your work is over, in the company of those close to you, your parents, your wife, your children; concern yourselves with your house and home. Let that be your policy: it will bring you happiness. As for politics (*die grosse Landespolitik*), spare yourselves that worry. Engaging in politics requires more time and experience than it is possible for the worker to have.' True, we do come across the odd example of the opposite point of view. As early as 1863, a certain number of Bohemian industrialists took the initiative — short-lived as it happened — of organising the German workers at Reichenberg. Whatever its premisses, however, the active paternalism seen in these few examples remained the exception. The general policy continued to be that of producing the goods as cheaply as possible and with maximum profits. Any concern for the workers' welfare, if it existed, was invariably subordinated to that policy.

These idealistic trends, widespread in the bourgeoisie and leading neither to concrete reforms nor to any positive education of the working mass, were matched by movements in the political field.

In France, these trends were expressed in a few of the more extremist tendencies of the Revolution. But the French Revolution was bourgeois. The industrial proletariat was still insignificant and attracted virtually no attention. Only Babeuf and his disciples seem to have perceived the force that it could become. But their attempt had no immediate follow up (it was later revived on several occasions and inspired, in Europe, the main anarchist movements). Moreover, the Empire, and the Restoration that succeeded it, left no room for the dissemination of ideas that were in any way subversive. Social thinking, or 'socialism', took refuge in idealism.

English society was solidly barricaded against the revolutionary notions of Jacobinism, and disposed of an efficient political police. Nonetheless Great Britain experienced, as early as the last decade of the eighteenth century, several political movements of a more or less clandestine nature that in the long run made their mark on the established regime. It was the political institutions that were challenged, rather than the social structures. But these ideas, originating in intellectual circles, met an echo from the lower levels of the population, the petty bourgeoisie of artisans, shopkeepers, and servants. Though expressed in various ways, these ideas were based on the common principle of 'liberty', whatever that meant: each individual, each social group, and soon each class claimed its own liberty which it attempted to impose as Liberty. Hence 'liberty' was mainly negative. It was opposition, especially to despotism: it was here that the political concern of a few intellectuals met and mingled with the aspirations of a large part of the population — with the exception of the working mass, which was still inert. Thomas Paine's strongly radical pamphlet *The Rights of Man*, published in 1791–2, sold 200,000 copies. Jacobin radicalism in Great Britain did not last for more than a few years, because the excesses of the French Revolution rapidly discredited it. Sentence was passed on its leaders amid popular indifference and the clubs were suppressed. But it had sown the first seeds of political awareness among the people.

Yet the people did not remain passive. On all sorts of occasions they rioted and rebelled. Sometimes spontaneously, without leadership, under the effects of famine. Sometimes more coherently and consciously, for wage demands. In the second instance, of course, there were leaders, whose own aims were political. This is why it is often difficult to distinguish between the social awareness of a rioting mass and the political aspirations of an élite of artisans and petty bourgeois attempting to lead it.

The shortlived movement known as Luddism was an illustration of this ambiguity. Its ill-defined platform was a mixture of rejection of the political regime, purely material labour demands, and protest against laissez-faire legislation that favoured industrial capitalism. Well organised and well led, it prefigured the labour movement. But it did not have much support from the mass: its members were artisans or skilled workers, mainly from the textile industry. This explains its hostility towards the new techniques and its deliberate smashing of the machines which, the Luddites believed, would result in unemployment and above all (here the fears were nearer to the truth) in upheavals in the traditional methods of production. It was an odd movement, revolutionary and conservative at once: this contradiction proved fatal to it after the outbreaks of rioting in the industrial North and Northwest in 1811 and 1812. But the Luddite leaders did not lay down their arms: many of them joined together again, fifteen or so years later, as the leaders of Chartism. In its most elementary form, blind revolt and destruction, Luddism had its equivalent in just about all the industrialising countries, e.g. the anti-machine riot of the weavers of Uster, near

Zurich, in November 1832, or similar movements in Germany in the 1840s and after. Outside England, however, these risings were spontaneous, non-political affairs which showed no sign, as yet, of social awareness.

Despite its contradictions, its limited social impact, and its short life, English Luddism was nonetheless an essential stage on the road to working-class consciousness. From then on, things moved faster. The grave economic crisis that affected the British economy in the years that followed the Napoleonic Wars, famine, decreases in wages insufficiently matched by decreases in prices, unemployment resulting from industrial bankruptcies, and inadequate government invervention aroused the ill humour, then the anger, of the mass. This time, popular feelings met with appropriate political and ideological leadership. Intellectual radicals such as Thomas Spence, the ardent publicist William Cobbett, and the orator Henry Hunt took the head of the movement, though with unequal success. Strikes, minor riots and mass meetings spread, without achieving a great deal apart from enlightening and mobilising the masses. The bloody Peterloo incident (August 15, 1819) put an end to this period of unrest because, with the crisis over, normal life and industrial growth set in again. But Peterloo was a decisive turning point. For the first time, workers and bourgeois had clashed head on: the class struggle had begun. And the stir created by the massacre was enormous.

Henceforth all the working mass was concerned and knew it. True, it was not capable of appreciating the ideological motives — which were very vague in any case — or the political aims of its leaders. The meetings organised throughout the country attracted only a fraction of the workers. But the mass was shaken to the core. In the inns, which played a central role in this process, the workers sang of their growing awareness of their misery and of their glimmer of hope.

The fight continued on the same two fronts: political, in the parliamentary activity of the radical leaders; and social, in the periodic strikes or riots into which the workers were driven in times of crisis. But the common purpose was henceforth recognised, and each of the two groups used the other in pursuit of its aims or demands. Meanwhile, the workers organised themselves by trades and by regions. Between 1824 and 1834 the first trade unions appeared. A few had already been in existence illegally for some years; others were new. Their common interests as regards wages and hours of work led them to combine their efforts. The Irishman Doherty (in 1830) and especially Robert Owen (in 1832) worked hard for trade union federation, but achieved only partial and short-lived results, doubtless because the gap was too wide between the utopian socialism that was the philosophical basis of these efforts and the practical needs of the infant working class. But the class, *qua* class, henceforth existed.

Its struggle found its first expression, and simultaneously its first success, in the Chartist movement (the 'Charter' was published in 1838). The demands of Chartism were political and parliamentarian (universal male suffrage, election reform, franchise reform), for the very reason that they expressed the political maturity, if not of the working class as a whole, at least of its élite. With Chartism (which petered out after 1848) we reach, in Great Britain, the end of the second phase and the start of the third phase that we defined earlier. The industrial bourgeoisie and the working class were henceforth in direct competition for political power. The struggle was to go through outbreaks of bitter conflict and periods of calm. Revolutionary at its birth, strongly influenced by Marxism around 1860–80, the labour movement subsequently inclined towards the reformist objectives put forward by the Fabian Society. After 1880, the Fabians dominated, not only British trade-unionism, but labour policy as a whole down to the founding of the Labour Party in 1906.

THE AWAKENING OF CLASS CONSCIOUSNESS ON THE CONTINENT

We may now ask whether the British model outlined above holds for the other industrial countries. Did the continental working classes follow the same pattern of development, gradually becoming self-conscious, then organised, and eventually institutionalised? If we limit ourselves to the barest outline and adjust our chronology to suit the varying degrees of industrial backwardness, we are bound to conclude that the processes were fairly analogous. Wherever it occurred, industrialisation unmistakably opposed a class of bourgeois entrepreneurs to a class of workers. The former held the reins of government and had great economic power; allied by common interest if not completely merged with the other groups of the bourgeoisie — the high bourgeoisie marked off by its wealth and management function — they were the masters of society, for better or for worse. The working class, by contrast, had no power at all. Its function was to work. Low in numbers at the outset, it grew steadily, at what seems to have been more or less the same rate everywhere. Everywhere, too, it became self-conscious, and formed itself into a political force (not without difficulty), as the result of outside incitation, intellectual and bourgeois.

This said, we are also bound to conclude that from one country to another, many fine distinctions must be made; historical conditions peculiar to the development of each one introduced different hues into the common pattern of social evolution. For the picture to be complete, we should need to bring in at this point as many short monographs as there are nations (even regions), hence working· classes, to consider. For neither the efforts of Marx nor the First International (1864) succeeded in giving the labour movement the unity of aims and attitudes that they propounded. The working classes remained astonishingly national; the internationalist principles posited by Marx and many others after him became dead letters as soon as national interests came into play. This came across very clearly in 1914, when the socialist movement was unable to oppose the war because the masses accepted it and welcomed it. . .

Since we cannot, within the scope of this essay, study every working class in detail, we must now attempt to single out some characteristic variants from the English model.

Among the great nations on the continent, France was the one in which the rise of industry followed closest on that of Great Britain. We might reasonably expect to find, therefore, similar stages occurring in the formation of the working class. In fact, this process followed a somewhat different course.

To begin with, the mobilisation of the masses in favour of industry began later and occurred more slowly. At the time of the first trade unions in Britain, around 1825, the French proletariat was still not *in situ* — far from it. In addition, the twenty-five years of the revolutionary and imperial period had focussed the nation's attention on other problems and forms of struggle than social protest. And the same period had wrought so many social reforms already that the working population could not as yet feel frustrated. The aristocratic and reactionary policy of the Restoration (1815–30) and the July Monarchy (1830–48), which marked the advent to power of the high bourgeoisie, modified the situation. This was the epoch of the great development of industry and of the concentration of the masses in the towns and suburbs. But these few thirty years — the span of a single generation — were insufficient for the proletariat to become aware of its living conditions, which were even worse than those of its British counterpart. It lacked the means to do so, both intellectually and juridically. The social reformers so numerous in France at that time, from Saint-Simon to Constantin Pecqueur via Cabet, Fourier, and the rest, beguiled themselves with high-minded utopias, preparing a world of the future that had no impact on the present, least of all on the workers, their contemporaries. In addition, the labour legislation of the time was extremely repressive. The *Loi Le Chapelier* (1791) and the penal code forbade 'coalitions', i.e. any form of professional association, and the law was rigidly enforced where the workers were concerned. There were tolerated mutual aid societies, guild societies, and a few secret organisations. But their action was limited, and above all they consisted solely of artisans and skilled workers (such as the '*canuts*', Lyons silk-workers, whose rising in 1831 has remained famous). Hence they met with little response from the proletariat proper. The latter was subjected to the formidable obligation of the '*livret*', which every worker had to present to his new employer and which mentioned his conduct — i.e. his docility.

Things being what they were, no 'worker action' was possible except in the spontaneous and unorganised form of popular risings, riots against high prices in times of crisis, or strikes, which were numerous under the Restoration and the July Monarchy, but short-lived, local, and isolated. In fact, the working mass, at least until 1830, remained closely associated with the class that supplied it with a living, the bourgeoisie. July 1830 was at once the test of this fidelity and its culmination. The people had fought and won only to be cheated of their victory — and henceforth they sensed it. At Peterloo, bourgeois and proletarians had clashed; in Paris in 1830, they fought side by side against the forces of reaction. The two events could not be more dissimilar; and yet they both played their part in the emergence of the working class consciousness.

In France, however, this awareness continued to develop slowly, because it was not galvanised by leaders who could understand, inspire, and use the people. Those who emerged at its head for a few weeks in 1848 failed to make the grade and were soon swept aside by a unanimous and anxious bourgeoisie. Repressive legislation, the source of worker passivity, was established by the second Empire.

Yet the ground gained had been gained for good. The proletariat could no longer be ignored. Legislation passed in 1864 at last allowed it to form associations; at the same time came the founding of the First International, whose success among French workers was remarkable (250,000 members in 1870).

Thereafter, the door stood open for the labour movement and its long-repressed political ambitions. These ambitions were to develop — slowly as yet, after the Commune outburst — during the Third Republic.

As we have seen, Germany entered the ranks of the industrial nations much later on. Up to around 1850, its industrial centres were few and far between. But even then the living conditions of the German workers were poor, though they varied a lot from one state or industry to another. As in France, the states' legislation was repressive and prevented any organisation of labour. Around 1840, however, a definite awareness of the situation and certain political aspirations existed in the artisan and skilled-worker milieux, which stood on the border-line between the incipient proletariat and the petty bourgeoisie (impoverished but better educated than the working mass). With the possible exception of Prussia, the states were small enough for the individual to feel the full weight of their cumbersome administration. Extremist, sometimes anarchist ideas found a ready hearing in this group. Weitling and Hess, soon followed by Marx and Lassalle, were heard or read by those who could do so. Press censorship was severe, the police were active. Hence the first associations (the Ligue des Justes of 1837, which became the League of Communists in 1847) were formed in exile, in Switzerland, Paris, Brussels, or London. Their premisses were intellectual, their aspirations political; their plans of action were largely influenced by the utopias of French socialist thinking. Not surprisingly, they made little impact on the masses.

Up to 1848, the German states had monarchical regimes in which power was invested in the landed nobility. The bourgeoisie itself had a restricted part to play; Marx saw clearly that the dictatorship of the proletariat would have to be preceded in Germany by a bourgeois revolution. Though that of 1848 did not go far enough, it at least allowed the entrepreneurial class to accelerate the industrialisation of Germany and, between 1850 and 1870, behind the well-protected barriers of the Zollverein, to turn their country into a great power. Large industry and the railways attracted a considerable mass of workers into the towns, where they were subjected to the conditions mentioned above. As in Britain at the start of the century or pre-1848 France, this mass, whose standard of living knew no improvement, remained largely unaware. But it had the advantage of being taken in hand by extremely dynamic leaders — all of bourgeois origin. Lassalle, its hero, organised, as early as 1863, the first labour party, the Allgemeiner Deutscher Arbeiterverein, but was killed in a duel near Geneva the following year. In 1869, two (disowned) disciples of Marx, Wilhelm Liebknecht and August Bebel, founded the Social-Democrat Party.

Two parties were no doubt too many, when neither Britain nor France had as yet any organised labour or 'socialist' parties: the working class would have nothing to do with them until they agreed on a common, non-revolutionary platform at Gotha in 1875, after which their membership gradually grew. In the meanwhile, a minority of workers had organised themselves into trade unions (as early as 1848, then again from 1860 onwards); but those concerned were as yet limited to the marginal branches of the young working class, privileged like the printers or on the contrary completely neglected like the tobacco workers. The more liberal co-operatives of Schulze-Delitzsch or Raiffeisen did not have much impact either. The mass was still passively subjected to the 'alienation' of repressive legislation, of entrepreneurial paternalism, and of the division of its leaders. Social democracy did not become a truly popular movement until after the period of economic recession from 1870 to 1890 — at virtually the same moment as the labour movement was reaching maturity in the other countries as well. For indeed, however diverse the national chronologies of the labour movement and the evolution of the various countries, the culmination — i.e. the entry of the labour parties into the political life of their countries — occurred (give or take a few years) at the same point in time.

Switzerland was no exception. The first socialist party (restricted to German Switzerland) was formed in 1870, and the first trade union federations occurred at around the same time. However, the preliminaries had taken a somewhat different course.

In a few regions with an ancient tradition of cottage industry and a high demographic density, industry (textiles and clocks, then mechanical instruments and, much later, chemicals) had got off the mark very early and had developed rapidly, without ever reaching a very high degree of labour concentration. Swiss industry remained either extremely specialised (clocks, in the Jura), with a low call on unskilled labour, or extremely dispersed. Even if home work, performed by the peasants in the time left over from the land, did not attain the proportions ascribed to it by national historiographic tradition — and this point needs to be verified — it certainly hindered the development of a collective consciousness. The living conditions of the workers, women and children included, were certainly no better than those obtaining in the neighbouring countries; but the number of people subjected to them, in the reduced context of the villages and the low complements of labour employed, probably made them less appreciable. In other respects, the same hindrances as those obtaining in the English proletariat delayed the development of awareness.

In Switzerland, however, the impulsion did not come, as it did elsewhere, from progressive elements of the bourgeoisie, but from the workers themselves. Or rather from two precise and limited categories of worker: the French and German political refugees that the liberal governments of the cantons tolerated on their territory; and the skilled workers, particularly those of the clock industry, whose level of culture was high, sometimes remarkably so. Inspired by the former, and by the delegates to the congresses of the First International that met in Switzerland, it was the latter who created class consciousness among their less fortunate comrades and led the labour movement, with varying shades of leftism (Bakunin-type anarchism played an important part) and with varying degrees of success. But it was thanks to them that the Swiss labour movement aligned itself, in the closing decades of the 19th century, on that of the great industrial nations, while continuing to be less revolutionary than reformist in its mood and ambitions. Class warfare, in the violent sense of the term, can hardly be said to have gained a foothold in Switzerland.

CONCLUSION

Later starters, such as Italy, may have known further types of social evolution, more rapid but also more confused. The struggle of the classes came late in these countries, but it was all the more acute as the mutations of the economy were violent and as the encouraging examples set by the more advanced working classes were appreciable. The social and political stagnation of Italy ultimately threw the door open to Fascism, when the older industrial countries seemed, prior to 1914 or even 1929, to be finding a better solution.

But within the framework of this essay particular circumstances have less weight than the route which, generally speaking, led the working populations towards class-consciousness and political action. The examples, or models, used to describe this process are significant. They bring out how difficult it was for the uneducated and degraded mass to achieve self-consciousness. They illustrate the ignorance, the impotence, and then the distrust of the bourgeoisie with regard to the labour problem. They underline the role of a politically-minded avant-garde of the working class who came to it from outside — from the petty bourgeoisie and the artisan class, repeatedly active, dominant even, in English Chartism, French or German socialism, or Swiss trade-unionism. And lastly they reveal how, despite the ambiguity between the political aims of some and the material and social aspirations of others, despite its contradictions, the working class slowly took form from a shapeless mass, became organised, and ultimately institutionalised.

BIBLIOGRAPHY

There is a mass of published material on the social history of the industrial era, and the list of books and articles gets longer every year. The labour movement is a particular favourite with both historians and sociologists; but much is available on other topics as well: the rise of the industrial bourgeoisie, the birth of the working class, the living conditions of the workers, 19th-century social philosophy and social science, etc. What follows is merely a severely limited choice of readings. Like any choice, it is arbitrary; but it should enable the non-specialist to find his bearings. Most of the recent works cited have more or less extensive bibliographies of their own.

The authors of the period must naturally be consulted first of all. Many of them were remarkably well informed and have left us first-hand and first-class sources of information. But they are too numerous and varied to be cited here, from philosophers and reformers like Saint-Simon, Fourier, Proudhon, Marx, Engels, Bakunin, and so on, to novelists like Balzac, Dickens, Eugène Sue, the Brontës, Jeremias Gotthelf, and many others. The least famous are not necessarily the least interesting.

Works of economic and social history, of which there are many series, and general or national studies of the Industrial Revolution will also be consulted with profit. As the more important of them are listed in the other chapters of Vols. 3 & 4 of the *Fontana Economic History of Europe*, there is no point in giving them again here; it should be noted, however, that many of them make important contributions to our subject.

Extremely specialised works have not been included.

On the societies immediately prior to the Industrial Revolution, see (in addition to the publishers' series of manuals and the general histories): Braudel, F., *Civilisation matérielle et capitalisme (XVe—XVIIIe siècle)*, Vol. I, Paris, 1967; Léon, P., *Economies et sociétés préindustrielles*, Vol. II: *1650–1780*, Paris, 1970; and for France: Goubert, P.,

L'Ancien Régime, Vol. I: *La Société*, Paris, 1966. On the birth of the industrial society, the general essay of: Nef, J. U., *La naissance de la civilisation industrielle dans le monde contemporain*, Paris, 1954; and most of the histories of the Industrial Revolution.

On the bourgeoisie, its rise to power, its attitudes at the start of the industrial era, see first the classic study by Sombart, W., *Der Bourgeois. Zur Geistesgeschichte des modernen Wirtschaftsmenschen*, München-Leipzig, 1913 (often reprinted and translated); more recent works: Morazé, C., *Les bourgeois conquérants*, Paris, 1957; Ponteil, F., *Les classes bourgeoises et l'avènement de la démocratie, 1815–1914*, Paris, 1968; Epsztein, L., *L'économie et la morale aux débuts du capitalisme industriel en France et en Grande-Bretagne*, Paris, 1966; on the French bourgeoisie, the socio-political study by Lhomme, J., *La grande bourgeoisie au pouvoir* (1830–1880), Paris, 1960; and the brilliant essay by Palmade, G., *Capitalisme et capitalistes français au XIXe siècle*, Paris, 1961. On the entrepreneurs, besides the famous works of Schumpeter J. (*Theorie der wirtschaftlichen Entwicklung*, Berlin, 1912; *Capitalism, Socialism and Democracy*, New York, 1942: available in recent reprints and in translation) and Perroux F. (*Le Capitalisme*, Paris, 1951, etc.), see: Redlich, F., *Der Unternehmer, Wirtschafts- und Sozialgeschichtliche Studien*, Göttingen, 1964.

On the working class, its origins, its rise, its living conditions, see the general works on the period and the monumental work: Kuczynski, J., *Die Geschichte der Lage der Arbeiter unter dem Indusirie-Kapitalismus*, 37 vols., Berlin, 1946–68. By the same author, in French translation, and much more succinct: *Les origines de la classe ouvrière*, Paris, 1967.

Other works of a general nature: Fohlen, C., *Le travail au XIXe siècle*, Paris, 1967, brief but useful; Fischer, W., ed., *Wirtschaftsund Sozialgeschichtliche Probleme der frühen Indusirialisierung*, Berlin, 1968, a collection of essays including important contributions to social history (definition of the entrepreneur by R. Braun, B. Hoselitz, F. Redlich; working classes and labour movements by R. Bendix, H. Freudenberger, A. Klima—the last two on Bohemia; etc.). However, most studies on this topic are cast more or less as monographs on one particular country.

For England, see (in addition to the classical but rather outdated studies by the Webbs, the Hammonds, *et hoc genus omne*): Hobsbawm, E. J., *Labouring Men. Studies in the History of Labour*, London, 1964, a collection of previously-published essays; also of importance is Thompson, E., *The Making of the English Working Class*, London, 1965.

For France: Duveau, G., *La vie ouvrière en France sous le Second Empire*, Paris, 1946; Chevalier, L., *Classes laborieuses et classes dangereuses pendant la première moitié du XIXe siècle*, Paris, 1958; Coornaert, E., *Les compagnonnages en France du moyen âge à nos jours*, Paris, 1966.

For Switzerland: Gruner, E., *Die Arbeiter in der Schweiz im 19. Jahrhundert. Soziale Lage, Organisation, Verhältnis zur Arbeitgeber und Staat*, Bern, 1968 (over 1,000 pages!); Braun, R., *Industrialisierung und Volksleben. Veranderungen der Lebensformen unter Einwirkung der verlagsindustriellen Heimarbeit in einem landlichen Industriegebiet (Zurcher Oberland) vor 1800*, Winterthur, 1960; by the same author, *Sozialer und kultureller Wandel in einem ländlichen Industriegebiet, Zürich-Stuttgart, 1965*.

For Germany, several recent books on the labour movement have given much space in their opening chapters to the constitution of the working class and its living conditions; such are: Grebing, H., *Geschichte der deutschen Arbeiterbewegung. Ein Ueberblick*, München, 1966; Wachenheim, H., *Die deutsche Arbeiterbewegung, 1844 bis 1914*, Köln–Opladen, 1967; and, on a limited but interesting problem: Noyes, P. H., *Organization and Revolution. Working-Class Associations in the German Revolutions of 1848–1849*, Princeton, N.J., 1966.

As for Italy, the fact that the emergence of its working class (after a late start in industrialisation) coincided with the great developments in European socialism, roughly speaking between 1860 and 1914, has meant that the Italian working class and Italian socialism have been studied simultaneously. See: (a) general works on the Italian economy since unification, in particular *L'economia italiana dal 1860 al 1961*, Milano, 1961, a collective work with a section on social history; Luzzatto, G., *L'economia italiana dal 1861 al 1914*, Vol. I, Milano, 1963, published by the Banca Commerciale Italiana; Caracciolo, A., ed., *La formazione dell'Italia industriale*, Bari, 1969, a collection of essays; (b) works on Italian socialism, such as: Romano, A., *Storia del movimento socialista in Italia*, 3 vols., Milano-Roma, 1954–55; Valliani, L., *Questioni di storia del socialismo*, Torino, 1958; Hostetter, R., *The Italian Socialist Movement*, Vol. I: (*1860–1882*), Princeton, N.J., 1958, and the Italian edition of the same book, Milano, 1963.

8. Agriculture and the Industrial Revolution 1700–1914

Paul Bairoch

INTRODUCTION

The term 'industrial revolution' denoting the period from the middle of the eighteenth century onwards, of gradual transition from traditionally agricultural societies to a type of economy in which industry was predominant has often been criticised on the ground that the idea of 'revolution' conflicts with the idea of gradual transition. But the term is open to a much more justifiable objection, for the industrial revolution was really first and foremost an agricultural revolution which, in the societies where it occurred, permitted and fostered an unprecedented development of the industrial and mining sectors.

Some nine or ten thousand years ago (or even much longer according to some sources), the transition to the neolithic civilisation—that is, broadly speaking, from an economy based on gleaning, hunting, and fishing to an economy based on agriculture and live-stock rear ng—had for the first time in the history of mankind afforded a durable surplus of food production secured per worker, and had thus made possible a significant consumption of other than purely food products. This situation led in turn to the initiation of specialised forms of work and the creation of an urban life that brought together certain non-agricultural producers; and this urban existence itself furthered an intellectual and technical development from which were born the c vilisations of antiquity.

But this agricultural surplus was still very meagre, even after the progress accomplished successively by the ancient and western civilisations. Thus, on the eve of the industrial revolution, at the beginning of the eighteenth century, the most highly developed societies still had to keep some 75 to 80% of their labour force employed in agriculture. At the same time the average consumption of food products was not only low in terms of calories but also consisted almost entirely of calories of vegetable origin. Consumption of calories of animal origin (meat, dairy products) was very low since it was costly; at that time it took about eight vegetable calories to produce one animal calorie.

Thus, in simplified terms, we may say that in traditional societies the average agricultural worker produced an amount of foodstuff only about 20 to 30% in excess of his family's consumption. We put it at 20 to 30% (rather than 15 to 25%, as might be deduced from the percentages of employment) so as to take into account the definitely higher food consumption of most of the other social groups. These percentages—this 20 to 30% surplus—acquire special meaning if we take into account a factor often omitted from theories of economic development, namely, the yearly fluctuations of agricultural yields, which even at a national level could amount to an average of over 25%. Consequently, periodical subsistence crises became inevitable, crises greater or less in degree but which at their worst could produce a decline in economic life and hence in the civilisation it supported. For this reason, as long as agricultural productivity had not progressed beyond that stage, it was practically impossible to conceive of a continuous progress in the development of civilisations, let alone of the accelerated scientific and technical progress that is an essential characteristic of modern times.

The profound changes in the system of agricultural production that preceded the industrial revolution brought that particular deadlock to an end. The consequent increase in productivity led in the space of 40 to 60 years to the transition from an average surplus of the order of 25% to something more like 50% or over, thus surpassing—for the first time in the history of mankind—what might be called the the risk-of-famine limit; in other words, a really bad harvest no longer meant, as in the past, serious shortage or actual famine. The agricultural revolution—for so these profound changes in rural life have been rightly called—

ended the deadlock, broke the stranglehold, and thus prepared the way for the industrial revolution.

The aim here is to trace the process through which the agricultural revolution first aroused and then fostered that industrial revolution which has so profoundly and irrevocably influenced the destiny not only of Europe, where it was born, but also of the world. For certain positive or, more usually, negative transformations in the societies of the 'Third World' have arisen directly from the industrialisation of the developed countries; and in this way the whole world has been affected in a relatively short time by the industrial revolution.

It is, moreover, because of these characteristics of irrevocability and depth, together with the suddenness of the phenomenon when compared with the evolution in the centuries that went before, that modern agricultural and industrial developments can be rightly called revolutionary.

The study will consist of three parts. The first part will describe the background of the agricultural revolution and the way in which it was carried out. The second part will study the causes tending to give agriculture a primary role in the development of the industrial revolution. The third and most important part will indicate and describe the numerous ways in which agricultural progress first aroused and then fostered the industrial revolution.

England was the cradle of the industrial revolution and as such will naturally occupy a foremost place in our study. For it was from the British Isles that the industrial revolution penetrated first to Europe and then to North America and Japan.

In order to lighten the text and conform to the usual rules of this series, footnotes have been reduced to a minimum. Consequently, it will not always be possible to give all the sources. The selected bibliography will assist readers who want to pursue the subject further. As to sources, as a general rule authors will be cited in footnotes only when more than one work of theirs is given in the bibliography or when the particular work referred to is only marginally concerned with this study and therefore does not appear in the bibliography.

THE AGRICULTURAL REVOLUTION

Before embarking, in the two following parts, on the effects of agricultural development on the industrial revolution, let us first consider the nature of what has for more than a century been termed the 'agricultural revolution.'[1] This involves answering two questions, already briefly touched on in the Introduction:

    i Was there really a profound change and break in the evolution of agricultural life in Western Europe, and if so, when did it occur?

   ii What are the characteristic features of the 'agricultural revolution'?

FACTS AND DATES

That an important break occurred in the technical conditions, and hence in the productivity, of agriculture in Western Europe, and first of all in England, between 1600 and 1800 is an established fact.

From 1800 onwards the labour productivity of agriculture[2] increased at an annual rate of around 1%; this rate varied according to the period and the country but on a long term (70 to 100 years) in no country engaged in agricultural development did it fall below 0.5% or rise above 2%. These figures, however, refer to the nineteenth

1. This term would seem to have been in use for at least a century, for though it does not figure in Adam Smith's *The Wealth of Nations* or in David Ricardo's *The Principles of Political Economy and Taxation*, Marx uses it in *Das Kapital*. Further research might even disclose an earlier use of the term.

2. In general, 'productivity' in this study will be taken to mean the gross labour productivity. On the other hand, calculations of productivity for periods before the twentieth century obviously do not include the concept of annual amount of work; these calculations are always based on the importance of the workers in the sectors under consideration. Even today, assessing variations in the amount of work raises serious problems of data, especially in the case of agriculture.

century; for since the middle of the twentieth century most of the developed countries have experienced a considerable acceleration in the rate of increase of agricultural productivity, even surpassing 5% per annum in many countries and, remarkably and unprecedented, exceeding the average rate of increase in industrial productivity.

Up to 1600 any long-term advance in agricultural productivity was almost non-existent, or at the most extremely slow and coupled with alternating phases of advance or regression. It can fairly certainly be affirmed that the level of agricultural productivity in Western Europe at the beginning of the seventeenth century was fundamentally no different from that of twenty centuries earlier, in other words from Roman times. It is even possible that Roman agriculture had reached a technical, and therefore a productivity, level higher than that prevailing in a great part of Europe in the seventeenth century. This does not, however, imply that no progress at all was made in Europe, for we must not forget the difference prevailing at the dawn of our era between what might then have been termed the developed regions of the Roman Empire and the 'underdeveloped regions,' a description covering most of Europe except for the Italian peninsula. It is obviously almost impossible to evaluate the difference between the average productivity of agriculture in Gaul or Britain at the beginning of the Roman Empire and that of French or British agriculture at the time of Louis XIII or Charles I, but it was certainly not more than 50%—a difference, in other words, which in the eighteenth and nineteenth centuries could have been produced within fifty years, and within less than ten years in the second half of the twentieth century.

Between the Latin treatises on agriculture of Cato, Columella, Palladio, and Varro and those of Fitzherbert, Tusser, Tarello, Serres or Weston there is a gap in time of seventeen to nineteen centuries, but very little difference in the level of the agrarian knowledge they expound. Moreover, the agricultural handbooks of the Renaissance in Europe derive their substance from the manuals of the Roman Empire. If we except the island formed by Flanders

—whence, incidentally, most of the ideas and principles of
of the agricultural revolution came—and a few other
restricted areas (notably the Palatinate and the Po valley),
European agriculture in the early seventeenth century from
the technical point of view still closely resembled that of the
beginning of our era, and was in any case not superior to
that of the Roman world from which its civilisation derived.

The break in Europe's agricultural evolution also becomes
apparent with the almost total disappearance, from the
second half of the nineteenth century onwards, of famines in
Western Europe. Before the beginning of the seventeenth
century England experienced an average of twelve famines
per century. We know a good deal more about the subsequent period, but even so, only four famines can be attributed to the seventeenth century, five to the eighteenth,
and just one (in 1812) to the nineteenth. Thus it can be said
that between 1600 and 1800 a definite break occurred in the
evolution of conditions of agricultural production.

We must now try to date this break rather more precisely. There is a general tendency today, in the light of
recent research, to assign an earlier date than used to be
thought likely to both the agricultural revolution and most
of the significant modifications in the economic structure.
Given the inevitably gradual nature of the agricultural
revolution, a gap of ten to twenty years can normally be
expected in the interpretation given by different authors
trying to localise the point of inflection of a given curve. It
may even differ by as much as fifty to a hundred years,
according to whether the beginning of a phenomenon is
taken to be its earliest manifestations or the point at which it
began to exercise a perceptible influence, a criterion which
we ourselves would adopt and which is also the one more
generally used. For examples can always be found of a
limited early application of new techniques or methods of
production that, however, have very little influence on the
general conditions of economic life or even on the particular sector they affect. Remote precedents can be found
for every invention or innovation introduced by the agricultural or the industrial revolutions. The method of dating a

phenomenon from its earliest manifestations would, if strictly applied, lead to ante-dating those revolutions by at least twenty centuries.

As far as the agricultural revolution is concerned, though fresh research may still cause the generally accepted timing to be revised, it seems almost unthinkable that it can have begun much before the early eighteenth century. A simple example will suffice to prove this. In the England of that time, by all accounts, the rural population was very dominant: some three-quarters of the labour force was still engaged in agriculture. National per capita consumption of calories was still very low, at most about 2,400, which, together with exported surplus, would represent a domestic production of some 2,450 calories per person. Now, if agricultural production had advanced from the beginning of the seventeenth century at an average yearly rate of 0.7% (the rate in the nineteenth century was about 1%), English agriculture in 1600, with even as much as 80% of the working population engaged in it, and without exports, could have produced only 1,400 calories per head (the figure for 1650 would be 1,800 calories, and for 1550 only 1,000). Since the minimum physiological consumption of calories per person is around 1,900, and since our estimates for the early 1700's were deliberately put high, we may conclude that the phase when agricultural productivity began to increase at a relatively high rate must certainly have begun later than 1650, even if we allow for a gradual rise at the outset.

On the other hand, and here we can be even more definite, the outset must have been before 1750, for by that time, as we shall see, important surpluses of agricultural products already existed. This confirms us in thinking that the majority of historians are probably right in assigning the start of the English agricultural revolution to the early years of the eighteenth century. Moreover, while qualitative estimates are always open to doubt, good quantitative data are also available to demonstrate the progress of agricultural production between 1700 and 1750: for foreign trade statistics show an increasing surplus of cereal exports, which expanded so greatly that England could even be described as the 'granary of Europe.' English cereal exports were quite insignificant throughout the seventeenth century, but from 1700 onwards sales of cereals and flour rose sharply and steadily to reach, in 1750, a total of 200,000 tons, or 30 kg. per head, which, on a basis of a daily per capita consumption of 2,500 calories, would represent 13% of the country's total food needs.

The fact that agriculture in England had by 1750 reached a level of production which permitted the export of 13% of domestic food consumption, is in itself sufficient proof of the great changes it had undergone. Moreover, the population itself had probably increased during the years 1700 to 1750 (by 5 to 7%, according to recent estimate), per capita consumption according to available indicators had also increased, and the proportion of the labour force engaged in agriculture had diminished. Yet in those fifty years there was no fall in the export of other agriculture or livestock products; wool products, in particular, even showed a marked increase, thus proving that cereal exports were not replacing other items of agricultural production.

Thus it can be stated with reasonable certainty that the agricultural revolution began in England about 1700, or at most a quarter of a century earlier. True, Kerridge's recent and well-documented study, unlike that of Chambers and Mingay, inclines to an even earlier date. The choice of the early eighteenth century does not, of course, exclude the possibility of progress or the introduction and application of certain new agricultural techniques in England even before that date; but it does mean that from that date onwards such progress was sufficiently widespread to exercise a perceptible influence on the English agricultural economy as a a whole.

It is much more difficult to establish a chronology for the start of the agricultural revolution in other countries. Not only are there far fewer studies of the subject than in the case of England, but also the regional differences in most of the countries are much more marked. To say, for example, that the agricultural revolution reached Italy in 1820-30 could be quite misleading, given the present state of under-development of agriculture in large parts of the South and the high level already reached in the seventeenth century in the Po valley. In addition, the absence of political unity in many of the European countries before the mid-nineteenth century further complicates the question. For those reasons the dates given below must be taken as only approximate and subject to revision in the light of studies now being undertaken for most of those countries.

Approximate dates for the outset of the agricultural revolution in various countries are: England, 1690-1700; France, 1750-60; United States, 1760-70; Switzerland, 1780-90; Germany, Denmark, 1790-1800; Austria, Italy, Sweden, 1820-30; Russia, Spain, 1860-70.

For Belgium and the Netherlands it would be quite arbitrary to assign a date, for, as we shall see in the next section, it was from Flanders and Brabant (the territories forming the Low Countries in the past) that the majority of the ideas originated on which the first stages of the agricultural revolution were based.

WAYS AND MEANS OF THE AGRICULTURAL REVOLUTION

Put briefly, the onset of the agricultural revolution consisted in the accelerated application, in sparsely populated territories, of agricultural techniques that had been gradually developed in regions confronted with the problem of a high-density population.

It is difficult to determine whether the development of the Low Countries in the sixteenth and seventeenth centuries, based largely on international trade, made possible a population density higher than in the rest of Europe,[3] or whether it was that density itself that led to the economic

3. In 1800, population density for the whole of Europe was 31 inhabitants per sq. km., as compared with 85 for the Low Countries. At the beginning of the eighteenth century, population density in the Low Countries had been of the order of 70 to the sq. km. as compared with 40 in England and France.

policy adopted. The same question can be asked for agriculture; but in that case it seems likely that since the Low Countries, thanks to their foreign trade, were no longer bound by restrictions of food supplies (having by then become a net importer of cereals), the increase in population led to intensified demand, and this in turn furthered a gradual development of agricultural techniques. But whatever the reason, the fact remains that from the sixteenth century onwards the densely populated plains of Flanders and Brabant had become, as Slicher van Bath notes, the Mecca of European agricultural experts.

During the seventeenth and eighteenth centuries the whole of England, in a sense, learnt from the Flemish school and, by applying its agricultural techniques in a much less densely populated countryside, achieved a strikingly higher increase of productivity in this vital sector of the economy. For though agriculture in the Low Countries had reached a relatively advanced technical level, with yields two or three times above those in the rest of Europe, the difference in productivity was not directly related to the difference in yields, since the shortage of land per worker led to a level of productivity fairly close to that of the other Western and Central European countries. It is important to avoid the frequent error of confusing 'level of yield' with 'level of productivity.' In agriculture extensive cultivation makes it possible to achieve a high level of productivity in spite of fairly low yields. The example of North America today, though falsified by the presence of elaborate agricultural machinery, illustrates this point. Yields of wheat in North America are about 16 quintals per hectare (16 cwt., U.S., per 2.5 acres or 24 bushels per acre), as compared with 30 quintals in France (or 45 bushels per acre). Now agricultural productivity in North America is about three times that of France; with a comparable yield this would make North American productivity six times greater. If we compare the situation of North American wheat with that of Indian rice, we find similar yields, although North American agriculture has some fifty times the productivity of Indian agriculture. When conditions more closely resembled those that concern us here, around 1840, cereal yields in Belgium were 50% higher than in France, although according to our estimates (see Part II, section c) agricultural productivity in France was then slightly higher.

We have dwelt at some length on this distinction because it is probably this that explains why Flanders and Brabant, despite their high level of agricultural techniques, were not the birthplace of the industrial revolution: the level of productivity there was probably insufficient to engender an important industrial development. As to why it was in England that the new techniques spread more rapidly, that is another and more complicated story, which falls outside this study, and one in which the question marks would be far more frequent than the affirmations, even the conditional ones. Suffice it to say that it was perhaps in part a result of the frequent contacts between England and the Low Countries, in particular the influx of Protestant émigrés turned out of Flanders under the Spanish domination. A hundred and fifty years later English Catholics played a similar role in exporting the industrial revolution to the Continent where, as W. O. Henderson notes, English entrepreneurs and, more particularly, technicians played a considerable part in industrialisation.

But if in the earliest stages of the agricultural revolution England merely copied Flemish methods, local innovations nevertheless soon gained the upper hand; and from about 1730 down to the middle of the nineteenth century it was England that became the Mecca of agricultural experts, and its example was the model for the agricultural revolution in the rest of Europe, as well as the United States.

Let us now consider what were the new techniques of the agricultural revolution whose geographical itinerary has been briefly outlined above. The first phases of this revolution were characterised by certain methods, presented here in a very summarised form and listed under six headings. The order in which they are given is not chronological—for most of these innovations were simultaneous if viewed in historical perspective—but rather reflects their relative influence; though too much importance should not be attached to that criterion, since their actual impact is very difficult to determine.

Gradual elimination of fallow land and its replacement by continuous rotation of crops. Throughout most of Europe traditional agriculture was based, in order to avoid exhausting the soil, on two main types of rotation: biennial rotation, a year of cultivation alternating with a year of fallow; and triennial rotation, or two years of cultivation followed by a year of fallow. Progress consisted in the diffusion of a system of crop rotation usually extending over a period of three or four years (though sometimes as much as six to twelve years) during which fallow completely disappeared. The soil was regenerated through planting a sequence of crops, each of which had a different consumption, at a different depth, of various chemical substances from the soil; through the introduction of plants having a regenerative effect; and, above all, through more lavish manuring, which was furthered by the expansion of live-stock-rearing made possible by the inclusion of fodder crops in the system of rotation. This type of exploitation of the land, involving as it did an effective integration between farming and herding, led to the gradual elimination of the fallow lands and hence to an increase, if not in agricultural productivity, at least in the productivity of the land itself.

Here we must touch briefly on the reorganisation of the systems of land ownership, and in particular the disappearance, varying in time but general throughout Europe, of certain quasi-collective forms of property and labour, affecting different proportions of the land in each country. While the changes in the methods of cultivation did not always lead to such reorganisation, they obviously furthered it everywhere; and reorganisation of land ownership, in turn, furthered the introduction of new agricultural techniques. It is interesting to note how, 150 to 200 years later, the appearance of agricultural machinery, viable only over large areas, resulted in pressure in Europe towards more collective forms for certain kinds of work (harvesting, threshing, etc.) and installations (dairies, oil or wine presses, etc.); for the sizes of the farms were much smaller in Europe than in the United States, where most of the machinery was first developed.

Lastly, mention must be made of a certain synchronisation between the agricultural revolution and the disappearance of serfdom in the regions of Europe where it still survived.

Introduction or extension of new crops. This aspect of the agricultural revolution was to a great extent a direct result of point 1, for continuous rotation implies the inclusion of new crops in the cycle. It is difficult and arbitrary to establish a distinction between the introduction of new crops and their wider cultivation; the economic effects are in any case the same, so we shall treat them together. Among the food or fodder crops that were new to most of Europe or that now became more widely grown there, the main ones were the 'famous' turnips, clover and other less important fodder crops, colza, hops, buckwheat, maize, carrots, cabbages, and, lastly, potatoes, the economic importance of which has been insufficiently stressed (as far as I know the only book on the subject is Salaman's).[4]

Improvement of traditional farm implements and introduction of new implements. First and foremost came the improvement of the plough (and also, in certain more backward areas, the replacement of the hoe by the plough), for it was here that the greatest efforts were made. Progress was carried out on two complementary fronts: improvements in the form and structure of the plough, and the increasing use of iron. Other innovations were the scythe, which gradually replaced the sickle, the sower, replacing broadcast sowing, and the horse-hoe. These innovations contributed towards increasing the productivity of agriculture, but the machine era itself was still to come (see end of this chapter).

Selection of seed and breeding animals. This period saw the be-

4. R. N. Salaman, *The History and Social Influence of the Potato*, Cambridge, 1949.

ginning of a long, patient, and methodical effort, still in progress today, in the selection of seed and of breeding animals. In the early stages the most mportant advances were in live-stock-breeding, resulting in rapid increases in weight and in milk yields.

Extension and improvement of arable land. Land clearance is obviously a constant feature in agrarian history, but in this period the process was speeded up and new techniques were used to drain marshy areas. At this time, too, drainage of humid land was introduced or became much more widely practised.

Extension of the use of horses for farm work. The horse's speed of traction is on average 50% above that of oxen, and their greater use in agriculture consequently led to a corresponding rise in productivity in a great deal of farm work. Thus, whereas in the seventeenth century using oxen it was possible to plough 0.4 hectares (about one acre) a day, with horses the figure rose to 0.5 to 0.6 hectares; improvements in the plough itself brought that figure up to 0·8 hectares towards the end of the eighteenth century, and by the middle of the nineteenth century steam traction increased it to 5 hectares a day (today a good tractor-driver with a modern machine can plough 60 hectares—about 168 acres —in 12 hours).

These, briefly, and in simplified terms, are the main innovations characterising the agricultural revolution. A second group of innovations was introduced later. These consisted of new agricultural machines[5] (chiefly reapers and threshers), improvements in traditional implements, the first use of non-animal traction, and the introduction of chemical fertilisers. At this point, too, the geographical

5. Here again we can see a typical example of the early date of certain inventions. To take the case of cereal reaping, a first advance was the replacement of the sickle by the scythe (sickles are indeed still widely used in many under-developed countries), reaping machines came only much later. Now, it seems that the Gauls already made use of a sort of reaper.

centre of impulse for these innovations moved over from England to the United States (except for fertilisers, where Germany played a prime role); the enormous extent of land available in the United States[6] favoured the development of cultivation by machinery, which was to initiate the second great change in the conditions of agricultural work and productivity. According to calculations made for the United States, in 1800 it took an average of 373 hours of work to produce 100 bushels of wheat; the figure fell to 233 in 1840, 152 in 1880, and 108 in 1900 (and to 34 in 1945-49, and 10 in 1966-70). But with this new group of innovations we have already reached the mid-nineteenth century, which is outside the scope of our study's historical framework.

REASONS FOR AGRICULTURE'S PRIMARY ROLE

'Ploughing and pasture are the two breasts of France.' This quotation, attributed to Henry IV's minister Sully, and familiar to all French children from their history books, reappears in a more generalised and systematised form a century and a half later in the '*Tableau economique*' of the physiocrats. This scheme, regarded today as the first attempt to provide a plan of distribution of the national income, was at the time considered to be a major, indeed inspired, discovery of Quesnay. It aimed to demonstrate statistically that the only source of wealth lay in agriculture, whose total production, and above all the surplus resulting from the difference between the farmers' consumption and their production, was the determining factor in the volume of all other economic activity. This prime role of agriculture is recognised, if less explicitly, by the so-called father of political economy, perhaps more justly to be termed the apostle of industrialisation, Adam Smith, who, incidentally,

6. Around 1880 available agricultural land (including pasture) per male worker employed in agriculture was as follows 71 hectares (175·5 acres) in the United States, 8 hectares (19·8 acres) in Great Britain, 6 hectares (14·8 acres) in France and Germany, 5 hectares (12·4 acres) in Italy, 3 hectares (7·4 acres) in Belgium.

himself owed much to the physiocrats: 'The capital employed in agriculture, therefore, not only puts into motion a greater quantity of productive labour than any equal capital employed in manufactures, but in proportion too to the quantity of productive labour which it employs, it adds a much greater value to the annual produce of the land and labour of the country, to the real wealth and revenue of its inhabitants. Of all the ways in which a capital can be employed, it is by far the most advantageous to society.'[7]

The attribution to agriculture of this prime role is a natural consequence of its economic importance in pre-industrial-revolution societies or 'traditional' societies, as we shall call them. The first of this part's four sections will be devoted to this major fact, a fact that tends to be forgotten in the more developed societies of today, where farming has become only one among a score of other forms of employment. The next two sections will deal with chronological developments in most of the European countries, and with the relationship between the levels of agricultural and industrial development. The fourth will be a more theoretical essay demonstrating the impossibility, up to the middle of the nineteenth century, of any important industrial growth without previous, or at any rate concomitant, agricultural development.

THE IMPORTANCE OF AGRICULTURE IN TRADITIONAL SOCIETIES

As we have just said, in highly developed societies today farming is only one among a score of other forms of employment; but in traditional societies 16 out of every 20 people were engaged in agriculture. Detailed statistics of the employed population are a sort of by-product of development, and they are obviously difficult to secure for the traditional societies of the past. Estimates or statistics available for some countries before their industrialisation (e.g. England in 1688, where some 75% of the working population was

7. Adam Smith, *The Wealth of Nations*, 1777 (London, Dent, Everyman edition, 1960, vol. I, p. 325).

employed in agriculture; France, c. 1700, 80-85%; Finland, 1754, 81%) tend to suggest that an average of about 80% of the working population was in agricultural employment. Adjusted figures[8] drawn from the earliest censuses in European countries and the U.S.A. are given in Table 1.

TABLE 1   Adjusted percentages[8] of working population employed in agriculture; from earliest available censuses.

	Date	%		Date	%
Austria	1869	68	Italy	1871	64
Belgium	1846	51	Netherlands	1849	53
Bulgaria	1910	82	Norway	1891	57
Czechoslovakia	1921	40	Poland	1897	70
Denmark	1850	60	Portugal	1890	65
Finland	1754	82	Rumania	1913	80
France	1856	54	Spain	1860	72
Germany	1882	47	Sweden	1860	67
Great Britain	1841	26	Switzerland	1880	42
Greece	1920	69	Russia	1926	82
Hungary	1857	74	United States	1850	65
Ireland	1841	53	Yugoslavia	1921	82

Source: International Historical Statistics, vol. I: 'The Working Population and its Structure,' by T. Deldycke, H. Gelders, J. M. Limbor, under the supervision of P. Bairoch; Brussels, Institut de Sociologie, 1968; Gordon and Breach, New York, 1969.

These figures confirm the estimates cited above, taking into account the relative stage of development of the different countries. It should also be noted that the percentage of the working population engaged in agriculture

8. The percentages of population employed in agriculture have been adjusted by us so as to take into account the frequent over-estimate of services arising from the inclusion under this heading of domestic servants working on farms. This has been done by calculating the average importance of services at different stages of development on the basis of the least dubious statistics. Calculation of percentages also includes unemployed persons and ill-defined activities.

in under-developed countries (including China) in 1930 was around 78 (75 in 1950, 73 in 1960).

It is obviously dangerous to use concepts and classifications of our present-day society to describe traditional societies with a much greater interpenetration of economic activities. For example, textile work in those societies was mainly rural, and this was also true, if to a lesser extent, of building and certain activities connected with transport and distribution; the farmer often delivered and sold his surplus produce himself. But such activities were generally subsidiary and represented only a small proportion of the farmers' total work, as can be deduced from the various estimates on the structure of consumption. Here food occupies by far the most important place (around 70 to 80%). And, while clothing accounts for 12 to 14%, it must not be forgotten that the raw materials for it were provided by agriculture or livestock-breeding. This was also the case for other non-food products, such as candles, soap, rope, etc.

Within such an economic structure, agriculture must clearly have played a major role in the process of development. Without the participation of such a large part of the population and, consequently, of consumers and production, it is impossible to conceive of profound changes such as were introduced by the industrial revolution. But while agriculture played an essential part in this development, the point of departure of the development might conceivably, in theory at least, have lain outside agriculture. This theoretical possibility, slender enough in itself (as we shall see in the fourth section of this part), appears even less likely when we examine the timing of the development in the different countries that became industrialised.

CHRONOLOGY OF AGRICULTURAL AND INDUSTRIAL DEVELOPMENT

We have already examined the chronological development of the agricultural revolution in various countries. We shall now compare the course of that development with the corresponding features in industrial development. It is by no means easy to demonstrate the absence of synchronisation between two interdependent phenomena. For example, in so far as agricultural development led to the expansion and speeding up of industrialisation, the consequences followed hard on the heels of the causes. And if, in the case of industrialisation, one compares the earliest dates with the most advanced dates in agricultural progress, one runs the risk of seriously reducing the very gap one is trying to demonstrate. In the following pages, therefore, to avoid this danger we shall try to take the earliest dates in each case.

To take England first. There, as we have seen, the start of the agricultural revolution can be put at about 1700. Now the traditional and generally accepted date for the beginning of the industrial revolution is 1760. Give or take ten years either way, the conclusion remains that the two revolutions were separated by about half a century.

In France, the beginning of the agricultural revolution was around 1750-60. Accelerated development of industry began only about 20 or 30 years later. Despite the organised efforts of the public authorities from 1747 onwards to make known Kay's flying shuttle, it aroused only fleeting interest, and not until 1787 that it began to be widely used. The spinning jenny was first introduced in 1761, and the expansion of the cotton industry began around 1770. That date also saw the beginning of a greater demand for iron (as can be seen from statistics of iron imports from Sweden). The bad harvest years preceding the Revolution of 1789 slowed down agricultural progress. The revolutionary period itself, as well as the First Empire, periods when war commandeered a high proportion of men and resources, witnessed virtual stagnation in agriculture and industry. After 1815 the textile industry developed rapidly; and it was then, too, rather than later, that agriculture once again began to progress. Thus, from the standpoint of economic evolution, these years represent a period of pause rather than retreat, since there was no reduction in the per capita supplies of food available.

France and England are the two main countries for which data and studies are the most available on this crucial period of development. This interest is justified by the important role these countries played—England as the cradle of the industrial revolution, and France as the first great continental European country to follow her example. Italy and Germany, of course, were not unified politically, hence not statistically, either, until after they had embarked on the process of development. Belgium, a country to which industrialisation came early, did not become a State until 1830. For these reasons we shall deal only briefly with the chronological development in other countries, especially since historical research will probably in due course provide more accurate data.

In Germany, agriculture made rapid progress from the beginning of the nineteenth century, while industry advanced only slowly. By 1850, when industry really began to develop, agriculture had effected great advances.

As we have seen, Flanders and certain parts of the Walloon regions were the place of origin for a number of technical innovations in agriculture in the seventeenth century. Agriculture in the regions later to form Belgium reached a very high level, and between 1760 and 1790 they were net exporters of cereals. There is as yet no detailed overall study on the industrial revolution in Belgium, but the available data suggest that this country can be regarded as the first to have imitated England's example and embarked, in the late eighteenth or early nineteenth century, on the industrial revolution.

Thus in general the speeding-up of agricultural development preceded that of industry by 30 to 50 years, so suggesting the propulsive role of agriculture in the process of the industrial revolution.

RELATIONSHIP BETWEEN AGRICULTURAL AND INDUSTRIAL LEVELS OF DEVELOPMENT

Setting out from the postulate that an increase in the level of agricultural productivity led to an industrial develop-

TABLE 2 Index of level of development of agriculture in various European countries and the U.S.A.

Note. 100=net annual production of 10 million vegetable-based calories per male worker in agriculture. The figures are rounded off to the nearest 5.

	1810	1840	1860	1880	1900
Austria	—	75	85	100	110
Belgium	—	100	110	130	150
France	70	115	145	140	155
Germany	—	75	105	145	220
Italy	—	40	50	60	60
Russia	—	70	75	70	90
Spain	—	—	110	70	75
Sweden	65	75	105	115	130
Switzerland	—	80	90	120	150
United Kingdom	140	175	200	235	225
United States	—	215	225	290	310

TABLE 3 Level of Industrial Development in various European countries and the U.S.A.

Rank	1810	1840	1860	1880	1900
1	U.K.	U.K.	U.K.	U.K.	U.K.
2	Belgium	Belgium	Belgium	Belgium	U.S.A.
3	U.S.A.	Switzerland	U.S.A.	U.S.A.	Belgium
4	France	U.S.A.	Switzerland	Switzerland	Switzerland
5	Switzerland	France	France	Germany	Germany
6	Austria	Austria	Austria	France	France
7	Germany	Germany	Germany	Austria	Sweden
8	Sweden	Sweden	Sweden	Sweden	Austria
9	Italy	Italy	Spain	Spain	Spain
10	Russia	Russia	Italy	Italy	Italy
11	Spain	Spain	Russia	Russia	Russia

Note. Where several countries fall in the same rank they are given in alphabetical order.

ment, it is logical to seek a relationship between the levels of productivity in agriculture and development in industry. In one of our studies[9] we have calculated an index figure for agricultural productivity comparable in time and space for eleven developed countries of today; and with the aid of six different indices we have classified these countries according to their level of industrial development.

The index of agricultural productivity is based on a calculation of the net production of calories of vegetable origin per male worker employed in agriculture (see Table 2, p. 472).

The classification of countries by level of industrial development is given in Table 3, based on an analysis of the ranks of countries according to the following indices: per capita consumption of raw cotton, per capita production of smelted iron, index of level of development of the railways, per capita consumption of coal, and per capital fixed motive power.

Comparing the two classifications given in Tables 2 and 3—by level of agricultural productivity and of industrial development—we find a close relationship. This relationship appears even closer in a dynamic perspective, comparing the agricultural classification for a particular date with the industrial classification for subsequent dates. Thus, calculating the rate of correlation between the two classifications on a basis of the year 1880 (where the margin of error is lower than for earlier dates) we arrive at the positive figure of 0.89. This positive correlation rises to 0.93 if we compare the agricultural classification of 1880 with that for industry of 1900. This close relationship provides an important additional proof of the historical existence of a cause-and-effect link between agricultural and industrial development in Europe.

9. 'Niveaux de développement économique de 1810 à 1910,' in *Annales, Economies, Sociétés, Civilisations*, 1965, No. 6. For the present study we have completed the data in this article by adding Austria; on the other hand, data for 1910 and for Japan are omitted here.

IMPOSSIBILITY OF SIGNIFICANT INDUSTRIAL GROWTH
WITHOUT A PRIOR, OR AT LEAST CONCOMITANT,
DEVELOPMENT IN AGRICULTURE

The period under consideration falls, let us remember, within the framework of the economic, social, and above all technical structure that pertained in European societies in the seventeenth and eighteenth centuries.

The three points just examined (the role of agriculture in traditional societies; chronological developments; and the relationship between the levels of agriculture and of industry) have enabled us to demonstrate the primary role played by agriculture in the industrial revolution. But this merely confirms the conclusions from a logical consideration of structural conditions before the agricultural revolution. The low level of agricultural productivity in fact constituted an obstacle to any significant expansion of the industrial sector: for an expansion of that sector presupposes, at least in the early stages, an increase in its working population, which would obviously lead to an equivalent reduction in the proportion of the agricultural working population. Now, a reduction in agricultural employment would have meant a fall in agricultural supplies at least equal to the proportion of workers taken away from agriculture. We say 'at least equal,' because most agricultural concerns had probably not reached the stage of diminishing returns. And in that case a fall in the amount of agricultural work done would have resulted in a more than proportionate fall in production. Such a fall would have led not only to undernourishment, with corresponding repercussions on the productivity of labour in both agriculture and industry, but also to a diminution of resources, thereby reducing the possibilities of sale of surplus industrial production.

Indeed the effects of lowering agricultural resources for long handicapped the possibilities of sale of industrial products. Thus in France up to about 1850 an industrial crisis habitually followed on a bad harvest; and up to the end of the nineteenth century there was a close correlation between the volume of agricultural and of industrial production. This aspect of the problem emerged also in all the other countries of nineteenth-century Europe where there was a high proportion of farming population (and it still exists in under-developed countries today).

In theory it might have been possible to overcome the difficulty by means of foreign trade, by exporting part of the surplus industrial production created by the increase of employment in the secondary sector in exchange for imports of an amount of agricultural produce equal to the loss sustained through the decline in agricultural employment. But to do that on any permanent scale would have involved a combination of favourable conditions: in particular, the difference in productivity between the agricultural and industrial sectors would need to be large enough to cover the expenses of transport.

In the case of wheat, for instance, available data suggest that before the industrial revolution total costs of transport (including insurance, handling, etc.) represented 100% of the value of the product when transferred from one country to another. For industrial products, transport costs can be estimated at about a third of those for agricultural produce (given the higher specific value of industrial products). For such trade exchanges to be practicable, therefore, the difference in productivity would need to be sufficient to cover the transport costs both of the agricultural produce and of the industrial products supplied in return. And whatever theoretical combinations might be envisaged in the relative levels of agricultural and industrial productivity so as to get round the obstacle of high transport costs (even taking into account the theory of comparative costs), each one presupposes a quite significant difference in the level of productivity of agriculture and industry. Consequently, a fairly advanced degree of previous economic development would be necessary to permit large-scale foreign exchanges.

There is, of course, in theory another possibility, that of a big reduction in transport costs. But, like the earlier assumption, this hypothesis demands a previous stage of development.

These conclusions might seem at first sight to be contradicted by the existence before the industrial revolution of a
flourishing international trade in cereals. This trade fulfilled
a dual function. The first, which might be termed episodic,
does not concern us here: this was the import trade conducted sporadically by most countries in order to alleviate
serious shortages resulting from a fall in domestic production due to climatic or other causes. The second function, on
the other hand, falls within our terms of reference and merits
consideration. It concerns those countries or regions that
regularly had recourse to foreign trade to provide part of
their food consumption in exchange for industrial goods or
services.

A common characteristic of all these cereal-importing
countries or regions is their relatively small demographic
importance, e.g., the Low Countries, the trading towns of
Italy. On the other hand, imported foodstuffs represented
only a small part of their consumption. These two factors
combined meant that this particular trade had only limited
importance within the framework of European economy
as a whole. Thus in the Mediterranean basin, Braudel
calculates that in the sixteenth century cereal trade represented at most 1% of the region's consumption; in the
seventeenth century it might have reached 3% in exceptional years. The percentage is naturally much higher for
regions that imported extensively. Thus, farther north, the
other deficient region, the Low Countries, according to
Slicher van Bath, imported some 13 to 14% of its cereal
consumption in the sixteenth century. But its population
represented only about 3% of the European total.

Thus on a continental scale these imports had only
negligible significance; for before the eighteenth century
less than 1% of total cereal production went into international trade. Trade in other food products was also very
limited.

On the other hand, these purchases of cereals did not
come within the classic network of trade exchanges, based
fundamentally on the import of agricultural products paid
for by export of domestic industrial products. In the trade

network before the industrial revolution, the great majority of products sold in Europe were in fact re-exports, in particular spices and silks from the Far East, or precious metals and sugar from the Americas.

Thus, the only regions to evade the economic constraint imposed by high transport costs and low level of development were those with small populations, situated by the sea and possessing, for historical or geographical reasons, a relatively important fleet and a monopoly or semi-monopoly of purchase trade in extra-European goods. For a real network of exchanges between agricultural and industrial products to become established on a broad and permanent scale, a large part of Europe needed, as we noted earlier, to become engaged in the industrial revolution.

It is, moreover, significant that England waited until after 1840, or some eighty years after the start of her industrial revolution, before she began to import an appreciable part of her foodstuffs. Her real dependence on foreign supplies began only around 1850. Imported wheat represented only 3% of the United Kingdom's consumption in 1811-30, rising to 13% in 1831-51, 30% in 1851-60, and reaching 79% in 1891-95. The Corn Laws, aiming to protect domestic agricultural production, were repealed only in 1846. In France, foodstuff imports were of no significant importance throughout the whole period of development. In Germany around 1890 they represented only 10% of total food needs In Belgium domestic agriculture provided the entire needs in food up to 1870. Even in Japan, it was not until about 1925, or forty-five years after what can be considered as the start of her industrial revolution, that rice imports became significant in relation to consumption.

This late dependence on imported food in certain countries is, moreover, connected with the settlement in certain extra-European regions (notably the United States), of a population that had acquired a high technical level in agriculture, and this development, combined with the availability of vast and fertile stretches of land, made possible the production of cereals at a very low cost. Thus for the period 1866-75 the difference between production costs in the U.S.A. and in France was about 53%, rising to 56% in 1876-85 and to 78% in 1886-95.

In short, to seek a solution by means of international trade signified in a sense transferring the problem, for the country importing industrial goods needed to have sufficient agricultural productivity to allow an important part of its agricultural resources to be allocated for export. Obviously, this condition could only be realised sporadically, when harvests were particularly good; to do so permanently would involve a profound modification in the conditions of agricultural production, including a significant and permanent rise in productivity.

It follows that an increase in agricultural productivity proved to be not only the main cause of the impulse towards industrialisation in England, the cradle of the industrial revolution, and probably in the eight or ten countries that first followed her example, but it was also the principal limiting factor for industrial progress in general in all countries then in course of development, until such time as at least two of the three following conditions could be fulfilled:

    i a significant lowering of transport costs;

    ii a clear-cut lead in productivity of industrially developed countries over countries still largely agricultural;

    iii development of agriculture in certain countries of recent European immigration, with or without a parallel development of industry.

It was when these three factors were realised almost simultaneously that England was able to move over from an importation of wheat insignificant in relation to her consumption, which had prevailed up to 1840, to an almost total dependence on imported supplies after 1880. But that came about a century after her industrial take-off.

It might have been possible for countries other than England to move over more quickly (in relation to their own evolution) to the stage of dependence on foreign sources of foodstuffs, seeing that the first two of the three conditions mentioned above were in process of being realised as an indirect result of England's development. For both the reduction in transport costs and the rise in agricultural production in new countries were consequences of British development, the transport reduction as a result of technical progress and expanding trade, the new agriculture arising from the use of British techniques and from England's demand for agricultural produce. A third factor was population pressure in England resulting from her agricultural and industrial revolutions, which caused numbers of people to emigrate to the new countries, providing the basis for their development.

This possibility, however, did not really materialise until about 1870-80, for it was not till then that transport costs reached a low enough level to cease impinging too unfavourably on the cost of imported foodstuffs. From that date, in consequence, the amount of foodstuffs coming from the 'new' countries of the Western hemisphere became really significant and began to replace more traditional sources (notably Russia).[10]

But another factor intervened to reduce the possibilities of utilising this pattern of development: industrial products came up against British competition, which continued to

10. The following table shows wheat production in the main European-peopled overseas countries, as compared with world production (yearly averages, in million metric tons)

	About 1850	1868-72	1878-82	1898-1902	1909-13
United States	2·7	7·3	12·3	17·3	18·3
Canada	0·2	0·5	0·9	2·1	5·4
Argentina			0·5	2·1	4·0
Australia	10·1	0·4	0·6	1·1	2·5
TOTAL above	3·1	8·5	14·3	22·5	30·6
World	30·0	50·0	62·0	81·0	102·9

After 1900 the same trend continued, but the rate of increase slowed down considerably. Production in those countries was 45·8 million tons in 1928-32, 71·4 million tons in 1963-67 (world production, 148·5 and 277·7 million tons).

Sources: *Historical Statistics of the United States*, Washington 1960; Retrospective section of the *Annuaire Statistique de la France*; MULHALL M. G., *A Dictionary of Statistics*, London, 1898; *Production Year Book*, F.A.O.; SUNDBARG G., *Aperçus statistiques internationaux*, Stockholm, 1908; MALENBAUM W., *The World Wheat Economy*, Harvard, 1953.

be an obstacle until the other countries reached a stage of industrial development approaching that of Britain.

We therefore reach the conclusion that a rapid passage towards a trading system that would free the economy from dependence on agriculture was virtually impossible for any country whose development began before the last years of the nineteenth century, in other words for any of the major developed economies. And it is interesting to note that that date, which in theory marks the opening of a period characterised by lower transport costs, also provides another im-important landmark: the closure, for the next forty or fifty years, of the list of countries embarking on development. Modifications in the cost of transport were obviously not the only reason for this check in development 'take-off.' Other contributing factors include population inflation, the complexity of modern techniques, and the high cost of industrial investments. But this problem falls outside the present study.[11]

THE INFLUENCE OF AGRICULTURE IN INDUSTRIAL DEVELOPMENT

An essential characteristic of the agricultural revolution, as of all economic progress, is the increase in productivity. For this reason we shall here use the terms 'agricultural development' and 'increase in agricultural productivity' as synonymous.

In this chapter we shall examine the following four aspects of the direct influence of agriculture: the start of the first demographic revolution, the increase in the demand for consumer goods, the birth of the modern iron and steel industry, and the financing of industrialisation.

---

11. Readers wishing to follow up this question may refer to Paul Bairoch's *Révolution industrielle et sous-développement*, Paris, SEDES, 1964, and *Diagnostic de l'évolution économique du Tiers-Monde, 1900-1968* (4th edition) Paris, Gauthier-Villars, 1970 (English translation to be published by Methuen, London) and *Le Tiers-Monde dans l'impasse. Le démarrage économique du XVIIIᵉ au XXᵉ siècle*, Paris, Gallimard, 1971.

THE AGRICULTURAL REVOLUTION AND THE FIRST
DEMOGRAPHIC REVOLUTION

Up to the present there have been three main stages in mankind's demographic evolution. The first came with the great increase in population that probably followed the neolithic revolution wherever it occurred. The transition from a gleaning and hunting economy to a cultivation and livestock-rearing economy made possible a much denser human population. From the neolithic revolution to the beginning or the middle of the eighteenth century, demographic evolution was characterised by three constant features: high rates of birth and mortality; high fluctuations in those rates as a result of wars, famines, and epidemics; and a low rate of long-term advance or decline in population, with high fluctuations in the short or medium term.

In the first half of the eighteenth century the first signs of the second demographic stage appeared in certain countries of Europe, especially in England: mortality rates began permanently to decline and short-term fluctuations in the population disappeared to make way, for the first time in history, for a steady increase. From an average gross mortality rate of some 35 to 40 ‰ in traditional societies, the rate in England fell to 30 ‰ in 1760-80 and reached 25 ‰ at the beginning of the nineteenth century. The annual rate of population increase reached and surpassed 0.5% during the first fifty years of this new stage, to approach 1% in the two following centuries, equivalent to a doubling of the population every 70 years, whereas previously the world population had taken about sixteen centuries to double itself since the beginning of our era.

This is still obviously a long way from the inflationary rates characteristic of the under-developed countries today (between 2 and 4% according to the country; 2.6% for all those regions together, or a doubling of the population every 27 years). But at the low rate of 0.5%, the descendants of the Pharaoh Cheops and only one of his wives would have produced today a population of 100 milliard (100 billion,

U.S. terms); now the world population in 1968 is $3\frac{1}{2}$ milliard ($3\frac{1}{2}$ billion, U.S.), and the estimated population for the year 2000 is between $5\frac{1}{2}$ and $7\frac{1}{2}$ milliard, according to the hypotheses of fecundity adopted. This break in the traditional demographic evolution has been termed by some demographers the first demographic revolution, to distinguish it from the modifications undergone by population movements a century and a half later as a result of the spread of birth control in the developed countries, which was to lead, for the first time among large groups of human beings, to a steep decline in the birth rate.

But we must return to the other 'first demographic revolution,' the one that concerns us here. As we have said, around 1740-60 the first signs of a new demographic era appeared in England. The population, which in more than a century, 1630-1740, had increased by only 8 to 10%, between 1740 and 1850 rose by over 150%. The same break in demographic evolution occurred around 1770 in France, but not until about 1820 in Italy and Sweden and even later in Finland (the northern countries provide the best population statistics for the eighteenth century) or other countries where the agricultural revolution occurred later.

Let us now see what part agriculture, or rather progress in food production, played in this demographic revolution.

First of all, a sharp distinction must be made between the predominant cause of the decline in mortality in the eighteenth century and the causes of that decline in the two subsequent centuries. From the last years of the eighteenth century in England and a little later in the other European countries, advances in medicine unquestionably saved the lives of a steadily increasing percentage of children and adults. But throughout all the earlier decades of the eighteenth century it was a very different matter. The level of medicine at that time was so low, and made such slight progress up to the century's third quarter, that we cannot seek to find the main cause of the demographic changes there. In fact, three different broad types of explanation have been successively advanced to account for the population increase in the eighteenth century.

Contemporaries, including the most illustrious 'demographer' of the day, Malthus, seem to have looked no further than economic causes; it was widely believed that population increase tended to be in proportion to the increase in production of food supplies. The ravages caused by periodic famines provided a justification, if such were needed, for this explanation.

The spectacular successes of medicine, thanks in particular to vaccines, and the great development of medical science from the middle of the nineteenth century made Molière's image of a doctor, portrayed as a figure of fun with a store of medical apparatus as limited as it was ineffective, seem thoroughly antiquated. These successes had the obvious and natural effect of supporting the theory that attributed to medicine a major role in the decline of mortality, and hence in population increase, even as far back as the middle of the eighteenth century.

Today the debate on the question falls broadly into two camps, one side supporting the 'economic' and the other the 'medical' explanation. But even the medical camp has to admit that though reduction in deaths from smallpox through inoculation played an important part in population increase, it was greater resources that enabled people to survive. And whatever part medicine may have played in the second half of the eighteenth century, its role was certainly insignificant in England up to 1760. The question is, therefore, to what extent was there a break in demographic evolution before that date? Available estimates of the population in England suggest such a break around 1740, but some demographers contest this though without being able, in the present state of demographic historical research, to provide more positive evidence. But while it is difficult to define the precise role played by medicine in population developments in the latter decades of the eighteenth century, it seems beyond doubt that the increase in food resources resulting from changes in English agriculture in the first half of that century was a vital factor in sustaining, if not in initiating, the demographic revolution. The fact that England experienced no serious food shortage during that century's first sixty years, even though cereal exports were increasing steadily to represent, by the middle of the century, about 13% of the country's total caloric needs, is sufficient proof that agricultural progress had for the first time put a permanent end to the classic pattern of a growing population periodically coming up against the problem of food supplies.

Thus progress in agriculture, by making possible the demographic revolution or more probably, in our view, by actually causing it, initiated a profound change in the rate of population increase, which was to lead to a great increase in the demand not only for agricultural but also for manufactured goods. This demand was to prove a powerful stimulus in the development of artisans' workshops, which the industrial revolution was gradually to transform into factories.

INCREASE IN THE DEMAND FOR CONSUMER GOODS

Given the structure of the societies studied here, societies where, as we have seen, some 80% of the working population was engaged in agriculture, it can easily be understood that advance in agricultural productivity had a wide impact. This important increase in productivity soon resulted in additional resources. Available sources suggest that in England production per worker in agriculture rose by about 100% between 1700 and 1800. In France, according to I.S.E.A. estimates the final product per male agricultural worker increased by 24% between 1751-60 and 1803-12, and by 38 per cent between 1803-12 and 1855-64, or by a total of around 70% during the century that corresponds, agriculturally, to the period 1700-1800 in England, but which in France included the adverse conditions brought on by the Revolution and the Napoleonic wars. According to our calculations, between 1840 and 1900 agricultural productivity increased by 30% in Russia, 45% in Austria, 50% in Belgium and Italy, 75% in Sweden, 90% in Switzerland, and 190% in Germany (see Table 2, page 472), or by an average of 75%, which signifies an annual rate of 0.9%.

Differences in types of tenure naturally lead to variations in the proportion of the population that profits by this increase in supplies. But if we except farm workers, for whom an increase in available supplies is not necessarily the result of progress in agricultural productivity, the peasants as a whole, if in differing degrees, must have benefited by this increase, especially since at that time the spread of more equitable systems of farm rents and tenure accelerated in most places.

In theory it might be supposed that the sole effect of increase in supplies would be a parallel variation in the level of food consumption; in that case, it would make little difference whether the change lay in an increase in the number of calories absorbed or in an improvement in the type of food consumed, through changing over from cheap, or vegetable-based, calories (cereals) to dear, or animal-based, calories (meat), or even, as was actually the case, from a diet based on a secondary cereal (rye, barley, etc.) to one based on wheat combined with an increase in consumption of partly sifted flour instead of black flour. A pure and simple increase in caloric consumption, however, comes up fairly soon against the ceiling of the physiological limit: an average daily consumption of 3,500 calories per person being taken as the upper limit.[12] In the case of a gradual progress towards greater consumption of calories of animal origin, the ceiling would obviously be considerably raised, but here one soon comes up against limitations of a psychological kind, for the scale of value of products makes too high a consumption of such products appear wasteful. Consequently, although a transition towards consumption of calories of animal origin certainly occurred to some extent at this time, it must soon have met a psychological, rather than a physiological, resistance. In short, as one of the precursors of econometry, Ernst Engel, had already de-

12. Calculations of the availability of calories per person, made by the F.A.O. in respect of recent years (*Production Yearbook, 1966*, Rome, 1967), show that no country reaches this figure. The average for European countries in the last few years is 3,020 (for the under-developed countries 2,300, and slightly under 2,000 around 1950).

duced, the elasticity of food consumption in relation to income is very slight.

Thus, in practice a regular increase in agricultural productivity leads fairly quickly to additional availability of resources. The choice of goods in which these new resources find an outlet depends on economic and social or political factors. In Europe, where climatic conditions make clothing an important item, a large part of such new resources would normally be spent on clothes. Since supplies of traditional textiles were by nature somewhat inelastic (for instance, increased wool production required an increase in livestock), the importation of cotton, first as woven material and later as raw material, received a strong stimulus from this demand.

During the first fifty years of agricultural development, imports of raw cotton to England more than doubled. Consumption in France went up even more rapidly because the point of departure was lower. Annual consumption of raw cotton for these two countries was as follows (in grams per capita): England, 1698-1710, 90 grs.; 1750-60, 200 grs.; France, around 1750, 50 grs.; 1790-1802, 180 grs.

Taking into account their respective dates of 'take-off,' similar evolution can be seen in most of the industrialised countries of today for which relevant statistics are available. But the later the 'take-off.' the more rapid the advance in consumption of cotton goods. Thus, cotton (which, it must be remembered, had been known for a long time) became an important commodity in the West where it was to play a major role in industrial development.

Cotton had a dual importance. The first part was quantitative. In England around 1840 textiles accounted for 75% of industrial employment, and within that figure cotton accounted for half. Cotton goods represented 40% of exports. Comparable percentages for other countries are lower because England alone, thanks to her advanced techniques, exported such large amounts of cotton goods; but in the other European countries cotton also had a foremost place in the development of industrialisation, which, indeed, it came to symbolise. Just as, ten to twenty years ago, the silhouette of the blast-furnace was the concrete image of industrialisation, so in the eighteenth century and the first half of the nineteenth the cotton mill—that huge squat building pierced by scores of small windows to which hordes of workers, mostly women and children, trooped as each day dawned—was the visual expression of the new economic age.

But cotton also played an important qualitative role. For its fibres particularly lend themselves to mechanical treatment, and this was the impulse for mechanisation of the textile industry. When we consider the difficulties of adapting cotton-spinning machines (which their inventors did not of course think of as solely for cotton) to wool, or even more to flax, we soon realise that the mechanisation of textile work, which marked and profoundly influenced the start of the industrial revolution, would probably never have come about but for this particular fibre, so uniquely suited to mechanical treatment. But for that early success with cotton, it is indeed unlikely that such tremendous efforts would have been made to develop machines capable of dealing with the traditional textile fibres. The consequent check to the use of machinery would probably have endangered, or at least seriously handicapped, the whole process of development.

Thus, agricultural development, by arousing an increased demand for consumer goods and especially for textile products, provided an important stimulus towards the launching of the industrial revolution. But for that stimulus to prove so productive another sector had also to undergo upheavals—namely, the iron and steel industry. For without the availability of low-cost iron all the technical advances that characterised the industrial revolution would have been gravely handicapped or even made impossible through economic non-viability. Now, as we shall see, agriculture appears to have played a major part in the birth of the modern iron and steel industry.

AGRICULTURE AND THE BIRTH OF THE MODERN IRON AND STEEL INDUSTRY

We will now attempt to define the part played by agriculture in the development of the iron and steel industry during the thirty to sixty years that preceded the industrial revolution. What follows will be a summarised version of another study on this subject by the present author.[13] But before embarking on that period which particularly concerns us here, it may be opportune to destroy a myth that still often finds a place in explanatory accounts of industrialisation, the myth of railways as an essential element in the start of the modern iron and steel industry.

It is in fact true that in a certain number of countries where industrial development came fairly late the demand created by railway construction was the basis for a modern iron and steel industry. This was not the case, however, in England, the birthplace of the industrial revolution, or in most of the European countries which experienced that revolution a little later. Indeed, it could hardly have been otherwise, for railways were the outcome of the gradual development of the steam-engine, which had itself been fostered by the growing needs of industrialisation.

In 1824, when no public railways yet existed in England, only 30% of the country's labour force was still employed in agriculture, and its iron industry already produced some 550,000 tons of pig iron a year; this was five times as much as the output of the whole world in 1700, and twenty times England's own production in 1720. In France, during the period 1828-41, iron consumption for railways represented according to our estimations only 2% of total production. In Belgium, in the years 1832-34, when the country was still without railways, cast-iron production amounted to some 100,000 tons, or 25 kg. per head of population, whereas the estimated annual per capita consumption of iron in the

---

13. 'Le rôle de l'agriculture dans la création de la sidérurgie moderne,' in *Revue d'Histoire Economique et Sociale*, vol. XLIV, 1966, No. 1.

traditional economies of seventeenth and eighteenth century Europe was only 1 to 3 kg.

But let us return to the period that particularly concerns us here, the thirty to sixty years before the beginning of the industrial revolution. During those years, in the countries undergoing the agricultural revolution, and especially in England and France, there was a notable increase in the consumption of iron products; but the demand for iron in non-agricultural sectors was relatively low and slow to increase.

Available data for England show that between 1720 and 1760 iron consumption increased from 41,000 to 63,000 tons, i.e. by over 50%, whereas the population increased by only about 10%.

In the various iron-using sectors apart from agriculture, the rate of increase and structural modifications are found to be too insignificant to account for this increase in the demand for iron. For example, the index of industrial production (including coalmining) calculated by Hoffman[14] increased in the years 1720-60 by only 15%. The increase in the output of the shipping industry was probably not much higher. On the basis of the evolution of the tonnage of English owned ships (and taking into account the fact that a sizeable proportion of the ships were produced by non-English shipyards) it can be estimated that the shipping industry increased its production by less than 20% between 1720 and 1760. And since only minor changes occurred in the technique of shipbuilding during that period, it seems likely that the consumption of iron products did not increase at a much higher rate than the tonnage. Estimates of the impact made by the advent of the steam-engine between 1720 and 1760 show a consumption of iron of around 1,500 tons, or less than 1 ‰ of the total consumption. Finally, we recall that these years fall within one of the rare periods of relative peace, for, as Ashton[15] notes, the effects

14. W. G. Hoffmann, *British Industry, 1700-1950* (translated by W. O. Henderson and W. H. Chaloner), Oxford, 1955.
15. T. S. Ashton, *Iron and Steel in the Industrial Revolution*, Manchester, 1924.

of the Seven Years War, beginning in 1756, were only felt towards the end of that decade.

Thus, as far as non-agricultural sectors were concerned, no sufficient development occurred to account for the great increase in the demand for iron. The rural sector, on the other hand—still employing, we must remember, some 75 to 80% of the working population—had, as we have seen, embarked on the agricultural revolution in England by the beginning of the eighteenth century. Now most of the innovations characteristic of that revolution had a direct impact on iron consumption—for example, the gradual elimination of fallow land, clearance and improvement of neglected land, improved equipment, new types of implements, and the wider use of horses and horse-shoeing. We will now examine briefly each of these factors in relation to their effect on the demand for iron products.

The elimination of fallow land resulted in practice in a considerable increase in farmwork and especially in ploughing; abandoning the system of biennial rotation, with its alternating years of fallow, would in fact imply a 100% increase in the land surface cultivated each year. That hypothesis naturally represents the extreme case, which, however, occurred very widely. Broadly speaking, traditional agriculture, as we have seen earlier, was characterised by two main types of crop rotation, the biennial and the triennial. Transition from triennial rotation including fallow to a rotation without fallow would increase the area to be cultivated by 50%. In practice it can be calculated that at the outset of the agricultural revolution some 45% of arable land was given up to fallow, while 60 to 50 years later that percentage had fallen to around 20%: this would mean an increase of 45% in ploughing and related farmwork. This in turn implied a greater use of implements and a proportionate increase in iron consumption.

The effects of land clearance resembled those of abandoning fallow, since it also led to an increase in the area cultivated. Though clearance also involved a large amount of labour and the extended use of new types of implements.

Improvements in agricultural implements had an even

more evident effect on the demand for iron, for they consisted essentially in the gradual replacement of wooden parts
in implements by iron ones. Such replacement affected first
the part of the implement most exposed to wear and
breakage, and then gradually extended to the whole
instrument. This was especially true of the plough, in which
at the end of the seventeenth century iron was used only for
the ploughshare but which during the eighteenth century
gradually incorporated more and more iron, until by the
middle of the nineteenth century it was made wholly of iron.
Fussell, studying the evolution of agricultural implements
in England, finds the first mention of an iron mould-board
in a work of 1716. The so-called Rotherham plough,
incorporating much more iron in its make-up than the
traditional plough, was introduced in England around 1730
and was soon widely used. The same pattern of change
applies also to the other agricultural implements.

We shall not insist on the effects of the introduction of new
implements since its impact on the demand for iron is
evident.

On the other hand, the wider use of horses for farmwork,
and of the practice of shoeing them, may at first sight seem
to be of no great significance in that connection. But in the
long run it was very important for, calculating on a basis
of the number of horses at work and the average use of iron
involved in their shoeing, our estimates suggest that the
demand thus created represented in the England of 1760,
about 15% of total iron consumption.

Thus, the combined effect of these various factors resulted
in a great increase in agriculture's demand for iron. At the
same time, the agricultural revolution provided farmers
with the economic means to acquire all this new equipment
through the increased yields they secured by the change in
methods. The relative demand for iron from agricultural
sources at this time was very high. Excluding the farmers'
private consumption, it can be estimated at between 30 and
50% of the total demand for iron. It can therefore easily be
seen that the constantly rising demand from agriculture
produced strong pressure on the iron industry. In England

this demand provided a powerful stimulus towards eliminating the main bottleneck in the domestic iron industry—the shortage of combustibles, specifically wood. This was how, as a result of the increased demand from agriculture, the major technical innovation in the iron industry came to be introduced—namely, the use of coal instead of wood as the basic combustible for blast-furnaces: it spread rapidly, opening the way for the numerous technical inventions that made the industrial revolution possible. For, though the economic role of the iron industry was not as important as that of cotton in the early stages of that revolution, iron nevertheless played a major and decisive part in carrying out technical innovations in all spheres of activity. Without supplies of low-cost iron it would have been impossible to extend widely the use of machines in which iron played an important part. And it was because of the greater use of iron that more productive machines could be built. Thus, the agricultural revolution contributed decisively to industrialisation by promoting changes in a vital part of mechanisation, which is itself the essence of the industrial revolution.

AGRICULTURE, ENTREPRENEURS, AND THE FINANCING OF INDUSTRIALISATION

The biographies of industrial entrepreneurs in the early stages of industrialisation show that the great majority of them came of modest origins and often of farming stock. Thus, Mantoux, investigating the origins of textile industrialists in England, writes: 'One general fact emerges: most of them came from the countryside; they came from that half-agricultural, half-industrial class that till then had formed a notable part, perhaps the majority, of the English population. If one goes further back, one nearly always arrives at a peasant stock, at the old vanished but not dead race of yeomen.'

In the case of metallurgy, Mantoux stresses that 'many of them came from small local workshops . . . but going further back in their families' origins one very often finds the land and the peasantry.'

E. L. Jones, in his recent study of the role of agriculture in English economic progress,[16] opens his section on investment by saying: 'The industrialisation of a predominantly rural society will understandably draw where possible on agrarian resources of capital, entrepreneurial talent, and technical skill. If these do not originate in agriculture proper, they may well come from its penumbra of servicing and processing trades'; and he concludes: 'Aggregating the fragments of evidence on the exchanges of capital and entrepreneurship between agriculture and industry is hazardous. It does seem that agriculturists contributed handsomely to the earlier industrial enterprises.' We for our part would incline to be rather less cautious, for the same predominance of agriculture is evident in the other European countries. In France, the conclusions reached by historians of this subject agree widely in finding among the entrepreneurs a great majority of modest people, especially former farmers, both in the textile industries and in other sectors. In Russia, Yatsunsky[17] notes the large preponderance of farmers among the textile industrialists; thus, in the textile town of Ivanovo, in 1828, out of 107 entrepreneurs 102 were peasants. In Switzerland, Braun[18] stresses the primary role played by rural environment and the small amount of capital behind the original enterprises in the industrialisation of that pole of development, the Zurich-Oberland region. Thus, to quote only two examples, the father of the great spinning magnate Heinrich Kunz still worked part-time on the land, and set up his spinning-mill in his own barn. The industrial fortune of another important family in the region, the Wilds, was similarly of rural origin, and their move into industry began with two spinning jennys.

Many other such examples could be given and other Euo-

16. E. L. Jones (ed.) *Agriculture and Economic Growth in England, 1760-1815*, London, 1967 editor's introduction, pp. 1-48.
17. V. K. Yatsunsky, 'Formation en Russie de la grande industrie textile sur la base de la production rurale,' in *Second International Congress of Economic History*, 1962, vol. II, Paris, 1965, pp. 365-7.
18. R. Braun, 'The rise of a rural class of industrial entrepreneurs,' in *Journal of World History*, Vol. X, No. 3, 1967, pp. 556-66.

pean countries could be quoted, but, to sum up, it can be said that recent research into the origins of industrialists tends increasingly to confirm the predominant place of the rural milieu at the outset of industrialisation, especially in textiles, which was not only the most important branch of industry but also the motive branch in the first stages of the industrial revolution in Europe.

The role of agriculture as the supplier of capital and entrepreneurs in the first stages of the industrial revolution calls for some explanation. The first question to be raised concerns the capitalist classes and what became of them; for to say that the great majority of entrepreneurs in the industrial revolution came from an agricultural background implies that the old capitalist class, contrary to many theories about the indistrial revolution, played a lesser role in its financing. The minor influence of commercial and financial capitalism in the sixteenth and seventeenth centuries can moreover be demonstrated by a simple comparison of the geographical areas of accumulation of finance capital and the areas of the industrial revolution. There is a marked divergence between these two types of region. At country level, it will suffice to cite, on the one hand, Holland, Italy, Spain and Portugal, and on the other Great Britain, France, and Germany, and to observe that of these two groups of countries the one in which the industrial revolution first gained a footing was in fact the one where accumulation of commercial capital was relatively less important.

This divergence between the countries that were seats of merchant capital accumulation and those that became seats of the industrial revolution appears even more marked when we consider more restricted areas. In France, it was not Marseilles, Bordeaux, or Nantes that became poles of the industrial revolution. The same is true of Venice and Genoa, of Bristol, Plymouth, and Dover, not to mention the Hanseatic towns.

The objection may be raised that capital accumulated in the 'commercial' towns might perhaps have been transferred to investment in regions where geological, climatic, or even demographic conditions were more favourable to industrialisation. Studies of the provenance of capital for this period, however, indicate that very little of it was not from local sources; for it seems that whenever an entrepreneur required more capital than he himself possessed, he found it locally. Moreover, a glance back to the conditions then prevailing will suffice to convince us of the unlikelihood of transfers of capital. Methods did, indeed, exist for making such transfers, but they were used almost entirely for commercial transactions. In addition there was the problem of guarantees and even of securing the necessary information. The whole banking system needed to be improved and expanded before transfers of savings to industrial investment could be carried out on any large scale. And that came about only as a result of the economic development, and at a relatively late stage. In fact, historians of financial institutions agree in stressing the mino part played by the banking systems at the outset of the industrial revolution in the sphere of industrial credit. This is equally true for England and France, and for all the countries whose development began in the nineteenth century. Even in Belgium, a pioneer in this sphere, the banks played no role in the beginning of industrial development.

Moreover, on a more general plane, Pirenne[19] commented more than half a century ago: 'I have observed, in surveying this history (the nature of capitalists and their origins) from the beginning of the Middle Ages to our own times, a very interesting phenomenon to which, so it seems to me, attention has not yet been sufficiently called. I believe that, for each period into which our economic history may be divided, there is a distinct and separate class of capitalists. In other words, the group of capitalists of a given epoch does not spring from the capitalist group of the preceding epoch. At every change in economic organisation we find a breach of continuity . . . there are as many classes of capitalists as there are epochs in economic history.'

This absence of 'capitalists from a preceding epoch' has,

19. H. Pirenne, 'The Stages in the Social History of Capitalism,' in *The American Historical Review*, vol. XIX, No. 3, April 1914, pp. 494-515.

in part, sociological explanations. It is very difficult to induce social groups to change their field of activity completely as long as their resources still allow them to lead a fairly satisfactory life. And since the industrial revolution did not cause a reduction in the activities carried on by the old groups of capitalists—indeed rather the reverse—there was little inducement to change.

This does not, however, imply that farmers alone played a part in the beginning of the new industries. Obviously, in many cases entrepreneurs from the traditional capitalist classes of the old regime (merchants and even quite often nobles) played an important part in certain branches (more frequently in the iron and steel industry than in textiles). But in the first stages the main body of capital and more particularly of entrepreneurs that produced the upheavals of the industrial revolution was of modest and nearly always agricultural origin.

If the lack of continuity of the traditional capitalist classes is to be explained largely by social factors, the emergence of the new class of entrepreneurs can be accounted for principally by economic factors, which we will now briefly review. The chief explanation lies in the low value of industrial capital and the difference in the value of capital per worker employed in agriculture as compared with that in industry. For the period that concerns us here, researches and calculations based on available estimates[20] suggest that the total capital (fixed and circulating) needed to employ a worker in industry in England in 1800 represented about 4 to 5 months' wages for a male worker at that time. In France, the corresponding figure for the period 1800-20 was 6 to 8 months' wages. The difference between the ratios for England and for France is explained by the different stages of development of the two countries. France, which started her development later than England, had to take into account the technical level England had reached. She was less advanced in the production of equipment goods, and, thus, prices for equipment comparable to that produced by

20. See the present author's *Révolution industrielle et sous-développement*, *op. cit.*, pp. 54–63.

the technically more proficient English industry could not be competitive. This low value of capital is obviously due to the relatively undeveloped level of techniques in the early nineteenth century. On the other hand, and this is very important, a much greater amount of capital was needed to put a man to work in agriculture than in industry. The difference between the two amounts obviously varied both according to the degree of development in agriculture or industry and to the availability of agricultural land; land represented the major part of capital in agriculture at that time.

Estimates of the difference in the value of capital per worker in industry and in agriculture in various countries are as follows:

United Kingdom	around 1810	1 to 9
France	,, 1850	1 to 8
Belgium	,, 1850	1 to 6
United States	,, 1880	1 to 2·5
Japan	,, 1905	1 to 8

The low ratio in the United States is accounted for by the very high availability of land. Apart from that, the average difference is around 1 to 8. This means that the sale of an average farm employing one labourer would produce enough capital to employ eight workers in industry. This very value of industrial capital is to be explained, as we have already said, by the low level of technical development at that time. No more need be said here about that aspect of the problem; but it is worth noting that technical level also conditioned the size of firms in which the economic optimum was very low, and this enabled small firms to be competitive. This also meant that the sale of a single-labourer farm with a below-average income would produce enough capital to make possible a start in industry.

Farmers were the more inclined to make use of that opportunity because the agricultural revolution tended to make many farms less remunerative, and consequently some farmers, especially those who owned their land, decided to change their occupation and go into industry, particularly into textiles; for we must not forget one very important structural aspect of pre-industrial Western societies and and indeed of all traditional societies, namely, the close link of interdependence between textile and agricultural work. Even since the end of the Middle Ages there had, of course, been important urban centres in which a high proportion of the working population was employed in textiles, but they provided only a fraction (greater or smaller according to the region) of the total consumption; the remainder was produced by the 'rural' textile industry. The amount of time spent on textile work in the countryside varied considerably, ranging from the domestic spinning-wheel working occasionally for family consumption only to spinning and weaving as practically whole-time activities on a commercial scale, producing goods sold with or without the aid of a middleman. Thus, the interdependence of the textile and agricultural sectors facilitated the transition of both workers and entrepreneurs from agriculture to the newly developing industry, in the case of the entrepreneurs especially because of this difference between the levels of agricultural and industrial capital.

We have stressed the role of the smaller farmer in this development; but big landowners also often played an important part in industrial investment, aided by the higher rent incomes from land that were a concomitant feature of the agricultural revolution in most European countries.

Thus agriculture not only set free the food resources and workers needed for that big adventure that was the industrial revolution; it not only made possible or even fostered the demographic revolution and generated the birth of the modern textile and iron industries; but it also provided in the early stages a large part of the capital and entrepreneurs that animated the motive sectors of that revolution.

We have surveyed the main effects of agricultural progress on the process of industrialisation. But, before concluding this study, we must glance very briefly at some of the interactions between agricultural and industrial development.

For if, as we have just seen, agriculture did much to awaken and further industrialisation, it is obvious that industrialisation also exercised a favourable influence on agriculture and so by a cumulative process contributed to economic growth. Thus the fall in the price of iron, a direct result of the technical progress in the iron industry caused by agriculture's increased demand for iron, furthered a wider use of iron in agricultural implements, which in turn brought about an increase in the productivity of farmwork.

Even more important, however, were the effects of the mechanisation of textile work, itself, as we recall, brought about by the increased demand for consumer goods that resulted from increased agricultural resources. The mechanisation of the textile industry inevitably, of course, meant the gradual disappearance of rural textile work, which was manual. This disappearance had varying effects, according to the particular farm and the extent to which rural textile work had taken hold there. That last was in inverse proportion to the profitability of the farm. Where a farm had proved profitable, the time formerly devoted to textile work was generally now transferred to agriculture. On less profitable farms, on the other hand, low revenues inclined the farmer to give up agriculture altogether, since it could not bring in enough to provide a living. And the net result of this divergent evolution was an increase in agricultural productivity, for it led to an increase in the amount of work done in the more profitable farms and a reduction of work in the less profitable ones.

These interactions had their main effect on supply in the agricultural sector; but demand too was favourably influenced by industrialisation, for it produced an increase in consumption both of food products and of agricultural raw materials.

Thus was set in motion that complex process, the industrial revolution, with all its multifarious interactions and its vast economic, technical, and social consequences. That revolution in less than two centuries radically transformed the life of mankind as a whole. For—and this is one of the negative aspects of this evolution—even the three-quarters of mankind living in societies that remained outside it have been touched by expansion from the small proportion of countries that have become industrialised. True, among the one-quarter of mankind represented by the developed countries the net balance of the industrial revolution can be regarded as positive, thanks to the economic, social, and cultural benefits it has made possible, and despite the tremendous suffering it entailed in the early stages of inhuman working conditions and low wages for the workers. But for all the other regions its net effect has been definitely negative. It can be summed up today in the agonising problem of the so-called under-developed countries. The introduction into those countries of medical techniques (the result of scientific progress made possible by the industrial revolution), together with aid in food supplies, has for the first time fostered an expansion of population that far surpasses any increase in resources and increasingly takes on the dimensions of a catastrophic inflation. The large-scale penetration of industrial goods from the developed countries has, among other things, accentuated still further the rupture in the balance of these traditional societies where economic development now becomes no longer a matter of choice but an absolute necessity in view of this demographic inflation. And while agricultural development still remains an urgent need and prime objective—if only because it provides a living for 70% of the population—the agricultural path is no longer, as in the past, the royal road leading almost automatically, via the industrialisation it encourages, to a general development of the economy. For in addition to the serious problem created by demographic inflation, which considerably restricts the possibilities of increasing agricultural productivity, other structural changes also complicate the economic mechanism. It is not possible here to describe them in detail but we would merely mention that, for instance, the cost of industrial capital per worker is no longer in this case lower than in agriculture, and that complex techniques and sharper competition from more advanced industries as a result of lower transport costs combine with other factors to render the spontaneous emergence of entrepreneurs and industrialists extremely difficult, if not impossible.

It is on this note, the reverse side of the medal of the industrial revolution's consequences, that we end this brief study of the close relationship that existed in Europe between agriculture and the birth of the industrial revolution.

BIBLIOGRAPHY

Up to the present only a few works exist having a direct bearing on the relationship between developments in agriculture and the industrial revolution. This is probably due to the fact that the earliest school of economists, the physiocrats, based its analysis on the fundamental role played by agriculture in economic life. Later on the science of economics, developing under the strong impression created by tremendous advances in industry and commerce, tended at least to neglect, if not to deny, the significance of physiocratic theories. Time merely served to reinforce this attitude. On the other hand numerous works both on the industrial revolution and on agricultural history touch on this problem. We will first consider these two types of studies.

Most studies of the industrial revolution contain references to the part played by agriculture in that far-reaching change in economic life; but they do not analyse systematically the close relationship between the two branches. Among such works the first to be mentioned is P. Mantoux, *La Révolution Industrielle au XVIII° siècle*, Paris, 1906 (reprinted 1959), English edition *The Industrial Revolution in the Eighteenth Century* (1928), which, though it first appeared over fifty years ago, still retains its value and is perhaps the book most closely concerned with our particular problem. Other works of a similar kind are: T. S. Ashton, *The Industrial Revolution, 1760-1830* (Oxford, 1948); H. L. Beales, *The Industrial Revolution 1750-1850* (London, 1928); and H. Heaton's article on 'Industrial Revolution' in the *Encyclopaedia of the Social Sciences*, New York, 1948 (reproduced in the symposium edited by Hartwell, mentioned below). For a more modern approach see P. Deane, *The First Industrial Revolution*, Cambridge, 1965, a study which is largely based on this author's earlier works in the field of quantitative economic history (especially P. Deane and W. Cole, *British Economic Growth, 1688-1959*, Cambridge, 2nd ed. 1967) and the excellent synthesis of E. J. Hobsbaum, *Industry and Empire*, London, 1968; and of P.

Mathias, *The First Industrial Nation*, London 1969.

Coming closer to our subject, though still without a special focus on the part played by agriculture, are various articles or short studies on the causes of the industrial revolution in England: M. W. Flynn, *The Origins of the Industrial Revolution* (London, 1966); J. T. Krause, 'Some neglected factors in the English Industrial Revolution,' in *The Journal of Economic History*, vol. XIX (1959); R. M. Hartwell, 'The Causes of the Industrial Revolution. An essay in Methodology,' in *The Economic History Review*, vol. XVIII, No. I, 1965, also reprinted in Hartwell ed., *The Causes of the Industrial Revolution in England* (London, 1967). That symposium also includes the following articles: E. W. Gilboy, 'Demand as a Factor in the Industrial Revolution,' and F. Crouzet, 'England and France in the Eighteenth Century: A Comparative Analysis of Two Economic Growths' (first appeared in French in *Annales*, vol. XXI, No. 2, 1966).

Besides these studies dealing specifically with the industrial revolution in England, which is rightly regarded as the main field for research on the subject, it would be logical to mention also works on the economic history o every other country that experienced the industrial revolution in the nineteenth century. But this, involving some twenty countries, would mean too detailed a treatment for the present bibliography, since apart from general works and the particular case of England overall studies on the industrial revolution in individual countries are the exception rather than the rule. However, this is no longer the case if we recall here Volume 4 of the *Fontana Economic History of Europe* which, in almost all cases are excellent syntheses of the Industrial Revolution in the principal European countries. Mention should, however, be made of the following works which, in going beyond the geographical framework of England and, in some cases, the historical framework of the industrial revolution, provide a broader conspectus of the process of development: F. Braudel, *Civilisation Matérielle et Capitalisme*, Paris 1967; C. Cipolla, *The Economic History of World Population*, London 1962; A.

Gerschenkron, *Economic Backwardness in Historical Perspective*, Cambridge, Mass., 1962; W. O. Henderson, *Britain and Industrial Europe 1750-1870*, Leicester 1954 (2nd ed. London 1965); D. S. Landes, *Technological Change and Industrial Development in Western Europe, 1750-1914*, in *The Cambridge Economic History of Europe*, vol. VI (ed. by H. J. Habakkuk and M. Postan), Cambridge, 1965; M. Niveau, *Histoire des faits économiques contemporains*, Paris 1966; W. W. Rostow, *The Stages of Economic Growth*, Cambridge, 1960. See also P. Bairoch, *Révolution Industrielle et sous-développement*, Paris, 1963 (3rd ed. 1969, Spanish translation, Mexico, 1967; Italian translation, Rome 1966) and 'Niveaux de développement économique de 1810 x 1910' in *Annales*, No. 6, Nov.-Dec. 1965.

On agricultural developments in England during our particular period, an excellent recent work is J. D. Chambers and G. E. Mingay, *The Agricultural Revolution, 1750-1880*, London 1966; and also E. Kerridge's less ambitious but well-documented essay, *The Agricultural Revolution*, London, 1967; also W. G. Hoskins' short study, 'English Agriculture in the 17th and 18th Centuries,' in *Relazioni del 10 Congresso Internazionale di Scienze Storiche*, vol. IV, Florence, 1955. See also the following recent articles, E. Kerridge, 'The Agricultural Revolution Reconsidered,' in *Agricultural History*, Vol. XLIII, No. 4, October 1969; and in the same issue G. E. Mingay, 'Dr. Kerridge's Agricultural Revolution, a Comment.'

For rural history, not centred solely on the case of England, first to be mentioned is an excellent synthesis, though too short in relation to the period covered— B. H. Slicher van Bath, *The Agrarian History of Western Europe A.D. 500-1850*, London, 1963; and, by the same author, his recent article 'Eighteenth Century Agriculture on the Continent of Europe: Evolution or Revolution' in *Agricultural History*, Vol. XLII, No. 1, January 1969. See also M. Auge-Laribe, *La révolution agricole*, Paris, 1955; F. Dovring, 'The Transformation of European Agriculture,' in *The Cambridge Economic History of Europe*, vol. VI (ed. by H. J. Habakkuk and M. Postan, Cambridge, 1965); D.

Faucher, 'Les techniques agricoles,' in *Histoire Générale des Techniques*, vol. 2, Paris, 1965; G. B. Masefield, 'Crops and Livestock,' in *The Cambridge Economic History of Europe*, vol. IV (ed. E. E. Rich and C. H. Wilson, Cambridge, 1967); J. Meuvret, 'L'agriculture en Europe aux XVIIe et XVIIIe siècles,' in *Relazioni del 10 Congresso Internazionale di scienze storiche*, vol. IV, Florence, 1955. Last but not least, mention must be made of the valuable works of G. E. Fussell in the sphere of history of agricultural equipment, especially *The Farmer's Tools, A.D. 1500-1900*, London 1952.

The recent appearance of a volume of seven articles edited by E. L. Jones, *Agriculture and Economic Growth in England 1750-1815* (London, 1967), greatly facilitates the study of literature on the relationship between agriculture and the industrial revolution in England. Among these articles, of special interest for our subject are: A. H. John, 'Agricultural Productivity and Economic Growth in England 1700-1760 (with a postscript)'; J. D. Chambers, 'Enclosure and Labour Supply in the Industrial Revolution'; E. L. Jones, 'Agriculture and Economic Growth in England 1660-1750: Agricultural Change'; and, especially, E. L. Jones's valuable introduction to the volume.

On the same problem but not specially for England, see E. Boserup, *The Conditions of Agricultural Growth: the Economics of Agrarian Change under Population Pressure*, London, 1965; E. L. Jones and S. Woolf (ed.), *Agrarian Change and Economic Development: the Historical Problems*, London, New York, 1970; T. W. Schultz, *The Economic Organization of Agriculture*, New York, 1953; J. W. Mellor, *The Economics of Agricultural Development*, New York, 1966; C. Eicher and L. Witt, eds., *Agriculture in Economic Development*, New York, 1964 (especially Part I); and articles by J. Craeybeckx, 'De Agrarische Wortels van de Industriele omwenteling,' in *Revue Belge de Philologie et d'Histoire*,' 1963, No. 2; F. Crouzet, 'Agriculture de Révolution Industrielle. Quelques réflexions,' in *Cahiers d'Histoire*, tome II, vol. 1-2, 1967; B. F. Johnston and J. W. Mellor, 'The Role of Agriculture in Economic Development,' in *The American Economic Review*, September, 1961; H. J. Habakkuk, 'Economic

Functions of English Land-owners in the 17th and 18th Centuries,' in *Explorations in Entrepreneurial History*, VI, 2 (1953-4); and P. Bairoch: *Révolution Industrielle et sous-développement* (op. cit., especially Part II, Les Mécanismes du développement, pp. 71-137); 'Le rôle de l'agriculture dans la sidérurgie moderne,' in *Revue d'Histoire Economique et Sociale*, XLIV, vol., année 1966, No. 1; 'Original Characteristic and Consequences of the Industrial Revolution,' in *Diogenes*, 54 (Summer, 1966).

9. The Emergence of Economics as a Science 1750–1870

Donald Winch

INTRODUCTION

By the middle of the eighteenth century a new mode of writing about economic questions had been established in many parts of Europe which was regarded by its practitioners as a science—the science of political economy. Although the original scientific impulse has not worked with equal strength at all times, the tradition which links the work of the early economic system-builders of the latter half of the eighteenth century to that of their modern counterparts in the twentieth century is a remarkably continuous one. It is a tradition that has always been of interest to economic historians whether or not they have been in sympathy with the latest manifestation of the discipline. Several reasons can be given for this. For historians of economics as diverse as Alfred Marshall and Karl Marx, the development of economics was a by-product of the sequence of agrarian and industrial revolutions which spread through Europe after 1750. Thus Marshall believed that it was associated with the conditions of industrial life, and more especially with the growth of a system of free enterprise which had helped to emancipate men's economic arrangements from custom and impulse. Marx, on the other hand, saw it as a way of thinking that was intimately connected with the rise of the bourgeoisie under capitalism. Alternatively, the emergence of the scientific study of economic processes and behaviour can be regarded as an important example of what Professor David Landes has referred to as 'the rationality principle and Faustian spirit of mastery'.[1] Belief in this principle not only distinguishes Western European culture from many others, but has been responsible for promoting and sustaining European econ-

1. D. Landes, *The Unbound Prometheus* (1969), p. 32.

omic advance through the continuous process of rational adaptation of means to ends.

Whether one views the rise of economics as an outcome of, or as an autonomous factor in, the process of industrialisation, therefore, the phenomenon itself is likely to engage the interest of those concerned with economic change. And since such systems of political economy as mercantilism, physiocracy, and classical economics can be identified with schemes of state action or inaction which have been influential at different times and places, it is also possible that economic historians will find in the literature of economics interpretations or rationalisations which are still of value in understanding European economic development in its various forms. Even if, as Professor Alexander Gerschenkron has recently argued, the pressure of circumstance has exercised a greater impact on the actual course of change than economic science, the literature of economics comprises ideologies as well as scientific theories—ideologies which have often fortified those groups in society most anxious to promote change along particular lines.[2]

There is room for almost indefinite dispute as to how and when a particular science began. For while it is possible to agree on a number of attributes of science as an on-going activity or as a completed body of knowledge, there are no necessary and sufficient conditions, applicable at all times and places, for distinguishing 'science' from other forms of knowledge. And if this is true of the natural sciences how much more likely is it to be true of economic science, where the degree of involvement with 'common-sense' observation, ethical and political norms, and the activities of special interest groups is much closer? There is also no clear answer as to whether economic science should be treated as a conscious invention occurring at a specific time and place, or as a body of knowledge accumulated over long periods. Nevertheless, there is general agreement that something happened to change the character of economic writings around the middle of the eighteenth century. The main

2. A Gerschenkron, 'History of Economic Doctrines and Economic History,' *American Economic Review*, May, 1969.

line of disagreement as to what this 'something' was can be drawn between those who believe that the emergence of economic science since 1750 can best be treated as an autonomous shift of perception and philosophical outlook, such that familiar transactions and institutions were seen in a different light; and those who maintain that the new science can be regarded as the outcome of changes in the nature of the economic world—a response to new economic problems and interests which excited criticism, explanation, and justification.

The former school of thought deals with the emergence of economics mainly as an intellectual phenomenon having its origins in conscious attempts to emulate the achievement of natural science by applying the methods of Bacon, Newton, Locke, and Descartes to economic questions. The latter school concentrates more on the social and economic changes which took place in the late eighteenth century and served as a basis for the industrial revolution. The idealist versus the materialist view of the *emergence* of economic science is related to another dispute between absolutists and relativists on the *development* of economics. The absolutist interprets the history of economics as a story involving the progressive development of an intellectually coherent and autonomous body of theory, where progress is judged in terms of conceptual refinement and explanatory power. The relativist is not concerned with this type of progress and may even deny that standards exist by which such progress can be determined; he treats the history of economics more as a reflection of, or reaction against, features of the changing contemporary environment. A further set of permutations is possible once distinctions are made between histories that concentrate on economic analysis as a set of tools that can be separated from the philosophical preconceptions and personal and political evaluations of the writers concerned; and histories of economic thought which deal, in Schumpeter's words, with 'the sum total of all the opinions and desires concerning economic subjects', whether or not they have scientific pretensions. Between these two extremes there is an intermediate form of history, namely the history of systems of political economy. This takes as its province systematic attempts to construct a coherent picture of the contemporary economic world, while acknowledging that the results often embody a vision of what that world might become, or how it might be improved by adopting various courses of action.

Each of these positions has its own characteristic strengths and weaknesses. For example, while there is a fairly obvious sense in which it is true to say that contemporary material conditions determine *what* it is that economic observers write about and *when* they do so, it is less easy to use the same approach to establish *why* and *how* they wrote as they did. 'Science', it could be argued, is more concerned with the 'how' and 'why' questions. It is also usual to distinguish 'science' as a systematic pursuit from casual observation-statements about empirical reality on the one side, and metaphysical statements about the nature and intelligibility of the universe on the other. Indeed, one definition of science might be that it comes into being when a dialogue is established between these two levels of discourse—when instances and later rules of correspondence are consciously sought. Similarly, it is usual to make a distinction between systems of moral or political principles and 'science', where the latter is thought of as an objective search for empirically verifiable knowledge. Neither of these distinctions is easy to apply in studying the history of economics. Contributions to 'science' in the strict sense have frequently arisen out of inquiries that were either philosophical in character or motivated by practical expediency, moral precept, or even mercenary gain. Economists who have gone out of their way to disentangle economic science from its practical or ideological applications have often merely exchanged one system of values for another that is merely less explicit.

A brief essay like the present one could be halted indefinitely at the threshold of its subject by these methodological problems. It seems best to begin, therefore, with a summary statement of intentions. This essay treats economic science as a succession of systems of political economy, where these are interpreted to include analytical concepts, empirical generalisations, institutional assumptions, and policy prescriptions. To be more precise, a large part of the essay will be concerned with the fortunes of one of the dominant forms which the new science assumed during the first half of the nineteenth century, namely English classical political economy. Apart from its intrinsic significance to the history of economics, classical political economy was addressed to the contemporary problems of the British economy during the early stages of the first industrial revolution. As will be shown later, the development of political economy in Britain and its reception on the Continent was strongly influenced by this conjunction; a fact which may help to link this essay more closely with others in this series. While an attempt will be made to relate economic science to its social and economic environment, no commitment to the view that one is the simple result of the other is intended. In fact, the assumption throughout will be that ideas and intellectual traditions have a momentum of their own, especially when they become the property of men who hold a self-conscious belief in their scientific status and promise. The first section is devoted to the origins and emergence of a self-conscious tradition, while the rest deal with the modification, diffusion, and rejection of classical political economy both in England and on the Continent.

ORIGINS AND EMERGENCE

Even those who regard economic science as an organic growth, whose origins can be found in the writings of the Greeks, the mediaeval scholars, and in the works of individual authors in the sixteenth and seventeenth centuries, acknowledge that there was a remarkable concentration of scientific effort in the three decades after 1750. A number of works which have acquired a permanent place in the history of economics were published in this period. In 1756 François Quesnay, the founder of the physiocratic sect, published his first economic essay; two years later his *Tableau Économique* appeared. In 1755 Richard Cantillon's *Essay on the Nature of Commerce in General*, written nearly twenty years before, was published for the first time. A few years earlier David Hume had brought out his penetrating essays on some leading economic topics as part of an attempt 'to improve the method of reasoning on these subjects, which of all others are the most important'. In 1766 Turgot committed to paper his *Réflexions sur la formation et la distribution des richesses;* and in the following year Sir James Steuart published his *Inquiry into the Principles of Political Economy.* Finally, in 1776, as a culmination to this burst of activity there came the work which borrowed from, synthesised, and in many respects surpassed these earlier writings, Adam Smith's *Inquiry into the Nature and Causes of the Wealth of Nations.*

The appearance of works of this character in such a relatively brief period of time indicates some kind of conjuncture in the history of economics. It makes it possible to speak of forerunners giving way to founders, of pre-history giving way to history. But it is important to recognise that there was a pre-history.

In Britain it was embodied in an amorphous literature extending back over two centuries and written largely by those engaged in trade and finance—a literature which is usually collected under the term 'mercantilism'. This term derives ultimately from Adam Smith, who spoke of the 'mercantile system' as one which maintained that the chief source of a nation's wealth lay in its ability to acquire specie through a favourable balance of trade by means of strategic state intervention in the form of exclusive monopolies, embargoes, tariffs, and bounties. There has been considerable debate as to whether the label 'mercantilism' is a useful one to describe either the policies practised or the doctrines preached during the sixteenth and seventeenth centuries. Economic historians have concluded that there was insufficient consistency of purpose behind the policies pursued by European nations in this period to warrant the use of any single term to designate a *system.* Similarly, doubts have been expressed as to whether Adam Smith and his successors were correct in describing mercantilism simply as an erroneous body of economic ideas. Indeed, can any consistent system of ideas be said to have emerged from the writings of the merchant-pamphleteers? Was there any continuity of concern beyond that furnished by the recurrence of certain types of practical problem and common traits of business mentality?

If we cannot speak as confidently as Adam Smith did when he coined the term 'mercantile *system*', it is still possible to retain the adjective to describe the main interests and outlook of the bulk of the economic commentators in the pre-Smithian period in Britain. It is not helpful, however, to say as R. H. Tawney did in his *Religion and the Rise of Capitalism* that 'economic science developed in England as the interpreter of the practical interests of the City'. The forerunners of the *science* were isolated writers who approached the established mercantile questions concerning trade, tariffs, taxes, population, coinage, and interest in a different spirit. They may have shared the utilitarian, or even mercenary, interests of their contemporaries; but they sought to strengthen their case by employing methods of reasoning and presenting evidence derived from the more highly respected branches of knowledge, namely natural science and philosophy. By this means such writers as William Petty, John Locke and Dudley North were frequently able to go beyond the common-sense observations and isolated insights of their contemporaries to envisage a wider range of conceptual connections between the various economic phenomena studied. The result was something that took the form of an objective and scientific demonstration around which a tradition could coalesce.[3]

In addition to the mercantile tradition an important contributory element in the pre-history of the science of political economy can be found in the writings of the philosophers of natural law. Locke stands at the junction of these two influences as one who consistently applied a secularised version of natural law to economic affairs as a means of contrasting appearance with underlying reality, and of showing where positive laws conflicted with Nature's

3. This case is argued with great finesse by W. Letwin in *The Origins of Scientific Economics; English Economic Thought, 1660–1776* (1963).

laws. Through other natural law philosophers, notably
Pufendorf and Francis Hutcheson, Adam Smith's mentor,
the science of political economy retained links with the
ethical teachings of the medieval scholars on such questions
as exchange value and the 'just price' links which cut across
the intervening mercantile period.

In France, the forerunners of the science are chiefly to be
found among those whom Schumpeter has aptly called the
'consultant administrators'—public servants with experience
of the fiscal and economic affairs of large parts of the Kingdom. Into this category fall Melon, the Abbé de St. Pierre,
Vauban, Boisguillebert and the Marquis d'Argenson. A
more codified version of this tradition, concentrating on
public finance and administration, flourished in Germany
under the title of cameralism. The leading feature of all
these writings was their practical concern with ways in
which the policies of the state in matters involving trade,
manufacture, agriculture, and taxation could be so conducted as to augment the wealth of the sovereign and his
subjects.

By the middle of the eighteenth century, therefore, a
foundation existed on which scientific tradition could be
constructed. It consisted of a number of diverse elements:
pamphlets and tracts on currency, commerce, population,
and the rate of interest; assemblages of statistical material
which went under the title of Political Arithmetic; and
commentaries on the principles of fiscal and economic administration. On specific topics the work of some forerunners
was equal to—if it did not surpass—that produced later.
But an extra infusion was needed to bring these elements
together to form a coherent subject-matter that could be
treated systematically. This extra infusion came when political economy was absorbed into the wider programme of
philosophical and historical studies which was characteristic
of the secular intellectual movement known as the Enlightenment. Many of the leading economists of the second half
of the eighteenth century—Hume, Smith, Quesnay, and
Turgot for example—were prominent members of this move-

ment, and contributed not only to political economy but to other aspects of the movement's programme.

It is important to note than in becoming an integral part of the Enlightenment political economy did not undergo a change in its subject-matter, nor did it shed its practical or normative character. For Adam Smith it was still 'a branch of the science of the statesman or legislator' designed to 'enrich both the people and the sovereign'. Hume's economic essays deal with those topics around which much of the economic inquiry of the previous two centuries had revolved. And while Hume opposed orthodox mercantilist opinion on many of these topics, he clearly believed that it raised serious questions, and made several important concessions to what is traditionally regarded as the mercantilist point of view. The full significance of the change which took place in the middle of the eighteenth century does not lie here. Rather it is to be found in the concepts, methods, and values which the philosophers of the Enlightenment brought to the study of political economy.

The ambitious attempt by members of the Enlightenment to construct a science of man in society provides material for a separate volume. Newton's discovery of the laws underlying movement and order in the physical universe acted as a challenge and a model to those concerned with social phenomena. Together with Locke's philosophy of experience, it furnished the eighteenth century philosophers with a methodological conviction that a proper combination of 'reason' and 'just observation' would yield comparable natural laws of individual and social behaviour. One of the most characteristic aspects of Enlightenment thought was the belief that man was poised to achieve mastery in his struggle with Nature. In intellectual, moral, and technical matters man was on the point of overcoming forces which had stunted his achievements in the past. Of all the branches of the science of man political economy was most closely concerned with man's direct confrontation with physical or natural resources. It was widely recognised that one of the fundamental clues to an understanding of man's past and prospects for improvement lay in his material circumstances—in the realm of economic necessity and the ways which men had devised for dealing with it. In simplified form a common train of Enlightenment speculation went as follows: If we assume that human nature is fundamentally the same wherever and at whatever epoch it is to be observed, why is it that historical and ethnographic evidence point to enormous diversity of custom, practice, and achievement? What circumstances external to human nature have produced such variety? How are the different social states related to one another? By what processes or stages did men and societies arrive at their present state?

In answering such questions several of the Scottish philosophers, including Adam Smith, adopted a materialist interpretation of the laws of social development which attempted to relate legal and political institutions, and the characteristic habits and virtues of different societies, to the basic economic facts of life in society. They depicted societies in terms of the mode of subsistence; they traced the development from hunting to nomadic shepherd societies, from settled agriculture up to the commercial society emerging in their own day. A similar approach can be found in the writings of Turgot and the physiocrats. Scottish and French writers also paid special attention to the size of the social surplus over subsistence or maintenance needs, to the hands into which control of the surplus passed, and to the ways in which the surplus was spent in different societies.

Political economy acquired a distinctive naturalist methodology from its absorption in the Enlightenment—a methodology which, in the hands of a thinker like Adam Smith, provided a means of bringing together the partial insights of previous economic writers into a system of connected principles. Without losing its claim to furnish practical guidance, political economy also took on the values associated with the Enlightenment pattern of philosophical inquiry. These values were partly the instrumental ones important to all branches of scholarly or scientific enterprise

—dedication to the pursuit of objective knowledge as far as was humanly possible. In addition, however, there were the other values which were part and parcel of the Enlightenment—reason, tolerance, respect for individual freedom, and humanity. David Hume the philosopher might draw attention to the distinction between facts and values, to the need to separate what is from what ought to be, but to him and his contemporaries the natural sciences of man were intended to serve the cause of enlightenment. It was in this respect, more than any other, that the economic writings of the Enlightenment differed from those of the mercantilist era.

Reason had been applied to economic question in the seventeenth century; and some of the mechanisms underlying the production of wealth had been discovered. Nevertheless, the Enlightenment view was that mistakes had been made in assigning basic causes; and that much of the mercantilist tradition was vitiated by its acceptance of national power as the aim of policy, and rivalry between nation-states as the proper framework of analysis. Earlier economic writers had been guilty of concentrating on too narrow a view of economic transactions; they had accepted too much of the ordinary businessman's outlook. Adam Smith's use of the term 'mercantile' was a pejorative one. It described an attitude which had led to production and the acquisition of specie being treated, or spoken of, as though they were sufficient ends in themselves. Furthermore, under the guise of serving the nation or the sovereign the mercantile interest had gained privileges at the expense of the population at large. For Smith mercantilism meant the association of the science of economics with the restricted aims of political expediency rather than with the interests of society and common humanity. The good society was one which guaranteed the fruits of their labour to all regardless of their social position. It was also likely to be a progressive society in which higher standards of living filtered down to all members; and one in which the prospects of a wider range of goods and higher wages acted as a more effective stimulus to work than the whiplash of poverty. But the good and progressive society could only be achieved by removing constraints and privileges belonging to less enlightened systems of polity, thereby giving the maximum scope for what Smith, in a famous phrase, described as 'the uniform, constant and uninterrupted effort of every man to better his condition'. From a cosmopolitan point of view it would be a world in which nations ceased to exploit their colonial possessions and hedge round their trade with devices conceived in jealousy of other nations' prosperity. The emergence of a free commercial society was prized not merely, or even mainly, for its immediate economic benefits. This type of society, in spite of certain drawbacks, was more likely than any other to bring civilisation in the broadest sense in its train. Economic progress and liberty, it was hoped, would not only enrich people, but make them more tolerant, more independent, and more capable of enjoying the fruits of the social union.

The combination of a methodology which emphasised the existence of an underlying natural order with a scheme of values which set great store by economic liberty for the individual imparted a *laissez-faire* bias to the earliest systematic expositions of economic principles. There had been no general presumption on the part of mercantilist writers that the unimpeded pursuit of private interests was compatible with the interest of the nation, though instances of harmony were cited and frequently given great prominence. The emphasis of their successors was the reverse: instances of conflict were noted, but there was a general presumption that within the appropriate institutional framework of competition and justice the pursuit of self-interest would not degenerate into mere licence. It is important to stress the fact that *laissez-faire* was a by-product of certain features of the philosophical outlook of the early economic system-builders rather than the essence of the new science. It was taken up in the nineteenth century as a slogan by popularisers and by the middle-class audience for whom they wrote. Its origins, however, are to be found in the natural law tradition, and its use by the early econo mists was, if anything, directed against the mercantile in terest groups surrounding government. The shift from mercantilism to *laissez-faire* was a subtle one in Britain, where the semblance of representative government had existed for some time and the state was either unable or unwilling to undertake ambitious tasks of intervention in economic affairs. On the Continent, where stronger *étatiste* traditions prevailed, *laissez-faire* made even less impact—except as a slogan.

The connections between economic and social circumstance and the economic writings of the second half of the eighteenth century are difficult to establish except in the most general terms. Unlike the mercantilist writers the founders of economic science cannot readily be characterised as a class. Quesnay was a physician at the French court; Hume and Smith held minor state offices, but are best described as philosophers or academics; Turgot was an administrator. It is, of course, possible to connect the intellectual preoccupations of the physiocratic movement with the state of French agriculture under the *ancien régime*. The fundamental feature of the physiocratic system was its belief that only in agriculture did the application of capital and labour give rise to a net surplus. In manufacturing, commerce, and the service trades the return was sufficient simply to give a 'normal' return over necessary costs. Quesnay's *tableau économique* was an attempt to show how, through expenditure of the surplus, the circular flow of economic activity was maintained and increased; and how further application of the surplus in the form of investment in agriculture would contribute to the expansion of the economy. The growth of agricultural output and the maintenance of agricultural prices at a level which would encourage production and investment provided the key to growth of the system as a whole. From this system the physiocrats deduced certain policy conclusions. Since all taxes were eventually met from the society's net surplus they argued that it would be better to impose taxes only and directly on landowners. They also advocated free internal and foreign trade in agricultural products on the grounds that this would guarantee a fair return to agriculture, the sole source of the net surplus.

These conclusions are clearly related in some sense to the parlous state of the French finances and agriculture, to the vexatious inheritance of Colbert's policies to stimulate French industry, and to the monetary disorder which followed the collapse of John Law's schemes. It is also possible to describe physiocracy as an attempt to rationalise and further the interests of a particular type of capitalistic agriculture. But even when true, such statements do not add greatly to our understanding of physiocracy. They tell us something about its most obvious assumptions and preoccupations, but very little about its inner logic and dynamic. The most penetrating materialist interpretation of physiocracy was that provided by Karl Marx, who regarded it as the 'first system which contains an analysis of capitalist production'. The peculiarity of the system is that the physiocrats selected agriculture as the sole representative form of capitalist production. Moreover, although agriculture was, in spite of Colbert's efforts, the dominant productive sphere, they chose to stress a type of capitalist agriculture that was more common in England than in France at the time. They were more concerned to depict agriculture as it should or might be organised than with simply describing the small-scale, under-capitalised, type of farming which then predominated. Professor Ronald Meek has argued convincingly that physiocracy can best be interpreted as an answer to the problem of France's under-development, as judged by her own past, her potential, and England's present state. Recognition of the problem was facilitated by the striking, if isolated, success of an improving type of farmer-capitalist in some of the northern provinces.[4]

A similar problem of interpretation faces the relativist when dealing with the fact that it was against the background of a fairly backward economy—that of Scotland—that Adam Smith wrote his account of the principles underlying the causes of the wealth of nations. Here again Professor Meek's hypothesis can be applied to show that evi-

4. See his *Economics of Physiocracy* (1962), pp. 23–7, and 364 ff.

dence of change and improvement, produced in this case by the spurt of commercial activity associated with the union with England and access to the colonial trade, is likely to be more striking against the background of a largely traditional form of economic organisation.

The *Wealth of Nations* is an unruly book held together by the author's espousal of 'the obvious and simple system of natural liberty'. From the outset Smith makes clear his intention to deal with the causes of economic growth as measured by the rise of national income per head in real terms. This depends on two broad factors: increases in the physical productivity of labour and the proportion of the labour force employed 'productively', which in turn depends on capital accumulation. The first two books of the *Wealth of Nations* deal with these 'causes' of growth. Book I contains the famous discussion of the division of labour and most of Smith's contribution to the theory of value and distribution. On market prices he argued that only in the short run were they determined by demand and supply: the long run 'natural' price was regulated by costs of production, which obliged him to put forward theories to explain the long and short run determinants of the components of cost, namely wages, rent, and profits. Book II emphasises the crucial importance of capital accumulation in maintaining the 'progressive state' and, in modern terms, lays the foundation for classical macro-economics in its discussion of the relationship between saving and investment. Book III is an exercise in conjectural economic history and deals with 'the progress of opulence among different nations' with special attention being paid to the earning and disposal of the social surplus in the different stages of development. Book IV is mainly a critique of mercantilism and physiocracy as systems of political economy; it also contains a detailed review of the mercantile system in practice from a free trade point of view. Book V is devoted to the general theme of taxation and state expenditure, and takes the form of a series of connected observations on the proper conduct of what we would now call the public sector. The whole is a rambling *tour de force*, placing economic theory firmly within a framework of moral philosophy and history. Of all the classic works in economics, it is the least 'specialised'. It is at one and the same time the crowning achievement of the attempt by the Scottish Enlightenment in the eighteenth century to create a Newtonian science of man in society, and the foundation stone for the separate development of political economy as a science in the nineteenth century.

Schumpeter has said that Smith was 'thoroughly in sympathy with the humours of his time'. The optimistic, generous, and enlightened temper of the book, together with the fact that it was written in an accessible style and copiously illustrated with telling examples, certainly helped to make the work popular with a wide public. It was not so much that Smith told his readers what they wanted to believe—there was much in the book with the opposite tendency—as that he told them things that were daily becoming clearer before their own eyes. The success of the book, the fact that its readership grew with the years, can be explained by Smith's skill in constructing a theoretical system which dealt with emergent forms—emergent in his own time, dominant later.

Modern economics, with its distinction between the micro-economics of optimal allocation and efficiency and the macro-economics of aggregate income-determination and growth, has wavered in its interpretation of the 'real' contribution of the founder. Does it lie in his extended treatment of spontaneous market mechanisms acting through relative prices and factor rewards? Or is it to be found in his analysis of the irreversible processes of change and growth acting through capital accumulation, the division of labour, and increases in productive employment and physical productivity? The possibility of conflict between allocative mechanisms on the one side and growth processes on the other may simply be a product of modern sophistication. Smith's eclecticism in dealing with the interdependence and self-regulatory character of individual markets that were becoming national and even international in scope, together with the problems of accumulation and the growth of opulence over long periods of time, corresponded with features of contemporary economic life in Britain which had not yet become distinct, and indeed were only partially in evidence when he wrote. The same can be said of his treatment of various sources of income, and more specifically of his identification of profit on capital used in employing wage-labour as a distinct species of economic reward.

One of the weaknesses of adopting the relativist point of view is that while it stresses points of correspondence between theoretical schemes and emergent reality, the points of dissonance which inevitably result from the fact that theories simplify reality are overlooked. In the case of successful works like the *Wealth of Nations* it is always possible to argue that the elements stressed were more 'representative' than those overlooked. The danger here lies in the tautology that success is explained by success. Features of a later stage of industrialism are read back into a work which, though frequently prophetic, remains firmly rooted in the eighteenth century. It is worth bearing in mind that Adam Smith and many of his English followers either overlooked or chose not to stress features of industrialism that we think of as important today. They minimised the role of fixed capital and technical innovation in agriculture and industry; they did not detect the emergence of a separate entrepreneurial class; and they consistently (and falsely) assumed that landowners (as distinct from capitalist-farmers) spent their rent-incomes 'unproductively'; unlike profit-recipients they could not be relied on to invest in productive enterprises. Finally, as a group— certainly up to the 1830's—they consistently devoted more attention to agricultural, monetary, and commercial problems than to factories, machinery, and industrialisation.

Before dealing with the special features of post-Smithian political economy in Britain, however, it is worth considering briefly some of the uses to which the new science was put on the Continent before and immediately after the French revolution.

The history of the science of political economy in many

European countries during the latter half of the eighteenth century is interwoven with the history of the phenomenon known as 'enlightened absolutism'. Throughout Europe various monarchs embarked on programmes of administrative reform with the underlying aim of improving the efficiency and cohesion of their regimes. The attempt to focus power on themselves and increase the taxable resources at their disposal frequently brought these absolute rulers into conflict with the Church and the anti-centralising interests of the old aristocracy, whose feudal privileges they sought to curb. Self-interest, and in some cases genuine conviction, combined to make absolute monarchs the sponsors of 'enlightened' government, putting themselves forward as direct custodians of the prosperity and happiness of their subjects, and calling upon the services of a new class of thinkers and administrators to help them carry out the task of managing increasingly centralised bureaucracies. The challenge provided by these efforts to modernise *anciens régimes* was responded to by many intellectuals prominent in the Enlightenment. It offered an opportunity to advance their cause by improving systems of legislation, taxation, education, and justice through the gentlemanly means of royal patronage. The role of adviser to rulers of territories as diverse as France, Russia, India and Latin America was not daunting to those who considered their principles to be universally applicable; it accorded well with their cosmopolitan sympathies and pretensions.

The connection between physiocracy and enlightened absolutism was particularly strong. The political ideas of the physiocratic movement entailed whole-hearted acceptance of absolute monarchy. Their ideal political system was one of 'legal despotism' with a single Leviathan or philosopher-king at its head. The duty of the king was not to 'create' law but to promulgate those laws which the science of man had discovered in Nature itself. Hence the slogan *laissez-faire, laissez-passer*. To realise the benefits of the 'natural' state of affairs, however, it was necessary for the absolute monarch to create a minimum framework of justice, security, and efficient administration. More important still, it was necessary to dismantle much of the existing apparatus of laws which impeded the beneficial operation of the underlying natural order.

At Versailles enthusiasm for agricultural improvement and rusticity acquired a cult status. Physiocratic advice was also sought by Catherine II and the Margrave of Baden. Beyond mere fashion, the problems to which physiocracy was addressed were crucial to the modernising ambitions of monarchs whose kingdoms derived their wealth and revenue very largely from agriculture. Although problems differed according to circumstance certain common features prevailed: serfdom; absentee and *un*improving landlordism; the burden of non-productive classes in the form of the clergy, the nobility, and the unemployed peasantry; overstrained exchequers; and a chaotic feudal and mercantile inheritance of local restrictions, exactions, privileges, and guilds. The physiocrats and other philosophers offered liberal, rationalist, and humanitarian solutions to all of these problems. For a time at least, their solutions were discussed and in some cases implemented.

As Intendant of Limousin for thirteen years and Controller-General of Finances under Louis XVI, Turgot provides the classic example of the philosopher-administrator. His downfall in 1776 was a direct result of the unpopularity aroused by his attempt to abolish the *corvée* and many guild-privileges, to establish internal free trade in grain, and to place the finances of the kingdom on a sound footing. The king's infirmity of purpose when faced with opposition from the vested interests effected by Turgot's reforms is also indicative of a general inability on the part of the *anciens régimes* to achieve radical transformation from within. In France revolution achieved what Turgot had left unfinished —and much more besides.

The success of Turgot's counterparts in other European countries was in some cases made possible, in others retarded, by the fears aroused by the revolution in France and later by the effects of the Napoleonic Wars. In some of the Italian states before the French revolution economist-administrators were encouraged and employed by absolute monarchs. The best examples are Beccaria and Pietro Verri in Milan, both of whom held university and administrative posts under the Austrian government; and Genovesi, Galiani, and Filangieri in Naples. A number of economic and adminstrative reforms were achieved which entailed an attack on the feudal powers of the clergy and aristocracy. But Napoleon's invasion of Italy in 1796 and the advent of French rule were more powerful in destroying much of the feudal apparatus of the old regime, and in introducing modern methods of law and government which, in spite of the heavy taxes imposed by the conqueror, were favourable to economic change. After the Congress of Vienna in 1815 Italy was once more divided into a multiplicity of states, each with its own customs barriers. A conscious effort was made to turn the clock back by revoking the Napoleonic codes. Nevertheless, some gains were permanent; and it was upon these that a subsequent generation of economic liberals and reformers, chiefly in the more advanced states of Lombardy and Piedmont, were able to build later in their efforts to bring Italy into the mainstream of European economic and intellectual life.

The introduction of new ideas into Spain during the eighteenth century faced severe obstacles, not least of which was the Inquisition. It would not have been possible without the support of an absolute monarch. Under the Bourbons, and notably under Charles III, a fairly typical regime of enlighted absolutism was established in Spain which enabled those in touch with the ideas of economists in France and Britain to operate with a certain amount of freedom and even encouragement. The chief rival to the establishment of a unified regime around the King was the Church. In a country in which a high proportion of the population was in holy orders of one kind or another, and where religious foundations had alienated extensive tracts of agricultural land, the Church was also the main obstacle to agrarian and other economic reforms. In tackling these problems Charles III called on the services of energetic and enlightened administrators. Support was also given to the diffusion of foreign ideas through the medium of the 'economic societies' that were formed in many provinces and cities at this time. One of the leading economic lights in the Spanish Enlightenment was the poet and administrator, Gaspar Jovellanos, through whose works many of the ideas of French and English economists filtered into Spanish discussions of the reform of land tenure and agrarian conditions. Political economy seemed to offer to Spanish reformers a scientific guide towards prosperity and social justice. The fears aroused by the French Revolution led to a retreat from these ideals. As in the case of Italy, Napoleonic rule and the upheavals of war produced the next major opportunity for building on the foundations laid by the enlightened administrators of the pre-revolutionary period—even though, initially, Napoleon's defeat was the signal for reaction.

Although Frederick the Great is rightly classed as one of the leading exponents of enlightened absolutism by virtue of his conception of the state as one in which the ruler was 'the first servant of the people', his views on political economy were quite untouched by the newer currents flowing from France. Unlike his Italian and Spanish counterparts, however, Frederick left behind him a self-perpetuating, bureaucratic autocracy, increasingly capable of taking the legislative initiative. The hand of bureaucratic reformers was decisively strengthened by the collapse of the old order produced by the Napoleonic Wars and Prussia's humiliating defeat at Jena in 1806. The next eight years constitute the Stein-Hardenberg reform era—a period during which a determined if limited assault was made on some of the more glaring feudal relics of aristocratic power and mercantile restriction. The importance of the Stein-Hardenberg era to the history of economics in Germany lies in the fact that it has frequently been linked with the introduction of Adam Smith's ideas into Germany at the turn of the century. It was certainly from those universities in Göttingen, Halle, and Königsberg, where Smith's work was modifying the cameralistic tradition, that many of the civil servants responsible for the reforms were educated. Smith's economic liberalism, as applied to agricultural reform and the removal of guild restrictions and internal trade barriers, provided a new and invigorating element within an established pattern of studies. But in the process of naturalisation a new blend of ethical and paternalistic liberalism was formed which was tailored to Prussian conditions. Even in this modified form 'Smithianism' can hardly be said to have made a lasting impact on the separate native tradition.

CLASSICAL POLITICAL ECONOMY IN BRITAIN AFTER ADAM SMITH

Although the liberal ideas of the early economic system-builders proved valuable to those members of the ruling élite in European countries who were trying to achieve modernisation from above, it was only in Britain that the new science of political economy put down roots that were more than merely academic in character. It is tempting, and to some extent valid, to explain this fact by reference to the relatively advanced state of the British economy. No royal or bureaucratic absolutism was necessary to establish the pre-conditions for an agricultural revolution. By the end of the eighteenth century British agriculture was already well-established on a capitalistic basis; and the rise in food prices during the Napoleonic wars completed the process by encouraging the last major step towards enclosure. At the same time, though less obvious, the process of industrialisation and urbanisation had begun. By the end of the war in 1815 Britain had established a decisive lead over France, her nearest rival, as a manufacturing and trading nation. More important, perhaps, Britain was the only country in which the economic revolution was accompanied by changes towards the kind of society later associated with industrialism. Although denied direct access to political power until the mid-nineteenth century, the middle classes in Britain became an identifiable and distinct force long before this.

Another obvious reason for the success of political economy in England is the fact that the *Wealth of Nations* provided the subject with a systematic text which served as a common point of departure for later writers. No work of equal comprehensiveness was produced until nearly seventy years later when John Stuart Mill completed his *Principles of Political Economy with Some of Their Applications to Social Philosophy* in 1848. The tradition was never a purely academic one, as it became in some Continental universities, with faithful pupils succeeding to the Chair held by their masters. As early as 1797 a proposal was made that the study of political economy should be part of the syllabus of the English universities. Apart from isolated lectures, this proposal came to little until Nassau Senior took the newly founded Drummond Chair of Political Economy at Oxford in 1825, and J. R. McCulloch the equivalent Chair at University College, London in 1827. Even so, neither of these tenures proved lasting: no major figure in English classical political economy during its formative stages held a university post.

The secret of the continuity and penetration of political economy into English public life during the first third of the nineteenth century is to be found outside the universities. One possible exception to this statement can be found in Scotland, where one of Smith's pupils, Dugald Stewart, kept up the Scottish tradition by lecturing on political economy as part of his duties as Professor of Moral Philosophy in Edinburgh. The list of Stewart's pupils is an impressive one; it includes James Mill, J. R. McCulloch, Lord Lauderdale, Thomas Chalmers, Henry Brougham, Francis Jeffrey, and Francis Horner. But this list also shows why the exception is only a partial one: all of these men made their reputations as journalists, publicists, and politicians. The leading contributors to the science were gifted amateurs like Malthus, a clergyman (albeit holding a teaching post at Haileybury College), Henry Thornton, a banker, and Ricardo, a stockbroker. There were scholarly treatises, and later several textbooks, but many of the central ideas of the new discipline were first worked out in pamphlets and memoranda of evidence to Select Committees designed as contributions to public debate on the burning issues of the day. The proponents of political economy proved highly skilful in finding ways of bringing home the 'truths' of their subject to the educated public at large. The *Edinburgh Review*, founded in 1802 by Sydney Smith, Francis Jeffrey and Francis Horner, carried regular articles on political economy by every one of the leading authorities or their disciples. In Parliament too, as well as in Select Committees, and behind the scenes in such crucial ministries as the Board of Trade, the economists found a platform which was used by Henry Brougham, Joseph Hume, Henry Parnell and David Ricardo. The fact that political economy consistently dealt with questions which lay at the heart of public debate—food prices, the causes of poverty, taxation, monetary instability—meant that the subject could not be ignored, even by those (and they were an increasing number after 1800) who found its conclusions gloomy and unpalatable.

Between Smith and John Stuart Mill the most important scientific contribution was that of Ricardo, whose *Principles of Political Economy and Taxation* was first published in 1817. The period marked out by the last edition of the *Wealth of Nations* to appear in Smith's lifetime in 1789 and Ricardo's death in 1823 was a crucial one in the history of the new science. It encompasses one of the critical phases in Britain's process of industrialisation, the Napoleonic Wars, and the difficult years of post-war distress and stagnation. In the course of dealing with the economic problems associated with these developments classical political economy acquired many of its leading characteristics.

Those who accepted the Smithian framework shared his conception of the economic problem as one of seeking the causes of growth. They believed that one of the main clues to an understanding of this phenomenon lay in capital accumulation. In dealing with this problem they took over Smith's general presumption in favour of competitive markets and economic individualism and his distrust of government intervention. They also made use of and sharpened many of Smith's tools of analysis: the labour theory of value, the tripartite division of income into rent, profits, and wages, and the concept of progress towards a stationary state. But in the hands of his successors, particularly those of Ricardo, Smithian political economy developed into a more rigorous, more narrowly deductive, more urgent type of inquiry. To a large extent this change of emphasis can be explained in terms of the pressing nature of the problems to which the next generation of economists felt called upon to address themselves.

For the most part Smith had maintained a fairly detached stance, sceptical but basically optimistic. This was no longer possible for his successors, living as they did through a period in which the conflicts between the interests of the dominant land-owning classes and the new industrial and commercial classes were becoming sharper. Smith had taken an optimistic view with respect to the effect of economic progress on the standards of living of the mass of society. His successors, faced with the problems of an economy at war, recurrent grain scarcity, the spread of pauperism, monetary disorder, rising prices, an increase in the National Debt and in the burden of direct and indirect taxation, began to question whether this was necessarily the case. Was the source of capital accumulation in jeopardy as a result of rising food prices and consequently wages, and also as a result of high taxes and the volume of 'unproductive' spending by the government? Was the need to provide for the necessities of a growing population an insuperable obstacle to any improvement in the wage-earner's standard of life, even when, according to some definitions, the aggregate wealth of the nation was increasing?

This was the form in which those most sympathetic to the Smithian framework posed the questions. The orthodox version of classical political economy took its shape from the answers they provided. But the same problems were open to a different interpretation, which led those who adopted it to formulate a counter-tradition. The general respect accorded to Smith's work in many circles did not mean that alternative systems of theory and policy in political economy were ruled out of court. Indeed, the exigencies of war and its aftermath kept alive or revived aspects of both mercantilism and physiocracy in Britain.

The future of the Navigation Acts and of the old colonial system was extensively debated after the breakaway of the American colonies in 1783. Adam Smith conceded that the Navigation Acts were beneficial in so far as they helped to maintain Britain's naval defences, but he denounced the colonial system as a prime example of the malignant and misguided nature of mercantilist thinking. None of the efforts made in the 1780's to relax the system was successful. Smith was quite right in predicting that the interest groups associated with it would be powerful enough to prevent any decisive moves in favour of freer trade. The outbreak of war in 1793 put paid to the Anglo-French commercial treaty negotiated by William Eden in 1786, and made it unlikely that any further attempts would be made to dismantle a tried-and-trusted system which promised self-sufficiency within the remaining empire. War, in fact, merely reinforced the views of such influential writers as Lord Sheffield when he argued that, as in the past, Britain's power and wealth depended on 'inviolably maintaining' the existing policy.

Another effect of Napoleon's attempted economic blockade was to dramatise issues which had already given cause for concern during the years of grain scarcity between 1795 and 1804. In the course of the latter half of the eighteenth century, and in spite of improvements in domestic farming methods, it became clear to many commentators that Britain was no longer a net exporter of grain products. The causes of this important economic change, and the appropriate action to be taken by the state in the face of it, provided the subject for heated debate during the intermittent periods of extreme scarcity, when food prices rose alarmingly and emergency relief measures were implemented, either locally or nationally, to deal with the problem. Among the many short term measures discussed, the one that was to become the centre of a long-standing debate in the first third of the nineteenth century was the 'allowance' system, whereby local Poor Law administrators made relief available to employed and unemployed alike according to the discrepancy between wages and the price of provisions. While Smith dealt with the relationship between subsistence and population increase, and had been critical of some features of the English Poor Law, notably the Law of Settlement, the *Wealth of Nations* gives little idea of the extent to which such questions were later to dominate political economy in Britain. They left an indelible mark on the methods and conclusions of the science which persisted long after the early crisis decades of the century had passed.

In its early stages the debate on cures for pauperism took place within an intellectual context which can loosely be described as Smithian: it dealt with methods of Poor Law relief or pauper management in terms of whether or not they were legitimate extensions or infringements of the principles of economic liberalism. Many of the leading protagonists, including Pitt, Fox, Whitbread, Burke and F. M. Eden, considered themselves to be adherents of Smith's system of economic liberty even though they differed considerably over feasible solutions to the problem. Eden's careful factual study of *The State of the Poor* (1797) was critical of many features of the administration of the Poor Laws where it seemed to involve paternalism and interference with the benevolent law of the market; but the general tone of the work is optimistic in the Smithian vein. Civil and religious liberty, respect for private property, education of the poor—these were the conditions which would encourage the advancement of wealth and independence, and lead to general improvement in living conditions for all. Burke's *Thoughts and Details on Scarcity*, published in the same year, was of a quite different character, though it proclaimed support for Smith's principles on almost every page. It was a virulent diatribe against all remedies—for example, wage regulation and public granaries—which break 'the laws of commerce, which are the laws of nature, and consequently the laws of God'. Any effort to relieve poverty by redistributing wealth or by interfering with the free market was doomed to failure. Burke's pamphlet is best seen as a counter-revolutionary

tract designed to underline the way in which economic
necessity reinforced the existing social order. As a recent
commentator has said, Burke's 'obsession with social order
and hatred of revolution led him to elevate Smith's system
of economic liberty into a dogmatic faith which the author
might scarcely have recognised'.[5] It is certainly true that
Burke's treatment of the wage relationship contains none
of the sympathy for the labouring classes that is such a
marked characteristic of the *Wealth of Nations*.

Burke's tract is an early example of one of the ideological
uses to which the new science could be put. It also provides
a foretaste of one aspect at least of the work which, more
than any other, was to change the tone and content of
English political economy in the nineteenth century;
Thomas Malthus's *Essay on the Principles of Population*, first
published in 1798 but considerably expanded and modified
in 1803. The counter-revolutionary side of Malthus's *Essay*
was more apparent in the first edition. By shifting the competition between the means of subsistence and population
to the centre of the stage and treating it as an immutable
law of nature, Malthus hoped to refute the egalitarian and
perfectibilist ideas of Godwin and Condorcet. This aspect
of the Malthusian position was widely taken up by those
who wished to believe that very little could be done to
amend the situation of the poor. The case for abolishing
the Poor Laws, as it developed in the next two decades,
was considerably strengthened by Malthus's population
theory. The Poor Laws, it was argued, merely encouraged
population growth, depressed wages, and kept the poor in
a demoralising state of dependence.

As a contribution to the science of political economy the
significance of the Malthusian challenge lies elsewhere. By
emphasising the subsistence minimum towards which wages
tended as a result of population pressure, and by treating
the stock of subsistence goods as though it was fixed independently of demand, Malthus laid the foundation for
the classical wage-fund theory. This theory stated that

5. J. R. Poynter, *Society and Pauperism; English Ideas on Poor Relief,
1795–1834* (1969), pp. 52–3.

wages are determined by the relationship between the labouring population and the volume of circulating capital available for its support. Moreover, by comparing the geometric rate of increase in population with the arithmetical rate of increase in food production, Malthus pointed clearly towards the law of diminishing returns in agriculture which was later to provide the underpinning for Ricardo's reformulation of Smithian economics. Malthus had drawn attention to global pressures which affected the standard of living of the bulk of the population. All the leading writers in the English classical tradition were Malthusians in this respect; they also shared his condemnation of the existing Poor Law. What they did not share, however, was Malthus's unwillingness to go far beyond hoping that the population dilemma could be solved by education and moral restraint; they also looked to the expansion of the British economy, and of industry in particular, to provide incentives and opportunities which would overcome the problem in the long term; and they supported shorter term remedies which Malthus refused to countenance—emigration, birth control, and notably, the abolition of the Corn Laws.

Under conditions of war and rising food prices, the Malthusian challenge gave prominence to the possibility of conflict between the interests of landowners and those of society at large. The defenders of the landowning interest argued that a policy of agricultural protection and export bounties on grain products was necessary to encourage domestic production. Those who adopted this position attacked Adam Smith and his followers by reviving various physiocratic doctrines which suggested that agriculture, rather than industry and commerce, was the true foundation of Britain's prosperity. Increased protection was granted to agriculture by the Corn Laws of 1791 and 1804, but the debate was resumed in more virulent form at the end of the war in 1814 and 1815 when the fall of the agricultural prices led to renewed demands for greater protection. It was during this debate that four writers, Malthus, West, Torrens, and Ricardo, enunciated the law of diminishing returns in agriculture. This law suggested that a country in which population was growing, with no offsetting improvement in agricultural techniques, would face increasing food prices and consequently money wages. From this Ricardo went on to derive a theory of rent which stated that as food prices rose the owners of intra-marginal land would receive a bonus in the form of increased rents. Restrictions on the free importation of foodstuffs would therefore enable the owners of land to benefit at the expense of those in receipt of wage and profit incomes.

When further elaborated these propositions not only provided a powerful argument against the Corn Laws but the cornerstone of Ricardo's *Principles*. His aim in this book was to treat Smith's problem of economic growth in terms of the likely effects of progress on the distribution of the national product between landowners, capitalists, and labourers. Instead of being a side-issue, the shares going to each of the factors of production became central to the whole scheme of things. Ricardo's *Principles* contains none of Smith's breadth of outlook or learning. It was written largely in the form of a commentary on those of Smith's doctrines that Ricardo considered were erroneous or unclear. At its core lay a series of propositions organised into a deductive model designed to prove 'that in all countries, and all times, profits depend on the quantity of labour requisite to provide the necessaries for the labourers on that land or with that capital which yields no rent'. The problem raised by Malthus was further dramatised by being made the key to future economic growth. Profits were the source and motive for further capital accumulation; if they were brought to a minimum by the rise in rent and money wages no further accumulation could take place. The stationary state would have arrived and the prospect for raising the living standards of the labouring population would have run out. In spite of Smith's criticisms of the physiocrats and the attention he paid to improvements in productivity in manufacturing, he clearly regarded agriculture as occupying a primary place in determining a nation's capacity for progress. By emphasising rising domestic food costs as the chief bottleneck to further growth Ricardo reached a similar conclusion, albeit via a different route.

In the process of trying to make his model determinate Ricardo found it necessary—as Smith had done before him —to wrestle with the labour theory of value, both as an explanation of relative prices at a given moment of time, and as an invariable measure of changing values over time. No other economist went so far in displaying both the virtues and drawbacks of a theory which seeks to explain the prices of goods in terms of relative labour inputs. By a roundabout process of reasoning, Ricardo's adherence to a version of the labour theory made it necessary for him to invent a special explanation for the values of goods traded internationally: the theory of comparative costs, which showed that free trade between two nations could still be profitable even if one of them possessed an absolute cost advantage in all tradeable goods. Like the theory of rent, comparative costs retains a place in the modern literature of economics. But the real significance of the labour theory lies in the fact that it suggested grounds for a socialist critique of capitalism, first by the so-called Ricardian socialists, who made it the basis for the claim that labour had a right to the whole produce, and later by Karl Marx, for whom it contained the fundamental clue to the exploitation of labour under capitalism.

On the question of the Corn Laws Smith's orthodox followers were defeated in 1815. It was not until 1846, after a nation-wide campaign by Cobden and Bright, that the Corn Laws were abolished. By this time, however, the connection between the free trade movement and political economy had become more tenuous; or rather perhaps, more overtly political, and therefore less closely connected with the working out of vital scientific propositions. But this should not be taken to imply that the economists of Ricardo's generation were without influence on public policy. One of the earliest victories for the free-trade position came in 1812 when the Orders in Council by means of which the British government had sought to maintain the semblance of the old colonial system were abolished.

On this occasion the economists found themselves speaking for a sizable body of opinion from the distressed manufacturing and trading interests in the new urban centres. The next significant victory was to come in the 1820's when two successive Presidents of the Board of Trade, Robinson and Huskisson, took decisive steps to lower tariffs and to dismantle the remaining apparatus of mercantilism. At the same time economists and their political spokesmen were successful in achieving the abolition of the Combination Acts and the laws restricting the emigration of skilled labour.

There were powerful economic reasons why the case for free trade gained in cogency after 1815. It became clear that Britain had emerged as the world's leading commercial and manufacturing power. Protected colonial markets were no longer necessary, especially if the *quid pro quo* took the form of paying high prices for colonial raw materials and running the risk of retaliatory tariffs in markets that were increasingly important to Britain's growing industries. Each bout of industrial distress, as in the immediate post-war period and later in 1825 when a speculative boom collapsed, strengthened the support from industrial areas for a policy which promised wider access to foreign markets, especially in North and South America, and cheaper imported raw materials.

The fact that the conclusions (but not necessarily the theoretical arguments) of the economists on free trade gathered increasing support from the new manufacturing classes in Britain has been interpreted as showing that the new science was chiefly a rationalisation of the interests of these classes and of Britain's unique position of industrial leadership and commercial dominance. As a popular movement, later diffused as a national mood, free trade certainly has this characteristic. It is worth pointing out, however, that in its formative stages orthodox political economy frequently adopted positions that were at variance with what were thought to be the interests of the manufacturing classes. This was true, for example, of what became the orthodox position on the currency question and on the causes and remedies for post-Napoleonic distress.

Throughout the war a dispute raged around the consequences of the suspension of cash payments by the Bank of England in 1793. Had this led to an over-issue of paper currency? Was non-convertibility of the currency into gold responsible for rising prices and the fall in the exchanges? The dispute between those who maintained that rising prices and falling exchanges were prima facie evidence of currency mismanagement by the Bank, and those who argued that they were primarily the result of such 'real' factors as war expenditure abroad, poor harvests, and the disruption of trade, gave rise to a literature which clarified and extended earlier contributions to monetary theory and practice. The official victory of the bullionist view, and the effort made after the war to restore the gold standard in 1819 by monetary deflation, had serious consequences for all debtors, which at this time included both agricultural and manufacturing interests. While it is wrong to regard the crude quantity theory reasoning of the Bullion Report as a full and accurate reflection of the classical position, their attitude was certainly hostile to schemes for positive monetary management, chiefly of an inflationist variety, designed to overcome unemployment and raise profits. The main opposition to 'sound money' and the gold standard came from such spokesmen for the depressed manufacturing trades as Thomas Attwood. For a time at least working-class radicalism added its support to the opponents of monetary orthodoxy. With the rejection of Attwood's ideas by the Chartists in the 1840's, however, the prospects for a populist monetary movement in Britain were cut short. The passage of the Bank Charter Act in 1844 brought this phase of monetary discussion to an end; it endowed Britain with a banking system designed to facilitate economic growth and curb speculative excess by means that involved the minimum positive intervention and interpenetration of banking and industry.

Post-Napoleonic agricultural and manufacturing distress provided the backdrop for another important debate in which orthodoxy was eventually triumphant. This was the famous 'glut controversy' between Malthus and other 'underconsumptionists' on the one side, and Ricardo and his followers on the other. Echoes of this controversy can be found in the works of a number of authors writing during the war who took issue with Smith's unqualified support for 'parsimony' or capital accumulation as the basis for continued economic expansion. In Malthus's hands the argument—never clearly joined—became one in which concern was expressed about the pace of Britain's industrialisation and the extent to which capital was flowing into industry and commerce. Unlike Ricardo, Malthus did not regard rent as a form of income earned at the expense of others; he believed, with the physiocrats, that agriculture and the 'unproductive' expenditure of landowners occupied a crucial role in determining the economic (and implicitly, the political) stability of the nation. Protection for agriculture was just one of the measures that he regarded as necessary to restore the balance by maintaining landowners' incomes and encouraging investment in agriculture. Malthus believed that special measures might be needed to ensure that the expansion of effective demand kept pace with Britain's growing population and industrial capacity if general overproduction and stagnation were to be avoided. Ricardo and his followers responded by invoking what became known as Say's Law of Markets to show that capital accumulation in itself could never be the cause of general overproduction. They did not deny that unemployment could be caused by 'sudden changes in the channels of trade', and, in Ricardo's case, by technological displacement of labour by machines; but they believed that self-regulatory forces could be relied on to preserve the overall stability of the economic system. Once the early post-war years of deflation and readjustment had passed, and the shock of such commercial crises as occurred in 1825 had been absorbed, underconsumptionist views survived only in the underground literature of economics until they were brought to the surface by Keynes in the twentieth century.

Largely as a result of the proselytising activities of two vigorous disciples, James Mill and J. R. McCulloch, by the 'twenties the Ricardian version of political economy had triumphed over rival interpretations. In semi-popular form Ricardo's ideas were publicised through articles in the *Edinburgh* and *Westminster Reviews* and the *Encyclopaedia Britannica*; and an even larger audience was reached through the highly simplified writings of Mrs Marcet, Harriet Martineau, and others who felt that the working classes would benefit from being taught the realities of their situation via the medium of political economy. It was this body of literature, with its dogmatism, apologetics, and facile transformation of theories into policy conclusions, that was responsible for the chorus of abuse directed at the subject from all directions—from working class and Tory radicals, from aristocratic humanitarians, and from the spokesmen for the Romantic movement. As we shall see, in its basic forms, if not with the same emphases imparted by the master, Ricardian political economy survived unpopularity as well as attacks on specific doctrines from within the small circle of devotees of the discipline. But first it is necessary to consider the fate of political economy on the Continent.

THE SPREAD OF CLASSICAL POLITICAL ECONOMY IN EUROPE AND SOME OF ITS CRITICS

In a lecture given in 1870, J. E. Cairnes felt able to make the following confident claim:

'Great Britain, if not the birthplace of Political Economy, has at least been its early home, as well as the scene of the most signal triumphs of its manhood. Every great step in the progress of economic science (I do not think an important exception can be named) has been won by English thinkers; and while we have led the van in economic speculation, we have also been the first to apply with boldness our theories to practice. Our foreign trade, our colonial policy, our fiscal system, each has in turn been reconstructed from the foundation upwards under the inspiration of economic ideas; and the population and the commerce of the country, responding to the impulse given by the new principles operating through those changes, have within a century multiplied themselves manifold.'[6]

It is possible to quarrel with this statement on several grounds. The role of ideas—as opposed to interest groups and circumstance—in producing changes in policy is exaggerated. In speaking of contributions to economic science it is also clear that Cairnes has in mind only the orthodox view of its subject matter. Nevertheless, there is a substantial element of truth in the claim, and it is one that many Continental writers, friend and foe, would have accepted. As written today, the history of economic analysis records many original contributions to the science made by Frenchmen and Germans, whose work went unnoticed at the time;[7] but the dominant scientific tradition in the first half of the nineteenth century was an English one. Cairnes' association of scientific leadership with Britain's industrial and commercial success was a fairly common one: success in the industrial sphere lent prestige and relevance to the writings and policy prescriptions of British economists. British experience and the views of her economists could neither be ignored by those in the less industrialised countries of Europe, nor entirely separated from one another. To those on the Continent who wished to emulate British successes, the 'English' science frequently served as an ideology of economic liberation and modernisation.

After the initial phase of widespread enthusiasm for Smithian liberalism at the end of the eighteenth century and the beginning of the nineteenth century, a more cautious attitude to the English recipe for economic progress set in. Britain's example was frequently held up as

6. *Essays in Political Economy* (1873), p. 232.
7. For example, the work of von Thünen, Cournot, Dupuit and Gossen.

a warning of the dire consequences of allowing economic individualism its head. Doubts were expressed as to whether it was desirable or feasible to expect market forces and private enterprise to lead to the same results in the more backward circumstances of most European countries, where the state had always been a more active force in economic affairs. In England too by the 1830's it was recognised that increased state intervention was required in order to create the necessary pre-conditions for a liberal order; the new Poor Law of 1834 and the Factory Acts can both be interpreted as movements in this direction. For these and other reasons several Continental writers began to formulate alternatives to the English version of political economy which accorded more with their hopes and national circumstances. The very 'Englishness' of the science became its weakness: perhaps it was simply a rationalisation of the peculiarities of Britain's unique position as the first of the industrialised nations—an uncertain guide to those arriving later and less fortunately endowed.

Before illustrating these points it is necessary to consider the special case of France, Britain's nearest industrial rival and the country which already had a firmly-established native tradition in political economy. By the end of the eighteenth century, if not before, physiocracy was in disarray. Indeed, it had already lost a good deal of ground before the appearance of the *Wealth of Nations*. Even during its heyday in the 1760's the physiocratic sect had been subjected to attack. By 1770 Quesnay had retired from the movement; and the fall of Turgot in 1776 was a serious blow to hopes temporarily revived by his appointment to high office. The French revolution carried through many of the liberal reforms which Turgot and the physiocrats had championed, but the association of physiocracy with the concept of legal despotism and with high prices for agricultural products did little to make the sect popular in revolutionary circles. Turgot's analysis of capital and of rates of return in different pursuits in his *Réflexions* was an advance on the treatment previously given to manufactur-

ing by the physiocrats; it may even have been helpful to
Adam Smith when formulating his own position. But the
basic doctrine proved incapable of accommodating itself
to new ideas without succumbing to internal contradictions.
The overwhelming concern with removing obstacles to the
development of a capitalistic form of agriculture had led to
neglect of the distinctive problems of industry and trade
which were to occupy the centre of the stage during the
nineteenth century.

The *Wealth of Nations* was quickly and frequently translated into French. After the first translation in 1779, six
editions of three different translations appeared before
Germain Garnier produced a fourth, and more definitive,
translation in 1801. The rambling structure of the book
might have limited its success in France had it not been for
the fact that Smith found an able interpreter in the person
of Jean Baptiste Say, the first edition of whose *Traité
d'Économie Politique* appeared in 1803. It was left to Say
to exorcise remaining physiocratic elements in French
thinking and to continue the battle for economic liberalism
against the dominant *étatiste* tradition of his native country.
In other parts of Europe too, Say's systematisation of
Smith's doctrines became the chief medium for their
diffusion.

The label 'Smithian' is an inadequate one to describe
Say's contribution. He made use of ideas derived from
physiocracy, Cantillon, Turgot, Condillac *and* Smith to destroy physiocracy and move beyond the work of Smith
himself. By extending an idea of Condillac that all production of material products or services, in manufacturing as
well as in agriculture, consists in the creation of utilities, he
countered both the physiocratic theory of exclusive productivity in agriculture and the remnants of this theory
that remained in the *Wealth of Nations*. In adumbrating his
famous Law of Markets he brought together the physiocratic conception of the circular flow of income and Smith's
doctrine that saving is merely a different way of spending to
combat the view that consumption in the aggregate could
fall short of total production. As noted earlier, Say's Law

of Markets was taken over by James Mill and Ricardo to form an essential part of the orthodox classical economists' theoretical and ideological armoury against the notion that systematic factors were at work in the process of capital accumulation which could lead to general glut and commercial crisis if left unchecked by special action to increase unproductive consumption. Say's Law confirmed the primacy of saving and production, the secondary importance to be attached to monetary as opposed to 'real' flows, and the self-adjusting nature of the liberal economic system.

On other matters Say was not in harmony with his English *confrères*, notably in his treatment of exchange value in terms of utility, and in his refusal to accept Ricardo's theory of rent as a differential payment due to varying fertility. Moreover, Say, in common with most French writers, devoted more attention at an earlier stage to industry and machinery than did Smith and Ricardo. One personal reason for this may have been that unlike the English writers he had practical experience of managing a textile factory. Say was also responsible for re-introducing Cantillon's concept of entrepreneurship as a distinct function earning a distinct form of income. English classical writers made little or no use of the idea: for them entrepreneurship and the ownership of capital were largely inseparable.

Say was also the founder of the French classical school as an academic entity. After the fall of Napoleon he was appointed to the first academic post devoted to political economy (significantly and safely re-entitled 'industrial economy') at the Conservatoire des Arts et Métiers in 1819; and he was subsequently honoured by an appointment to a Chair at the Collège de France which remained in the hands of his followers until the end of the century. According to Say, political economy was a pure science divorced from ethical principles and political applications. He was one of the first to make this self-denying ordinance, and went further towards the explicit aim of value-neutrality than any English economist before Nassau Senior. Like many others after him—certainly his immediate followers in France—he was unable to maintain this stance in practice. Nevertheless the aim is of some interest in its own right as evidence of growing scientific, and hence methodological, self-consciousness. There is in fact something paradoxical about the aim as pursued by French classical writers. They claimed to have made a rigid distinction between economics and politics which in practice amounts to a fusion of the two. Economic science discovers and proclaims the universal and spontaneous principles which underly the economic order; the economist does not concern himself with the 'accidents' of this or that instance of political intervention. But since Say also points out that governments which ignore the unalterable principles of the economic order suffer in consequence, this amounts to saying that politics should merely reflect the economic order.

The assertion of the hegemony of economic laws over politics became a marked characteristic of French classicism. By the middle of the nineteenth century, as evidenced by the work of Charles Dunoyer and Frédéric Bastiat, orthodox French economics was identified with an intransigent belief in an extreme form of *laissez-faire*. The retreat begun by Say (and continued in England by Ricardo) from the more expansive approach of the *Wealth of Nations* laid the science open to charges of narrowness and indifference on the wider questions of social justice. Similar charges were made against Say's English counterparts, but the French writers were more vulnerable on this score because they rejected the more pessimistic (realistic?) aspects of Ricardian doctrines. One obvious explanation for this contrast is the difference in the situations of the two countries. By 1846, when the Corn Laws were abolished, English exponents of economic liberalism had achieved considerable success; they could even regret the crudities and enthusiasm with which the middle classes had taken up the *laissez-faire* principle. In France the academic liberal economists were more closely engaged in popular polemics against *étatisme* and protectionism on the one side, and socialist ideas on the other. Ironically, this situation meant that they were unable to adopt the detached stance which Say had claimed was essential.

The history of political economy in France during the nineteenth century, and in Britain also, is one of growing division between a narrowly circumscribed and deductive science of wealth on the one side, and an ethico-historical approach to society on the other. Political economy was liberal (sometimes radical), unsentimental, and, within limits, reformist. It was opposed by a wide variety of critics, many of whom had in common a belief in the necessity for a more comprehensive and historical (later called sociological) approach to the science of society as the only proper basis for total social reconstruction. Here we shall deal with two French representatives from this large dissenting literature, Sismondi and Saint-Simon. Both writers began as economic liberals of the Smith-Say variety; and both later developed positions which formed a basis for two of the more influential social and intellectual movements in the nineteenth century, namely socialism and positivism.

Simonde de Sismondi provides an interesting example of an economist who began and finished his career as a disciple of Adam Smith but was increasingly drawn into opposition to Smith's orthodox followers. His first economic work, *Richesse Commerciale*, published in 1803, belongs to the initial phase of enthusiasm for Smithian ideas of commercial freedom on the Continent. When Sismondi returned to the subject in 1815 his views had undergone a transformation as a result of his observation of the disruptive effects of the new industrial order on the lives of urban and agricultural workers in several European countries, but above all in England. The work which he then set out to write, *Nouveaux Principes d'Économie Politique*, was an attempt to reconstruct the science so as to bring it to bear more closely on the practical and humanitarian problems created by industrial and agricultural change. In his search for clues as to what had gone wrong Sismondi laid great stress on the change in the aim and methods of political economy; he believed that in abandoning the historical dimension,

Smith's followers had narrowed the inquiry to a concern with wealth alone.

The true significance of Sismondi's work does not lie in his methodological criticisms, his 'humanitarian' emphasis (he had no monopoly in this matter), or his practical remedies. As far as the latter are concerned, although he envisaged an important protective role for the state, and expressed nostalgia for an economy composed of independent agriculturists and artisans in which property and labour would be united, he confessed himself unable to see how his ideals could be realised. His contribution lay in the attention he paid to flaws in the liberal assumption of the spontaneous identification of individual and social interests under emerging industrial conditions. He was one of the first to highlight snags in the process of adjustment from one equilibrium situation to another; to show how competition could break down by virtue of the concentration of wealth and lead to a lowering of wages and working conditions as well as to cheaper goods for the consumer; to draw attention to the effect of machinery on specific groups of workers; to indicate the benefits in terms of security of independent proprietorship; and to question whether commercial crises were not the result of flaws in the process of capital accumulation itself. In all these respects Sismondi provides a foretaste of positions that many later critics of political economy and the new industrial order, both in Britain and on the Continent, were to adopt.

Like Sismondi, Henri de Saint-Simon's early views on political economy have roots in Adam Smith. In his search for principles according to which a new order could be created in Europe following the disruption of revolution and war, Saint-Simon turned to the new science of political economy. While Sismondi concentrated on flaws in the process of industrial change, Saint-Simon adopted a more optimistic, even Utopian attitude towards the potentialities of an industrial civilisation. Suitably harnessed, with control placed in the right hands, industrialism provided a blueprint for a 'positive' re-ordering of society. Saint-Simon's own work, therefore, represents an exaggerated form of economic liberalism—exaggerated because he believed that an administrative technocracy, which would replace the state and politics as then understood, could be built on the principles of political economy. Under Saint-Simon's new industrial dispensation only those who performed a clear economic function would remain—workers, peasants, artists, scientists, manufacturers, and bankers. With the nation turned into a gigantic workshop dedicated to the supreme end of production, the state would become unnecessary.

Already in the works of Saint-Simon himself the spontaneous economic order had given way to control by a new élite charged with responsibility for co-ordinating all activities conducive to production and with the working out of a system of distributive justice. In the hands of his followers the doctrine acquired a quasi-religious flavour with definite socialistic and moral regenerative leanings. Their critique of property relationships and inheritance, their emphasis on man as producer rather than as consumer, brought them into conflict with the English science of political economy, which they considered was too specialised, too concerned with negative freedoms, and insufficiently organic and evolutionary in its approach to the problems of creating a new industrial order. Once more, as in the case of Sismondi, Saint-Simonianism was important in pointing out alternative solutions to those suggested by economic liberalism. On a purely intellectual plane the fecundity of Saint-Simonianism can be seen in several different directions; it led into the world of Auguste Comte, one of the founders of sociology as a rival to political economy; it influenced the views of Friederich List on industrial development, though it acquired a more nationalistic flavour in the process; and it influenced the thinking of two of the most important later exponents of political economy, Karl Marx and John Stuart Mill—of whom more later. There were also more practical results of Saint-Simonianism. Followers of Saint-Simon were prominent in many of the important industrial enterprises of France during the Second Empire and notably in the fields of railway construction and private investment banking. At an early stage it was clear to Saint-Simonians, like Emil Péreire, co-founder with his brother of the Credit Mobilier in 1852, that some kind of restructuring of the financial system would be needed if France was to make the most of her industrial resources. In seeking a French equivalent to the English system of country banks a new instrumentality was fashioned, the investment banker-cum-entrepreneur. It marked a radical departure from the English pattern but was found to fit the needs of several European countries.

Just as at an earlier stage political economy in many European countries was associated with enlightened absolutism so later it became involved with the fluctuating fortunes of liberalism as a social and political movement— a movement that encompassed the rise of an industrial bourgeoisie, demands for constitutional reform, and in the cases of Italy and Germany, the cause of national unity. Even so, the connections were neither necessary nor permanent, and certain parallels with the earlier period of enlightened absolutism remained. In the case of Prussia, for example, it could be argued that economic liberalism frequently served as a substitute for what passed for political liberalism in other countries. And in Italy the importation of liberal ideas associated with political economy was by no means a straightforward example of finding support for a bourgeois ideology. In the first half of the nineteenth century the movement was chiefly sponsored by progressive-minded aristocrats who preached the virtues of enterprise, thrift, and free trade in an effort to galvanise the commercial classes into action.

Although the importation of Smithian ideas into Italy in the early years of the century seems not to have been a very whole-hearted affair, political economy and economic liberalism later played an interesting contributory role in the *Risorgimento* as a practical philosophy of modernisation designed to bring political unity and freedom from foreign domination in its train. As early as 1819, Gioia, an economist of the classical type, was advocating the removal of internal customs barriers as the best means of fostering Italian unity; and the same theme was taken up by several Italian economic commentators later, notably by Romagnosi, Cattaneo, Balbo and Scialoja. Perhaps the best example of the contribution of English political economy to Italian unity, however, can be found in the career of Cavour, the Prime Minister of Piedmont, who was a devotee of the subject and once described it as 'the science of the love of country'. Cavour paid two visits to England in 1835 and 1843, and followed English political and economic debates closely. One of his earliest publications was a commentary on Nassau Senior's Report on the Poor Laws, and few years later, after having observed the final stage of the campaign for the abolition of the Corn Laws, he drew the following lessons from English experience for his compatriots.

'The time approaches when England will offer for the first time the spectacle of a great nation in which the laws which regulate foreign commerce will be in complete accord with economic principles. This example will exercise a most salutary effect upon the economic world. Science, supporting its theories upon the example of a great nation, will acquire greater authority in men's minds, and its maxims, finding daily a greater support amongst those classes which, profiting by the opening of the English market, have an interest in widening their inter-relationships, will end by triumphing upon the Continent over the prejudices and false economic doctrines whose empire today still appears unassailable. Such at least is our profound conviction'.[8]

From the moment that he joined the Piedmontese Cabinet in 1830 Cavour exerted himself on behalf of a full-scale modernising programme on liberal lines, which included free trade, agricultural improvement, railway construction, banking reform, and sound public finances. As far as Cavour was concerned the English influence was a peculiarly direct

8. As cited in A. J. Whyte, *The Early Life & Letters of Cavour* (1925), p. 299.

one, though it is noticeable that to achive similar ends he found it necessary to make greater use of state initiative in establishing the institutional pre-conditions for agricultural and industrial progress than was the case in England. This was true of most European countries, particularly where railways and banking facilities were concerned. English ideas and example were appealed to, but only after significant modification to fit local circumstance. Economic liberals in Italy and elsewhere were also alive to the dangers of uncontrolled individualism in the form of rapacity, speculation, poor working conditions, and economic instability; such excesses would need to be tempered by philanthropy and government control.

The situation in Germany resembles that of Italy in some particulars, except that earlier progress was made towards internal free trade with the formation in 1818 of the *Zollverein*, which by the 1840's united most German states behind what was originally conceived of as a liberal external tariff. As in Italy and France there were academic exponents of liberal doctrines like Karl Heinrich Rau. There were also publicists like John Prince Smith, an Englishman turned Prussian, who drew inspiration and encouragement from Cobden's victory in 1846. But while Malthusian ideas and the principles of the amended Poor Law Act of 1834 were sympathetically received in some circles in Germany, Prince Smith's attempt to emulate Cobden by building a popular political movement around free trade met with limited success. The great triumph of Cobdenism on the Continent was the signing of the Cobden-Chevalier treaty in 1860. But even in France, it could be argued, this victory for free trade was largely imposed on a reluctant nation by an autocratic Emperor, Napoleon III.

Although economic liberalism took a more paternalist form in most European countries, stronger resistance to the methods and conclusions of the English science of political economy was encountered in Germany than elsewhere. This was partly due to the unfortunate effects of earlier liberal reforms introduced during the Stein-Hardenberg reform era on agriculture and some manufacturing trades;

the rapid growth of population in some states; the sluggish and uneven growth of manufacturing industry before 1850; and the disastrous results of the influx of British goods over the comparatively low Prussian tariff when the protection and stimulus provided by Napoleon's economic blockade was removed. These developments put economic liberals in Germany on the defensive; they made it necessary for them to put forward a modified version of economic individualism which accorded a greater protective role to the state.

Liberal ideas in Germany also had to make headway against the views of an entrenched school of writers who made an organic concept of nationality the starting point for political and economic speculation. We are here concerned not so much with the views of the more extreme Romantic nationalists, Fichte and Müller, or with the views of the German historical school which made their influence felt later in the period—as with those of Friederich List. While it is possible to exaggerate the significance of List's *National System of Political Economy* (1841) to the history of economic science, and the extent of its influence on German thinking and practice, there is no doubt that it represents in a peculiarly clear form one type of reaction against the application of the English science to European conditions.

List believed that political economy *à la* Smith was both a reflection and a means of widening the sphere of England's industrial hegemony. Free trade within nations had clearly to be distinguished from free trade between nations at different stages of industrial development. Whereas the former was desirable, the latter would have to be curtailed by means of protective tariffs if those nations which had already reached industrial maturity were not to prevent others from following the same path. The cosmopolitan claims of the English science had to be resisted. What was in the interests of England, and might ultimately be true for all nations once those with manufacturing potential had achieved maturity, was actively harmful to nations like Germany and the United States at their present stage of development.

As List himself was at pains to point out, his conclusions

related to the specific historical situation in which a disunited Germany found itself in the period between the
formation of the *Zollverein* in 1818, when the infant industries of Germany came under heavy competitive pressure from English goods, and the abolition of English restrictions on the import of grain products, Prussia's chief
export. He was animated by a patriotic desire to foster
Germany's industrial well-being, and by a corresponding
suspicion that under existing conditions there could be no
equal dealing with England in matters of trade. But List's
jealousy was a true jealousy in that it sprang from a genuine
desire to emulate England's success. He was certainly correct in detecting enlightened self-interest, if not perfidious
Albion, behind England's espousal of universal free trade.

List's campaign against the English science began with
an attack on its assumption that individuals or the whole
human race were the basic units of economic discourse,
rather than nations treated as historic entities. His own
theory was based on an appreciation of the lessons of history
and the realities of national power conceived of as dynamic
force by means of which new productive resources could be
acquired and defended. In contrast to the views of the
'cosmopolitan school' he wished to construct a science
'which correctly appreciating the existing interests and the
individual circumstances of nations, teaches how *every separate nation* can be raised to that stage of industrial development in which union with other nations equally well-
developed, and consequently freedom of trade, can become
possible and useful to it'.[9] List distinguished between wealth
and productive powers, and between the interests of individual merchants and those of the nation. His enthusiasm—
which took Saint-Simonian proportions—for the potentialities of an industrial civilisation led him to stress the wider
social benefits of establishing 'manufacturing power' and
an 'industrial ethic' in a nation by means of 'educational'
tariffs. Agricultural power belonged to an earlier and lower
stage in a nation's development; agriculture itself could only
acquire a commercial character by the presence of manu-

9. *National System of Political Economy* (1885 edn.), p. 127.

facturing power in a nation. Since ordinary market forces were unable to achieve this balanced pattern of development, a national policy of protecting the home market was needed to promote equality between nations. Unlike the classical school and Saint-Simon, therefore, List wished to make economics subservient to politics rather than vice-versa. Nevertheless, his choice of the tariff as the chief means of exerting an influence on national development, his recognition that universal free trade might be desirable as an ultimate goal, and his antagonism towards a return to a regulated, autarkic, and feudal past placed him closer to the liberal position than to either the romantic nationalists or some of the representatives of the German Historical school who, in the final stages of Germany's unification, saw in the mercantilism of the past—and implicitly in the present—a praiseworthy system of state-building.

The fate of English political economy on the Continent, therefore, was very much under the influence of whether or not some of its policy conclusions on freedom of enterprise and trade were considered by bureaucrats and particular interest groups to coincide with their assessment of the needs of the moment. Smithianism, Malthusianism, and to a lesser extent, Ricardianism, acquired a limited following at different periods. But there was always an air of wearing borrowed clothes, which lends some justification to Marx's contemptuous judgment on the German professors of political economy, that they 'remained mere schoolboys, imitators and followers, petty retailers and hawkers in the service of the great foreign wholesale concern'.[10]

THE CULMINATION OF CLASSICAL POLITICAL ECONOMY: KARL MARX AND JOHN STUART MILL

By the 1840's there were signs that the original scientific impulse behind classical political economy had lost much of its momentum. In England, as on the Continent, after the formative post-Napoleonic war years had passed, the

10. *Capital* (Moscow edn.), p. 12.

science became better known for certain policy conclusions and attitudes—notably *laissez-faire* and free trade—than for its theoretical insights. As a science the subject had acquired a dangerously fixed appearance. Indeed, those practitioners who were anxious to achieve definite policy goals actually had an interest in stressing that the science from which they drew support was no longer at a provisional stage of development. Hence the emphasis on catechisms, dictionaries, elementary text-books, and historical surveys of the development of science, which were designed to present conclusions rather than raise questions of a critical nature. In presenting a new dictionary of political economy to the French public in 1854, for example, Ambroise Clément claimed that the subject was ripe for codification because,

'. . . we are convinced that [political economy] is now sufficiently advanced to leave no legitimate doubt as to its essential principles, and that the truths expressed by these principles will not be any more disturbed by subsequent research or discoveries than have been the elements of geometry or the universal laws of gravitation by the work of Lagrange of Laplace.'[11]

In England the appearance of fixity was related not so much to hopes as to actual successes. It is possible to argue, as Cairnes did in the lecture cited earlier, that political economy, especially after the victory of free trade in 1846, had become too successful for its own good as an intellectual enterprise; it had become part of the conventional wisdom of the middle-classes, businessmen, and politicians in all parties. While it had proved apposite to the problems of a society passing through an unprecedented period of transition from being a largely agricultural economy towards one characterised by rapid industrialisation, population growth, and increasing reliance on foreign trade, its relevance was less clear to a society in which manufacturing industry, concentrated more and more in large cities, was part of the

11. Introduction to *Dictionnaire de l'Économie Politique*, edited by Coquelin and Guillaumin (1854).

established order. It was no longer obvious that political economy was capable of coming to terms with the new problems of the second phase of industrialisation, even in the country of its origin.

In their separate ways two contrasting authors, Karl Marx and John Stuart Mill, recognised the situation into which political economy had fallen. With quite different ends in view they both made an effort to extend the life of Ricardian economics by showing its relevance to the new industrial civilisation. Indeed, the main reason for the survival of the Ricardian model of economic inquiry beyond the middle of the nineteenth century lies in the fact that both Marx and Mill retained it as the basis for their influential critique and restatement of the principles of the science. Only in recent years has it been recognised that 'Marx and Mill have more in common with each other than either has with the representative thinkers of the next generation, let alone those of our own troubled age'.[12] Among the many points of contact between the two writers considered as economists is the fact that both can accurately be described as the last of the classical line.

It was Marx's view that the bourgeois science of political economy had reached its peak with the work of Ricardo in England and Sismondi in France. It had investigated the 'real relations of production in bourgeois society' and had laid bare many of the mechanisms and sources of conflict involved in the supersession of feudalism by capitalism in its earlier stages. Its chief fault lay in treating capitalism as 'the absolutely final form of social production, instead of as a passing historical phase of its evolution'. After Ricardo's death the development of class antagonism within capitalism made further objective examination of the laws of capitalist development by the bourgeoisie impossible. Scientific bourgeois economy gave way to 'vulgar economy', to sophistry and apologetics on behalf of the interests of capital. In countries like Germany the later development of modern industry and of the bourgeoisie not only made it

12. The words are George Lichtheim's in *Marxism, An Historical & Critical Study* (1961), p. 404.

necessary to import the science ready-made from England and France, but under conditions in which impartial investigation was no longer feasible. Marx saw it as his task to develop a socialist critique of capitalism and of political economy in order to reveal the 'laws of motion' and inner contradictions of capitalist society—contradictions which would eventually prove fatal to the continuity of the system.

The economic materials from which such a critique could be constructed—the labour theory of value, subsistence wages, declining profits—were all to be found in the writings of Smith and Ricardo. What was needed then was a modification and rearrangement of these building blocks so as to emphasise the connection between the mode of production and class relationships. Marx saw that the labour theory of value was capable of supporting an edifice far more imposing than that of the early Ricardian socialists. He realised that it could be made the centre-piece of an explanation of the social origins of surplus value and a theory of class exploitation. When linked with capital accumulation, the labour theory of value could be made to yield a picture of the capitalist dynamic which conformed to the Hegelian dialectic and led not to the classical stationary state but to revolution and the expropriation of the expropriators. Once this was accomplished the antagonism of capital and labour would stand out more clearly, and the self-defeating nature of efforts by capital to expand and retain its hold on surplus value could be demonstrated. In extending the logic of the Ricardian model Marx also claimed that he was able to take fuller account than earlier writers in the bourgeois tradition had done of the realities of 'machinufacture', technical innovation, and cyclical breakdowns in the process of capitalist expansion.

Marx applied the same type of approach to his predecessors in the socialist tradition. Their works belonged to an immature stage of capitalism and the class struggle. Consequently, the remedies which earlier socialists had proposed were also immature. Because they were unable to discern the outline of the new society within the existing capitalist society, they had been forced to construct Utopias based on reason rather than on the revealed laws of historical change. It was one of the virtues of Marx's system, as he saw it, that it avoided the errors of the Utopian socialists by demonstrating that capitalism was inherently self-destructive and could not be reformed by the elimination of specific injustices and abuses.

Among the many works criticised by Marx in *Capital* (1867) was John Stuart Mill's *Principles of Political Economy* (1848)—though it can now be shown that Marx was more indebted to Mill than he cared to acknowledge. Mill was criticised not as a vulgar apologist but as a 'shallow syncretist'; as one who had tried to 'reconcile irreconcilables' by attempting 'to harmonise the Political Economy of Capital with the claims, no longer to be ignored, of the proletariat'.[13] Needless to say, Mill's own assessment of what he set out to achieve was different. It was a product of his attempt to reconcile the Ricardianism and utilitarianism of his original upbringing with the manifold intellectual influences of his early manhood, which included Coleridge, Carlyle, the Saint-Simonians, and Comte. On the narrower economic front, Mill set out to show that political economy was not in a state of stagnation and disintegration; that— suitably qualified and supplemented by other branches of knowledge—it was capable of useful service as a guide to the new problems facing an established industrial society at the mid-point of the century. The object then of the *Principles* was to incorporate recent speculations by 'bringing them into harmony with the principles previously laid down by the best thinkers on the subject'; and to do what the *Wealth of Nations* had done for an earlier generation by combining systematic exposition of scientific principles with applications to contemporary problems.

On matters of abstract theory Mill followed Ricardo fairly closely. This does not mean that he was incapable of recognising new ideas or of making important modifications of his own, merely that he continued to regard the questions posed by the Ricardian framework as being the

13. *Capital* (Moscow edn.), p. 15.

important ones. In spite of the abolition of the Corn Laws and of evidence that diminishing returns in agriculture had been overcome—temporarily at least—Mill still felt that the Malthusian problem posed a real threat to hopes of raising the living standards of the majority. He was less concerned than Ricardo about the sources of further capital accumulation in Britain, and less worried about the effect of new machinery in generating technological unemployment. Nevertheless, he was also more pessimistic about the effects of economic growth—unaccompanied by radical interference in the system of income and wealth distribution—in raising the living standards of the masses; and he thought it questionable 'if all the mechanical inventions yet made have lightened the day's toil of any human being'.

In deference to Comte and Saint-Simonians, Mill distinguished between the laws of production, which 'partake of the character of physical truth', and the laws governing distribution, which were matters involving human will and institution. For this reason, in contrast with earlier writers in the orthodox classical tradition, Mill included a treatment of societies in which custom rather than competition determined economic relationships, and a full discussion of 'different modes of distributing the produce of land and labour, which have been adopted in practice, or may be conceived in theory'. It was here that Mill, with increasing sympathy over the years, discussed the various alternatives put forward by the socialists. Mill's famous eulogy of the stationary state as one in which more attention would be paid to the quality of life as opposed to economic striving, and his detailed analysis of the functions of government, place him among the forerunners of modern welfare thinking in affluent societies today.

In its Marxian and Millian forms classical political economy survived well into the second half of the nineteenth century. But in spite of the enormous readership of Mill's *Principles* in England and elsewhere, and Marx's following on the Continent, the works of these two authors constitute the effective end of the classical mode of scientific inquiry in the nineteenth century.[14] In the case of both writers, it was not the corpus of scientific reasoning that accounted for their subsequent influence but the ethical and political doctrines with which the economic theory was associated. Mill showed that it was possible to be an economist and still be sympathetic towards different ways of studying society and radical alternatives to the status quo. His attitude towards 'purely abstract investigations' was that they were 'of very minor importance compared with the great practical questions which the progress of democracy and the spread of socialist opinions are pressing on'. His statement that 'happily there is nothing in the laws of Value which remains for the present or any future writer to clear up' was treated as a monument to complacency by a later generation of economists concerned precisely with the 'laws of Value'. There is a good deal of truth in the charge that Mill's authority and air of finality on theoretical questions stifled, rather than provoked, inquiry—which had certainly not been the case with Smith and Ricardo. Similarly with Marx: his followers were more concerned to propagate the ideological and revolutionary content of his writings. For as Professor Gerschenkron has said:

'What was received and worked as intellectual yeast was not the theory in any reasonable sense of the word, but the ethical norm in conjunction with a gospel-like promise of delivery. All the talk about scientific socialism could not change the fact that what was created was an ideology which contained, along with other things, paratheoretical elements and did so probably to a somewhat higher degree than most ideologies'.[15]

By the 1870's, therefore, economic science as originally conceived by Adam Smith and developed by his successors

14. With the revival of interest in the political economy of growth and development in the middle of the twentieth century has come a revival of interest in the classical-type models. And while Marx's theories have not proved particularly helpful in understanding developments in communist countries today. the Marxian approach to the analysis of capitalism has of course always had its adherents.

15. Op. cit., p. 14.

I.R.

in the classical tradition was suffering from a definite hardening of the arteries. For his own generation, Mill had partially succeeded in answering the charges levelled against political economy by its earlier critics—that it was a narrow-minded, abstract, and bloodless type of inquiry which took no account of ethical questions or social bonds. He had also given a powerful defence of the necessity for deductive reasoning, while stressing the qualified or hypothetical character of economic theory, and acknowledging that 'for practical purposes, Political Economy is inseparably inter-twined with many other branches of social philosophy'. Nevertheless, by the 1870's political economy faced a re-newed onslaught on its methods and aims. It was criticised for its concentration on one aspect of human behaviour separated from the rest; for its reliance on abstract deductive methods based on premises which were inadequately grounded on concrete, historical, and other inductive evi-dence; and for its inability to take full account of the ele-ments of change and diversity in society. Most of these criticisms had been made earlier in the century when the subject was more vigorous, by Sismondi and the Saint-Simonians, and by writers such as Richard Jones. By the 1870's, however, the critics were able to attack an en-feebled citadel from academic strongholds of their own.

The most obvious symbol of internal decay was Mill's recantation in 1869 on the wage-fund theory, which had come to be regarded as crucial to the integrity of the classical model. When Stanley Jevons denounced the Mill-Ricardo school of thought on the theory of value in his *Theory of Political Economy* (1871) for having 'shunted the car of Economic Science on to a wrong line', the impression of a crumbling edifice was confirmed. Jevons in fact had fired the first shot in the marginal revolution, as it later became known—a revolution which was to show the way forward out of an *impasse*, and was to herald the transforma-tion of classical political economy into neo-classical economics.

Although economic science was eventually to be renewed from within, there were those who felt that the whole enterprise should be abandoned or subsumed in a broader, more historically-oriented, study of the evolution of social and economic institutions. The reaction against political economy came from several different directions at once. From France there came the influence of Comte's positivism, with its programme for an organic and unified social science. Judged by Comtist criteria political economy belonged to the pre-positivist, or metaphysical, stage of human thought. It ignored the consensus of different social functions, and was at best merely a fragment of the territory to be annexed in the name of sociology. From Germany there came the influence of a long tradition of historians with an impressive array of monographs to its credit, devoted to the detailed study of economic conditions, ancient and modern, stressing national diversity, and attacking either implicitly or explicitly the 'universalism' and 'atomism' of the Ricardian method. Faced with the complexity and social tensions of the industrial order, and with the rise of working-class movements dedicated to socialism in one form or another, there was a need to find a more positive collective ideal than that embodied in the liberal pleas for individual freedom in economic affairs. The German historical school promised something that was at the same time broader, more realistic, and more overtly practical and ethical than that offered by classical political economy.

These Continental ideas were either taken up by British disciples or matched by native counterparts; by Toynbee and other ethico-historical writers like Thorold Rogers, J. K. Ingram, W. J. Ashley, T. C. Cliffe-Leslie and W. Cunningham. They were quickly joined by a new brigade of statistical investigators concerned with the 'social question', who also took issue with the *a priori* method. Here again there was a parallel with the work of those members of the German historical school who formed the *Verein für Sozialpolitik* in 1874 with the object of collecting material to guide the state in its new protective and interventionist role. The cosmopolitan character of this movement in itself constituted an implied criticism of political economy, which more and more seemed like an insular discipline concerned only with the peculiar conditions ruling in one country at one stage of its historical development. This stage had passed by 1870. Just as Britain's industrial leadership was being challenged by Germany, so, it seemed, were the ideas of her economists. Britain's period of uniqueness was passing; she was now being urged to pay closer attention to the ideas and experience of nations with similar social problems but longer traditions of paternalist government and centralised bureaucracy, where economic liberalism had never taken strong hold. Walter Bagehot summarised this trend against the 'English' science when he said that 'no theory, economical or political, can now be both insular and secure; foreign thoughts come soon and trouble us; there will always be doubt here as to what is only believed here'.[16] Moreover, just as the achievement of Newton had fortified the early economic scientists in their search for natural laws of society so the achievements of Darwin could be cited in support of the virtues of an evolutionary or historical approach based on close attention to specific forms of social life.

The reconstruction of the theoretical basis of economics went on side by side with the disputes over method. This too was an international movement. Almost at the same time as Jevons published his attack on the classical labour theory of value, Karl Menger in Austria and Leon Walras in Switzerland published works reaching essentially similar conclusions. And once the new theory had been propounded an international pedigree was soon assembled, consisting of all those writers whose works anticipated the three major 'marginalists' but were submerged beneath the classical consensus.

In essence and in its early stages the new approach consisted mainly in focusing attention on the subjective determinants which underlie the demand for goods, rather than on the objective factors which determine the cost and supply of goods. The proper foundation for a new economics, it was argued, lay in the quasi-psychological law of diminish-

16. *Economic Studies* (1880).

ing marginal utility—a law which posited a definite (if subjective) relationship between the quantities of goods possessed and the extra satisfaction to be derived from additional amounts of them. With such a law in his possession the economist was able to explain the market behaviour of buyers faced with an array of prices, their responses to changes in price, the gains to be made from exchange, and the optimal allocation of a given stock of resources among alternative uses. The whole system turned on the effect of marginal variations, and proved capable of being extended beyond variations in degrees of satisfaction to other economic quantities, notably costs, revenues, and physical products.

The classical approach to economics was dominated by the problems of capital accumulation, population growth, and diminishing returns in agriculture. The interest of the classical theorists in the economics of allocation and value in exchange, though it was profound and led them to make permanent contributions to our understanding of these questions, was largely subservient to their interest in economic growth and macro-distribution. After the marginal revolution attention shifted away from such grand speculations towards a narrower and more precise inquiry into the determination of relative prices. Economics became a quasi-mathematical discipline in which the important questions were posed as scarcity or choice-problems involving the maximisation or minimisation of strategic economic quantities under specified conditions.

In spite of the vigour of Jevons's attack in 1871, the transition from classical political economy to neo-classical economics was a slow process. It did not prove easy, in England at least, to abandon classical dispositions entirely. By 1890, however, when Alfred Marshall published his *Principles of Economics*, the process was complete. Jevons had thought that 'it would be as well to discard, and as quickly as possible, the old troublesome double-worded name of our Science',[17] but Marshall was the first major economist to do so in the title of his book. The change of name was meant to

17. Preface to 2nd edition of *Theory of Political Economy* (1879), p. xiv.

convey a new sense of scientific purpose and to help dissociate the new and more precise discipline from the old, with all its inherited political and doctrinal entanglements. Having made the distinction, Marshall, in contrast to Jevons, was anxious to stress the remaining links with what was valuable in the older English tradition. He also made a determined effort to overcome methodological dissension by recognising the claims of the historical approach, and by making extensive use of it in his own work. It is, in fact, significant that the end of our period not only witnessed the demise of political economy and the birth of economics, but also saw the inauguration of economic history as an academic study.

BIBLIOGRAPHY

There are so many comprehensive histories of economic thought covering this period that any recommendation is bound to be rather arbitrary. J. A. Schumpeter's *History of Economic Analysis* (1954) is not only comprehensive but magisterial. Mark Blaug's *Economic Theory in Retrospect* (2nd ed. 1968) is the best of the recent histories of economic analysis and contains valuable bibliographies. Of the numerous histories of economic doctrines—a popular genre in France—that by C. Gide and C. Rist, originally published in French in 1909 and available in a second edition in English since 1948, is still very useful and readable. Many of the articles on individual figures and schools of thought in the new *International Encyclopaedia of the Social Sciences* are worth reading.

ORIGINS AND EMERGENCE

There is now one very good book on this subject by W. L. Letwin, *The Origins of Scientific Economics* (1963) which deals with the English founders of the science before Adam Smith from the point of view of someone who believes that 'there can be no period when a science is partly in existence'. A thoroughly relativist view of this question can be found in W. Stark's, *The History of Economics In Its Relation to Social Development* (1944). The first chapter of J. A. Schumpeter's *Economic Doctrine and Method* (English edn. 1954), contains many suggestive ideas on this subject and deals with European-wide developments; see also J. H. Hollander, 'The Dawn of a Science' in J. M. Clark et al, *Adam Smith, 1776–1926* (1928). As examples of how this question was tackled by two of the earliest historians of economics see J. R. McCulloch, *A Discourse on the Rise, Progress, Peculiar Objects, and Importance of Political Economy* (1824) and A. Blanqui, *Histoire de l'économie politique* (1837).

Another approach is to consider the claims of individual authors as founders. On Cantillon see J. J. Spengler, 'Richard Cantillon: First of the Moderns', *Journal of Political*

Economy, vol. 62, 1954. G. Weulersse considers the French precursors of the physiocrats in *Les Physiocrates* (1931). For an example of a consultant administrator treated at length see P. Harsin, "L'abbé de St-Pierre, économiste', *Revue d'histoire économique et sociale* (1932). The claims of Steuart are championed by S. R. Sen, *The Economics of Sir James Steuart* (1957), though this should now be supplemented by A. Skinner's introduction to his edition of Steuart's *Inquiry* published for the Scottish Economic Society in 1967.

The main issues in the debate on mercantilism are clearly rehearsed in D. C. Coleman (ed.) *Revisions in Mercantilism* (1969). Another brief introduction to the subject can be found in C. Wilson's *Mercantilism* (Historical Association Pamphlet: 1958). On the natural law tradition and economic science see O. H. Taylor's *Economics and Liberalism* (1955). The connection between the Enlightenment and the social sciences in general has given rise to a large literature. For a good summary treatment see P. Gay, *The Enlightenment, An Interpretation* (1970), chapter 7. On the Scottish Enlightenment view of history as related to economics see R. L. Meek, 'The Scottish Contribution to Marxist Sociology', reprinted in the author's *Economics and Ideology* (1967), and A. Skinner, 'Economics and History—The Scottish Enlightenment', *Scottish Journal of Political Economy*, February 1965.

PHYSIOCRACY

The standard work on the subject is G. Weulersse, *Le Mouvement Physiocratique en France, de 1756 à 1770*, (1910). By far the best modern study in exposition and interpretation can be found in R. L. Meek's *The Economics of Physiocracy* (1962). A rather crude exercise in relating physiocracy to its economic and ideological environment can be found in N. J. Ware, 'The Physiocrats: A Study in Economic Rationalisation', *American Economic Review*, Dec. 1931. For an examination of the connection of physiocracy with some of the wider philosophical themes of the Enlightenment see T. P. Neill, 'The Physiocrats' Concept of Economics',

Quarterly Journal of Economics, Nov. 1949, and by the same author, 'Quesnay and Physiocracy', *Journal of the History of Ideas*, April, 1958.

ADAM SMITH

A useful start can still be made from *Adam Smith, 1776–1926* (1928), which contains several useful essays including a seminal one by J. Viner on 'Adam Smith and Laissez-faire'. It also includes a long survey by M. Palyi on 'The Introduction of Adam Smith on the Continent'. The economic background is discussed by R. Koebner, 'Adam Smith and the Industrial Revolution', *Economic History Review* April 1959; by J. Viner in his introduction to the Kelley reprint of J. Rae's *Life of Adam Smith* (1965); and, from a Marxian point of view, by R. L. Meek in 'Adam Smith and the Classical Concept of Profit' in his *Economics & Ideology* (1967). The reinterpretation of Smith and his followers as being primarily concerned with economic growth started effectively with H. Myint, *Theories of Welfare Economics* (1948); for a sample of essays on this subject see B. Hoselitz (ed.) *Theories of Economic Growth* (1960).

POLITICAL ECONOMY AND ENLIGHTENED ABSOLUTISM

Most of the sources already cited on physiocracy deal with their concept of legal despotism. The facts of Turgot's public career and its ending can be found in D. Dakin, *Turgot and the Ancien Regime* (1939).

For Spain see R. Herr, *The Eighteenth Century Revolution in Spain* (1958) and R. Carr, *Spain 1808–1939* (1966). There is also a valuable pair of articles by R. S. Smith on 'Economists and the Enlightenment in Spain, 1750-1800', *Journal of Political Economy*, vol. 63, 1955 and on 'The *Wealth of Nations* in Spain and Latin America, 1780–1800', *Journal of Political Economy*, vol. 65, 1957. The same author has written on 'English Economic Thought in Spain, 1776–1848' for C. D. Goodwin and I. B. Holley (eds.) *The Transfer of Ideas:*

Historical Essays (1968). For a study of one of the ways in which new economic ideas were propagated see R. J. Shafer, *The Economic Societies in the Spanish World, 1763– 1821* (1958). On the general Prussian background the most penetrating book is by H. Rosenberg, *Bureaucracy, Aristocracy and Autocracy, The Prussian Experience, 1660–1815.* For the Stein-Hardenberg period of reform see G. S. Ford, *Stein & the Era of Reform in Prussia, 1807–1815* (1965), and C. W. Hasek. *The Introduction of Adam Smith's Doctrines into Germany,* (1925).

CLASSICAL POLITICAL ECONOMY IN BRITAIN AFTER ADAM SMITH

The period between the publication of the *Wealth of Nations* and Ricardo's *Principles* has not been treated as a whole by any historian of economic thought, though there are plenty of works dealing with individual authors and topics. On the historical background and Napoleon's economic blockade in particular see E. Heckscher, *The Continental System* (1922), and F. Crouzet, *Le Blocus Continental et l'Economie Britannique* (1958). On some of the leading issues debated by economists during the Napoleonic Wars see R. L. Meek, *Economics of Physiocracy* (1962), pp. 313–63 on early theories of under-consumption and physiocracy in Britain. The literature concerned with grain scarcity and pauperism has now been treated comprehensively by J. R. Poynter, *Society & Pauperism, English Ideas on Poor Relief, 1795–1834* (1969). The best survey of the Corn Law debate is still that by D. G. Barnes, *A History of the English Corn Laws, 1660–1846* (1930), though on the post-Napoleonic war debates and their significance for economics this needs to be supplemented by E. Cannan, *Theories of Production and Distribution in English Political Economy* (1893), pp. 116– 23 and G. J. Stigler, 'The Ricardian Theory of Value and Distribution', *Journal of Political Economy*, June 1952. The literature on the bullionist controversy is vast: for two recent works see B. A. Corry, *Money, Saving and Investment in English*

Economics, 1800–1850 (1962) and F. W. Fetter, *The Development of British Monetary Orthodoxy, 1797–1815* (1965).

The dissemination of the views of political economists to a wider public is dealt with by F. W. Fetter in his articles on the authorship of economic articles in the *Edinburgh Review* (J.P.E. Feb. 1958) and the *Westminster Review* (J.P.E. Dec. 1962). See also J. Clive, *Scotch Reviewers* (1962), and R. K. Webb, *The British Working Class Reader* (1955).

The best single work on Ricardo and his followers is M. Blaug's *Ricardian Economics* (1958), and the same author deals with the glut controversy with great clarity in his *Economic Theory in Retrospect* (2nd ed. 1968). James Mill as an expositor of Ricardian ideas is discussed in the introductions by D. Winch to *James Mill; Selected Economic Writings* published for the Scottish Economic Society in 1966. On J. R. McCulloch see D. P. O'Brien's *J. R. McCulloch, A Study in Classical Economics* (1970).

CLASSICAL POLITICAL ECONOMY IN EUROPE AND ITS CRITICS

French classicism is considered at length in such standard French texts as those written by R. Gonnard (1947), E. James (1959), and H. Denis (1967). The best treatment is still that of Gide and Rist. Saint-Simon and Sismondi also feature in these texts and in more broadly-gauged works on the history of socialism and social ideas such as that by M. Leroy, *Histoire des Idées Sociales en France* vol. 2, (1950) and F. E. Manuel, *The Prophets of Paris* (1962). The liberal origins of both Sismondi and Saint-Simon are stressed in essays by E. Halevy reprinted in his *The Era of Tyrannies* (1967).

Some of the works referred to above under enlightened absolutism also cover German, Spanish and Italian developments in the later period. On Italy the most relevant work is that by K. R. Greenfield, *Economics & Liberalism in the Risorgimento* (1965 revised edn.). The modified form which liberalism took in Germany is the subject of D. Röhr's book on *The Origins of Social Liberalism in Germany* (1963).

The role played by John Prince Smith is considered by W. O. Henderson in his *Britain and Industrial Europe, 1750–1850* (1954). The formation of and debate within the Zollverein forms one essential background to German developments: see A. H. Price, *The Evolution of the Zollverein* (1949) and W. O. Henderson, *The Zollverein* (2nd edn. 1959). The standard biography of List is that by F. Lenz published in 1936; see also M. Bouvier-Ajain, *Frédéric List* (1938).

THE CULMINATION OF CLASSICAL POLITICAL ECONOMY

The connections between Mill and Marx mentioned in the text are dealt with in detail by B. Balassa, 'Karl Marx & J. S. Mill', *Weltwirt schaftliches Archiv*, Band 83, Heft II, 1959, and B. Shoul, 'Similarities in the Work of J. S. Mill and Karl Marx', *Science & Society*, vol. XXIX, 1965. Of the many works on Marxian economics the following samples are particularly helpful: M. Blaug's chapter in his *Economic Theory in Retrospect*; R. L. Meek's essays on Marx in his *Economics & Ideology*; J. Robinson's *Essay on Marxian Economics* (1946); and D. Horowitz (ed.) *Marx and Modern Economics* (1968). On J. S. Mill's role as an expositor of Ricardo's system see M. Blaug, *Ricardian Economics* (1958), Chapter 9, and his article on 'The Empirical Content of Ricardian Economics', *Journal of Political Economy*, Feb. 1956. W. J. Ashley's introduction to his edition of Mill's *Principles*, though written in 1909, is still a good place to begin consideration of Mill's attempt to blend new and old ideas.

The state of classical political economy around 1890 and the related methodological disputes can be conveniently studied by reference to R. L. Smyth (ed.) *Essays in Economic Method* (1962), a collection of Presidential addresses to Section F of the British Association for the Advancement of Science. T. W. Hutchison begins his *Review of Economic Doctrine, 1870–1929* (1953) with an excellent chapter on the subject; see also S. G. Checkland, 'Economic Opinion in England as Jevons Found It', *Manchester School*, May 1951, and A. W. Coats, 'The Historist Reaction in English Political Economy', *Economica*, May 1954.

I should like to acknowledge financial assistance given by the Nuffield Foundation in the course of writing this essay.

10. Industrial Archaeology

M. J. T. Lewis

Archaeology, it has been said, is the handmaid of history. By extension, industrial archaeology should be the hand-maid of industrial history. It is not an end in itself, but a means to an end. Like the archaeology of other periods of history, it can clothe with flesh the dry bones of the written record, and sometimes help to restore the documentary skeleton where it is lacking. Technical and economic historians have long had recourse to surviving remains of earlier industry; but in its present form industrial archaeo-logy is still a young study, born of an urgency engendered by the great wave of urban redevelopment, road-building, suburban expansion and plain vandalism that has charac-terised the post-war years. Because it is so new, its full potential has hardly yet been achieved, and certainly not yet fully appreciated.

Industrial archaeology can operate on two distinct planes. At one level it can act as an educator and an eye-opener. The man in the street may read about the economic and social impact of the industrial revolution, but he will probably acquire only a blurred two-dimensional picture unless he can actually see something of the buildings and machinery involved. Even if the sites are in ruins, a little imagination can often bring the third dimension into play, endow the written word with life and meaning. By means of museum exhibits and preserved monuments, industrial archaeology can help to balance the historical picture by preventing the economic past from being swamped in the public mind by the military, ecclesiastical and artistic past. Nor is this educative process restricted to the public at large. By pointing out examples of early technology, be it old machine tools or suspension bridges, industrial archaeo-logy can lead the engineer to a greater appreciation of his profession. By explaining the workings and limitations of, say, the Bessemer converter and supplying actual dimensions of nineteenth-century housing, it can offer the economic and social historian a better understanding of his material.

On a higher level, industrial archaeology can make a more positive contribution to knowledge, in cases where the serious worker tackles individual sites or groups of sites, documents them fully, asks meaningful questions and tries to answer them, and interprets his findings in the light of written sources. A concise definition of industrial archaeology is hard to find because it is, or should be, as wide-ranging in its approach as in its subject matter. Dr Buchanan has described it as 'a field of study concerned with the investigation, surveying, recording and sometimes the preservation of industrial monuments. It aims, moreover, at assessing the significance of such monuments in the context of social and technological history'.[1] He goes on to interpret 'monuments' very widely, including the sites, structures and layouts of all kinds of industrial buildings, machinery and engineering features, as well as the surrounding landscape of workers' houses, inns, chapels and the like. These monuments may be of any date, although by implication they are obsolete or obsolescent. The early Iron Age pottery kiln and the plastics factory of the 1930s should alike be grist to the industrial archaeologist's mill, though the great bulk of his material comes from the Industrial Revolution or Revolutions—whatever dates one cares to assign them—simply because of the scale of industrialisation involved.

The work of the industrial archaeologist lies primarily in the field: assessing, clearing where necessary, surveying in as much or as little detail as circumstances demand, recording in a permanent form for future reference. In all this he resembles his more traditional archaeological colleague; the main difference is that the one normally has to rely on careful excavation and stratigraphy, while the other—usually—has more upstanding evidence to work on. But, in any kind of archaeology, a bare record is rarely useful in a vacuum. The site needs to be interpreted and

1. R. A. Buchanan, *The Theory and Practice of Industrial Archaeology*, Bath (1968), 1.

located in the context of comparable sites and of documentary evidence. If there is any real distinction between the industrial archaeologist and the industrial historian, it is that one starts from a tangible, the other from a documentary, basis. Ideally, the two approaches should be united. In the words of an archivist, 'It is a fallacy to suppose that "archaeology" stops, or becomes less useful, when historical and documentary sources begin . . . The more we have documentary sources to help us, the more we can hope to get out of the material remains, and *vice versa*'.[2]

One of the great virtues of industrial archaeology is that it is interdisciplinary. It may draw upon, and contribute to, not only economic history, but technological, social, architectural and local history as well. It can open up vistas which might otherwise remain closed. The economic historian and the engineer will regard a site with different eyes and with different results: both valid, but complementary. As things stand at present, the number of professional practitioners of industrial archaeology is small. The vast bulk of the work—in Britain, though not elsewhere—is done by amateurs or, to use a more suitable label, part-time workers. The study is not yet institutionalised: an asset in that the diverse non-specialist approach is still fresh and not yet desiccated by academic aridity. Parochialism and lack of facilities for documentary research among part-time workers are possible pitfalls; and the regular and urgent need to beat the bulldozer—the equivalent of the rescue dig of other brands of archaeologist —can create the inevitable situation where recording has to take priority and interpretation goes to the wall. But those who criticise industrial archaeology for making only a meagre contribution to historical knowledge are expecting workers in this new field to run before they walk. The subject is a mammoth jigsaw puzzle, where many of the pieces are already lost for good; the more that can be saved before they too are destroyed, the more complete the final picture will be. Rescue of the pieces must take priority

2. W. A. Pantin, 'Monuments or Muniments?', *Medieval Archaeology*, ii (1958), 158f.

over the completion of the puzzle: recording must come before interpretation.

The pursuit of industrial archaeology in Europe is decidedly uneven.[3] This is in part because the history of industrialisation in the various countries has been uneven: one would naturally expect more interest to be shown, and more profound results obtained, in Germany and Britain than in Greece or Portugal. The main sphere of activity, taking Europe as a whole, is preservation, whether in museums or *in situ*. Most countries have their national and provincial museums of general industry and technology, with more numerous museums of particular industries in the appropriate districts. There are, too, notable museums maintained by individual firms, though their number varies widely from country to country. It is impossible to make truly fair comparisons, but, allowing for the size of the country and the degree of its industrialisation, Poland, Czechoslovakia, Holland and Sweden seem to boast the best traditional museums of industry. Open-air museums, to which buildings and machinery are removed bodily, are increasing in number, and the scope of the Dutch and Scandinavian prototypes—folk life, crafts, and the more rural branches of industry like cornmills, small-scale textiles and pottery— is becoming ever wider.

The preservation of industrial buildings *in situ* is no easy task. In the smaller heavily-populated countries where space is at a premium, commercial considerations are overwhelming, especially where urban redevelopment is under way. The costs of restoration and maintenance can be astronomical, and local or national authorities are often unable or unwilling to shoulder the burden. There is clearly a strict limit to the sites where preservation can reasonably

3. The name Industrial Archaeology does not find much favour on the Continent, where people tend to refer simply to 'technological monuments'. In German-speaking lands the compromise *technische Archäologie* is found. *Industrie-Archäologie* usually means the study of ancient industry by traditional archaeological methods: see R. Pittioni, 'Industrie-Archäologie: ein neuer Forschungszweig für Ur- und Frühgeschichte', *Wissenschaft und Weltbild*, Jg.23 H.1 (1970), 32–7.

be expected, but a representative selection of typical and outstanding examples must be kept, if the past is to be illustrated in a truthful and balanced way. Nations with a tradition of private—even family—enterprise come off worst in this respect, communist countries with a political interest in the history of production the best.

In recording, the honours are yet more unequal. Several countries have begun to compile inventories of industrial monuments, the value of which depends on their completeness. In any event, they generally consist of little more than lists of monuments with the bare essentials described. Their primary purpose is as a guide to deciding priorities for preservation and as an index to be consulted by researchers. In the more detailed recording—and interpretation—of industrial remains, Britain, with its army of amateur workers, undoubtedly leads the way; elsewhere the recording of sites is, on the whole, limited, the position being akin to that in Britain in the 1950s. Europe—especially Western Europe—is well endowed with local history societies, many of which do now include industrial studies among their other interests. There are, too, a number of national journals of technical history,[4] though Britain is the only country with a journal devoted solely to industrial archaeology.

Britain, as the cradle of the industrial revolution in many of its aspects, is rich in industrial monuments. It is not, as a nation, as conscious of this wealth as it might be. A moth-eaten fragment of medieval castle can still be safeguarded while a national monument like Euston Station is consigned to the demolition contractor. With some notable exceptions, individual firms and nationalised undertakings are careless of their past. Apart from many excellent national and local museums of technology, whether run by state or local authority, the established practice of continental Europe is now being imitated, after too long a delay, in the form of

4. Such as *Technikgeschichte* (Germany), *Blätter für Technikgeschichte* (Austria), *Sbornik pro dějiny přírodnich věd a techniky* (Czechoslovakia), and *Transactions of the Newcomen Society* (Britain).

new open-air museums devoted to industry. Complete industrial units are now preserved, such as the eighteenth-century Abbeydale steelworks at Sheffield, as well as many smaller structures. An inventory of sites, compiled on standard cards, is well under way, supplied with most of its material by numerous and enthusiastic amateurs. Britain has seen an outburst of industrial archaeology groups and societies in the past ten years: there are now something like sixty of them, not counting those bodies formed specifically for the preservation or restoration of an individual site. Their members have assumed the Herculean task of field-work, and in some degree of library and archive work. In museums and in preservation Britain may still lag behind some of her progressive neighbours; but she is far ahead in the equally urgent and vital, if less visible, task of recording.[5] To illustrate the scale of this activity and something of the raw material available, a generous selection of recent projects seems justified.

There are tremendous problems involved in studying and presenting the industrial archaeology of a large region with a wide range of industries and vast numbers of sites of significance. Owen Ashmore, faced with the daunting task of describing the industrial archaeology of Lancashire, has produced a book which is outstanding among its kind.[6] Lancashire was arguably one of the hubs of the industrial revolution; and in its sprawling conurbations it still possesses huge, though dwindling, numbers of potentially interesting monuments. The textile industries dominate the scene, but metal trades, engineering, coal mining, corn milling and

5. The two most authoritative works on industrial archaeology in Britain are A. Raistrick, *Industrial Archaeology: an Historical Survey*, London (1972), and R. A. Buchanan, *Industrial Archaeology in Britain*, Harmondsworth (1972). *Industrial Archaeologists' Guide* (edited Neil Cossons and Kenneth Hudson), Newton Abbot (1971) is a useful guide to museums, societies, preserved sites, etc. Mention may also be made of the series of regional studies in industrial archaeology published by David & Charles (14 titles to date), and the series arranged by subject published by Longmans (eight titles).

6. Owen Ashmore, *The Industrial Archaeology of Lancashire*, Newton Abbot (1969).

numerous other industries, as well as the complex ramifications of transport, all claim their place. Mr Ashmore paints a general industrial portrait of the county, drawing on ordinary historical sources and on the results of archaeological fieldwork alike. Since much detail is impossible and undesirable, he highlights phases and aspects by pointing to just a few surviving buildings and machines. In these few instances he can afford, without becoming bogged down in niceties, to give some details, to compare them with their counterparts elsewhere, to ask questions which cannot yet be answered. In the space of a compact but illuminating book he shows forcefully that history does not exist only in the library and the archives—as some industrial historians would have us believe—but also in the grimy townscape of mills and back-to-back houses and foul-watered canals.

The study of a more limited area offers obvious advantages to the part-time worker or local group. A good example is the survey of the industrial archaeology of the London borough of Enfield,[7] renowned for the Royal Small Arms Factory which dates back (in the form of gunpowder mills) to the seventeenth century. But there have been other industries besides: survivals from an early period like corn watermills, as well as the unrelated miscellany of processes which tend to spring up around the fringes of a large city. Sir Hugh Myddelton's New River (opened in 1613 for supplying London with water) passes through the borough; so do the ancient Lee Navigation and later railways. A record of the remains of all these undertakings and an account of their history is a valuable contribution to local studies and especially to an understanding of the economic foundations of the area.

More often, single industries are picked out for treatment, either on a national or a local scale. Coal mining is one such topic, where early records are distressingly reticent on details. Although Professor Nef's *Rise of the British Coal Industry* has given us a solid foundation to build on, early

7. *Industrial Archaeology in Enfield,* Enfield Arch. Soc. Research Report No. 2 (1971).

documents just do not contain details of bell-pit workings: how close they were dug to each other, how wide and how deep they were, what proportion of the coal seam was extracted from them, how they were drained. Similar questions can be asked (but rarely answered) of the early stage of the next development, where headings were driven out from the bottom of deeper pits. Now, indeed, we can only hope to find the answers by examining old mine workings exposed by opencast operations, which advance at such a speed that evidence can be destroyed, unrecorded, within hours of its first appearance. Dr A. R. Griffin of the National Coal Board has taken a step towards resolving this problem by arranging with opencast officials to notify him the moment their excavators reveal old pits and headings, so that he can take measurements and photographs. His activities have shown the very low extraction rate of about 25% in some Derbyshire seams worked in the mid-eighteenth century; they have cast light on the spread of the more productive Shropshire method of longwall mining as opposed to the north-eastern pillar and stall practice which caused less ground subsidence; and they have produced some unexpectedly deep soughs to drain mines in the pre-steam era.[8]

A paragon of its kind is a survey of the lime industry in the Lothians of Scotland,[9] covering the limestone quarries, mines, and kilns of that region. The economic and technical information derived from documents is married to the evidence of the structures themselves; one would be incomplete without the other. The Lothians produced large quantities of stone for roads and for the ironworks around Glasgow, and of burnt lime for mortar, limewashing and especially for agriculture. The evolution of the kiln from clamp to stone structure is illustrated by existing specimens; the different types of kiln are compared with the theories of the early nineteenth-century agriculturists; the mechanisa-

8. A. R. Griffin, 'Bell-Pits and Soughs: some East Midlands Examples', *Industrial Archaeology*, vol. 6 No. 4 (Nov. 1969), 392–7; *idem, Coalmining*, London (1971), especially pp. 3–6.

9. B. C. Skinner, *The Lime Industry of the Lothians*, Edinburgh (1969).

tion of the industry is traced from horse gin to windmill, waterwheel and steam engine; the sites are related to transport routes; and the output of the kilns, the cost of production and wages of the workmen are logically welded together and set against the fluctuations of the market and the rise and decline of the industry.

An industry which has been unjustly neglected is slate quarrying in North Wales: unjustly because it was not only the mainstay of much of Caernarvonshire and Merioneth, but played a vital part in roofing the new houses of the industrial revolution. A survey of Rhosydd slate mine near Blaenau Ffestiniog therefore breaks new ground as a case study of one particular concern. Stretching over a mile and a half of remote mountainside, it was of medium size as quarries went and had a working life of 80 years from the 1850s. The slate was at first worked in an open quarry, but was later pursued underground in a deep mine, the regular practice of that district. Power for the pumps and dressing machinery was provided by waterwheels fed from a dozen reservoirs. Evidence survives of more advanced equipment in the form of hydraulic drills and Pelton wheels adopted towards the end of the mine's life, when depression in the slate trade made cheaper production essential. Transport of the finished slate was originally by packhorse and by cart down an extremely steep track to the nearest railway for carriage to the port; but later a private tramway was built, with a cable-worked incline which is one of the engineering wonders of Britain. It soars up the valley head like Jacob's ladder, with a vertical height of 700 feet and a final gradient rather steeper than 45 degrees. The site being so remote, many of the quarrymen went home only at weekends, living in barracks at the quarry during the week. Into these barracks, which were notorious in their day and still exist as ruins, they were crammed like sardines. In a room 18 by 14 feet, for example, nine men lived, cooked, ate and slept. A graphic picture can be built up by fieldwork of life and work at Rhosydd, which is all the more necessary as the quarry papers have perished and very few of the men who worked there still survive. A single case study of this kind can be illuminating by itself, but it is even more so if similar surveys are done of other quarries for comparison.[10]

Still in the realm of the extractive industries, Robert Clough's pioneer study of the Yorkshire lead smelting mills,[11] while not above criticism in detail, is valuable because it recorded the architecture of these mills before many of them were overtaken by ruin and demolition. The enormous and magnificent octagonal mill at Arkengarthdale, for instance, must have been among the very largest industrial buildings of the early eighteenth century. Clough also recorded details of the waterwheels, crushers, buddles, bellows and hearths and flues, and related them to developments in dressing and smelting techniques. The long survival of the small and simple ore-hearth is noteworthy in view of the early introduction elsewhere of the reverberatory furnace; it seems that the ore-hearth was more suited to the needs of the small and scattered operators of the dales, the larger reverberatory furnace to the larger, more centralised, concerns. The widespread installation of long flues—up to a mile and a half long—is comprehensible less as an attempt to safeguard the smelt mill workers' health by leading the poisonous fumes away, than as an economy measure. These flues served as elongated condensers for recovering lead held in suspension in the fumes, and it was not unknown for a mill to derive 6% of its output from scraping the flues.[12]

Many more cases could be quoted where the historian of tomorrow will be forced to rely on the archaeologist of today. To continue for a moment with the lead industry, the Redcliff shot tower in Bristol was built about 1786 by William Watts, the patentee of the process of high-fall shot making; an extension and adaptation of his own house—half tower, half well—it was the first shot tower in the world. It remained in continuous use until demolished for road-

10. Report forthcoming.

11. R. T. Clough, *The Lead Smelting Mills of the Yorkshire Dales*, privately published (1962).

12. A. Raistrick and B. Jennings, *A History of Lead Mining in the Pennines*, London (1965), based largely on documentary sources, is an excellent complement to Clough's mainly archaeological work.

widening in 1968. Another tower, at Elswick near Newcastle, built in 1797 and a much more sophisticated structure, was knocked down in 1969. Both were fully recorded before it was too late, and good drawings and photographs were published in local journals.[13] Whoever comes to undertake the task—not yet attempted in any detail—of tracing the history of lead shot making on a national basis will find himself indebted to these articles. Without them two historic and important buildings would have been no more than names.

The work of members of the Historical Metallurgy Group (published in its Bulletin) well illustrates how light can be shed on the early development of ironmaking. Later periods are reasonably well documented in general terms, if not in specific instances; but since few written records survive of furnaces up to the end of the eighteenth century, archaeology is often the only means of discovering the type of furnace used, the sources of raw materials, even the length of life of the works. Excavations by Dr R. F. Tylecote, for example, in 1963–4 of seventeenth- and eighteenth-century charcoal blast furnaces at Melbourne in Derbyshire (a rescue dig in advance of flooding by a new reservoir) and at Coed Ithel on the banks of the Wye have added considerably to our knowledge of these ironworks. Previously, only their existence and sporadic figures of their output were on record. Now, their structure is known; so is their place in the evolution of blast furnace design (Coed Ithel is unique in its lines), the ore used (Coed Ithel was fed partly with bloomery slag) and the power supply for their bellows. A similar piece of work[14] has increased the evidence available for assessing Dud Dudley's famous claim that he smelted iron with coal in the 1630s. The site of his furnace at Himley

13. John Mosse, 'Redcliff Shot Tower', *Bristol Industrial Archaeology Society Journal*, 2 (1969), 4–5; Ian Glendenning, 'Shot Making and the Shot Tower at Elswick', *Proceedings of Soc. of Antiquaries of Newcastle upon Tyne*, 5th series, 9 (1955), 351–61; R. M. Higgins, 'Lead Shot Tower at Elswick', *Ind. Arch. Soc. for North East Bulletin*, 10 (1970), 9–16.

14. G. R. Morton and M. D. G. Wanklyn, 'Dud Dudley, a new appraisal', *Journal of West Midlands Regional Studies*, 1 (1967), 48–65.

was located and the slag analysed, the result suggesting that his claim was at least partly justified and that it deserves better than the outright rejection which it has so often received. Abraham Darby, therefore, who introduced coke smelting in 1709, was not necessarily the unrivalled pioneer, although his fame for beginning the effective smelting of iron with coke remains untarnished.

Between 1968 and 1971 two glass furnaces were discovered and excavated at Rosedale and Hutton-le-Hole in north Yorkshire, which proved to be almost the only examples in Britain of the type of furnace introduced in the second half of the sixteenth century by immigrant glass workers from France and Flanders. The activities of these Huguenots in, for example, Stourbridge and Newcastle are reasonably well known from documents; but the presence of the industry in the North Riding was hitherto quite unsuspected. We can now see that it explains the foreign names which occur in the late Elizabethan registers at the local church. Some fresh light is thus shed on the movement and works of these craftsmen and on the history of this type of furnace which, when adapted to burn coal after the use of wood as fuel was forbidden in 1615, became the central feature of the English-type glasshouse.[15]

Post-medieval pottery has been much studied from the aesthetic angle, little (until recently) from the archaeological side. Part of the productive but admittedly not very high class Bellevue Pottery at Hull, of early nineteenth century date, was excavated in 1970.[16] The main find was a cellar full of wasters, from which it transpired that only a small percentage of Hull products was stamped with the pottery mark. This general anonymity had meant that very few patterns had previously been recognised as Hull ones; after the excavation the known number of anonymous but indubitably Hull-made patterns was increased many-fold. Of particular interest was the presence of several fragments of Don Pottery ware, and the stylistic (but inferior) resem-

15. Excavations by F. A. Aberg and D. W. Crossley.
16. J. Bartlett and D. Brooks, *Hull Pottery*, Kingston upon Hull Museums Bulletin No. 5 (1970).

blance of some Hull designs to Sunderland and Minton ones. It seems likely that the Hull artists were to some extent imitators. Another line was well represented: garish souvenir plates for the export market, adorned with German mottoes. On a higher artistic plane, a large-scale excavation at the site of the original Royal Worcester pottery had profound repercussions that echoed through the antique trade. Several patterns that had been regarded as the work of Caughley pottery and therefore, to the connoisseur, far less desirable, were now proved to be genuine Worcester; with grave effect on sale-room prices.

The application of water power to the flax and the linen industries of Northern Ireland has formed a fruitful subject of research and fieldwork.[17] From 1698 the government brought over a number of Huguenot experts who helped to transform what had previously been a small-scale manual craft into a nascent mechanised industry. In the 1710s and 1720s the first water-powered flax scutching and beetling machines were installed in the province, and a century later water-powered spinning and weaving began to prevail. The remains of many mills, especially from the great nineteenth-century expansion, survive to help out documentary sources in plotting the growth of the industry and the size of its units. Power spinning on a large scale appeared mainly in Belfast, while other areas proved to be slow in developing the factory system; the mills sometimes remained small simply because of the limitations of the power available. This is a clear case where the use of water power led to considerable social and economic advance, encouraged improvements in agriculture by increasing the demand for flax, and raised what had been a traditional craft to the level of industrial production.

A fundamental study of a technical advance pioneered

17. E. R. R. Green, *The Industrial Archaeology of County Down*, Belfast (1963); W. A. McCutcheon, 'The Application of Water Power to Industrial Purposes in the North of Ireland', *Industrial Archaeology*, vol. 2 No. 3 (Oct. 1965), 69–81; idem, 'Water Power in the North of Ireland', *Trans. Newcomen Soc.*, xxxix (1966–7), 67–94; H. B. Gribbon, *History of Water Power in Ulster*, Newton Abbot (1969).

very largely by one man concerns the introduction of fireproof structures for mills and warehouses where the risk of fire was great.[18] The old method of supporting wooden floors and beams on wooden posts was first modified by William Strutt in three buildings he had built for his Derbyshire textile empire between 1793 and 1795. These were Derby calico mill, Milford warehouse and Belper West Mill, where brick vaults and cast iron pillars replaced the wooden floors and uprights, and where the floor beams, still of wood, were coated with plaster to protect them from flames. The next step, where the beams themselves were made of cast iron, was first taken at Charles Bage's Shrewsbury flax mill of 1797, in whose design Strutt gave much assistance. Strutt himself used the same method in his Belper North and South Mills of 1804 and 1812. Except for Shrewsbury and Belper North Mill, all of these buildings have now been demolished, but some of them survived recently enough for precise details of the beams and floors to be recorded and to play a part in the elucidating of this highly important stage in the history of structures. Shrewsbury mill is the first father of the steel-framed skyscraper.

In the field of transport, though railways (and to a lesser extent canals) have received much attention from 'documentary' historians, much still remains to be found in the field. A national survey that may be mentioned deals with flashlocks on English river navigations.[19] It was common knowledge that, in the days before the double-gated pound lock was introduced, boats could navigate rivers which were obstructed by mill weirs, shallows and rapids only by means of the single-barrier flashlock, a dangerous device that was exceedingly wasteful of time and water. General books on inland navigation tended to dismiss these flashlocks in a few sentences as long-obsolete affairs of merely

18. H. R. Johnson and A. W. Skempton, 'William Strutt's Cotton Mills 1793–1812', *Trans. Newcomen Soc.*, xxx (1955–7), 179–205.

19. M. J. T. Lewis, W. N. Slatcher, P. N. Jarvis, 'Flashlocks on English Waterways', *Industrial Archaeology*, vol. 6 No. 3 (Aug. 1969), 209–53; 'Flashlocks: an Addendum', *Industrial Archaeology*, vol. 7 No. 2 (May 1970), 190–4.

588   *The Industrial Revolution*

remote historical interest. In fact flashlocks survived in use
well into the twentieth century on some rivers, and a survey
in 1967–9 that embraced the whole of England revealed no
less than 57 sites where something of the structure remained
(although the number has been reduced by demolition since
then). When these structures were drawn up and compared,
it could be seen that one type was generally adopted to
allow passage through a mill weir, another where shallows
or a ford obstructed the river; and further that, inside this
pattern, there was another marked pattern of regional
variation in design. It also became clear that, whereas
flashlocks survived on some rivers, in spite of the demands
of traffic, because of the vested interest of millers, they
remained on others because the amount of traffic did not
justify the bigger capital expenditure necessary for the far
more efficient pound lock. As always, though the pioneer
innovation may hit the headlines, the antique survival does
not.

Some mystery too, surrounds the origin and early
evolution of pound locks on British waterways. It is assumed,
no doubt correctly, that they were imitated from their
predecessors on the Continent, where this branch of civil
engineering was already well established. But which
particular Continental waterways? And who brought the
basic idea across—Dutchmen, Frenchmen, Italians, or
Britons? So little is known about the engineers of early
British navigations and their contacts abroad that our
greatest hope of advance lies in archaeological work. A
detailed comparison of early locks that survive, on both
sides of the Channel, may, by revealing relationships, allow
an evolutionary tree to be compiled. Is there, for instance,
anything in common between the locks with oval or
circular chambers on the Stecknitz Canal, the Canal du
Midi, the River Brenta, and the Warwickshire Avon?
Here, as in so many cases, not only national but international cooperation holds the promise of useful discovery.

One would have expected historians to know from
documentary evidence which rivers were improved with
navigation works in the past few centuries. Not so; within

the past fifty years locks have been found on two tributaries of the Severn where no written sources at all have been discovered. One of these navigations served a blast furnace probably of the 1650s, the other two forges which were active in the first half of the 18th century.[20] One stream was navigable for half a mile, the other for one and a half. These may seem very paltry discoveries, but their implications are rather more wide-reaching. Both add to our meagre knowledge of traffic on that great highway the Severn, for these works were evidently supplied by water with ore, charcoal and pig iron. This traffic would cause no problem were it not that the locks on both streams are far too small to accommodate the ordinary Severn trow or barge. Was there, therefore, an extensive but otherwise unknown trade on the Severn in small boats hardly bigger than punts; or were the raw materials brought by trow for the bulk of their journey, and then expensively transhipped into small craft for the final short leg to the works? The question is unanswered; but at least it can now be asked.

On the revolution in society and in living conditions which is part of the industrial revolution, much has been written, especially on workers' housing in the more squalid cities like Nottingham and Manchester at the nadir of overcrowding and jerry-building in the 1830s and 1840s. The most scarifying and commonly quoted sources are the reports of the sanitary reformers and the parliamentary commissioners; but how generally true was their picture of gloom? Although much of the material evidence—the housing itself—has mercifully been demolished, enough remains to throw some light on the methods of industrialists and speculative builders and on the density of population in individual houses and streets.

Historians tend to emphasise the role of the railways as creators of new towns. This is right and proper; but the

20. T. C. Cantrill and M. Wight, 'Yarranton's Works at Astley', *Trans. Worcs. Arch. Soc.*, new series, vi (1929), 92–115; R. Chaplin, 'Discovering lost ironworks', *The Local Historian*, vol. 9 No. 2 (1970), 83–4; idem, 'A forgotten industrial valley', *Shropshire News Letter*, 36 (1969), 1–6; and unpublished surveys.

canal company towns which preceded them are less well known. An outstanding example of the type has recently been examined. Goole was the creation of the Aire & Calder Navigation, a planned town erected between 1825 and 1840 at the docks where the newly-cut Knottingley and Goole canal met the River Ouse. As the site was low-lying and prone to flooding, the streets were raised with material dug from the docks, but the houses were built at the original level. The front doors were thus one storey above the back doors, which gave access to low-ceilinged cellars that were regularly flooded by water backing up the sewers. Some houses had six rooms on three floors, some only three, and even in the smaller ones there were cases of families doubling up. Nonetheless, although the population was extremely cramped in 1826 when the main building programme was still under way—eleven persons per dwelling on average— by 1828 the pressure had been eased to 6·2 persons per dwelling. The size and appearance of the houses accurately reflected the social standing of their occupants. Public buildings—inns, institute, chapel and church—were added. The Aire & Calder Navigation was certainly paternalistic in providing for its employees, but its attitude was a far cry from the avowed philanthropy that motivated such magnates as Salt at Saltaire, Akroyd at Halifax, even de Gorge-Legrand at Le Grand-Hornu. Almost the whole of the company town of Goole has now been demolished, and the rest may well follow soon.[21]

Not so far from Goole is New Holland, the southern terminal of the Humber ferry from Hull which was bought up by the Manchester Sheffield & Lincolnshire Railway in 1845. At this date New Holland boasted only three cottages and three inns (for the benefit of ferry passengers); six years later it had developed into a railway village of some significance, with 83 houses and 401 inhabitants, which has been grandly described as the Swindon or Crewe of Lincolnshire. Part of this housing was built by private

21. J. D. Porteous, 'Goole: a pre-Victorian Company Town', *Industrial Archaeology*, vol. 6 No. 2 (May 1969), 105–13; *idem, The Company Town of Goole*, Hull (1969).

enterprise, but most of it by the railway company. The dominant feature is the three-sided Manchester Square, which contains forty terrace houses almost identical in design. Each covers the reasonably generous ground area of 336 sq ft (inside), with two rooms on each of two floors and a large but low attic. Each has a small yard with washhouse and coalshed. The 1851 census returns show that certainly 73, probably 83, out of the 87 wage-earners who lived in the square were employed directly or (like the schoolmaster) indirectly by the railway. The occupancy of the houses varied widely, from two (a fireman and his wife) to eleven (a pointsman, his wife and five children, and four lodgers). The standard of these terraces is good enough for them to survive, modernised, in use. New Holland has remained too small to be well endowed with public buildings; early on, a chapel was built; but Church of England services, held originally in the station waiting room, were later transferred to the schoolroom and only in this century to a proper church. [22]

It would be tedious to rehearse details of industrial archaeological exercises in the rest of Europe at such length as has been permitted for Britain. For one thing, the main point has perhaps been made; for another, it would in some sense be misleading. The countries of mainland Europe are, many of them, in advance of Britain in the sphere of museums and preservation policy, but none can boast more than a tithe of the solid down-to-earth fieldwork that this country has achieved. Since these practical researches are our main concern, let our survey of the European scene be correspondingly brief. [23]

Norway and Finland, both barren and thinly populated, do not have a great deal to offer the industrial archaeologist;

22. A. Harris, 'The Humber Ferries and the Rise of New Holland', *East Midland Geographer*, 15 (1961), 11–19; and unpublished surveys.

23. Kenneth Hudson, *A Guide to the Industrial Archaeology of Europe*, Bath (1971) contains invaluable lists of the major museums and preserved sites, though it has nothing to say about published work and little about fieldwork.

but what they do have—notably industries connected with timber and the sea—is well treated in museums. Sweden is a different matter. Its industries, which go back many centuries, were often in small decentralised units set in rural surroundings, and have thus been spared the pressures which urban development exerts. At the same time, an unusually large proportion of present-day industrial firms, taking a pride and interest in the history of their concerns, have preserved the old structures at the core of their works and created company museums. The most shining example of this practice is the great Falun copper mine in Dalarna, owned by the Stora Kopparberg Company which claims to be the oldest corporation in the world. Continuous production began before 1288, and the mine grew until in the seventeenth century it dominated the copper trade of Europe. Around the great open pit caused by the partial collapse of the underground workings in 1687, old shaft houses are preserved, together with the eighteenth-century office building which now contains the company museum. Among the exhibits are contemporary models of the revolutionary pumping and hoisting machines introduced by the famous Christopher Polhem, engineer to the company from 1700 to 1716.[24] Stora Kopparberg extended its operations in the nineteenth century to include ironworks and forestry.

Perhaps the crowning glory of industrial archaeology in Sweden is the *bruks* or iron-working communities, complete with furnaces, forges, owner's house, workers' housing, shops, church, and often warehouse and harbour. In these *bruks* the world-famous Swedish iron was produced. Some are now defunct, some have developed into large works, and many are preserved to display not only the complete surroundings of former industrial life but also the many technical processes which were initiated or developed in the *bruks*. Ramnäs Bruk, where charcoal iron is still refined in Lancashire hearths, is almost the only works in Europe which still produces wrought iron. The *bruks*, taken together, give an almost unparalleled insight into the

24. Sven Lindroth, *Gruvbrytning och Kopparhantering vid Stora Kopparberget intill 1800-talets början*, Uppsala (1955).

technological and social history of the industry which put Sweden prominently on the economic map of Europe.

Denmark and Holland have much in common economically in their long agrarian tradition and their lack of mineral resources (apart from the Limburg coalfield). They are also similar in their provision of fine museums; especially those specialising in such industries as glass and brewing. In both countries, too, the chief industrial monuments are mills: watermills in Denmark, windmills in both. In Denmark, the survival of over fifty of them is due largely to the efforts of the Danish Mill Preservation Board; in Holland, where roughly two thousand are still at work, the Dutch Windmill Society wields great influence, with much assistance from the tourist interests. In neither country were the mills used solely for corn-grinding; many were for gunpowder, paper-making, sawing and especially in Holland for drainage. Molinology, as its *aficionados* call it, is one of the few branches of technology that is being thoroughly studied on an international scale. This broad treatment can reveal points of contact and influences that might well remain obscured in purely local studies. It is regular practice in Central Europe, where scholars of neighbouring countries are happy to ignore the artificial modern frontiers which defy natural boundaries; but elsewhere there is still a sad tendency among researchers to stick to their own cabbage patch. A broader view of technical history can only prove a more enlightening one. With windmills, more fieldwork has probably been done than on any other kind of machinery, although watermills lag some way behind them. Long and patient work by such men as Rex Wailes in England, Anders Jespersen in Denmark, and J. M. dos Santos Simões in Portugal has yielded an unparalleled record of windmill types, distribution and technology. Detailed answers can be given, on a national basis, to such questions as the use of structural materials, the advance of mechanical design, the spheres of activity of local millwrights and their adoption (or rejection) of other millwrights' methods. Answers to such questions are now being sought—and found—on an international basis too.[25] But although mill technology is well catered for, there are still gaps which need filling, especially in the economic and social role of mills and millers.

Belgium also does well for its old industry. It makes up for the lack of a national technical museum by some excellent local and specialist ones, especially of glass and iron, and by the intelligent and active interest taken in industrial archaeology and fostered by private companies. One outstanding site which has been well studied is Le Grand-Hornu, a planned industrial settlement of unusually early date for the Continent.[26] It was laid out by Henri de Gorge-Legrand between 1819 and 1832 to accommodate (and deliberately to attract) workers at his expanding empire of coal mines, workshops and steam engine factory. By the time of his death in 1832, 425 houses had been built for 2,500 people. The architecture is modest, but by no means inelegant by the idiom of the period. The houses are all two-storey, with three rooms on each, the average floor area being 617 sq ft. Each has a cellar and small garden with coalhouse. A family of between six and ten people, and sometimes a lodger too, inhabited each house in comparative comfort. De Gorge-Legrand further improved the amenities with a dance-hall, baths with piped hot water, schools, library and hospital. Compared with the English company towns mentioned earlier, Le Grand-Hornu was near the acme of its type; New Holland was some way below, and Goole was considerably lower down the scale, yet still well above the normal standard of the day. All three instances serve to emphasize that not all employers were money-grubbing exploiters of their workpeople.

France has a long industrial history. Its extensive textile

25. *Transactions of the Second International Symposium on Molinology*, edited Anders Jespersen, Brede (Denmark) (1971) contains articles on mills in Britain, France, Holland, Germany, Denmark, Portugal, Poland, Rumania, Israel and Brazil.

26. M. Bruwier, A. Meurant and C. Piérard, 'Le Grand-Hornu', *Industrie*, Jan. 1968, translated in *Industrial Archaeology*, vol. 6 No. 4 (Nov. 1969), 354–68.

industries and its iron and steel works were responsible for
important technical innovations, and it led the world in its
encouragement of the engineering profession. But France is
strangely disappointing to the industrial archaeologist.
Firms show little of the pride in their corporate past which
is so visible in West Germany and Sweden; although there
are some very reasonable museums, the state does not display
any deep care for preservation, and countless monuments
of significance have been destroyed unsung and unrecorded.
There are exceptions indeed: the restoration of the grand
but futile eighteenth-century Saline de Chaux near
Bescançon, for example, and the active interest shown in
the old iron industry. Perhaps the most outstanding
monuments are engineering ones, like the famous Canal du
Midi, finished in 1681, and the series of great bridges, a
study of which is fundamental to an understanding of
engineering history: the Roman Pont du Gard, the fine
medieval span at Ceret, the eighteenth-century works of
Perronet, the father of modern bridge-building (though his
chef d'oeuvre at Neuilly was recently demolished), the
pioneering concrete structures by Hennebique and Freyssinet. Most significantly, France is in the process of compil-
ing, under the aegis of the Ministry of Culture, an inventory
of all outstanding monuments—industrial and otherwise—
with a view to scheduling the best of them and to educating
the public. The labour force involved in this scheme, as in
Britain, is largely composed of volunteers. Nonetheless, for
its potential, France may be said to lag behind.

West Germany, by contrast, is a treasury of industrial
monuments—well-cared-for in spite of wartime tribulations
—and of fine museums. This richness is a reflection of the
natural wealth of the country, of the comparatively early
industrialisation of Prussia, and of the standard of education
and historical responsibility. The German Engineers
Association has long fostered historical research and
preservation. Although a considerable amount of recording
work is carried out and published in the many local and
national journals, yet the bulk of it seems to be in the hands
of professionals—museum and university men—rather

than amateurs: the reverse of current practice in Britain. In the realm of engineering, some important bridges survive, though decimated by war, as well as early canals and harbour works. The early days of the iron industry on the Ruhr, though not as old as in some areas, is represented by the preserved Wocklum charcoal iron furnace and Margarethental forge. As in some neighbouring countries, mining is a favourite and profitable topic of study. Old timbered buildings set among the forested hills of the metal-mining Harz (where the preservation of the outstanding St Andreasberg mine deserves mention) contrast strongly with the more recent industrial valley of the Ruhr; but both played their essential part in the creation of Germany. In the mid-nineteenth century the cotton and silk mills of the Rhineland and South Germany, together with their counterparts in what is now East Germany, formed perhaps the most important industry in the country; but textile history does not attract as much attention as it deserves.

As an instance of the work being done in Germany, Schulz has studied two neighbouring saltworks in Würt-temberg, owned by the same company and founded at almost the same time.[27] The Schwenningen works was opened in 1823, and closed in 1865 on the loss of its Swiss market, where it had disposed of 97% of its output. In addition to this commercial failure there were technical drawbacks too, the bore being extremely deep, the water supply poor, fuel dear and transport difficult. In contrast, its neighbour at Rottweil survived the loss of its main market—just—being saved by its better technical situation and by the acquisition of new and more distant markets with the opening up of the railway system. Its ultimate closure was due to corrosion of the plant and the impossi-bility of replacing it during and immediately after the second world war. Schulz obtained access to the works archives and the equipment just before it closed, and his investigation into both sources in conjunction is a valuable

27. Günter Schulz, *Geschichte der ehemaligen Königlich Württembergischen Saline Wilhelmshall bei Schwenningen am Neckar 1823–1865*, Schwenningen (1967); idem, *Die Saline Wilhelmshall bei Rottweil*, Rottweil (1970).

record which caters equally for the interests of the economist, the engineer and the social historian. All that survives
now of the Rottweil works is two brine tanks, scheduled as
ancient monuments, and an early borehole house whose
future is in the balance. Quite apart from their technical
significance, the two works were of major economic
importance, for between them they produced close on a
million tons of salt in their lifetime.

The Alpine countries of Switzerland and Austria have a
number of good museums, with specialities such as glass-
making and watch-making. Several old silver, iron and salt
mines are open to the public, notably the impressive
Hallstatt salt mine in the Salzkammergut. Because of the
terrain, railway engineering is often spectacular, and there
are many historically important bridges, from the wooden
Kapellbrücke in Lucerne of 1333 to Maillart's concrete
masterpiece at Schwandbach built exactly six centuries
later. But fewer obsolete buildings and machines have been
preserved—or even survive—than one might at first
thought expect. Among the most important old industries
of either country are the ironworks of Carinthia and
Styria. They have been the subject of much archival
research which has elucidated a great deal of their history.
But until recently the actual remains of the roasting ovens,
blast furnaces, fineries and steelworks had never been
systematically recorded and compared.[28] A few buildings,
much altered, still survive from the Middle Ages, but the
great period of expansion in the Austrian iron industry was
1820–75. Some of the equipment of this vintage was later
replaced by more modern plant, but when the industry
was freed from its bondage to wood and water in the late
nineteenth century, others of the old structures were simply
abandoned and forgotten. Dr Wehdorn's survey comprises
four parts. First he studies the architectural development

28. Manfred Wehdorn, *Die Baudenkmäler des Eisenhüttenwesens in
Österreich*, dissertation, Vienna Technical High School, 1969. Some
aspects are elaborated upon by the same author in 'Zur Baugeschichte
der Eisenhüttengebäude in Österreich', *Der Anschnitt*, Jg. 22 No. 2
(1970), 3–16, and Jg. 23 No. 1 (1971), 12–18.

of the buildings and establishes their typology—a fundamental piece of work which, though not necessarily applicable to other countries, does provide essential comparative material. He lists the surviving structures, giving detailed descriptions and technical explanations. He then evaluates the sites historically and makes suggestions for the preservation of some of them. Finally he provides illustrations and drawings taken both from old plans and from his own surveys. All this has resulted in a basic study which contains such information as the dates when the different types of furnace were introduced, regional variations, and foreign influences.

On this last point, the links between Austria and Silesia seem to have been strong, even long after Silesia was lost by the Empire to Prussia in 1742. Furnace buildings in the two areas have much in common architecturally—especially in the exuberant Gothic and Tudor styles they favoured—which is confirmed by the activity in Austria of Silesian industrial architects such as the Wedding family and Graf Hugo Henckel. St Gertraud furnace in Carinthia (1847-8) belongs to the same family as Chorzow foundry in Silesia (c. 1794). Silesian ironworks architecture is said to owe much—and clearly does—to French sources, just as in technical design the influence of England was predominant.[29] From the late eighteenth century, the export to Europe of the technical expertise acquired by industrial Britain became a commonplace. William Gascoigne of Carron erected the Alexandrovsk foundry for Catherine the Great; William Wilkinson advised the French in constructing their foundries at Indret and Le Creusot; Graf von Reden visited Britain three times and invited John Baildon, also of Carron, to help in building furnaces in Silesia. From documents and archaeology, between them, can be discerned something of the direction of international influences; but the potential of this broad approach has hardly yet been tapped.

29. J. Pazdur, 'Postęp techniczny w hutnictwie polskim na tle rewolucji technicznej w Anglii', *Studia i materiały z dziejów nauki polskiej*, serie D nr 6 (1971), 57–87.

Industrialisation came late to the Mediterranean countries of Greece, Italy, Spain and Portugal, in some of which, indeed, the economy is still largely agrarian. Industrial monuments are therefore comparatively few, though by no means non-existent. Spain and Italy in particular boast some highly important civil engineering works: dams, harbours, and such bridges as the Roman Alcántara in Spain and the Ponte Santa Trinità of 1567 in Florence. The glories of the classical, medieval and renaissance past, however, so overshadow the historical scene that interest in industrial monuments is marginal. Few industrial museums exist, and very few industrial buildings are preserved, the most outstanding exception in both cases being the wine industry.

The southern countries of Eastern Europe form a marked contrast. Industrial development in Yugoslavia, Bulgaria, Rumania and Hungary began, on any worthwhile scale, only after 1945, though here too there was limited industrial activity for centuries before. But Communism has brought about a certain revulsion from castles and palaces, those symbols of capitalism and imperialism, and the state encourages an interest in the history of production. There are national technical museums at Zagreb, Bucharest and Budapest, several transport museums, and a whole host of regional museums where the role of industry and the worker in the local scene is emphasized—some might say over-emphasized. A considerable effort is made to record and to preserve examples of the multitudinous small grain mills, of wine presses and cellars, of mining remains and in Rumania of the highly important oil industry. Hungary in particular may be picked out for its preservation of small ironworks dating from the Middle Ages to the nineteenth century.[30]

In the more northerly nations of the communist bloc the industrial archaeology scene is similar but more intensive. There is considerable state protection for technical monu-

30. Many reports on projects concerning mines and ironworks may be found in *Bányászati és Kohászati Lapok* (Budapest).

ments, often in association with the local museum, and a more catholic interest is visible in the preservation of all kinds of historical monuments. For the industrial archaeologist, if he can move around freely, this policy makes East Germany, Poland and Czechoslovakia extremely fruitful hunting-grounds. For the man in the street, it offers a more basic view of history than the traditional showmanship of Western Europe which focuses on great art, warfare and the olde-worlde picturesque; and it avoids the opposite extreme, sometimes apparent in south-eastern Europe, of over-emphasizing recent socialist advances and underplaying earlier history. Russia is the main exception to this trend. Partial industrialisation came to it earlier than to its neighbours, with important industrial centres in Moscow and St Petersburg, and with considerable textile mills and ironworks. But much has been destroyed by war; and much more preservation is now based on museums than on monuments *in situ*, while historians tend to concentrate more on documentary than on archaeological sources.

Poland contains within its present boundaries the great mining and iron-working districts of Silesia and Galicia, where the enlightened state policy on industrial monuments is to be seen in full flower. A national survey, sponsored in the first instance by the Polish Academy of Science, recorded the sites; a selection of the most important was then scheduled for preservation by law; and now a number of monuments are open to the public, backed up by excellent regional museums. As a result, in spite of the depredations of war, a corpus of knowledge has been built up of this region that abounds with lead, silver, salt and iron mines, blast furnaces and hammer works.[31] Nor is the south the only part of Poland to receive this treatment: workers' housing is preserved at the textile centres of Żyrardów and

31. A typical Polish example of recording and publishing concerns an ironworks built in 1784 with waterwheel and 11 finery hammers, to which plate rolls were added in 1839: Z. Olszewski, 'Zapomniany zabytek hutniczy w Malencu', *Wiadomości hutnicze*, Jg. 27 nr. 5 (1971), 165ff.

Łódź; and the historical potential of Baltic ports like Danzig is not forgotten.

Czechoslovakia is almost as far advanced in its provision of museums and in the associated preservation of outstanding structures. At Banská Štiavnica (Schemnitz), for instance, the centre of the Slovakian ore-field, the local mining museum is in the process of setting up an open-air annexe at the nearby site of an old mine, where various types of headgear and winding engines, as well as more portable equipment, can be seen in the setting of the original shaft (which is 1,411 feet deep) and levels, backed by the great Klinger dam, 74 feet high and built in 1742 by Jozef Karol Hell to impound water for powering the mine. Hell, an engineer little known in Western Europe, is an example of the contribution that industrial archaeology can make to our understanding of the work of a single man.[32] Several of his large engineering works—like the Klinger dam and deep drainage tunnels—survive to show the scale of his operations, on which the written sources are either silent or missing. It was he, too, who introduced the hydraulic or water-pressure engine to the mines of what was then Lower Hungary, for pumping and later for winding. A Newcomen steam engine—the first on the Continent—was installed to drain the mines at Nová Baňa (Königsberg) in 1721; but the steam engine was slow in finding favour in a hilly, indeed mountainous, country where water was available in large quantities for prime movers. Since the steam engine was more expensive to instal and to run, engineers in those parts preferred ordinary waterwheels or—where greater efficiency and more compact design were needed—Hell's high-pressure hydraulic engine. After a somewhat unsatisfactory attempt in 1738, Hell installed his first successful

32. Much has been written about Hell's machines, e.g. J. Schenk, 'Důlní vodotězné stroje Josefa Karla Hella', *Sborník pro dějiny přírodních věd a techniky*, 1 (1954), 48–69; J. Voda, *Jozef Karol Hell*, Martin (1957); idem, 'Strojnícka konstrukčná činnost Jozefa Karola Hella', *Zbornik Slovenského Banského Múzea*, vii (1971), 143–67; O. Wagenbreth, 'Über eine Wassersäulenmaschine im Bergbau von Schlaggenwald...', *Cín v dějinách vědy, techniky a umení*, Prague, ii (1970), 63–74.

engine in 1749 at Banská Štiavnica, where his successors developed the concept which was to remain in widespread use until recent times, when electricity gradually drove it out. Examples still survive to shed light on the design. Nonetheless, Hell did draw on steam engine design—with which he was well acquainted in his early career—in that his original water engine transmitted the motion by rocking beam just like the Newcomen type. A similar machine was invented independently in the Harz in 1748, but ultimately it was the Hell design which prevailed in Germany, being introduced to Saxony in 1816. In Britain, the hydraulic engine was applied to metal mines in several areas from 1765—an excellent water-balance engine survives at Wanlockhead in Scotland—but nobody has yet traced its ancestry. It may well prove that the inspiration came directly or indirectly from the Hell engines.

In Czechoslovakia as in Poland, though mining receives, quite properly, the lion's share of interest, other industries are not ignored. Much fieldwork has been done—and some sites preserved—in the Bohemian and Moravian iron-working districts, where techniques were highly advanced for their time: their heyday was the eighteenth and early nineteenth centuries. Again, though many countries of Europe boast transport or railway museums, with the emphasis on locomotives and moveable equipment, little attention has been paid to the buildings and engineering. Czechoslovakia provides an exception with the pioneer Budweis–Linz railway, opened in 1832, where a length of line has been restored to show the engineering features involved, and where the station at Česke Budějovice (Budweis) is preserved as a small museum. An excellent history of the railway[33] deals much more fully with its archaeological side and places it better in its international context that is usual with such studies.

East Germany, too, has a forward-looking policy towards industrial archaeology. Here again, technical history is taken very seriously and museums are fostered as an essential part of education. As in Poland, a national survey

33. Karl Feiler, *Die alte Schienenstrasse Budweis-Gmunden*, Vienna (1952)

of industrial monuments has been undertaken, from which many sites have been selected for preservation by the state. Nonetheless, much was lost during and after the war. Interest centres on heavy engineering, ironworks, and on mining for coal and metals, especially in the Erzgebirge. Once more, this devotion to mining history is not misplaced, since Saxony was the main breeding-ground of the miners who in medieval, renaissance and even later times carried their expertise and their machines to almost every mining field of Europe from Cumberland to the Urals. It was perhaps the earliest, and certainly among the most significant, of technological diffusions in European history; and a comparison of the remains of mining techniques in Saxony (taken together with such basic sources as Agricola's great treatise) with those of areas colonised by its offspring can shed much light on the movements of these miners, the acknowledged masters of their craft, and on the development of their methods. Other important German industries, however, like wool, silk and cotton in Saxony and Brandenburg, are neglected by comparison with the mines.

Industrial archaeology is still in its infancy; technological history has reached adolescence; economic history is in its maturity. There is therefore a tendency, perhaps made inevitable by the background of most of its practitioners, for industrial archaeology to concentrate on the technical angle. Its most valuable contribution to knowledge probably lies in this field. But industrial archaeology can have a bearing on economic matters, either indirectly *via* technical history, or directly by illustrating documentary sources, expanding on them, and sometimes by filling gaps in the archives. Either way, it is a tool which should not be overlooked. Its value is the greater as much of its raw material, unlike most other brands of archaeology which demand excavation, is there to be seen by all and recorded and interpreted by those who will. He that hath eyes to see, let him see.

Notes on the Authors

C. M. CIPOLLA
is Professor of Economic History at the University of Pavia and at the University of California at Berkeley. Born in 1922 at Pavia, Italy, he graduated from Pavia University, then proceeded to Paris and London where he continued his studies from 1945 to 1948. Since 1949 he has lectured at various European and American Universities on economic history. His publications in English include *Money, Prices and Civilisation* (1956), *The Economic History of World Population* (1962), *Guns and Sails in the Early Phase of European Expansion* (1965), *Clocks and Culture* (1967) and *Literacy and Development in the West* (1969).

ANDRE ARMENGAUD
was born in 1920 at Castres (Tarn) and was Professor of Economic and Social History at the University of Dijon. He is now Professor of Historical and Social Demography at the University of Toulouse, as well as organiser of courses at the Sorbonne and the Institute of Demography, University of Paris. He is also vice-president of the Society of Demographical History. His principal publications are *Les Populations de l'Est-Aquitain au début de l'époque contemporaine* (Paris and The Hague 1961), *La Population française au XXe siècle* (Paris 1965, 2nd ed. 1967), *Démographie et Sociétés* (Paris 1966), and in collaboration with Marcel Reinhard and Jacques Dupâquier, *Histoire générale de la population mondiale* (Paris 1968).

WALTER MINCHINTON
has been professor of economic history at the University of Exeter since 1964. He was educated at Queen Elizabeth's Hospital, Bristol, and the London School of Economics. From 1948 to 1964 he taught at the University College of Swansea. He has published books on *The British Tinplate Industry: a history* (1957); *The Trade of Bristol in the Eighteenth Century* (1957); *Politics and the Port of Bristol in the Eighteenth Century* (1962); *Industrial South Wales, 1750–1914: essays in*

Welsh economic history (1969); *Mercantilism: system or expediency?* (1969); *The Growth of English Overseas Trade in the Seventeenth and Eighteenth Centuries* (1969), and *Wage Regulation in Pre-industrial England* (1972).

SAMUEL LILLEY

was born in 1914 at Belfast and educated at the University of that city and then at Cambridge—where he was a fellow of St John's College, 1945-48. Originally a mathematician, he later turned to the study of the history of science and technology in its relations to social development, though he retains a strong interest in presenting the Theory of Relativity (even including its mathematics!) in terms comprehensible to the layman. He is now Staff Tutor in Science at the University of Nottingham Department of Adult Education. His publications include *Automation and Social Progress* (1957) and *Men, Machines and History* (2nd edition 1965).

BERTRAND GILLE

was born in 1920 and studied both in the Arts and Law Faculties of the Sorbonne. A palaeographer, he served as Head of the Commercial section of the Archives Nationaux from 1950-1957. In 1958 he was appointed to his present position as Professor in the Faculté des Lettres of the University of Clermont. Among his publications are *La banque et le crédit en France de 1815 à 1848* (Paris 1959) *Histoire de la Maison Rothschild* (Geneva 1965-67).

BARRY SUPPLE

is Professor of Economic and Social History at the University of Sussex. He studied at the London School of Economics and at Cambridge University, and subsequently taught business and economic history at the Harvard Business School from 1955 to 1960, and at McGill University from 1960 to 1962. He has published books on *Commercial Crisis and Change in England 1600–1642* (1959), *The Experience of Economic Growth: Case Studies in Economic History* (1963), *Boston Capitalists and Western Railroads* (1967) and *The Royal*

Exchange Assurance: A History of British Insurance 1720–1970 (1970).

R. M. HARTWELL
was born in Australia in 1921 and is Reader in Recent Social and Economic History of Nuffield College, University of Oxford. He was educated at the Universities of New England and Sydney, and in England at Balliol and Nuffield Colleges, Oxford. He has been a high-school teacher, Teaching Fellow of Economics, University of Sydney, and Professor of Economic History and Dean of the Faculty of Humanities at the University of New South Wales. From 1957 to 1972 he was in turn assistant editor, editor and book review editor of the *Economic History Review*. Besides contributing to professional journals, he has written *The Economic History of Van Dieman's Land* (1954), *The Industrial Revolution and Economic Growth* (1971), and with R. W. Breach, *British Economy and Society 1870–1970* (1972), and edited *The Causes of the Industrial Revolution* (1967), *The Industrial Revolution* (1970) and *On the Principles of Political Economy and Taxation* by David Ricardo (1971).

J-F. BERGIER
was born in Lausanne in 1931 and graduated there in 1954. He subsequently worked at the Ecole des Chartes in Paris and at the universities of Munich and Oxford. He became Professor of Economic History and Social Economy at the University of Geneva in 1963 and now holds the History Chair at the Swiss Institute of Technology, Zurich. He has been on the editorial board of the Revue Suisse d'Histoire since 1964 and in 1965 became Secretary General of the International Association of Economic History. Among his publications are *Genève et l'économie européenne de la Renaissance* (Paris 1963), *Registres de la Compagnie des Pasteurs de Genève au temps de Calvin*, 2 vols. (Geneva 1962 and 1964) and *Problèmes de l'histoire économique de la Suisse* (Berne 1968).

PAUL BAIROCH
was born in 1930 and studied in Paris and Brussels. He

began his research in the field of economic development in 1956 with a memoir for the Ecole Pratique des Hautes Etudes (Sorbonne) on the growth of France in the 19th century. He subsequently researched at the Institut de Sociologie and taught at the University of Brussels and is now Professor of Economics at Sir George Williams University, Montreal, and Directeur d'Etudes associé a l'Ecole Pratique des Hautes Etudes, Sorbonne. His publications include *Révolution industrielle et sous-développement* (3rd ed. Paris 1969, Spanish and Italian translations), *Diagnostic de l'évolution économique du Tiers Monde 1900–1968* (4th ed. Paris 1970, Spanish and English translations), and *Le Tiers Monde dans l'impasse: Le démarrage économique du XVIIIe au XXe siecle* (Paris 1971).

DONALD WINCH

was born in London in 1935. He was educated at the London School of Economics and Princeton University. He has taught economics at the University of California at Berkeley, Edinburgh University, and the University of Sussex, where he is Professor of the History of Economics and Dean of the School of Social Sciences. He is the author of *Classical Political Economy and Colonies* (1965) and *Economics and Policy: A Historical Study* (1970); he also edited and introduced *James Mill, Selected Economic Writings* (1966) and has written several articles on the history of economic thought.

M. J. T. LEWIS

was born in London in 1938 After reading classics and researching in classical archaeology at Corpus Christi College, Cambridge, he changed horses to industrial archaeology on becoming a research fellow of that college in 1963. He is now Senior Staff Tutor in industrial archaeology in the Department of Adult Education at the University of Hull. As well as articles on industrial archaeology and transport history in various journals, he has written *Temples in Roman Britain* (1966), *The Pentewan Railway* (1960), *How Ffestiniog got its Railway* (2nd ed. 1968), and *Early Wooden Railways* (1970).

Index of Persons

Abel 130
Agricola 190, 603
Akroyd 590
Alexander II, Tsar of Russia 347
André and Cottier (bankers) 288
Arago, Etienne 270, 289
Arenberg, Duke of 31
Argenson, Marquis d' 514
Arkwright, Sir Richard 192, 193, 195, 409
Arlès—Dufour, Jean Barthélemy 284
Aron (engineer) 290
Ashley, W. J. 563
Ashmore, Owen 579, 580
Ashton, T. S. 113, 429, 489
Attwood, Thomas 539
Avenel, d' 381

Babeuf, François Noël 398, 437
Bacon, Francis 509
Baden, Margrave of 525
Baeyer, J. F. W. A. von 248
Bage, Charles 587
Bagehot, Walter 381, 564
Baildon, John 312, 598
Bakewell, Robert 131
Bakunin, M. 446, 448
Balbo, Cesare 551
Balzac, Honoré de 428, 448
Barber 221
Baring family 266
Basset 284
Bastiat, Frédéric 546
Baudart de Saint-James 259
Bebel, August 445
Beccaria, Cesare 526
Beethoven, Ludwig van 365
Beeton, Isabella 123

Bell, Alexander Graham 240
Bentham, Jeremy 173, 314
Belioz, Hector 160
Bernal, J. D. 241
Berthollet, C. L. 229
Bessemer, Sir Henry 237, 238, 574
Bismarck, Otto von 99, 107, 348
Black, Joseph 227, 231, 233, 234
Bleichröder (banker) 292
Boisguillebert, Pierre de 514
Bontoux 290
Borsig, firm of 167, 285, 427
Boswell, James 158
Boulton, Matthew 144, 166, 213, 220, n 45, 221, 234, 258, 410, 415, 417
Bouthier 284
Bouvier, J. 290
Bowley, A. L. 124
Boyle, Robert 233
Bramah, Joseph 168
Braudel, Fernand 476
Braun, R. 493
Bright, John 537
Bristol, Earl of 170
Brölemann 284
Bronte sisters 125, 448
Brougham, Henry 529, 530
Brownlee, J. 43
Buchanan, Dr R. A. 575
Burke, Edmund 533-4

Cabet, Etienne 442
Cadbury, firm of 150
Cairnes, J. E. 541-2, 556
Calla, firm of 167
Callon, Professor 290
Cantillon, Richard 511, 544, 545

Carlyle, Thomas 559
Carr-Saunders, A. M 381
Cartwright, Edmund 194, 221
Catherine II 8, 62, 311, 525, 598
Cato 456
Cattaneo, Carlo 551
Catullus 9
Cavour, Count 339, 551
Cederna 8
Chalmers, Thomas 529
Chamberlain. Joseph 107
Chambers, J. D. 424, 459
Chapman, S. 150
Charles I 456
Charles III (of Spain) 526
Chenery, H. B. 388
Chevalier, Michel 332
Citroën, André 278
Clapham, J. H. 113, 128, 178
Clapham, T. 429
Clark, Colin 36, 358, 382, 387, 391
Clément, Ambroise 556
Cliffe-Leslie, T. C. 563
Clough, Robert 583
Cobbett, William 439
Cobden, Richard 537, 552
Cockerill, John (and firm) 105, 167, 279
Colbert, Jean-Baptiste 24, 311, 520
Coleridge, S. T. 159
Columella, L. J. M. 9, 456
Comte, Auguste 549, 559, 563
Condilhac, Etienne de 544
Connell, Professor K. G. 129
Cook, Thomas, firm of 171
Copland, Patrick 229
Cort, Henry 201, 202, 212
Crawshay, Richard 410
Crescenzi, Pietro 8
Crompton, Samuel 192, 193, 195
Crowley 258
Cullen, William 227
Cunningham, W. 563

Darby, Abraham (and firm) 197,

200. 201, 202, 204, 205, 212, 220. 258, 410, 585
Darwin, Charles 564
Davies, David 116
Davy, Sir Humphry 239
Deane, Phyllis 389
Dehaynin (contractor) 284
Delahante 284
Delhaize Frères 93
Descartes, René 509
Desseilligny 284
Dicey A. V. 99
Dickens, Charles 448
Dietrich family 402
Doherty 440
Dudley, Dud 584
Duhamel du Monceau, Henri-Louis 231
Dundonald, 9th Earl of 231, 232
Dunnoyer. Charles 546

Eden, F. M. 533
Eden. William 532
Edison, Thomas Alva 240 *n* 73, 241-2
Egells, firm ot 167
Eichhorn, firm ot 259
Eichthal (banker) 292
Elgar, Sir Edward 160
Enfantin, Prosper (Père) 417
Engel, Ernest 115, 117, 485
Engels, Friedrich 178, 448
Escher family 410

Fairbairn, William 166, 167
Faraday, Michael 240, 241
Faucher 158
Ferouillat 284
Fichte, J. G. 553
Filangieri, Gaetano 526
Fisher, A. G. B. 386
Fitzherbert, John 456
Fohlen, C. 390, 410
Fordyce, A and G. 231
Fourier. Claude 96, 442, 448
Fox, Charles James 533

Francis I of France 23
Frederick II, the Great 62, 311, 527
Freyssinet, Eugène 595
Fussell, G. E. 491

Galbraith, J. K. 13
Galen 8, 9
Galiani, Ferdinando 526
Galileo, Galilei 233
Garbett, Samuel 228
Garibaldi, Giuseppe 140
Garnier, Germain 544
Gascoigne, William 598
Gascoyne, Charles 312
Gautier, Etienne 50
Genovesi, Antonio 526
Germain, Henri 284
Gerschenkron, Professor A. 351, 352, 508, 561
Gille, Professor Bertrand 163
Giooia, Melchiorre 550
Goldsmith, Oliver 424
Goldsmith, R. W. 380-1
Gorge-Legrand, Henri de 590, 594
Gotthelf, Jeremias 448
Gouin, firm of 167
Griffin, Dr A. R. 581
Gropius, Walter 176
Guericke, Otto von 233
Guyton de Morveau, Baron L. B. 231

Habakkuk, H. J. 424
Hakort, firm of 167
Hall 239
Hammond, J. L. and B. 113, 145, 429
Hargreaves, James 193, 195
Hartwell, R. M. 113, 129, 132
Haussmann, Baron Georges 8, 37, 332
Hawks, William 410
Heckscher, Eli F. 125
Hegel, Georg Wilhelm Friedrich 558

Hell, Jozef Karl 601, 602
Henckel, Count Hugo 598
Henderson, W. O. 462
Hennebique 595
Henry IV (of France) 466
Henry, Louis 50
Hentsch (banker) 266
Héroult, Paul 239, 296
Hertz, Heinrich Rudolf 240
Hess 444
Higgins, Brian 231
Hippocrates 8, 9
Hitler, Adolf 249
Hobbes, Thomas 7
Hobsbawm, E. J. 113, 429
Hobson, J. A. 96
Hochet 284
Hoffmann A. W. 247, 248
Hoffmann, W. G. 371, 489
Hogarth, William 134
Holker, John 312
Holt, Alfred 211
Home, Francis 229
Honnecourt 10
Horace 9
Horner, Francis 529, 530
Horrocks, William 194 n 13
Hoselitz, Professor B. F. 307
Hottinger family 410
Hume, David 512, 517, 519
Hume, Joseph 530
Hunt, Henry 439
Huskisson, William 538
Hutcheson, Francis 514
Huygens, Christian 233

Ingram, J. K. 563
Irving (banker) 266
Isoard 418

Jeffrey, Francis 529, 530
Jenner, Dr Edward 42
Jevons, Stanley 562, 564, 565
Jones, E. L. 493
Jones, Richard 562
Jovellanos, Gaspar 527
Jullien 284

Kaskel (banker) 292
Kay, John 192, 195 *n* 15, 470
Keir, James 231, 232, 235
Kelvin, Lord 240
Kerridge, E. 459
Keynes, J. M. 374, 540
Kindelberger, C. P. 389
King, Gregory 157
Klöckner 294
Krupp family 113, 146, 277, 427, 436
Kunz, Heinnch 493
Kuznets, Professor S. 108, 387-8

Laënnec, R. T. H. 43
Laffitte, Jacques, 266, 267, 269-70, 283, 289
Landes, Professor David 128, 258, 507
Landry, Adolf 59
Lassalle, Ferdinand 444, 445
Lauderdale, 6th Earl of 529
Lavoisier, Antoine Laurent 231
Law, John 520
Lazard (banker) 278
Leblanc, Nicholas 232
Lengelle, M. 359
Leonardo da Vinci 10
Lesseps, Ferdinand de 277, 332
Lever Brothers 113, 150
Liebig, Justus 247, 248
Liebknecht, Wilhelm 445
Lipton, Sir Thomas 93
List, Friedrich 322, 323-4, 348, 549, 553-5
Lloyds Bank 258
Locke, John 509, 513, 515
Louis XIII 456
Louis XIV 62
Louis XV 61
Louis XVI 525
Louis-Philippe 32, 327, 331, 416

McCulloch, J. R. 529, 541
Machiavelli, Niccolò 8
Macintosh, Charles 230
Macpherson, David 141

Mahler, Gustav 160
Maillart, Robert 597
Malherbe 231
Malthus, Thomas Robert 216, 372, 420, 435, 483, 529, 534-5, 536, 540, 552, 560
Mantoux, Paul 411, 416, 424, 429, 492
Marcet, Jane 541
Marconi, Guglielmo 241
Maria Theresa, Empress 311
Marks and Spencer 94
Marshall, Alfred 359, 507, 565-6
Martineau, Harriet 541
Marx, Karl 398, 412, 418, 428, 429, 430, 433, 444, 445, 448, 507, 520, 537, 549, 555, 557-9, 560
Maudslay, Henry 168, 194
Maxwell, James Clark 240
Mayhew, Henry 133
Meek, Professor R. L. 520
Melon, Jean François 514
Mendelssohn, Felix 160
Mendelssohn, Moses (banker) 292
Menger, Karl 564
Métherie, Jean Claude de la 231
Mevissen (banker) 272, 294
Mill, James 529, 541, 545
Mill, John Stuart 529, 530, 549, 557, 559, 561, 562
Milleret (banker) 291
Mingay, J. E. 459
Molière, J. B. 483
Montané (ship builder) 284
Montagu, Lady Mary Wortley 42
Montague, C. E. 176
Morazé, Charles 403
Morse, Samuel F. B. 240
Müller, Johann Gottlieb 553
Muspratt, James 232, 233 *n* 62
Myddelton, Sir Hugh 580
Mylne, Robert 171

Napoleon I 25, 26, 54, 90, 104, 317, 330, 331, 334, 397, 526, 532, 545, 553,

Napoleon III (Louis) 37, 328, 329, 331, 332, 552
Nasmyth, James 168
Net, Professor J. U. 203, 580
Newcomen, Thomas 164, 200, 203-4, 212, 220, 233, 397, 601, 602
Newton, Sir Isaac 10, 509, 515, 522, 564
Nightingale, Florence 105, 126
North, Dudley 513

Oersted, Hans Christian 239
Oppenheim (banker) 257, 292
Owen, Robert 439, 440

Paine, Thomas 398, 438
Palladio, Andrea 8, 456
Palmade, Guy 407
Papin, Denis 233
Paracelsus 8
Parent 284
Parnell, Henry 530
Pasteur, Louis 46
Paul, Lewis 192, 193, 195 *n* 15, 221
Peabody, Samuel 150
Péchiney, firm o⟩ 296
Pecqueur, Constantin 417, 442
Peel, Dorothy 158
Peel, Sir Robert 144, 404, 409, 410
Péreire, Emile or Isaac 271, 272, 273, 274, 276, 279, 290, 332, 550
Perier, firm of 259
Perkin, Professor 173
Perkin, William Henry 243, 245, 247
Perronet, Jean Rodolphe 595
Perroux, François 406
Peter I, the Great 8, 311
Petty, Sir William 358, 513
Peugeot family 409
Pirenne, H. 495
Pitt, William 136, 533
Poisat, Michel 289
Polhem, Christopher 592

Poncelet 164
Pourtalès family 260
Priestley, Joseph 234-5
Proudhon, Jean-Baptiste Victor 448
Pufendorf, Samuel von 514

Quesnay, François 466, 511, 519, 543

Radcliffe, William 409
Raiffeisen 445
Ramsden Jesse 168
Rathenau, Emil and Walther 285
Rau, Karl Heinrich 552
Reden, Count von 598
Redlich, Fritz 406
Ricardo, David 266, 304, 372, 529, 530, 531, 535-6, 537, 540, 541 545, 546, 555, 557, 558, 559, 560, 561, 562
Robins, Benjamin 104
Robinson, Frederick John 538
Roebuck, John 221, 228, 231
Rogers, J. E. Thorold 563
Romagnesi, Giovanni Domenico 551
Roscher 129
Rostow, W. W. 309
Rothschild family 113, 273, 278, 288, 289, 290, 292
Rowntree, B. S. 140

Saint-Pierre, Abbé de 514
Saint-Simon, Claude Henri, Comte de 328, 331, 417, 442, 448, 547, 548-9, 554, 555, 559, 560, 562
Salaman, R. N. 464
Salt, Sir Titus 590
Santos Simes, J. M. dos 593
Sartoris (banker) 288
Say, Jean Baptiste 540, 544-6
Schaafhausen, Abraham 294, 295
Scheele, Karl 229, 231
Schneider family 113, 167, 284, 289, 297, 402

Schulz, Günter 596
Schulze-Delitzsch 445
Schumpeter, Joseph 406, 509, 511, 522
Schwabe 147
Scialoja Vittorio 551
Seillière family 289, 292
Senior, Nassau 529, 545, 551
Serres, Olivier de 456
Sheffield, Lord 532
Shelley, Frances, Lady 435
Siemens, Georg 285
Siemens, Werner von 237, 238
Sismondi, Jean Charles Simonde de 547-8, 549, 551, 562,
Slicher van Bath, B. H. 461, 476
Small, William 234
Smeaton, John 200, 204, 233
Smiles, Samuel 99, 417
Smith, Adam 89, 109, 123, 304, 359, 466, 512-13, 514, 515, 516-19, 520-3, 527, 530-4, 535, 536, 537, 540, 543, 545, 547, 548, 553, 555, 558, 561
Smith, A. D. 388
Smith, Dr Edward 124
Smith, John Prince 552
Smith, Sydney 130
Solvay, Ernest 285
Spence, Thomas 439
Stendhal. Henri 17
Stephenson, George 205, 206, 221
Steuart, Sir James 512
Stewart, Dugald 529
Stinnes, Hugo 286, 289
Stolypin, P. A. 350
Strutt, William 587
Stubs, Peter 410
Sue, Eugène 428, 448
Sully, Duc de 466
Swan, Sir Joseph 241

Talabot, Paulin 289
Talcott, Parsons 382
Tarello 456
Tawney, R. H. 375, 513

Tennant, Charles 230, 233
Terray, Joseph Marie 24
Thomas, Sidney Gilchrist 238
Thompson, E. P. 113, 435
Thornton, Henry 529
Thyssen 286
Torrens, R. R. 535
Torricelli, Evangelista 233
Tracy, Michael 101
Trevithick, Richard 205
Turgot, Anne Robert Jacques 129, 512, 516, 519, 525, 543, 544
Tusser, Thomas 456
Tylecote, Dr R. F. 584

Varro 456
Vassal (banker) 292
Vauban, Marshal 104, 514
Verri, Pietro 526
Villermé, Dr 429
Volta, Alessandro 239
Voltaire, François Marie Arouet de 100

Wailes, Rex 593
Wakefield, Edward Gibbon 66
Walker, Aaron 258, 410
Walpole, Horace 9
Walras, Leon 564
Ward, Joshua 228
Watt, James 11, 164, 166, 171, 190, 200, 204, 213, 220 *n* 40, 221, 229, 231, 234, 397
Watts, William 583
Webb, Beatrice and Sidney 424
Weber, Max 406
Wedgwood, Joshua 415, 417
Wehdorn, Dr M. 597
Weitling, Wilhelm 444
Wendel family 280, 285
West, 284, 535
Weston, Richard 456
Wheatstone, Sir Charles 240
Whitbread, Samuel 533
White, John 228
Whitehead 11
Whiteley, William 93

Whitworth, Joseph 168
Wilkinson, John 200, 212, 258, 410
Wilkinson, William 312, 598
William I (of Netherlands) 267
Wilson, P. A. 381
Withering, W. 234

Witte, Count 348, 349
Woolf 165
Woolworth, Frank 94
Worth, Charles Frederick 142

Yatsunsky, V. K. 493
Young, Arthur 136

Index of Places

Note.—All references to Britain (England and United Kingdom) have been omitted as they are far too numerous to be of any help to the reader.

Similarly, only principal references are given for France, Germany and Italy.

Abbeydale steel works (Sheffield) 579
Aberdeen 229
Africa 13, 28, 72, 105
Aix-en-Provence 172
Alais 283, 289, 291
Algeria 69
Alsace 402, 417
Althoff 93
America 28, 61, 63, 81, 127, 315, 380
America (North) 17, 23, 69, 72, 81, 454, 461, 538; *see also* Canada, U.S.A.
America (South) 62, 275, 524, 538
Amsterdam 174, 273, 402
Antwerp 273
Argentina 13, 69, 70, 132, 479
Ascot 161
Asia 28, 29, 70, 72, 315
Augsburg 146
Australia (Australasia) 23, 66, 72, 81, 132, 479
Austria (-Hungary) 26, 27, 29, 30, 33, 35, 46, 47, 53, 56, 58, 62, 67, 70, 86, 100, 132, 136, 141, 165, 282, 287, 292, 293, 311, 336, 369, 385, 404, 460, 468, 472, 484, 526, 564, 597, 598

Baigorry 259
Balkans 36, 70, 78, 114
Banska Stiavnica 601, 602
Barcelona 152

Basle 262
Bavaria 26, 104, 124
Belfast 586
Belgium 12, 13, 18, 29, 30, 35, 36, 44, 46, 49, 53, 56, 58, 59, 61, 72, 73, 78, 93, 100, 101, 102, 105, 107, 111, 117, 118, 128, 130, 132, 135, 136, 138, 139, 146, 165, 167, 172, 258, 259, 260, 262, 267-9, 278-9, 281, 285, 292, 297, 318, 322, 324, 327, 329, 339, 340, 369, 379, 404, 425, 460, 468, 471, 472, 477, 484, 488, 495, 497, 594; *see also* Flanders
Belper 168, 587
Birmingham 33, 173, 228, 235, 414
Bishop Auckland 206
Blackpool 162
Bohemia 36, 44, 86, 426, 436, 602; *see also* Czechoslovakia
Bologna 34
Bolton 146
Bonn 248
Bordeaux 174, 399, 400, 402, 494
Boulogne 162
Brabant 460, 461, 462
Brandenburg 31, 603
Brazil 69, 70
Bremen 100
Breslau 33, 148, 149, 153, 259
Bristol 33, 494, 583
Brittany 123, 124, 135
Brussels 173, 275, 444
Bucharest 599

Budapest 599
Budweis 602
Bulgaria 29, 30, 56, 60, 100, 120, 468, 599

California 66
Canada 15, 61, 70, 178, 479
Carron 202, 598
Catalonia 50, 62
Ceylon 93
China 8, 9, 13, 17, 188 *n* 2, 469
Coalbrookdale 197, 258
Coed Ithel 584
Cologne 33, 34, 175, 270, 272, 292, 294
Constantinople 42
Copenhagen 125, 175
Crewe 146. 590
Croydon 205
Crulai (Normandy) 50-2
Czechoslovakia 468, 577, 600, 601, 602

Dalarna 592
Dalmatia 139
Danzig 601
Darlington 206, 207
Dartmoor 173
Decazeville, 280, 283. 284, 291
Decize 259
Denmark 26, 29, 30, 46, 48, 56, 60, 61, 101, 114, 115, 137, 158, 369, 385, 460, 468, 593
Derbyshire 581, 584, 587
Doncaster 161
Dortmund 34
Dover 494
Dresden 33, 34, 148, 149, 174, 292
Duisberg 34
Düsseldorf 33, 34

Edinburgh 33, 171, 278, 529
Egypt 275
Elba 342
Enfield 580
Epsom 161
Essen 33, 34

Finland 8, 26, 29, 30, 31, 46, 70, 385, 468, 582, 591
Firminy steel plant 284
Flanders 10, 49, 456, 460, 461, 462, 471; *see also* Belgium
Florence 34, 599
Fourchambault 283, 284
France (principal reierences only)
    15, 23, 24-6, 27, 29, 30, 31, 32, 33 35, 36, 37, 39, 45, 46, 47, 48, 50-3, 54, 55, 56, 57-8, 61, 62, 63, 71, 73, 88, 93, 100, 101, 102, 106, 108, 111. 118, 124, 128, 130, 131, 132, 136, 138, 141, 156, 164, 165, 222, 258-60, 271-2, 274-8, 280-1, 283-4, 288-94, 295-6, 316-17, 327-9, 330-4, 399-400, 417-18, 420, 437, 442-4, 460, 461, 462, 466, 468, 470, 472, 484, 486, 488, 494-5, 496-7, 514, 519-20, 525, 543-50, 594-5
Frankfurt 175, 402

Geneva 47, 53, 260, 262, 275, 297, 400, 402, 403
Genoa 34, 172, 494
Germany (principle references only) 15 26, 27, 29, 30, 31, 33-4, 36, 37, 45, 46, 47, 48, 53, 55, 56, 58, 61-2, 63, 66, 68, 69-70, 72, 85, 88, 93, 100, 101, 102, 106, 108, 111, 115, 118, 124, 128, 130, 131, 132, 134, 136, 138, 141, 148-9, 153, 156, 165, 243-9, 270, 272-4, 275, 285-7, 294-5, 296, 318-19, 323-6, 329-30, 335-7, 426-8, 436, 444-5, 460, 466, 468, 472, 484, 527-8, 552-5, 595-6
Ghent 105
Glasgow 33, 232, 233, 234, 322, 581
Goole 590, 594
Gotha 445
Göttingen 527
Greece 35, 70, 178, 379, 468, 599

Grenoble 259

Hainault 31
Halifax 590
Halle 527
Hamburg 33, 34, 148, 149
Hanover 31
Hanseatic towns 494
Hesse 26
Himley 584
Holland 10, 11, 29, 30, 31, 61, 62,
    130, 136, 137, 216, 267, 322,
    324, 327, 369, 494, 577, 593;
    see also Low Countries and Neth-
    erlands
Homburg 160
Hull 158, 585-6
Hungary 24, 25, 30, 44, 46,
    47, 53, 56, 58, 70, 86, 130, 169,
    385, 404, 468, 601; *see also*
    Austria

India 13, 143, 244, 461, 524
Ireland 29, 30, 31, 35, 39, 53, 54,
    56, 60, 61, 63, 67, 68, 71, 72, 86,
    87, 114, 120, 129, 132, 144, 150,
    417, 468, 586
Italy (principal references only)
    15, 26, 29, 31, 34, 35, 39, 45, 46,
    47, 48, 55, 56, 58, 66, 67, 69,
    73, 85, 100, 108, 128, 130, 131,
    132, 134, 136, 138, 141, 156,
    165, 275, 339, 341-3, 426, 447,
    460-1, 468, 472, 484, 525-6,
    550-2

Japan 13, 14, 15, 18, 341, 350,
    379, 454, 477, 497

Karlskrona 174
Karlstadt 93
Kazan 34
Kiev 34, 35
Königsberg 33, 527

Lancashire 192, 227, 230, 322,
    579, 592

Le Creusot 259, 284, 285, 289, 292,
    402, 598
Leeds 173
Le Grand Hornu 146, 590, 594
Leipzig 34, 91, 148, 149
Letchworth 151
Leyden 228
Liège 105, 112, 146, 322
Lille 112, 278, 414
Liverpool 33, 172, 173, 175, 206,
    207, 210, 232
Lodz 601
Lombardy 426, 526
London 9, 32, 33, 37, 91, 93, 134,
    135, 137, 150, 151, 152, 157,
    158, 159, 171, 173, 174, 175,
    206, 258, 381, 402, 415, 422,
    435, 444, 529, 580
Lothians 581
Low Countries 9, 10, 325, 460,
    461, 462, 476; *see also* Belgium,
    Holland and Netherlands
Lübeck 149
Lyons 33, 260, 270, 284, 400, 402,
    415, 420, 443

Madrid 152, 273
Magdeburg 149, 175
Manchester 33, 146, 158, 161, 167,
    172, 175, 206, 207, 210, 322,
    414, 589
Marseilles 33, 39, 123, 400, 402,
    494
Mauritius 211
Melbourne (Derbyshire) 584
Merstham 205
Messina 34, 39
Middlesborough 146, 207
Milan 34, 171, 415, 526
Minden 100
Mons 259
Montbéliard 409
Monte Carlo 160
Moravia 426, 602
Moscow 34, 39, 104, 600
Mulhouse 105, 406, 415, 435
Munich 33, 34, 174, 248, 292

Namur 31
Nantes 402, 494
Naples 34, 273, 288, 426, 526
Netherlands 26, 30, 35, 46, 53, 56, 58, 62, 88, 100, 110, 165, 169, 318, 379, 385, 404, 460, 468; *see also* Holland
Neuchâtel 260
Newcastle 205, 410, 584, 585
Newfoundland 133
New Holland 590-1, 594
New Lanark 146, 168
Newmarket 161
Nîmes 289
Norway 23, 26, 29, 31, 43, 46, 50, 54, 56, 60, 108, 136, 156, 158, 296, 369, 468, 591
Nottingham 161, 230, 589
Nova Bana 601
Nüremberg 146

Odessa 34, 35
Ostend 162

Paisely 158
Palatinate 457
Palermo 34
Paris 24, 32, 33, 37, 39, 97, 105, 141, 152, 158, 159, 171, 174, 175, 259, 266, 270, 273, 275, 288, 289, 291, 292, 293, 294, 332, 399, 402, 415, 419, 420, 443, 444
Pen-y-Darran 205
Perigueux 400
Piedmont 426, 526, 551
Plymouth 494
Po Valley 457, 460
Poland 44, 63, 66, 70, 86, 404, 468, 577, 600
Portugal 29, 36, 46, 56, 61, 67, 69, 72, 100, 144, 369, 468, 494, 593, 599, 602
Prague 295
Prestonpans 228
Provence 124
Prussia 26, 56, 62, 92, 114, 115, 129, 158, 245, 248, 270, 309, 311, 318-19, 324-5, 329-30, 335-6, 426, 427, 444, 527-8, 550, 553, 595, 598; *see also* Germany

Ramnäs Bruk 592
Reichenberg 436
Rennes 135
Rhineland 86, 270, 410, 427, 428, 596
Rhosydd 582
Rome 34, 273
Rosedale 585
Rottweil 596-7
Rouen 322
Ruhr 34, 112, 294, 414, 596
Rumania 24, 31, 46, 47, 56, 60, 100, 140, 468
Russia 8, 13, 15, 17, 18, 26, 27, 29, 31, 34, 46, 47, 48, 56, 58, 60, 62, 63, 66, 67, 70, 71, 72, 86, 87, 95, 100, 105, 106, 107, 110, 111, 114, 120, 130, 132, 136, 137, 141, 142, 144, 155, 165, 170, 177, 249, 258, 273, 295, 296, 309, 310, 311, 312, 341, 343-50, 351, 379, 385, 400, 404, 413, 425, 433, 460, 468, 472, 479, 484, 493, 524, 600

Saar 112
Saint-Véran 260
Saltaire 146, 590
Saratov 34
Saxony 105, 114, 115, 137, 410, 426, 603, 604
Scandinavia 20, 23, 26, 31, 35, 36, 47, 49, 54, 62, 67, 174, 404
Schleswig-Holstein 31, 124
Schwenningen 596
Scotland 56, 68, 124, 146, 171, 202, 215, 220, 221, 222, 227, 228, 229, 230, 231, 233, 322, 516, 520, 522, 529, 581, 602
Serbia 46, 53, 56, 60; *see also* Yugoslavia
Sheffield 172, 579

Shrewsbury 587
Shropshire 581
Siberia 62
Silesia 311, 312, 324, 427, 598, 600
Southend 162
Spain 26, 27, 29, 30, 36, 42, 46, 47, 48, 50, 56, 58, 60, 61, 62, 63, 67, 69, 78, 100, 120, 161, 165, 170, 275, 294, 369, 379, 383, 404, 460, 462, 468, 472, 494, 526-7, 599
Stockton 206 207
Stourbridge 585
Suez Canal 211, 277, 332
Sweden 13, 18, 24, 26, 29, 31, 36, 39, 43, 46, 47, 48, 49, 50, 53, 54, 56, 57, 58, 60, 62, 85, 86, 88, 100, 108, 125, 136, 137, 156, 165, 167, 197, 229, 274, 287, 296, 341, 460, 468, 470, 472, 482, 484, 577, 590-2, 595
Swindon 146, 590
Switzerland 13, 14, 15, 18, 29, 44, 56, 62, 88, 100, 105, 128, 130, 132, 134, 137, 138, 260, 266, 274, 286, 296-7, 318, 385, 400, 404, 409, 413, 416, 421, 423, 425-6, 444, 445-7, 460, 468, 472, 484, 493, 564, 596, 597

Terni 342
Theiss River 170
Tietz 93
Toulon 174
Truro 175, 258

Tula 34
Turin 34, 273, 414
Turkey 62, 70, 106, 346
Tuscany 56, 426

Ukraine 39
U.S.A. 13, 14, 15, 17, 18, 26, 61, 67, 68, 69, 70, 71, 94, 127, 132, 137, 178, 210, 239, 240, 242, 249, 282, 325, 329, 368, 369, 376, 379, 394, 460, 461, 462, 464, 466, 468, 472, 477, 478, 479, 497, 532, 553
Uster 438

Venice 34, 50, 494
Versailles 145, 525
Vienna 32, 33, 159, 173, 175, 273, 289, 295, 322

Wales 68, 112, 582
Wandsworth 205
Wanlockhead 602
Weser River 100
Westphalia 270, 426
Wiener Neustadt 295
Wolverton 146
Woolwich 174

Yugoslavia 468, 599

Zagreb 599
Zola dam 171
Zürich 105, 286, 296, 414, 439, 493
Zyrardów 600

General Index

Note.—Many of the topics touched upon in this volume (e.g. agriculture, banking, capital, entrepreneurs, population, railways, technology, transport, etc.) are constantly referred to throughout, and so only principal references have been given. The same applies to many raw and manfactured commodities (e.g. coal, cotton, iron and steel, etc.).

Agriculture 17, 19, 31, 36, 38-9, 43, 72, 77, 80-1, 83, 95, 100, 112, 127, 131, 156, 169-70, 177, 222, 314, 320, 334, 345 *et seq.*, 371, 386, 389-90, 391, 423-4, 452-506, 519, 520, 523, 525, 528, 532, 535-6, 543, 544, 554, 556, 565, 581
aluminium industry 238-9
archaeology (industrial) 190, 574-603
architecture 8, 79, 175-6, 365, 366, 382, 576, 587, 594; *see also* housing
Auerstadt, battle of 318

Banking 14, 77, 90, 96, 98, 113, 162, 163, 169, 215, 246, 255-99, 331, 332, 360, 363, 378, 380-1, 405, 495, 539, 549-50, 552
bicycles 80, 83, 155
birth control, 22, 53, 535
birth rate 22, 23, 28, 30, 38, 54 *et seq.*, 61, 71
blast furnaces 201-2, 219, 412, 487, 492, 584-5, 600
bleaching 227 *et seq.*, 237
Boer War 140, 143
books, 16, 82, 93, 154
bourgeoisie 397, 398, 399-418, 507, 557-8, 574, 595
bridges 170, 200, 328, 597, 599
buses 171

Cable (oceanic) 95

canals 80, 189, 191, 205, 207, 212, 217, 221, 311, 337, 360, 376, 580, 587, 588-9, 590, 595
capital and investment 10, 14, 16, 77, 78, 80, 82, 83 *et seq.*, 90, 92, 94, 162-3, 169-70, 187, 214 *et seq.*, 222, 225, 246, 255 *et seq.*, 303, 307 *passim*, 353, 391, 407 *et seq.*, 412 *et seq.*, 467, 492 *et seq.*, 520, 522, 523, 537, 540, 549, 557 *et seq.*
census 24 *et seq.*
Chartists 433, 438, 440, 447, 539
chemical industry 166, 226, 227 *et seq.*, 242-9, 311
Christian socialism 434
clock industry (Swiss) 422, 446
clothes 79, 82, 93, 96 *et seq.*, 114, 116, 117, 120, 121, 140-4, 155, 162, 177, 178
coal (industry) 7, 11-12, 152, 172, 197, 201, 203, 206, 207, 211, 212, 224, 225, 230, 242, 286, 291, 294, 311, 324, 327, 331, 473, 579, 580-1, 600, 603
Cobden-Chevalier Treaty (1860) 100, 333, 552
coffee 82, 96, 103, 120, 124, 127, 136, 155
coke 197-8, 200, 201, 202, 220, 226, 312, 585
Commune (Paris 1870) 444
communism 444 *et seq.*, 599; *see also* Marx, Karl
communications 16, 77, 95, 363,

377; *see also* telegraph, telephone and transport

consumption 16, 77-185, 216, 224

Corn Laws 127, 320, 477, 535, 537, 546, 551, 560

cotton 81, 88, 105, 141, 142, 143, 164, 177, 190, 192 *et seq.*, 197, 203, 219, 220, 223, 225, 228, 408, 409, 411, 412, 416, 421, 470, 486-7, 596, 603

Crimean War 42, 105, 126, 344, 346

crime 38

Dams 171-2, 599, 601

demand *see* Patterns of Demand

disease 22, 37, 39 *et seq.*, 86, 105, 125, 126

domestic servants 80, 83, 98, 121, 147, 155, 157-8, 364, 383

drink 82-3, 97, 99, 120 *et seq.*, 134-7, 187; *see also* Food

dyeing 229 *et seq.*, 242-7; *see also* bleaching

dynamo 241

Economics (emergence as a science) 507-73

education 14, 19, 107, 119, 120, 121, 173, 246, 247, 308, 325, 337, 360, 363, 365, 366, 524, 535

electricity 7, 83, 107, 152-3, 164, 165, 171, 172, 226, 239-42, 285, 296

emigration 22-3, 54, 60 *et seq.*, 77, 86, 87-8, 320, 428

enclosures 131, 169, 222, 320, 391, 423, 424

Enlightenment, The 514 *et seq.*, 522, 524 *et seq.*

entertainment 117, 159 *et seq.*, 174-5, 364, 385-6

entrepreneurs 14, 94, 215, 217, 219-20, 221, 246, 309 *passim*, 351, 405, 406 *et seq.*, 416, 418,

422, 431, 435, 492 *et seq.*, 523, 545

exchanges 77, 91, 96, 381; *see also* banking

Fabianism 440

Factory Acts 543

factory conditions 429 *et seq.*, 523

fairs 91, 94, 159

famine 16, 22, 38, 39, 43, 44, 77, 85, 86, 87, 177, 439, 453, 457; *see also* Irish Potato Famine

fashion 95, 96 *et seq.*, 142

fish 123, 127, 132-4; *see also* food

flax industry 487, 586

flying shuttle 192, 470

food 16, 31, 79, 81, 82, 86-7, 88, 90, 91, 92, 93, 95, 96, 100, 101-2, 104, 110, 112, 115, 116, 117, 118, 120-40, 145, 154, 162, 163, 169, 177, 187, 216, 393, 420, 453, 458-9, 461, 470, 476 *et seq.*, 484 *et seq.*, 532, 535 *et seq.*

fortifications 104-6, 174

free trade 315, 317, 320 *et seq.*, 525, 532, 537 *et seq.*, 550 *et seq.*, 556; *see also* laissez-faire

French Revolution 53, 63, 100, 176, 247, 305, 316, 317, 318, 319, 400, 423, 437, 470, 484, 523, 527, 543

fruit 130-1; *see also* food

furniture 96, 114, 153-4

Gambling 160

gas industry 83, 107, 110, 152-3, 165, 168, 171, 172

Great Exhibition (1851) 91

Holidays 161-2

hospitals 144, 172-3

housing 96, 112, 113, 116, 121, 144-53, 170, 177, 580, 589 *et seq.*, 600

Huguenots 586

Illiteracy 12, 13, 19, 429
immigration 38, 60 *et seq.*
income, growth of 15-16, 81, 82, 88, 108-15, 148, 370 *et seq.*; *see also* wages
International, The First (1864) 441, 443, 446
international organisations 90-1
investment *see* capital
Irish Potato Famine 31, 63, 129
iron and steel industry 11, 15, 80, 81, 163, 164, 166, 169, 188, 189, 190, 191, 197, 200 *et seq.*, 205, 212, 224, 225, 237-9, 241, 291, 294, 296, 322, 324, 344, 402, 408, 410, 421, 464, 470, 488-92, 598, 600
iron works 311, 312, 410, 500, 584, 592, 594, 596, 597, 598

Jacobinism 435, 437, 438
Jena, battle of 318

Labour Party 440
laissez-faire 99-100, 222, 301-2, 321, 338, 340, 417, 437, 518 *et seq.*, 524, 546, 556
Law of Markets (Say's) 544-5
lead industry 583
lime industry 581-2
literacy 10, 82, 95, 107, 159
locks 587-8
Luddism 438-9

Machinery 18, 19, 80, 83, 92, 164 *et seq.*, 167 *et seq.*, 192 *et seq.*, 226 *et seq.*, 320, 360, 463, 464, 523, 560, 592
marriage 49 *et seq.*
meat 82, 102, 124, 128, 131-2, 177, 485; *see also* food
medicine 8, 9, 22, 39 *et seq.*, 105, 227, 364, 366, 383, 483
medieval inventions 188 *et seq.*, 214
mercantalism 311 *et seq.*, 512 *et seq.*, 517 *et seq.*, 521, 532, 538, 555

milk 102, 124, 126, 137, 138, 140, 177; *see also* food
mills 580, 583, 586, 587, 590
mortality rate 22, 23, 32, 38, 43-9, 59, 71, 85, 109, 431, 481, 482 *et seq.*; *see also* population
motor car 80, 83, 84, 155

Napoleonic Code 25, 90, 317, 318, 526
Napoleonic Wars 104, 105, 139, 143, 247, 316, 319, 423, 439, 484, 525, 528, 530, 555
Navigation Acts 217, 320, 532
newspapers 16, 82, 94-5, 98, 121

Oil industry 7, 11, 88, 152, 165

Paternalism 436-7, 528, 533, 590
Patterns of Demand 77-185
pawning 162-3
Peterloo Massacre 439, 443
petroleum 81
physiocracy 466-7, 507, 511 *et seq.*, 516, 519-20, 521, 524 *et seq.*, 532, 535, 536, 540, 543-4
piano 154
police 143, 144, 363
pollution 20
Poor Laws 422, 532, 533, 534, 535, 543, 551, 552
population 15, 16, 17, 22-76, 77, 85 *et seq.*, 89, 92, 109, 145, 216, 314, 378, 424-5, 467-8, 476, 481-4, 513, 533, 534 *et seq.*, 552, 556, 565
Positivism 547, 563
potato 86, 87, 102, 104, 120, 123, 124, 128-30
pottery 415, 585-6
prostitution 158-9
public utilities 171-2, 363; *see also* services

Radio 16, 195, 240-1
railways 16, 77, 80, 84, 105, 107, 143, 144, 166, 170-1, 175, 191,

202, 205-10, 212, 224-5, 226, 240, 241, 262, 265, 279, 283, 292, 293, 294, 308, 322, 326-30, 331, 332, 333, 334, 337, 340-1, 360, 376, 379, 444, 473, 488, 549, 551, 552, 580, 589, 602
refrigeration 77, 80
registration of population 23 *et seq.*
religion 38, 175, 384, 406, 417, 434-5
roads 16, 80, 170, 191, 205, 216, 327, 328, 331, 574, 581
rubber 81, 249

Saint Simonians 265-6, 267, 274, 332, 547
salt mines 596-7
schools 14, 107, 125, 143, 325; *see also* education
science (as aid to industry) 226-49
servants *see* domestic servants
services, revolution in 358-96
sewing machines 80, 83, 143, 155
shipping industry 16, 77, 80, 84, 90, 95, 191, 210-11, 213, 315, 324, 360, 376-8, 489
shops 91-4, 113
slate industry 582-3
slave trade 105
soap 103, 153, 166, 469
social services 88-9, 103-4, 106-7, 172 *et seq.*, 358-96
socialism 107, 437, 445 *et seq.*, 558
spinning 192 *et seq.*, 227, 409, 410, 413, 470, 493
sport 91, 160-1, 174
State (attitude to Industrial Revolution) 14, 19-20, 99 *et seq.*, 107, 222, 246, 258, 301-57; *see also* economics, bourgeoisie, services *and* working class
steam engine 164 *et seq.*, 203 *et seq.*, 213, 229, 233, 397, 412, 582, 601, 602
steam ship 211
steel industry *see* iron and steel industry

steel works 579
Stein-Hardenberg reforms 527, 552
sugar 102, 103, 124, 126, 127, 138-9, 166, 477
suicide 38

Tariffs 100-101, 303 *passim*, 351, 513, 538, 553, 555
taxation 102 *et seq.*, 302, 325, 513, 514, 519, 521 524, 530, 531
tea 82, 93, 96, 103, 120, 124, 127, 136
technology, progress in 14, 18, 19, 77, 80 *et seq.*, 86, 89, 98, 187-254
telegraph 77, 95, 171, 239, 240, 262, 363, 377
telephone 16, 95, 171, 240, 296
television 16
textile industry 80, 141, 163, 164, 165 *et seq.*, 224, 226 *et seq.*, 311, 322, 327, 409-10, 413, 470, 486-7, 494, 498, 499, 579, 600
timber 79, 81, 88, 144, 152, 164, 197, 212
tin 88, 203
tobacco 21, 139, 445
trade unions 320, 364, 384-5, 440 *et seq.*, 447
trams 151, 171, 582
Trans-Siberian railway 344
transport 8, 9, 16-17, 37, 80, 81, 82, 86, 89-90, 98, 151, 155, 170 *et seq.*, 187-8, 189, 205 *et seq.*, 216-17, 294, 310, 314, 324, 326 *et seq.*, 363, 367, 375-7, 475, 478, 500, 580, 587

Urban development 9, 10, 17, 32 *et seq.*, 36-7, 77, 87, 88-9, 92, 99, 106, 112, 145 *et seq.*, 172, 376, 378, 386, 393, 442, 528, 574, 577

Wages 95-6, 101, 112, 176, 178,

Wages [contd.]
315, 419-20, 439, 496 *et seq.*
war 22, 38, 104-5, 323
Wealth of Nations 512, 521-3, 528, 530, 533, 534, 543, 544, 546, 559
weaving 82, 227, 409, 413
windmills 169, 188, 200, 204, 582, 593

wool 81, 88, 131, 164, 192, 218, 412, 487, 603
women, employment of 157-8, 361
working class, emergence of 397, 398, 399, 418-51

Zollverein 100, 335-7, 444, 552, 554